k_e	Cost of equity capital given the firm's degree of leverage
k_I	Weighted cost of capital for a project
k^*	Cost of equity capital if all equity financed
L	Parent's target debt ratio
LC	Local currency
L/C	Letter of credit
LDC	Less-developed country
LIBOR	London interbank offer rate
MNC	Multinational corporation
NPV	Net present value
OFDI	Office of Foreign Direct Investment
P	(a) Put option premium or (b) Principle amount of foreign currency loan
P/E	Price-earnings ratio on a share of stock
PPP	Purchasing power parity
r	Effective yield on a bond
r_h	Home currency interest rate
r_f	Foreign currency interest rate
r_{us}	U.S. interest rate
r_L	Local Currency interest rate
R_f	Risk-free rate of return
R_m	Required return on the market
s	Flotation cost, in percent, on long-term debt
S	Current spot rate
S_i	Interest subsidy in period i
SDR	Special drawing right
t	(a) Tax rate or (b) Time, when used as a subscript
t_a	Foreign affiliate tax rate
T_i	Tax savings in period I association with using debt financing
X_i	Home currency cash flow in period i

FOUNDATIONS OF MULTINATIONAL FINANCIAL MANAGEMENT

SIXTH EDITION

Alan C. Shapiro

UNIVERSITY OF SOUTHERN CALIFORNIA

Atulya Sarin

SANTA CLARA UNIVERSITY

WILEY

JOHN WILEY & SONS, INC.

VP & Executive Publisher	Don Fowley
Associate Publisher	Judith Joseph
Associate Editor	Jennifer Conklin
Editorial Assistant	Sarah Vernon
Executive Marketing Manager	Amy Scholz
Senior Production Editor	Sandra Dumas
Production Manager	Dorothy Sinclair
Cover Designer	Jeof Vita
Media Editor	Allison Morris
Production Management Services	Thomson Digital
Cover Photo	Superstock

This book was set in 10/12 Janson by Thomson Digital and printed and bound by R. R. Donnelley/Jefferson City. The cover was printed by R. R. Donnelley/Jefferson City.

This book is printed on acid free paper. ∞

To order books or for customer service please, call 1-800-CALL WILEY (225-5945).

ISBN-13   978-0470-12895-4

Printed in the United States of America

10   9   8   7   6   5   4   3   2   1

To our wives,
Diane and Seema,
for their encouragement,
support, and love

BRIEF CONTENTS

CONTENTS

APPROACH

The basic thrust of this sixth edition of *Foundations of Multinational Financial Management* is to provide a conceptual framework within which the key financial decisions of the multinational firm can be analyzed. This edition now has a co-author, Dr. Atulya Sarin, who brings his vast academic and consulting experience to bear on this significant revision from the previous edition. The approach followed in this book is to treat international financial management as a natural and logical extension of the principles learned in the foundations course in financial management. Thus, it builds on and extends the valuation framework provided by domestic corporate finance to account for dimensions unique to international finance.

Foundations focuses on decision making in an international context. Analytical techniques help translate the often vague rules of thumb used by international financial executives into specific decision criteria. The book offers a variety of real-life examples, both numerical and institutional, that demonstrate the use of financial analysis and reasoning in solving international financial problems. These examples have been culled from the thousands of illustrations of corporate practice that we have collected over the years from business periodicals and our consulting practice. By scattering the best of these examples throughout the text, students can see the value of examining decision-making problems with the aid of a solid theoretical foundation. Seemingly disparate facts and events can then be interpreted as specific manifestations of more general financial principles.

All the traditional areas of corporate finance are explored, including working capital management, capital budgeting, cost of capital, and financial structure. However, this is done from the perspective of a multinational corporation, concentrating on those decision elements that are rarely, if ever, encountered by purely domestic firms. These elements include multiple currencies with frequent exchange rate changes and varying rates of inflation, differing tax systems, multiple money markets, exchange controls, segmented capital markets, and political risks such as nationalization or expropriation. Throughout the book, we have tried to demystify and simplify multinational financial management by showing that its basic principles rest on the same foundation as does corporate finance.

The emphasis throughout this book is on taking advantage of being multinational. Too often companies focus on the threats and risks inherent in venturing abroad rather than on the opportunities that are available to multinational firms. These opportunities include the ability to obtain a greater degree of international diversification than security purchases alone can provide as well as the ability to arbitrage between imperfect capital markets, thereby obtaining funds at a lower cost than could a purely domestic firm.

AUDIENCE

The current edition of *Foundations of Multinational Financial Management* has been streamlined to fit with a regular semester-long course schedule. As such, it now contains only 16 chapters as compared to 20 in the previous edition. The book still retains the content that is important for a foundations course in multinational financial management and continues to emphasize broad concepts and practices rather than extensive quantitative material. Compared to *Multinational Financial Management (MFM)*, the graduate-level text by the first author, *Foundations* reduces the range and complexity of the subject matter covered. Although *Foundations* is intended primarily for an undergraduate audience, it is suitable for use in master's level courses where there is not enough time to cover the full range of topics dealt with in *MFM* or where the students do not have the necessary preparation for using *MFM*. It is also suitable for use in bank management and other executive development programs.

FEATURES

Foundations of Multinational Financial Management presumes a knowledge of basic corporate finance, economics, and algebra. However, it does not assume prior knowledge of international economics or international finance, and it is, therefore, self-contained in that respect. For those who are not familiar with *Multinational Financial Management*, here are some of the distinctive features that have led to its widespread adoption. These features have been incorporated and enhanced in *Foundations*.

- Extensive discussion of globalization and its consequences and reasons for the evolution and spread of multinational corporations. Elaboration of the basic concepts of absolute and comparative advantage as well as some insight into the gains and income redistributions associated with free trade and the consequences of barriers to trade are provided in Appendix 1A to the chapter under the title, "The Origins and Consequences of International Trade"
- Determination of exchange rates and the role of expectations in determining exchange rates (Chapter 2)
- Extensive discussion of the impacts of foreign exchange market intervention (Chapter 2)
- Extensive discussion of the causes and consequences of the Asian and other emerging market currency crises in 1997–1998 (Chapters 2 and 3)
- Analysis of the September 1992 and August 1993 European currency crises (Chapter 3)
- Discussion of monetary union, optimum currency areas, and the causes and consequences of the introduction of the euro (Chapter 3)
- Integrated discussion of the five key parity relationships in international finance and how they can be used to forecast exchange rates (Chapter 4)
- Discussion of recent research on biases in the forward exchange rate and possible causes, including the peso problem (Chapter 4)
- Discussion on linking currency forecasts to specific decision rules (Chapter 4)
- Use of the balance-of-payments framework to assess the economic links among nations (Chapter 5)
- Demonstration of double-entry bookkeeping in balance-of-payments accounting (Chapter 5)
- Comprehensive discussion of the foreign exchange market and its institutions and mechanisms, including electronic trading (Chapter 6)
- Understanding of currency futures and options contracts (Chapter 7), and their use in exchange risk management (Chapter 9)
- Presentation on how to compute gains, losses, and maintenance margins on a futures contract (Chapter 7)

- Use of interest rate and currency swaps to manage foreign exchange and interest rate risk (Chapter 8)
- Discussion of interest-rate risk management techniques, including forward rate agreements, forward forwards, and Eurodollar futures (Chapter 8)
- Discussion and comparison of the three basic types of exposure–accounting exposure, transaction exposure, and operating exposure (Chapter 9)
- Extended discussion on the design of a hedging strategy (Chapter 9)
- Discussion of managing the risk management function, including lessons learned from some highly publicized cases of derivatives-related losses (Chapter 9)
- Use of currency risk sharing in international contracts (Chapter 9)
- Comparison of hedging alternatives when there are transaction costs (Chapter 9)
- Discussion of cross-hedging using a simple regression analysis (Chapter 9)
- Discussion of how to structure and use currency collars (or range forwards) and currency cylinders to hedge exchange risk (Chapter 9)
- Identification of the economic, as opposed to accounting, aspects of foreign exchange risk (Chapter 10)
- Presentation on identifying and calculating economic exposure for several companies (Chapter 10)
- Development of marketing and production strategies to cope with exchange risk (Chapter 10)
- Analysis of how Japanese firms have coped with the appreciation of the yen (Chapter 10)
- Discussion of country risk analysis for both companies and banks, along with an analysis of the dramatic changes taking place throughout Latin America, Eastern Europe, and China and their implications for economic growth (Chapter 11)
- Discussion of strategies for managing political risk (Appendix 11A in Chapter 11)
- Discussion of the functions, consequences, and globalization of financial markets and the links between national and international capital markets (Chapter 12)
- Discussion of the Eurocurrency and Eurobond markets (Chapter 12)
- Discussion of how to calculate the effective costs of Eurocurrency loans and Eurocommercial paper and all-in costs of Eurobonds (Chapter 12)
- Understanding of the nature and consequences of international portfolio investment (Chapter 13)
- Discussion of the home bias in international portfolio investing and the effects of hedging on the efficient frontier for internationally diversified portfolios (Chapter 13)
- Analysis of exchange risk associated with foreign portfolio investments (Chapter 13)
- Extended discussion of calculating the cost of capital for multinational corporations (Chapter 14)
- Discussion of alternative approaches to estimating the cost of capital for foreign operations (Chapter 14)
- Detailed presentation on how to appraise foreign projects (Chapter 14)
- Analysis of cash flow and risk issues in foreign investments (Chapter 14)
- Discussion on the establishment of a worldwide capital structure (Chapter 14)
- Elaboration of payment terms, documentation, and financing techniques in international trade (Chapter 15)

- Calculation of the cost of acceptance financing and factoring (Chapter 15)
- Role of countertrade in financing international trade (Chapter 15)
- Elaboration of the key issues in short-term financing (Chapter 15)
- Costs and benefits of managing interaffiliate fund flows on a global basis (Chapter 16)
- Discussion of new transfer pricing issues and "earnings-stripping" charges involving foreign company operations in the United States (Chapter 16)
- Issues in the design of a global remittance policy (Chapter 16)

CHANGES TO THE SIXTH EDITION

Overall, the book has been updated and shortened. Specific changes that have been made to the sixth edition of *Foundations of Multinational Financial Management* include the following:

- The book is now divided into five parts rather than six, with integration of content from omitted chapters into other chapters. Part I on the Environment of International Financial Management has been modified to include discussion of multinational corporations in the very first chapter. The chapter on country risk has been moved now to Chapter 11. Other sections of the book have also been significantly modified and/or rearranged. Parts II and III remain titled Foreign Exchange and Derivatives Markets, and Foreign Exchange Risk Management, respectively. A new Part IV, Foreign Markets and Investments, now contains the chapters on country risk analysis, debt financing, portfolio investing, and evaluation of foreign investments. The new Part V titled Financing and Controlling Multinational Operations wraps up the edition with chapters on international financing and the management of the multinational financial system.

- Part I now contains only 5 chapters instead of 6. Chapter 1 has been modified to include discussion on the evolution and spread of multinational corporations from the previous Chapter 16, which has now been eliminated. Chapters 2 to 5 lay the foundations for understanding exchange rates, the international monetary system, currency forecasting, and balance of payments.

- Part II contains chapters that elaborate on the functions and functioning of foreign exchange markets, currency futures and options, and swaps and interest rate derivatives. Thus, Part II provides all the essential concepts and theories for understanding foreign exchange and derivatives markets, including strategies that would enable future managers to better manage their currency and interest rate risks.

- Part III contains important chapters on foreign exchange risk management, including the measurement and management of accounting and economic risks in foreign transactions and operations.

- Managing multinational financial decisions is the core focus of Parts IV and V. Part IV begins with the old chapter 6 on country risk, now renumbered as Chapter 11, and then uses these concepts in later chapters on financing options, portfolio investing and appraisal of foreign investment projects. Chapter 13 on Euromarkets in the previous edition has been merged with the revised Chapter 12 on International Financing and National Capital Markets in the current edition. A revised version of Chapter 15 on International Portfolio Investment from the previous edition is now the new Chapter 13. Also, Chapter 14 on the Cost of Capital and Chapter 17 on Capital Budgeting have been combined into an extensively revised Chapter 14 in the new edition under the title Capital Budgeting for the Multinational Corporation. Thus, the three chapters in Part V from the previous edition have now been incorporated into Part IV. As noted above, Chapter 15 is the new Chapter 13, and Chapter 17 has been merged with Chapter 14 to form the new Chapter 14. Parts of Chapter 16 have been merged into Chapter 1 in Part I.

- In the previous edition, Part VI contained three chapters covering foreign trade financing (Chapter 18), short-term financing (Chapter 19), and managing the multinational financial system (Chapter 20). The chapters on foreign trade financing and short-term financing have now been combined to form the new Chapter 15 on Foreign Trade and Short-term Financing. Chapter 20 in a revised form is now the new Chapter 16. All these chapters now comprise Part V of this edition.

At the same time that the book has been updated, reorganized, and shortened, new material has been added, including the following:

- Many new solved numerical problems in the body of the chapters to illustrate the application of the various concepts and techniques presented in the text, along with new end-of-chapter problems.
- Wherever applicable, illustrations involving exchange rates have been updated to reflect exchange rates current at the time of writing.
- Much more discussion of China, its new role in the world economy and its various economic policies, such as its weak yuan exchange rate policy (see Chapters 1, 2, 3, and 11).

The book also contains many new charts and illustrations of corporate practice that are designed to highlight specific techniques or teaching points. Again, the emphasis is on reinforcing and making more relevant the concepts developed in the body of each chapter. To make the text more suitable as a teaching vehicle, we have added numerous questions and problems at the end of each chapter, most of which are based on up-to-date information and real-life situations.

PEDAGOGY

The pedagogical thrust of the book is greatly enhanced by including the following learning and teaching aids:

1. Focus on Corporate Practice. Throughout the text, numerous real-world examples and vignettes provide actual applications of financial concepts and theories. They show students that the issues, tools, and techniques discussed in the book are being applied to day-to-day financial decision making.

2. Extensive Use of Examples and Illustrations. Numerous short illustrations and examples of specific concepts and techniques are scattered throughout the body of most chapters.

3. Lengthier Illustrations of Corporate Practice. A number of longer illustrations of actual company practices appear at the end of key chapters and are designed to demonstrate different aspects of international financial management.

4. Problems and Discussion Questions. There are hundreds of realistic end-of-chapter questions and problems that offer practice in applying the concepts and theories being taught. Many of these questions and problems relate to actual situations and companies.

5. Chapter Learning Objectives. Each chapter opens with a statement of its action-oriented learning objectives. This statement enhances learning by previewing and guiding the reader's understanding of the materials that will be encountered in the chapter.

6. Key Terms. The introduction to each chapter also contains a list of key terms. Placing these terms at the beginning of the chapter gives readers added preparation for what is to come.

7. Key Concepts. Most pages contain one or two key ideas in the margins next to the point where these ideas appear in the text. Highlighting these key ideas serves as an effective study and review tool for students.

8. Mini-cases. Each chapter now has at least one mini-case that briefly presents a situation that illustrates an important concept in that chapter and then has a series of questions to test student understanding of that concept.

9. Each chapter has a section called "Internet Resources and Exercises" that contains a set of relevant websites for that chapter and several exercises that use those websites to address various issues that arise in the chapter.

10. Glossary. The back of the book contains a Glossary that defines all the key terms appearing in the text.

11. Supplements. A complete set of ancillary materials to supplement the text is available for adopters of *Foundations*. One key addition to the ancillary materials for this revised edition is PowerPoint presentation slides for each chapter. The list of available supplements includes:

  • An Instructor's Manual containing detailed solutions to the end-of-chapter questions and problems and tips for teaching each chapter.

  • PowerPoint presentation slides covering each chapter.

  • A Testbank containing over 160 additional questions and problems suitable for use in multiple choice exams.

  • The Study Guide, available on the companion website, contains detailed chapter outlines and a number of solved questions and problems.

  • A companion website to the book that contains chapter summaries, key learning points, illustrative examples and cases and templates for the various formulae presented in the book.

THANKS

We have been greatly aided in developing *Foundations of Multinational Financial Management* by the helpful suggestions of the following reviewers: Robert Aubey, University of Wisconsin; James Baker, Kent State University; Donald T. Buck, Southern Connecticut State University; C. Edward Chang, Deanne Butchey, Florida International University, Mitch Charkiewicz, Central Connecticut State University, Pankaj K. Jain, University of Memphis, Jeong W. Lee, University of North Dakota, Suk Hun Lee, Loyola University Chicago, Ike Mathur, Southern Illinois University, Missouri State University; Jay Choi, Temple University; Robert C. Duvic, University of Texas, Austin; Janice Wickstead Jadlow, Oklahoma State University; Steve Johnson, University of Texas at

El Paso; Boyden C. Lee, New Mexico State University; Marc Lars Lipson, Boston University; Richard K. Lyons, University of California, Berkeley; Dileep Mehta, Georgia State University; Margaret Moore, Franklin University; William Pugh, Auburn University; Bruce Seifert, Old Dominion University; Jay Sultan, Bentley College; Paul J. Swanson, Jr., University of Cincinnati; and Steve Wyatt, University of Cincinnati.

In addition, Gopal Iyer, Florida Atlantic University, and Allen Shen, (CFA) contributed greatly to the revisions undertaken in this edition. Thanks are also due to Aileen Thomas for help in developing the author PowerPoint slides, to Joe Greco for developing additional PowerPoint Presentations and the Test Bank, and to John VanDolen for help in developing the website.

We also thank our families for their support and encouragement. Alan thanks his wife, Diane, as well as his mother and three brothers, for such continual support and encouragement. Likewise, Atulya thanks his wife, Seema, and his mother. We also thank our children (Thomas and Kathryn in the case of Alan and Natasha and Saagar in the case of Atulya) for the (usual) cheerfulness with which they endured the many hours spent revising the sixth edition of this text.

A.C.S.
Pacific Palisades
A.S.
Los Altos Hills

PART I
ENVIRONMENT OF INTERNATIONAL FINANCIAL MANAGEMENT

INTRODUCTION: MULTINATIONAL ENTERPRISE AND MULTINATIONAL FINANCIAL MANAGEMENT

What is prudence in the conduct of every private family can scarce be folly in that of a great kingdom. If a foreign country can supply us with a commodity cheaper than we ourselves can make it, better buy it of them with some part of the produce of our own industry employed in a way in which we have some advantage.

Adam Smith (1776)

CHAPTER LEARNING OBJECTIVES

- To understand the nature and benefits of globalization.
- To explain why multinational corporations are the key players in international economic competition today.
- To understand the motivations for foreign direct investment and the evolution of multinational corporations (MNCs).
- To identify the stages of corporate expansion overseas by which companies gradually become MNCs.

KEY TERMS

absolute advantage
comparative advantage
competitive advantage
creative destruction
economies of scale
efficient market
foreign direct investment (FDI)
global economy
global manager
globalization
global-scanning capability

international diversification
internalization
internationalization
investment decision
investment flows
licensing
market efficiency
market imperfections
multinational corporation (MNC)
terms of trade [from appendix]

A key theme of this book is that companies today operate within a global market-place and can ignore this fact only at their peril. The internationalization of finance and commerce has been brought about by the great advances in transportation, communications, and information processing technology. This development introduces a dramatic new commercial reality—the global market for standardized consumer and industrial products on a previously unimagined scale. It places primary emphasis on the one great thing all markets have in common: the overwhelming desire for dependable, world-class products at aggressively low prices. The international integration of markets also introduces the global competitor, making firms insecure even in their home markets.

The transformation of the world economy has dramatic implications for business. American management, for example, is learning that the United States can no longer be viewed as a huge economy that does a bit of business with secondary economies around the world. Rather, the United States is merely one economy, albeit a very large one, that is part of an extremely competitive, integrated world economic system. To succeed, U.S. companies need great flexibility; they must be able to change corporate policies quickly, as the world market creates new opportunities and challenges. Big Steel, which was virtually the antithesis of this modern model of business practice, paid the price for failing to adjust to the transformation of the world economy. Similarly, non-U.S. companies are finding that they must increasingly turn to foreign markets to source capital and technology and sell their products.

Today's financial reality is that money knows no national boundary. The dollar has become the world's central currency, with billions switched at the flick of an electronic blip from one global corporation to another, from one central bank to another. The international mobility of capital has benefited firms by giving them more financial options, while at the same time complicating the job of the chief financial officer by increasing its complexity.

Because we operate in an integrated world economy, all students of finance should have an international orientation. Indeed, rarely does a company today, in any country, not have a supplier, competitor, or customer located abroad. Moreover, its domestic suppliers, competitors, and customers likely have their own foreign choices as well. Thus, a key aim of this book is to help you bring to bear on key business decisions a global perspective, manifested by questions such as, where in the *world* should we locate our plants? which *global* market segments should we seek to penetrate? and where in the *world* should we raise our finances? The right answers to these questions would help a manager make decisions that utilize resources from around the world in order to operate efficiently and effectively, obtain superlative performance, and achieve competitive advantage in an increasingly competitive business world.

In this world-oriented corporation, a person's passport is not the criterion for promotion. Nor is a firm's citizenship a critical determinant of its success. Success depends on a new breed of businessperson: the **global manager**. In a world in which change is the rule and not the exception, the key to international competitiveness is the ability of management to adjust to change and volatility at an ever faster rate. In the words of General Electric's former Chairman Jack Welch, I'm not here to predict the world. "I'm here to be sure I've got a company that is strong enough to respond to whatever happens."[1]

The rapid pace of change means that new global managers need detailed knowledge of their operations. Global managers must know how to make the products, where the raw materials and parts come from, how they get there, the alternatives, where the funds come from, and what their changing relative values do to the bottom line. They must also

---

[1] Quoted in Ronald Henkoff, "How to Plan for 1995," *Fortune*, December 31, 1990, p. 70.

understand the political and economic choices facing key nations and how those choices will affect the outcomes of their decisions.

In making decisions for the global company, managers search their array of plants in various nations for the most cost-effective mix of supplies, components, transport, and funds. All this is done with the constant awareness that the options change and the choices must be made again and again.

The problem of constant change disturbs some managers. It always has. But today's global managers have to anticipate it, understand it, deal with it, and turn it to their company's advantage. The payoff to thinking globally is a quality of decision making that enhances the firm's prospects for survival, growth, and profitability.

1.1 GLOBALIZATION AND ITS CONSEQUENCES

During the past three decades, fundamental political, technological, regulatory, and economic forces have radically changed the global competitive environment. A brief list of some of these forces would include the following:

- Massive deregulation;
- The collapse of Communism;
- The sale of hundreds of billions of dollars of state-owned firms around the world in massive privatizations designed to shrink the public sector;
- The revolution in information technologies;
- The rise in the market for corporate control with its waves of takeovers, mergers, leveraged buyouts, and private equity transactions;
- The jettisoning of statist policies and their replacement by free-market policies in many Third World nations; and
- The unprecedented number of nations submitting themselves to the exacting rigors and standards of the global marketplace.

These forces have combined to usher in an era of brutal price and service competition. The United States is further along than other nations in adapting to this new world economic order, largely because its more open economy has forced its firms to confront rather than hide from competitors. Facing vicious competition at home and abroad, U.S. companies, including such corporate landmarks as IBM, General Motors, Walt Disney, Xerox, American Express, Coca-Cola, and Kodak, have been restructuring and investing heavily in new technologies and marketing strategies to boost their productivity and expand their markets. In addition, the United States has gone further than any other industrialized country in deregulating its financial services, telecommunications, airlines, and trucking industries. The result: Even traditionally sheltered U.S. industries have become far more competitive in recent years, and so has the U.S. workforce. The heightened competitiveness of U.S. firms has in turn compelled European and Japanese rivals to undergo a similar process of restructuring and renewal.

1.1.1 Criticism and Consequences of Globalization

Yet despite the many advantages of operating in a world economy, many powerful interest groups feel threatened by globalization and have fought it desperately. Politicians and labor leaders, unlike corporate leaders, usually take a more parochial view of globalization. Many instinctively denounce local corporations that invest abroad as job "exporters," even though most welcome foreign investors in their own countries as job

---

ILLUSTRATION   *General Electric Discusses the Risks and Benefits of Globalization*

In its 2006 Annual Report (p.57), General Electric (GE) explains the pluses and minuses of its global activities as follows:

> *Our global activities span all geographic regions and primarily encompass manufacturing for local and export markets, import and sale of products produced in other regions, leasing of aircraft, sourcing for our plants domiciled in other global regions and provision of financial services within these regional economies. Thus, when countries or regions experience currency and/or economic stress, we often have increased exposure to certain risks but also often have new profit opportunities. Potential increased risks include, among other things, higher receivables delinquencies and bad debts, delays or cancellation of sales and orders principally related to power and aircraft equipment, higher local currency financing costs and a slowdown in established financial services activities. New profit opportunities include, among other things, more opportunities for lower cost outsourcing, expansion of industrial and financial services activities through purchases of companies or assets at reduced prices and lower U.S. debt financing costs.*

---

creators. However, many U.S. citizens today view the current tide of American asset sales to foreign companies as a dangerous assault on U.S. sovereignty.[2] They are unaware, for example, that foreign-owned companies account for more than 20% of industrial production in Germany and more than 50% in Canada, and neither of these countries appears to have experienced the slightest loss of sovereignty. Regardless of their views, however, the global rationalization of production will continue, as it is driven by global competition. The end result will be higher living standards brought about by improvements in worker productivity and private sector efficiency.

The economic purpose of free trade is to allocate resources to their highest valued use. This process is not painless. Like technological innovation, globalization unleashes the forces of **creative destruction**, a process described by economist Joseph Schumpeter more than 50 years ago. Schumpeter's oft-repeated phrase conveys the essence of capitalism: continuous change—out with the old, in with the new. When competing for customers, companies adopt new technologies, improve production methods, explore new markets, and introduce new and better products. In this constantly churning world, some industries advance, others recede, jobs are gained and lost, businesses boom and go bust, some workers are forced to change jobs and even occupations. But the process of globalization creates more winners than losers. Consumers clearly benefit from lower prices and expanded choice. But workers and businesses overall also benefit from doing things that they are best suited for and by having new job and investment opportunities. The end result is economic progress, with economies emerging from the turmoil more efficient, more productive, and wealthier.

Ultimately, the consequences of globalization are an empirical issue. If the anti-free traders were right, the United States, with one of the most liberal trading regimes in the world and facing intense competitive pressure from low-cost imports across a range of industries, would be losing jobs by the millions. Instead, as Exhibit 1.1 shows,

---

[2] The importance of foreign investment in the United States is indicated by a few facts: Four of America's six major music labels are now foreign-owned; Goodyear is the last major American-owned tire manufacturer; in 2006, Japanese auto companies had the capacity to build 4.3 million cars a year in their U.S. plants, over 25% of the total in a typical sales year; four of Hollywood's largest film companies are foreign-owned; and in July 1995, Zenith, the last of the 21 American-owned, companies manufacturing televisions in the United States was purchased by the South Korean firm LG Group.

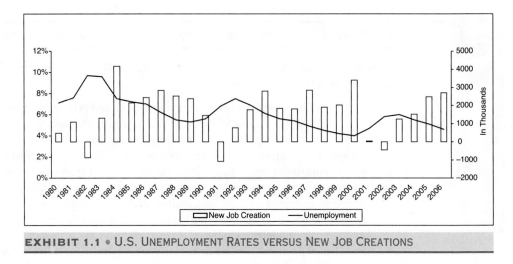

EXHIBIT 1.1 • U.S. UNEMPLOYMENT RATES VERSUS NEW JOB CREATIONS

the United States created over 45 million jobs since 1980, when the competitive pressure from foreign imports intensified dramatically. The unemployment rate also fell during this period, from 7.2% in 1980 to 4.5% in 2006. Moreover, according to the foes of globalization, intensifying competition from low-cost foreign workers is driving down average worker compensation (wages and benefits) in the United States, both in absolute terms and also relative to foreign workers. Once again, the facts are inconsistent with the claims. Exhibit 1.2 shows that U.S. worker compensation has steadily risen and it shows why. The answer is productivity: As output per hour (the standard measure of worker productivity) has gone up so has inflation-adjusted worker compensation. The key to higher compensation, therefore, is increased productivity, not trade protectionism. In fact, increased trade leads to higher productivity and, therefore, higher average wages and benefits. Moreover, Exhibit 1.3 shows that over time the income advantage Americans enjoy relative to the world overall has risen not fallen, from 5.4 in 1970 to 6.7 in 2006. These empirical facts point to a larger reality: Globalization is not a zero-sum game, where for some to win others must lose. Instead, international trade and investment expand the total economic pie, enabling nations to get richer together.

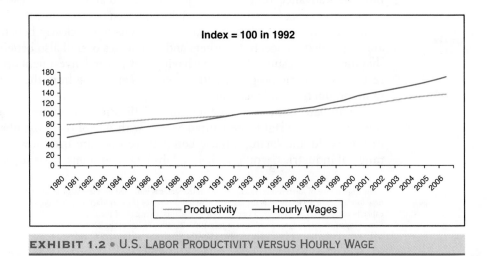

EXHIBIT 1.2 • U.S. LABOR PRODUCTIVITY VERSUS HOURLY WAGE

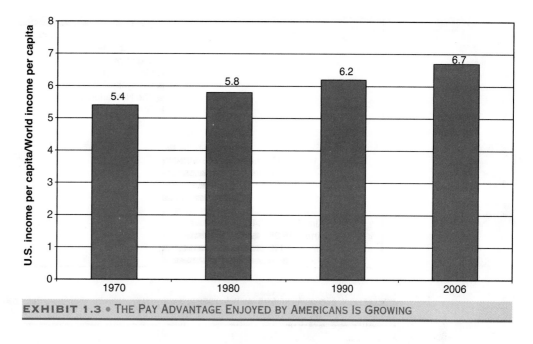

EXHIBIT 1.3 • THE PAY ADVANTAGE ENJOYED BY AMERICANS IS GROWING

🌐 **ILLUSTRATION** *The Myth of a Deindustrializing America*

The share of workers employed in manufacturing in the United States has declined steadily since 1960, from 26% then to about 10.8% in 2006. It is an article of faith among protectionists that these manufacturing jobs have been lost to low-cost labor in China, India, Mexico, Brazil, and the rest of the developing world. According to the doomsayers, the answer to these job losses and the hollowing out of American industry is protectionism.

The truth turns out to be more complex. In fact, manufacturing jobs are disappearing worldwide. A study of employment trends in 20 economies found that between 1995 and 2002, more than 22 million factory jobs disappeared.[3] Moreover, the United States

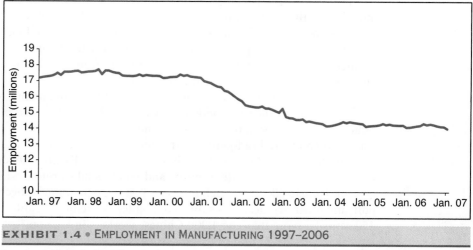

EXHIBIT 1.4 • EMPLOYMENT IN MANUFACTURING 1997–2006

http://www.bls.gov/iag/manufacturing.htm

---

[3] U.S. Economic and Investment Perspective—Manufacturing Payrolls Declining Globally: The Untold Story (Parts 1 and 2), New York, AllianceBernstein Institutional Capital Management, October 10 and 24, 2003.

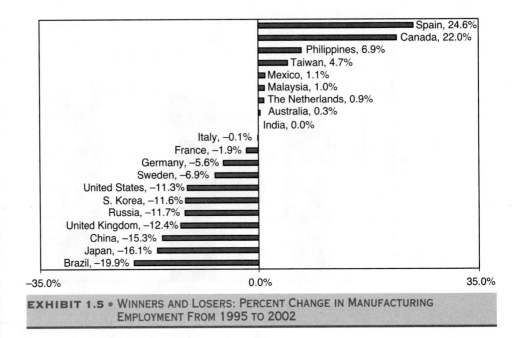

EXHIBIT 1.5 • WINNERS AND LOSERS: PERCENT CHANGE IN MANUFACTURING EMPLOYMENT FROM 1995 TO 2002

has not even been the biggest loser. As Exhibit 1.5 shows, the distinction goes to Brazil, which lost almost 20% of its manufacturing jobs during that period. China, the usual villain, saw a 15% drop. In fact, the real culprit is higher productivity.

All over the world, factories are becoming more efficient. With new equipment, better technology, and better manufacturing processes factories can turn out more products employing fewer workers. Indeed, between 1995 and 2002, factory production worldwide jumped by 30% even as factory employment fell by 11%. In the United States, even as millions of factory jobs were lost, factory output has more than doubled in the past 30 years. Indeed, despite China being acclaimed as the new workshop of the world, the United States remains the world's largest manufacturer. Because of its higher productivity, the United States manufactures twice as many goods as China even though China has around six times as many manufacturing workers.

Manufacturing is being transformed the same way that farming was. In 1910, one out of every three American workers was a farmer. By 2000, with the advent of tractors and other technology, it was less than one in 33 even as U.S. food output has increased dramatically. As such, postponing the expiration date of some U.S. manufacturing jobs through protectionist policies diverts resources from new, growing industries toward keeping dying U.S. industries alive for a little while longer.

It is also important to distinguish between the outsourcing of manufacturing and the outsourcing of the value added associated with manufactured products. Consider, for example, the wireless mouse named Wanda sold by Logitech International SA, a Swiss-American company headquartered in California. The mice are made in Suzhou, China, and sold to American consumers for around $40. As Exhibit 1.6 shows, of this amount, Logitech takes about $8, distributors and retailers take around $15, and parts suppliers get $14. China's take from each mouse is just $3, which must cover wages, power, transport, and other overhead costs. Indeed, Logitech's Fremont, California, marketing staff of 450 earns far more than the 4,000 Chinese workers in Suzhou.[4]

---

[4] Information on. Logitech's Wanda mouse appears in Andrew Higgins, 'As China Surges, It Also Proves a Buttress to American Strength, The *Wall Street Journal*, January 30, 2004, A1.

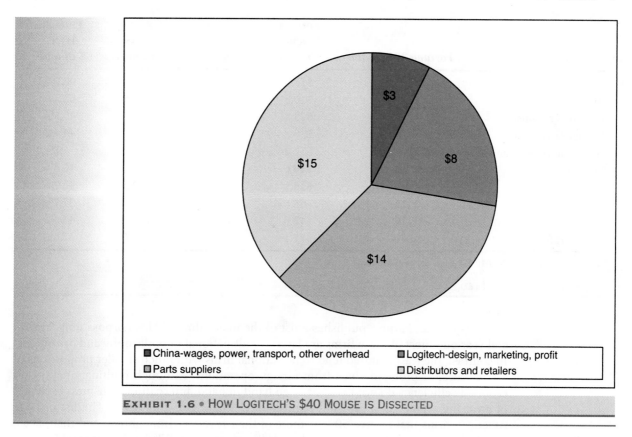

EXHIBIT 1.6 • HOW LOGITECH'S $40 MOUSE IS DISSECTED

1.2 THE RISE OF THE MULTINATIONAL CORPORATION

A **multinational corporation** (MNC) is a company engaged in producing and selling goods or services in more than one country. It ordinarily consists of a parent company located in the home country and at least five or six foreign subsidiaries, typically with a high degree of strategic interaction among the units. Some MNCs have upward of 100 foreign subsidiaries scattered around the world. The United Nations Conference on Trade and Development (UNCTAD) estimated in its World Investment Report for 2006 that at least 77,000 companies around the world can be classified as multinational. These parent companies, and their estimated 770,000 foreign affiliates, generated about $4.5 trillion in value added, employed 62 million people, and exported goods and services valued at more than $4 trillion in 2005.[5]

What differentiates the multinational enterprise from other firms engaged in international business is the globally coordinated allocation of resources by a single centralized management. MNCs make decisions about market-entry strategy; ownership of foreign operations; and design, production, marketing, and financial activities with an eye to what is best for the corporation as a whole. A true MNC emphasizes group performance rather than the performance of its individual parts. For example, in 2003, Whirlpool Corporation launched what it billed as the world's cheapest washing machine, with an eye on low-income consumers who never thought they could afford one. Whirlpool designed and developed the Ideale washing machine in Brazil, but it manufactures the Ideale in China and India, as well as Brazil, for sale in those and other developing countries.

---

[5] UNCTAD, World Investment Report 2006. New York and Geneva: United Nations, 2006, p. xviii.

	Fortune 2007 Rank	*Foreign Revenue ($ billions)*	*Foreign Revenue (% of total)*	*Foreign Assets ($ billions)*	*Foreign Assets (% of total)*
General Electric	1	$77.8	87.0%	$310.5	90.0%
Apple Computer	7	$10.8	53.6%	$1.5	62.3%
Johnson & Johnson	9	$23.5	44.2%	$18.8	45.5%
Procter & Gamble	10	$38.8	56.8%	$60.3	44.4%
Goldman Sachs Group	11	$17.3	45.9%	N/A	N/A
Microsoft	12	$14.6	32.9%	$0.8	10.6%
3M	14	$14.1	61.4%	$2.5	42.7%
American Express	17	$8.8	32.3%	$48.2	37.7%
PepsiCo	19	$13.0	36.9%	$11.3	45.4%
Wal-Mart Stores	19	$77.1	22.3%	$56.0	37.0%

Source: Company 2006–2007 10-K Filings. Segment Reporting.

EXHIBIT 1.7 • SELECTED LARGE U.S. MULTINATIONALS

Every year, *Fortune* publishes a list of the most admired U.S. corporations. Year in and year out, most of these firms are largely multinational in philosophy and operations. In contrast, the least admired tend to be national firms with much smaller proportions of assets, sales, or profits derived from foreign operations. Although multinationality and economic efficiency do not necessarily go hand in hand, international business is clearly of great importance to a growing number of U.S. and non-U.S. firms. The list of large American firms that receive 50% or more of their revenues from abroad and that have a sizable fraction of their assets abroad reads like a corporate *Who's Who*: General Electric, Apple Computer, Procter & Gamble, IBM Corp. Colgate-Palmolive, Coca-Cola Co., Nike Inc., Hewlett-Packard Co., McDonald's Corp., ExxonMobil Corp., Avon Products Inc, and 3M. In 2006, General Electric obtained 87% of its revenues from outside the U.S.

Industries differ greatly in the extent to which foreign operations are of importance to them. For example, oil companies and banks are far more heavily involved overseas than are tobacco companies and automakers. Even within industries, companies differ in their commitment to international business. For example, in 2006, ExxonMobil had 69.1% of its sales, 70.8% of its assets, and 71.6% of its profits abroad. The corresponding figures for Valero, the largest refiner in North America, were 12%, 13%, and 7.5%. Similarly, General Motors generated 37.8% of its revenues overseas, in contrast to the 49.3% of revenues from overseas operations for Ford. Other examples of the importance of foreign operations to U.S. business are shown in Exhibit 1.7.

The degree of internationalization of the American economy is often surprising. For example, Hollywood's revenues from foreign markets have been increasing in the past decade, with more films in recent years grossing upwards of $200 million from foreign markets alone.[6] The film industry illustrates other dimensions of internationalization as well, many of which are reflected in *Total Recall*, a film that was made by a Hungarian-born producer and a Dutch director, starred an Austrian-born leading man (now the governor of California) and a Canadian villain, was shot in Mexico, and was distributed by a Hollywood studio owned by a Japanese firm.

Exhibit 1.8 provides further evidence of the growing **internationalization** of American business. It shows that overseas investment by U.S. firms and U.S. investment by foreign firms are in the hundreds of billions of dollars each year. **Foreign direct**

---

[6] Hollywood's Global Warming, *Variety*, January 3–9, 2005.

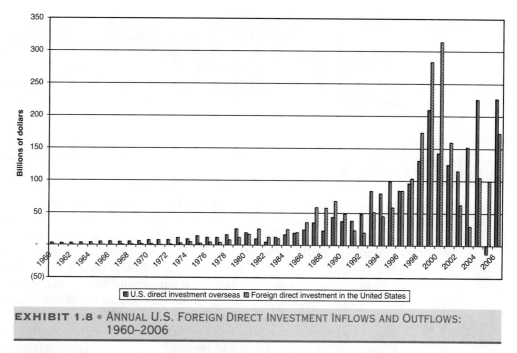

EXHIBIT 1.8 • ANNUAL U.S. FOREIGN DIRECT INVESTMENT INFLOWS AND OUTFLOWS: 1960–2006

Source: Bureau of Economic Analysis: U.S. Department of Commerce.

investment (FDI) is the acquisition abroad of companies, properties or physical assets such as plant and equipment. The stock of FDI by U.S. companies reached $2.05 trillion in 2005 while direct investment by foreign companies in the United States exceeded $1.625 trillion that year.[7] Worldwide, the stock of FDI reached $10.1 trillion in 2005, as shown in Exhibit 1.9. Moreover, these investments have grown steadily over time,

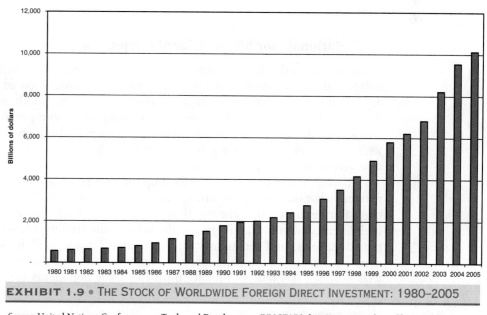

EXHIBIT 1.9 • THE STOCK OF WORLDWIDE FOREIGN DIRECT INVESTMENT: 1980–2005

Source: United Nations Conference on Trade and Development (UNCTAD). http//stats.unctad.org/dfi/eng/tableviewer

---

[7] UNCTAD, World Investment Report, 2006.

facilitated by a combination of factors: falling regulatory barriers to overseas investment; rapidly declining telecommunications and transport costs; and freer domestic and international capital markets in which vast sums of money can be raised, companies can be bought, and currency and other risks can be hedged. These factors have made it easier for companies to invest abroad, to do so more cheaply, and to experience less risk than ever before.

ILLUSTRATION *The Rise of China*

Perhaps the most dramatic change in the international economy over the past decade is the rise of China as a global competitor. From 1978, when Deng Xiaoping launched his country's economic reform program, to 2006, China's gross domestic product (GDP) rose by 9.67% annually, the most rapid growth rate of any country in the world during this 28-year period. Since 1991, China has attracted the largest amount of foreign investment among developing countries each year, with annual foreign investment by the late 1990s exceeding $50 billion. Since 2002, China has been the world's number-one destination for FDI, attracting $72.4 billion in FDI flows in 2005.[8] About 400 out of the world's 500 largest companies have now invested in China. It is estimated that by the end of 2006, about 590,000 foreign firms had invested in China.[9] The transformation of China from an insular nation to the world's low-cost site for labor-intensive manufacturing has had enormous effects on everything from Mexico's competitiveness as an export platform to the cost of furniture and computers in the United States to the value of the dollar to the number of U.S. manufacturing jobs.

The prime transmitter of competitive forces in this global economy is the multinational corporation. For example, in 2005, 58% of all exports from China were by foreign-owned companies manufacturing in China.[10]

1.2.1 Rationale for Multinational Corporations

Based in part on the development of modern communications and transportation technologies, the rise of the multinational corporation was unanticipated by the classical theory of international trade as first developed by Adam Smith and David Ricardo. According to this theory, which rests on the doctrine of **comparative advantage**, each nation should specialize in the production and export of those goods that it can produce with highest relative efficiency and import those goods that other nations can produce relatively more efficiently.

Underlying this theory is the assumption that goods and services can move internationally but factors of production, such as capital, labor, and land, are relatively immobile. Furthermore, the theory deals only with trade in commodities—that is, undifferentiated products; it ignores the roles of uncertainty, economies of scale, transportation costs, and technology in international trade; and it is static rather than dynamic. Despite all these defects, however, it is a valuable theory, and it still provides a well-reasoned theoretical foundation for free-trade arguments (see Appendix 1A). But

---

[8] World Investment Report 2006, p. 51.

[9] Investment Shanghai, "China's GDP Grows Annual Average of 9.67% from 1978 to 2006," http://www.investment.gov.cn/2007-05-08/1175476363888.html

[10] Salil Tripathi, "The Dragon Tamers," *The Guardian*, August 11, 2006.

the growth of the MNC can be understood only by relaxing the traditional assumptions of classical trade theory.

Classical trade theory implicitly assumes that countries differ enough in terms of resource endowments and economic skills for those differences to be at the center of any analysis of corporate competitiveness. Differences among individual corporate strategies are considered to be of only secondary importance; a company's citizenship is the key determinant of international success in the world of Adam Smith and David Ricardo.

This theory, however, is becoming increasingly irrelevant to the analysis of businesses in the countries currently at the core of the world economy—the United States, Japan, the nations of Western Europe, and to an increasing extent, the most successful East Asian countries. Within this advanced and highly integrated core economy, differences among corporations are becoming more important than aggregate differences among countries. Furthermore, the increasing capacity of even small companies to operate in a global perspective makes the old analytical framework even more obsolete.

Not only are the "core nations" more homogeneous than before in terms of living standards, lifestyles, and economic organization, but their factors of production tend to move more rapidly in search of higher returns. Natural resources have lost much of their previous role in national specialization as advanced, knowledge-intensive societies move rapidly into the age of artificial materials and genetic engineering. Capital moves around the world in massive amounts practically at the speed of light; increasingly, corporations raise capital simultaneously in several major markets. Labor skills in these countries no longer can be considered fundamentally different; many of the students enrolled in American business schools are foreign, while training has become a key dimension of many joint ventures between international corporations. Technology and know-how are also rapidly becoming a global pool, with companies like Microsoft, General Electric, Morgan Stanley, Electronic Data Systems, Cisco Systems, McKinsey & Co., and IBM shifting software writing, accounting, engineering, and other skilled services to countries like India and China.

Against this background, the ability of corporations of all sizes to use these globally available factors of production is a far bigger factor in international competitiveness than broad macroeconomic differences among countries. The very existence of the multinational enterprise is based on the international mobility of certain factors of production. Capital raised in London on the Eurodollar market may be used by a Swiss-based pharmaceutical firm to finance the acquisition of German equipment by a subsidiary in Brazil. A single Barbie doll is made in 10 countries—designed in California, with parts and clothing from Japan, China, Hong Kong, Malaysia, Indonesia, Korea, Italy, and Taiwan, assembled in Mexico—and sold in 144 countries. Information technology also makes it possible for worker skills to flow with little regard to borders. In the semiconductor industry, the leading companies typically locate their design facilities in high-tech corridors in the United States, Japan, and Europe. Finished designs are transported quickly by computer networks to manufacturing plants in countries with more advantageous cost structures. In effect, the traditional world economy in which products are exported has been replaced by one in which value is added in several different countries.

The movement and deployment of factors of production across borders, and therefore, the rise of the multinational corporation, may be prompted by several considerations, including the search for the best production locations in terms of cost-efficiency, or the best markets in terms of profitability. Below are some of the major reasons for the evolution of MNCs.

Search for Raw Materials Raw-material seekers were the earliest multinationals, the villains of international business. They were the firms—the British, Dutch, and French

East India Companies, the Hudson's Bay Trading Company, and the Union Miniere Haut-Katanga—that first grew under the protective mantle of the British, Dutch, French, and Belgian colonial empires. Their aim was to exploit the raw materials that could be found overseas. The modern-day counterparts of these firms, the multinational oil and mining companies, were the first to make large foreign investments, beginning in the early years of the twentieth century. Hence, large oil companies such as British Petroleum and Standard Oil, which went where the dinosaurs died, were among the first true multinationals. Hard-mineral companies such as International Nickel, Anaconda Copper, and Kennecott Copper were also early investors abroad.

Market Seeking   The market seeker is the archetype of the modern multinational firm that goes overseas to produce and sell in foreign markets. Examples include IBM, Volkswagen, and Unilever. Similarly, branded consumer-products companies such as Nestlé, Levi Strauss, McDonald's, Procter & Gamble, and Coca-Cola have been operating abroad for decades and maintain vast manufacturing, marketing, and distribution networks from which they derive substantial sales and income.

While foreign markets may be attractive in and of themselves, MNCs possess certain firm-specific advantages, which may include unique products, processes, technologies, patents, specific rights or specific knowledge, and skills. MNCs find that the advantages that were successfully applied in domestic markets can also be profitably used in foreign markets. Firms such as Wal-Mart, Toys 'R' Us, and Price/Costco take advantage of unique process technologies, largely in the form of superior information gathering, organizational, and distribution skills, to sell overseas.

The exploitation of additional foreign markets may be possible at considerably lower costs. For example, after developing a drug successfully, pharmaceutical companies enter several markets, obtain relevant patents and permissions, and begin marketing the product in several countries within a short period of time. Marketing of the product in multiple countries enables the pharmaceutical company to extract revenues from multiple markets and therefore, cover the high costs of drug development in a shorter period of time as compared to marketing within a single country.

In some industries, foreign market entry may be essential for obtaining **economies of scale**, or the unit cost decreases that are achieved through volume production. Firms in industries characterized by high fixed costs relative to variable costs must engage in volume selling just to break even. These large volumes may be forthcoming only if the firms expand overseas. For example, companies manufacturing products such as computers that require huge R&D expenditures often need a larger customer base than that provided by even a market as large as the United States in order to recapture their investment in knowledge. Similarly, firms in capital-intensive industries with enormous production economies of scale may also be forced to sell overseas in order to spread their overhead over a larger quantity of sales.

L.M. Ericsson, the Swedish manufacturer of telecommunications equipment, is an extreme case. The manufacturer is forced to think internationally when designing new products because its domestic market is too small to absorb the enormous R&D expenditures involved and to reap the full benefit of production scale economies. Thus, when Ericsson developed its revolutionary AXE digital switching system, it geared its design to achieve global market penetration.

Some companies, such as Coca-Cola, McDonald's, Nestlé, and Procter & Gamble, take advantage of enormous advertising expenditures and highly developed marketing skills to differentiate their products and keep out potential competitors that are wary of the high marketing costs of new-product introduction. Expansion into emerging markets enables these firms to enjoy the benefits of economies of scale as well as exploit

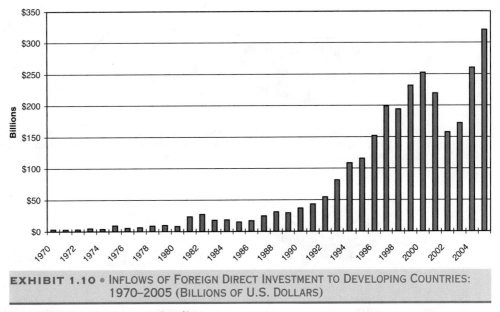

EXHIBIT 1.10 • INFLOWS OF FOREIGN DIRECT INVESTMENT TO DEVELOPING COUNTRIES: 1970–2005 (BILLIONS OF U.S. DOLLARS)

Source: UNCTAD at http://stats.unctad.org/fdi

the premium associated with their strong brand names. Companies such as Nestle and Procter & Gamble expect sales of brand-name consumer goods to soar as disposable incomes rise in developing countries in contrast to the mature markets of Europe and the United States. The costs and risks of taking advantage of these profitable growth opportunities are also lower today now that their more free-market-oriented governments have reduced trade barriers and cut regulations. In response, foreign direct investment in emerging markets by multinationals has soared over the past decade (see Exhibit 1.10).

Cost Minimization   Over time, if competitive advantages in product lines or markets gets eroded due to local and global competition, MNCs seek and enter new markets with little competition or seek out lower production cost sites through their global-scanning capability. Costs can then be minimized by combining production shifts with **rationalization** and **integration** of the firm's manufacturing facilities worldwide. This strategy usually involves plants specializing in different stages of production, for example, in assembly or fabrication, as well as in particular components or products.

Necessary complements to the integration of worldwide operations are flexibility, adaptability, and speed. Indeed, speed has become one of the critical competitive weapons in the fight for world market share. The ability to develop, manufacture, and distribute products or services quickly enables companies to capture customers who demand constant innovation and rapid, flexible response. Exhibit 1.11 illustrates the combination of globally integrated activities and rapid response times of Dell Inc., which keeps not more than 2 hours of inventory in its plants, while sourcing for components across the globe and assembling built-to-order computers for its customers within 5 days.

One strategy that is often followed by firms for which cost is the key consideration is to develop a **global-scanning capability** to seek out lower-cost production sites or production technologies worldwide. In fact, firms in competitive industries have to continually seize new, nonproprietary, cost-reduction opportunities, not to earn excess returns but to make normal profits and survive.

Customer places an order for a Dell computer through the phone or Internet.

Order is analyzed for financial (customer credit checks) and sent to manufacturing facility.

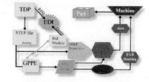

Manufacturing facility analyzes technical configuration details for component requirements and requests component parts from suppliers

Suppliers located in other countries send components by air. Component parts are aggregated on specific flights with an average of three flights daily from Asia. (One Boeing 747 can carry enough parts to manufacture 10,000 PCs)

Manufacturing facility receives the parts and assembles computers as per each customer's order specifications

Assembled computer is ready for shipping to the consumer no later than 5 days after receiving the order. If a customer requests next-day delivery, a built-to-order computer is delivered on the sixth day.

EXHIBIT 1.11 • HOW DELL REDUCES THE ORDER-TO-DELIVERY CYCLE

ILLUSTRATION   *Honda Builds an Asian Car Factory*

Honda and other automakers attempting to break into Asia's small but potentially fast-growing auto markets face a problem: it is tough to start small. Automakers need big volumes to take full advantage of economies of scale and justify the cost of building a modern car plant. But outside of Japan and China, few Asian countries offer such scale. Companies such as General Motors and Ford are relying on an export strategy in all but the largest Asian markets to overcome this hurdle GM, for example, exports cars throughout Asia from a large plant in Thailand. However, the success of an export strategy depends on Asian countries fully embracing free trade, something that may not happen soon. Honda has decided to follow a different strategy. It is essentially building a car factory that spans all of Asia, putting up plants for different components in small Asian markets all at once: a transmission plant in Indonesia, engine-parts manufacturing in China, and other components operations in Malaysia. Honda assembles cars at its existing plants in the region. Its City subcompact, for example, is assembled in Thailand from parts made there and in nearby countries. By concentrating production of individual components in certain countries, Honda expects to reap economies of scale that are unattainable by setting up major factories in each of the small Asian markets. A sharp reduction in trade barriers across Asia that took effect in 2003 has made it easier for Honda to trade among its factories in Asia. Nonetheless, Asian countries are expected to still focus on balancing trade so that, in any given nation, an increase in imports is offset by an increase in exports. If so, Honda's web of Asian manufacturing facilities could give it an advantage over its rivals in avoiding trade friction.

Cost minimizer is a fairly recent category of firms doing business internationally. These firms seek out and invest in lower cost production sites overseas (for example, Hong

Kong, Taiwan, and Ireland) to remain cost-competitive both at home and abroad. Many of these firms are in the electronics industry. Examples include Texas Instruments, Intel, and Seagate Technology. Increasingly, companies are shifting services overseas, not just manufacturing work. For example, as of June 2007, GE has about 13,000 employees in India to handle local market sales, software operations, accounting, claims processing, customer service, and sourcing of components for GE's global manufacturing locations. Similarly, companies such as AOL (customer service), American Express (finance and customer service), and British Airways (accounting) have set up call centers and are shifting work to countries such as India, Jamaica, Hungary, Morocco, and the Philippines for savings of up to 60%.

The offshoring of services can be done in two ways: internally, through the establishment of wholly owned foreign affiliates, or externally, by outsourcing a service to a third-party provider. Exhibit 1.12 categorizes and defines different variants of offshoring and outsourcing.

Location of Production	Internalized	Internalized or Externalized Production Externalized ("Outsourcing")
Home Country	Production kept in-house at home	Production outsourced to third-party service provider at home.
Foreign Country	Production by foreign affiliate, e.g., Infineion's center in Dublin	Production outsourced to third-party provider abroad To local company e.g.,
	DHL's IT center in Prague British Telecom's call centers in Bangalore and Hyderabad "Intra-firm (captive) offshoring"	Bank of America's outsourcing of software development to Infosys in India To Foreign affiliate of another MNC e.g., A U.S. company outsourcing data processing services to ACS in Ghana

EXHIBIT 1.12 • OFF SHORING AND OUTSOURCING: SOME DEFINITIONS

MINI-CASE   *The Debate Over Outsourcing*

In early 2004, White House economist Gregory Mankiw had the misfortune of stating publicly what most economists believe privately—that outsourcing of jobs is a form of international trade and is good for the U.S. economy because it allows Americans to buy services less expensively abroad. Critics of outsourcing immediately called on President Bush to fire Dr. Mankiw for being insensitive to workers who have lost their jobs. It is obvious to these critics that outsourcing, exporting white-collar American jobs to foreign countries, is a major cause of U.S. unemployment. Related criticisms are that outsourcing costs the U.S. good jobs and is a one-way street, with the U.S. outsourcing jobs to foreign countries and getting nothing in return.

These critics fail to see the other side of the coin. First, outsourcing increases U.S. productivity and enables U.S. companies to realize net cost savings on the order of 30 to 50%. Through outsourcing, a firm can cut its costs while improving its quality, time-to-market, and capacity to innovate, and use the abilities of its remaining workers in other, more productive tasks, thereby making it more competitive. Second, it will come as a real surprise to most critics that far more private services are outsourced by foreigners to the United States than away from it. In other words, just as U.S. firms use the services of foreigners, foreign firms make even greater use of the services of U.S. residents. Private services include computer programming, management consulting, engineering, banking, telecommunications, legal work, call centers, data entry, and so on. Exhibit 1.13 shows that in 2006, for example, U.S. firms bought about $114 billion of those services from foreigners but the value of the services Americans sold to foreigners was far higher, over $177 billion, resulting in a trade surplus in private services of about $63 billion. Lastly, outsourced jobs are responsible for less than 1% of unemployment. Recent estimates are that white-collar outsourcing costs the United States about 100,000 jobs each year.[11] In contrast, the U.S. economy loses an average of 15 million jobs annually. However, those jobs are typically replaced by even more jobs, with about 17 million new jobs created each year.[12]

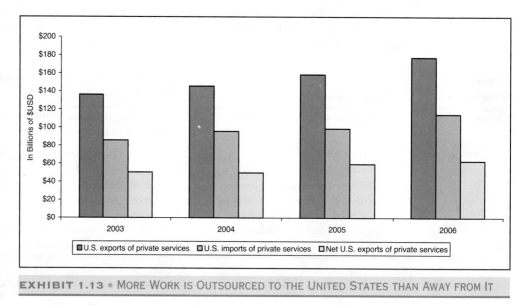

EXHIBIT 1.13 • MORE WORK IS OUTSOURCED TO THE UNITED STATES THAN AWAY FROM IT

Source: Bureau of Economic Analysis: US International Trade in Goods and Services 2005 and 2007, U.S. Department of Commerce.

This creation of new jobs and workers' ability to move into them are the hallmarks of a flexible economy—one in which labor and capital move freely among firms and industries to where they can be most productive. Such flexibility is a significant strength of the U.S. economy and results in higher productivity, which is the only way to create higher standards of living in the long run. Protectionism would only diminish that flexibility. Rather, the focus should be on increasing flexibility, which means improving the performance of the U.S. education system and encouraging the entrepreneurship and innovation that give the United States its competitive edge.

QUESTIONS

1. What are the pros and cons of outsourcing?
2. How does outsourcing affect U.S. consumers and producers?
3. What is the likely long-term impact of outsourcing on American jobs?
4. Several states are contemplating legislation to ban outsourcing of government work to foreign firms. What would be the likely consequences of such legislation?

---

[11] See, for example, Jon E. Hilsenrath, "Behind Outsourcing Debate: Surprisingly Few Hard Numbers," *The Wall Street Journal*, April 12, 2004, A1.

[12] These estimates appear in "Trade and Jobs," Remarks by Governor Ben S. Bernanke at the Distinguished Speaker Series, Fuqua School of Business, Duke University, Durham, North Carolina, March 30, 2004.

Knowledge Seeking   Some firms enter foreign markets to gain information and experience that are expected to prove useful elsewhere. For instance, Beecham, an English firm (now part of GlaxoSmithKline), deliberately set out to learn from its U.S. operations how to be more competitive, first in the area of consumer products and later in pharmaceuticals. This knowledge proved highly valuable in competing with American and other firms in its European markets.

The flow of ideas is not all one-way, however. As Americans have demanded better-built, better-handling, and more fuel-efficient small cars, Ford of Europe has become an important source of design and engineering ideas and management talent for its U.S. parent, notably with the hugely successful Taurus.

In industries characterized by rapid product innovation and technical breakthroughs by foreign competitors, it is imperative to track overseas developments constantly. Japanese firms excel here, systematically and effectively collecting information on foreign innovation and disseminating it within their own research and development (R&D), marketing, and production groups. The analysis of new foreign products as soon as they reach the market is an especially long-lived Japanese technique. One of the jobs of Japanese researchers is to tear down a new foreign product and analyze how it works as a base on which to develop a product of their own that will outperform the original. In a bit of a switch, Data General's Japanese operation is giving the company a close look at Japanese technology, enabling it to quickly pick up and transfer back to the United States new information on Japanese innovations in the areas of computer design and manufacturing.

Keeping Domestic Customers   Suppliers of goods or services to multinationals often will follow their customers abroad in order to guarantee them a continuing product flow. Otherwise, the threat of a potential disruption to an overseas supply line—for example, a dock strike or the imposition of trade barriers—can lead the customer to select a local supplier, which may be a domestic competitor with international operations. Hence, comes the dilemma: Follow your customers abroad or lose not only their foreign but also their domestic business. A similar threat to domestic market share has led many banks, advertising agencies, and accounting, law, and consulting firms to set up foreign practices in the wake of their multinational clients' overseas expansion.

Exploiting Financial Market Imperfections   An alternative explanation for foreign direct investment relies on the existence of financial market imperfections. The ability to reduce taxes and circumvent currency controls may lead to greater project cash flows and a lower cost of funds for the MNC than for a purely domestic firm.

An even more important financial motivation for FDI is likely to be the desire to reduce risks through international diversification. This motivation may be somewhat surprising because the riskiness inherent in the multinational corporation is usually taken for granted. Exchange rate changes, currency controls, expropriation, and other forms of government intervention are some of the risks that purely domestic firms rarely, if ever, encounter. Thus, the greater a firm's international investment, the riskier its operations should be.

Yet, there is good reason to believe that being multinational may actually reduce the riskiness of a firm. Much of the systematic or general market risk affecting a company is related to the cyclical nature of the national economy in which the company is domiciled. Hence, the diversification effect due to operating in a number of countries whose economic cycles are not perfectly in phase should reduce the variability of MNC earnings. Several studies indicate that this result, in fact, is the case.[13] Thus, because foreign cash

---

[13] See, for example, Benjamin I. Cohen, *Multinational Firms and Asian Exports* (New Haven, Conn.: Yale University Press, 1975); and Alan Rugman, "Risk Reduction by International Diversification," *Journal of International Business Studies*, Fall 1976, pp. 75–80.

flows generally are not perfectly correlated with those of domestic investments, the greater riskiness of individual projects overseas can well be offset by beneficial portfolio effects. Furthermore, because most of the economic and political risks specific to an MNC are unsystematic, they can be eliminated through diversification.

1.3 THE PROCESS OF OVERSEAS EXPANSION BY MULTINATIONALS

Studies of corporate expansion overseas indicate that firms become multinational by degree, with FDI being a late step in a process that begins with exports. For most companies, the *globalization process* does not occur through conscious design, at least in the early stages. It is the unplanned result of a series of corporate responses to a variety of threats and opportunities appearing at random abroad. From a broader perspective, however, the globalization of firms is the inevitable outcome of the competitive strivings of members of oligopolistic industries. Each member tries both to create and to exploit monopolistic product and factor advantages internationally while simultaneously attempting to reduce the competitive threats posed by other industry members.

To meet these challenges, companies gradually increase their commitment to international business, developing strategies that are progressively more elaborate and sophisticated. The sequence normally involves exporting, setting up a foreign sales subsidiary, securing licensing agreements, and eventually establishing foreign production. This evolutionary approach to overseas expansion is a risk-minimizing response to operating in a highly uncertain foreign environment. By internationalizing in phases, a firm can gradually move from a relatively low-risk, low-return, export-oriented strategy to a higher risk, higher return strategy emphasizing international production. In effect, the firm is investing in information, learning enough at each stage to improve significantly its chances for success at the next stage. Exhibit 1.14 depicts the usual sequence of overseas expansion.

1.3.1 Exporting

Firms facing highly uncertain demand abroad typically will begin by exporting to a foreign market. The advantages of exporting are significant: Capital requirements and start-up costs are minimal, risk is low, and profits are immediate. Furthermore, this initial step provides the opportunity to learn about present and future supply and demand conditions, competition, channels of distribution, payment conventions, financial institutions, and financial techniques. Building on prior successes, companies then expand their marketing organizations abroad, switching from using export agents and other intermediaries to dealing directly with foreign agents and distributors. As increased communication with customers reduces uncertainty, the firm might set up its own sales subsidiary and new service facilities, such as a warehouse, with these marketing activities culminating in the control of its own distribution system.

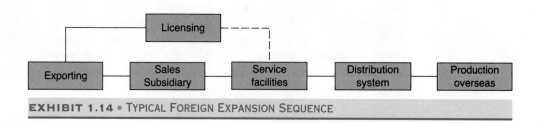

EXHIBIT 1.14 • TYPICAL FOREIGN EXPANSION SEQUENCE

1.3.2 Overseas Production

A major drawback to exporting is the inability to realize the full sales potential of a product. By manufacturing abroad, a company can more easily keep itself abreast of market developments, adapt its products and production schedules to changing local tastes and conditions, fill orders faster, and provide more comprehensive after-sales service. Many companies also set up R&D facilities along with their foreign operations; they aim to pick the best brains, wherever they are. The results help companies keep track of the competition and design new products. For example, the Japanese subsidiary of Loctite, a U.S. maker of engineering adhesives, devised several new applications for sealants in the electronics industry.

Setting up local production facilities also shows a greater commitment to the local market, a move that typically brings added sales and provides increased assurance of supply stability. Certainty of supply is particularly important for firms that produce intermediate goods for sale to other companies. A case in point is SKF, the Swedish ball-bearing manufacturer. It was forced to manufacture in the United States to guarantee that its product, a crucial component in military equipment, would be available when needed. The Pentagon would not permit its suppliers of military hardware to be dependent on imported ball bearings because imports could be halted in wartime and are always subject to the vagaries of ocean shipping.

Thus, most firms selling in foreign markets eventually find themselves forced to manufacture abroad. Foreign production covers a wide spectrum of activities from repairing, packaging, and finishing to processing, assembly, and full manufacture. Firms typically begin with the simpler stages, for example, packaging and assembly, and progressively integrate their manufacturing activities backward—to production of components and subassemblies.

Because the optimal entry strategy can change over time, a firm must continually monitor and evaluate the factors that bear on the effectiveness of its current entry strategy. New information and market perceptions change the risk-return trade-off for a given entry strategy, leading to a sequence of preferred entry modes, each adapted on the basis of prior experience to sustain and strengthen the firm's market position over time.

Associated with a firm's decision to produce abroad is the question of whether to *create* its own affiliates or to *acquire* going concerns. A major advantage of an acquisition is the capacity to effect a speedy transfer overseas of highly developed but underutilized parent skills, such as a novel production technology. Often the local firm also provides a ready-made marketing network. This network is especially important if the parent is a late entrant to the market. Many firms have used the acquisition approach to gain knowledge about the local market or a particular technology. The disadvantage is the cost of buying an ongoing company. In general, the larger and more experienced a firm becomes, the less frequently it uses acquisitions to expand overseas. Smaller and relatively less-experienced firms often turn to acquisitions.

Regardless of its preferences, a firm interested in expanding overseas may not have the option of acquiring a local operation. Michelin, the French manufacturer of radial tires, set up its own facilities in the United States because its tires are built on specially designed equipment; taking over an existing operation would have been out of the question.[14] Similarly, companies moving into developing countries often find they are forced to begin from the ground up because their line of business has no local counterpart.

---

[14] Once that equipment became widespread in the industry, Michelin was able to expand through acquisition which it did in 1989, when it acquired Uniroyal Goodrich.

1.3.3 Licensing

An alternative, and at times a precursor, to setting up production facilities abroad is to *license* a local firm to manufacture the company's products in return for royalties and other forms of payment. The principal advantages of **licensing** are the minimal investment required, faster market-entry time, and fewer financial and legal risks. But the corresponding cash flow is also relatively low, and there may be problems in maintaining product quality standards. The licensor may also face difficulty controlling exports by the foreign licensee, particularly when, as in Japan, the host government refuses to sanction restrictive clauses on sales to foreign markets. Thus, a licensing agreement may lead to the establishment of a competitor in third-country markets, with a consequent loss of future revenues to the licensing firm. The foreign licensee may even become such a strong competitor that the licensing firm will face difficulty entering the market when the agreement expires, leading to a further loss of potential profits.

For some firms, licensing alone is the preferred method of penetrating foreign markets. Other firms with diversified innovative product lines follow a strategy of trading technology for both equity in foreign joint ventures and royalty payments.

1.3.4 Trade-offs Between Alternative Modes of Overseas Expansion

There are certain general circumstances under which each approach, exporting, licensing, or local production, will be the preferred alternative for exploiting foreign markets.

Multinationals often possess **intangible capital** in the form of trademarks, patents, general marketing skills, and other organizational abilities.[15] If this intangible capital can be embodied in the form of products without adaptation, then exporting generally will be the preferred mode of market penetration. Where the firm's knowledge takes the form of specific product or process technologies that can be written down and transmitted objectively, then foreign expansion usually will take the licensing route.

Often, however, this intangible capital takes the form of organizational skills that are inseparable from the firm itself. A basic skill involves knowing how best to service a market through new product development and adaptation, quality control, advertising, distribution, after-sales service, and the general ability to read changing market needs and translate them into salable products. Because it would be difficult, if not impossible, to unbundle these services and sell them apart from the firm, the firm would attempt to exert control directly via the establishment of foreign affiliates. However, internalizing the market for an intangible asset by setting up foreign affiliates makes economic sense if, and only if, the benefits from circumventing market imperfections outweigh the administrative and other costs of central control.

A useful means to judge whether a foreign investment is desirable is to consider the type of imperfection that an investment is designed to overcome.[16] **Internalization**, and hence FDI, is most likely to be economically viable in those settings where the possibility of contractual difficulties make it especially costly to coordinate economic activities via arm's-length transactions in the marketplace.

Such "market failure" imperfections lead to both vertical and horizontal direct investment. **Vertical integration**—direct investment across industries that are related to different stages of production of a particular good—enables the MNC to substitute internal production and distribution systems for inefficient markets. For instance, vertical

---

[15] Richard E. Caves, "International Corporations: The Industrial Economics of Foreign Investment," *Economica*, February 1971, pp. 1–27.

[16] These considerations are discussed by William Kahley, "Direct Investment Activity of Foreign Firms," *Economic Review*, Federal Reserve Bank of Atlanta, Summer 1987, pp. 36–51.

integration might allow a firm to install specialized cost-saving equipment in two locations without the worry and risk that facilities may be idled by disagreements with unrelated enterprises. **Horizontal direct investment**—investment that is cross-border but within an industry—enables the MNC to utilize an advantage such as know-how or technology and avoid the contractual difficulties of dealing with unrelated parties. Examples of contractual difficulties are the MNC's inability to price know-how or to write, monitor, and enforce use restrictions governing technology-transfer arrangements. Thus, FDI makes most sense when a firm possesses a valuable asset and is better off directly controlling the use of the asset rather than selling or licensing it.

1.4 THEME AND ORGANIZATION OF THE BOOK

Although all functional areas can benefit from a global perspective, this book concentrates on developing financial policies that are appropriate for a multinational firm. The main objective of multinational financial management is to maximize shareholder wealth as measured by share price. This means making financing and investment decisions that add as much value as possible to the firm. It also means that companies must manage effectively the assets under their control.

The focus on shareholder value stems from the fact that shareholders are the legal owners of the firm and management has a fiduciary obligation to act in their best interests. Although other stakeholders in the company do have rights, these are not coequal with the shareholders' rights. Shareholders provide the risk capital that cushions the claims of alternative stakeholders. Companies that build shareholder value also find it easier to attract equity capital. Equity capital is especially critical for companies that operate in a riskier environment and for companies that are seeking to grow.

This book considers the links between financial management and other functional areas. Financial management is traditionally separated into two basic functions: the acquisition of funds and the investment of those funds. The first function, also known as the **financing decision**, involves generating funds from internal sources or from sources external to the firm at the lowest long-run cost possible. The **investment decision** is concerned with the allocation of funds over time in such a way that shareholder wealth is maximized. Many of the concerns and activities of multinational financial management, however, cannot be categorized so neatly.

Internal corporate fund flows such as loan repayments often are undertaken to access funds that are already owned, at least in theory, by the MNC itself. Other flows, such as dividend payments, may take place to reduce taxes or currency risk. Capital structure and other financing decisions frequently are motivated by a desire to reduce investment risks as well as financing costs. Furthermore, exchange risk management involves both the financing decision and the investment decision. Throughout this book, therefore, the interaction between financing and investment decisions is stressed because the right combination of these decisions is the key to maximizing the value of the firm to its shareholders.

This book also concentrates on the development of analytical approaches to deal with the major environmental problems and decisions involving overseas investment and financing. In carrying out these financial policies, however, conflicts between corporations and nation-states will inevitably arise. Therefore, this book also examines the modifications to financial policies that may be necessary for better alignment with national objectives in an effort to reduce such conflicts.

Financial executives in MNCs face many factors that have no domestic counterparts. These factors include exchange and inflation risks; international differences in tax rates; multiple money markets, often with limited access; currency controls; and political risks, such as sudden or creeping expropriation.

In summary, this book emphasizes the many opportunities associated with being multinational without neglecting the corresponding risks.

This book is divided into five parts.

- Part I: Environment of International Financial Management
- Part II: Foreign Exchange and Derivatives Markets
- Part III: Foreign Exchange Risk Management
- Part IV: Foreign Markets and Investments
- Part V: Financing and Controlling Multinational Operations

The following sections briefly discuss these parts and their chapters.

1.4.1 Environment of International Financial Management

Part I examines the environment in which international financial decisions are made. Chapter 2 in Part I discusses the basic factors that affect currency values. It also explains the basics of central bank intervention in foreign exchange markets, including the economic and political motivations for such intervention. Chapter 3 describes the international monetary system and shows how the choice of system affects the determination of exchange rates. Chapter 4 is crucial because it introduces five key equilibrium relationships among inflation rates, interest rates, and exchange rates in international finance that form the basis for much of the analysis in the remainder of the book. Chapter 5 analyzes the balance of payments and links between national economies.

1.4.2 Foreign Exchange and Derivatives Markets

Part II explores the foreign exchange and derivative markets used by multinational corporations to manage their currency and interest rate risks. Chapter 6 describes the foreign exchange market and how it functions. Foreign currency futures and options contracts are discussed in Chapter 7. Chapter 8 analyzes interest rate and currency swaps, interest rate forwards and futures, and how these derivatives can be used to manage risk.

1.4.3 Foreign Exchange Risk Management

Part III discusses foreign exchange risk management, a traditional area of concern that is receiving even more attention today. Chapter 9 discusses the likely impact that an exchange rate change will have on a firm (its exposure) from an accounting perspective and then analyzes the costs and benefits of alternative financial techniques to hedge against those exchange risks. Chapter 10 examines exposure from an economic perspective and presents marketing, logistic, and financial policies to cope with the competitive consequences of currency changes. As part of the analysis of economic exposure, the relationship between inflation and currency changes and its implications for corporate cash flows is recognized.

1.4.4 Foreign Markets and Investment

Part IV analyzes the foreign investment decision process. Chapter 11 discusses the subject of country risk analysis, the assessment of the potential risks and rewards associated with making investments and doing business in a foreign country. Chapter 12 describes the alternative external, medium- and long-term debt financing options available to a multinational corporation, with a special focus on eurocurrency and eurobond markets. Chapter 13 begins by discussing the nature and consequences of international portfolio investing—the purchase of foreign stocks and bonds. Chapter 14 presents techniques for evaluating foreign investment proposals, emphasizing how to adjust cash flows for the various political and economic risks encountered abroad, such as inflation, currency fluctuations, and expropriations. It also discusses how companies can manage political risks by appropriately structuring the initial investment and making suitable modifications to subsequent operating decisions.

1.4.5 Financing and Controlling Multinational Operations

Part V examines topics related to managing an MNC's finances. Chapter 15 covers international financing decisions, including trade financing and short-term financing. Chapter 16 describes the mechanisms available to an MNC to shift funds and profits among its various units, while considering the tax and other consequences of these maneuvers. The aim of these maneuvers is to create an integrated global financial planning system.

QUESTIONS

1. Explain how globalization may affect even a small business in your local area.

2. Opponents of globalization and outsourcing argue that locating manufacturing activities abroad causes a loss of U.S. jobs. However, when total employment figures are tallied, it is found that rather than a net loss of jobs, employment has actually increased. Also, the average wages of workers has also increased. How would you account for this discrepancy between what the critics say and what statistics reveal?

3. Elaborate on the benefits of a proactive approach to globalization and global competition.

4. What are the various reasons for the emergence of multinational firms?

5. Given the added political and economic risks that appear to exist overseas, are multinational firms more or less risky than purely domestic firms in the same industry? Consider whether a firm that decides not to operate abroad is insulated from the effects of economic events that occur outside the home country.

6. How is the nature of IBM's competitive advantages related to its becoming a multinational firm?

7. If capital markets were perfect, that is, capital could move freely across national borders, would MNCs still exist? Why? Or, why not?

8. What are the various ways in which domestic firms enter international markets? What are the benefits and risks of each strategy of foreign market entry?

9. Why do firms from each of the following categories become multinational? Identify the competitive advantages that a firm in each category must have to be a successful multinational.
   a. Raw-materials seekers
   b. Market seekers
   c. Cost minimizers

10. What factors help determine whether a firm will export its output, license foreign companies to manufacture its products, or set up its own production or service facilities abroad? Identify the competitive advantages that lead companies to prefer one mode of international expansion over another.

11. Time Warner is trying to decide whether to license foreign companies to produce its films and records or to set up foreign sales affiliates to sell its products directly. What factors might determine whether it expands abroad via licensing or by investing in its own sales force and distribution network?

INTERNET RESOURCES

http://www.wto.org Web site of the World Trade Organization (WTO). Contains news, information, and statistics on international trade.

http://www.worldbank.org Web site of the World Bank. Contains economic and demographic data on 206 countries (organized in "Country At-A-Glance" tables), various economic forecasts, and links to a number of other data sources.

http://www.bea.doc.gov Web site of the Bureau of Economic Analysis (BEA). Contains data and articles on U.S. international trade, capital flows, and other international economic matters.

http://online.wsj.com/public/us Web site of the *Wall Street Journal*, the foremost business newspaper in the United States. Contains domestic and international business news.

http://www.ft.com/home/us Web site of the *Financial Times*, the foremost international business newspaper, published in London. Contains a wealth of international financial news and data.

http://www.economist.com Web site of *The Economist*. Contains stories on the economic and political situations of countries and international business developments, along with various national and international economic and financial data.

http://www.oecd.org Web site of the Organisation for Economic Co-operation and Development (OECD). Contains news, analyses, and data on international finance and economics.

http://fisher.osu.edu/fin/fdf/osudata.htm Web site run by the Finance Department of Ohio State University. Contains a detailed listing of and links to many different Web sites related to finance and economics.

http://www.census.gov/ Contains the International Data Base (IDB), which is a computerized data bank with statistical tables of demographic, and socioeconomic data for 227 countries and areas of the world.

http://www.economy.com/dismal/ Covers over 65 economic releases from over 15 countries. Also contains numerous stories dealing with international finance and economics.

http://www.reportgallery.com Web site that contains links to annual reports of over 2,200 companies, many of which are multinationals.

http://www.sec.gov/ Website of U.S. Securities and Exchange Commission. Contains company filings of companies including 10-K and 10-Q.

http://www.unctad.org/Templates/StartPage.asp?intItemID = 2068 Website of the United Nations Conference on Trade and Development. Contains information on international trade statistics.

http://epp.eurostat.ec.europa.eu/portal/page?_pageid=1090,30070682,1090_33076576&_dad=portal&_schema=PORTAL Website Eurostat Database from European Commission. Contains economic data for EU and Non-EU nations.

http://www.bls.gov/ Website of the Bureau of Labor Statistics within U.S. Department of Labor. Contains historical U.S. labor, productivity, and inflation data.

INTERNET EXERCISES

1. Who are the major trading partners of the United States? Which countries are the top five exporters to the United States? Which countries are the top five importers of U.S. goods? Good references are the WTO site and the BEA site.

2. Who are the major recipients of U.S. overseas investment? Which countries are the major sources of foreign investment in the United States? A good reference is the BEA site.

3. Go to the Web sites of companies such as the ones listed below and examine their international business activity. For example, what importance do these companies appear to place on international business? What percentage of sales revenues, assets, and income do these companies derive from their foreign operations? What percentage of their sales and income comes from exports? Is their foreign activity increasing or decreasing? How many countries and continents do these companies operate on? Which countries are listed as locations of the company's foreign

subsidiaries? What is the headquarters country of each company? Much of this information can be gleaned from the annual reports of the companies, which can be found at http://www.reportgallery.com.

Ford Motor Company

Walt Disney Company

General Electric

DaimlerChrysler

Philips Electronics

Unilever

IBM

Sony

Nestlé

Microsoft

Coca-Cola

ExxonMobil

4. Based on your review of *The Economist*, the *Wall Street Journal*, and the *Financial Times*, which countries appear to be giving foreign investors concerns? What are these concerns?

5. Visit the Bureau of Labor Statistics website at http://www.bls.gov. What are the sectors that have added the most jobs in the period 1990 to 2005?

6. Visit the website of Dell Inc. (www.dell.com). From the home page, visit Dell's site for three other countries. What similarities and differences do you see in the products, prices and other details when comparing the various country sites? How would you account for these similarities and differences?

APPENDIX 1A

THE ORIGINS AND CONSEQUENCES OF INTERNATIONAL TRADE

Underlying the theory of international trade is the doctrine of comparative advantage. This doctrine rests on certain assumptions:

- Exporters sell undifferentiated (commodity) goods and services to unrelated importers.
- Factors of production cannot move freely across countries. Instead, trade takes place in the goods and services produced by these factors of production.

As noted at the beginning of Chapter 1, the doctrine of comparative advantage also ignores the roles of uncertainty, economies of scale, and technology in international trade; and it is static rather than dynamic. Nonetheless, this theory helps to explain why nations trade with each other, and it forms the basis for assessing the consequences of international trade policies.

To illustrate the main features of the doctrine of comparative advantage and to distinguish this concept from that of absolute advantage, suppose the United States and the United Kingdom produce the same two products, wheat and coal, according to the following production schedules, where the units referred to are units of production (labor, capital, land, and technology). These schedules show how many units it costs to produce each ton in each country:[17]

	Wheat	*Coal*
U.S.	2 units/ton	1 unit/ton
U.K.	3 units/ton	4 units/ton

These figures show clearly that the United States has an **absolute advantage** in both mining coal and growing wheat. That is, in using fewer units of production per ton produced, the United States is more efficient than the United Kingdom in producing both coal and wheat.

---

[17] The traditional theory of international trade ignores the role of technology in differentiating products, but it leaves open the possibility of different production technologies to produce commodities.

However, although the United Kingdom is at an absolute disadvantage in both products, it has a **comparative advantage** in producing wheat. Put another way, the United Kingdom's absolute disadvantage is less in growing wheat than in mining coal. This lesser disadvantage can be seen by redoing the production figures above to reflect the output per unit of production for both countries:

	Wheat	Coal
U.S.	0.5 tons/unit	1 ton/unit
U.K.	0.33 tons/unit	0.25 tons

Productivity for the United States relative to the United Kingdom in coal is 4:1 (1/0.25), whereas it is only 1.5:1 (0.5/0.33) in wheat.

In order to induce the production of both wheat and coal prior to the introduction of trade, the profitability of producing both commodities must be identical. This condition is satisfied only when the return per unit of production is the same for both wheat and coal in each country. Hence, prior to the introduction of trade between the two countries, the exchange rate between wheat and coal in the United States and the United Kingdom must be as follows:

U.S. 1 ton wheat = 2 tons coal

U.K. 1 ton wheat = 0.75 tons coal

THE GAINS FROM TRADE

Based on the relative prices of wheat and coal in both countries, there will be obvious gains to trade. By switching production units from wheat to coal, the United States can produce coal and trade with the United Kingdom for more wheat than those same production units can produce at home. Similarly, by specializing in growing wheat and trading for coal, the United Kingdom can consume more coal than if it mined its own. This example demonstrates that trade will be beneficial even if one nation (the United States here) has an absolute advantage in everything. As long as the degree of absolute advantage varies across products, even the nation with an across-the-board absolute disadvantage will have a comparative advantage in making and exporting some goods and services.

The gains from trade for each country depend on exactly where the exchange rate between wheat and coal ends up following the introduction of trade. This exchange rate, known as the **terms of trade**, depends on the relative supplies and demands for wheat and coal in each country. However, any exchange rate between 0.75 and 2.0 tons of coal per ton of wheat will still lead to trade because trading at that exchange rate will allow both countries to improve their ability to consume. By illustration, suppose the terms of trade end up at 1:1—that is, one ton of wheat equals one ton of coal.

Each unit of production in the United States can now provide its owner with either one ton of coal to con-

sume or one ton of wheat or some combination of the two. By producing coal and trading for wheat, each production unit in the United States now enables its owner to consume twice as much wheat as before. Similarly, by switching from mining coal to growing wheat and trading for coal, each production unit in the United Kingdom will enable its owner to consume 0.33 tons of coal, 33% (0.33/0.25 = 133%) more than before.

SPECIALIZED FACTORS OF PRODUCTION

So far, we have assumed that the factors of production are unspecialized. That is, they can easily be switched between the production of wheat and coal. However, suppose that some factors such as labor and capital are specialized (that is, relatively more efficient) in terms of producing one commodity rather than the other. In that case, the prices of the factors of production that specialize in the commodity that is exported (coal in the United States, wheat in the United Kingdom) will gain because of greater demand once trade begins, whereas those factors that specialize in the commodity that is now imported (wheat in the United States, coal in the United Kingdom) will lose because of lower demand. This conclusion is based on the economic fact that the demand for factors of production is derived from the demand for the goods those factors produce.

The gains and losses to the specialized factors of production will depend on the magnitude of the price shifts after the introduction of trade. To take an extreme case: suppose the terms of trade become 1 ton of wheat equals 1.95 tons of coal; at this exchange rate, trade is still beneficial for both countries but far more so for the United Kingdom than the United States. The disparity in the gains from trade can be seen as follows: by producing coal and trading it for wheat, the United States can now consume approximately 2.5% more wheat per ton of coal than before.[18] However, the United Kingdom gains enormously, too. Each unit of wheat traded for coal will now provide it 1.95 tons of coal, a 160% (1.95/0.75 − 1) increase relative to the earlier ratio.

These gains are all to the good. However, with specialization comes costs. In the United States, the labor and capital that specialized in growing wheat will be hurt. If they continue to grow wheat (which may make sense because they cannot easily be switched to mining coal), they will suffer approximately a 2.5% loss of income because the wheat they produce now will buy about 2.5% less coal than before (1.95 tons instead of 2 tons). At the same time, U.S. labor and capital that specializes in mining coal will be able to buy about 2.5% more wheat. Although gains and losses for specialized U.S. factors of production exist, they are relatively small. But the same cannot be said for U.K. gains and losses.

---

[18] With trade, the United States can now consume 1/1.95 = 0.5128 tons of wheat per ton of coal, which is 2.56% more wheat than the 0.5 tons it could previously consume (0.5128/0.50 = 1.0256).

As we saw earlier, U.K. labor and capital that specialize in growing wheat will be able to buy 160% more coal than before, a dramatic boost in purchasing power. Conversely, those factors that specialize in mining coal will see their wheat purchasing power plummet, from 1.33 (4/3) tons of coal before trade to 0.5128 (1/1.95) tons of wheat now. These figures translate into a drop of about 62% (0.5128/1.33 = 38%) in wheat purchasing power.

This example illustrates a general principle of international trade: *The greater the gains from trade for a country overall, the greater the cost of trade to those factors of production that specialize in producing the commodity that is now imported.* The reason is that in order for trade to make sense, imports must be less expensive than the competing domestic products. The less expensive these imports are, the greater will be the gains from trade. By the same token, however, less expensive imports drive down the prices of competing domestic products, thereby reducing the value of those factors of production that specialize in their manufacture.

It is this redistribution of income—from factors specializing in producing the competing domestic products to consumers of those products—that leads to demands for protection from imports. However, protection is a double-edged sword. These points are illustrated by the experience of the U.S. auto industry.

As discussed in the chapter, the onslaught of Japanese cars in the U.S. market drove down the price and quantity of cars sold by American manufacturers, reducing their return on capital and forcing them to be much tougher in negotiating with the United Auto Workers. The end result was better and less expensive cars for Americans but lower profits for Detroit automakers, lower wages and benefits for U.S. autoworkers, and fewer jobs in the U.S. auto industry.

The U.S. auto industry responded to the Japanese competition by demanding, and receiving, protection in the form of a quota on Japanese auto imports. The Japanese response to the quota, which allowed them to raise their prices (why cut prices when you can't sell more cars anyway?) and increase their profit margins, was to focus on making and selling higher quality cars in the U.S. market (as these carried higher profit margins) and shifting substantial production to the United States. In the end, protection did not help U.S. automakers nearly as much as improving the quality of their cars and reducing their manufacturing costs. Indeed, to the extent that protection helped delay the needed changes while boosting Japanese automaker profits (thereby giving them more capital to invest), it may well have hurt the U.S. auto industry.

MONETARY PRICES AND EXCHANGE RATES

So far, we have talked about prices of goods in terms of each other. To introduce monetary prices into the example we have been analyzing, suppose that before the opening of trade between the two nations, each production unit costs $30 in the United States and £10 in the United Kingdom. In this case, the prices of wheat and coal in the two countries will be as follows:

	Wheat	Coal
U.S.	$60/ton	$30/ton
U.K.	£30/ton	£40/ton

These prices are determined by taking the number of required production units and multiplying them by the price per unit.

Following the introduction of trade, assume the same 1:1 terms of trade as before and that the cost of a unit of production remains the same. The prices of wheat and coal in each country will settle at the following, assuming that the exported goods maintain their prices and the prices of the goods imported adjust to these prices so as to preserve the 1:1 terms of trade:

	Wheat	Coal
U.S.	$30/ton	$30/ton
U.K.	£30/ton	£30/ton

These prices present a potential problem in that there will be equilibrium at these prices only if the exchange rate is $1 = £1. Suppose, however, that before the introduction of trade, the exchange rate is £1 = $3. In this case, dollar-equivalent prices in both countries will begin as follows:

	Wheat	Coal
U.S.	$60/ton	$30/ton
U.K.	$90/ton	$120/ton

This is clearly a disequilibrium situation. Once trade begins at these initial prices, the British will demand both U.S. wheat and coal, whereas Americans will demand no British coal or wheat. Money will be flowing in one direction only (from the United Kingdom to the United States to pay for these goods), and goods will flow only in the opposite direction. The United Kingdom will run a massive trade deficit, matched exactly by the U.S. trade surplus. Factors of production in the United Kingdom will be idle (because there is no demand for the goods they can produce) whereas U.S. factors of production will experience an enormous increase in demand for their services.

This is the nightmare scenario for those concerned with the effects of free trade: One country will sell everything to the other country and demand nothing in return (save money), leading to prosperity for the exporting nation and massive unemployment and depression in the importing country. However, such worries ignore the way markets work.

Absent government interference, a set of forces will swing into play simultaneously. The British demand for dollars (to buy U.S. coal and wheat) will boost the value of the dollar, making U.S. products more expensive to the British and British goods less expensive to Americans. At the same time, the jump in demand for U.S. factors of production will raise their prices and hence the cost of producing U.S. coal and wheat. The rise in cost will force a rise in the dollar price of U.S. wheat and coal. Conversely, the lack of demand for U.K. factors of production will drive down their price and hence the pound cost of producing British coal and wheat. The net result of these adjustments in the pound:dollar exchange rate and the cost of factors of production in both countries is to make British products more attractive to consumers and U.S. products less competitive. This process will continue until both countries can find their comparative advantage and the terms of trade between coal and wheat are equal in both countries (say, at 1:1).

TARIFFS

Introducing tariffs (taxes) on imported goods will distort the prices at which trade takes place and will reduce the quantity of goods traded. In effect, tariffs introduce a wedge between the prices paid by domestic customers and the prices received by the exporter, reducing the incentive for both to trade. To see this, suppose Mexican tomatoes are sold in the United States at a price of $0.30 per pound. If the United States imposes a tariff of, say, $0.15 per pound on Mexican tomatoes, then Mexican tomatoes will have to sell for $0.45 per pound to provide Mexican producers with the same pretariff profits on their tomato exports to the United States. However, it is likely that at this price, some Americans will forgo Mexican tomatoes and either substitute U.S. tomatoes or do without tomatoes in their salads. More likely, competition will preclude Mexican tomato growers from raising their price to $0.45 per pound. Suppose, instead, that the price of Mexican tomatoes, including the tariff, settles at $0.35 per pound. At this price, the Mexican tomato growers will receive only $0.20 per pound, reducing their incentive to ship tomatoes to the American market. At the same time, the higher price paid by American customers will reduce their demand for Mexican tomatoes. As a result fewer Mexican tomatoes will be sold in the U.S. market. Such a result will benefit American tomato growers (who now face less competition and can thereby raise their prices) and farmworkers (who can now raise their wages without driving their employers out of business) while harming U.S. consumers of tomatoes (including purchasers of Campbell's tomato soup, Ragu spaghetti sauce, Progresso ravioli, and Heinz ketchup).

Ultimately, the effects of free trade are beneficial for an economy because it promotes increased competition among producers. This leads to lower prices for consumers, greater productivity and rising wages for workers, increased innovation, and higher living standards for the country overall.

Questions

1. In a satirical petition on behalf of French candlemakers, Frederic Bastiat, a French economist, called attention to cheap competition from afar: sunlight. A law requiring the shuttering of windows during the day, he suggested, would benefit not only candlemakers but "everything connected with lighting" and the country as a whole. He explained: "As long as you exclude, as you do, iron, corn, foreign fabrics, in proportion as their prices approximate to zero, what inconsistency it would be to admit the light of the sun, the price of which is already at zero during the entire day!"

   a. Is there a logical flaw in Bastiat's satirical argument?

   b. Do Japanese automakers prefer a tariff or a quota on their U.S. auto exports? Why? Is there likely to be consensus among the Japanese carmakers on this point? Might there be any Japanese automakers who would prefer U.S. trade restrictions? Why? Who are they?

   c. What characteristics of the U.S. auto industry have helped it gain protection? Why does protectionism persist despite the obvious gains to society from free trade?

2. Review the arguments both pro and con on NAFTA. What is the empirical evidence so far?

3. Given the resources available to them, countries A and B can produce the following combinations of steel and corn.

Country A		Country B	
Steel (tons)	Corn (bushels)	Steel (tons)	Corn (bushels)
36	0	54	0
30	3	45	9
24	6	36	18
18	9	27	27
15	12	18	36
6	15	9	45
0	18	0	54

   a. Do you expect trade to take place between countries A and B? Why?

   b. Which country will export steel? Which will export corn? Explain.

THE DETERMINATION OF EXCHANGE RATES

Experience shows that neither a state nor a bank ever have had the unrestricted power of issuing paper money without abusing that power.

David Ricardo (1817)

CHAPTER LEARNING OBJECTIVES

- To explain the concept of an equilibrium exchange rate
- To identify the basic factors affecting exchange rates in a floating exchange rate system
- To calculate the amount of currency appreciation or depreciation associated with a given exchange rate change
- To describe the motives and different forms and consequences of central bank intervention in the foreign exchange market
- To explain how and why expectations affect exchange rates

KEY TERMS

appreciation	liquidity
ask rate	monetary base
asset market model	monetize the deficit
bid rate	moral hazard
central bank	nominal exchange rate
currency board	open-market operation
depreciation	pegged currency
devaluation	real (inflation-adjusted)
dollarization	exchange rate
equilibrium exchange rate	real interest rate
exchange rate	reference currency
fiat money	revaluation
floating currency	seigniorage
foreign exchange market intervention	spot rate
forward rate	sterilization
freely floating exchange rate	unsterilized intervention

Economic activity today is globally unified to an unprecedented degree. Changes in one nation's economy are rapidly transmitted to that nation's trading partners. These fluctuations in economic activity are reflected, almost immediately, in fluctuations in currency values. Consequently, multinational corporations (MNCR), with their integrated cross-border production and marketing operations, continually face devaluation or revaluation worries somewhere in the world. The purpose of this chapter and the next one is to provide an understanding of what an exchange rate is and why it might change. Such an understanding is basic to dealing with currency risk.

This chapter first describes what an exchange rate is and how it is determined in a **freely floating exchange rate** regime, that is, in the absence of government intervention. Next, the chapter discusses the role of expectations in exchange rate determination. It also examines the different forms and consequences of central bank intervention in the foreign exchange market. Chapter 3 describes the political aspects of currency determination under alternative exchange rate systems and presents a brief history of the international monetary system.

Before proceeding further, here are definitions of several terms commonly used to describe currency changes. Technically, a **devaluation** refers to a decrease in the stated par value of a **pegged currency**, one whose value is set by the government; an increase in par value is known as a **revaluation**. By contrast, a **floating currency**, one whose value is set primarily by market forces, is said to **depreciate** if it loses value and to **appreciate** if it gains value. However, discussions in this book will use the terms *devaluation* and *depreciation* and *revaluation* and *appreciation* interchangeably.

2.1 SETTING THE EQUILIBRIUM SPOT EXCHANGE RATE

An **exchange rate** is, simply, the price of one nation's currency in terms of another currency, often termed the **reference currency**. For example, the yen/dollar exchange rate is just the number of yen that one dollar will buy. If a dollar will buy 100 yens, the exchange rate would be expressed as ¥100/$ and the yen would be the reference currency. Equivalently, the dollar/yen exchange rate is the number of dollars one yen will buy. Continuing with the previous example, the exchange rate would be $0.01/¥ (1/100) and the dollar would now be the reference currency.

Exchange rates can be for spot or forward delivery. A **spot rate** is the price at which currencies are traded for immediate delivery, or in two days in the interbank market. A **forward rate** is the price at which foreign exchange is quoted for delivery at a specified future date. The foreign exchange market, where currencies are traded, is not a physical place; rather, it is an electronically linked network of banks, foreign exchange brokers, and dealers whose function is to bring together buyers and sellers of foreign exchange.

To understand how exchange rates are set, it helps to recognize that they are market-clearing prices that equilibrate supplies and demands in the foreign exchange market. The determinants of currency supplies and demands are first discussed with the aid of a two-currency model featuring the U.S. dollar and the euro, the official currency of the 13 countries that participate in the European Monetary Union (EMU). The members of EMU are often known collectively as the Eurozone or Euroland. Euroland is the term used here. Later, the various currency influences in a multicurrency world will be studied more closely.

2.1.1 Demand for a Currency

The demand for the euro in the foreign exchange market (which in this two-currency model is equivalent to the supply of dollars) derives from the American demand for Euroland goods and services and euro-denominated financial assets. Euroland prices are set in euros, so in order for Americans to pay for their Euroland purchases they must first exchange their dollars for euros. That is, they will demand euros.

An increase in the euro's dollar value is equivalent to an increase in the dollar price of Euroland products. This higher dollar price normally will reduce the U.S. demand for Euroland goods, services, and assets. Conversely, as the dollar value of the euro falls, Americans will demand more euros to buy the less-expensive Euroland products, resulting in a downward-sloping demand curve for euros. As the dollar cost of the euro (the exchange rate) falls, Americans will tend to buy more Euroland goods and so will demand more euros.

2.1.2 Supply of a Currency

Similarly, the supply of euros (which for the model is equivalent to the demand for dollars) is based on Euroland demand for U.S. goods and services and dollar-denominated financial assets. In order for Euroland residents to pay for their U.S. purchases, they must first acquire dollars. As the dollar value of the euro increases, thereby lowering the euro cost of U.S. goods, the increased Euroland demand for U.S. goods will cause an increase in the Euroland demand for dollars and, hence, an increase in the amount of euros supplied.[1]

In Exhibit 2.1, e is the spot exchange rate (dollar value of one euro, that is, €1 = e), and Q is the quantity of euros supplied and demanded. Since the euro is expressed in terms of dollars, the dollar is the reference currency. The euro supply (S) and demand (D) curves intersect at e_0, the **equilibrium exchange rate**. The foreign exchange market is said to be in equilibrium at e_0 because both the demand for euros and the supply of euros at this price is Q_0.

Before continuing, it should be noted that the notion of a single exchange rate is a convenient fiction. In reality, exchange rates, both spot rates and forward rates, are quoted in pairs, with a dealer (usually a bank foreign exchange trader) standing willing to buy foreign exchange at the **bid rate** or to sell foreign exchange at the **ask rate**. As might be expected, the bid rate is always less than the ask rate, enabling dealers to profit from the spread between the bid and ask rates by buying low and selling high. Chapter 6 describes the mechanics of the foreign exchange market in great detail.

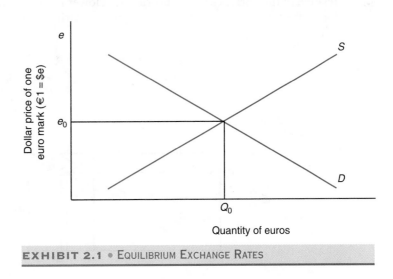

EXHIBIT 2.1 • Equilibrium Exchange Rates

---

[1] This statement holds provided the price elasticity of Euroland demand, E, is greater than 1. In general, $E = (\Delta Q/Q)/(\Delta P/P)$, where Q is the quantity of goods demanded, P is the price, and ΔQ is the change in quantity demanded for a change in price, ΔP. If $E > 1$, then total spending goes up when price declines.

2.1.3 Factors that Affect the Equilibrium Exchange Rate

Money has value because people are willing to accept it in exchange for goods and services. The value of money, therefore, depends on its purchasing power. Money also provides **liquidity**—that is, you can readily exchange it for goods or other assets, thereby facilitating economic transactions. Thus, money represents both a *store of value* and a *store of liquidity*. The demand for money, therefore, depends on money's ability to maintain its value and on the level of economic activity.

As the supply and demand schedules for a currency change over time, the equilibrium exchange will also change. Some of the factors that influence currency supply and demand are inflation rates, interest rates, economic growth, and political and economic risks. Section 2.2 shows how expectations about these factors also exert a powerful influence on currency supplies and demands and, hence, on exchange rates.

Relative Inflation Rates   Suppose that the supply of dollars increases relative to its demand. This excess growth in the money supply will cause inflation in the United States, which means that U.S. prices will begin to rise relative to prices of goods and services in Euroland. Euroland consumers are likely to buy fewer U.S. products and begin switching to Euroland substitutes, leading to a decrease in the amount of euros supplied at every exchange rate. The result is a leftward shift in the euro supply curve to S' as shown in Exhibit 2.2. Similarly, higher prices in the United States will lead American consumers to substitute Euroland imports for U.S. products, resulting in an increase in the demand for euros as depicted by D'. In effect, both Americans and residents of Euroland are searching for the best deals worldwide and will switch their purchases accordingly as the prices of U.S. goods change relative to prices in Euroland. Hence, a higher rate of inflation in the United States than in Euroland will simultaneously increase Euroland exports to the United States and reduce U.S. exports to Euroland.

A new equilibrium rate $e_1 > e_0$ results. In other words, a higher rate of inflation in the United States than in Europe will lead to a depreciation of the dollar relative to the euro or, equivalently, to an appreciation of the euro relative to the dollar. In general, a nation running a relatively high rate of inflation will find its currency declining in value relative to the currencies of countries with lower inflation rates. This relationship will be formalized in Chapter 4 as purchasing power parity (PPP).

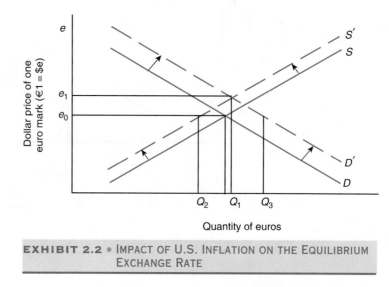

EXHIBIT 2.2 • IMPACT OF U.S. INFLATION ON THE EQUILIBRIUM EXCHANGE RATE

Relative Interest Rates   Interest rate differentials will also affect the equilibrium exchange rate. A rise in U.S. interest rates relative to Euroland rates, all else being equal, will cause investors in both nations to switch from euro- to dollar-denominated securities to take advantage of the higher dollar rates. The net result will be depreciation of the euro in the absence of government intervention.

It should be noted that the interest rates discussed here are real interest rates. The **real interest rate** equals the nominal or actual interest rate minus the rate of inflation. The distinction between nominal and real interest rates is critical in international finance and will be discussed at length in Chapter 4. If the increase in U.S. interest rates relative to Euroland rates just reflects higher U.S. inflation, the predicted result will be a weaker dollar. Only an increase in the real U.S. interest rate relative to the real Euroland rate will result in an appreciating dollar.

Relative Economic Growth Rates   Similarly, a nation with strong economic growth will attract investment capital seeking to acquire domestic assets. The demand for domestic assets, in turn, results in an increased demand for the domestic currency and a stronger currency, other things being equal. Empirical evidence supports the hypothesis that economic growth should lead to a stronger currency. Conversely, nations with poor growth prospects will see an exodus of capital and weaker currencies.

Political and Economic Risk   Other factors that can influence exchange rates include political and economic risks. Investors prefer to hold lesser amounts of riskier assets; thus, low-risk currencies—those associated with more politically and economically stable nations—are more highly valued than high-risk currencies.

ILLUSTRATION   *The Ruble is Rubble*

Since the breakup of the former Soviet Union in 1991, the Russian government had difficulty managing its finances. By spending more than it was collecting in revenues, Russia faced persistent budget deficits financed by issuing short-term treasury bills and printing rubles. By late 1997, the combination of rapidly increasing debt issuance and falling commodity prices (a major source of Russia's revenue and foreign exchange comes from exports of oil, timber, gold, and other commodities) increased investors' doubts that Russia would be able to service its growing debt burden, including $160 billion in foreign debt. Sensing blood, speculators launched a series of attacks against the Russian ruble. The Russian government responded by repeatedly raising interest rates, which eventually reached 150% by the middle of May 1998. To help support the ruble, the International Monetary Fund (IMF) put together a $23 billion financial package, contingent on Russia implementing an adjustment program that stressed boosting tax revenues. When the Russian Parliament balked at the tax collection measures, the IMF withheld its funds. Despite the high interest rates it was paying, the government had difficulty persuading investors to roll over their short-term government debt. The stock market sank to new lows, interest rates remained high, and investors began transferring money out of Russia.

Facing accelerating capital flight and mounting domestic problems, the Russian government announced a radical policy shift on August 17, 1998. The key measures included abandonment of its currency supports, suspension of trading in treasury bills combined with a mandatory restructuring of government debt, and a 90-day moratorium on the repayment of corporate and bank debt to foreign creditors (that is, default).

In response, the Russian ruble plunged in value (see Exhibit 2.3). Rather than dealing with the root causes of the financial crisis, the government reverted to previously discarded administrative measures. It imposed extensive controls on the foreign exchange market, increasingly financed its debt by printing more rubles, and forced exporters to surrender 75% of their export earnings. The crisis and the government's subsequent actions resulted in a steep rise in inflation and a deep recession in Russia, causing a continuing sharp decline in the ruble's value, shown in Exhibit 2.3.

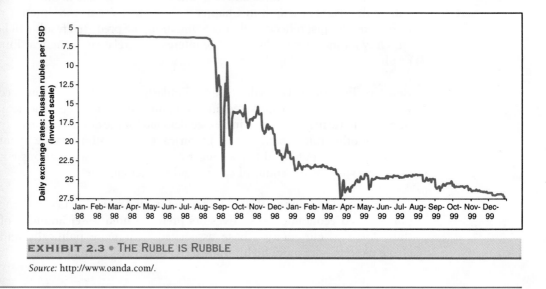

EXHIBIT 2.3 • THE RUBLE IS RUBBLE

Source: http://www.oanda.com/.

2.1.4 Calculating Exchange Rate Changes

Depending on the current value of the euro relative to the dollar, the amount of euro appreciation or depreciation is computed as the fractional increase or decrease in the dollar value of the euro. For example, if the €/$ exchange rate goes from €1 = $1.25 to €1 = $1.35, the euro is said to have appreciated by the change in its dollar value, which is $(1.35 - 1.25)/1.25 = 8\%$.

The general formula by which we can calculate the euro's appreciation or depreciation against the dollar is as follows:

$$\text{Amount of euro appreciation (depreciation)} = \frac{\text{New dollar value of euro} - \text{Old dollar value of euro}}{\text{Old dollar value of euro}}$$

$$= \frac{e_1 - e_0}{e_0} \tag{2.1}$$

Substituting in the numbers from the previous example (with $e_0 = \$1.250$ and $e_1 = \$1.35$) yields the 8% euro appreciation.

Alternatively, we can calculate the change in the euro value of the dollar. We can do this by recognizing that if e equals the dollar value of a euro (dollars per euro), then the euro value of a dollar (euros per dollar) must be the reciprocal, or $1/e$. For example, if the euro is worth $1.25, then the dollar must be worth €0.80 (1/1.25). The change in the euro value of the dollar between time 0 and time 1 equals $1/e_1 - 1/e_0$. In percentage terms, the dollar is said to have depreciated (appreciated) against the euro by the fractional decrease (increase) in the euro value of the dollar.

$$\text{Amount of dollar depreciation (appreciation)} = \frac{\text{New euro value of dollar} - \text{Old euro value of dollar}}{\text{Old euro value of dollar}}$$

$$= \frac{1/e_1 - 1/e_0}{1/e_0} = \frac{e_0 - e_1}{e_1} \tag{2.2}$$

Employing Equation 2.2, we can find the increase in the euro exchange rate from $1.25 to $1.35 to be equivalent to a dollar depreciation of 7.41% [(1.25 − 1.35)/1.35 = −0.0741]. (Why do the two exchange rate changes not equal each other?)[2]

ILLUSTRATION   *Calculating British Pound Appreciation Against the Dollar*

During 2006, the British pound went from 1.7188 to 1.9586 against the U.S. dollar. By how much did the pound appreciate against the dollar?

Solution. Using Equation 2.1, the pound has appreciated against the dollar by an amount equal to (1.9586 − 1.7188) / 1.7188 = 13.95%

By how much has the dollar depreciated against the pound?

Solution. An exchange rate of £1 = $1.9586 translates into an exchange rate of $1 = £0.51 (1/1.9586). Similarly, the exchange rate of £1 = $1.7188 is equivalent to an exchange rate of $1 = £ 0.58. Using Equation 2.2, the dollar has depreciated against the pound by an amount equal to (0.51 − 0.58)/0.58 = −12.07%.

ILLUSTRATION   *Calculating Dollar Appreciation Against the Turkish Lira*

On February 22, 2001, the Turkish lira lost 41.18% of its value against the U.S. dollar following a political and financial crisis that forced the government to abandon exchange controls. By how much did the dollar appreciate against the lira that day?

Solution. If e_0 is the initial dollar value of the lira and e_1 is the postdevaluation exchange rate, then we know from Equation 2.1 that $(e_1 - e_0)/e_0 = -41.18\%$. Solving for e_1 in terms of e_0 yields $e_1 = 0.5882e_0$. From Equation 2.2, we know that the dollar's appreciation against the lira equals $(e_0 - e_1)/e_1$ or $(e_0 - 0.5882e_0)/0.5882e_0 = 0.4118/0.5882 = 70.01\%$.

2.2 EXPECTATIONS AND THE ASSET MARKET MODEL OF EXCHANGE RATES

Although currency values are affected by current events and current supply and demand flows in the foreign exchange market, they also depend on expectations or forecasts about future exchange rate movements. And exchange rate forecasts, as we will see in Chapter 4, are influenced by every conceivable economic, political, and social factor.

---

[2] The reason the euro appreciation is unequal to the amount of dollar depreciation depends on the fact that the value of one currency is the inverse of the value of the other one. Hence, the percentage change in currency value differs, because the base off which the change is measured differs.

The role of expectations in determining exchange rates depends on the fact that currencies are financial assets and that an exchange rate is simply the relative price of two financial assets—one country's currency in terms of another's. Thus, currency prices are determined in the same manner as the prices of assets such as stocks, bonds, gold, or real estate are determined. Unlike the prices of services or products with short storage lives, asset prices are influenced comparatively little by current events. Rather, they are determined by people's willingness to hold the existing quantities of assets, which in turn depends on their expectations of the future worth of these assets. Thus, for example, frost in Florida can bump up the price of oranges, but it should have little impact on the price of the citrus groves producing the oranges; instead, longer-term expectations of the demand and supply of oranges govern the values of these groves.

Similarly, the value today of a given currency, say, the dollar, depends on whether or not–and how strongly–people still want the amount of dollars and dollar-denominated assets they held yesterday. According to this view–known as the **asset market model** of exchange rate determination, the exchange rate between two currencies represents the price that just balances the relative supplies of, and demands for, assets denominated in those currencies. Consequently, shifts in preferences can lead to massive shifts in currency values.

For example, during the 1990s, the Cold War ended and the United States became the sole global power. Following a brief recession, the U.S. economy innovated and grew rapidly while Japan and Europe largely stagnated. Capital was attracted to the United States by the strength of its economy, the high after-tax real rate of return, and the favorable political climate—conditions superior to those attainable elsewhere. Foreigners found the United States to be a safer and more rewarding place in which to invest than elsewhere, so they added many more U.S. assets to their portfolios. In response, the dollar soared in value against other currencies.

The desire to hold a currency today depends critically on expectations of the factors that can affect the currency's future value; therefore, what matters is not only what is happening today but also what markets expect will happen in the future. Thus, currency values are forward looking; they are set by investor expectations of their issuing countries' economic prospects rather than by contemporaneous events alone. Moreover, in a world of high capital mobility, the difference between having the right policies and the wrong ones has never been greater. This point is illustrated by the Asian currency crisis of 1997.

MINI-CASE   *Asian Currencies Sink in 1997*

During the second half of 1997, and beginning in Thailand, currencies and stock markets plunged across East Asia, while hundreds of banks, builders, and manufacturers went bankrupt. The Thai baht, Indonesian rupiah, Malaysian ringgit, Philippine peso, and South Korean won depreciated by 40% to 80% apiece. All this happened despite the fact that Asia's fundamentals looked good: low inflation, balanced budgets, well-run central banks, high domestic savings, strong export industries, a large and growing middle class, a vibrant entrepreneurial class, and industrious, well-trained, and often well-educated workforces paid relatively low wages. But investors saw signs of impending trouble since many East Asian economies were characterized by large trade deficits, huge short-term foreign debts, overvalued currencies, and financial systems that were rotten at their core. Each of these ingredients played a role in the crisis and its spread from one country to another.

LOSS OF EXPORT COMPETITIVENESS

To begin, most East Asian countries depend on exports as their engines of growth and development. Along with Japan, the United States is the most important market for these exports. Partly because of this, many of them had tied their currencies to the dollar. This served them well until 1995, promoting low inflation and currency stability. It also boosted exports at the expense of Japan as the dollar fell against the yen, forcing Japanese companies to shift production to East Asia to cope with the strong yen. Currency stability also led East Asian banks and companies to finance themselves with dollars, yen, and Deutsche marks—some $275 billion worth, much of it short term—because dollar and other foreign currency loans carried lower interest rates than did their domestic currencies. The party ended in 1995, when the dollar began recovering against the yen and other currencies. By mid-1997, the dollar had risen by over 50% against the yen and by 20% against the German mark. Dollar appreciation alone would have made East Asia's exports less price competitive. But their competitiveness problem was greatly exacerbated by the fact that during this period, the Chinese yuan depreciated by about 25% against the dollar.[3] China exported similar products, so the yuan devaluation raised China's export competitiveness at East Asia's expense. The loss of export competitiveness slowed down Asian growth and caused utilization rates, and profits, on huge investments in production capacity to plunge. It also gave the Asian central banks a mutual incentive to devalue their currencies. According to one theory, recognizing these altered incentives, speculators attacked the East Asian currencies almost simultaneously and forced a round of devaluations.[4]

MORAL HAZARD AND CRONY CAPITALISM

Another theory suggests that **moral hazard**—the tendency to incur risks that one is protected against—lies at the heart of Asia's financial problems. Specifically, most Asian banks and finance companies operated with implicit or explicit government guarantees. For example, the South Korean government directed the banking system to lend massively to companies and industries that it viewed as economically strategic, with little regard for their profitability. When combined with poor regulation, these guarantees distorted investment decisions, encouraging financial institutions to fund risky projects in the expectation that the banks would enjoy any profits, while sticking the government with any losses. (These same perverse incentives underlie the savings and loan fiasco in the United States during the 1980s.) In Asia's case, the problem was compounded by the crony capitalism that is pervasive throughout the region, with lending decisions often dictated more by political and family ties than by economic reality. Billions of dollars in easy-money loans were made to family and friends of the well-connected. Without market discipline or risk-based bank lending, the result was overinvestment—financed by vast quantities of debt—and inflated prices of assets in short supply, such as land.[5]

This financial bubble persists as long as the government guarantee is maintained. The inevitable glut of real estate and excess production capacity leads to large amounts of nonperforming loans and widespread loan defaults. When reality strikes, and investors realize that the government doesn't have the resources to bail out everyone, asset values plummet and the bubble is burst. The decline in asset values triggers further loan defaults, causing a loss of the confidence on which economic activity depends. Investors also

---

[3] For a discussion of the role that the Chinese yuan devaluation played in the Asian crisis, see Kenneth Kasa, "Export Competition and Contagious Currency Crises," *Economic Letter*, Federal Reserve Bank of San Francisco, January 16, 1998.

[4] See C. Hu and Kenneth Kasa, "A Dynamic Model of Export Competition, Policy Coordination, and Simultaneous Currency Collapse," Working Paper, Federal Reserve Bank of San Francisco, 1997.

[5] This explanation for the Asian crisis is set forth in Paul Krugman, "What Happened to Asia?" MIT Working Paper, 1998.

worry that the government will try to inflate its way out of its difficulty. The result is a self-reinforcing downward spiral and capital flight. As foreign investors refuse to renew loans and begin to sell off shares of overvalued local companies, capital flight accelerates and the local currency falls, increasing the cost of servicing foreign debts. Local firms and banks scramble to buy foreign exchange before the currency falls further, putting even more downward pressure on the exchange rate. This story explains why stock prices and currency values declined together and why Asian financial institutions were especially hard hit. Moreover, this process is likely to be contagious, as investors search for other countries with similar characteristics. When such a country is found, everyone rushes for the exit simultaneously and another bubble is burst, another currency is sunk.

The standard approach of staving off currency devaluation is to raise interest rates, thereby making it more attractive to hold the local currency and increasing capital inflows. However, this approach was problematic for Asian central banks. Raising interest rates boosted the cost of funds to banks and made it more difficult for borrowers to service their debts, thereby further crippling an already sick financial sector. Higher interest rates also lowered real estate values, which served as collateral for many of these loans, and pushed even more loans into default. Thus, Asian central banks found their hands were tied and investors recognized that.

THE BUBBLE BURSTS

These two stories—loss of export competitiveness and moral hazard in lending combined with crony capitalism—explain the severity of the Asian crisis. Appreciation of the dollar and depreciation of the yen and yuan slowed down Asian economic growth and hurt corporate profits. These factors turned ill-conceived and overleveraged investments in property developments and industrial complexes into financial disasters. The Asian financial crisis then was touched off when local investors began dumping their own currencies for dollars and foreign lenders refused to renew their loans. It was aggravated by politicians, such as in Malaysia and South Korea, who preferred to blame foreigners for their problems rather than seek structural reforms of their economies. Both foreign and domestic investors, already spooked by the currency crisis, lost yet more confidence in these nations and dumped more of their currencies and stocks, driving them to record lows.

This synthesized story is consistent with the experience of Taiwan, which is a net exporter of capital and whose savings are largely invested by private capitalists without government direction or guarantees. Taiwanese businesses also are financed far less by debt than by equity. In contrast to its Asian competitors, Taiwan suffered minimally during 1997, with the Taiwanese dollar (NT$) down by a modest 15% (to counteract its loss of export competitiveness to China and Japan) and its stock market actually up by 17% in NT$ terms.

"The way out," said Confucius, "is through the door." The clear-exit strategy for East Asian countries was to restructure their ailing financial systems by shutting down or selling off failing banks (for example, to healthy foreign banks) and disposing of the collateral (real estate and industrial properties) underlying their bad loans. Although the restructuring has not gone as far as it needs to, the result so far is fewer but stronger and better-capitalized banks and restructured and consolidated industries and a continuation of East Asia's strong historical growth record. However, progress has been slow in reforming bankruptcy laws, a critical element of reform. Simply put, governments must step aside and allow those who borrow too much or lend too foolishly to fail. Ending government guarantees and politically motivated lending will transform Asia's financial sector and force cleaner and more transparent financial transactions. The result will be better investment decisions—decisions driven by market forces rather than personal connections or government whim—and healthier economies that attract capital for the right reasons.

QUESTIONS

1. What were the origins of the Asian currency crisis?
2. What role did expectations play in the Asian currency crisis?
3. How did the appreciation of the U.S. dollar and depreciation of the yuan affect the timing and magnitude of the Asian currency crisis?
4. What is moral hazard and how did it help cause the Asian currency crisis?
5. Why did so many East Asian companies and banks borrow dollars, yen, and Deutsche marks instead of their local currencies to finance their operations? What risks were they exposing themselves to?

2.2.1 Central Bank Reputations and Currency Values

Another critical determinant of currency values is central bank behavior. A **central bank** is the nation's official monetary authority; its job is to use the instruments of monetary policy, including the sole power to create money, to achieve one or more of the following objectives: price stability, low interest rates, or a target currency value. As such, the central bank affects the risk associated with holding money. This risk is inextricably linked to the nature of a **fiat money**, which is nonconvertible paper money. Until 1971, every major currency was linked to a commodity. Today no major currency is linked to a commodity. With a commodity base, usually gold, there was a stable, long-term anchor to the price level. Prices varied a great deal in the short-term, but they eventually returned to where they had been.

With a fiat money, there is no anchor to the price level—that is, there is no standard of value that investors can use to find out what the currency's future value might be. Instead, a currency's value is largely determined by the central bank through its control of the money supply. If the central bank creates too much money, inflation will occur and the value of money will fall. *Expectations* of central bank behavior also will affect exchange rates today; a currency will decline if people *think* the central bank will expand the money supply in the future.

Viewed this way, money becomes a brand-name product whose value is backed by the reputation of the central bank that issues it. And just as reputations among automobiles vary—from Mercedes-Benz to Yugo—so currencies come backed by a range of quality reputations—from the dollar, Swiss franc, and Japanese yen on the high side to the Mexican peso, Thai baht, and Russian ruble on the low side. Underlying these reputations is trust in the willingness of the central bank to maintain price stability.

The high-quality currencies are those expected to maintain their purchasing power because they are issued by reputable central banks. A reputable central bank is one that the markets trust to do the right thing, and not merely the politically expedient thing, when it comes to monetary policy. This trust, in turn, comes from history: reputable banks, like the Bundesbank (Germany's central bank prior to the European Monetary Union), have developed their credibility by having done hard, cruel, and painful things for years in order to fight inflation. In contrast, the low-quality currencies are those that bear little assurance that their purchasing power will be maintained. As in the car market, high-quality currencies sell at a premium, and low-quality currencies sell at a discount (relative to their values based on economic fundamentals alone). That is, investors demand a risk premium to hold a riskier currency, whereas safer currencies will be worth more than their economic fundamentals would indicate.

Price Stability and Central Bank Independence Because good reputations are slow to build and quick to disappear, many economists recommend that central banks adopt rules for price stability that are verifiable, unambiguous, and enforceable along with the independence and accountability necessary to realize this goal.[6] Focus is also important. A central bank whose responsibilities are limited to price stability is more likely to achieve this goal. For example, the Bundesbank—a model for many economists—managed to maintain such a low rate of German inflation because of its statutory commitment to price stability, a legacy of Germany's bitter memories of hyperinflation in the 1920s, which peaked at 200% in 1923. Absent such rules, the natural accountability of central banks to government becomes an avenue for political influence. For example, even though the U.S. Federal Reserve is an independent central bank, its legal responsibility to pursue both full employment and price stability (aims that conflict in the short-term) can hinder its effectiveness in fighting inflation. The greater scope for political influence in central banks that do not have a clear mandate to pursue price stability will, in turn, add to the perception of inflation risk.

This perception stems from the fact that government officials and other critics routinely exhort the central bank to follow "easier" monetary policies, by which they mean boosting the money supply at lower interest rates. These officials and critics believe (1) that the central bank can trade off a higher rate of inflation for more economic growth, and (2) that the central bank determines the rate of interest independently of the rate of inflation and other economic conditions. Despite the questionable merits of these beliefs, central banks—particularly those not independent—often respond to these demands by expanding the money supply.

Central banks that lack independence are also often forced to **monetize the deficit**, which means financing the public-sector deficit by buying government debt with newly created money. Whether monetary expansion stems from economic stimulus or deficit financing, it inevitably leads to higher inflation and a devalued currency.

Independent central bankers, on the other hand, are better able to avoid interference from politicians concerned by short-term economic fluctuations. With independence, a central bank can credibly commit itself to a low-inflation monetary policy and stick to it. Absent such a credible commitment, households and businesses will rationally anticipate that monetary policy would have an inflationary bias, resulting in high inflation becoming a self-fulfilling prophecy.[7]

The link between central bank independence and sound monetary policies is borne out by the empirical evidence.[8] Exhibit 2.4a shows that countries whose central banks are less subject to government intervention tend to have lower and less volatile inflation rates and vice versa. The central banks of Germany, Switzerland, and the United States, identified as the most independent in the post–World War II era, also showed the lowest inflation rates from 1951 to 1988. Least independent were the central banks of Italy, New Zealand, and Spain, countries wracked by the highest inflation rates in the industrial world. Moreover, Exhibit 2.4b indicates that this lower inflation rate is not achieved at the expense of economic growth; rather, central bank independence and economic growth seem to go together.

The idea that central bank independence can help establish a credible monetary policy is being put into practice today, as countries that have been plagued with high inflation rates are enacting legislation to reshape their conduct of monetary policy. For example, New Zealand, England, Mexico, Canada, Chile, and Bolivia all have passed laws that mandate an explicit inflation goal or that give their central banks more independence. The focus on creating credible institutions, by granting central banks independence and substituting rules for discretion over monetary policy, has caused inflation to abate worldwide.

---

[6] See, for example, W. Lee Hoskins, "A European System of Central Banks: Observations from Abroad," *Economic Commentary*, Federal Reserve Bank of Cleveland, November 15, 1990.

[7] In 2004, Edward Prescott and Finn Kydland won the Nobel prize in economics for, among other things, their insights into the relationship between central bank credibility and a low-inflation monetary policy.

[8] See, for example, Alberto Alesina, "Macroeconomics and Politics," in *NBER Macroeconomic Annual, 1988*. Cambridge, Mass.: MIT Press, 1988.

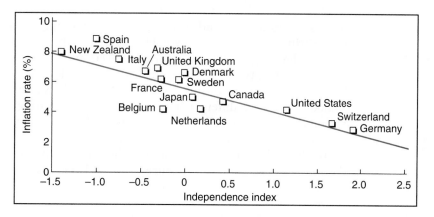

(a) Central Bank Independence versus Inflation

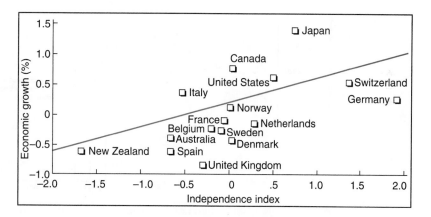

(b) Central Bank Independence versus Economic Growth

EXHIBIT 2.4 ● CENTRAL BANK INDEPENDENCE, INFLATION, AND
ECONOMIC GROWTH

* Inflation and economic growth rates calculated for the period 1951–1988.
Source: Adapted from J. Bradford DeLong and Lawrence H. Summers. "Macroeconomic Policy and
Long-Run growth," *Economic Review*, Federal Reserve Bank of Kansas City, Fourth quarter 1992,
pp. 14–16.

Evidence that even the announcement of greater central bank independence can
boost the credibility of monetary policy comes from England. This example shows that
institutional change alone can have a significant impact on future expected inflation rates.

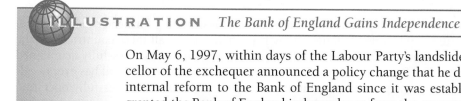

ILLUSTRATION   *The Bank of England Gains Independence*

On May 6, 1997, within days of the Labour Party's landslide victory, Britain's new chancellor of the exchequer announced a policy change that he described as "the most radical
internal reform to the Bank of England since it was established in 1694." The reform
granted the Bank of England independence from the government in the conduct of monetary policy, meaning that it is now free to pursue its policy goals without political interference, and charged it with the task of keeping inflation to 2.5%. The decision was a
surprise, coming as it did from the Labour Party, a party with a strong socialist history that
traditionally was unsympathetic to low-inflation policies, which it viewed as destructive

of jobs. Investors responded to the news by revising downward their expectations of future British inflation. This favorable reaction can be seen by examining the performance of index-linked gilts, which are British government bonds that pay an interest rate that varies with the British inflation rate. One can use the prices of these gilts to estimate the inflation expectations of investors.[9] Exhibit 2.5 shows how the expected inflation rate embodied in three different index-linked gilts—maturing in 2001, 2006, and 2016—responded to the chancellor's announcement of independence. Over the two-week period surrounding the announcement, the expected inflation rate dropped by 0.60% for the 2016 gilt and by somewhat less for the shorter-maturity gilts. These results indicate that the market perceived that enhanced central bank independence would lead to lower future inflation rates. Consistent with our earlier discussion on the inverse relation between inflation and currency values, the British pound jumped in value against the U.S. dollar and the Deutsche mark on the day of the announcement.

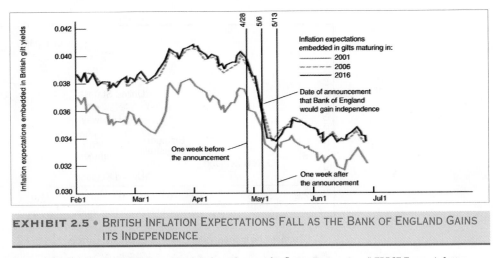

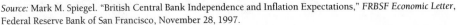

EXHIBIT 2.5 • BRITISH INFLATION EXPECTATIONS FALL AS THE BANK OF ENGLAND GAINS ITS INDEPENDENCE

Source: Mark M. Spiegel. "British Central Bank Independence and Inflation Expectations," *FRBSF Economic Letter*, Federal Reserve Bank of San Francisco, November 28, 1997.

Currency Boards Some countries, like Argentina, have gone even further and established what is in effect a currency board. Under a **currency board** system, there is no central bank. Instead, the currency board issues notes and coins that are convertible on demand and at a fixed rate into a foreign reserve currency. As reserves, the currency board holds high-quality, interest-bearing securities denominated in the reserve currency. Its reserves are equal to 100%, or slightly more, of its notes and coins in circulation. The board has no discretionary monetary policy. Instead, market forces alone determine the money supply.

Over the past 150 years, more than 70 countries (mainly former British colonies) have had currency boards. As long as they kept their boards, all these countries had the same rate of inflation, as the country issuing the reserve currency successfully maintained convertibility at a fixed exchange rate into the reserve currency; no board has ever devalued its currency against its anchor currency. Currency boards are successfully operating today in Estonia, Hong Kong, and Lithuania. Argentina dropped its currency board in January 2002.

---

[9] The methodology used to compute these inflation expectations is described in detail in Mark M. Spiegel, "Central Bank Independence and Inflation Expectations: Evidence from British Index-Linked Gilts," *Economic Review*, Federal Reserve Bank of San Francisco, 1998, No. 1, pp. 3–14.

In addition to promoting price stability, a currency board also compels government to follow a responsible fiscal (spending and tax) policy. If the budget is not balanced, the government must convince the private sector to lend to it; it no longer has the option of forcing the central bank to monetize the deficit. By establishing a monetary authority that is independent of the government and is committed to a conservative monetary policy, currency boards are likely to promote confidence in a country's currency. Such confidence is especially valuable for emerging economies with a past history of profligate monetary and fiscal policy.

The downside of a currency board is that a run on the currency forces a sharp contraction in the money supply and a jump in interest rates. High interest rates slow economic activity, increase bankruptcies, and batter real estate and financial markets. For example, Hong Kong's currency board weathered the Asian storm and delivered a stable currency but at the expense of high interest rates (300% at one point in October 1997), plummeting stock and real estate markets, and deflation. Short of breaking the Hong Kong dollar's peg to the U.S. dollar, the government can do nothing about deflation. Instead of being able to ease monetary policy and cut interest rates during a downturn, Hong Kong must allow wages and prices to decline and wait for the global economy to recover and boost demand for the city's goods and services. Argentina, on the other hand, abandoned its currency board in an attempt to deal with its recession.

Exchange rate arrangements are no substitute for good macroeconomic policy that in turn takes discipline and a willingness to say no to special interests. The peso and its currency board collapsed once domestic and foreign investors determined that Argentina's fiscal policies were unsound, unlikely to improve, and incompatible with the maintenance of a fixed exchange rate. Another lesson is that a nation cannot be forced to maintain a currency arrangement that has outlived its usefulness. As such, no fixed exchange rate system, no matter how strong it appears, is completely sound and credible.

Dollarization The ultimate commitment to monetary credibility and a currency as good as the dollar is **dollarization**—the complete replacement of the local currency with the U.S. dollar. The desirability of dollarization depends on whether monetary discipline is easier to maintain by abandoning the local currency altogether than under a system in which the local currency circulates but is backed by the dollar. The experience of Panama with dollarization is instructive. Dollarization began in Panama almost 100 years ago, in 1904. Annual inflation has averaged 1.7% for the past 30 years, lower than in the United States; there is no local currency risk; and 30-year mortgages are readily available. These are unusual conditions for a developing country, and they stem from dollarization. The downside of dollarization is the loss of **seigniorage**, the central bank's profit on the currency it prints. However, this loss is acceptable if the alternative is monetary chaos.

That is what Ecuador decided in 2000. Ecuador's new government—faced with a plunging currency, accelerating capital flight, a bankrupt banking system, huge budget deficits, in default to foreign creditors, and with its economy in a nosedive—unveiled an economic reform package on January 9, 2000. The centerpiece of the program was the planned replacement of the currency it had used for the past 116 years, the sucre, with the U.S. dollar. As Exhibit 2.6 demonstrates, the announcement of dollarization was enough, by itself, to stabilize the foreign exchange market. The next day, the sucre traded at the new official level of 25,000 per dollar. It remained there, despite nationwide strikes and two changes of government, until September 9, 2000 when Ecuador officially replaced the sucre with the dollar. During the period leading up to that date, some capital returned to Ecuador and the economy began to grow again.

Dollarization by itself, of course, is no guarantee of economic success. It can provide price stability, but like a currency board it is not a substitute for sound economic policies. Even the United States, which by definition is dollarized, has its economic ups

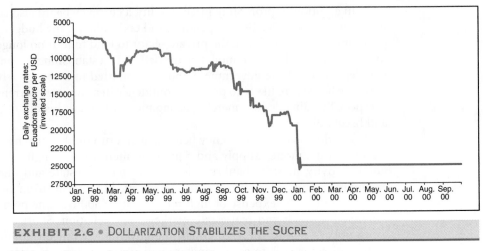

EXHIBIT 2.6 • DOLLARIZATION STABILIZES THE SUCRE

Source: http://www.oanda.com/

and downs. But what dollarization can do is to provide the macroeconomic stability that will enhance the impact of these reforms.

Expectations and Currency Values   The importance of expectations and central bank reputations in determining currency values was dramatically illustrated on June 2, 1987, when the financial markets learned that Paul Volcker was resigning as chairman of the Federal Reserve Board. Within seconds after this news appeared on the ubiquitous video screens used by traders to watch the world, both the price of the dollar on foreign exchange markets and the prices of bonds began a steep decline. By day's end, the dollar had fallen by 2.6% against the Japanese yen, and the price of Treasury bonds declined by 2.3%—one of the largest one-day declines ever. The price of corporate bonds fell by a similar amount. All told, the value of U.S. bonds fell by more than $100 billion.

The response by the financial markets reveals the real forces that are setting the value of the dollar and interest rates under our current monetary system. On that day, there was no other economic news of note. There was no news about American competitiveness. There was no change in Federal Reserve (Fed) policy or inflation statistics; nor was there any change in the size of the budget deficit, the trade deficit, or the growth rate of the U.S. economy.

What actually happened on that announcement day? Foreign exchange traders and investors simply became less certain of the path U.S. monetary policy would take in the days and years ahead. Volcker was a known inflation fighter. Alan Greenspan, the incoming Fed chairman, was an unknown quantity. The possibility that he would emphasize growth over price stability raised the specter of a more expansive monetary policy. Because the natural response to risk is to hold less of the asset whose risk has risen, investors tried to reduce their holdings of dollars and dollar-denominated bonds, driving down their prices in the process.

The import of what happened on June 2, 1987, is that prices of the dollar and those billions of dollars in bonds were changed by nothing more or less than investors changing their collective assessment of what actions the Fed would or would not take. A critical lesson for businesspeople and policy makers alike surfaces: A shift in the trust that people have for a currency can change its value now by changing its expected value in the future. The level of interest rates is also affected by trust in the future value of money. All else being equal, the greater the trust in the promise that money will maintain its purchasing power, the lower the interest rates will be. This theory is formalized in Chapter 4 as the Fisher effect.

M I N I - C A S E   *The U.S. Dollar Sells Off*

On September 3, 2003, the finance ministers of the Group of Seven (G-7) industrialized countries endorsed "flexibility" in exchange rates, a code word widely regarded as an encouragement for China and Japan to stop managing their currencies.[10] Both countries had been actively intervening in the foreign exchange market to weaken their currencies against the dollar and thereby improve their exports. China and Japan had been seen buying billions of dollars in U.S. Treasury bonds. The G-7 statement prompted massive selling of the U.S. dollar and dollar assets. The dollar fell 2% against the yen, the biggest one-day drop that year, and U.S. Treasury bonds saw a steep decline in value as well.

QUESTIONS

1. How did China and Japan manage to weaken their currencies against the dollar?
2. Why did the U.S. dollar and U.S. Treasury bonds fall in response to the G-7 statement?
3. What is the link between currency intervention and China and Japan buying U.S. Treasury bonds?
4. What risks do China and Japan face from their currency intervention?

2.3 THE FUNDAMENTALS OF CENTRAL BANK INTERVENTION

The exchange rate is one of the most important prices in a country because it links the domestic economy to the rest-of-world economy. As such, it affects relative national competitiveness.

2.3.1 How Real Exchange Rates Affect Relative Competitiveness

We already have seen the link between exchange rate changes and relative inflation rates. The important point for now is that an appreciation of the exchange rate beyond what is necessary to offset the inflation differential between two countries raises the price of domestic goods relative to the price of foreign goods. This rise in the **real** or **inflation-adjusted exchange rate**—measured as the **nominal** (or actual) **exchange rate** adjusted for changes in relative price levels—proves to be a mixed blessing. For example, the rise in the value of the U.S. dollar from 1980 to 1985 translated directly into a reduction in the dollar prices of imported goods and raw materials. As a result, the prices of imports and of products that compete with imports began to ease. This development contributed significantly to the slowing of U.S. inflation in the early 1980s.

However, the rising dollar had some distinctly negative consequences for the U.S. economy as well. Declining dollar prices of imports had their counterpart in the increasing foreign currency prices of U.S. products sold abroad. As a result, American exports became less competitive in world markets, and American-made import substitutes

---

[10] The G-7 consists of Canada, France, Germany, Italy, Japan, the United Kingdom, and the United States.

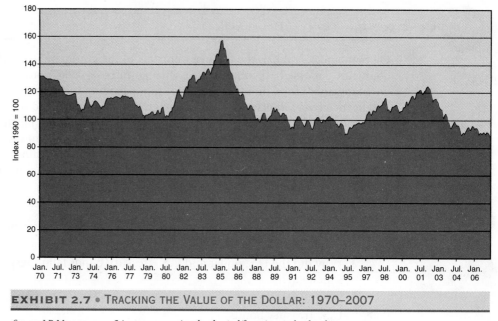

EXHIBIT 2.7 • TRACKING THE VALUE OF THE DOLLAR: 1970–2007

Source: J.P. Morgan. www.2.jpmorgan.com/marketdataind/forex/currindex.html

became less competitive in the United States. Domestic sales of traded goods declined, generating unemployment in the traded-goods sector and inducing a shift in resources from the traded- to the nontraded-goods sector of the economy.

Alternatively, home currency depreciation results in a more competitive traded-goods sector, stimulating domestic employment and inducing a shift in resources from the nontraded- to the traded-goods sector. The bad part is that currency weakness also results in higher prices for imported goods and services, eroding living standards and worsening domestic inflation.

From its peak in mid-1985, the U.S. dollar fell by more than 50% during the next few years, enabling Americans to experience the joys and sorrows of both a strong and a weak currency in less than a decade. The weak dollar made U.S. companies more competitive worldwide; at the same time, it lowered the living standards of Americans who enjoyed consuming foreign goods and services. The dollar hit a low point in 1995 and then began to strengthen, largely based on the substantial success that the United States had in taming inflation and the budget deficit and in generating strong economic growth. Exhibit 2.7 charts the value of the U.S. dollar from 1970 to 2006. Despite its substantial rise in the late 1990s, the dollar is still below its level achieved back in 1970 (partly due to its recent decline).

2.3.2 Foreign Exchange Market Intervention

Depending on their economic goals, some governments will prefer an overvalued domestic currency, whereas others will prefer an undervalued currency. Still others just want a correctly valued currency, but economic policy makers may feel that the rate set by the market is irrational; that is, they feel they can better judge the correct exchange rate than the marketplace can. The tradeoffs faced by governments in terms of their exchange rate objectives are illustrated by the example of China's yuan.

MINI-CASE   *A Yen for Yuan*

On April 6, 2005, the U.S. Senate voted 67–33 to impose a 27.5% tariff on all Chinese products entering the United States if Beijing did not agree to revalue the yuan by a like amount. Almost 2 years earlier, on September 2, 2003, U.S. Treasury Secretary John Snow had traveled to Beijing to lobby his Chinese counterparts to revalue what was then and still is widely regarded as an undervalued yuan. In the eyes of U.S. manufacturers and labor unions, a cheap yuan gives China's exports an unfair price advantage over American competitors in the world market and is accelerating the movement of manufacturing jobs to China. One evidence of this problem is the widening U.S. trade deficit with China, which had reached $162 billion in 2004 (on about $200 billion in total imports from China).[11] Similarly, Japan, South Korea, and many European and other nations are pushing for China to abandon its fixed exchange rate because a weak U.S. dollar, which automatically lowered the yuan against other currencies, was making already-inexpensive Chinese goods unfairly cheap in global markets, hurting their own exports.

China rejected calls for it to revalue its currency and said it would maintain the stability of the yuan. Since 1996, China has fixed its exchange rate at 8.28 yuan to the dollar. In the past year, the dollar has depreciated significantly against the euro, giving Chinese companies a competitive advantage against European manufacturers. A massive rise in China's foreign exchange reserves in recent years (reserves rose 47% in 2004, to reach $609.9 billion by the end of the year) is evidence that the Chinese government has been holding its currency down artificially. Politicians and businesspeople in the United States and elsewhere have been calling for the yuan to be revalued, which it almost certainly would in a free market. (Economists estimate that the yuan is currently undervalued by 20% to 30% against the dollar.)

The Chinese government has been resisting the clamor for yuan revaluation because of the serious problems it faces. China is often referred to as a "bicycle economy," meaning that it needs to keep moving forward just to avoid falling down. As the country becomes more market-oriented, its money-losing state-owned enterprises must lay off millions of workers. Only flourishing businesses can absorb this surplus labor. The Chinese government is concerned that allowing the yuan to appreciate would stifle the competitiveness of its exports, hurt farmers by making agricultural imports cheaper, and imperil the country's fragile banking system, resulting in millions of unemployed and disgruntled Chinese wandering the countryside and threatening the stability of the communist regime. It also justified a weak yuan as a means of fighting the threat of deflation.

Nonetheless, keeping China's currency peg is not risk free. Foreign currency inflows are rising as investors, many of whom are ordinary Chinese bringing overseas capital back home, bet that China will be forced to revalue its yuan. They are betting on the yuan by purchasing Chinese stocks, real estate, and treasury bonds. To maintain its fixed exchange rate, the Bank of China must sell yuan to buy up all these foreign currency inflows. This intervention has boosted China's foreign exchange reserves but at the expense of a surging yuan money supply, which rose 19.6% in 2003 and 14.6% in 2004. For a time, a rising domestic money supply seemed an appropriate response to an economy that appeared to be on the verge of deflation. More recently, however, rapid money supply growth threatens inflation, and has led to roaring asset prices, including fears of a speculative bubble in real estate, and excessive bank lending. The latter is particularly problematic as Chinese banks are estimated to already have at least $500 billion in nonperforming loans to bankrupt state companies and unprofitable property developers.

---

[11] U.S. Census Bureau, Foreign Trade Statistics, http://www.census.gov/foreign-trade/balance/c5700.html#2007. Corresponding figures for 2006 are a trade deficit of $232.5 billion on imports from China of about $288 billion.

Another risk in pursuing a cheap currency policy is the possibility of stirring protectionist measures in its trading partners. For example, ailing U.S. textile makers are lobbying the Bush administration for emergency quotas on Chinese textiles imports, while other manufacturers are seeking trade sanctions if Beijing won't allow the yuan to rise. Similarly, European government officials have spoken of retaliatory trade measures to force a revalued yuan.

On July 21, 2005, the People's Bank of China (PBOC) announced a revaluation of the yuan (from 8.28 to 8.11 to the dollar) and a reform of the exchange rate regime. Under the reform, the PBOC would incorporate a reference basket of currencies when choosing its target rate for the currency. On May 18, 2007, China announced that it is expanding the trading band for the yuan to plus or minus 0.5% from the previous 0.3%.

QUESTIONS

1. Why is China trying to hold down the value of the yuan? What evidence suggests that China is indeed pursuing a weak currency policy?

2. What benefits does China expect to realize from a weak currency policy?

3. Other things being equal, what would a 27.5% tariff cost American consumers annually on $200 billion in imports from China?

4. Currently, imports from China account for about 10% of total U.S. imports. A 25% appreciation of the yuan would be the equivalent of what percent dollar depreciation? How significant would such a depreciation likely be in terms of stemming America's appetite for foreign goods?

5. What policy tool is China using to maintain the yuan at an artificially low level? Are there any potential problems with using this policy tool? What might China do to counter these problems?

6. Does an undervalued yuan impose any costs on the Chinese economy? If so, what are they?

7. Suppose the Chinese government were to cease its foreign exchange market intervention and the yuan climbed to five to the dollar. What would be the percentage gain to investors who measure their returns in dollars?

8. Currently, the yuan is not a convertible currency, meaning that Chinese individuals are not permitted to exchange their yuan for dollars to invest abroad. Moreover, companies operating in China must convert all their foreign exchange earnings into yuan. Suppose China were to relax these currency controls and restraints on capital outflows, what would happen to the pressure on the yuan to revalue? Explain.

9. By how much did the yuan appreciate against the dollar on July 21, 2005?

10. What has happened to the yuan exchange rate since May 18, 2007 and how has it affected the U.S. trade deficit with China?

No matter what category they fall in, most governments will be tempted to intervene in the foreign exchange market to move the exchange rate to the level consistent with their goals or beliefs. **Foreign exchange market intervention** refers to official purchases and sales of foreign exchange that nations undertake through their central banks to influence their currencies.

For example, review Section 2.1 and suppose the United States and Euroland decide to maintain the old exchange rate e_0 in the face of the new equilibrium rate e_1. According to Exhibit 2.2, the result will be an excess demand for euros equal to Q_3-Q_2; this euro shortage is the same as an excess supply of $(Q_3$-$Q_2)e_0$ dollars. Either the Federal Reserve (the American central bank), or the ECB (the central bank for Euroland), or both will then have to intervene in the market to supply this additional quantity of euros (to buy up the excess supply of dollars). Absent some change, the United States will face a perpetual balance-of-payments deficit equal to $(Q_3$-$Q_2)e_0$ dollars, which is the dollar value of the Euroland balance-of-payments surplus of $(Q_3$-$Q_2)$ euros.

Mechanics of Intervention   Although the mechanics of central bank intervention vary, the general purpose of each variant is basically the same: to increase the market demand for one currency by increasing the market supply of another. To see how this purpose can be accomplished, suppose in the previous example that the ECB wants to reduce the value of the euro from e_1 to its previous equilibrium value of e_0. To do so, the ECB must sell an additional $(Q_3$-$Q_2)$ euros in the foreign exchange market, thereby eliminating the shortage of euros that would otherwise exist at e_0. This sale of euros (which involves the purchase of an equivalent amount of dollars) will also eliminate the excess supply of $(Q_3$-$Q_2)e_0$ dollars that now exists at e_0. The simultaneous sale of euros and purchase of dollars will balance the supply and demand for euros (and dollars) at e_0.

If the Fed also wants to raise the value of the dollar, it will buy dollars with euros. Regardless of whether the Fed or the ECB initiates this foreign exchange operation, the net result is the same: The U.S. money supply will fall, and Euroland money supply will rise.

Sterilized versus Unsterilized Intervention   The two examples just discussed are instances of **unsterilized intervention**; that is, the monetary authorities have not insulated their domestic money supplies from the foreign exchange transactions. In both cases, the U.S. money supply will fall, and the Euroland money supply will rise. As noted earlier, an increase (decrease) in the supply of money, all other things held constant, will result in more (less) inflation. Thus, the foreign exchange market intervention will not only change the exchange rate, it will also increase Euroland inflation, while reducing U.S. inflation. Recall that it was the jump in the U.S. money supply that caused this inflation. These money supply changes will also affect interest rates in both countries.

To neutralize these effects, the Fed and/or the ECB can *sterilize* the impact of their foreign exchange market intervention on the domestic money supply through an **open-market operation**, which is just the sale or purchase of Treasury securities. For example, the purchase of U.S. Treasury bills by the Fed supplies reserves to the banking system and increases the U.S. money supply. After the open-market operation, therefore, the public will hold more cash and bank deposits and fewer Treasury securities. If the Fed buys enough T-bills, the U.S. money supply will return to its preintervention level. Similarly, the ECB could neutralize the impact of intervention on the Euroland money supply by subtracting reserves from its banking system through sales of euro-denominated securities.

For example, during a 3-month period in 2003 alone, the Bank of China issued 250 billion yuan in short-term notes to commercial banks to sterilize the yuan created by its foreign-exchange market intervention. The Bank of China also sought to mop up excess liquidity by raising its reserve requirements for financial institutions, forcing banks to keep more money on deposit with it and make fewer loans.

The net result of sterilization should be a rise or fall in the country's foreign exchange reserves but no change in the domestic money supply. These effects are shown in Exhibit 2.8a, which displays a steep decline in Mexico's reserves during 1994 while its money supply, measured by its **monetary base** (currency in circulation plus bank reserves), followed its usual growth path with its usual seasonal variations. As mentioned earlier, Banco de Mexico sterilized its purchases of pesos by buying back government securities. Conversely, Argentina's currency board precluded its ability to sterilize changes

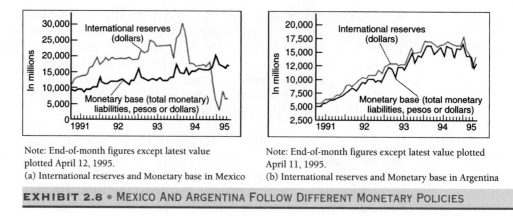

Note: End-of-month figures except latest value
plotted April 12, 1995.
(a) International reserves and Monetary base in Mexico

Note: End-of-month figures except latest value plotted
April 11, 1995.
(b) International reserves and Monetary base in Argentina

EXHIBIT 2.8 • MEXICO AND ARGENTINA FOLLOW DIFFERENT MONETARY POLICIES

in reserves, forcing changes in Argentina's monetary base to closely match changes in its dollar reserves, as can be seen in Exhibit 2.8b.

2.3.3 The Effects of Foreign Exchange Market Intervention

The basic problem with central bank intervention is that it is likely to be either ineffectual or irresponsible. Because sterilized intervention entails a substitution of foreign currency-denominated securities for domestic currency securities,[12] the exchange rate will be permanently affected only if investors view domestic and foreign securities as being imperfect substitutes. If this is the case, then the exchange rate and relative interest rates must change to induce investors to hold the new portfolio of securities. For example, if the Bank of Japan sells yen in the foreign exchange market, investors would find themselves holding a larger share of yen assets than before. At prevailing exchange rates, if the public considers assets denominated in yen and in dollars to be imperfect substitutes for each other, people would attempt to sell these extra yen assets to rebalance their portfolios. As a result, the value of the yen would fall below its level absent the intervention.

If investors consider these securities to be perfect substitutes, however, then no change in the exchange rate or interest rates will be necessary to convince investors to hold this portfolio. In this case, sterilized intervention is ineffectual. This conclusion is consistent with the experiences of Mexico as well as those of the United States and other industrial nations in their intervention policies. For example, Exhibit 2.9 shows that a sequence of eight large currency interventions by the Clinton administration between 1993 and 2000 had little effect on the value of the dollar or its direction; exchange rates appear to have been moved largely by basic market forces. Similarly, Mexico ran through about $25 billion in reserves in 1994, and Asian nations ran through more than $100 billion in reserves in 1997 to no avail.

Sterilized intervention could affect exchange rates by conveying information or by altering market expectations. It does this by signaling a change in monetary policy to the market, not by changing market fundamentals, so its influence is transitory.

On the other hand, unsterilized intervention can have a lasting effect on exchange rates, but insidiously—by creating inflation in some nations and deflation in others. In the example presented above, Euroland would wind up with a permanent (and inflationary) increase in its money supply, and the United States would end up with a deflationary decrease in its money supply. If the resulting increase in Euroland inflation and decrease

---

[12] Central banks typically hold their foreign exchange reserves in the form of foreign currency bonds. Sterilized intervention, therefore, involves selling off some of these foreign currency bonds and replacing them with domestic currency ones. Following the intervention, the public will hold more foreign currency bonds and fewer domestic currency bonds.

The Clinton administration's currency-market interventions, shown with JP Morgan's index of the U.S. dollar against 18 major currencies.

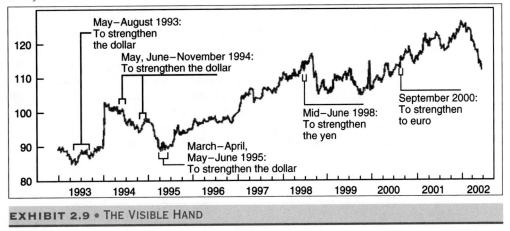

EXHIBIT 2.9 • THE VISIBLE HAND

Note: Episodes typically involved more than one sale or purchase of dollars over days or weeks.
Source: WSJ Market Data Group; Jeffrey A. Frankel, *Wall Street Journal*, July 23, 2002, p. A2.

in U.S. inflation were sufficiently large, the exchange rate would remain at e_0 without the need for further government intervention. But it is the money supply changes, and not the intervention by itself, that affect the exchange rate. Moreover, moving the nominal exchange rate from e_1 to e_0 should not affect the real exchange rate because the change in inflation rates offsets the nominal exchange rate change.

If forcing a currency below its equilibrium level causes inflation, it follows that devaluation cannot be of much use as a means of restoring competitiveness. A devaluation improves competitiveness only to the extent that it does not cause higher inflation. If the devaluation causes domestic wages and prices to rise, any gain in competitiveness is quickly eroded.

Of course, when the world's central banks execute a coordinated surprise attack, the impact on the market can be dramatic, though for a short period. Early in the morning on February 27, 1985, for example, Western European central bankers began telephoning banks in London, Frankfurt, Milan, and other financial centers to order the sale of hundreds of millions of dollars; the action—joined a few hours later by the Federal Reserve in New York—panicked the markets and drove the dollar down by 5% that day.

But keeping the market off balance requires credible repetitions. Shortly after the February 27 blitzkrieg, the dollar was back on the rise. The Fed intervened again, but it was not until clear signs of a U.S. economic slowdown emerged that the dollar turned down in March.

2.4 SUMMARY AND CONCLUSIONS

This chapter studied the process of determining exchange rates under a floating exchange rate system. We saw that in the absence of government intervention, exchange rates respond to the forces of supply and demand, which in turn are dependent on relative inflation rates, interest rates, and GDP growth rates. Monetary policy is crucial here. If the central bank expands the money supply at a faster rate than the growth in money demand, the purchasing power of money declines both at home (inflation) and abroad (currency depreciation). In addition, the healthier the economy is, the stronger the currency is likely to be. Exchange rates also are crucially affected by expectations of future currency changes, which depend on forecasts of future economic and political conditions.

In order to achieve certain economic or political objectives, governments often intervene in the currency markets to affect the exchange rate. Although the mechanics of such interventions vary, the general purpose of each variant is basically the same: to increase the market demand for one currency by increasing the market supply of another. Alternatively, the government can control the exchange rate directly by setting a price for its currency and then restricting access to the foreign exchange market.

A critical factor that helps explain the volatility of exchange rates is that with a fiat money there is no anchor to a currency's value, nothing around which beliefs can coalesce. In this situation, where people are unsure of what to expect, any new piece of information can dramatically alter their beliefs. Thus, if the underlying domestic economic policies are unstable, exchange rates will be volatile as traders react to new information.

QUESTIONS

1. Describe how these three typical transactions should affect present and future exchange rates:
   a. Seagram imports a year's supply of French champagne. Payment in French francs is due immediately.
   b. MCI sells a new stock issue to Alcatel, the French telecommunications company. Payment in dollars is due immediately.
   c. Korean Airlines buys five Boeing 747s. As part of the deal, Boeing arranges a loan to KAL for the purchase amount from the U.S. Export-Import Bank. The loan is to be paid back over the next 7 years with a 2-year grace period.

2. The maintenance of money's value is said to depend on the monetary authorities. What might the monetary authorities do to a currency that would cause its value to drop?

3. For each of the following six scenarios, state whether the value of the dollar will appreciate, depreciate, or remain the same relative to the Japanese yen. Explain each answer. Assume that exchange rates are free to vary and that other factors are held constant.
   a. The growth rate of national income is higher in the United States than in Japan.
   b. Inflation is higher in the United States than in Japan.
   c. Prices in Japan and the United States are rising at the same rate.
   d. Real interest rates in the United States rise relative to real rates in Japan.
   e. The United States imposes new restrictions on the ability of foreigners to buy American companies and real estate.
   f. U.S. wages rise relative to Japanese wages, while American productivity falls behind Japanese productivity.

4. The Fed adopts an easier monetary policy. How is this likely to affect the value of the dollar and U.S. interest rates?

5. Comment on the following news from the *Wall Street Journal* (April 3, 2007, p. C12): "The dollar was little changed against the euro and yen, but weakened versus the currencies of Australia and the United Kingdom as investors mulled possible further rate increases in those countries."

6. On November 28, 1990, Federal Reserve Chairman Alan Greenspan told the House Banking Committee that despite possible benefits to the U.S. trade balance, "a weaker dollar also is a cause for concern." This statement departed from what appeared to be an attitude of benign neglect by U.S. monetary officials toward dollar's depreciation. He also rejected the notion that the Fed should aggressively ease monetary policy, as some treasury officials had been urging. At the same time, Mr. Greenspan did not mention foreign exchange market intervention to support the dollar's value.
   a. What was the likely reaction of the foreign exchange market to Mr. Greenspan's statements? Explain.
   b. Could Mr. Greenspan support the value of the U.S. dollar without intervening in the foreign exchange market? If so, how?

7. Many Asian governments have attempted to promote their export competitiveness by holding down the values of their currencies through foreign exchange market intervention.
   a. What is the likely impact of this policy on Asian foreign exchange reserves, on Asian inflation, on Asian export competitiveness, and on Asian living standards?
   b. Some Asian countries have attempted to sterilize their foreign exchange market intervention by selling bonds. What are the likely consequences of sterilization on interest rates? On exchange rates in the longer term and on export competitiveness?

8. As mentioned in the chapter, Hong Kong has a currency board that fixes the exchange rate between the U.S. and H.K. dollars.

a. What is the likely consequence of a large capital inflow for the rate of inflation in Hong Kong? For the competitiveness of Hong Kong business? Explain.

b. Given a large capital inflow, what would happen to the value of the Hong Kong dollar if it were allowed to freely float? What would be the effect on the competitiveness of Hong Kong business? Explain.

c. Given a large capital inflow, will Hong Kong business be more or less competitive under a currency board or with a freely floating currency? Explain.

9. In 1994, an influx of drug money to Colombia coincided with a sharp increase in its export earnings from coffee and oil.

a. What was the likely impact of these factors on the value of the Colombian peso and the competitiveness of Colombia's legal exports? Explain.

b. In 1996, Colombia's president, facing charges of involvement in his country's drug cartel, sought to boost his domestic popularity by pursuing more expansionary monetary policies. Standing in the way was Colombia's independent central bank—Banco de la Republica. In response, the president and his supporters discussed the possibility of returning central bank control to the executive branch. Describe the likely economic consequences of ending Banco de la Republica's independence.

PROBLEMS

1. On August 1, 2006, Zimbabwe changed the value of the Zim dollar from Z$101/U.S.$ to Z$250/U.S.$.

a. What was the original U.S. dollar value of the Zim dollar? What is the new U.S. dollar value of the Zim dollar?

b. By what percent has the Zim dollar devalued (revalued) relative to the U.S. dollar?

c. By what percent has the U.S. dollar appreciated (depreciated) relative to the Zim dollar?

2. In 2002 , one dollar bought ¥125. In 2006, it bought about ¥115.

a. What was the dollar value of the yen in 2002? What was the yen's dollar value in 2006?

b. By what percent has the yen risen in value between 2002 and 2006?

c. By what percent has the dollar fallen in value between 2002 and 2006?

3. On February 1, the euro is worth $1.2966. By May 1, it has moved to $1.3634.

a. By what percent has the euro appreciated or depreciated against the dollar during this 3-month period?

b. By what percent has the dollar appreciated or depreciated against the euro during this period?

4. In early August 2002 (the exact date is a state secret), North Korea reduced the official value of the won from $0.465 to $0.0067. The black market value of the won at that time was $0.005.

a. By what percent did the won devalue?

b. Following the initial devaluation, what further percentage devaluation would be necessary for the won to equal its black market value?

5. On March 29, 2007, the Indian rupee was worth $0.023270. The next day, it was worth $0.022980.

a. By how much had the rupee depreciated against the dollar?

b. By how much had the dollar appreciated against the rupee?

6. On June 14, 2001, Domingo Cavallo, Argentina's treasury secretary announced a new exchange rate policy designed to stimulate Argentina's slumping economy. Under the new policy, exporters and importers would be able to convert between dollars and pesos at an exchange rate that was an average of the dollar and the euro exchange rates, that is, P1 = $0.50 + €0.50. At that time, the euro was trading at $0.85.

a. How many pesos would an exporter receive for one dollar under the new system?

b. How many dollars would an importer receive for one peso under the new system?

BIBLIOGRAPHY

Frenkel, J. A. and H. G. Johnson, eds. *The Economics of Exchange Rates.* Reading, Mass.: Addison–Wesley, 1978.

Levich, R. M. "Empirical Studies of Exchange Rates: Price Behavior, Rate Determination and Market Efficiency." In *Handbook of International Economics*, Vol. II. Ronald W. Jones and Peter B. Kenen, eds. Netherlands: Elsevier B.V., 1985, pp. 980–1040.

Marrinan, J. "Exchange Rate Determination: Sorting Out Theory and Evidence." *New England Economic Review*, November-December 1989, pp. 39–51.

INTERNET RESOURCES

http://pacific.commerce.ubc.ca/xr/plot.html Contains current and historical foreign exchange rate data for all currencies that you can download into preformatted time series charts.

http://www.ny.frb.org Web site of the Federal Reserve Bank of New York. Contains information on U.S. interventions in the foreign exchange market.

http://www.bis.org/ Web site of the Bank for International Settlements (BIS) that takes you directly to links with the various central banks of the world.

http://www.bis.org/ Contains a collection of articles and speeches by senior central bankers.

http://www2.jpmorgan.com/MarketDataInd/Forex/currIndex.html Web site of J.P. Morgan that contains historical data on real and nominal foreign exchange rate indexes that go back to 1970.

http://research.stlouisfed.org/ Web site of the Federal Reserve Bank of St. Louis that takes you directly to current and historical foreign exchange rate data that you can download into spreadsheets.

http://www.federalreserve.gov/ Web site of the Federal Reserve Bank that takes you directly to historical foreign exchange rate data that you can download into spreadsheets.

http://www.oanda.com/ Contains current and historical foreign exchange rate data for all currencies.

INTERNET EXERCISES

1. Plot the nominal and real values of the dollar over the past 10 years using the J.P. Morgan data.

2. How closely correlated are changes in the real and nominal values of the dollar over this period? That is, do the real and nominal exchange rates tend to move together?

3. By how much has the dollar changed in real terms over this period?

4. By how much has the dollar changed in nominal terms over this period?

5. Plot the following exchange rates over the past 5 years: dollar/yen, dollar/DM, and dollar/pound. Are these exchange rates closely correlated with each other? You can use foreign exchange data from the Federal Reserve for this assignment.

6. Based on your review of several recent currency interventions, what reasons were given by the monetary authorities for these interventions? How much money was expended during these interventions? You can find stories of these interventions by searching the Web site of the Federal Reserve Bank of New York and the Web sites of other central banks linked through the BIS Web site.

7. Based on your review of *The Economist*, the *Wall Street Journal*, and the *Financial Times*, which countries are having currency problems? What are the causes of those currency problems?

THE INTERNATIONAL MONETARY SYSTEM

The monetary and economic disorders of the past fifteen years . . . are a reaction to a world monetary system that has no historical precedent. We have been sailing on uncharted waters and it has been taking time to learn the safest routes.

Milton Friedman
Winner of Nobel Prize in Economics

CHAPTER LEARNING OBJECTIVES

- To distinguish between a free float, a managed float, a target-zone arrangement, and a fixed-rate system of exchange rate determination
- To describe how equilibrium in the foreign exchange market is achieved under alternative exchange rate systems, including a gold standard
- To identify the three categories of central bank intervention under a managed float
- To describe the purposes, operation, and consequences of the European Monetary System
- To describe the origins, purposes, and consequences of European Monetary Union and the euro
- To identify the four alternatives to devaluation under a system of fixed exchange rates
- To explain the political realities that underlie government intervention in the foreign exchange market
- To describe the history and consequences of the gold standard
- To explain why the postwar international monetary system broke down
- To describe the origins of and proposed mechanisms to deal with the various emerging market currency crises that have occurred during the past decade

KEY TERMS

austerity
Bank for International Settlements
  (BIS)
"beggar-thy-neighbor" devaluation
Bretton Woods Agreement
Bretton Woods system
clean float
Common Market
conditionality
dirty float
euro
European Central Bank
European Currency Unit (ECU)

European Community (EC)
European Monetary System (EMS)
European Monetary Union (EMU)
exchange-rate mechanism (ERM)
fiat money
fixed-rate system
free float
G-5 nations
G-7 nations
gold standard
International Bank for Reconstruction
  and Development (World Bank)
International Monetary Fund (IMF)

international monetary system
lender of last resort
Louvre Accord
Maastricht criteria
Maastricht Treaty
managed float
monetary union
optimum currency area

par value
Plaza Agreement
price-specie-flow mechanism
privatization
seigniorage
Smithsonian Agreement
Special Drawing Right (SDR)
target-zone arrangement

Over the past five decades, increasing currency volatility has subjected the earnings and asset values of multinational corporations (MNCs), banks, and cross-border investors to large and unpredictable fluctuations in value. These currency problems have been exacerbated by the breakdown of the postwar international monetary system that was established at the Bretton Woods Conference in 1944. The main features of the **Bretton Woods system** were the relatively fixed exchange rates of individual currencies in terms of the U.S. dollar and the convertibility of the dollar into gold for foreign official institutions. These fixed exchange rates were supposed to reduce the riskiness of international transactions, thus promoting growth in world trade.

However, in 1971 the Bretton Woods system fell victim to the international monetary turmoil it was designed to avoid. It was replaced by the present regime of rapidly fluctuating exchange rates, resulting in major problems as well as opportunities for multinational corporations. The purpose of this chapter is to help managers, both financial and nonfinancial, understand what the international monetary system is and how the choice of system affects currency values. It also provides a historical background of the international monetary system to enable managers to gain perspective when trying to interpret the likely consequences of new policy moves in the area of international finance. After all, although the types of government foreign-exchange policies may at times appear to be limitless, they are all variations on a common theme.

3.1 ALTERNATIVE EXCHANGE RATE SYSTEMS

The **international monetary system** refers primarily to the set of policies, institutions, practices, regulations, and mechanisms that determine the rate at which one currency is exchanged for another. This section considers five market mechanisms for establishing exchange rates: free float, managed float, target-zone arrangement, fixed-rate system, and the current hybrid system.

As we shall see, each of these mechanisms has costs and benefits associated with it. Nations prefer economic stability and often equate this objective with a stable exchange rate. However, fixing an exchange rate often leads to currency crises if the nation attempts to follow a monetary policy that is inconsistent with that fixed rate. At the same time, a nation may decide to fix its exchange rate in order to limit the scope of monetary policy, as in the case of currency boards described in Chapter 2. Although economic shocks can be absorbed more easily when exchange rates are allowed to float freely, freely floating exchange rates may exhibit excessive volatility, which hurts trade and stifles economic growth. The choice of a particular exchange rate mechanism depends on the relative importance that a given nation at a given point in time places on the trade-offs associated with these different systems.

3.1.1 Free Float

We already have seen that free-market exchange rates are determined by the interaction of currency supplies and demands. The supply-and-demand schedules, in turn, are influenced by price level changes, interest differentials, and economic growth. In a **free float**, as these economic parameters change—for example, because of new government policies or acts of nature—market participants will adjust their current and expected future currency needs. In the two-country example of Euroland and the United States, the shifts in the euro supply-and-demand schedules will, in turn, lead to new equilibrium positions. Over time, the exchange rate will fluctuate randomly as market participants assess and react to new information, as much as security and commodity prices in other financial markets respond to news. These shifts and oscillations are illustrated in Exhibits 3.1 and 3.2a for the dollar/euro exchange rate; D_t and S_t are the hypothetical euro demand and supply curves, respectively, for period t. Exhibit 3.2b shows how the dollar/euro exchange rate actually changed during a 7-day period in May 2007. Such a system of freely floating exchange rates is usually referred to as a **clean float**.

3.1.2 Managed Float

Not surprisingly, few countries have been able to long resist the temptation to intervene actively in the foreign exchange market in order to reduce the economic uncertainty associated with a clean float. The fear is that too abrupt a change in the value of a nation's currency could imperil its export industries (if the currency appreciates) or could lead to a higher rate of inflation (if the currency depreciates). Moreover, the experience with floating rates has not been encouraging. Instead of reducing economic volatility, as they were supposed to do, floating exchange rates appear to have increased it. Exchange rate uncertainty also reduces economic efficiency by acting as a tax on trade and foreign investment. Therefore, most countries with floating currencies have attempted, through central bank intervention, to smooth out exchange rate fluctuations. Such a system of managed exchange rates, called a **managed float**, is also known as a **dirty float**.

Managed floats fall into three distinct categories of central bank intervention. The approaches, which vary in their reliance on market forces, are as follows:

1. *Smoothing out daily fluctuations.* Governments following this route attempt only to preserve an orderly pattern of exchange rate changes. They occasionally enter the market on the buy or sell side to ease the transition from one rate to another,

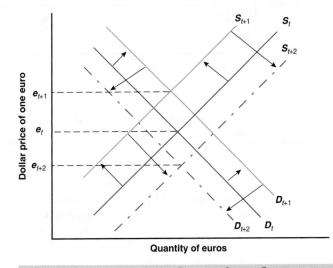

Quantity of euros

EXHIBIT 3.1 • SUPPLY AND DEMAND CURVE SHIFTS

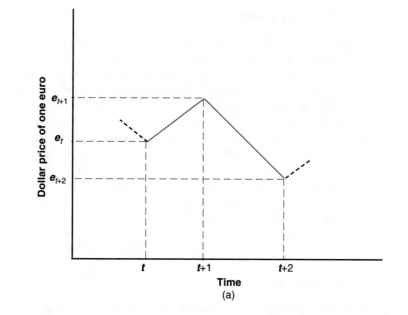

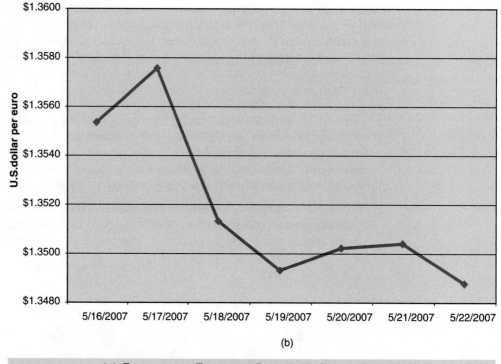

EXHIBIT 3.2 • (A) FLUCTUATING EXCHANGE RATES; (B) ACTUAL CHANGES IN THE DOLLAR/ EURO EXCHANGE RATE: MAY 16–22, 2007

www.oanda.com

rather than resist fundamental market forces, tending to bring about longer-term currency appreciation or depreciation. One variant of this approach is the "crawling peg" system that was used in some countries, such as Poland, Russia, and Brazil, especially in the 1990s. Under a crawling peg, the local currency depreciates against a reference currency or currency basket on a regular, controlled basis. For example, the Brazilian *real* and Russian ruble were allowed to depreciate monthly by about 0.6% and 0.5%, respectively, against the dollar and the Polish zloty was allowed to depreciate by 1% a month against a basket of currencies. However, after the various financial crises of the late 1990s and early 2000s, including in some Asian countries, Russia, Brazil, Argentina, and Turkey, the number of countries adopting an intermediate system between hard pegs and free floats has declined sharply. In 2006, only five countries, including Azerbaijan, Botswana, Costa Rica, Iran, and Nicaragua had a crawling peg system in place.

2. *"Leaning against the wind."* This approach is an intermediate policy designed to moderate or prevent abrupt short- and medium-term fluctuations brought about by random events whose effects are expected to be only temporary. The rationale for this policy, which is primarily aimed at delaying, rather than resisting, fundamental exchange rate adjustments, is that government intervention can reduce for exporters and importers the uncertainty caused by disruptive exchange rate changes. It is questionable, however, whether governments are more capable than private forecasters of distinguishing between fundamental and temporary (irrational) values.

3. *Unofficial pegging.* This strategy evokes memories of a fixed-rate system. It involves resisting fundamental upward or downward exchange rate movements for reasons clearly unrelated to exchange market forces. Thus, Japan historically has resisted revaluation of the yen for fear of its consequences for Japanese exports. With unofficial pegging, however, there is no publicly announced government commitment to a given exchange rate level.

3.1.3 Target-Zone Arrangement

Many economists and policymakers have argued that the industrialized countries could minimize exchange rate volatility and enhance economic stability if the United States, Germany, and Japan linked their currencies in a target-zone system. Under a **target-zone arrangement**, countries adjust their national economic policies to maintain their exchange rates within a specific margin around agreed-upon, fixed central exchange rates. Such a system existed for the major European currencies participating in the European Monetary System and was the precursor to the euro, discussed later in this chapter.

3.1.4 Fixed-Rate System

Under a **fixed-rate system**, such as the Bretton Woods system, governments are committed to maintaining target exchange rates. Each central bank actively buys or sells its currency in the foreign exchange market whenever its exchange rate threatens to deviate from its stated **par value** by more than an agreed percentage. The resulting coordination of monetary policy ensures that all member nations have the same inflation rate. Put another way, for a fixed-rate system to work, each member country must accept the group's joint inflation rate as its own. A corollary is that monetary policy must become subordinate to exchange rate policy. In the extreme case, those who fix their exchange rate via a currency board system surrender all control of monetary policy. The money supply is determined solely by people's willingness to hold the domestic currency.

With or without a currency board system, there is always a rate of monetary growth (it could be negative) that will maintain an exchange rate at its target level. If it involves monetary tightening, however, maintaining the fixed exchange rate could mean a high interest rate and a resultant slowdown in economic growth and job creation.

Restriction or prohibition of certain remittance categories such as dividends or royalties

Ceilings on direct foreign investment outflows (e.g., the elaborate U.S. Office of Foreign Direct Investment controls in effect 1968–1975)

Controls on overseas portfolio investments

Import restrictions

Required surrender of hard-currency export receipts to central bank

Limitations on prepayments for imports

Requirements to deposit in interest-free accounts with central bank, for a specified time, some percentage of the value of imports and/or remittance

Foreign borrowings restricted to a minimum or maximum maturity

Ceilings on granting of credit to foreign firms

Imposition of taxes and limitations on foreign-owned bank deposits

Multiple exchange rates for buying and selling foreign currencies, depending on category of goods or services each transaction falls into

EXHIBIT 3.3 • TYPICAL CURRENCY CONTROL MEASURES

Under the Bretton Woods system, whenever the commitment to the official rate became untenable, it was abruptly changed and a new rate was announced publicly. Currency devaluation or revaluation, however, was usually the last in a string of temporizing alternatives for solving a persistent balance-of-payments deficit or surplus. These alternatives, which are related only in their lack of success, ranged from foreign borrowing to finance the balance-of-payments deficit, wage and price controls, and import restrictions to exchange controls. The latter have become a way of life in many developing countries. Nations with overvalued currencies often ration foreign exchange, whereas countries facing revaluation (an infrequent situation) may restrict capital inflows.

In effect, government controls supersede the allocative function of the foreign exchange market. The most drastic situation occurs when all foreign exchange earnings must be surrendered to the central bank, which, in turn, apportions these funds to users on the basis of government priorities. The buying and selling rates need neither be equal nor be uniform across all transaction categories. Exhibit 3.3 lists the most frequently used currency control measures. These controls are a major source of market imperfection, providing opportunities as well as risks for multinational corporations.

Austerity brought about by a combination of reduced government expenditures and increased taxes can be a permanent substitute for devaluation. By reducing the nation's budget deficit, austerity will lessen the need to monetize the deficit. Lowering the rate of money supply growth, in turn, will bring about a lower rate of domestic inflation (disinflation). Disinflation will strengthen the currency's value, ending the threat of devaluation. However, disinflation often leads to a short-run increase in unemployment, a cost of austerity that politicians today generally consider to be unacceptable.

3.1.5 The Current System of Exchange Rate Determination

The current international monetary system is a hybrid, with major currencies floating on a managed basis, some currencies freely floating, and other currencies moving in and out of various types of pegged exchange rate relationships. Exhibit 3.4 presents a currency map that describes the various zones and blocs linking the world's currencies as July 31, 2006.

	Another Currency as Legal Tender	CFA Franc Zone	Euro Area	ECCU
Exchange arrangements with no separate legal tender (41)	Ecuador El Salvador Kiribati Marshall Islands Micronesia Palau Panama San Marino Timor-Leste	Benin Burkin a Faso Cameroon Central African Republic Chad Congo Cote d'Ivoire Equatorial Guinea Gabon Guinea-Bissau Mali Niger Senegal Togo	Austria Belgium Finland France Germany Greece Ireland Italy Luxembourg Netherlands Portugal Spain	Antigua & Barbuda Dominica Grenada St. Kitts & Nevis St. Lucia St. Vincent & the Grenadines
Currency board arrangement (7)	Bosnia and Herzegovina Djibouti Brunei Darussalam Estonia Bulgaria Hong Kong Lithuania			

	Against a Single Currency		Against a Composite
Other conventional fixed peg arrangements (including de facto peg arrangements under managed floating) (52)	Aruba Bahamas Bahrain Barbados Belarus Belize Bhutan Bolivia Cape Verde China, P.R. Comoros Egypt Eritrea Ethiopia Guynea Honduras Iraq Jordan Kuwait Latvia Lebanon Lesotho Macedonia Maldives	Malta Mauritania Namibia Nepal Netherlands Antilles Oman Pakistan Qatar Rwanda Saudi Arabia Seychelles Sierra Leone Solomon Islands Suriname Swaziland Syrian Arab Trinidad and Tobago Turkmenistan Ukraine United Arab Emirates Venezuela Vietnam Zimbabwe	Fiji Libyan Arab Morocco Samoa Vanuatu

Source: IMF staff reports; IMF Recent Economic Developments; and IMF staff estimates.

(Continues)

EXHIBIT 3.4 • EXCHANGE RATE REGIME (AS OF JULY 31, 2006)

Pegged exchange rates within horizontal bands (6) Crawling pegs (5)	*Within a Cooperative*		*Other Band Arrangements*	
	Cyprus	Slovak Rep.	Hungary	
	Denmark	Slovenia	Tonga	
	Azerbaijan	Costa Rica	Iran	
	Botswana	Nicaragua		
Managed floating with no preannounced path for exchange rate (51)	Afghanistan	Georgia	Malawi	Sao Tome
	Algeria	Ghana	Mauritius	Tunisia
	Angola	Guatemala	Moldova	Singapore
	Argentina	Guinea	Mongolia	Papua New Guinea
	Armenia	Haiti	Mozambique	Sudan
	Bangladesh	India	Myanmar	Serbia
	Burundi	Liberia	Nigeria	Tajikistan
	Cambodia	Madagascar	Malaysia	Thailand
	Croatia	Jamaica	Paraguay	Uzbekistan
	Czech Republic	Kazakhstan	Peru	Uruguay
	Columbia	Kenya	Romania	Zambia
	Dominican Rep.	Kyrgyz	Russia	Yemen
	Gambia	Laos	Sri Lanka	
Independently floating (25)	Albania	Indonesia	Philippines	Turkey
	Australia	Israel	Poland	Uganda
	Brazil	Japan	Somalia	United Kingdom
	Canada	Korea	South Africa	United States
	Chile	Mexico	Sweden	
	Congo	New Zealand	Switzerland	
	Iceland	Norway	Tanzania	

Exchange rate arrangements with no separate legal tender: The currency of another country circulates as the sole legal tender or the member belongs to a monetary or currency union in which the same legal tender is shared by the members of the union.

Currency board arrangements: A monetary regime based on an implicit legislative commitment to exchange domestic currency for a specified foreign currency at a fixed exchange rate.

Other conventional fixed peg arrangements: The country pegs its currency at a fixed rate to a major currency or a basket of currencies where the exchange rate fluctuates within a narrow margin of at most ±1% around a central rate.

Pegged exchange rates within horizontal bands: The value of the currency is maintained within margins of fluctuations around a fixed peg that are wider than ±1% around a central rate.

Crawling peg: The currency is adjusted periodically in small amounts at a fixed preannounced rate or in response to changes in selective quantitative indicators.

Exchange rates within crawling bands: The currency is maintained within certain fluctuation margins around a central rate that is adjusted periodically at a fixed preannounced rate or in response to changes in selective quantitative indicators.

Managed floating with no preannounced path for the exchange rate: The monetary authority influences the movements of the exchange rate through active intervention in the foreign exchange market without specifying or precommitting to a preannounced path for the exchange rate.

Independent floating: The exchange rate is market determined, with any foreign exchange intervention aimed at moderating the rate of change and preventing undue fluctuations in the exchange rate, rather than establishing a level for it.

EXHIBIT 3.4 • (CONTINUED)

3.2 A BRIEF HISTORY OF THE INTERNATIONAL MONETARY SYSTEM

Almost from the dawn of history, gold has been used as a medium of exchange because of its desirable properties. It is durable, storable, portable, easily recognized, divisible, and easily standardized. Another valuable attribute of gold is that short-run changes in its stock are limited by high production costs, making it costly for governments to manipulate. Most important, because gold is a commodity money, it ensures a long-run tendency toward price stability. The reason is that the purchasing power of an ounce of gold, or what it will buy in terms of all other goods and services, will tend toward equality with its long-run cost of production.

For these reasons, most major currencies, until fairly recently, were on a gold standard, which defined their relative values or exchange rates. The **gold standard** essentially involved a commitment by the participating countries to fix the prices of their domestic currencies in terms of a specified amount of gold. The countries maintained these prices by being willing to buy or sell gold to anyone at that price. For example, from 1821 to 1914, Great Britain maintained a fixed price of gold at £4.2474 per ounce. The United States, during the 1834–1933 period, maintained the price of gold at $20.67 per ounce (with the exception of the Greenback period from 1861–1878). Thus, over the period 1834–1914 (with the exception of 1861–1878), the dollar:pound exchange rate, referred to as the par exchange rate, was perfectly determined at

$$\frac{\$20.67/\text{ounce of gold}}{£4.2474/\text{ounce of gold}} = \$4.8665/£1$$

The value of gold relative to other goods and services does not change much over long periods of time, so the monetary discipline imposed by a gold standard should ensure long-run price stability for both individual countries and groups of countries. Indeed, there was remarkable long-run price stability in the period before World War I, during which most countries were on a gold standard. As Exhibit 3.5 shows, price levels at the start of World War I were roughly the same as they had been in the late 1700s before the Napoleonic Wars began.

This record is all the more remarkable when contrasted with the post–World War II inflationary experience of the industrialized nations of Europe and North America. As shown in Exhibit 3.6, 1995 price levels in all these nations were several times as high as they were in 1950. Even in Germany, the value of the currency in 1995 was only one-quarter of its 1950 level, whereas the comparable magnitude was less than one-tenth for France, Italy, and the United Kingdom. Although there were no episodes of extremely rapid inflation, price levels rose steadily and substantially.

3.2.1 The Classical Gold Standard

A gold standard is often considered an anachronism in our modern, high-tech world because of its needless expense; on the most basic level, it means digging up gold in one corner of the globe for burial in another corner. Nonetheless, until recently, discontent with the current monetary system, which produced more than two decades of worldwide inflation and widely fluctuating exchange rates, prompted interest in a return to some

Year	Belgium	Britain	France	Germany	United States
1776	n/a	101	n/a	n/a	84
1793	n/a	120	n/a	98	100
1800	n/a	186	155	135	127
1825	n/a	139	126	76	101
1850	83	91	96	71	82
1875	100	121	111	100	80
1900	87	86	85	90	80
1913	100	100	100	100	100

EXHIBIT 3.5 • WHOLESALE PRICE INDICES: PRE–WORLD WAR I

form of a gold standard. (This interest has abated somewhat with the current low inflation environment.)

To put it bluntly, calls for a new gold standard reflect a fundamental distrust of government's willingness to maintain the integrity of fiat money. **Fiat money** is nonconvertible paper money backed only by faith that the monetary authorities will not cheat (by issuing more money). This faith has been tempered by hard experience; the 100% profit margin on issuing new fiat money has proved to be an irresistible temptation for most governments.

By contrast, the net profit margin on issuing more money under a gold standard is zero. The government must acquire more gold before it can issue more money, and the government's cost of acquiring the extra gold equals the value of the money it issues. Thus, expansion of the money supply is constrained by the available supply of gold. This fact is crucial in understanding how a gold standard works.

Under the classical gold standard, disturbances in the price level in one country would be wholly or partly offset by an automatic balance-of-payments adjustment mechanism called the **price-specie-flow mechanism**. (*Specie* refers to gold coins.) To see how this adjustment mechanism worked to equalize prices among countries and automatically bring international payments back in balance, consider the example that is illustrated in Exhibit 3.7.

Suppose a technological advance increases productivity in the non-gold-producing sector of the U.S. economy. This productivity will lower the price of other goods and services relative to the price of gold, and the U.S. price level will decline. The fall in U.S. prices will result in lower prices of U.S. exports; export prices will decline relative to

Nation	CPI 1950	CPI 2005	Loss of Purchasing Power During Period 1950–2005
Belgium	100	697	85.6%
France	100	1510	93.4%
Germany	100	448	77.7%
Italy	100	2748	96.4%
Netherlands	100	759	86.8%
United Kingdom	100	1881	94.7%
United States	100	797	87.5%

EXHIBIT 3.6 • CONSUMER PRICE INDICES (CPI): POST–WORLD WAR II

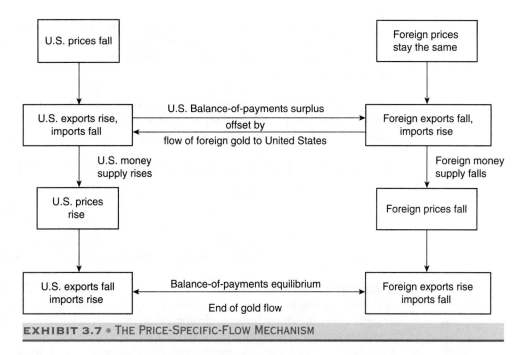

EXHIBIT 3.7 • THE PRICE-SPECIFIC-FLOW MECHANISM

import prices (determined largely by supply and demand in the rest of the world). Consequently, foreigners will demand more U.S. exports, and Americans will buy fewer imports.

Starting from a position of equilibrium in its international payments, the United States will now run a balance-of-payments surplus. The difference will be made up by a flow of gold into the United States. The gold inflow will increase the U.S. money supply (under a gold standard, more gold means more money in circulation), reversing the initial decline in prices. At the same time, the other countries will experience gold outflows, reducing their money supplies (less gold, less money in circulation) and, thus, their price levels. In final equilibrium, price levels in all countries will be slightly lower than they were before because of the increase in the worldwide supply of other goods and services relative to the supply of gold. Exchange rates will remain fixed.

Thus, the operation of the price-specie-flow mechanism tended to keep prices in line for those countries that were on the gold standard. As long as the world was on a gold standard, all adjustments were automatic, and although many undesirable things might have happened under a gold standard, enduring inflation was not one of them.

Gold does have a cost, however—the opportunity cost associated with mining and storing it. By the late 1990s, with inflation on the wane worldwide, the value of gold as an inflation hedge had declined. Central banks also began selling their gold reserves and replacing them with U.S. Treasury bonds that, unlike gold, pay interest. The reduced demand for gold has lowered its usefulness as a monetary asset.

3.2.2 How the Classical Gold Standard Worked in Practice: 1821–1914

In 1821, after the Napoleonic Wars and associated inflation, England returned to the gold standard. From 1821 to 1880, more and more countries joined the gold standard. By 1880, most nations of the world were on some form of gold standard. The period from 1880 to 1914, during which the classical gold standard prevailed in its most pristine form, was a remarkable period in world economic history. The period was characterized by a rapid expansion of virtually free international trade, stable exchange rates and prices, a free flow of labor and capital across political borders, rapid economic growth, and, in general, world peace. Advocates of the gold standard harken back to this period as illustrating the standard's value.

Opponents of a rigid gold standard, in contrast, point to some less-than-idyllic economic conditions during this period: a major depression during the 1890s, a severe economic contraction in 1907, and repeated recessions. Whether these sharp ups and downs could have been prevented under a fiat money standard cannot be known.

3.2.3 The Gold Exchange Standard and Its Aftermath: 1925–1944

The gold standard broke down during World War I and was briefly reinstated from 1925 to 1931 as the Gold Exchange Standard. Under this standard, the United States and England could hold only gold reserves, but other nations could hold both gold and dollars or pounds as reserves. In 1931, England departed from gold in the face of massive gold and capital flows, owing to an unrealistic exchange rate, and the Gold Exchange Standard was finished.

Competitive Devaluations   After the devaluation of sterling, 25 other nations devalued their currencies to maintain trade competitiveness. These **"beggar-thy-neighbor" devaluations**, in which nations cheapened their currencies to increase their exports at others' expense and to reduce their imports, led to a trade war. Many economists and policymakers believed that the protectionist exchange rate and trade policies fueled the global depression of the 1930s.

Bretton Woods Conference and the Postwar Monetary System   To avoid such destructive economic policies in the future, the Allied nations agreed to a new postwar monetary system at a conference held in Bretton Woods, New Hampshire, in 1944. The conference also created two new institutions, the **International Monetary Fund (IMF)** and the **International Bank for Reconstruction and Development (World Bank)**, to implement the new system and to promote international financial stability. The IMF was created to promote monetary stability, whereas the World Bank was set up to lend money to countries so they could rebuild their infrastructure that had been destroyed during the War.

Role of the IMF   Both agencies have seen their roles evolve over time. The IMF now oversees exchange rate policies in member countries (currently totaling 182 nations) and advises developing countries about how to turn their economies around. In the process, it has become the **lender of last resort** to countries that get into serious financial trouble. It is currently exploring new ways to monitor financial health of member nations so as to prevent another Mexico-like surprise. Despite these efforts, the IMF was blindsided by the Asian crisis and ended up leading a $118-billion attempt to shore up Asian financial systems. It was also blindsided by the Russian crisis a year later. Critics argue that by bailing out careless lenders and imprudent nations, IMF rescues make it too easy for governments to persist with bad policies and for investors to ignore the risks these policies create. In the long run, by removing from governments and investors the prospect of failure, which underlies the market discipline that encourages sound policies, these rescues magnify the problem of moral hazard and so make imprudent policies more likely to recur.[1] **Moral hazard** refers here to the perverse incentives created for international lenders and borrowers by IMF bailouts. Anticipating further IMF bailouts, investors underestimate the risks of lending to governments who persist in irresponsible policies.

---

[1] As economist Allan H. Meltzer puts it, "Capitalism without failure is like religion without sin. It doesn't work. Bankruptcies and losses concentrate the mind on prudent behavior."

In theory, the IMF makes short-term loans conditional on the borrower's implementation of policy changes that will allow it to achieve self-sustaining economic growth. This is the doctrine of **conditionality**. However, a review of the evidence suggests that the IMF creates long-term dependency. For example, between 1971 and 2000, as many as 51 countries were long-term users of IMF loans, and by late 2002, there were still 30 countries with such long-term IMF loans.[2] This evidence explains why IMF conditionality has little credibility.

Role of the World Bank   The World Bank is looking to expand its lending to developing countries and to provide more loan guarantees for businesses entering new developing markets. But here too there is controversy. Specifically, critics claim that World Bank financing allows projects and policies to avoid being subject to the scrutiny of financial markets and permits governments to delay enacting the changes necessary to make their countries more attractive to private investors.

Role of the Bank for International Settlements   Another key institution is the **Bank for International Settlements (BIS)**, which acts as the central bank for the industrial countries' central banks. The BIS helps central banks manage and invest their foreign exchange reserves, and, in cooperation with the IMF and the World Bank, helps the central banks of developing countries, mostly in Latin America and Eastern Europe. The BIS also holds deposits of central banks so that reserves are readily available.

ILLUSTRATION   *Competitive Devaluations in 2003*

Unfortunately, despite Bretton Woods, competitive devaluations have not disappeared. According to *the Wall Street Journal* (June 6, 2003, p. B12), "A war of competitive currency devaluations is rattling the $1.2 trillion-a-day global foreign exchange market . . . The aim of the devaluing governments: to steal growth and markets from others, while simultaneously exporting their problems, which in this case is the threat of deflation."

Currency analysts argue that the environment in 2003—of slow growth and the threat of deflation—has encouraged countries such as Japan, China, and the United States to pursue a weak currency policy. For example, analysts believe that the Bush administration is looking for a falling dollar to boost U.S. exports, lift economic growth, battle deflationary pressure, push the Europeans to cut interest rates, and force Japan to overhaul its stagnant economy.

The weapons in this war include policy shifts, foreign exchange market intervention, and interest rates. For example, the foreign exchange market widely views the Bush administration as having abandoned the long-standing strong-dollar policy and welcoming a weaker dollar. Japan has tried to keep its currency from rising against the dollar by selling a record ¥3.98 billion ($33.4 billion) in May 2003 alone. A strong yen hurts Japanese exports and growth and aggravates deflationary tendencies. If Japan succeeds in pushing down the yen sufficiently, South Korea and Taiwan could also try to devalue their currencies to remain competitive.

China, meanwhile, has stuck with an undervalued yuan to bolster its economy. Another currency analyst attributed Canada's growth over the past decade to an undervalued Canadian dollar: "They've been the beggar-thy-neighbor success story."[3] On June 5,

---

[2] David Goldsbrough, Kevin Barnes, Isabelle Mateos y Lago and Tsidi Tsikata, "Prolonged Use of IMF Loans," *Finance & Development,* December 2002, pp. 34–37.

[3] Michael R. Sesit, "Currency Conflict Shakes Market," *Wall Street Journal,* June 6, 2003, B12.

2003, the European Central Bank entered the competitive devaluation fray by cutting the euro interest rate by a half percentage point. This came as a response to the fact that over the past one year, the euro had appreciated by 27% against the dollar, making European business less profitable and less competitive and hurting European growth. From June 2002 to end-May 2007, the Euro had appreicated about 38% against the dollar.

The ultimate fear: an ongoing round of competitive devaluations that degenerates into the same kind of pre-Bretton Woods protectionist free-for-all that brought on the Great Depression.

3.2.4 The Bretton Woods System: 1946–1971

Under the **Bretton Woods Agreement**, implemented in 1946, each government pledged to maintain a fixed, or pegged, exchange rate for its currency vis-à-vis the dollar or gold. As one ounce of gold was set equal to $35, fixing a currency's gold price was equivalent to setting its exchange rate relative to the dollar. For example, the Deutsche mark was set equal to 1/140 of an ounce of gold, meaning it was worth $0.25 ($35/140). The exchange rate was allowed to fluctuate only within 1% of its stated par value (usually less in practice).

The fixed exchange rates were maintained by official intervention in the foreign exchange markets. The intervention took the form of purchases and sales of dollars by foreign central banks against their own currencies whenever the supply-and-demand conditions in the market caused rates to deviate from the agreed par values. The IMF stood ready to provide the necessary foreign exchange to member nations defending their currencies against pressure resulting from temporary factors.[4] Any dollars acquired by the monetary authorities in the process of such intervention could then be exchanged for gold at the U.S. Treasury, at a fixed price of $35 per ounce.

These technical aspects of the system had important practical implications for all trading nations participating in it. In principle, the stability of exchange rates removed a great deal of uncertainty from international trade and investment transactions, thus promoting their growth for the benefit of all the participants. Also, in theory, the functioning of the system imposed a degree of discipline on the participating nations' economic policies.

For example, a country that followed policies leading to a higher rate of inflation than that experienced by its trading partners would experience a balance-of-payments deficit as its goods became more expensive, reducing its exports and increasing its imports. The necessary consequences of the deficit would be an increase in the supply of the deficit country's currency on the foreign exchange markets. The excess supply would depress the exchange value of that country's currency, forcing its authorities to intervene. The country would be obligated to "buy" with its reserves the excess supply of its own currency, effectively reducing the domestic money supply. Moreover, as the country's reserves were gradually depleted through intervention, the authorities would be forced, sooner or later, to change economic policies to eliminate the source of the reserve-draining deficit. The reduction in the money supply and the adoption of restrictive policies would reduce the country's inflation, thus bringing it in line with the rest of the world.

The reluctance of governments to change currency values or to make the necessary economic adjustments to ratify the current values of their currencies led to periodic foreign

---

[4] The IMF supplemented its foreign exchange reserves by creating a new reserve asset, the **Special Drawing Right** (SDR), which serves as the IMF's unit of account. It is a currency basket whose value is the weighted average of the currencies of five nations (United States, Germany, France, Japan, and Great Britain; the euro is the currency used for France and Germany). The weights, which are based on the relative importance of each country in international trade, are updated periodically.

exchange crises. Dramatic battles between the central banks and the foreign exchange markets ensued. Those battles invariably were won by the markets. However, because devaluation or revaluation was used only as a last resort, exchange rate changes were infrequent and large.

In fact, Bretton Woods was a fixed exchange-rate system in name only. Of 21 major industrial countries, only the United States and Japan had no change in par value during the period 1946–1971. Of the 21 countries, 12 devalued their currencies more than 30% against the dollar, four had revaluations, and four were floating their currencies by mid-1971 when the system collapsed. The deathblow to the system came on August 15, 1971, when President Richard Nixon, convinced that the "run" on the dollar was reaching alarming proportions, abruptly ordered U.S. authorities to terminate convertibility even for central banks. At the same time, he devalued the dollar to deal with America's emerging trade deficit.

The fixed exchange-rate system collapsed along with the dissolution of the gold standard. There are two related reasons for the collapse of the Bretton Woods system. First, inflation reared its ugly head in the United States. In the mid-1960s, the Johnson administration financed the escalating war in Vietnam and its equally expensive Great Society programs by, in effect, printing money instead of raising taxes. This lack of monetary discipline made it difficult for the United States to maintain the price of gold at $35 an ounce.

Second, the fixed exchange-rate system collapsed because some countries, primarily West Germany, Japan, and Switzerland, refused to accept the inflation that a fixed exchange rate with the dollar would have imposed on them. Thus, the dollar depreciated sharply relative to the currencies of those three countries.

3.2.5 The Post-Bretton Woods System: 1971 to the Present

In December 1971, under the **Smithsonian Agreement**, the dollar was devalued to 1/38 of an ounce of gold, and other currencies were revalued by agreed values vis-à-vis the dollar. After months of such last-ditch efforts to set new fixed rates, the world officially turned to floating exchange rates in 1973. The dollar's ups and downs started soon after with the oil crisis of 1973 (see illustration).

ILLUSTRATION *OPEC and the Oil Crisis of 1973–1974*

October 1973 marked the beginning of successful efforts by the Organization of Petroleum Exporting Countries (OPEC) to raise the price of oil. By 1974, oil prices had quadrupled. Nations responded in various ways to the vast shift of resources to the oil-exporting countries. Some nations, such as the United States, tried to offset the effect of higher energy bills by boosting spending, pursuing expansionary monetary policies, and controlling the price of oil. The result was high inflation, economic dislocation, and a misallocation of resources without bringing about the real economic growth that was desired. Other nations, such as Japan, allowed the price of oil to rise to its market level and followed more prudent monetary policies.

The first group of nations experienced balance-of-payments deficits because their governments kept intervening in the foreign exchange market to maintain overvalued currencies; the second group of nations, along with the OPEC nations, wound up with balance-of-payments surpluses. These surpluses were recycled to debtor nations, setting the stage for the international debt crisis of the 1980s.

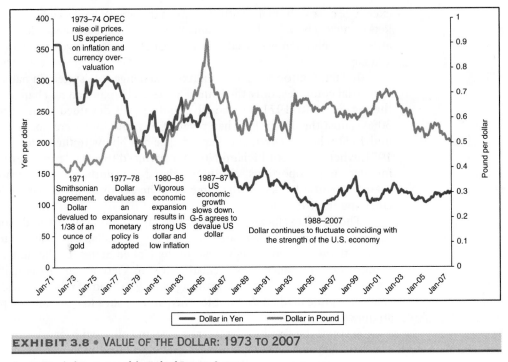

EXHIBIT 3.8 • VALUE OF THE DOLLAR: 1973 TO 2007

Source: Board of Governors of the Federal Reserve System.

Exhibit 3.8 charts the value of the dollar against the Japanese yen and British pound for the period 1973 to mid-2007. During 1977–1978, the value of the dollar plummeted, and on October 6, 1979, the Federal Reserve (under its new chairman, Paul Volcker) announced a major change in its conduct of monetary policy. From here on, in order to curb inflation, it would focus its efforts on stabilizing the money supply, even if that meant more volatile interest rates. Before this date, the Fed had attempted to stabilize interest rates, indirectly causing the money supply to be highly variable.

This shift had its desired effect on both the inflation rate and the value of the U.S. dollar. Inflation plummeted and the dollar rebounded extraordinarily. The dollar peaked in March 1985 and then began a long downhill slide. The dollar's rebound has been attributed to vigorous economic expansion and high real interest rates, while the slide has been largely attributed to changes in government policy and the slowdown in U.S. economic growth relative to growth in the rest of the world.

By September 1985, the dollar had fallen about 15% from its March high, but this decline was considered inadequate to dent the growing U.S. trade deficit. In late September of 1985, the Group of Five, or **G-5 nations** (the United States, France, Japan, Great Britain, and West Germany), met at the Plaza Hotel in New York City. The outcome was the **Plaza Agreement**, a coordinated program designed to force down the dollar against other major currencies and thereby improve American competitiveness.

The policy to bring down the value of the dollar worked too well. The dollar slid so fast during 1986 that the central banks of Japan, West Germany, and Britain reversed their policies and began buying dollars to stem the dollar's decline. Believing that the dollar had declined enough and in fact showed signs of "overshooting" its equilibrium level, the United States, Japan, West Germany, France, Britain, Canada, and Italy—also known as the Group of Seven, or **G-7 nations**—met again in February 1987 and agreed to an ambitious plan to slow the dollar's fall.[5] The **Louvre Accord**, named for the Paris landmark

---

[5] With the inclusion of Russia in 1998, the group is now known as the G-8.

where it was negotiated, called for the G-7 nations to support the falling dollar by pegging exchange rates within a narrow, undisclosed range, while they also moved to bring their economic policies into line.

As always, however, it proved much easier to talk about coordinating policy than to change it. The hoped-for economic cooperation faded, and the dollar continued to fall (see Exhibit 3.8). Beginning in early 1988, the U.S. dollar rallied somewhat and then maintained its strength against most currencies through 1989. It fell sharply again in 1990, remained somewhat stable in 1991 and 1992, before falling again in 1993. The dollar rallied again in 1996 and continued its upward direction through December 2001 owing to the sustained strength of the U.S. economy. Even after the U.S. economy began to slow down in late 2000, it still looked strong compared to those of its major trading partners. However, in 2002, the sluggishness of the U.S. economy and low U.S. interest

---

ILLUSTRATION *Swiss Franc Provides a Safe Haven After September 11*

Following the terrorist attacks on the World Trade Center and the Pentagon, the Swiss franc soared in value as investors sought a safe haven no longer provided by the United States. The Swiss franc rose still further after Afghanistan's Taliban leaders declared a holy war against the United States and the United States faced a bio-terrorism threat from anthrax (see Exhibit 3.9). However, the ensuing war in Afghanistan and military successes there, combined with renewed prospects for a U.S. recovery, brought a reminder of American strength—and a stronger dollar. As the Swiss franc lost some of its luster, it fell toward its pre-September 11 value.

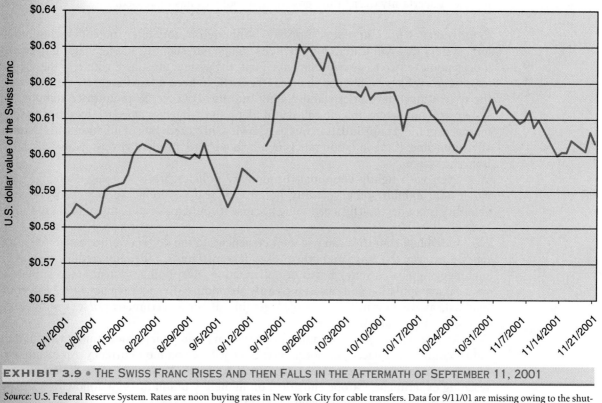

EXHIBIT 3.9 • THE SWISS FRANC RISES AND THEN FALLS IN THE AFTERMATH OF SEPTEMBER 11, 2001

Source: U.S. Federal Reserve System. Rates are noon buying rates in New York City for cable transfers. Data for 9/11/01 are missing owing to the shutdown of financial trading in New York City following the destruction of the World Trade Center.

rates, combined with the fear of war in Iraq (and later the actual war), resulted in a significant decline in the value of the dollar relative to euro and other currencies. This decline has continued through 2007. The dollar's future course is unpredictable given the absence of an anchor for its value.

3.2.6 Assessment of the Floating-Rate System

At the time floating rates were adopted in 1973, its proponents said that the new system would reduce economic volatility and facilitate free trade. In particular, floating exchange rates would offset international differences in inflation rates so that trade, wages, employment, and output would not have to adjust. High-inflation countries would see their currencies depreciate, allowing their firms to stay competitive without having to cut wages or employment. At the same time, currency appreciation would not place firms in low-inflation countries at a competitive disadvantage. Real exchange rates would stabilize, even if permitted to float in principle, because the underlying conditions affecting trade and the relative productivity of capital would change only gradually; and if countries would coordinate their monetary policies to achieve a convergence of inflation rates, then nominal exchange rates would also stabilize.

Currency Volatility Has Increased   The experience to date, however, is disappointing. The dollar's ups and downs have had little to do with actual inflation and a lot to do with expectations of future government policies and economic conditions. Put another way, real exchange rate volatility has increased, not decreased, since floating began. This instability reflects, in part, nonmonetary (or real) shocks to the world economy, such as changing oil prices and shifting competitiveness among countries, but these real shocks were not obviously greater during the 1980s or 1990s than they were in earlier periods. Instead, uncertainty over future government policies has increased.

Requirements for Currency Stability   Although history offers no convincing model for a system that will lead to long-term exchange rate stability among major currencies, it does point to two basic requirements. First, the system must be credible. If the market expects an exchange rate to be changed, the battle to keep it fixed is already lost. Second, the system must have price stability built into its very core. Without price stability, the system will not be credible. Recall that under a fixed-rate system, each member country must accept the group's inflation rate as its own. Only a zero rate of inflation will be mutually acceptable. If the inflation rate is much above zero, prudent governments will defect from the system.

Even with tightly coordinated monetary policies, freely floating exchange rates would still exhibit some volatility because of real economic shocks. However, this volatility is not necessarily a bad thing because it could make adjustment to these shocks easier.

Individual countries can peg their currencies to the dollar or other benchmark currency. However, the Asian and other crises demonstrate that the only credible system for such pegging is a currency board or dollarization. Every other system is too subject to political manipulation and can be too easily abandoned. Even a currency board can come unglued, as we saw in the case of Argentina, if the government pursues sufficiently wrong-headed economic policies.

An alternative system for a fixed-rate system is **monetary union**, under which, individual countries replace their local currencies with a common currency. An example of monetary union is the United States, with all 50 states sharing the same dollar. In a far-reaching experiment, Europe embarked on monetary union in 1999, following its experiences with the European Monetary System.

3.3 THE EUROPEAN MONETARY SYSTEM AND MONETARY UNION

The **European Monetary System** (EMS) began operating in March 1979. Its purpose is to foster monetary stability in the **European Community** (EC, or the **Common Market**). As part of this system, the members established the European Currency Unit, which played a central role in the functioning of the EMS. The **European Currency Unit**, or ECU, was a composite currency consisting of fixed amounts of the 12 European Community member currencies. The quantity of each country's currency in the ECU reflects that country's relative economic strength in the EC. The ECU functioned as a unit of account, a means of settlement, and a reserve asset for the members of the EMS. In 1992, the EC became the European Union (EU). With the inclusion of Bulgaria and Romania on January 1, 2007, the EU currently has 27 member states.

3.3.1 The Exchange Rate Mechanism

At the heart of the EMS was an **exchange rate mechanism** (ERM), which allowed each member country to determine a mutually agreed central exchange rate for its currency; each rate was denominated in currency units per ECU. These central rates attempted to establish equilibrium exchange values, but members could seek adjustments to the central rates.

Central rates established a grid of bilateral cross-exchange rates between the currencies. Nations participating in the ERM pledged to keep their currencies within a 15% margin on either side of these central cross-exchange rates ($\pm 2.25\%$ for the DM/guilder cross rate). The upper and lower intervention levels for each currency pair were found by applying the appropriate margin to their central cross-exchange rate.

The original intervention limits were set at 2.25% above and below the central cross rates (Spain and Britain had 6% margins) but were later changed. Despite good intentions, the ERM came unglued in a series of speculative attacks that began in 1992. By mid-1993, the EMS had slipped into a two-tiered system. One tier consisted of a core group of currencies tightly anchored by the DM. That tier included the Dutch guilder, the French, Belgian, and Luxembourg francs, and possibly the Danish krone. The other tier consisted of weaker currencies such as those of Spain, Portugal, Britain, Italy, and Ireland.

3.3.2 Lessons from the European Monetary System

A review of the EMS and its history provides valuable insights into the operation of a target-zone system and illustrates the problems that such mechanisms are likely to encounter. Perhaps the most important lesson the EMS illustrates is that the exchange rate stability afforded by any target-zone arrangement requires a coordination of economic policy objectives and practices. Nations should achieve convergence of those economic variables that directly affect exchange rates—variables such as fiscal deficits, monetary growth rates, and real economic growth differentials.

Although the system helped keep its member currencies in a remarkably narrow zone of stability between 1987 and 1992, it had a history of ups and downs. During this time, the values of the EMS currencies were realigned 12 times despite heavy central bank intervention.

The experience of the EMS demonstrates that foreign exchange market intervention not supported by a change in a nation's monetary policy has only a limited influence on exchange rates.

3.3.3 The Exchange Rate Mechanism Is Abandoned in August 1993

Another currency crisis was touched off on July 29, 1993, when the Bundesbank left its key lending rate, the discount rate, unchanged. Traders and investors had been expecting

ILLUSTRATION *The Currency Crisis of September 1992*

The attempt to maintain increasingly misaligned exchange rates in the EMS led to the breakdown of the system in September 1992. The catalyst for the September currency crisis was the Bundesbank's decision to tighten monetary policy and force up German interest rates both to battle inflationary pressures associated with the spiraling costs of bailing out the former East Germany and to attract the inflows of foreign capital needed to finance the resulting German budget deficit. To defend their currency parities with the DM, the other member countries had to match the high interest rates in Germany (see Exhibit 3.10). The deflationary effects of high interest rates were accompanied by a prolonged economic slump and even higher unemployment rates in Britain, France, Italy, Spain, and most other EMS members.

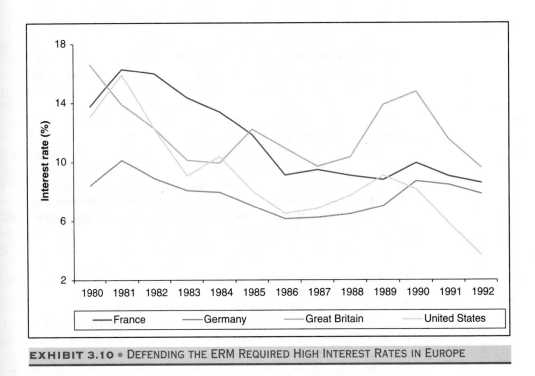

EXHIBIT 3.10 • DEFENDING THE ERM REQUIRED HIGH INTEREST RATES IN EUROPE

As the costs of maintaining exchange rate stability rose, the markets began betting that some countries with weaker economies would devalue their currencies or withdraw from the ERM altogether rather than maintain painfully high interest rates at a time of rising unemployment.

The High Cost of Intervention To combat speculative attacks on their currencies, nations had to raise their interest rates dramatically: 15% in Britain and Italy, 13.75% in Spain, 13% in France, and an extraordinary 500% in Sweden. They also intervened aggressively in the foreign exchange markets. British, French, Italian, Spanish, and Swedish central banks together spent the equivalent of roughly $100 billion trying to prop up their currencies, with the Bank of England reported to have spent $15 billion to $20 billion in just one day to support the pound. The Bundesbank spent another $50 billion in DM to support the ERM. All to no avail.

On September 14, the central banks capitulated but not before losing an estimated $4 billion to $6 billion in their mostly futile attempt to maintain the ERM. Despite these costly efforts, Britain and Italy were forced to drop out of the ERM, and Spain, Portugal, and Ireland devalued their currencies within the ERM. In addition, Sweden, Norway, and Finland were forced to abandon their currencies' unofficial links to the ERM.

the Bundesbank to cut the discount rate to relieve pressure on the French franc and other weak currencies within the ERM. When the Bundesbank refused to cut its discount rate, speculators reacted logically.

They dumped the French franc and other European currencies and bought DM, gambling that economic pressures, such as rising unemployment and deepening recession, would prevent these countries from keeping their interest rates well above those in Germany. In other words, speculators bet—rightly, as it turned out—that domestic priorities would ultimately win out despite governments' pledges to the contrary.

Without capital controls or a credible commitment to move to a single currency in the near future, speculators could easily take advantage of a one-sided bet. The result was massive capital flows that overwhelmed the central banks' ability to stabilize exchange rates. Over the weekend of July 31–August 1, the EC finance ministers agreed essentially to abandon the defense of each other's currencies and the EMS became a floating-rate system in all but name only.

A Postmortem on the EMS   The currency turmoil of 1992–1993 showed once again that a genuinely stable European Monetary System, and eventually a single currency, requires the political will to direct fiscal and monetary policies at that European goal and not at purely national one. In showing that they lacked that will, European governments proved once again that allowing words to run ahead of actions is a recipe for failure.

Despite its problems, however, the EMS did achieve some significant success. By improving monetary policy coordination among its member states, the EMS succeeded in narrowing inflation differentials in Europe. Inflation rates tended to converge toward Germany's lower rate as other countries adjusted their monetary policies to closely mimic Germany's low-inflation policy (see Exhibit 3.11).

3.3.4 European Monetary Union

Many politicians and commentators pointed to the turmoil in the EMS as increasing the need for the European Community to move toward **monetary union**. This view prevailed and was

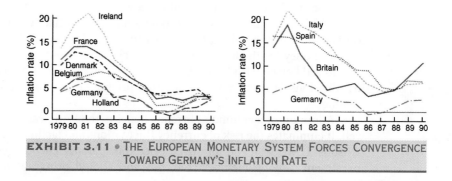

EXHIBIT 3.11 • THE EUROPEAN MONETARY SYSTEM FORCES CONVERGENCE TOWARD GERMANY'S INFLATION RATE

formalized in the **Maastricht Treaty**. Under this treaty, the EC nations would establish a single central bank with the sole power to issue a single European currency called the **euro** as of January 1, 1999. On that date, conversion rates would be locked in for member currencies, and the euro would become a currency, although euro coins and bills would not be available until 2002. All went as planned. Francs, marks, guilders, schillings, and other member currencies were phased out until the euro replaced them all on January 1, 2002.

Maastricht Convergence Criteria   In order to join the **European Monetary Union** (EMU), European nations were supposed to meet tough standards on inflation, currency stability, and deficit spending. According to these standards, known as the **Maastricht criteria**, government debt could not go beyond 60% of gross domestic product (GDP), the government budget deficit could not exceed 3% of GDP, the inflation rate could not be more than 1.5 percentage points above the average rate of Europe's three lowest-inflation nations, and long-term interest rates could not be more than 2 percentage points higher than the average interest rate in the three lowest-inflation nations. It should be noted that most countries, including Germany, fudged some of their figures through one-time maneuvers (redefining government debt or selling off government assets) or fudged the criteria (Italy's debt/GDP ratio was 121%) in order to qualify. Nonetheless, on May 2, 1998, the European Parliament formally approved the historic decision to launch the euro with 11 founder nations—Germany, France, Italy, Spain, the Netherlands, Belgium, Finland, Portugal, Austria, Ireland, and Luxembourg. Britain, Sweden, and Denmark opted out of the launch. On January 1, 2001, Greece became the 12th country to join the euro-zone when it was finally able to meet the economic convergence criteria. Slovenia became the 13th country to adopt the euro, on January 1, 2007. Britain is still debating whether to join EMU and retire the pound sterling.

Launch of the Euro   As planned, on January 1, 1999, the 11 founding member countries of the **European Monetary Union** (EMU) surrendered their monetary autonomy to the new **European Central Bank** (ECB) and gave up their right to create money; only the European Central Bank is now able to do so. Governments can issue bonds denominated in euros, just as individual American states can issue dollar bonds. However, like California or New York, member nations are unable to print the currency needed to service their debts. Instead, they can only attract investors by convincing them they have the financial ability (through taxes and other revenues) to generate the euros to repay their debts.

Consequences of EMU   Although the full impact of the euro has yet to be felt, its effects have already been profound. Business clearly benefits from EMU through lower cross-border currency conversion costs. For example, Philips, the giant Dutch electronics company, estimates that a single European currency saves it $300 million a year in currency transaction costs. Overall, the EC Commission estimates that prior to the euro, businesses in Europe spent $13 billion a year converting money from one EC currency to another. Ordinary citizens also bore some substantial currency conversion costs. A tourist who left Paris with 1,000 francs and visited the other 11 EC countries, exchanging her money for the local currency in each country but not spending any of it, would have found herself with fewer than 500 francs when she returned to Paris. Multinational firms will also find corporate planning, pricing, and invoicing easier with a common currency.

Adoption of a common currency benefits the European economy in other ways as well. It eliminates the risk of currency fluctuations and facilitates cross-border price comparisons. Lower risk and improved price transparency encourages the flow of trade and investments among member countries and should bring about greater integration of

Europe's capital, labor, and commodity markets and a more efficient allocation of resources within the region as a whole. Increased trade and price transparency, in turn, has intensified Europe-wide competition in goods and services and spurred a wave of corporate restructurings and mergers and acquisitions.

Moreover, monetary union—such as the one that exists among the 50 states of the United States, where the exchange rate between states is immutably set at 1—provides the ultimate in coordination of monetary policy. Inflation rates under monetary union converges, but not in the same way as in the EMS. The common inflation rate is decided by the monetary policy of the ECB. It would tend to reflect the average preferences of the people running the bank, rather than giving automatic weight to the most anti-inflationary nation as in the current system. Thus, for the EMU to be an improvement over the past state of affairs, the new ECB must be as averse to inflation as Europe's previous de facto central bank, the Bundesbank.

To ensure the EMU's inflation-fighting success, the new central bankers must be granted true independence along with a statutory duty to devote monetary policy to keeping the price level stable. However, absent a political union among the member states, the ECB shoulders all the responsibility for the fiscal and monetary success of the euro. Contrast this to the United States, where both the Federal Reserve and the federal government use their respective instruments to stabilize the business cycle. The ECB has to work alone to keep inflation low, manage expectations, and maintain financial stability. However, each country's financial stability rests on the fiscal policies they adopt as well as on their own financial institutions.[6] The ECB will find it difficult to be tough on inflation without the benefit of a uniformly prudent fiscal policy across all its member countries.

Another important issue in forming a monetary union is that of who gets the benefits of **seigniorage**—the profit to the central bank from money creation. In other words, who gets to spend the proceeds from printing money? In the United States, the answer is the federal government. In the case of Europe, however, this issue has not been resolved.

Performance of the Euro   The euro was born in optimism given the size and economic potential of the European Union (see Exhibit 3.12). However, reality set in quickly. Although many commentators felt the euro would soon replace the U.S. dollar as the world's *de facto* currency, Exhibit 3.13 shows that until 2002 the euro mostly fell against the dollar. The euro's decline during this period has been attributed to the continued robustness of the

	Euro 13	*United States*	*Japan*
Population	313 million	301 million	127 million
GDP	$9.3 trillion	$12.98 trillion	$4.22 trillion
Share of world GDP	14%	20%	6%
Exports	$1,330 billion	$1,024 billion	$590 billion
Imports	$1,466 billion	$1,869 billion	$524 billion
Share of world total trade (% of world export)	10.7%	8.2%	4.7%

EXHIBIT 3.12 • COMPARATIVE STATISTICS FOR THE EMU COUNTRIES

Source: CIA World Factbook, 2006 Estimate.

---

[6] Paul De Grauwe, "Review: Flaws in the Design of the Eurosystem?" *International Finance*, Vol. 9, No. 1, 2006, pp. 137–144.

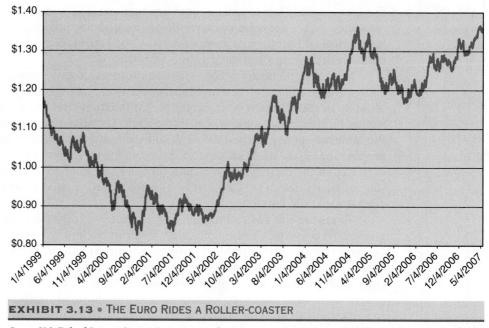

EXHIBIT 3.13 • THE EURO RIDES A ROLLER-COASTER

Source: U.S. Federal Reserve System. Rates are noon buying rates in New York City for cable transfers. Data for 9/11/01 are missing owing to the shutdown of financial trading in New York City following the destruction of the World Trade Center.

U.S. economy combined with the slowness of many European countries in performing the necessary restructuring of their economies that the euro was supposed to initiate.

Following the terrorist attacks on the United States on September 11, the euro rose briefly as the United States looked to be a relatively riskier place to invest in. But the euro soon reversed course again as it became clear that Euroland's economic environment was worse than earlier thought and investors became more optimistic about U.S. economic recovery. Beginning in 2002, however, continuing sluggish U.S. growth and aggressive Fed lowering of U.S. interest rates, combined with higher yields on euro-denominated securities and signs of structural reform in European economies, led to a dramatic rise in the value of the euro. This rise has been greater than many expected, particularly given the sluggish European economic growth and the U.S. economic recovery since 2002.

One explanation for the dollar's large decline has been the large and growing U.S. trade deficit. This deficit has now reached a point where it is unsustainable and so must be corrected. One such correction is a large fall in the value of the dollar, which translates into a rise in the euro. Moreover, the euro has likely risen more than it otherwise would have because it must shoulder a disproportionate share of dollar's decline. The reason is that, as we have already seen, several U.S. trading partners, such as China and Japan, have resisted a rise in their currencies. In the interlocking world of foreign exchange, if the yuan cannot appreciate against the dollar, then other currencies, and especially the euro, have to compensate by appreciating even more to make up for the fixed yuan. Suppose, for example, that the dollar must decline by 10% to reach its appropriate trade-weighted value. If the yuan remains pegged to the dollar, then other currencies must rise by more than 10% against the dollar to achieve overall balance. To prevent overheating, the ECB raised its key financing rate seven times, by 25 basis points each, between the period December 2005 and March 2007. The continuing influence of political factors on the value of the euro is illustrated by its reaction to the rejection by France and the Netherlands of a proposed European constitution in 2005.

ILLUSTRATION   *The French Say* Non *to a European Constitution and the Euro Responds*

On Sunday, May 29, 2005, French voters resoundingly rejected a proposed constitution for the European Union. The concern expressed by most of these *non* voters was that the constitution would force open their borders wider, accelerating economic competition and further threatening their treasured welfare state and protections against onerous toil. Three days later, Dutch voters rejected the constitution by an even larger margin. In response, the euro fell dramatically against the dollar (see Exhibit 3.14). The rejection of

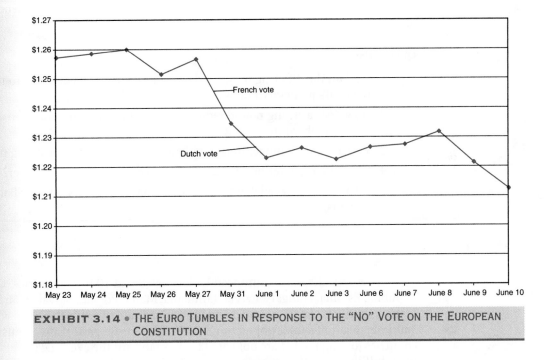

EXHIBIT 3.14 • THE EURO TUMBLES IN RESPONSE TO THE "NO" VOTE ON THE EUROPEAN CONSTITUTION

the European constitution underscored Europe's political woes and the myriad challenges facing the euro and the Euroland economies. Sunday's *non* by 55% of French voters led investors to reassess the prospects of Europe's ability to manage a common currency without a unified government to back it up. Most importantly, currency traders worried that the French and Dutch votes were part of a broader populist protest against free trade and free markets that would slow down the pace of economic integration and reform in Euroland. That would make Europe a less desirable place to invest, reducing the demand for euros. The French and Dutch votes reinforced the view that Europe was unwilling and unable to make tough economic and political decisions. We saw earlier that even before the constitution problems arose, EMU countries had fudged rules to limit government spending considered key to underpinning the currency. They had also fought over a rule to remove cross-border barriers to services industries, with France and other nations seeking protection from low-cost service providers. As can be seen in Exhibit 3.14, the fear that Europe would reverse course on economic liberalization in response to persistently high unemployment and stagnant economic growth had already resulted in a falling euro earlier in the year.

MINI-CASE *The Euro Reacts to New Information*

According to an article in the *Wall Street Journal* (October 8, 1999), "The European Central Bank left interest rates unchanged but made clear it is seriously considering tightening monetary policy. The euro fell slightly on the ECB's announcement around midday that it would hold its key refinancing rate steady at 2.5%. But it rebounded as ECB President Wim Duisenberg reinforced expectations that a rate rise is in the works." In the same story, the journal reported that "the Bank of England didn't elaborate on its decision to leave its key repo rate unchanged at 5.25%." At the same time, "sterling remains strong, which reduces the threat of imported inflation as well as continuing to pressure U.K. manufacturers. That could work against higher interest rates, which could send sterling even higher."

QUESTIONS

1. Explain the differing initial and subsequent reactions of the euro to news about the ECB's monetary policy.
2. How does a strong pound reduce the threat of imported inflation and work against higher interest rates?
3. Which U.K. manufacturers are likely to be pressured by a strong pound?
4. Why might higher pound interest rates send sterling even higher?
5. What tools are available to the European Central Bank and the Bank of England to manage their monetary policies?

On May 1, 2004, the European Union welcomed 10 new countries, Cyprus, Czech Republic, Estonia, Hungary, Latvia, Lithuania, Malta, Poland, Slovakia, and Slovenia. On January 1, 2007, the EU was expanded to 27 countries, with the inclusion of Bulgaria and Romaina, for a total population of 493 million. As part of the admissions bargain, countries joining the EU are obligated to strive toward the eventual adoption of the euro upon fulfillment of the convergence criteria. Integration into the monetary union represents a key step toward full economic integration within the EU and has the potential to deliver considerable economic benefits to the new members. In particular, it helps countries to reap the full benefits of the EU's single market, as it works in parallel with the free movement of goods, labor, services, and capital, favoring an efficient allocation of resources. Moreover, the process and prospect of joining EMU may contribute to anchor expectations and support the implementation of sound macroeconomic and structural policies.

3.3.5 Optimum Currency Area

Most discussion of European monetary union has highlighted its benefits, such as eliminating currency uncertainty and lowering the costs of doing business. The potential costs of currency integration have been overlooked. Suppose, for example, France had not joined the monetary union. If the worldwide demand for French goods falls sharply, France must make its goods less expensive and attract new industries to replace its shrinking old ones. The quickest way to do this is to reduce French wages, thereby making its workers more competitive. But this reduction is unlikely to be accomplished quickly. Eventually, high unemployment might persuade French workers to accept lower pay. But in the interim, the social and economic costs of reducing wages by, say, 10% will be high. In contrast, a 10% depreciation of the franc would achieve the same thing quickly and relatively painlessly.

Conversely, a worldwide surge in demand for French goods could give rise to French inflation, unless France allowed the franc to appreciate. In other words, currency changes can substitute for periodic bouts of inflation and deflation caused by various economic shocks. Once France enters the monetary union, and replaces the franc with the euro, it no longer has the option of changing its exchange rate to cope with these shocks. This option would have been valuable to the ERM, which instead came unglued because of the huge economic shock to its fixed parities brought about by the absorption of East Germany into the German economy.

Taking this logic to its extreme would imply that not only should each nation have its own currency, but so should each region within a nation. Why not a southern California dollar, or indeed a Los Angeles dollar? The answer is having separate currencies brings costs as well as benefits.

The more currencies there are, the higher the costs of doing business and the more currency risks exist. Both factors impair the functions of money as a medium of exchange and a store of value, so maintaining more currencies acts as a barrier to international trade and investment, even as it reduces vulnerability to economic shocks.

According to the theory of the **optimum currency area**, this trade-off becomes less and less favorable as the size of the economic unit shrinks. The key idea is that money is more useful the more widely it is used. So how large is the optimum currency area? No one knows. But some economists argue that Europe might be better off with four or five regional currencies than with only one.[7]

The great hope of enthusiasts for Europe's single currency, as for its single market, was that it would unleash pressures that would force its members to reform their rigid economies to make them more flexible and competitive. Such competitive pressures were unleashed but the core euro countries, especially France, Germany, and Italy, have responded by first initiating and then resisting the reforms that the euro and single market made necessary. As predicted, the result has been greater vulnerability to economic shocks and difficult economic times.

Such difficulty brought speculation in 2005 that EMU would break apart over its handling of monetary policy. The ECB is trying to steer the economy of a region in which the four largest nations, Germany, France, Italy, and Spain, are growing at very different rates. As a result, the ECB cannot apply an optimal interest rate for any one country. For example, some economists argue that Italy, being in a recession, could use interest rates close to zero, and France and Germany with their slow growth could use interest rates of 1% to 1.5%. Booming Spain, on the other hand, might be better off with an interest rate of 3%. Instead, the ECB's key short-term rate is 2%, too low for Spain and too high for Italy, Germany, and France. Viewing these problems, some economists claim that Britain has benefited from staying out of the euro because the Bank of England can still set interest rates in line with its own particular facts and circumstances.

[7] See, for example, Geoffrey M. B. Tootell, "Central Bank Flexibility and the Drawbacks to Currency Unification," *New England Economic Review*, May–June 1990, pp. 3–18; and Paul Krugman, "A Europe-Wide Currency Makes No Economic Sense," *Los Angeles Times*, August 5, 1990, p. D2.

MINI-CASE *Britain—In or Out for the Euro*

The interminable debate in Britain over whether to join the European Monetary Union (EMU) reached a feverish pitch in early 2003. That was when Prime Minister Gordon Brown, the then chancellor of the exchequer had promised to make his recommendation to the then Prime Minister Tony Blair as to whether economic conditions were such as to warrant the move. Although Prime Minister Blair was likely to accept Chancellor Brown's judgment, he also had to pay attention to the intense debate over the euro. This debate went way beyond party lines, splitting political parties and raising passions in a way few other issues do. Business was similarly divided over the merits of EMU. The economy, and how it could be affected by joining the euro, was central to this debate.

Euro skeptics pointed out that by adopting the euro, Britain would trade control over its own interest rates and monetary policy for a single vote on the governing council of the ECB in Frankfurt, which sets interest rates for Euroland as a whole. Shocks to the economy, like the terrorist attacks of September 11 or a drop in the housing market, make it harder for the ECB to find the right rate. After euro entry, given the limitation on deficits, the British government could face a stark choice between cutting public spending or raising taxes. For many opponents, monetary union would also mean more EU-generated regulation. Moreover, skeptics argued, the benefits of EMU were not readily apparent insofar as Britain had lower unemployment, lower inflation, and higher growth than Euroland.

Despite this dismal view of Britain's prospects if it joined EMU, equally passionate euro enthusiasts argued that Britain was paying a high price for its economic isolation. They pointed out that foreign investment, a cornerstone of Britain's economic prosperity, was in jeopardy. Thousands of foreign businesses, employing hundreds of thousands of workers, had brought new skills and innovations to Britain, raising productivity and boosting prosperity. However, since the advent of the euro, Britain's share of foreign investment in Europe had fallen precipitously. The pro-euro camp's explanation for this sharp decline was that multinationals locating in Britain now had to bear transaction costs and exchange rate uncertainty that they could avoid by basing themselves in EMU countries. Similarly, euro supporters argued that Britain's trade with the EU, half its overall trade, was stagnating because of these same currency costs and risks. Meanwhile, euro countries are seeing their trade with each other rise dramatically. Supporters, therefore, argued that joining EMU would lead to greater stability and shared growth in the EU. If EMU would also facilitate greater economic efficiency and increase competition by allowing British companies and consumers to more easily compare prices and wages with their Euroland counterparts. Skeptics, however, argued that Britain's lighter regulatory and tax burden were more important for investors and businesses than the euro and these advantages would be lost if Britain joined EMU.

QUESTIONS

1. Discuss the pros and cons for Britain of joining EMU.
2. Commentators pointed to the fact that many people in Britain have variable rate mortgages, as opposed to the fixed-rate mortgages more common in Europe. Britain also has the most flexible labor markets in Europe. How would these factors likely affect Britain's economic costs and benefits of joining the euro?
3. What types of British companies would most likely benefit from joining EMU?
4. Some large multinationals warned that they only chose to invest in Britain on the assumption that it would ultimately adopt the euro. Why would multinationals be interested in Britain joining the euro?

3.4 EMERGING MARKET CURRENCY CRISES

As we saw in Chapter 2, the decade of the 1990s was punctuated by a series of currency crises in emerging markets. First was the Mexican crisis in 1994–1995. That crisis was followed by the Asian crisis 2 years later in 1997, then the Russian crisis of 1998, and the Brazilian crisis of 1998–1999.

3.4.1 Transmission Mechanisms

The problem with these currency crises is that they tend to be contagious, spreading from one nation to another. There are two principal routes of contagion: trade links and the financial system. Contagion is exacerbated by a reliance on short-term U.S. dollar-linked debt.

Trade Links   Contagion can spread from one emerging market to another through trade links. For example, when Argentina is in crisis, it imports less from Brazil, its principal trading partner. As Brazil's economy begins to contract, its currency is likely to weaken. At the same time, the contagion will spread from Brazil to its other emerging market trade partners.

Financial System   The second and more important transmission mechanism is through the financial system. As we saw in the case of the Asian currency crisis, trouble in one emerging market often can serve as a "wake-up call" to investors who seek to exit other countries with similar risky characteristics. For example, Argentina's problems, which stem from its large budget deficit, focused investor attention on Brazil's unresolved fiscal problems. Financial contagion can also occur, because investors who are leveraged up start selling assets in other countries to make up for their initial losses. Investors may also become more risk averse and seek to rebalance their portfolios by selling off a portion of all their risky assets.

Debt Policy   Crisis-prone countries tend to have one thing in common that promotes contagion: They issue too much short-term debt that is closely linked to the U.S. dollar. When times are good, confident investors gladly buy short-term emerging market bonds and roll them over when they come due. However, when the bad times come and currencies tumble, the cost of repaying dollar-linked bonds soars, savvy investors rush for the exits, and governments find their debt-raising capacity vanishes overnight. Things quickly spiral out of control.

3.4.2 Origins of Emerging Market Crises

The sequence of currency crises has prompted policy makers to seek ways to deal with them. Many of their crisis-fighting proposals involve increasing the IMF's funding and giving it and possibly new international agencies the power to guide global financial markets. However, these proposals could exacerbate the two principal sources of these crises.

Moral Hazard   A number of economists believe that by bailing out first Mexico and then the Asian countries, the IMF actually helped fuel these crises by creating a moral hazard in lending behavior. For example, the Mexican bailout encouraged investors to lend more money on less stringent terms to the Asian countries than they would have otherwise because of their belief that the IMF would bail them out if trouble hit. The $118-billion Asian bailout by the IMF ($57 billion for South Korea alone) reinforced the view of foreign investors that they were operating with an implicit guarantee from the IMF, which led to the Russian currency crisis and then the Brazilian crisis. At the same time, the provision of an IMF safety net gives recipient governments less incentive to adopt responsible fiscal and monetary policies.

Fundamental Policy Conflict   Underlying the emerging market currency crises is a fundamental conflict among policy objectives that the target nations have failed to resolve and that IMF assistance has only allowed them to drag out. These three objectives are a fixed exchange rate, independent domestic monetary policy, and free capital movement. As we saw in Chapter 2, any two of these objectives are possible; all three are not. Speculators recognized that the attempts by Mexico, Indonesia, Thailand, South Korea, Brazil, Russia, and other countries to achieve these three objectives simultaneously were unsustainable and attacked their currencies, resulting in the inevitable breakdowns in their systems.

3.4.3 Policy Proposals for Dealing with Emerging Market Crises

There are three possible ways to avoid these financial crises. One is to impose currency controls, another is to permit currencies to float freely, and the third is to permanently fix the exchange rate by dollarizing, adopting a common currency as the participants in EMU have done, or establishing a currency board.

Currency Controls   Some economists have advocated abandoning free capital movement, as Malaysia has done, as a means of insulating a nation's currency from speculative attacks. However, open capital markets improve economic welfare by channeling savings to where they are most productive. Moreover, most developing nations need foreign capital and the know-how, discipline, and more efficient resource allocation that come with it. Finally, the long history of currency controls should provide no comfort to its advocates. Currency controls have inevitably led to corruption and government misallocation of foreign exchange, hardly prescriptions for healthy growth.

Freely Floating Currency   With a freely floating currency, the exchange rate is set by the interplay of supply and demand. As Milton Friedman pointed out, with a floating exchange rate, there never has been a foreign exchange crisis. The reason is simple: The floating rate absorbs the pressures that would otherwise build up in countries that try to peg the exchange rate while simultaneously pursuing an independent monetary policy. For example, the Asian currency crisis did not spill over to Australia and New Zealand because the latter countries had floating exchange rates.

Permanently Fixed Exchange Rate   Through dollarization, establishment of a currency board, or monetary union, a nation can fix its exchange rate permanently. The key to this system's viability is the surrender of monetary independence to a single central bank: the ECB for the countries using the euro and the Federal Reserve for countries like Ecuador and Panama that have dollarized. The Federal Reserve is also the *de facto* central bank for countries such as Argentina (until 2002) and Hong Kong that have dollar-based currency boards.

Adherence to either a truly fixed or a floating exchange rate will help avert foreign exchange crises. Which mechanism is superior depends on a variety of factors. For example, if a country has a major trading partner with a long history of a stable monetary policy, then tying the domestic currency to the partner's currency would probably be a good choice. In any event, the choice of either system will eliminate the need for the IMF or other international agency to intervene in or usurp the market.

Better Information   Information about emerging markets is improving, allowing investors to distinguish good ones from the bad. As such, the best way to reduce financial market contagion in the future is to develop and disseminate better information about emerging market policies and their consequences. This course of action is exactly what one would expect free markets to undertake on their own, without the need for government intervention.

3.5 SUMMARY AND CONCLUSIONS

This chapter studied the process of exchange rate determination under five market mechanisms: free float, managed float, target-zone system, fixed-rate system, and the current hybrid system. In the last four systems, governments intervene in the currency markets in various ways to affect the exchange rate.

Regardless of the form of intervention, however, fixed rates do not remain fixed for long. Neither do floating rates. The basic reason that exchange rates do not remain fixed in either a fixed- or floating-rate system is that governments subordinate exchange rate considerations to domestic political considerations.

We saw that the gold standard is a specific type of fixed exchange-rate system, one that required participating countries to maintain the value of their currencies in terms of gold. Calls for a new gold standard reflect a fundamental lack of trust that monetary authorities will desist from tampering with the integrity of fiat money.

Finally, we concluded that intervention to maintain a disequilibrium rate is generally ineffective or injurious when pursued over lengthy periods of time. Seldom have policymakers been able to outsmart, for any extended period, the collective judgment of currency buyers and sellers. The current volatile market environment, which is a consequence of unstable U.S. and world financial conditions, cannot be arbitrarily directed by government officials for long.

Examining the U.S. experience since the abandonment of fixed rates, we found that free-market forces did correctly reflect economic realities thereafter. The dollar's value dropped sharply between 1973 and 1980 when the United States experienced high inflation and weakened economic conditions. Beginning in 1981, the dollar's value rose when American policies dramatically changed under the leadership of the Federal Reserve and a new president, but fell when foreign economies strengthened relative to the U.S. economy. Nonetheless, the resulting shifts in U.S. cost competitiveness have led many to question the current international monetary system.

The principal alternative to the current system of floating currencies with its economic volatility is a fixed exchange-rate system. History offers no entirely convincing model for how such a system should be constructed, but it does point to two requirements. To succeed in reducing economic volatility, a system of fixed exchange rates must be credible, and it must have price stability built into its very fabric. Otherwise, the market's expectations of exchange rate changes combined with an unsatisfactory rate of inflation will lead to periodic battles among central banks and between central banks and the financial markets. The recent experiences of the European Monetary System (EMS) point to the costs associated with the maintenance of exchange rates at unrealistic levels. These experiences also point out that, in the end, there is no real escape from market forces. Most European nations have responded to this reality by forming a monetary union and adopting the euro as their common currency. Some developing nations have gone further and abandoned their currencies altogether by dollarizing, either explicitly or implicitly through a currency board.

A final lesson learned is that one must have realistic expectations of a currency system. In particular, no currency system can achieve what many politicians expect of it—a way to keep all the benefits of economic policy for their own nation while passing along the costs to foreigners (who do not vote) or to future generations (who do not vote yet). The recent series of emerging market crises points to the futility of this exercise.

QUESTIONS

1. What are the five basic mechanisms for establishing exchange rates?
   a. How does each mechanism work?
   b. What costs and benefits are associated with each mechanism?
   c. Have exchange rate movements under the current system of managed floating been excessive? Explain.

2. Find a recent example of a nation's foreign exchange market intervention and note what the government's justification was. Does this justification make economic sense?

3. Gold has been called "the ultimate burglar alarm." Explain what this expression means.

4. Suppose nations attempt to pursue independent monetary and fiscal policies. How will exchange rates behave?

5. The experiences of fixed exchange-rate systems and target-zone arrangements have not been entirely satisfactory.
   a. What lessons can economists draw from the breakdown of the Bretton Woods system?
   b. What lessons can economists draw from the exchange rate experiences of the EMS?

6. How did the EMS limit the economic ability of each member nation to set its interest rate to be different from Germany's?

7. Historically, Spain has had high inflation and has seen its peseta continuously depreciate. In 1989, however, Spain joined the EMS and pegged the peseta to the DM. According to a Spanish banker, EMS membership means that "the government has less capability to manage the currency but, on the other hand, the people are more trusting of the currency for that reason."
   a. What underlies the peseta's historical weakness?
   b. Comment on the banker's statement.
   c. What are the likely consequences of EMS membership on the Spanish public's willingness to save and invest?

8. In discussing EMU, a recent government report stressed a need to make the central bank accountable to the "democratic process." What are the likely consequences for price and exchange rate stability in the EMS if the ECB becomes accountable to the "democratic process"?

9. In 1996, Britain's Chancellor of the Exchequer Kenneth Clarke called for a national debate on whether Britain should join the European Monetary Union (EMU). Discuss the pros and cons for Britain of joining EMU.

10. Comment on the statement: "With monetary union, the era of protection for European firms and workers has come to an end."

PROBLEMS

1. During the currency crisis of September 1992, the Bank of England borrowed DM 33 billion from the Bundesbank when a pound was worth DM 2.78, or $1.912. It sold these DM in the foreign exchange market for pounds in a futile attempt to prevent a devaluation of the pound. It repaid these DM at the postcrisis rate of DM 2.50:£1. By then, the dollar:pound exchange rate was $1.782:£1.
   a. By what percentage had the pound sterling devalued in the interim against the Deutsche mark? Against the dollar?
   b. What was the cost of intervention to the Bank of England in pounds? In dollars?

2. Suppose the central rates within the ERM for the French franc and DM are FF 6.90403:ECU 1 and DM 2.05853:ECU 1, respectively.
   a. What is the cross-exchange rate between the franc and the mark?
   b. Under the former 2.25% margin on either side of the central rate, what were the approximate upper and lower intervention limits for France and Germany?
   c. Under the new 15% margin on either side of the central rate, what are the current approximate upper and lower intervention limits for France and Germany?

3. A Dutch company exporting to France had FF 3 million due in 90 days. Suppose that the spot exchange rate was FF 1 = DFl 0.3291.
   a. Under the exchange rate mechanism, and assuming central rates of FF 6.45863/ECU and Dfl 2.16979/ECU, what was the central cross-exchange rate between the two currencies?
   b. Based on the answer to Part (a), what was the most the Dutch company could lose on its French franc receivable, assuming that France and the Netherlands stuck to the ERM with a 15% band on either side of their central cross rate?
   c. Redo Part (b), assuming the band was narrowed to 2.25%.

d. Redo Part (b), assuming you know nothing about the spot cross-exchange rate.

4. Panama adopted the U.S. dollar as its official paper money in 1904. Currently, $400 million to $500 million in U.S. dollars is circulating in Panama. If interest rates on U.S. Treasury securities are 7%, what is the value of the seigniorage that Panama is forgoing by using the U.S. dollar instead of its own-issue money?

5. By some estimates, $185 billion to $260 billion in currency is held outside the United States.

a. What is the value to the United States of the seigniorage associated with these overseas dollars? Assume that dollar interest rates are about 6%.

b. Who in the United States realizes this seigniorage?

BIBLIOGRAPHY

Bordo, M. D. "The Classical Gold Standard: Some Lessons for Today." *Federal Reserve Bank of St. Louis Review*, May 1981, pp. 2–17.

Coombs, C. A. *The Arena of International Finance*. New York: John Wiley & Sons, 1976.

De Grauwe, P. "Review: Flaws in the Design of the Eurosystem?" *International Finance*, Vol. 9, No. 1, 2006, pp. 137–144.

Eichengreen, B. and R. Razo-Garcia, "The International Monetary System in the Last and Next 20 Years," *Economic Policy*, June 2006, pp. 393–442.

Friedman, M. and R. V. Roosa, "Free versus Fixed Exchange Rates: A Debate." *Journal of Portfolio Management*, Spring 1977, pp. 68–73.

Goldsbrough, D., K. Barnes, I. Mateos y Lago, and T. Tsikata, "Prolonged Use of IMF Loans," *Finance & Development*, December 2002, pp. 34–37.

Mundell, R. A. "A Theory of Optimum Currency Areas." *American Economic Review*, September 1961, pp. 657–663.

INTERNET RESOURCES

http://www.imf.org Web site of the International Monetary Fund (IMF) that takes you directly to information on the IMF, SDRs, exchange rates, position of each country in the IMF, and lending arrangements with member nations.

www.ex.ac.uk/~RDavies/arian/llyfr.html Contains a detailed history of money from ancient times to the present.

www.ecb.int Web site of the European Central Bank (ECB). Contains press releases and publications put out by the ECB along with exchange rate data and other euro area-related economic and financial statistics.

europa.eu.int Web site of the European Union (EU). Contains news, information, and statistics on the EU and its member nations and the euro.

www.sysmod.com/eurofaq.htm Contains answers to frequently asked questions about the euro and EMU as well as links to related Web sites.

http://www.ny.frb.org/ Website of the Federal Reserve Bank of New York. Contains information on U.S. interventions in the foreign exchange market.

http://www.oanda.com/ Contains current and historical foreign exchange rate data for all currencies.

http://www.oecd.org/ Website of the Organization for Economic Co-operation and Development. Contains news, analyses, and data on international finance and economics including interest rates and foreign exchange rates (including PPP rates)

https://www.cia.gov/library/publications/the-world-factbook/index.html Website of CIA: The World Factbook. Contains demographic, social, political, and economic data for every country.

INTERNET EXERCISES

1. Plot the dollar value of the euro since its inception. How has the euro fared in the past year?
2. What explanations have been given for the decline of the euro in the first 3 years of its existence?
3. What are the objectives of the ECB? What policy trade-offs does the ECB have to consider?
4. According to the IMF, what are its main purposes?
5. What proposals have been made by the IMF to reduce the incidence and severity of international financial crises?

4

PARITY CONDITIONS IN INTERNATIONAL FINANCE AND CURRENCY FORECASTING

It is not for its own sake that men desire money, but for the sake of what they can purchase with it.

Adam Smith (1776)

CHAPTER LEARNING OBJECTIVES

- To describe the meaning of "the law of one price" and its importance to the study of international finance
- To explain how arbitrage links goods prices and asset returns internationally
- To list and describe the five key theoretical relationships among spot exchange rates, forward exchange rates, inflation rates, and interest rates that result from international arbitrage activities
- To differentiate between the real and nominal exchange rate and the real and nominal interest rate
- To list and describe the four requirements for successful currency forecasting
- To identify a five-stage procedure for forecasting exchange rates in a fixed-rate system
- To describe how to forecast exchange rates in a floating-rate system using the predictions already embodied in interest and forward rates
- To describe the meaning and likelihood of forecasting success in both fixed-rate and floating-rate systems

KEY TERMS

arbitrage
black-market exchange rate
capital market integration
capital market segmentation
charting
covered interest arbitrage
covered interest differential
currency forecasting
Fisher effect (FE)
forward discount
forward premium
fundamental analysis
inflation differential
interest rate differential
interest rate parity

international Fisher effect (IFE)
law of one price
market-based forecasts
model-based forecasts
nominal exchange rate
nominal interest rate
parity conditions
peso problem
purchasing power parity (PPP)
real exchange rate
real interest rate
technical analysis
trend analysis
unbiased forward rate (UFR)
unbiased predictor

On the basis of the flows of goods and capital discussed in Chapter 2, this chapter presents a simple yet elegant set of equilibrium relationships that should apply to product prices, interest rates, and spot and forward exchange rates if markets are not impeded. These relationships, or **parity conditions**, provide the foundation for much of the remainder of this book; these should be clearly understood before you proceed further. The final section of this chapter examines the usefulness of a number of models and methodologies in profitably forecasting currency changes under both fixed-rate and floating-rate systems.

4.1 ARBITRAGE AND THE LAW OF ONE PRICE

Arbitrage is one of the most important concepts in all of finance. It is ordinarily defined as the simultaneous purchase and sale of the same assets or commodities on different markets to profit from price discrepancies. The concept of arbitrage is of particular importance in international finance because so many of the relationships between domestic and international financial markets, exchange rates, interest rates, and inflation rates depend on arbitrage for their existence. Indeed, by linking markets together, arbitrage underlies the globalization of markets.

One of the central ideas of international finance stems from arbitrage: In competitive markets, characterized by numerous buyers and sellers having low-cost access to information, exchange-adjusted prices of identical tradable goods and financial assets must be within transaction costs of equality worldwide. This idea, referred to as the **law of one price**, is enforced by international arbitrageurs who follow the profit-guaranteeing dictum of "buy low, sell high" and prevent all but trivial deviations from equality. Similarly, in the absence of market imperfections, risk-adjusted expected returns on financial assets in different markets should be equal.

Five key theoretical economic relationships, which are depicted in Exhibit 4.1, result from these arbitrage activities:

- Purchasing power parity (PPP)
- Fisher effect (FE)
- International Fisher effect (IFE)

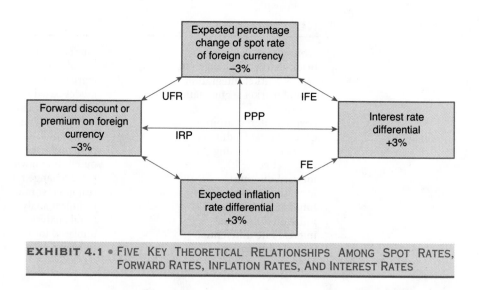

EXHIBIT 4.1 • FIVE KEY THEORETICAL RELATIONSHIPS AMONG SPOT RATES, FORWARD RATES, INFLATION RATES, AND INTEREST RATES

- Interest rate parity (IRP)
- Forward rates as unbiased predictors of future spot rates (UFR)

The framework of Exhibit 4.1 emphasizes the links among prices, spot exchange rates, interest rates, and forward exchange rates. Before proceeding, some terminology is in order. Specifically, a foreign currency is said to be at a **forward discount** if the forward rate expressed in dollars is below the spot rate, whereas a **forward premium** exists if the forward rate is above the spot rate. The forward discount or premium is expressed in annualized percentage terms as follows:

$$\begin{array}{l} \text{Forward premium} \\ \text{or discount} \end{array} = \frac{\text{Forward rate} - \text{Spot rate}}{\text{Spot rate}} \times \frac{360}{\begin{array}{c} \text{Forward contract} \\ \text{number of days} \end{array}} \quad (4.1)$$

where the exchange rate is stated in domestic currency units per unit of foreign currency.

According to the diagram in Exhibit 4.1, if inflation in, say, Mexico is expected to exceed inflation in the United States by 3% for the coming year, then the Mexican peso should decline in value by about 3% relative to the dollar. By the same token, the 1-year forward Mexican peso should sell at a 3% discount relative to the U.S. dollar. Similarly, 1-year interest rates in Mexico should be about 3% higher than 1-year interest rates on securities of comparable risk in the United States.

The common denominator of these parity conditions is the adjustment of the various rates and prices to inflation. As the supply of money increases relative to the supply of goods and services, the purchasing power of money—the exchange rate between goods and services—must decline.

The mechanism that brings this adjustment about is simple and direct. Suppose, for example, that the supply of U.S. dollars exceeds the amount that individuals wish to hold. In order to reduce their excess holdings of money, individuals increase their spending on goods, services, and securities, causing U.S. prices to rise. Moreover, as we saw in Chapter 2, this price inflation will cause the value of the dollar to decline.

A further link in the chain relating money-supply growth, inflation, interest rates, and exchange rates is the notion that money is neutral. That is, money should have no impact on real variables. Thus, for example, a 10% increase in the supply of money relative to the demand for money should cause prices to rise by 10%. This view has important implications for international finance. Specifically, although a change in the quantity of money will affect prices and exchange rates, this change should not affect the rate at which domestic goods are exchanged for foreign goods or the rate at which goods today are exchanged for goods in the future. These ideas are formalized as purchasing power parity and the Fisher effect, respectively. We will examine them here briefly and then in greater detail in the next two sections.

The international analogue to inflation is home currency depreciation relative to foreign currencies. The analogy derives from the observation that inflation involves a change in the exchange rate between the home currency and domestic goods, whereas home currency depreciation—a decline in the foreign currency value of the home currency—results in a change in the exchange rate between the home currency and foreign goods.

That inflation and currency depreciation are related is no accident. Excess money-supply growth, through its impact on the rate of aggregate spending, affects the demand for goods produced abroad as well as goods produced domestically. In turn, the domestic demand for foreign currencies changes, and, consequently, the foreign exchange value of the domestic currency changes. Thus, the rate of domestic inflation and changes in the exchange rate are jointly determined by the rate of domestic money growth relative to the growth of the amount that people, domestic and foreign, want to hold.

If international arbitrage enforces the law of one price, then the exchange rate between the home currency and domestic goods must equal the exchange rate between the home currency and foreign goods. In other words, a unit of home currency (HC) should have the same purchasing power worldwide. Thus, if a dollar buys a pound of bread in the United States, it should also buy a pound of bread in Great Britain. For this to happen, the foreign exchange rate must change by (approximately) the difference between the domestic and foreign rates of inflation. This relationship is called **purchasing power parity** (PPP).

Similarly, the **nominal interest rate**, the price quoted on lending and borrowing transactions, determines the exchange rate between current and future dollars (or any other currency). For example, an interest rate of 10% on a 1-year loan means that one dollar today is being exchanged for 1.1 dollars a year from now. But what really matters, according to the **Fisher effect (FE)**, is the exchange rate between current and future purchasing power, as measured by the real interest rate. Simply put, the lender is concerned with how many more goods can be obtained in the future by forgoing consumption today, whereas the borrower wants to know how much future consumption must be sacrificed to obtain more goods today. This condition is the case regardless of whether the borrower and lender are located in the same or different countries. As a result, if the exchange rate between current and future goods—the **real interest rate**—varies from one country to the next, arbitrage between domestic and foreign capital markets, in the form of international capital flows, should occur. These flows will tend to equalize real interest rates across countries. By looking more closely at these and related parity conditions, we can see how they can be formalized and used for management purposes.

4.2 PURCHASING POWER PARITY

Purchasing power parity (PPP) has been widely used by central banks as a guide to establishing new par values for their currencies when the old ones were clearly in disequilibrium. From a management standpoint, PPP is often used to forecast future exchange rates, for purposes ranging from deciding on the currency denomination of long-term debt issues to determining in which countries to build plants.

In its *absolute* version, PPP states that price levels should be equal worldwide when expressed in a common currency. In other words, a unit of home currency (HC) should have the same purchasing power around the world. This theory is just an application of the law of one price to national price levels rather than to individual prices. (That is, it rests on the assumption that free trade will equalize the price of any good in all countries; otherwise, arbitrage opportunities would exist.) However, absolute PPP ignores the effects on free trade of transportation costs, tariffs, quotas and other restrictions, and product differentiation.

The Big Mac index, a light-hearted guide to whether currencies are at their "correct" levels against the dollar, illustrates the law of one price and absolute PPP. It is calculated by comparing the prices of Big Macs worldwide (they are produced in almost 120 countries). The Big Mac PPP, put together by *The Economist*, is the exchange rate that would leave hamburgers costing the same overseas as in the United States. By comparing Big Mac PPPs with actual exchange rates, which is done in Exhibit 4.2, we can see whether a currency is over- or undervalued by this standard.

	Big Mac prices		Implied PPP* Exchange Rate of the Dollar	Actual Dollar Exchange Rate Jan 31, 2007	Under (−)/Over (+) Valuation** Against the Dollar, %
	In Local Currency (LC)	In Dollars			
United States	$3.22	3.22	—	—	—
Argentina	Peso 8.25	2.65	2.56	3.11	−17.7
Australia	A$3.45	2.67	1.07	1.29	−17.1
Brazil	Real 6.40	3.01	1.99	2.13	−6.5
Britain	£1.99	3.90	2.37	1.96	21.1
Canada	C$3.63	3.08	1.13	1.18	−4.3
Chile	Peso 1670	3.07	518.66	544	−4.7
China	Yuan 11.0	1.41	3.40	7.77	−56.2
Denmark	DKr27.75	4.84	8.63	6	50.3
Euro area	€ 2.94	3.82	1.54	1.30	18.6
Hong Kong	HK$12.00	1.54	3.74	7.81	−52.2
Hungary	Forint 590	3.00	183.54	197.00	−6.8
Indonesia	Rupiah 15,900	1.75	4,945.65	9,100.0	−45.7
Japan	¥280	2.31	86.96	121.36	−28.3
Malaysia	M$5.50	1.57	1.71	3.50	−51.2
Mexico	Peso 29.0	2.66	9.00	10.90	−17.4
New Zealand	NZ$4.60	3.16	1.42	1.45	−1.9
Poland	Zloty 6.90	2.29	2.14	3.01	−28.9
Russia	Ruble 49.00	1.89	15.22	25.88	−41.2
Singapore	S$3.60	2.34	1.12	1.54	−27.3
South Africa	Rand 15.5	2.14	4.82	7.25	−33.5
South Korea	Won 2,900	3.08	901.04	942.00	−4.3
Sweden	SKr 32.0	4.59	9.94	6.97	42.5
Switzerland	SFr 6.30	5.05	1.96	1.25	56.8
Taiwan	NT$75.00	2.28	23.30	32.90	−29.2
Thailand	Baht 62.0	1.78	19.18	34.70	−44.7

* Purchasing power parity: local currency price divided by dollar price in the United States
** Under/over valuation: (implied PPP rate—actual exchange rate)/actual exchange rate
[1] Average of New York, Chicago, San Francisco, and Atlanta prices
Source: The Economist, Feb. 27, 2007 Study.

EXHIBIT 4.2 • THE BIG MAC HAMBURGER STANDARD AS OF FEB, 2007

For example, a Big Mac in Britain cost £1.99 on January 31, 2007. Dividing this price through by its U.S. price of $3.22 implies a PPP exchange rate of £0.62/$:

$$\frac{£1.99}{3.22} = £0.62/\$$$

The actual exchange rate on that date was £0.51. By this measure, the pound was 21% overvalued on January 31, 2007:

$$\frac{£0.62 − £0.51}{£0.51} = +21\%$$

Alternatively, with a dollar PPP of R1.99/S (R6.40/$3.22), the Brazilian *real* appeared to be undervalued by 6% (R1.99/R2.13 − 1 = − 6%).

The Big Mac standard is somewhat misleading because you are buying not just the hamburger but the location. Included in the price of a Big Mac is the cost of real estate, local taxes, and local services, which differ worldwide and are not traded goods. When the items being compared contain a bundle of traded and nontraded goods and services, as in the case of a Big Mac, it should not be surprising that absolute PPP and the law of one price fail to hold. Despite its flaws, the Big Mac index has had some success. For example, in 1999, it signaled that the euro was overvalued at its launch and the euro fell, notwithstanding expectations to the contrary. In 2002, it signaled that the U.S. dollar was more overvalued than at any other time in the life of the Big Mac index; shortly thereafter, the dollar plummeted in value. In 2007, it has indicated that despite the Japanese yen's rise in value, it is still 28% undervalued against the dollar (Exhibit 4.2).

The *relative* version of PPP, which is used more commonly now, states that the exchange rate between the home currency and any foreign currency will adjust to reflect changes in the price levels of the two countries. For example, if inflation is 5% in the United States and 1% in Japan, then the dollar value of the Japanese yen must rise by about 4% to equalize the dollar price of goods in the two countries.

Formally, if i_h and i_f are the periodic price-level increases (rates of inflation) for the home country and the foreign country, respectively; e_0 is the dollar (HC) value of one unit of foreign currency at the beginning of the period; and e_t is the spot exchange rate in period t, then

$$\frac{e_t}{e_0} = \frac{(1 + i_h)^t}{(1 + i_f)^t} \tag{4.2}$$

If Equation 4.2 holds, then

$$e_t = e_0 \times \frac{(1 + i_h)^t}{(1 + i_f)^t} \tag{4.3}$$

The value of e_1 appearing in Equation 4.3 is known as the *PPP rate*. For example, if the United States and Switzerland are running annual inflation rates of 5% and 3%, respectively, and the spot rate is SFr 1 = $0.75, then according to Equation 4.3 the PPP rate for the Swiss franc in 3 years should be

$$e_3 = 0.75 \left(\frac{1.05}{1.03}\right)^3 = \$0.7945$$

If PPP is expected to hold, then $0.7945/SFr is the best prediction for the Swiss franc spot rate in 3 years. The one-period version of Equation 4.3 is commonly used. It is

$$e_1 = e_0 \times \frac{1 + i_h}{1 + i_f} \tag{4.4}$$

> **ILLUSTRATION**   *Calculating the PPP Rate for the Swiss Franc*

Suppose the current U.S. price level is at 112 and the Swiss price level is at 107, relative to base price levels of 100. If the initial value of the Swiss franc was $0.58, then according to PPP, the dollar value of the franc should have risen to approximately $0.6071 [0.58 × (112/107)], an appreciation of 4.67%. On the contrary, if the Swiss price level now equals 119, then the franc should have depreciated by about 5.88%, to $0.5459 [0.58 × 112/119)].

PPP is often represented by the following approximation of Equation 4.4.[1]

$$\frac{e_1 - e_0}{e_0} = i_h - i_f \qquad (4.5)$$

That is, the exchange rate change during a period should equal the **inflation differential** for that same time period. In effect, PPP says that *currencies with high rates of inflation should depreciate relative to currencies with lower rates of inflation.*

Equation 4.5 is illustrated in Exhibit 4.3. The vertical axis measures the percentage currency change, and the horizontal axis shows the inflation differential. Equilibrium is reached on the parity line, which contains all those points at which these two differentials are equal. At point A, for example, the 3% inflation differential is just offset by the 3% appreciation of the foreign currency relative to the home currency. Point B, on the other hand, depicts a situation of disequilibrium, where the inflation differential of 3% is greater than the appreciation of 1% in the HC value of the foreign currency.

4.2.1 The Lesson of Purchasing Power Parity

Purchasing power parity bears an important message: Just as the price of goods in one year cannot be meaningfully compared with the price of goods in another year without adjusting for interim inflation, so exchange rate changes may indicate nothing more than the reality that countries have different inflation rates. In fact, according to PPP, exchange rate movements should just cancel out changes in the foreign price level relative to the domestic price level. These offsetting movements should have no effects on the relative competitive positions of domestic firms and their foreign competitors. Thus, changes in the **nominal exchange rate**, that is, the actual exchange rate, may be of little significance in determining the true effects of currency changes on a firm and a nation. The focus must instead be on the real purchasing power of one currency relative to another. Here we consider the concept of the real exchange rate.

The **real exchange rate** is the nominal exchange rate adjusted for changes in the relative purchasing power of each currency since some base period. In technical terms, the

---

[1] Dividing both sides of Equation 4.4 by e_0 and then subtracting 1 from both sides yields

$$\frac{e_1 - e_0}{e_0} = \frac{i_h - i_f}{1 + i_f}$$

Equation 4.5 follows if i_f is relatively small.

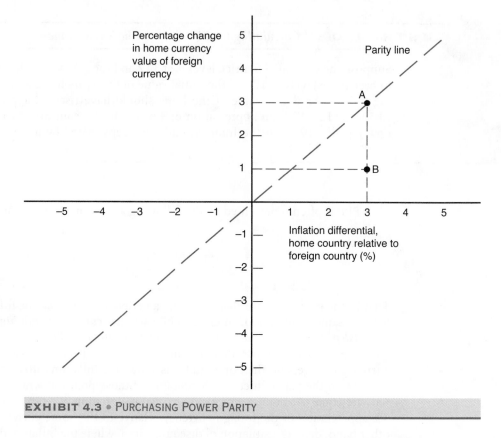

EXHIBIT 4.3 • PURCHASING POWER PARITY

real exchange rate at time t (dollars or HC per unit of foreign currency), e_t', relative to the base period (specified as time 0) is defined as

$$e_t' = e_t - \frac{P_f}{P_h} \tag{4.6}$$

where P_f is the foreign price level and P_h the home price level at time t, both indexed to 100 at time 0.

By indexing these price levels to 100 as of the base period, their ratio reflects the change in the relative purchasing power of these currencies since time 0. Note that increases in the foreign price level and foreign currency depreciation have offsetting effects on the real exchange rate. Similarly, home price-level increases and foreign currency appreciation offset each other.

An alternative, and equivalent, way to represent the real exchange rate is to directly reflect the change in relative purchasing powers of these currencies by adjusting the nominal exchange rate for inflation in both countries since time 0, as follows:

$$e_t' = e_t \times \frac{(1 + i_f)^t}{(1 + i_h)^t} \tag{4.7}$$

where the various parameters are the same as those defined previously.

If changes in the nominal exchange rate are fully offset by changes in the relative price levels between the two countries, then the real exchange rate remains unchanged.

(Note that the real exchange rate in the base period is just the nominal rate e_0.) Specifically, if PPP holds, then we can substitute the value of e_t from Equation 4.2 into Equation 4.6. Making this substitution yields $e_t' = e_0$; that is, the real exchange rate remains constant at e_0. Alternatively, a change in the real exchange rate is equivalent to a deviation from PPP.

ILLUSTRATION   *Calculating the Real Exchange Rate for the Japanese Yen*

Between 1982 and 2006, the ¥/$ exchange rate moved from ¥249.05/$ to ¥116.34. During this same 25-year period, the consumer price index (CPI) in Japan rose from 80.75 to 97.72 and the U.S. CPI rose from 56.06 to 117.07.

a. If PPP had held over this period, what would the ¥/$ exchange rate have been in 2006?

Solution. According to Equation 4.2, in 2006, the ¥/$ exchange rate should have been ¥144.32/$:

$$\text{¥/\$ PPP rate} = 249.05 \times \frac{(97.72/80.75)}{(117.07/56.06)} = \text{¥}144.32/\$$$

In working this problem, note that Equation 4.3 was inverted because we are expressing the exchange rate in ¥/$ terms rather than $/¥ terms. Note too that the ratio of CPIs is equal to the cumulative price-level increase. Comparing the PPP rate of ¥144.32/$ to the actual rate of ¥116.34/$, we can see that the yen has appreciated more than PPP would suggest.

b. What happened to the real value of the yen in terms of dollars during this period?

Solution. To estimate the real value of the yen, we convert the exchange rate from ¥/$ terms to $/¥ terms and apply Equation 4.5 (using the yen quoted in ¥/$ terms would yield us the real value of the U.S. dollar in terms of yen):[2]

$$e_t' = e_t \frac{P_f}{P_h} = \frac{1}{116.34} \times \frac{(97.72/80.75)}{(117.07/56.06)} = \$0.004981/\text{¥}$$

To interpret this real exchange rate and see how it changed since 1982, we compare it to the real exchange rate in 1982, which just equals the nominal rate at that time of $1/249.05 = \$0.004015/\text{¥}$ (because the real and nominal rates are equal in the base period). This comparison reveals that during the 25-year period 1982–2006 the yen appreciated in real terms by $(0.004981 - 0.004015)/0.004015 = 24\%$. This dramatic appreciation in the inflation-adjusted value of the Japanese yen put enormous competitive pressure on Japanese exporters as the dollar prices of their goods rose far more than the U.S. rate of inflation would justify.

---

[2] Dividing both current price levels by their base levels effectively indexes each to 100 as of the base period.

Alternative to above:

ILLUSTRATION   *Competitive Pressures Due to the Difference Between Real and Nominal Exchange Rates*

The competitive pressures on Japanese exporters due to the difference between real and nominal exchange rates is illustrated by comparing the real and nominal exchange rates between Japan and the U.S. for the period 1980 to 1995. During this period, the ¥/$ exchange rate moved from ¥226.63/$ to ¥93.96. During this same 15-year period, the CPI in Japan rose from 91.0 to 119.2 and the U.S. CPI rose from 82.4 to 152.4.

If PPP had held over this period, the ¥/$ exchange rate, according to Equation 4.2, should have been ¥160.51/$:

$$\text{¥/\$ PPP rate} = 226.63 \times \frac{(119.2/91.0)}{(152.4/82.4)} = \text{¥160.51/\$}$$

Note that Equation 4.3 was inverted because we are expressing the exchange rate in ¥/$ terms rather than $/¥ terms. Note too that the ratio of CPIs is equal to the cumulative price-level increase. Comparing the PPP rate of ¥160.51/$ to the actual rate of ¥93.96/$, we can see that the yen had appreciated more than PPP would suggest.

The real value of the yen in terms of the dollar during this period can be calculated from Equation 4.5. Using the yen quoted in ¥/$ terms would yield us the real value of the U.S. dollar in terms of yen.[3] Thus, we convert the exchange rate from ¥/$ terms to $/¥ terms and apply Equation 4.5:

$$e_t' = e_t \frac{P_f}{P_h} = \frac{1}{93.96} \times \frac{(119.2/91.0)}{(152.4/82.4)} = \$0.007538/\text{¥}$$

To interpret this real exchange rate and see how it changed since 1980, we compare it to the real exchange rate in 1980, which just equals the nominal rate at that time of $1/226.63 = \$0.004412/\text{¥}$ (because the real and nominal rates are equal in the base period). This comparison reveals that during the 15-year period 1980–1995 the yen appreciated in real terms by $(0.007538 - 0.004412)/0.004412 \approx 71\%$. This dramatic appreciation in the inflation-adjusted value of the Japanese yen put enormous competitive pressure on Japanese exporters as the dollar prices of their goods rose far more than the U.S. rate of inflation would justify.

The distinction between the nominal exchange rate and the real exchange rate has important implications for foreign exchange risk measurement and management. As we will see in Chapter 10, if the real exchange rate remains constant (i.e., if PPP holds), currency gains or losses from nominal exchange rate changes will generally be offset over time by the effects of differences in relative rates of inflation, thereby reducing the net impact of nominal devaluations and revaluations. Deviations from PPP, however, will lead to real exchange gains and losses. In the case of Japanese exporters, the real appreciation of the yen forced them to cut costs and develop new products less subject to pricing pressures. We will discuss their responses in more detail in Chapter 10.

---

[3] Dividing both current price levels by their base levels effectively indexes each to 100 as of the base period.

4.2.2 Expected Inflation and Exchange Rate Changes

Changes in expected, as well as actual, inflation will cause exchange rate changes. An increase in a currency's expected rate of inflation, all other things being equal, makes that currency more expensive to hold over time (because its value is being eroded at a faster rate) and less in demand at the same price. Consequently, the value of higher-inflation currencies will tend to be depressed relative to the value of lower-inflation currencies, other things being equal.

4.2.3 Empirical Evidence

The strictest version of PPP—that all goods and financial assets obey the law of one price—is demonstrably false. The risks and costs of shipping goods internationally, as well as government-erected barriers to trade and capital flows, are at times high enough to cause exchange-adjusted prices to systematically differ among countries. On the other hand, there is clearly a relationship between relative inflation rates and changes in exchange rates. In particular, over time, as shown in Exhibit 4.4, those currencies with the largest relative decline (gain) in purchasing power saw the sharpest erosion (appreciation) in their foreign exchange values.

The general conclusion from empirical studies of PPP is that the theory holds up well in the long run, but not as well over shorter time periods.[4] The difference between the short-run and long-run effects can be seen in Exhibit 4.5, which compares the actual dollar exchange rate for six currencies with their PPP rates. Despite substantial short-run deviations from PPP, currencies have a distinct tendency to move toward their PPP-predicted rates.

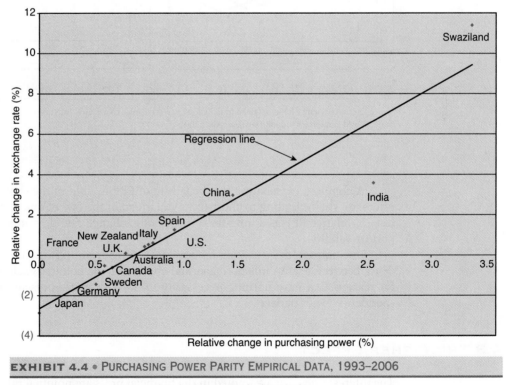

EXHIBIT 4.4 • Purchasing Power Parity Empirical Data, 1993–2006

Source: International Monetary Fund; Federal Reserve Bank of New York.

---

[4] Perhaps the best known of these studies is Henry J. Gailliot's, "Purchasing Power Parity as an Explanation of Long-Term Changes in Exchange Rates," *Journal of Money, Credit, and Banking,* August 1971, pp. 348–357.

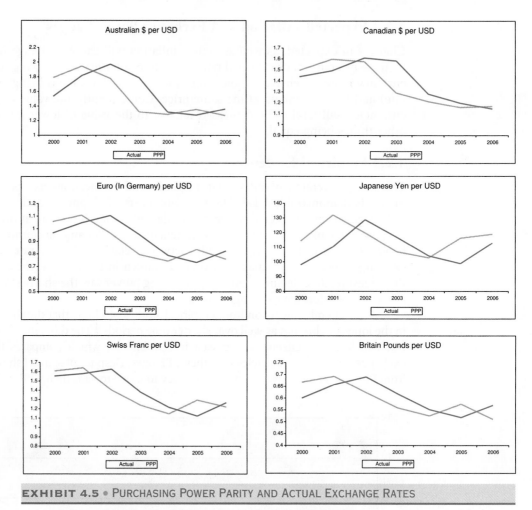

EXHIBIT 4.5 • PURCHASING POWER PARITY AND ACTUAL EXCHANGE RATES

Source: Actual Exchange Rates obtained from Federal Reserve Bank of New York. Inflation data from International Monetary Fund, World Economic Outlook Database, April 2007.

A common explanation for the failure of PPP to hold in the short-run is that goods prices are sticky, leading to short-term violations of the law of one price. However, most tests of relative PPP as a long-term theory of exchange rate determination seem to support its validity.

In summary, despite often lengthy departures from PPP, there is a clear correspondence between relative inflation rates and changes in the nominal exchange rate. However, for reasons that have nothing necessarily to do with market disequilibrium, the correspondence is not perfect.

4.3 THE FISHER EFFECT

The interest rates that are quoted in the financial press are nominal rates. That is, they are expressed as the rate of exchange between current and future dollars. For example, a nominal interest rate of 8% on a 1-year loan means that $1.08 must be repaid in 1 year for $1.00 loaned today. But what really matters to both parties to a loan agreement is the real interest rate, the rate at which current goods are being converted into future goods.

Looked at one way, the real rate of interest is the net increase in wealth that people expect to achieve when they save and invest their current income. Alternatively, it can be viewed as the added future consumption promised by a corporate borrower to a lender in return for the latter's deferring current consumption. From the company's standpoint, this exchange is worthwhile as long as it can find suitably productive investments.

However, because virtually all financial contracts are stated in nominal terms, the real interest rate must be adjusted to reflect expected inflation. The *Fisher effect* states that the nominal interest rate r is made up of two components: (1) a real required rate of return a and (2) an inflation premium equal to the expected amount of inflation i. Formally, the Fisher effect is

$$1 + Nominal\ rate = (1 + Real\ rate)(1 + Expected\ inflation\ rate)$$

$$1 + r = (1 + a)(1 + i)$$

or

$$r = a + i + ai \qquad (4.11)$$

Equation 4.11 is often approximated by the equation $r = a + i$.

The Fisher equation says, for example, that if the required real return is 3% and expected inflation is 10%, then the nominal interest rate will be about 13% (13.3%, to be exact). The logic behind this result is that $1 next year will have the purchasing power of $0.90 in terms of today's dollars. Thus, the borrower must pay the lender $0.103 to compensate for the erosion in the purchasing power of the $1.03 in principal and interest payments, in addition to the $0.03 necessary to provide a 3% real return.

ILLUSTRATION   *Brazilians Shun Negative Real Interest Rates on Savings*

In 1981, the Brazilian government spent $10 million on an advertising campaign to help boost national savings, which dropped sharply in 1980. According to the *Wall Street Journal* (January 12, 1981, p. 23), the decline in savings occurred "because the pre-fixed rates on savings deposits and treasury bills for 1980 were far below the rate of inflation, currently 110%." Clearly, the Brazilians were not interested in investing money at interest rates less than the inflation rate.

The generalized version of the Fisher effect asserts that real returns are equalized across countries through arbitrage—that is, $a_h = a_f$, where the subscripts h and f refer to home and foreign real rates, respectively. If expected real returns were higher in one currency than another, capital would flow from the second to the first currency. This process of arbitrage would continue, in the absence of government intervention, until expected real returns were equalized.

In equilibrium, then, with no government interference, it should follow that the nominal **interest rate differential** will approximately equal the anticipated inflation differential between the two currencies, or

$$r_h - r_f = i_h - i_f \qquad (4.12)$$

where r_h and r_f are the nominal home and foreign currency interest rates, respectively. The exact form of this relationship is expressed by Equation 4.13:[5]

$$\frac{1 + r_h}{1 + r_f} = \frac{1 + i_h}{1 + i_f} \qquad (4.13)$$

---

[5] Equation 4.13 can be converted into Equation 4.12 by subtracting 1 from both sides and assuming that r_f and i_f are relatively small.

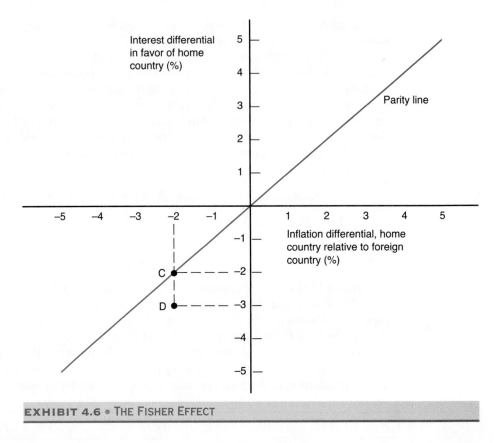

EXHIBIT 4.6 • THE FISHER EFFECT

In effect, the generalized version of the Fisher effect says that *currencies with high rates of inflation should bear higher interest rates than currencies with lower rates of inflation.*

For example, if inflation rates in the United States and the United Kingdom are 4% and 7%, respectively, the Fisher effect says that nominal interest rates should be about 3% higher in the United Kingdom than in the United States. A graph of Equation 4.12 is shown in Exhibit 4.6. The horizontal axis shows the expected difference in inflation rates between the home country and the foreign country, and the vertical axis shows the interest differential between the two countries for the same time period. The parity line shows all points for which $r_h - r_f = i_h - i_f$.

Point C, for example, is a position of equilibrium because the 2% higher rate of inflation in the foreign country ($i_h - i_f = -2\%$) is just offset by the 2% lower HC interest rate ($r_h - r_f = -2\%$). At point D, however, where the real rate of return in the home country is 1% lower than in the foreign country (an inflation differential of 2% versus an interest differential of 3%), funds should flow from the home country to the foreign country to take advantage of the real differential. This flow will continue until expected real returns are again equal.

4.3.1 Empirical Evidence

Exhibit 4.7 illustrates the relationship between interest rates and inflation rates for 27 countries as of May 2007. It is evident from the graph that nations with higher inflation rates generally have higher interest rates. Thus, the empirical evidence is consistent with the hypothesis that most of the variation in nominal interest rates across countries can be attributed to differences in inflationary expectations.

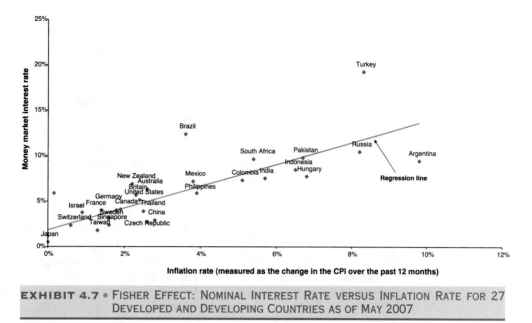

EXHIBIT 4.7 • FISHER EFFECT: NOMINAL INTEREST RATE VERSUS INFLATION RATE FOR 27 DEVELOPED AND DEVELOPING COUNTRIES AS OF MAY 2007

Inflation = Change in 2007 Consumer Price
Nominal Rate = 3-Month Money Market Rate
Source: The Economist, May 17, 2007.

Moreover, significant real interest differentials would not survive long in the increasingly internationalized capital markets. Most market participants agree that arbitrage, via the huge pool of liquid capital that operates in international markets these days, is forcing pretax real interest rates to converge across all the major nations.

To the extent that arbitrage is permitted to operate unhindered, capital markets are integrated worldwide. **Capital market integration** means that real interest rates are determined by the global supply and demand for funds. This is in contrast to **capital market segmentation**, where real interest rates are determined by local credit conditions. The difference between capital market segmentation and capital market integration is depicted in Exhibit 4.8. With a segmented capital market, the real interest rate in the United States, a_{us}, is based on the national demand D_{us} and national supply S_{us} of credit. Conversely, the real rate in the rest of the world, a_{rw}, is based on the rest-of-world supply S_{rw} and demand D_{rw}. In this example, the U.S. real rate is higher than the real rate outside the United States, or $a_{us} > a_{rw}$.

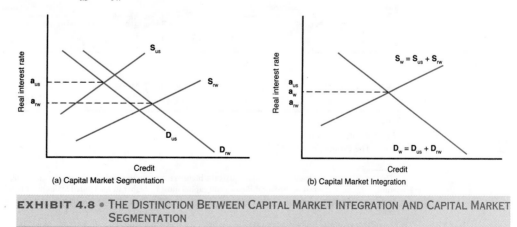

EXHIBIT 4.8 • THE DISTINCTION BETWEEN CAPITAL MARKET INTEGRATION AND CAPITAL MARKET SEGMENTATION

Once the U.S. market opens up, the U.S. real interest rate falls (and the rest-of-world rate rises) to the new world rate a_w, which is determined by the world supply S_w (S_{us} + S_{rw}) and world demand D_w (D_{us} + D_{rw}) for credit. The mechanism whereby equilibrium is brought about is a capital inflow to the United States. It is this same capital flow that drives up the real interest rate outside the United States.[6]

As shown by Exhibit 4.8, in an integrated capital market, the domestic real interest rate depends on what is happening outside as well as inside the United States. For example, a rise in the demand for capital by German companies to finance investments in Eastern Europe will raise the real interest rate in the United States as well as in Germany. Similarly, a rise in the U.S. savings rate, other things being equal, will lower the real cost of capital both in the United States and in the rest of the world. Conversely, a fall in U.S. inflation will lower the nominal U.S. interest rate (the Fisher effect), while leaving unchanged real interest rates worldwide.

Capital market integration has homogenized markets around the world, eroding much, though not all, of the real interest rate differentials between comparable domestic and offshore securities, and strengthening the link between assets that are denominated in different currencies but carry similar credit risks.[7] To the extent that real interest differentials do exist, they must be due to either currency risk or some form of political risk.

A real interest rate differential could exist without being arbitraged away if investors strongly preferred to hold domestic assets in order to avoid currency risk, even if the expected real return on foreign assets were higher. There could be extended periods of apparent differences in real interest rates between nations as shown in Exhibit 4.9.

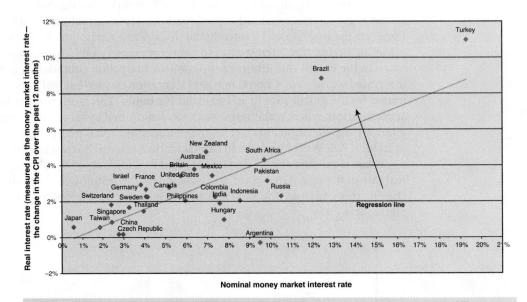

EXHIBIT 4.9 • REAL INTEREST RATE VERSUS NOMINAL INTEREST RATE FOR 27 DEVELOPED AND DEVELOPING COUNTRIES AS OF MAY 2007

Inflation = Change in 2007 Consumer Price
Nominal Rate = 3-Month Money Market Rate
Source: The Economist, May 17, 2007

---

[6] The net gain from the transfer of capital equals the higher returns on the capital imported to the United States less the lower returns forgone in the rest of the world. Returns on capital must be higher in the United States prior to the capital inflow, because the demand for capital depends on the expected return on capital. Thus, a higher real interest rate indicates a higher real return on capital.

[7] An offshore security is one denominated in the home currency but issued abroad. They are generally referred to as Eurosecurities.

This exhibit compares real interest rates (measured as the nominal interest rate minus the past year's inflation rate as a surrogate for the expected inflation rate) as of May 2007 versus nominal rates for the same 27 countries shown in Exhibit 4.7. According to this exhibit, countries with higher nominal interest rates (implying higher expected inflation and greater currency risk) tend to have higher real interest rates, resulting in large real rate differentials among some countries.

In addition to currency and inflation risk, real interest rate differentials in a closely integrated world economy can stem from countries pursuing sharply differing tax policies or imposing regulatory barriers to the free flow of capital.

ILLUSTRATION *France Segments Its Capital Market*

Throughout the European Monetary System's September 1992 crisis, the French franc managed to stay within the ERM. Exhibit 4.10 suggests why. It plots two interest rate differentials: (1) the gap between 3-month domestic money-market rates and the corresponding Eurofranc rate, which is the rate on francs deposited in London in the Eurocurrency market (to be discussed in Chapter 12); and (2) the gap between the domestic money-market rate and the bank prime rate.

France supposedly has ended capital market controls, so arbitrage should ensure that the first of these interest differentials (shown by the solid black line) should be approximately zero, as it was until the crisis that began in mid-September. Once trouble began, however, the Euromarket rate exceeded the domestic rate by a big margin for almost two weeks, indicating that the French government was impeding the flow of capital out of France.

The other series sheds more light on what was going on during this period. Until pressures began building in the spring, the prime lending rate slightly exceeded the money-market rate—as you might expect because money-market rates help determine the banks' cost of funds. In May, however, the money-market rates rose above the prime lending rate, widening to more than 4 percentage points at the height of the crisis.

The obvious conclusion is that the French government was using high money-market rates to defend the franc, while forcing banks to lend money at a loss in order to avoid the adverse impact of high interest rates on the French economy.

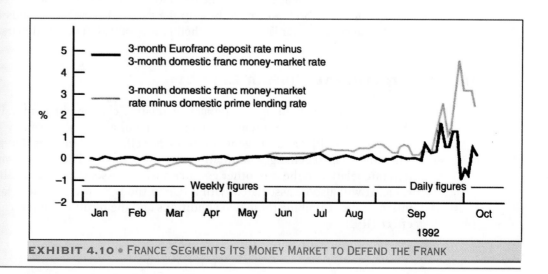

EXHIBIT 4.10 ● FRANCE SEGMENTS ITS MONEY MARKET TO DEFEND THE FRANK

In many developing countries, however, currency controls and other government policies impose political risk on foreign investors. In fact, political risk can drive a wedge between the returns available to domestic investors and those available to foreign investors. For example, if political risk in Brazil causes foreign investors to demand a 7% higher interest rate than they demand elsewhere, then foreign investors would consider a 10% expected real return in Brazil to be equivalent to a 3% expected real return in the United States. Hence, real interest rates in developing countries can exceed those in developed countries without presenting attractive arbitrage opportunities to foreign investors. The combination of a relative shortage of capital and high political risk in most developing countries is likely to cause real interest rates in these countries to exceed real interest rates in the developed countries. Indeed, the countries in Exhibit 4.9 with the highest real rates of interest are all developing countries.

Investors' tolerance of economic mismanagement in developed nations also has fallen dramatically, as financial deregulation, abolition of foreign exchange controls, and the process of global portfolio diversification have swollen the volume of international capital flows. With modern technology enabling investors to move capital from one market to another at low cost and almost instantaneously, the pressure on central banks to seem to "do the right thing" is intense. Conversely, those nations that must attract a disproportionate amount of global capital to finance their national debts and that have no credible policies to deal with their problems in a noninflationary way will be forced to pay a rising risk premium.

We must keep in mind that there are numerous interest differentials just as there are many different interest rates in a market. The rate on bank deposits, for instance, will not be identical to that on Treasury bills. In computation of an interest differential, therefore, the securities on which this differential is based must be of identical risk characteristics save for currency risk. Otherwise, there is the danger of comparing apples with oranges (or at least temple oranges with navel oranges).

Adding Up Capital Markets Internationally   Central to the understanding how we can add yen and Euro and dollar capital markets together is to recognize that money is only a veil: All financial transactions, no matter how complex, ultimately involve exchanges of goods today for goods in the future. You supply credit (capital) when you consume less than you produce; you demand credit when you consume more than you produce. Thus, the supply of credit can be thought of as the excess supply of goods and the demand for credit as the excess demand for goods. When we add up the capital markets around the world, we are adding up the excess demands for goods and the excess supplies of goods. A car is still a car, whether it is valued in yen or dollars.

4.4 THE INTERNATIONAL FISHER EFFECT

The key to understanding the impact of relative changes in nominal interest rates among countries on the foreign exchange value of a nation's currency is to recall the implications of PPP and the generalized Fisher effect. PPP implies that exchange rates will move to offset changes in inflation rate differentials. Thus, a rise in the U.S. inflation rate relative to those of other countries will be associated with a fall in the dollar's value. It will also be associated with a rise in the U.S. interest rate relative to foreign interest rates. Combine these two conditions and the result is the **international Fisher effect** (IFE):

$$\frac{(1 + r_h)^t}{(1 + r_f)^t} = \frac{\bar{e}_t}{e_0} \tag{4.14}$$

where $\bar{e}_t$ is the expected exchange rate in period t. The single-period analogue to Equation 4.14 is

$$\frac{1 + r_h}{1 + r_f} = \frac{\bar{e}_1}{e_0} \tag{4.15}$$

According to Equation 4.15, the expected return from investing at home, $1 + r_h$, should equal the expected HC return from investing abroad, $(1 + r_f)\,\bar{e}_1/e_0$. As discussed in the previous section, however, despite the intuitive appeal of equal expected returns, domestic and foreign expected returns might not equilibrate if the element of currency risk restrained the process of international arbitrage.

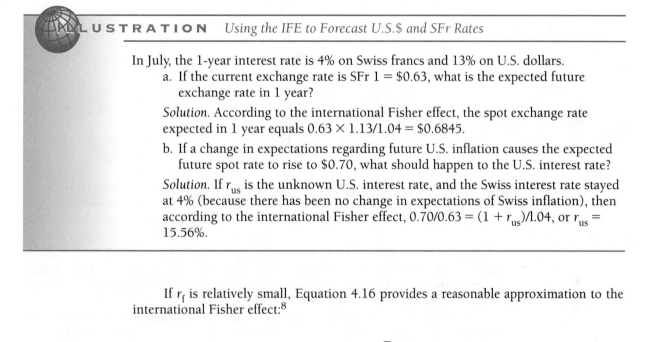

ILLUSTRATION   *Using the IFE to Forecast U.S.$ and SFr Rates*

In July, the 1-year interest rate is 4% on Swiss francs and 13% on U.S. dollars.
   a. If the current exchange rate is SFr 1 = $0.63, what is the expected future exchange rate in 1 year?

Solution. According to the international Fisher effect, the spot exchange rate expected in 1 year equals $0.63 \times 1.13/1.04 = \$0.6845$.

   b. If a change in expectations regarding future U.S. inflation causes the expected future spot rate to rise to $0.70, what should happen to the U.S. interest rate?

Solution. If r_{us} is the unknown U.S. interest rate, and the Swiss interest rate stayed at 4% (because there has been no change in expectations of Swiss inflation), then according to the international Fisher effect, $0.70/0.63 = (1 + r_{us})/1.04$, or $r_{us} = 15.56\%$.

If r_f is relatively small, Equation 4.16 provides a reasonable approximation to the international Fisher effect:[8]

$$r_h - r_f = \frac{\bar{e}_1 - e_0}{e_0} \tag{4.16}$$

In effect, the IFE says that *currencies with low interest rates are expected to appreciate relative to currencies with high interest rates.*

A graph of Equation 4.16 is shown in Exhibit 4.11. The vertical axis shows the expected change in the home currency value of the foreign currency, and the horizontal axis shows the interest differential between the two countries for the same time period. The parity line shows all points for which $r_h - r_f = (e_1 - e_0)/e_0$.

Point E is a position of equilibrium because it lies on the parity line, with the 4% interest differential in favor of the home country just offset by the anticipated 4% appreciation in the HC value of the foreign currency. Point F, however, illustrates a situation of disequilibrium. If the foreign currency is expected to appreciate by 3% in terms of the

---

[8] Subtracting 1 from both sides of Equation 4.15 yields

$$\frac{\bar{e}_1 - e_0}{e_0} = \frac{r_h - r_f}{1 + r_f}$$

Equation 4.16 follows if r_f is relatively small.

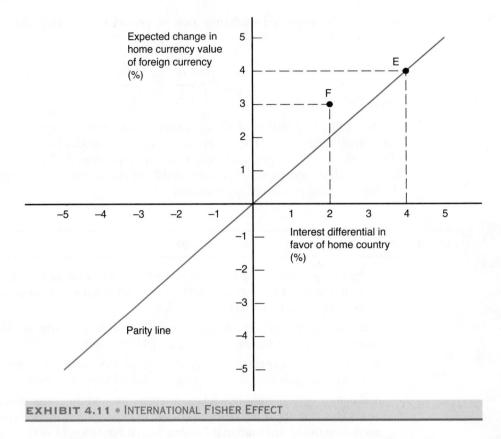

EXHIBIT 4.11 • INTERNATIONAL FISHER EFFECT

HC, but the interest differential in favor of the home country is only 2%, then funds would flow from the home to the foreign country to take advantage of the higher exchange-adjusted returns there. This capital flow will continue until exchange-adjusted returns are equal in the two nations.

Essentially, what the IFE says is that arbitrage between financial markets—in the form of international capital flows—should ensure that the interest differential between any two countries is an **unbiased predictor** of the future change in the spot rate of exchange. This condition does not mean, however, that the interest differential is an especially accurate predictor; it just means that prediction errors tend to cancel out over time. Moreover, an implicit assumption underlying IFE is that investors view foreign and domestic assets as perfect substitutes. To the extent that this condition is violated (see the discussion on the Fisher effect) and investors require a risk premium (in the form of a higher expected real return) to hold foreign assets, IFE will not hold exactly.

4.4.1 Empirical Evidence

As predicted, there is a clear tendency for currencies with high interest rates (for example, Mexico and Brazil) to depreciate and those with low interest rates (for example, Japan and Switzerland) to appreciate. The ability of interest differentials to anticipate currency changes is supported by several empirical studies that indicate the long-run tendency for these differentials to offset exchange rate changes.[9] The international

[9] See, for example, Ian H. Giddy and Gunter Dufey, "The Random Behavior of Flexible Exchange Rates," *Journal of International Business Studies,* Spring 1975, pp. 1–32; and Robert A. Aliber and Clyde P. Stickney, "Accounting Measures of Foreign Exchange Exposure: The Long and Short of It," *The Accounting Review,* January 1975, pp. 44–57.

Fisher effect also appears to hold even in the short run in the case of nations facing very rapid rates of inflation. Thus, at any given time, currencies bearing higher nominal interest rates can be reasonably expected to depreciate relative to currencies bearing lower interest rates.

IFE may not hold in the short run since changes in the nominal interest differential can be due to changes in either the real interest differential or relative inflationary expectations. These two possibilities have opposite effects on currency values. For example, suppose that the nominal interest differential widens in favor of the United States. If this spread is due to a rise in the real interest rate in the United States relative to that of other countries, the value of the dollar will rise. Alternatively, if the change in the nominal interest differential is caused by an increase in inflationary expectations for the United States, the dollar's value will drop.

The key to understanding short-run changes in the value of the dollar or other currency, then, is to distinguish changes in nominal interest rate differentials that are caused by changes in real interest rate differentials from those caused by changes in relative inflation expectations. Historically, changes in the nominal interest differential have been dominated, at times, by changes in the real interest differential; at other times, they have been dominated by changes in relative inflation expectations. Consequently, there is no stable, predictable relationship between changes in the nominal interest differential and exchange rate changes.

4.5 INTEREST RATE PARITY THEORY

Spot and forward rates are closely linked to each other and to interest rates in different currencies through the medium of arbitrage. Specifically, the movement of funds between two currencies to take advantage of *interest rate differentials* is a major determinant of the spread between forward and spot rates. In fact, the forward discount or premium is closely related to the interest differential between the two currencies.

According to *interest rate parity* (IRP) theory, the currency of the country with a lower interest rate should be at a forward premium in terms of the currency of the country with the higher rate. More specifically, in an efficient market with no transaction costs, the interest differential should be (approximately) equal to the forward differential. When this condition is met, the forward rate is said to be at **interest rate parity**, and equilibrium prevails in the money markets.

IRP ensures that the return on a hedged (or "covered") foreign investment will just equal the domestic interest rate on investments of identical risk, thereby eliminating the possibility of having a money machine. When this condition holds, the **covered interest** differential, the difference between the domestic interest rate and the hedged foreign rate, is zero. To illustrate this condition, suppose an investor with $1,000,000 to invest for 90 days is trying to decide between investing in U.S. dollars at 8% per annum (2% for 90 days) or in euros at 6% per annum (1.5% for 90 days). The current spot rate is €0.7400/$, and the 90-day forward rate is €0.7370/$. Exhibit 4.12 shows that regardless of the investor's currency choice, her hedged return will be identical. Specifically, $1,000,000 invested in dollars for 90 days will yield $1,000,000 × 1.02 = $1,020,000. Alternatively, if an investor chooses to invest in euros on a hedged basis, she will

1. Convert the $1,000,000 to euros at the spot rate of €0.7400/$. This yields €740,000 available for investment.
2. Invest the principal of €740,000 at 1.5% for 90 days. At the end of 90 days, the investor will have €751,100.
3. Simultaneously with the other transactions, sell the €751,100 in principal plus interest forward at a rate of €0.73640/$ for delivery in 90 days. This transaction will yield €751,1000.7364 = $1,020,000 in 90 days.

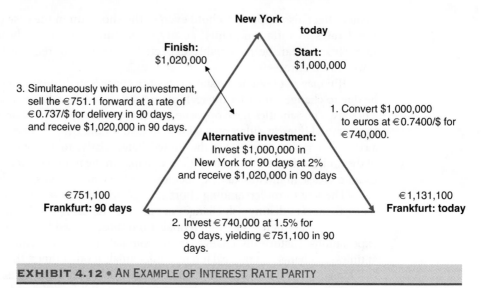

EXHIBIT 4.12 ● AN EXAMPLE OF INTEREST RATE PARITY

If the covered interest differential between two money markets is nonzero, there is an arbitrage incentive to move money from one market to the other. This movement of money to take advantage of a covered interest differential is known as **covered interest arbitrage.**

ILLUSTRATION   *Covered Interest Arbitrage Between London and New York*

Suppose the interest rate on pounds sterling is 12% in London, and the interest rate on a comparable dollar investment in New York is 7%. The pound spot rate is $1.95, and the 1-year forward rate is $1.88. These rates imply a forward discount on sterling of 3.6% [(1.88 − 1.95)/1.95] and a covered yield on sterling approximately equal to 8% (12% − 4%). Because there is a covered interest differential in favor of London, funds will flow from New York to London.

To illustrate the profits associated with covered interest arbitrage, we will assume that the borrowing and lending rates are identical and the bid–ask spread in the spot and forward markets is zero. Here are the steps the arbitrageur can take to profit from the discrepancy in rates based on a $1 million transaction. Specifically, as shown in Exhibit 4.13, the arbitrageur will

1. Borrow $1,000,000 in New York at an interest rate of 7%. This means that at the end of 1 year, the arbitrageur must repay principal plus interest of $1,070,000.

2. Immediately convert the $1,000,000 to pounds at the spot rate of £1 = $1.95. This yields £512,820.5 available for investment.

3. Invest the principal of £512,820.5 in London at 12% for 1 year. At the end of the year, the arbitrageur will have £574,358.9.

4. Simultaneously with the other transactions, sell the £574,358.9 in principal plus interest forward at a rate of £1 = $1.88 for delivery in 1 year. This transaction will yield $1,079,395 next year.

5. At the end of the year, collect the £ £574,358.9, deliver it to the bank's foreign exchange department in return for $1,079,395, and use $1,070,000 to repay the loan. The arbitrageur will earn $9,395 on this set of transactions.

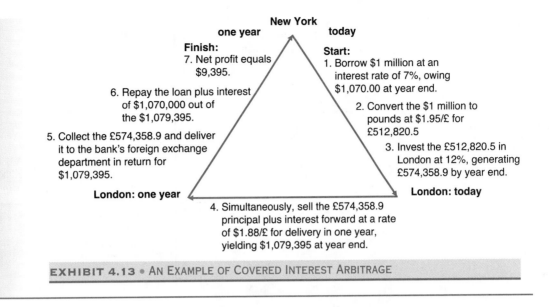

New York

one year   **today**

Finish:
7. Net profit equals
$9,395.

6. Repay the loan plus interest
of $1,070,000 out of
the $1,079,395.

5. Collect the £574,358.9 and deliver
it to the bank's foreign exchange
department in return for
$1,079,395.

Start:
1. Borrow $1 million at an
interest rate of 7%, owing
$1,070.00 at year end.

2. Convert the $1 million to
pounds at $1.95/£ for
£512,820.5

3. Invest the £512,820.5 in
London at 12%, generating
£574,358.9 by year end.

London: one year   **London: today**

4. Simultaneously, sell the £574,358.9
principal plus interest forward at a rate
of $1.88/£ for delivery in one year,
yielding $1,079,395 at year end.

EXHIBIT 4.13 • AN EXAMPLE OF COVERED INTEREST ARBITRAGE

The transactions associated with covered interest arbitrage will affect prices in both the money and foreign exchange markets. In the previous example, as pounds are bought spot and sold forward, boosting the spot rate and lowering the forward rate, the forward discount will tend to widen. Simultaneously, as money flows from New York, interest rates there will tend to increase; at the same time, the inflow of funds to London will depress interest rates there. The process of covered interest arbitrage will continue until interest parity is achieved, unless there is government interference.

If this process is interfered with, covered interest differentials between national money markets will not be arbitraged away. Interference often occurs because many governments regulate and restrict flows of capital across their borders. Moreover, just the risk of controls will be sufficient to yield prolonged deviations from interest rate parity.

The relationship between the spot and forward rates and interest rates in a free market can be shown graphically, as in Exhibit 4.14. Plotted on the vertical axis is the interest differential in favor of the home country. The horizontal axis plots the percentage forward discount (negative) or premium (positive) on the foreign currency relative to the home currency. The interest parity line joins those points for which the forward exchange rate is in equilibrium with the interest differential. For example, if the interest differential in favor of the foreign country is 2%, the currency of that country must be selling at a 2% forward discount for equilibrium to exist.

Point G indicates a situation of disequilibrium. Here, the interest differential is 2%, whereas the forward premium on the foreign currency is 3%. The transfer of funds abroad with exchange risks covered will yield an additional 1% annually. At point H, the forward premium remains at 3%, but the interest differential increases to 4%. Now reversing the flow of funds becomes profitable. The 4% higher interest rate more than makes up for the 3% loss on the forward exchange transaction, leading to a 1% increase in the interest yield.

In reality, the interest parity line is a band because transaction costs, arising from the spread on spot and forward contracts and brokerage fees on security purchases and sales, cause effective yields to be lower than nominal yields. For example, if transaction costs are 0.75%, a covered yield differential of only 0.5% will not be sufficient to induce a flow of funds. For interest arbitrage to occur, the covered differential must exceed the transaction costs involved.

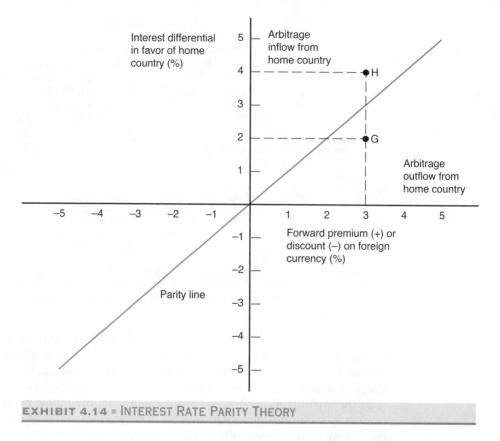

EXHIBIT 4.14 ● INTEREST RATE PARITY THEORY

The covered interest arbitrage relationship can be stated formally. Let e_0 be the current spot rate (dollar value of one unit of foreign currency) and f_1 the end-of-period forward rate. If r_h and r_f are the prevailing interest rates in New York and, say, London, respectively, then one dollar invested in New York will yield $1 + r_h$ at the end of the period; the same dollar invested in London will be worth $(1 + r_f)f_1/e_0$ dollars at maturity. This latter result can be seen as follows: One dollar will convert into $1/e_0$ pounds that, when invested at r_f, will yield $(1 + r_f)/e_0$ pounds at the end of the period. By selling the proceeds forward today, this amount will be worth $(1 + r_f)f_1/e_0$ dollars when the investment matures.

Funds will flow from New York to London if and only if

$$1 + r_h < \frac{(1 + r_f)f_1}{e_0}$$

Conversely, funds will flow from London to New York if and only if

$$1 + r_h > \frac{(1 + r_f)f_1}{e_0}$$

IRP holds when there are no covered interest arbitrage opportunities. On the basis of the previous discussion, this no-arbitrage condition can be stated as follows:

$$\frac{1 + r_h}{1 + r_f} = \frac{f_1}{e_0} \tag{4.17}$$

ILLUSTRATION *Using Interest Rate Parity to Calculate the $/¥ Forward Rate*

The interest rate in the United States is 10%; in Japan, the comparable rate is 7%. The spot rate for the yen is $0.008200. If interest rate parity holds, what is the 90-day forward rate?

Solution. According to IRP, the 90-day forward rate on the yen, f_{90}, should be $0.008260:

$$f_{90} = \$0.008200 \times \frac{1 + (0.10/4)}{1 + (0.07/4)} = \$0.0038260$$

In other words, the 90-day forward Japanese yen should be selling at an annualized premium of about 2.93% [$4 \times (0.008260 - 0.008200)/0.008200$].

IRP is often approximated by Equation 4.18:[10]

$$r_h - r_f = \frac{f_1 - e_0}{e_0} \qquad (4.18)$$

In fact, IRP says that *high interest rates on a currency are offset by forward discounts and that low interest rates are offset by forward premiums.*

Transaction costs in the form of bid–ask spreads make the computations more difficult, but the principle is the same: Compute the covered interest differential to see whether there is an arbitrage opportunity.

ILLUSTRATION *Computing the Covered Interest Differential When Transaction Costs Exist*

Suppose the annualized interest rate on 180-day dollar deposits is 6 7/16 − 5/16%, meaning that dollars can be borrowed at 6 7/16% (the ask rate) and lent at 6 5/16% (the bid rate). At the same time, the annualized interest rate on 180-day Thai baht deposits is 9 3/8 − 1/8%. Spot and 180-day forward quotes on Thai baht are B 31.5107 − 46/$ and B 32.1027 − 87/$, respectively. Is there an arbitrage opportunity? Compute the profit using B 10,000,000.

Solution. The only way to determine whether an arbitrage opportunity exists is to examine the two possibilities: Borrow dollars and lend Thai baht or borrow baht and lend dollars, both on a hedged basis. The key is to ensure that you are using the correct bid or ask interest and exchange rates. In this case, it turns out that there is an arbitrage opportunity from borrowing Thai baht and lending dollars. The specific steps to implement this arbitrage are as follows:

1. Borrow B 10,000,000 at the ask rate of 9 3/8% for 180 days. This interest rate translates into a 180-day rate of 0.09375/2 = 4.6875%, requiring repayment of B 10,468,750 in principal plus interest at the end of 180 days.

2. Immediately convert the B 10,000,000 to dollars at the spot ask rate of B 31.5146/$ (the baht cost of buying dollars on spot rate). This yields $317,313.25 ($10,000,000/31.5146) available for investment.

---

[10] Subtracting 1 from both sides of Equation 4.17 yields $(f_1 - e_0)/e_0 = (r_h - r_f)/(1 + r_f)$. Equation 4.18 follows if r_f is relatively small.

3. Invest the principal of $317,313.25 at 0.063125/2 = 3.15625% for 180 days. In 6 months, this investment will have grown to $327,328.44 ($317,313.25 × 1.0315625).

4. Simultaneously with the other transactions, sell the $327,328.44 in principal plus interest forward at the bid rate of B 32.1027 (the rate at which dollars can be converted into baht) for delivery in 180 days. This transaction will yield B 10,508,126.86 in 180 days.

5. At the end of 6 months, collect the $327,328.44, deliver it to the bank's foreign exchange department in return for B 10,508.126.86, and use B 10,468,750 of the proceeds to repay the loan. The gain on this set of transactions is B 39,376.86.

4.5.1 Empirical Evidence

Interest rate parity is one of the best-documented relationships in international finance. In fact, in the Eurocurrency markets, the forward rate is calculated from the interest differential between the two currencies using the no-arbitrage condition. Deviations from IRP do occur between national capital markets, however, owing to capital controls (or the threat of them), the imposition of taxes on interest payments to foreigners, and transaction costs. However, as we can see in Exhibit 4.15, these deviations tend to be small and short-lived.

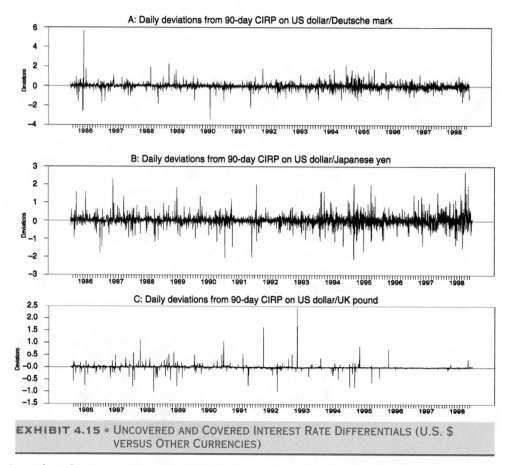

EXHIBIT 4.15 • UNCOVERED AND COVERED INTEREST RATE DIFFERENTIALS (U.S. $ VERSUS OTHER CURRENCIES)

Source: Bhar, Buk-Joogn, Kim, Ramprasad, and Toan M., Pham, "Exchange Rate Volatility and Its Impact on the Transaction Cost of Covered Interest Rate Parity." *Japan and the World Economy*. Vol. 16, 2004.

4.6 THE RELATIONSHIP BETWEEN THE FORWARD RATE AND THE FUTURE SPOT RATE

Our current understanding of the workings of the foreign exchange market suggests that, in the absence of government intervention in the market, both the spot rate and the forward rate are influenced heavily by current expectations of future events. The two rates move in tandem, with the link between them based on interest differentials. New information, such as a change in interest rate differentials, is reflected almost immediately in both spot and forward rates.

Suppose a depreciation of the pound sterling is anticipated. Recipients of sterling will begin selling sterling forward, and sterling-area dollar earners will slow their sales of dollars in the forward market. These actions will tend to depress the price of forward sterling. At the same time, banks will probably try to even out their long (net purchaser) positions in forward sterling by selling sterling spot. In addition, sterling-area recipients of dollars will tend to delay converting dollars into sterling, and earners of sterling will speed up their collection and conversion of sterling. In this way, pressure from the forward market is transmitted to the spot market, and vice versa.

Ignoring risk for the moment, equilibrium is achieved only when the forward differential equals the expected change in the exchange rate. At this point, there is no longer any incentive to buy or sell the currency forward. This condition is illustrated in Exhibit 4.16. The vertical axis measures the expected change in the home currency value of the foreign currency and the horizontal axis shows the forward discount or premium on the foreign currency. Parity prevails at point I, for example, where the expected foreign currency

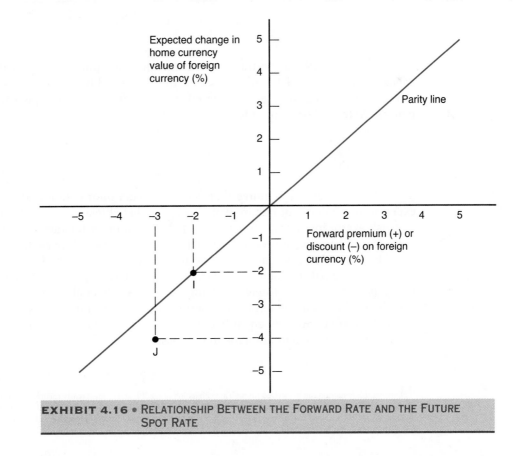

EXHIBIT 4.16 • RELATIONSHIP BETWEEN THE FORWARD RATE AND THE FUTURE SPOT RATE

depreciation of 2% is just matched by the 2% forward discount on the foreign currency. Point J, however, is a position of disequilibrium because the expected 4% depreciation of the foreign currency exceeds the 3% forward discount on the foreign currency. We would, therefore, expect to see speculators selling the foreign currency forward for home currency, taking a 3% discount in the expectation of covering their commitment with 4% fewer units of HC.

A formal statement of the **unbiased forward rate** (UFR) condition is that the forward rate should reflect the expected future spot rate on the date of settlement of the forward contract:

$$f_t = \bar{e}_t \tag{4.19}$$

where $\bar{e}_t$, is the expected future exchange rate at time t (units of home currency per unit of foreign currency) and f_t is the forward rate for settlement at time t.

ILLUSTRATION   *Using UFR to Forecast the Future $/€ Spot Rate*

If the 90-day forward rate is €1 = $1.3487, what is the expected value of the euro in 90 days?

Solution. Arbitrage should ensure that the market expects the spot value of the euro in 90 days to be about $1.3487.

Equation 4.19 can be transformed into the equation reflected in the parity line appearing in Exhibit 4.17, which is that the forward differential equals the expected change in the exchange rate, by subtracting (e_0/e_0), from both sides, where e_0 is the current spot rate (HC per unit of foreign currency):[11]

$$\frac{f_1 - e_0}{e_0} = \frac{\bar{e}_1 - e_0}{e_0} \tag{4.20}$$

Market efficiency requires that people process information and form reasonable expectations; it does not require that $f_1 = \bar{e}_1$. Market efficiency allows for the possibility that risk-averse investors will demand a risk premium on forward contracts, much the same way as they demand compensation for bearing the risk of investing in stocks. In this case, the forward rate will not reflect exclusively the expectation of the future spot rate.

The principal argument against the existence of a risk premium is that currency risk is largely diversifiable. If foreign exchange risk can be diversified away, no risk premium need be paid for holding a forward contract; the forward rate and expected future spot rate will be approximately equal. Ultimately, therefore, the unbiased nature of forward rates is an empirical, and not a theoretical, issue.

---

[11] Note that this condition can be derived through a combination of the IFE and interest parity theory. Specifically, IRP says that the interest differential equals the forward differential, whereas the IFE says that the interest differential equals the expected change in the spot rate. Things equal to the same thing are equal to each other, so the forward differential will equal the expected exchange rate change if both IRP and IFE hold.

4.6.1 Empirical Evidence

A number of studies have examined the relation between forward rates and future spot rates.[12] Of course, it would be unrealistic to expect a perfect correlation between forward and future spot rates because the future spot rate will be influenced by events, such as an oil crisis, that can be forecast only imperfectly, if at all.

The empirical data point to a common conclusion: Over time, currencies bearing a forward discount (higher interest rate) depreciate relative to currencies with a forward premium (lower interest rate). That is, on average, the forward rate is unbiased. However, at any point in time, the forward rate appears to be a biased predictor of the future spot rate. More specifically, the evidence indicates that one can profit on average by buying currencies selling at a forward discount (that is, currencies whose interest rate is relatively high) and selling currencies trading at a forward premium (that is, currencies whose interest rate is relatively low). Nonetheless, research also suggests that this evidence of forward market inefficiency may be difficult to profit from on a risk-adjusted basis. One reason is the existence of what is known as the peso problem as noted in the illustration.

ILLUSTRATION *The Peso Problem*

The **peso problem** refers to the possibility that during the time period studied investors anticipated significant events that did not materialize, thereby invalidating statistical inferences based on data drawn from that period. The term derives from the experience of Mexico during the period 1955–1975. During this entire period, the peso was fixed at a rate of $0.125, yet continually sold at a forward discount because investors anticipated a large peso devaluation. This devaluation eventually occurred in 1976, thereby validating the prediction embedded in the forward rate (and relative interest rates). However, those who limited their analysis on the relation between forward and future spot rates to data drawn only from the 1955–1975 period would have falsely concluded that the forward rate was a biased predictor of the future spot rate.

Even though foreign exchange markets may appear to be inefficient, the risk–return trade-off for a single currency is not very attractive, especially since traders would be unwilling to embrace complex and costly strategies to diversify the risk in the single currency. To summarize, the evidence suggests that the selective use of forward contracts— sell forward if the currency is at a forward premium and buy it forward if it is selling at a discount—may increase expected profits but at the expense of higher risk.

4.7 CURRENCY FORECASTING

Forecasting exchange rates has become an occupational hazard for financial executives of multinational corporations. The potential for periodic, and unpredictable, government intervention makes currency forecasting all the more difficult. But this difficulty has not dampened the enthusiasm for currency forecasts or the willingness of economists and others to supply them. Unfortunately, however, enthusiasm and willingness are not sufficient conditions for success.

---

[12] See, for example, Giddy and Dufey, "The Random Behavior of Flexible Exchange Rates"; and Bradford Cornell, "Spot Rates, Forward Rates, and Market Efficiency," *Journal of Financial Economics,* January 1977, pp. 55–65.

4.7.1 Requirements for Successful Currency Forecasting

Currency forecasting can lead to consistent profits only if the forecaster meets at least one of the following four criteria.[13] The successful forecaster

- Has exclusive use of a superior forecasting model;
- Has consistent access to information before other investors;
- Exploits small, temporary deviations from equilibrium; and
- Can predict the nature of government intervention in the foreign exchange market.

The first two conditions are self-correcting. Successful forecasting breeds imitators, while early access to information is unlikely to be sustained in the highly informed world of international finance. The third situation is how foreign exchange traders actually earn their living, but deviations from equilibrium are not likely to last long. The fourth situation is the one worth searching out. Countries that insist on managing their exchange rates and are willing to take losses to achieve their target rates present speculators with potentially profitable opportunities. Simply put, consistently profitable predictions are possible in the long run only if it is not necessary to outguess the market to win.

As a general rule, in a fixed-rate system, the forecaster must focus on the governmental decision-making structure, because the decision to devalue or revalue at a given time is clearly political. In the case of a floating-rate system, where government intervention is sporadic or nonexistent, currency prognosticators have the choice of using either market- or model-based forecasts, neither of which guarantees success.

4.7.2 Market-Based Forecasts

So far, we have identified several equilibrium relationships that should exist between exchange rates and interest rates. The empirical evidence on these relationships implies that, in general, the financial markets of developed countries efficiently incorporate expected currency changes in the cost of money and forward exchange. This means that currency forecasts can be obtained by extracting the predictions already embodied in interest and forward rates.

Forward Rates   **Market-based forecasts** of exchange rate changes can be derived most simply from current forward rates. Specifically, f_1—the forward rate for one period from now—will usually suffice for an unbiased estimate of the spot rate as of that date. In other words, f_1 should equal e_1, where e_1 is the expected future spot rate.

Interest Rates   Although forward rates provide simple and easy-to-use currency forecasts, their forecasting horizon is limited to about 1 year because of the general absence of longer-term forward contracts. Interest rate differentials can be used to supply exchange rate predictions beyond 1 year. For example, suppose 5-year interest rates on dollars and euros are 6% and 5%, respectively. If the current spot rate for the euro is $1.34 and the (unknown) value of the euro in 5 years is e_5, then $1.00 invested today in euros will be worth $(1.05)^5 e_5/1.34$ dollars at the end of five years; if invested in the dollar security, it will be worth $(1.06)^5$ in 5 years. The market's forecast of e_5 can be found by assuming that investors demand equal returns on dollar and euro securities, or

$$\frac{(1.05)^5 e_5}{1.34} = (1.06)^5$$

---

[13] These criteria were suggested by Giddy and Dufey, "The Random Behavior of Flexible Exchange Rates." Journal of International Business Studies, Spring 1975, pp. 1–52.

Thus, the 5-year euro spot rate implied by the relative interest rates is $e_5 = \$1,405$ ($1.34 \times 1.06^5/1.05^5$).

4.7.3 Model-Based Forecasts

The two principal model-based approaches to currency prediction are known as fundamental analysis and technical analysis. Each approach has its advocates and detractors.

Fundamental Analysis   Fundamental analysis is the most common approach to generating **model-based forecasts** of future exchange rates. It relies on painstaking examination of the macroeconomic variables and policies that are likely to influence a currency's prospects. The variables examined include relative inflation and interest rates, national income growth, and changes in money supplies. The interpretation of these variables and their implications for future exchange rates depend on the analyst's model of exchange rate determination.

The simplest form of fundamental analysis involves the use of PPP. We have previously seen the value of PPP in explaining exchange rate changes. Its application in currency forecasting is straightforward.

ILLUSTRATION   *Using PPP to Forecast the South African Rand's Future Spot Rate*

The U.S. inflation rate is expected to average about 4% annually, and the South African rate of inflation is expected to average about 9% annually. If the current spot rate for the rand is $0.1412, what is the expected spot rate in 2 years?

Solution. According to PPP (Equation 4.3), the expected spot rate for the rand in 2 years is $\$0.1412 \times (1.04/1.09)^2 = \$0.1285$.

Most analysts use more complicated forecasting models whose analysis usually centers on how the different macroeconomic variables are likely to affect the demand and supply for a given foreign currency. The currency's future value is then determined by estimating the exchange rate at which supply just equals demand—when any current-account imbalance is just matched by a net capital flow.

Forecasting based on fundamental analysis has inherent difficulties. First, you must be able to select the right fundamentals; then you must be able to forecast them—itself a problematic task (think about forecasting interest rates); and finally, your forecasts of the fundamentals must differ from those of the market. Otherwise, the exchange rate will have already discounted the anticipated change in the fundamentals. Another difficulty that forecasters face is the variability in the lag between when changes in fundamentals are forecast to occur and when they actually affect the exchange rate.

Technical Analysis   **Technical analysis** is the antithesis of fundamental analysis in that it focuses exclusively on past price and volume movements—while totally ignoring economic and political factors—to forecast currency winners and losers. Success depends on whether technical analysts can discover price patterns that repeat themselves and are, therefore, useful for forecasting.

There are two primary methods of technical analysis: **charting** and **trend analysis**. Chartists examine bar charts or use more sophisticated computer-based extrapolation techniques to find recurring price patterns. They then issue buy or sell recommendations if prices diverge from their past pattern. Trend-following systems seek to identify price trends via various mathematical computations.

4.7.4 Model Evaluation

The possibility that either fundamental or technical analysis can be used to profitably forecast exchange rates is inconsistent with the efficient market hypothesis, which says that current exchange rates reflect all publicly available information. Because markets are forward-looking, exchange rates will fluctuate randomly as market participants assess and then react to new information, much as security and commodity prices in other asset markets respond to news. Thus, exchange rate movements are unpredictable; otherwise, it would be possible to earn arbitrage profits. Such profits could not persist in a market, such as the foreign exchange market, that is characterized by free entry and exit and an almost unlimited amount of money, time, and energy that participants are willing to commit in pursuit of profit opportunities.

In addition to the theoretical doubts surrounding forecasting models, a variety of statistical and technical assumptions underlying these models have been called into question as well. For all practical purposes, however, the quality of a currency forecasting model must be viewed in relative terms. That is, a model can be said to be "good" if it is better than alternative means of forecasting currency values. Ultimately, a currency forecasting model is "good" only to the extent that its predictions will lead to better decisions.

Certainly, interest differentials and/or forward rates provide low-cost alternative forecasts of future exchange rates. At a minimum, any currency forecasting model should be able to consistently outperform the market's estimates of currency changes. In other words, one relevant question is whether *profitable* decisions can be made in the forward and/or money markets by using any of these models.

The success of any forecasting method can be evaluated by its accuracy and correctness. The accuracy measure focuses on the deviations between the actual and the forecasted rates, and the correctness measure examines whether the forecast predicts the right direction of the change in exchange rates. However, an accurate forecast may not be correct in predicting the direction of change, and a correct forecast may not be very accurate. The two criteria are sometimes in conflict. Which of these two criteria should be used in evaluation depends on how the forecasts are to be used.

ILLUSTRATION *The Distinction Between an Accurate Forecast and a Profitable Forecast*

Suppose that the ¥/$ spot rate is currently ¥110/$. A 90-day forecast puts the exchange rate at ¥102/$; the 90-day forward rate is ¥109/$. According to our decision rule, we should buy the yen forward. If we buy $1 million worth of yen forward and the actual rate turns out to be ¥108/$, then our decision will yield a profit of $9,259 [(109,000,000 − 108,000,000)/108]. In contrast, if the forecasted value of the yen had been ¥111/$, we would have sold yen forward and lost $9,259. Thus, an accurate forecast, off by less than 3% (3/108), leads to a loss; and a less accurate forecast, off by almost 6% (6/108), leads to a profitable decision.

When deciding on a new investment or planning a revised pricing strategy, however, the most critical attribute of a forecasting model is its accuracy. In the latter case, the second forecast would be judged superior.

4.7.5 Forecasting Controlled Exchange Rates

A major problem in currency forecasting is that the widespread existence of exchange controls, as well as restrictions on imports and capital flows, often masks the true pressures on a currency to devalue. In such situations, forward markets and capital markets are invariably nonexistent or subject to such stringent controls that interest and forward differentials are of little practical use in providing market-based forecasts of exchange rate changes. An alternative forecasting approach in such a controlled environment is to use **black-market exchange rates** as useful indicators of devaluation pressure on the nation's currency.

The black-market rate tends to be a good indicator of where the official rate is likely to go if the monetary authorities give in to market pressure. It seems to be most accurate in forecasting the official rate 1 month ahead and is progressively less accurate as a forecaster of the future official rate for longer time periods.[14]

ILLUSTRATION   *Zimbabwe Dollar Catches Up With the Black Market*

In 1983, the Zimbabwe Dollar (ZWD) was at par with the U.S. dollar. In 1999, the official exchange rate was pegged at ZWD 38 per U.S. dollar. However, later that year, a black market for foreign exchange started blossoming and the country responded with various currency devaluations in the period 1999 to 2006. In July 2006, it was estimated that the black market exchange rate was upwards of 300,000 ZWD per U.S. dollar. Finally, responding to a hyperinflation of almost 1200%, Zimbabwe's central bank introduced a new revalued Zimbabwe dollar on August 1, 2006. The new exchange rate was pegged at 250 revalued Zimbabwe dollars per U.S. dollar. The revalued Zimbabwe dollar was arrived at by dropping three zeros from the older currency. In other words, the new Zimbabwe dollar would be worth 1000 old Zimbabwe dollars. At the old currency values, this implied that Zimbabwe had officially accepted a rate of 250,000 old Zimbabwe dollars per U.S. dollar.

4.8 SUMMARY AND CONCLUSIONS

In this chapter, we examined five relationships, or parity conditions, that should apply to spot rates, inflation rates, and interest rates in different currencies: purchasing power parity (PPP), the Fisher effect (FE), the international Fisher effect (IFE), interest rate parity (IRP) theory, and the forward rate as an unbiased forecast of the future spot rate (UFR). These parity conditions follow from the law of one price, the notion that in the absence of market imperfections, arbitrage ensures that exchange-adjusted prices of identical traded goods and financial assets are within transaction costs worldwide.

The technical description of these five equilibrium relationships is summarized as follows:

- Purchasing Power Parity

$$\frac{e_t}{e_0} = \frac{(1 + i_h)^t}{(1 + i_f)^t}$$

---

[14] See, for example, Ian Giddy, "Black Market Exchange Rates as a Forecasting Tool," Working Paper, Columbia University, May 1978.

where

e_t = the home currency value of the foreign currency at time t

e_0 = the home currency value of the foreign currency at time 0

i_h = the periodic domestic inflation rate

i_f = the periodic foreign inflation rate

- Fisher effect

$$1 + r = (1 + a)(1 + i)$$

where

r = the nominal rate of interest

a = the real rate of interest

i = the rate of expected inflation

- Generalized version of Fisher effect

$$\frac{(1 + r_h)^t}{(1 + r_f)^t} = \frac{(1 + i_h)^t}{(1 + i_f)^t}$$

where

r_h = the periodic home currency interest rate

r_f = the periodic foreign currency interest rate

- International Fisher effect

$$\frac{(1 + r_h)^t}{(1 + r_f)^t} = \frac{\bar{e}_t}{e_0}$$

where

$\bar{e}_t$ = the expected home currency value of the foreign currency at time t

- Interest rate parity

$$\frac{(1 + r_h)^t}{(1 + r_f)^t} = \frac{f_t}{e_0}$$

where

f_t = the forward rate for delivery of one unit of foreign currency at time t

- Forward rate as an unbiased predictor of the future spot rate

$$f_t = \bar{e}_t$$

Despite the mathematical precision with which these parity conditions are expressed, they are only approximations of reality. A variety of factors can lead to significant and prolonged deviations from parity. For example, both currency risk and inflation risk may cause real interest rates to differ across countries. Similarly, various shocks can cause the real exchange rate—defined as the nominal, or actual, exchange rate adjusted for changes in the relative purchasing power of each currency since some base period—to change over time. Moreover, the short-run relation between changes in the nominal interest differential and changes in the exchange rate is not so easily determined. The lack of definiteness in this relation stems from the differing effects on exchange rates of purely nominal interest rate changes and real interest rate changes.

We examined the concept of the real exchange rate in more detail as well. The real exchange rate, e_t', incorporates both the nominal exchange rate between two currencies and the inflation rates in both countries. It is defined as follows:

$$e_1' = e \frac{P_f}{P_h}$$

where

P_f = the foreign price level at time t indexed to 100 at time 0

P_h = the home price level at time t indexed to 100 at time 0

We then analyzed a series of forecasting models that purport to outperform the market's own forecasts of future exchange rates as embodied in interest and forward differentials. We concluded that the foreign exchange market is no different from any other financial market in its susceptibility to profitable predictions.

Those who have inside information about events that will affect the value of a currency or a security should benefit handsomely. Those who do not have this access will have to trust either their luck or the existence of a market imperfection, such as government intervention, to assure themselves of above-average, risk-adjusted profits. Given the widespread availability of information and the many knowledgeable participants in the foreign exchange market, only the latter situation—government manipulation of exchange rates—holds the promise of superior risk-adjusted returns from currency forecasting. When governments spend money to control exchange rates, this money flows into the hands of private participants who bet against the government. The trick is to predict government actions.

QUESTIONS

1. a. What is purchasing power parity (PPP)?
   b. What are some reasons for deviations from PPP?
   c. Under what circumstances can PPP be applied?

2. One proposal to stabilize the international monetary system involves setting exchange rates at their PPP rates. Once exchange rates were correctly aligned (according to PPP), each nation would adjust its monetary policy so as to maintain them. What problems might arise from using the PPP rate as a guide to the equilibrium exchange rate?

3. Suppose the dollar/rupiah rate is fixed but Indonesian prices are rising faster than U.S. prices. Is the Indonesian rupiah appreciating or depreciating in real terms?

4. Comment on the following statement. "It makes sense to borrow during times of high inflation because you can repay the loan in cheaper dollars."

5. Which is likely to be higher, a 150% ruble return in Russia or a 15% dollar return in the United States?

6. The interest rate in England is 12%; in Switzerland it is 5%. What are the possible reasons for this interest rate differential? What is the most likely reason?

7. Over the period 1982–1988, Peru and Chile stood out as countries whose interest rates were not consistent with their inflation experience. Specifically, Peru's inflation and interest rates averaged about 125% and 8%, respectively, over this period, whereas Chile's

inflation and interest rates averaged about 22% and 38%, respectively.

   a. How would you characterize the real interest rates of Peru and Chile (e.g., close to zero, highly positive, highly negative)?

   b. What might account for Peru's low interest rate relative to its high inflation rate? What are the likely consequences of this low interest rate?

   c. What might account for Chile's high interest rate relative to its inflation rate? What are the likely consequences of this high interest rate?

   d. During this same period, Peru had a small interest differential and yet a large average exchange rate change. How would you reconcile this experience with the international Fisher effect and with your answer to Part (b)?

8. Over the period 1982–1988, a number of countries (e.g., Pakistan, Hungary, Venezuela) had a small or negative interest rate differential and a large average annual depreciation against the dollar. How would you explain these data? Can you reconcile these data with the international Fisher effect?

9. What factors might lead to persistent covered interest arbitrage opportunities among countries?

10. In early 1989, Japanese interest rates were about 4 percentage points below U.S. rates. The wide difference between Japanese and U.S. interest rates prompted some U.S. real estate developers to borrow in yen to finance their projects. Comment on this strategy.

11. In early 1990, Japanese and German interest rates rose while U.S. rates fell. At the same time, the yen and DM fell against the U.S. dollar. What might explain the divergent trends in interest rates?

12. In late December 1990, 1-year German treasury bills yielded 9.1%, whereas 1-year U.S. treasury bills yielded 6.9%. At the same time, the inflation rate during 2006 was 6.3% in the United States, double the German rate of 3.1%.

   a. Are these inflation and interest rates consistent with the Fisher effect?

   b. What might explain this difference in interest rates between the United States and Germany?

13. The spot rate on the euro is $0.91, and the 180-day forward rate is $0.91. What are the possible reasons for the difference between the two rates?

14. German government bonds, or Bunds, currently are paying higher interest rates than comparable U.S. treasury bonds. Suppose the Bundesbank eases the money supply to drive down interest rates. How is an American investor in Bunds likely to fare?

15. In 1993 and early 1994, Turkish banks borrowed abroad at relatively low interest rates to fund their lending at home. The banks earned high profits because rampant inflation in Turkey forced up domestic interest rates. At the same time, Turkey's central bank was intervening in the foreign exchange market to maintain the value of the Turkish lira. Comment on the Turkish banks' funding strategy.

PROBLEMS

1. From base price levels of 100 in 2000, Japanese and U.S. price levels in 2003 stood at 98 and 109, respectively.

   a. If the 2000 $:¥ exchange rate was $0.00928, what should be the exchange rate in 2006?

   b. In fact, the exchange rate in 2006 was ¥ 1 = $0.00860. What might account for the discrepancy? (Price levels were measured using the consumer price index.)

2. Two countries, the United States and England, produce only one good, wheat. Suppose the price of wheat is $3.25 in the United States and is £1.35 in England.

   a. According to the law of one price, what should the $:£ spot exchange rate be?

   b. Suppose the price of wheat over the next year is expected to rise to $3.50 in the United States and to £1.60 in England. What should the 1-year $:£ forward rate be?

   c. If the U.S. government imposes a tariff of $0.50 per bushel on wheat imported from England, what is the maximum possible change in the spot exchange rate that could occur?

3. If expected inflation is 100% and the real required return is 5%, what should be the nominal interest rate according to the Fisher effect?

4. Suppose the short-term interest rate in France is 3.7%, and forecast French inflation is 1.8%. At the same time, the short-term German interest rate is 2.6% and forecast inflation in Germany is 1.6%.

   a. Based on these figures, what are the real interest rates in France and Germany?

   b. To what would you attribute any discrepancy in real rates between France and Germany?

5. In July, the 1-year interest rate is 12% on British pounds and 9% on U.S. dollars.

   a. If the current exchange rate is $1.63:£1, what is the expected future exchange rate in 1 year?

b. Suppose a change in expectations regarding future U.S. inflation causes the expected future spot rate to decline to $1.52:£1. What should happen to the U.S. interest rate?

6. Suppose that in Japan the interest rate is 8% and inflation is expected to be 3%. Meanwhile, the expected inflation rate in France is 12% and the British interest rate is 14%. To the nearest whole number, what is the best estimate of the 1-year forward exchange premium (discount) at which the pound will be selling relative to the euro?

7. An economic analysis firm has just published projected inflation rates for the United States and Germany for the next 5 years. U.S. inflation is expected to be 10% per year, and German inflation is expected to be 4% per year.

   a. If the current exchange rate is $0.95/€, forecast the exchange rates for the next 5 years.

   b. Suppose that U.S. inflation over the next five years turns out to average 3.2%, German inflation averages 1.5%, and the exchange rate in 5 years is $0.99/€. What has happened to the real value of the euro over this 5-year period?

8. During 1995, the Mexican peso exchange rate rose from Mex$5.33/U.S.$ to Mex$7.64/U.S.$. At the same time, U.S. inflation was approximately 3% in contrast to Mexican inflation of about 48.7%.

   a. By how much did the nominal value of the peso change during 1995?

   b. By how much did the real value of the peso change over this period?

9. Suppose 3-year deposit rates on Eurodollars and Euro francs (Swiss) are 12% and 7%, respectively. If the current spot rate for the Swiss franc is $0.3985, what is the spot rate implied by these interest rates for the franc 3 years from now?

10. Assume that the interest rate is 16% on pounds sterling and 7% on euros. At the same time, inflation is running at an annual rate of 3% in Germany and 9% in England.

    a. If the euro is selling at a 1-year forward premium of 10% against the pound, is there an arbitrage opportunity? Explain.

    b. What is the real interest rate in Germany? In England?

    c. Suppose that during the year the exchange rate changes from €1.8:£1 to €1.77:£1. What are the real costs to a German company of borrowing pounds? Contrast this cost to its real cost of borrowing euros.

    d. What are the real costs to a British firm of borrowing euros? Contrast this cost to its real cost of borrowing pounds.

11. Suppose the Eurosterling rate is 15% and the Eurodollar rate is 11.5%. What is the forward premium on the dollar? Explain.

12. Suppose the spot rates for the euro, pound sterling, and Swiss franc are $1.34, $1.98, and $0,815, respectively. The associated 90-day interest rates (annualized) are 8%, 16%, and 4%; the U.S. 90-day rate (annualized) is 12%. What is the 90-day forward rate on an ACU (ACU 1 = € 1 + £1 + SFr 1) if interest rate parity holds?

13. Suppose that 3-month interest rates (annualized) in Japan and the United States are 7% and 9%, respectively. If the spot rate is ¥142:$1 and the 90-day forward rate is ¥139:$1,

    a. Where would you invest?

    b. Where would you borrow?

    c. What arbitrage opportunity do these figures present?

    d. Assuming no transaction costs, what would be your arbitrage profit per dollar or dollar-equivalent borrowed?

14. Here are some prices in the international money markets:

Spot rate	= $1.34:€
Forward rate (1 year)	= $ 1.36:€
Interest rate (€)	= 3.5% per year
Interest rate ($)	= 4.75% per year

    a. Assuming no transaction costs or taxes exist, do covered arbitrage profits exist in this situation? Describe the flows.

    b. Suppose now that transaction costs in the foreign exchange market equal 0.25% per transaction. Do unexploited covered arbitrage profit opportunities still exist?

    c. Suppose no transaction costs exist. Let the capital gains tax on currency profits equal 25% and the ordinary income tax on interest income equal 50%. In this situation, do covered arbitrage profits exist? How large are they? Describe the transactions required to exploit these profits.

15. Suppose today's exchange rate is $1.35/€. The 6-month interest rates on dollars and euros are 6% and 3%, respectively. The 6-month forward rate is $1.3672. A foreign exchange advisory service has predicted that the euro will appreciate to $1,375 within 6 months.

    a. How would you use forward contracts to profit in the above situation?

    b. How would you use money-market instruments (borrowing and lending) to profit?

    c. Which alternatives (forward contracts or money market instruments) would you prefer? Why?

BIBLIOGRAPHY

Aliber, R. A. and C. P. Stickney, "Accounting Measures of Foreign Exchange Exposure: The Long and Short of It," *The Accounting Review,* January 1975, pp. 44–57.

Cassel, G. "Abnormal Deviations in International Exchanges," *Economic Journal,* December 1918, pp. 413–415.

Cornell, B. "Spot Rates, Forward Rates, and Market Efficiency," *Journal of Financial Economics,* January 1977, pp. 55–65.

Cumby, R. "Is It Risk? Deviations from Uncovered Interest Parity," *Journal of Monetary Economics,* September 1988, pp. 279–300.

Dufey, G. and I. H. Giddy, "Forecasting Exchange Rates in a Floating World," *Euromoney,* November 1975, pp. 28–35.

———. *The International Money Market.* Englewood Cliffs, N.J.: Prentice Hall, 1978.

Frankel, Jeffrey. "Flexible Exchange Rates: Experience Versus Theory," *Journal of Portfolio Management,* Winter 1989, pp. 45–54.

Froot, K. A. and J. A. Frankel. "Forward Discount Bias: Is It an Exchange Risk Premium?" *Quarterly Journal of Economics,* February 1989, pp. 139–161.

Froot, K. A. and R. H. Thaler, "Anomalies: Foreign Exchange," *Journal of Economic Perspectives,* Summer 1990, pp. 179–192.

Gailliot, H. J. "Purchasing Power Parity as an Explanation of Long-Term Changes in Exchange Rates," *Journal of Money, Credit, and Banking,* August 1971, pp. 348–357.

Giddy, I. H. "An Integrated Theory of Exchange Rate Equilibrium," *Journal of Financial and Quantitative Analysis,* December 1976, pp. 883–892.

———. "Black Market Exchange Rates as a Forecasting Tool." Working Paper, Columbia University, May 1978.

Giddy, I. H. and G. Dufey, "The Random Behavior of Flexible Exchange Rates," *Journal of International Business Studies,* Spring 1975, pp. 1–32.

Hansen, L. P. and R. J. Hodrick. "Forward Rates as Optimal Predictions of Future Spot Rates," *Journal of Political Economy,* October 1980, pp. 829–853.

Levich, R. M. "Analyzing the Accuracy of Foreign Exchange Advisory Services: Theory and Evidence." In *Exchange Risk and Exposure,* Richard Levich and Clas Wihlborg, eds. Lexington, Mass.: D.C. Heath, 1980.

———. "The Use and Analysis of Foreign Exchange Forecasts: Current Issues and Evidence," paper presented at the Euromoney Treasury Consultancy Program, New York, September 4–5, 1980.

Lothian, J. R. and M. P. Taylor, "Real Exchange Rate Behavior: The Recent Float from the Perspective of the Past Two Centuries," *Journal of Political Economy,* June 1996.

Meese, R. A. and K. Rogoff, "Empirical Exchange Rate Models of the Seventies: Do They Fit Out of Sample?" *Journal of International Economics 14,* no. 1/2 (1983): 3–24.

Mishkin, F. S. "Are Real Interest Rates Equal across Countries? An International Investigation of Parity Conditions." *Journal of Finance,* December 1984, pp. 1345–1357.

Modjtahedi, B. "Dynamics of Real Interest Rate Differentials: An Empirical Investigation." *European Economic Review 32,* No. 6, 1988, pp. 1191–1211.

Officer, L. H. "The Purchasing-Power-Parity Theory of Exchange Rates: A Review Article." *IMF Staff Papers,* March 1976, pp. 1–60.

Osier, C. L. "Currency Orders and Exchange Rate Dynamics: An Explanation for the Predictive Success of Technical Analysis," *Journal of Finance,* October 2003, pp. 1791–1818.

Shapiro, A. C. "What Does Purchasing Power Parity Mean?" *Journal of International Money and Finance,* December 1983, pp. 295–318.

Strongin, S. "International Credit Market Connections," *Economic Perspectives,* July/August 1990, pp. 2–10.

Throop, A. "International Financial Market Integration and Linkages of National Interest Rates," *Federal Reserve Bank of San Francisco Economic Review,* No. 3, 1994, pp. 3–18.

INTERNET RESOURCES

http://www.oecd.org/ Contains data on **PPP** exchange rates for the OECD countries going back to 1970. The **PPP** exchange rate data is presented in a spreadsheet that can be saved.

www.oanda.com Contains current exchange rates along with currency forecasts and news.

http://mwprices.ft.com/custom/ft-com/html-marketsDataTools.asp Web site of the *Financial Times* that contains data on short-term Eurocurrency interest rates for the U.S. dollar, euro, Swiss franc, yen, pound, and several other currencies. This website also provide links to worldwide exchange rate data.

http://www.economist.com/index.html Website of *The Economist.* Contains stories on the economic and political situations of countries and international business development, along with various national and international economic and financial data.

http://www.imf.org/ Website of the International Monetary Fund. Contains information and data on the IMF, SDRs and exchange rates, position of each country in the IMF, and lending arrangements with member nations.

http://www.ny.frb.org/ Website of the Federal Reserve Bank of New York. Contains information on U.S. interventions in the foreign exchange market.

INTERNET EXERCISES

1. Using data from the OECD, compare the most recent PPP exchange rates for the pound, yen, and euro with their nominal exchange rates. What differences do you observe? What accounts for these differences?

2. Using OECD data, plot the PPP exchange rates for the pound, yen, Mexican peso, and Korean won. Have these PPP exchange gone up or down over time? What accounts for the changes in these PPP exchange rate over time?

3. Find the 90-day interest rates from the *Financial Times* Web site for the dollar, yen, euro, and pound. Are the yield differentials on these currencies consistent with the forward rates reported in the *Wall Street Journal?* What might account for any differences?

4. Examine forecasts from www.oanda.com for the pound, yen, and euro.

   a. Which of these currencies are forecast to appreciate and which to depreciate?

   b. Compare these forecasts to the forward rates for the same maturity. Are the predicted exchange rates greater or less than the corresponding forward rates?

   c. Compare these forecasts to the actual exchange rates. How accurate were these forecasts?

   d. If you had followed these forecasts (by buying forward when the forecast exchange rate exceeded the forward rate and selling forward when it was below the forward rate), would you have made or lost money?

5. How have forward premiums and discounts relative to the dollar changed over annual intervals during the past 5 years for the Japanese yen, British pound, and euro? Use beginning-of-year data.

THE BALANCE OF PAYMENTS AND INTERNATIONAL ECONOMIC LINKAGES

I had a trade deficit in 1986 because I took a vacation in France. I didn't worry about it; I enjoyed it.

> Herbert Stein
> Chairman of the Council of Economic
> Advisors under Presidents Nixon and Ford

We have almost a crisis in trade and this is the year Congress will try to turn it around with trade legislation.

> Lloyd Bentsen
> Former U.S. Senator from Texas

Despite all the cries for protectionism to cure the trade deficit, protectionism will not lower the trade deficit.

> Phil Gramm
> U.S. Senator from Texas

CHAPTER LEARNING OBJECTIVES

- To distinguish between the current account, the financial account, and the official reserves account and describe the links among these accounts.
- To calculate a nation's balance-of-payments accounts from data on its international transactions.
- To identify the links between domestic economic behavior and the international flows of goods and capital, and to describe how these links are reflected in the various balance-of-payments accounts.

KEY TERMS

balance of payments	national expenditure
basic balance	national income
capital account	national product
current account	net international wealth
direct investment	net liquidity balance
financial account	official reserve transactions balance
government budget deficit	portfolio investment
J-curve theory	protectionism
macroeconomic accounting identities	quota

real investment   tariff
reserve assets   trade deficit
statistical discrepancy   unilateral transfers

A key theme of this book, as noted, is that companies today operate within a global marketplace, and they can ignore this fact only at their peril. In line with that theme, the purpose of this chapter is to present the financial and real linkages between the domestic and world economies and examine how these linkages affect business viability. The chapter identifies the basic forces underlying the flows of goods, services, and capital between countries and relates these flows to key political, economic, and cultural factors.

Politicians and the business press realize the importance of these trade and capital flows. They pay attention to the balance of payments, on which these flows are recorded, and to the massive and continuing U.S. trade deficits. As we saw in Chapter 2, government foreign exchange policies are often geared toward dealing with balance-of-payments problems. However, as indicated by the three quotations that opened the chapter, many people disagree on the nature of the trade deficit problem and its solution. In the process of studying the balance of payments in this chapter, we will sort out some of these issues.

5.1 BALANCE-OF-PAYMENTS CATEGORIES

The **balance of payments** is an accounting statement that summarizes all the economic transactions between residents of the home country and residents of all other countries. Balance-of-payments statistics are published quarterly in the United States by the Commerce Department and include such transactions as trade in goods and services, transfer payments, loans, and short- and long-term investments. The statistics are followed closely by bankers and businesspeople, economists, and foreign exchange traders; the publication affects the value of the home currency if these figures are more, or less, favorable than anticipated.

Currency inflows are recorded as *credits*, and outflows are recorded as *debits*. Credits show up with a plus sign, and debits have a minus sign. There are three principal balance-of-payments categories:

1. **Current account**, which records imports and exports of goods, services, income, and current unilateral transfers.

2. **Capital account**, which includes mainly debt forgiveness and transfers of goods and financial assets by migrants as they enter or leave the United States.

3. **Financial account**, which shows public and private investment and lending activities. The naming of this account is somewhat misleading as it, rather than the capital account, records inflows and outflows of capital.

For most countries, only the current and financial accounts are significant.

Exports of goods and services are credits; imports of goods and services are debits. Interest and dividends are treated as services because they represent payment for the use of capital. Financial inflows appear as credits because the nation is selling (exporting) to foreigners valuable assets—buildings, land, stock, bonds, and other financial claims—and receiving cash in return. Financial outflows show up as debits because they represent purchases (imports) of foreign assets. The increase in a nation's official reserves also shows up as a debit item because the purchase of gold and other reserve assets is equivalent to importing these assets.

The balance-of-payments statement is based on double-entry bookkeeping; every economic transaction recorded as a credit brings about an equal and offsetting debit entry, and vice versa. According to accounting convention, a source of funds (either a decrease in assets or an increase in liabilities) is a credit, and a use of funds (either an increase in assets or a decrease in liabilities or net worth) is a debit. Suppose a U.S. company exports machine tools to Switzerland at a price of 2,000,000 Swiss francs (SFr). At the current exchange rate of SFr 1 = $0.75, this order is worth $1,500,000. The Swiss importer pays for the order with a check drawn on its Swiss bank account. A credit is recorded for the increase in U.S. exports (a reduction in U.S. goods—a source of funds), and because the exporter has acquired a Swiss franc deposit (an increase in a foreign asset—a use of funds), a debit is recorded to reflect a private capital outflow:

	Debit	**Credit**
U.S. exports		$1,500,000
Private foreign assets	$1,500,000	

Suppose the U.S. company decides to sell the Swiss francs it received to the Federal Reserve for dollars. In this case, a private asset would have been converted into an official (government) liability. This transaction would show up as a credit to the private asset account (as it is a source of funds) and a debit to the official assets account (as it is a use of funds):

	Debit	**Credit**
Private assets		$1,500,000
Official assets	$1,500,000	

Similarly, if a German sells a painting to a U.S. resident for $1,000,000, with payment made by issuing a check drawn on a U.S. bank, a debit is recorded to indicate an increase in assets (the painting) by U.S. residents, which is a use of funds, and a credit is recorded to reflect an increase in liabilities (payment for the painting) to a foreigner, which is a source of funds:

	Debit	**Credit**
Private liabilities to foreigners		$1,000,000
U.S. imports	$1,000,000	

In the case of **unilateral transfers**, which are gifts and grants overseas, the transfer is debited because the donor's net worth is reduced, whereas another account must be credited: exports, if goods are donated; services, if services are donated; or capital, if the recipient receives cash or a check. Suppose the American Red Cross donates $100,000 in goods for earthquake relief to Nicaragua, the balance-of-payments entries for this transaction would appear as follows:

	Debit	**Credit**
U.S. exports		$100,000
Unilateral transfer	$100,000	

Because double-entry bookkeeping ensures that debits equal credits, the sum of all transactions is zero. That is, the sum of the balance on the current account, the capital account, and the financial account must equal zero:

Current-account balance + Capital-account balance + Financial-account balance
= Balance of payments = 0

Credits: Sources of Foreign Exchange (+)		Debits: Uses of Foreign Exchange (−)		
a: Exports of goods	1,023.7	b: Imports of civilian goods	1,859.6	
	Trade balance	= Deficit of $835.9		($835.900)
c: Exports of services (Fees earned, transportation receipts, foreign tourism in United States, etc.)	413.1	d: Imports of services (Fees paid out, transportation charges, U.S. tourism abroad, etc.)	342.4	
		= Surplus of $70.7		70.7
e: Income receipts	622.0	f: Income payments	629.3	
	Income balance	= Deficit of $7.3		−7.3
		g: Net unilateral transfers (gifts)	84.1	
	Current-account balance	= a + c + e − (b + d + f + g)		(856.62)
		= Deficit of $856.7		
h: Capital account transactions, net	−3.9			
	Capital-account balance	= Deficit of $3.9		
i: Foreign private investment in the United States	1,464.4	j: U.S. private investment overseas	1,053.0	
k: Foreign official lending in the United States	300.5	l: U.S. government lending overseas	(5.2)	
		m: Net increase in U.S. official reserves	(2.4)	
	Financial-account balance	= i + k − (j+l+m)		
		= Surplus of $719.5		719.50
n: Statistical discrepancy	141.0			

[1]Numbers may not sum exactly owing to rounding.
Source: Data from the Bureau of Economic Analysis, U.S. Department of Commerce. Balance of Payment Release March 14, 2007.

EXHIBIT 5.1 • THE U.S. BALANCE OF PAYMENTS FOR 2006[1] (USD BILLIONS)

These features of balance-of-payments accounting are illustrated in Exhibit 5.1, which shows the U.S. balance of payments for 2006, and in Exhibit 5.2, which gives examples of entries in the U.S. balance-of-payments accounts.

5.1.1 Current Account

The balance on current account reflects the net flow of goods, services, income, and unilateral transfers. It includes exports and imports of merchandise (trade balance), service transactions (invisibles), and income transfers. The service account includes sales under military contracts, tourism, financial charges (banking and insurance), and transportation expenses (shipping and air travel). The income account was once part of the services account, but it has become so large in recent years that it is now shown separately. It includes investment income (interest and dividends) and employee compensation.

Credits	**Debits**
Current Account	
a: Sales of wheat to Great Britain; sales of computers to Germany	*b:* Purchases of oil from Saudi Arabia; purchases of Japanese automobiles
c: Sales of Phantom jets to Canada	*d:* Payments to German workers at U.S. bases in Germany
e: Licensing fees earned by Microsoft; spending by Japanese tourists at Disneyland	*f:* Hotel bills of U.S. tourists in Paris
g: Interest earnings on loans to Argentina; profits on U.S.-owned auto plants abroad	*h:* Profits on sales by Nestlé's U.S. affiliate
	i: Remittances by Mexican Americans to relatives in Mexico; Social Security payments to Americans living in Italy; economic aid to Pakistan
Capital Account	
j: Purchases by the Japanese of U.S. real estate; increases in Arab bank deposits in New York banks; purchases by the French of IBM stock; investment in plant expansion in Ohio by Honda	*k:* New investment in a German chemical plant by DuPont; increases in U.S. bank loans to Mexico; deposits in Swiss banks by Americans; purchases of Japanese stocks and bonds by Americans
l: Purchases of U.S. Treasury bonds by Bank of Japan; increases in holdings of New York bank deposits by Saudi Arabian government	*m:* Deposits of funds by the U.S. Treasury in British banks; purchases of Swiss-franc bonds by the Federal Reserve
Official Reserve Account	
	n: Purchases of gold by the U.S. Treasury; increases in holdings of Japanese yen by the Federal Reserve

EXHIBIT 5.2 • EXAMPLES OF ENTRIES IN THE U.S. BALANCE-OF-PAYMENTS ACCOUNTS

Unilateral transfers include pensions, remittances, and other transfers overseas for which no specific services are rendered. In 2006, for example, the U.S. balance of trade registered a deficit of $835.9 billion, not very different from the overall current-account deficit of $856.7 billion. Also, in 2006, the United States ran a *surplus* of $70.7 billion on its services account and deficits of $7.3 billion and $84.1 billion on the income account and unilateral transfers, respectively.

The U.S. current-account deficit at $856.7 billion in 2006 was the world's largest. In addition, as a percent of GDP, the deficit was 6.4%, and, as shown in Exhibit 5.3, one of the highest in the industrialized world.

5.1.2 Capital Account

The capital account records capital transfers that offset transactions that are undertaken, without exchange, in fixed assets or in their financing (such as development aid). For example, migrants' funds represent the shift of the migrants' net worth to or from the United States, and are classified as capital transfers. This a minor account for most purposes.

5.1.3 Financial Account

Financial-account transactions affect a nation's wealth and net creditor position. These transactions are classified as portfolio investment, direct investment, other investment, or reserve assets. **Portfolio investments** are purchases of financial assets with a maturity greater than 1 year; *short-term investments* involve securities with a maturity of less than 1 year. **Direct investments** are those where management control is exerted, defined under

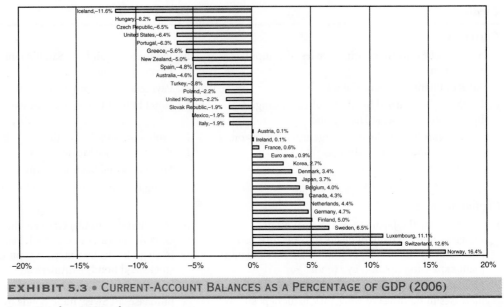

EXHIBIT 5.3 ● CURRENT-ACCOUNT BALANCES AS A PERCENTAGE OF GDP (2006)

Source: Data from OECD website.

U.S. rules as ownership of at least 10% of the equity. Government borrowing and lending are included in the balance on financial account. The financial account also includes changes in reserve assets, which are holdings of gold and foreign currencies by official monetary institutions. As shown in Exhibit 5.1, the U.S. financial-account balance in 2006 was a surplus of $719.5 billion.

5.1.4 Balance-of-Payments Measures

There are several balance-of-payments definitions. The **basic balance** focuses on transactions considered to be fundamental to the economic health of a currency. Thus, it includes the balance on current account and long-term capital, but it excludes such ephemeral items as short-term capital flows, mainly bank deposits, that are heavily influenced by temporary factors—short-run monetary policy, changes in interest differentials, and anticipations of currency fluctuations.

The **net liquidity balance** measures the change in private domestic borrowing or lending that is required to keep payments in balance without adjusting official reserves. Nonliquid, private, short-term capital flows, and errors and omissions are included in the balance; liquid assets and liabilities are excluded.

The **official reserve transactions balance** measures the adjustment required in official reserves to achieve balance-of-payments equilibrium. The assumption here is that official transactions are different from private transactions.

Each of these measures has shortcomings, primarily because of the increasing complexity of international financial transactions. For example, changes in the official reserve balance may now reflect investment flows as well as central bank intervention. Similarly, critics of the basic balance argue that the distinction between short- and long-term capital flows has become blurred. Direct investment is still determined by longer-term factors, but investment in stocks and bonds can be just as speculative as bank deposits and sold just as quickly. The astute international financial manager, therefore, must analyze the payments figures rather than rely on a single summarizing number.

MINI-CASE   *The Bank of Korea Reassesses Its Reserve Policy*

In April 2005, the Bank of Korea, South Korea's central bank, was reviewing its investment policy. It was looking at a range of higher-yielding investment options, including corporate bonds and mortgage-backed securities, to improve returns on its large and growing reserve holdings. At the end of March 2005, South Korea's foreign reserves were the fourth largest in the world, at $205.5 billion. Currency traders were suspicious that the bank's decision to invest more money in nontraditional assets was a cover for plans to diversify its reserves out of U.S. dollars and into euros, yen, and other currencies that have held their value better than the sinking dollar. The Bank of Korea's governor, Park Seung, said in response to these concerns that the bank had no plans to sell dollars because that would lead to a further appreciation of the South Korean won. The bank has been trying to slow the won's rise against the dollar to protect Korean exporters.

Historically, the Bank of Korea, like other central banks, has focused on safe, short-term investments so that money is available on short notice to intervene in currency markets or cope with sudden shifts in capital flows. It has paid little attention to maximizing returns. However, this policy is changing as foreign-exchange reserves pile up, exceeding the amount needed for policy reasons. For example, South Korea's reserves grew 28% in 2004.

One of the factors prompting the current review is the growing cost of maintaining such large reserves. This cost stems from the Bank of Korea's policy of sterilizing its currency market interventions. It has been selling government bonds to soak up the newly minted won it has been issuing to prop up the weakening dollar. The problem is that the South Korean government has been paying higher interest rates on these domestic bonds than it has been earning on the U.S. Treasury bonds and other dollar-denominated assets it has been buying with its dollar reserves. Moreover, the Bank of Korea has been suffering valuation losses as the dollar continues to fall against the won. The public and politicians have also been calling for South Korea's large reserves to be put to more productive use.

QUESTIONS

1. What is the link between South Korea's currency market interventions and its growing foreign exchange reserves?

2. What is the annualized cost to the Bank of Korea of maintaining $205.5 billion in reserves? Assume that the government of Korea is issuing bonds that yield about 4% annually while buying dollar assets that yield about 3.25%.

3. Suppose that during the year the won rose by 8% against the dollar and that the Bank of Korea kept 100% of its reserves in dollars. At a current exchange rate of W1,011/$, what would that do to the won cost of maintaining reserves of $205.5 billion?

4. What are some pros and cons of the Bank of Korea diversifying its investment holdings out of dollars and into other currencies, such as euros and yen?

5. How has the almost universal central bank preference for investing reserve assets in U.S. treasury bonds affected the cost of financing the U.S. budget deficit?

5.1.5 The Missing Numbers

In going over the numbers in Exhibit 5.1, you will note an item referred to as a **statistical discrepancy**. This number reflects errors and omissions in collecting data on international transactions. In 2006, that item was +$141 billion. Typically, a positive figure reflects a mysterious inflow of funds; a negative amount reflects an outflow.

5.2 THE INTERNATIONAL FLOW OF GOODS, SERVICES, AND CAPITAL

This section provides an analytical framework that links the international flows of goods and capital to domestic economic behavior. The framework consists of a set of basic **macroeconomic accounting identities** that link domestic spending and production to savings, consumption, and investment behavior, and thence to the financial-account and current-account balances. By manipulating these equations, we can identify the nature of the links between the U.S. and world economies and assess the effects on the domestic economy of international economic policies, and vice versa. As we see in the next section, ignoring these links leads to political solutions to international economic problems, such as the trade deficit, that create greater problems. At the same time, authors of domestic policy changes are often unaware of the effect these changes can have on the country's international economic affairs.

5.2.1 Domestic Savings and Investment and the Financial Account

The national income and product accounts provide an accounting framework for recording the national product and showing how its components are affected by international transactions. This framework begins with the observation that **national income**, which is the same as **national product**, is either spent on consumption or saved:

$$\text{National income} = \text{Consumption} + \text{Savings} \tag{5.1}$$

Similarly, **national expenditure**, the total amount that the nation spends on goods and services, can be divided into spending on consumption and spending on domestic real investment. **Real investment** refers to plant and equipment, research and development, and other expenditures designed to increase the nation's productive capacity. This equation provides the second national accounting identity:

$$\text{National spending} = \text{Consumption} + \text{Investment} \tag{5.2}$$

Subtracting Equation 5.2 from Equation 5.1 yields a new identity:

$$\text{National income} - \text{National spending} = \text{Savings} - \text{Investment} \tag{5.3}$$

This identity says that if a nation's income exceeds its spending, savings will exceed domestic investment, yielding surplus capital. The surplus capital must be invested overseas (if it were invested domestically there would not be a capital surplus). In other words, savings equals domestic investment plus net foreign investment. Net foreign investment equals the nation's net public and private capital outflows plus net capital transfers. The net private and public capital outflows equal the financial-account deficit if the outflow is positive (a financial-account surplus if negative); the net increase in capital transfers equals the balance in the capital account. Ignoring the minor impact of the capital account, excess savings equals the financial-account deficit. Alternatively, a national savings deficit will equal the financial-account surplus (net borrowing from abroad); this borrowing finances the excess of national spending over national income.

Here is the bottom line: A nation that produces more than it spends will save more than it invests domestically and will have a net capital outflow. This capital outflow will appear as a financial-account deficit. Conversely, a nation that spends more than it produces will invest domestically more than it saves and have a net capital inflow. This capital inflow will appear as a financial-account surplus.

5.2.2 The Link Between the Current and Financial Accounts

Beginning again with national product, we can subtract from it spending on domestic goods and services. The remaining goods and services must equal exports. Similarly, if we subtract spending on domestic goods and services from total expenditures, the remaining spending must be on imports. Combining these two identities leads to another national income identity:

$$\text{National income} - \text{National spending} = \text{Exports} - \text{Imports} \qquad (5.4)$$

Equation 5.4 says that a current-account surplus arises when national output exceeds domestic expenditures; similarly, a current-account deficit is due to domestic expenditures exceeding domestic output. Exhibit 5.4 illustrates this latter point for the United States. Moreover, when Equation 5.4 is combined with Equation 5.3, we have a new identity:

$$\text{Savings} - \text{Investment} = \text{Exports} - \text{Imports} \qquad (5.5)$$

According to Equation 5.5, if a nation's savings exceed its domestic investment, that nation will run a current-account surplus. This equation explains the Japanese current-account surplus: The Japanese have an extremely high savings rate, both in absolute terms and relative to their investment rate. Conversely, a nation such as the United States, which saves less than it invests, must run a current-account deficit. Noting that savings minus domestic investment equals net foreign investment, we have the following identity:

$$\text{Net foreign investment} = \text{Exports} - \text{Imports} \qquad (5.6)$$

Equation 5.6 says that the balance on the current account must equal the net capital outflow; that is, any foreign exchange earned by selling abroad must be either spent on imports or exchanged for claims against foreigners. The net amount of these IOUs

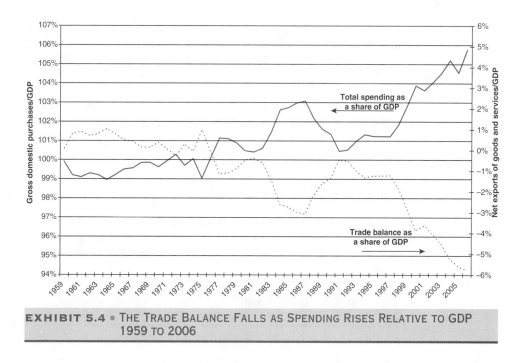

EXHIBIT 5.4 • THE TRADE BALANCE FALLS AS SPENDING RISES RELATIVE TO GDP 1959 TO 2006

equals the nation's capital outflow. If the current account is in surplus, the country must be a net exporter of capital; a current-account deficit indicates that the nation is a net capital importer. This equation explains why Japan, with its large current-account surpluses, is a major capital exporter, whereas the United States, with its large current-account deficits, is a major capital importer. Bearing in mind that trade is goods plus services, to say that the United States has a **trade deficit** with Japan is simply to say that the United States is buying more goods and services from Japan than Japan is buying from the United States, and that Japan is investing more in the United States than the United States is investing in Japan. Between the United States and Japan, any deficit in the current account is exactly equal to the surplus in the financial account. Otherwise, there would be an imbalance in the foreign exchange market, and the exchange rate would change.

Another interpretation of Equation 5.6 is that the excess of goods and services bought over goods and services produced domestically must be acquired through foreign trade and must be financed by an equal amount of borrowing from abroad (the financial-account surplus). Thus, the current-account balance and the financial-account and capital-account balances must exactly offset each other. That is, the sum of the current-account balance plus the capital-account balance plus the financial-account balance must be zero. These relations are shown in Exhibit 5.5.

These identities are useful because they allow us to assess the efficacy of proposed solutions for improving the current-account balance. It is clear that a nation can neither reduce its current-account deficit nor increase its current-account surplus unless it meets two conditions: (1) Raise national product relative to national spending and (2) increase savings relative to domestic investment. A proposal to improve the current-account balance by reducing imports (say, via higher tariffs) that does not affect national output/spending and national savings/investment leaves the trade deficit the same; and the proposal cannot achieve its objective without violating fundamental accounting identities. With regard to Japan, a clear implication is that chronic Japanese trade surpluses are not reflective of unfair trade practices and restrictive import policies, but rather are the natural effect of differing cultures and philosophies regarding saving and consumption. As long as the Japanese prefer to save and invest rather than consume, the imbalance will persist.

	Our national product (Y)	−	Our total spending (E)
minus	Our spending for consumption		minus Our spending for consumption

= | Our national savings (S) | − | Our investment in new real assets (Id) |

= Net foreign investment, or the net increase in claims on foreigners, and official reserve assets, e.g., gold (If)

	Our national product (Y)	−	Our total spending (E)
minus	Our spending on our own goods		minus Our spending on our own goods and services

= | Our exports of goods and services (X) | − | Our imports of goods and services (M) |

= Balance on current account

= − (Balance on capital and financial accounts)

$$Y - E = S - Id = X - M = If$$

Conclusions: A nation that produces more than it spends will save more than it invests, export more than it imports, and wind up with a capital outflow. A nation that spends more than it produces will invest more than it saves, import more than it exports, and wind up with a capital inflow.

EXHIBIT 5.5 ● Linking National Economic Activity with Balance-of-Payments Accounts: Basic Identities

These accounting identities also suggest that a current-account surplus is not necessarily a sign of economic vigor, nor is a current-account deficit necessarily a sign of weakness or of a lack of competitiveness. Indeed, economically healthy nations that provide good investment opportunities tend to run trade deficits, because this is the only way to run a financial-account surplus.

Note, too, that nations that grow rapidly will import more goods and services at the same time that weak economies will slow down or reduce their imports, because imports are positively related to income. As a result, the faster a nation grows relative to other economies, the larger its current-account deficit (or smaller its surplus). Conversely, slower-growing nations will have smaller current-account deficits (or larger surpluses). Hence, current-account deficits may reflect strong economic growth or a low level of savings, and current-account surpluses can signify a high level of savings or a slow rate of growth.

Because current-account deficits are financed by capital inflows, the cumulative effect of these deficits is to increase net foreign claims against the deficit nation and reduce that nation's net international wealth. Similarly, nations that consistently run current-account surpluses increase their **net international wealth**, which is just the difference between a nation's investment abroad and foreign investment domestically. Sooner or later, deficit countries like the United States become net international debtors, and surplus countries like Japan become net creditors. For example, Exhibit 5.6 shows that the inevitable consequence of continued U.S. current-account deficits was to turn U.S. net international wealth (computed on a current cost basis) negative. In 1987, the United States became a net international debtor, reverting to the position it was in at the start of the twentieth century. By the end of 2005, U.S. net international wealth was −$2.7 trillion.

5.2.3 Government Budget Deficits and Current-Account Deficits

Upto now, government spending and taxation have been included in aggregate domestic spending and income figures. By differentiating between the government and private sectors, we can see the effect of a government deficit on the current-account deficit.

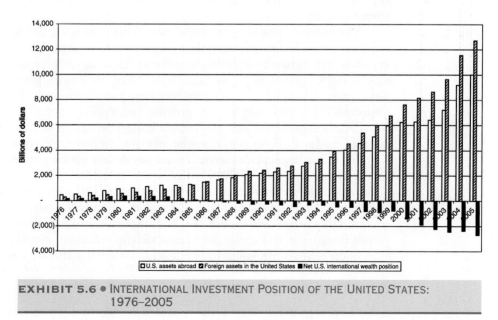

EXHIBIT 5.6 • INTERNATIONAL INVESTMENT POSITION OF THE UNITED STATES: 1976–2005

Source: Bureau of Economic Analysis. Data are investment positions calculated on a current cost basis by the U.S. Bureau of Economic Analysis.

National spending can be divided into household spending plus private investment plus government spending. Household spending, in turn, equals national income less the sum of private savings and taxes. Combining these terms yields the following identity:

$$\begin{aligned}
\frac{\text{National}}{\text{spending}} &= \frac{\text{Household}}{\text{spending}} + \frac{\text{Private}}{\text{investment}} + \frac{\text{Government}}{\text{spending}} \\
&= \frac{\text{National}}{\text{income}} - \frac{\text{Private}}{\text{savings}} - \text{Taxes} + \frac{\text{Private}}{\text{investment}} + \frac{\text{Government}}{\text{spending}}
\end{aligned} \qquad (5.7)$$

Rearranging Equation 5.7 yields a new expression for excess spending:

$$\frac{\text{National}}{\text{spending}} - \frac{\text{National}}{\text{Income}} = \frac{\text{Private}}{\text{Investment}} - \frac{\text{Private}}{\text{Savings}} + \frac{\text{Government}}{\text{budget deficit}} \qquad (5.8)$$

where the **government budget deficit** equals government spending minus taxes. Equation 5.8 says that excess national spending is composed of two parts: the excess of private domestic investment over private savings and the total government (federal, state, and local) deficit. Because national spending minus national product equals the net capital inflow, Equation 5.8 also says that the nation's excess spending equals its net borrowing from abroad.

Rearranging and combining Equations 5.4 and 5.8 provides a new accounting identity:

$$\frac{Current - account}{balance} = \frac{Private\ savings}{surplus} - \frac{Government}{budget\ deficit} \qquad (5.9)$$

Equation 5.9 reveals that a nation's current-account balance is identically equal to its private savings-investment balance less the government budget deficit. According to this expression, a nation running a current-account deficit is not saving enough to finance its private investment and government budget deficit. Conversely, a nation running a current-account surplus is saving more than it needs to finance its private investment and government deficit.

The increase in the U.S. current-account deficit during the 1980s, shown in Exhibit 5.7, was associated with an increase in the total government budget deficit and with a narrowing in private savings relative to private investment. As savings relative to investment rose beginning in 1989, the current-account deficit narrowed, even as the government deficit continued to grow. Conversely, even as strong economic growth during the 1990s eventually turned the federal deficit into a surplus, the current-account deficit continued to grow. Moreover, the twin-deficits hypothesis—that government budget deficits cause current-account deficits—does not shed any light on why a number of major countries, including Germany and Japan, continue to run large current-account surpluses despite government budget deficits that are similar in size (as a share of GDP) to that of the United States.

In general, a current-account deficit represents a decision to consume, both publicly and privately, and to invest more than the nation currently is producing. As such, steps taken to correct the current-account deficit can be effective only if they also change private savings, private investment, and/or the government deficit. Policies or events that fail to affect both sides of the relationship as shown in Equation 5.9 will not alter the current-account deficit.

5.2.4 The Current Situation

As we have seen in Exhibit 5.7, the United States has been generating ever-larger current-account deficits and worries about these deficits. By now, this deficit is of a sufficient magnitude

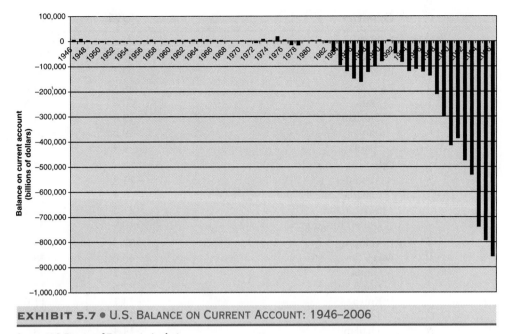

EXHIBIT 5.7 ● U.S. BALANCE ON CURRENT ACCOUNT: 1946–2006

Source: U.S. Bureau of Economic Analysis.

that it is unsustainable over the long term. In particular, since 2000, the U.S. current-account deficit has been running at 4% to over 6% of GDP At this rate, which exceeds the long-run rate of U.S. economic growth, the United States is piling up debt-servicing costs that will eventually exceed its GDP. Since that is an impossibility (the United States cannot pay more than its GDP in debt-servicing costs annually), something must change.

What must change depends on what has brought about the deficit. In this regard, it should be noted that a nation's current-account balance depends on the behavior of its trading partners as well as its own economic policies and propensities. For example, regardless of the U.S. propensity to consume or to save and invest, it can run a current-account deficit only if other nations are willing to run offsetting current-account surpluses. Hence, to understand the recent deterioration in the U.S. current account we must look beyond economic policies and other economic developments within the United States itself and take into account events outside the United States. One such explanation is provided by the then Federal Reserve governor and now Chairman of the Board of Governors, Ben Bernanke. That explanation holds that a key factor driving recent developments in the U.S. current account has been the very substantial shift in the current accounts of developing and emerging-market nations, a shift that has transformed these countries from net borrowers on international capital markets to large net lenders and created a significant increase in the global supply of saving.[1] The global saving glut, in turn, helps to explain both the increase in the U.S. current-account deficit and the relatively low level of long-term real interest rates in the world today.

As Exhibit 5.8 shows, the bulk of the $410 billion increase in the U.S. current-account deficit between 1996 and 2003 was balanced by changes in the current-account positions of developing countries, which moved from a collective deficit of $88 billion to a surplus of $205 billion, a net change of $293 billion, between 1996 and 2003. The surplus

---

[1] Ben S. Bernanke, "The Global Saving Glut and the U.S. Current Account Deficit," March 10, 2005. Much of the discussion in this section is based on this speech, which is available at www.federalreserve.gov/boarddocs/speeches/2005/200503102/default.htm.

Countries	1996	2003	2006
Industrial	46.2	−342.3	−741.68
United States	−120.2	−530.7	−862.3
Japan	65.4	138.2	174.4
Euro Area	88.5	24.9	−25.5
France	20.8	4.5	−38
Germany	−13.4	55.1	134.8
Italy	39.6	−20.7	−23.7
Spain	0.4	−23.6	−98.6
Other	12.5	25.3	−28.28
Australia	−15.8	−30.4	−41.6
Canada	3.4	17.1	20.56
Switzerland	21.3	42.2	50.44
United Kingdom	−10.9	−30.5	−57.68
Developing	**−87.5**	**205**	**564.2**
Asia	−40.8	148.3	210.8
China	7.2	45.9	179.1
Hong Kong	−2.6	17	20.9
Korea	−23.1	11.9	2
Taiwan	10.9	29.3	9.7
Thailand	−14.4	8	−0.9
Latin America	−39.1	3.8	18.9
Argentina	−6.8	7.4	6.8
Brazil	−23.2	4	13.5
Mexico	−2.5	−8.7	−0.4
Middle East and Africa	5.9	47.8	249.2
E. Europe and the former Soviet Union	−13.5	5.1	85.3
Statistical discrepancy	**41.3**	**137.2**	**177.5**

Source: Ben S. Bernanke, "the Global Saving Glut and the U.S. Current Account Deficit," March 10, 2005; 2006 Data from CIA World Factbook.

EXHIBIT 5.8 • GLOBAL CURRENT ACCOUNT BALANCES: 1996 AND 2006 (BILLIONS OF U.S. DOLLARS)

jumped to $562.2 billion in 2006. This shift by developing nations is attributable to a combination of financial crises that forced many emerging-market nations to switch from being net importers of financial capital to being net exporters; foreign exchange interventions by East Asian countries–intended to promote export-led growth by preventing exchange-rate appreciation—that led them to pile up reserves; and the sharp rise in oil prices that boosted the current-account surpluses of Middle East and other oil exporters. At the same time, the high saving propensities of Germany, Japan, and some other major industrial nations have resulted in a global saving glut. This increased supply of saving boosted U.S. equity values during the period of the stock market boom; the saving glut also lowered real interest rates and helped to increase U.S. housing prices after 2000, consequently reducing U.S. national savings and contributing to the rising current-account deficit. This explanation is consistent with the experience of other industrial countries besides the United States.

As shown in Exhibit 5.8, a number of key industrial countries other than the United States have seen their current accounts move substantially toward deficit since 1996, including France, Italy, Spain, Australia, and the United Kingdom. The principal exceptions to this trend among the major industrial countries are Germany and Japan, both of which saw substantial increases in their current-account balances between 1996 and 2003 (and significant further increases in 2006). A key difference between the two groups of countries is that the countries whose current accounts have moved toward deficit have generally experienced substantial housing appreciation and increases in household wealth, while Germany and Japan—whose economies have been growing slowly despite very low interest rates—have not. The latter group has increased its net savings while the former group has not.

5.3 COPING WITH THE CURRENT-ACCOUNT DEFICIT

Conventional wisdom suggests some oft-repeated solutions to unsustainable current-account deficits. The principal suggestions are currency devaluation and protectionism. There are important, though subtle, reasons, however, why neither is likely to work.

5.3.1 Currency Depreciation

An overvalued currency acts as a tax on exports and a subsidy to imports, reducing the former and increasing the latter. The result, as we saw in Chapter 2, is that a nation maintaining an overvalued currency will run a trade deficit. Permitting the currency to return to its equilibrium level will help reduce the trade deficit.

Many academics, politicians, and businesspeople also believe that devaluation can reduce a trade deficit in a floating-rate system. Key to the effectiveness of devaluation is sluggish adjustment of nominal prices, which translates changes in nominal exchange rates into changes in real (inflation-adjusted) exchange rates. This view of exchange rate changes implies a systematic relation between the exchange rate and the current-account balance. For example, it implies that the current U.S. trade deficit will be reduced eventually by a fall in the value of the dollar.

By contrast, we saw in Chapter 2 that all exchange rates do is to equate currency supplies and demands; they do not determine the distribution of these currency flows between trade flows (the current-account balance) and capital flows (the financial-account balance). This view of exchange rates predicts that there is no simple relation between the exchange rate and the current-account balance. Trade deficits do not *cause* currency depreciation, nor does currency depreciation by itself help reduce a trade deficit: Both exchange rate changes and trade balances are determined by more fundamental economic factors.

These diametrically opposed theories can be evaluated by studying evidence on trade deficits and exchange rate changes. A good place to start is with U.S. experience over the past 30 years.

From 1976 to 1980, the value of the dollar declined as the current-account deficit for the United States first worsened and then improved; but from 1980 to 1985, the dollar strengthened even as the current account steadily deteriorated. Many analysts attributed the rise in the U.S. trade deficit in the early 1980s to the sharp rise in the value of the U.S. dollar over that period. As the dollar rose in value against the currencies of America's trading partners, fewer dollars were required to buy a given amount of foreign goods, and more foreign currencies were needed to buy a fixed amount of U.S. goods. Responding to these price changes, Americans bought more foreign goods and foreign consumers reduced their purchases of U.S.-made goods. U.S. imports increased and exports declined.

After reaching its peak in early March 1985, the value of the dollar began to decline. This decline was actively encouraged by the United States and by several foreign governments in hope of reducing the U.S. trade deficit. Conventional wisdom suggested that the

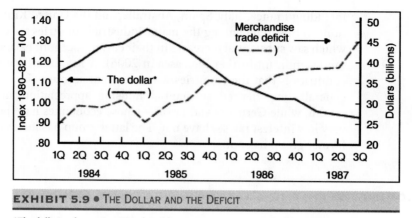

EXHIBIT 5.9 • THE DOLLAR AND THE DEFICIT

*The dollar's value against 15 industrial-country currencies weighted by trade.

very same basic economic forces affecting the trade account during the dollar's runup would now be working in the opposite direction, reducing the U.S. trade (current-account) deficit. As Exhibit 5.9 documents, however, the theory did not work. The U.S. trade deficit kept rising, reaching new record levels month after month. By 1987, it had risen to $167 billion. The 1988 trade deficit fell to $128 billion, but this figure still exceeded the $125 billion trade deficit in 1985. Even more discouraging from the standpoint of those who believe that currency devaluation should cure a trade deficit is that between 1985 and 1987 the yen more than doubled in dollar value without reducing the U.S. trade deficit with Japan. More recently, after peaking in value in 2002, the U.S. dollar fell dramatically against currencies worldwide while the U.S. current-account deficit reached record levels in both absolute terms as well as relative to U.S. GDP. What went wrong?

Lagged Effects   The simplest explanation is that time is needed for an exchange rate change to affect trade. Exhibit 5.10 shows that when the exchange rate is lagged 2 years (for example, the current-account balance for 1987 is matched against the value of the dollar in 1985), there is a closer correspondence between the current-account balance as a percent of GDP and the exchange rate. Despite this closer correspondence, however, in

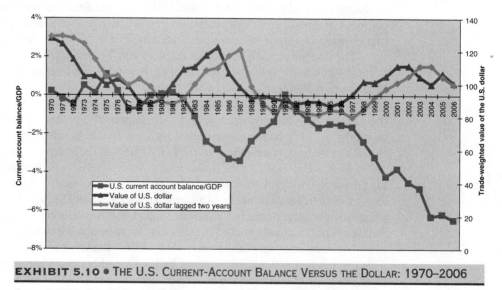

EXHIBIT 5.10 • THE U.S. CURRENT-ACCOUNT BALANCE VERSUS THE DOLLAR: 1970–2006

Source: OECD Statistical Release; Federal Reserve Statistical Release; Bureau of Economic Analysis.

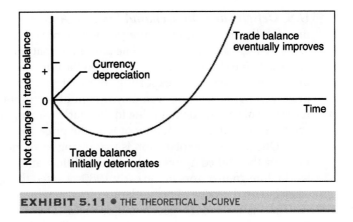

EXHIBIT 5.11 ● THE THEORETICAL J-CURVE

some years the dollar is falling and the current-account balance is worsening, and in other years the dollar is strengthening and the current-account balance is improving. Overall, changes in the dollar's value explain less than 5% of the variation in the U.S. current-account balance as a percentage of GDP over the period 1970–2006.

J-Curve Theory Another explanation, which is consistent with the presence of lagged effects, is based on the J-curve theory, illustrated in Exhibit 5.11. The letter J describes a curve that, viewed from left to right, goes down sharply for a short time, flattens out, and then rises steeply for an extended period. That's how J-curve proponents have been expecting the U.S. trade deficit to behave. According to the **J-curve theory**, a country's trade deficit worsens just after its currency depreciates because price effects will dominate the effect on volume of imports in the short run. That is, the higher cost of imports will more than offset the reduced volume of imports. Thus, the J-curve says that a decline in the value of the dollar should be followed by a temporary worsening in the trade deficit before its longer-term improvement.

The initial worsening of the trade deficit occurred as predicted in 1985, but not until 4 years later, in 1989, was the trade deficit below where it had been in 1985. Moreover, the improvement that occurred between 1985 and 1989 may owe more to the $59 billion drop in the federal budget deficit over this period than to depreciation of the dollar. Similarly, between 1970 and 1995, the yen rose from ¥360 to the dollar to ¥95 to the dollar. At the same time, America's trade deficit with Japan kept rising. In other words, the upturn of the J-curve has proved elusive. Part of the answer in the case of Japan is that Japanese manufacturers responded to currency appreciation by cutting costs and profit margins enough to keep their goods competitive abroad. Another confounding factor is that a strong yen makes Japanese raw material imports cheaper, offsetting some of their cost disadvantage.

The Japanese experience has been similarly disappointing to advocates of using currency changes to cure current-account imbalances. Between 1991 and 1995, when the yen was rising rapidly, Japan's current-account surplus widened. Since 1995, however, Japan's surplus has narrowed, even as the yen has fallen in value. One explanation for the recent turn of events is that the Japanese government's budget has moved into sizable deficit, reducing Japan's total domestic savings. Other things being equal, lower domestic savings will reduce a current-account surplus.

Devaluation and Inflation Devaluing to gain trade competitiveness can also be self-defeating because a weaker currency tends to result in higher domestic inflation, offsetting the benefits of devaluation. For example, higher inflation brought about by a lower dollar will make U.S. exports more expensive abroad and imports more competitive in the U.S. market.

U.S. Deficits and the Demand for U.S. Assets   Another possible reason for the failure of dollar devaluation to cure the persistent U.S. trade deficit is that the earlier analysis mixed up cause and effect. The argument that the strong dollar was the main culprit of the massive U.S. trade deficit rested on the obvious fact that the dollar's high price made importing cheaper than exporting. But that was not the complete picture. The dollar's price was not a cause or even a symptom of the problem. It is axiomatic that price is a reflection of a fundamental value in the market. To argue that the high dollar hurt the U.S. economy does not explain how or why the price got there.

One plausible explanation is that owing to an increasingly attractive investment climate in the United States and added political and economic turmoil elsewhere in the world, foreign investors in the early 1980s wanted to expand their holdings of U.S. assets. They bid up the value of the dollar to a level at which Americans were willing to exchange their assets for foreign goods and services. The result was a financial-account surplus balanced by a current-account deficit. In effect, the financial-account surplus drove the current-account deficit. The net result was excess American spending financed by borrowing from abroad.

Adding fuel to the current-account deficit, particularly after 1982, was the growth of the federal government's budget deficit. The U.S. budget deficit could be funded in only one of three ways: restricting investment, increasing savings, or exporting debt. The United States rejected the first alternative, was unable to accomplish the second, and thus relied heavily on the third. Accordingly, the trade deficit was the equilibrating factor that enabled the United States to satisfy its extra-large appetite for debt. The price of the dollar determined the terms on which the rest of the world was willing to finance that deficit. When foreigners wanted to hold U.S. assets, the terms were quite attractive (they were willing to pay a high price for dollars); when foreigners no longer found U.S. assets so desirable, the financing terms became more onerous (they reduced the price they were willing to pay for dollars).

This analysis suggests that the current-account deficit will disappear only if the U.S. savings rate rises significantly or the rate of investment falls. As such, currency devaluation will work only if some mechanism is in place that leads to a rise in private savings, a cut in private investment, or a further increase in the government budget surplus.

5.3.2 Protectionism

Another response to a current-account deficit is **protectionism**–that is, the imposition of tariffs, quotas, or other forms of restraint against foreign imports. A **tariff** is essentially a tax that is imposed on a foreign product sold in a country. Its purpose is to increase the price of the product, thereby discouraging purchase of that product and encouraging the purchase of a substitute, domestically produced product.[2] A **quota** specifies the quantity of particular products that can be imported to a country, typically an amount that is much less than the amount currently being imported. By restricting the supply relative to the demand, the quota causes the price of foreign products to rise. In both cases, the results are ultimately a rise in the price of products consumers buy, an erosion of purchasing power, and a collective decline in the standard of living.

These results present a powerful argument against selective trade restrictions as a way to correct a nation's trade imbalance. An even more powerful argument is that such restrictions do not work. Either other imports rise or exports fall. This conclusion follows

---

[2] The incidence of a tariff—that is, who pays it—depends on the relative elasticities of supply and demand. For example, the more elastic the demand the more of the tariff that will be absorbed by the exporter. On the other hand, an elastic supply means that more of the tariff will be paid by the consumer.

from the basic national income accounting identity: Savings − Investment = Exports − Imports. Unless saving or investment behavior changes, this identity says that a $1-reduction in imports will lead to a $1-decrease in exports.

The mechanism that brings about this result depends on the basic market forces that shape the supply and demand for currencies in the foreign exchange market. For example, when the U.S. government imposes restrictions on steel imports, the reduction in purchases of foreign steel effectively reduces the U.S. demand for foreign exchange. Fewer dollars tendered for foreign exchange means a higher value for the dollar. The higher-valued dollar raises the price of U.S. goods sold overseas and causes proportionately lower sales of U.S. exports. A higher-valued dollar also lowers the cost in the United States of foreign goods, thereby encouraging the purchase of those imported goods on which there is no tariff. Thus, any reduction in imports from tariffs or quotas will be offset by the reduction in exports and increase in other imports.

Restrictions on importing steel will also raise the price of steel, reducing the competitiveness of U.S. users of steel, such as automakers and capital goods manufacturers. Their ability to compete will be constrained both at home and abroad. Ironically, protectionism punishes the most efficient and internationally most competitive producers who are exporting or are able to compete against imports, whereas it shelters the inefficient producers.

5.3.3 Ending Foreign Ownership of Domestic Assets

One approach that would eliminate a current-account deficit is to forbid foreigners from owning domestic assets. If foreigners cannot hold claims on the nation, they will export an amount equal in value only to what they are willing to import, ending net capital inflows. The microeconomic adjustment mechanism that will balance imports and exports under this policy is as follows.

The cessation of foreign capital inflows, by reducing the available supply of capital, will raise real domestic interest rates. Higher interest rates will stimulate more savings because the opportunity cost of consumption rises with the real interest rate; higher rates will also cause domestic investment to fall because fewer projects will have positive net present values. The outcome will be a balance between savings/investment and elimination of the excess domestic spending that caused the current-account deficit in the first place. Although such an approach would work, most observers would consider the resulting slower economic growth too high a price to pay to eliminate a current-account deficit.

Many observers are troubled by the role of foreign investors in U.S. financial markets, but as long as Americans continue to spend more than they produce, there will be a continuing need for foreign capital. This foreign capital is helping to improve America's industrial base, while at the same time providing capital gains to those Americans who are selling their assets to foreigners. Foreign investors often introduce improved management, better production skills, or new technology that increases the quality and variety of goods available to U.S. consumers, who benefit from lower prices as well. Investment, even foreign investment, also makes labor more productive. And higher labor productivity leads to higher wages, whether the factory's owners live across town or across the Pacific. A recent study indicates that FDI is an especially powerful engine for stimulating the productivity of domestic industries.[3] The study demonstrates that domestic workers could achieve productivity levels on a par with leading foreign workers, and foreign investment spreads good practices as employees move from the foreign firm to local ones. For example, Japanese auto transplants have provided a closeup learning lab for U.S. automakers to grasp concepts such as lean production and just-in-time component

---

[3] "Manufacturing Productivity," McKinsey Global Institute, October 1993.

delivery. Restrictions on foreign investment will eliminate such productivity gains and may also provoke reciprocal restrictions by foreign governments.

5.3.4 Boosting the Savings Rate

We have seen that a low savings rate tends to lead to a current-account deficit. Thus, another way to reduce the current-account deficit would be to stimulate savings behavior. The data, however, indicate that the rate of U.S. private savings has declined over time, turning negative in 2000. Future U.S. wealth will be impaired if the low U.S. personal savings rate persists.

One possible explanation for the decline in personal savings is that Social Security benefits expanded greatly during the 1970s. By attenuating the link between savings behavior and retirement income, Social Security may have reduced the incentive for Americans to save for retirement. By contrast, Japan with only a rudimentary social security system and no welfare to speak of has an extraordinarily high personal savings rate. Presumably, the inability of the Japanese to throw themselves on the mercy of the state has affected their willingness to save for a rainy day. As people become aware that the Social Security system cannot pay its promised benefits, the odds are that U.S. savings will increase. Savings can also be boosted by creating further tax-favored saving vehicles or switching from an income tax to a consumption tax. At the same time, reducing the federal budget deficit would be a step in the right direction as well. Similarly, changes in tax regulations and tax rates may greatly affect savings and investment behavior and, therefore, the nation's trade and capital flows. Thus, purely domestic policies may have dramatic, and unanticipated, consequences for a nation's international economic transactions. The lesson is clear: In an integrated world economy, everything connects to everything else; politicians cannot tinker with one parameter without affecting the entire system.

MINI-CASE *Warren Buffett Offers a Solution to America's Trade Deficits*

In October 2003, Warren Buffett, the "Sage of Omaha" and one of the shrewdest investors of all time, announced that over the past year his company, Berkshire Hathaway, had made significant investments in other currencies.[4] He said that he made these investments in the belief that the large and growing U.S. trade deficit would result in a steep decline in the value of the U.S. dollar.

At the same time, Mr. Buffett offered a solution to America's trade deficit. He proposed issuing what he called Import Certificates (ICs) to all U.S. exporters in an amount equal to their exports. Each exporter would, in turn, sell the ICs to domestic importers or (foreign exporters) seeking to get goods into the U.S. market. For example, to import goods worth $1 million, an importer would need to buy ICs that were the byproduct of $1 million of U.S. exports. The inevitable result would be trade balance.

Competition among importers would determine the price of the ICs. The market for ICs would be huge and liquid, insofar as the U.S. exports about $80 billion in goods each month. Mr. Buffett acknowledged that his remedy was a tariff called by another name but insisted that it retained most free-market virtues, neither protecting specific industries nor punishing specific countries. He also explained that the U.S. government could introduce a transition period by auctioning a declining amount of "bonus" ICs every month for a period of several years.

---

[4] Warren E. Buffett, "America's Growing Trade Deficit Is Selling the Nation Out From Under Us. Here's a Way to Fix the Problem—And We Need to Do It Now," *Fortune*, October 26, 2003, www.Fortune.com.

QUESTIONS

1. In what way is Warren Buffett's plan the equivalent of a tariff? What will be its likely impact on American consumers?
2. What will be the likely effect of Mr. Buffett's plan on U.S. exports?
3. How would Mr. Buffett's plan likely affect savings, investment, and interest rates in the United States? The value of the U.S. dollar?
4. How would the "bonus" ICs affect the U.S. trade deficit?
5. Mr. Buffett's plan focuses on the U.S. trade deficit. What would be its likely impact on the U.S. current-account deficit?
6. What are some possible costs of Mr. Buffett's plan?

5.3.5 External Policies

As explained earlier, some key reasons for the large U.S. current-account deficit are likely to be external to the United States, implying that purely domestic policy changes are unlikely to resolve this issue. Dr. Bernanke explains what some of these policy changes might be:[5] *[A] more direct approach is to help and encourage developing countries to re-enter international capital markets in their more natural role as borrowers, rather than as lenders. For example, developing countries could improve their investment climates by continuing to increase macroeconomic stability, strengthen property rights, reduce corruption, and remove barriers to the free flow of financial capital. Providing assistance to developing countries in strengthening their financial institutions–for example, by improving bank regulation and supervision and by increasing financial transparency—could lessen the risk of financial crises and thus increase both the willingness of those countries to accept capital inflows and the willingness of foreigners to invest there. Financial liberalization is a particularly attractive option, as it would help both to permit capital inflows to find the highest-return uses and, by easing borrowing constraints, to spur domestic consumption. Other changes will occur naturally over time. For example, the pace at which emerging-market countries are accumulating international reserves should slow as they increasingly perceive their reserves to be adequate and as they move toward more flexible exchange rates.*

5.3.6 Current-Account Deficits and Unemployment

One rationale for attempting to eliminate a current-account deficit is that such a deficit leads to unemployment. Underlying this rationale is the notion that imported goods and services are substituting for domestic goods and services and costing domestic jobs. For example, some have argued that every million-dollar increase in the U.S. trade deficit costs about 33 American jobs, assuming that the average worker earns about $30,000 a year ($1,000,000/$30,000 = 33). Hence, it is claimed, reducing imports would raise domestic production and employment. However, the view that reducing a current-account deficit promotes jobs is based on single-entry bookkeeping.

If a country buys fewer foreign goods and services, it will demand less foreign exchange. As discussed earlier, this result will raise the value of the domestic currency, thereby reducing exports and encouraging the purchase of other imports. Jobs are saved

---

[5] See Bernanke, "The Global Saving Glut and the U.S. Current Account Deficit," op cit.

in some industries, but other jobs are lost by the decline in exports and rise in other imports. Following this line of reasoning, the net impact of a trade deficit or surplus on jobs should be nil.

According to the apocalyptic claims of some politicians, however, the recent economic performance of the United States should have been dismal because of its huge current-account deficits. However, if the alternative story that a current-account deficit reflects excess spending and has little to do with the health of an economy is correct, then there should be no necessary relation between economic performance and the current-account balance.

The appropriate way to settle this dispute is to examine the evidence. Research that examined the economic performance of the 23 OECD (Organization for Economic Cooperation and Development) countries during a 38-year period found no systematic relationship between trade deficits and unemployment rates.[6] This result is not surprising for those who have looked at the U.S. economic performance over the past 20 years or so. During this period, the trade deficit soared, but the United States created jobs three times as fast as Japan and 20 times as fast as Germany. Also, in the same time period, America's GDP grew 43% faster than that of Japan or Germany, even though both nations had huge trade surpluses with the United States.

In general, no systematic relationship between net exports and economic growth should be expected—and none is to be found.[7] The evidence shows that current-account surpluses—in and of themselves—are neither good nor bad. They are not correlated with jobs, growth, decline, competitiveness, or weakness. What matters is why they occur.

5.3.7 The Bottom Line on Current-Account Deficits and Surpluses

To summarize the previous discussion of current-account deficits and surpluses, consider the following stylized facts. Suppose the United States is a country whose citizens, for one reason or another, have a low propensity to save. And suppose also that for a variety of reasons, the United States is an attractive place to invest. Finally, suppose that in the rest of the world, people have high propensities to save but their opportunities for investment are less attractive. In these circumstances, there will be a flow of capital from the rest of the world and a corresponding net inflow of goods and services to the United States. The United States would have a current-account deficit.

In the above situation, the current-account deficit would not be viewed as a problem. Rather, it would be regarded as an efficient adaptation to different savings propensities and investment opportunities in the United States and the rest of the world. From this perspective, a current-account deficit becomes a solution, not a problem. This was the situation confronting the United States early in its history, when it ran almost continual trade deficits for its first 100 years. Nobody viewed that as a problem back then, and it still is not one.

The real problem, if there is one, is either too much consumption and thus too little savings or too much investment. Regardless of what one's opinions are, the situation confronting the United States and the rest of the world is an expression of national preferences, to which trade flows have adjusted in a timely manner. An economist has no further wisdom to shed on this matter.

What are the long-term consequences for the United States or for any other nation that runs a current-account deficit? Here an economist can speak with some authority. As

---

[6] See David M. Gould, Roy J. Ruffin, and Graeme L. Woodbridge, "The Theory and Practice of Free Trade," Federal Reserve Bank of Dallas *Economic Review*, Fourth Quarter, 1993, pp. 1–16.

[7] See, for example, David M. Gould and Roy J. Ruffin, "Trade Deficits: Causes and Consequences," Federal Reserve Bank of Dallas *Economic Review*, Fourth Quarter, 1996, pp. 10–20. After analyzing a group of 101 countries over a 30-year period, they conclude (p. 17) that "trade imbalances have little effect on rates of economic growth once we account for the fundamental determinants of economic growth."

we saw in Section 5.2, the cumulative effect of current-account deficits is to reduce that nation's net international wealth.

The consequences of a reduction in a nation's net international wealth depend on the nature of the foreign capital inflows that cause the erosion. If the capital inflows finance productive domestic investments, then the nation is better off; the returns from these added investments will service the foreign debts with income left over to increase living standards. Conversely, capital inflows that finance current consumption will increase the nation's well-being today at the expense of its future well-being, when the loans must be repaid. That trade-off, however, has little to do with the balance of payments per se.

In the case of the United States, a good portion of the inflows seems to have been of the productive variety. But a growing share of capital inflows, particularly since the late 1990s, appear to be financing consumption and government borrowing. If they are, the erosion of net U.S. international wealth will inflict new burdens on the U.S. economy in the future.

5.4 SUMMARY AND CONCLUSIONS

The balance of payments is an accounting statement of the international transactions of one nation over a specific period. The statement shows the sum of economic transactions of individuals, businesses, and government agencies located in one nation with those located in the rest of the world during the period. Thus, the U.S. balance of payments for a given year is an accounting of all transactions between U.S. residents and residents of all other countries during that year.

The statement is based on double-entry bookkeeping; every economic transaction recorded as a credit brings about an equal and offsetting debit entry, and vice versa. A debit entry shows a purchase of foreign goods, services, or assets, or a decline in liabilities to foreigners. A credit entry shows a sale of domestic goods, services, or assets, or an increase in liabilities to foreigners. For example, if a foreign company sells a car to a U.S. resident, a debit is recorded to indicate an increase in purchases made by the United States (the car); a credit is recorded to reflect an increase in liabilities to the foreigner (payment for the car).

The balance of payments is often divided into several components. Each shows a particular kind of transaction, such as merchandise exports or foreign purchases of U.S. government securities. Transactions representing purchases and sales of goods and services in the current period are called the current account; those representing capital transactions are called the financial account. Changes in official reserves appear on the official reserves account.

Double-entry bookkeeping ensures that debits equal credits; therefore, the sum of all transactions is zero. In the absence of official reserve transactions, a financial-account surplus must offset the current-account deficit, and a financial-account deficit must offset a current-account surplus.

The United States is currently running a large current-account deficit. Much public discussion about why the United States imports more than it exports has focused on claims of unfair trading practices or on the high value of the dollar. However, economic theory indicates that the total size of the current-account deficit is a macroeconomic phenomenon; there is a basic accounting identity that a nation's current-account deficit reflects excess domestic spending. Equivalently, a current-account deficit equals the excess of domestic investment over domestic savings. Explicitly taking government into account yields a new relation: The domestic spending balance equals the private savings-investment balance minus the government budget deficit. As private savings and investment have historically been in balance for the United States, the trade deficit until recently could be traced to the federal budget deficit. With the federal budget now in balance, the culprit today appears to be a low U.S. savings rate.

We saw that failure to consider the elementary economic accounting identities can mislead policymakers into relying on dollar depreciation, trade restrictions, or trade subsidies in order to reduce U.S. trade deficits without doing anything about excess domestic spending. The current-account deficit can be reduced only if domestic savings rise, private investment declines, or the government deficit is reduced. Absent any of those changes, the current-account deficit will not diminish, regardless of the imposition of trade barriers or the amount of dollar depreciation.

QUESTIONS

1. In a freely floating exchange-rate system, if the current account is running a deficit, what are the consequences for the nation's balance on financial account and its overall balance of payments?

2. a. As the value of the U.S. dollar rises, what is likely to happen to the U.S. balance on current account? Explain.

   b. What is likely to happen to the value of the dollar as the U.S. current-account deficit increases? Explain.

   c. A current-account surplus is not always a sign of health; a current-account deficit is not always a sign of weakness. Comment.

3. Suppose Lufthansa buys $400 million worth of Boeing jets in 2008 and is financed by the U.S. Eximbank with a 5-year loan that has no principal or interest payments due until 2009. What is the net impact of this sale on the U.S. current account, financial account, and overall balance of payments for 2008?

4. What happens to Mexico's ability to repay its foreign loans if the United States restricts imports of Mexican agricultural produce?

5. Suppose Brazil starts welcoming foreign investment with open arms. How is this policy likely to affect the value of the Brazilian *real*? The Brazilian current-account balance?

6. According to popular opinion, U.S. trade deficits indicate any or all of the following: a lack of U.S. competitiveness owing to low productivity or low-quality products and/or lower wages, superior technology,

and unfair trade practices by foreign countries. Which of those factors is likely to underlie the persistent U.S. trade deficits? Explain.

7. During the 1990s, Mexico and Argentina went from economic pariahs with huge foreign debts to countries posting strong economic growth and welcoming foreign investment. What would you expect these changes to do to their current-account balances?

8. Suppose the trade imbalances of the 2000s largely disappear during the next decade. What is likely to happen to the huge global capital flows of the 2000s? What is the link between the trade imbalances and the global movement of capital?

9. In the early 1990s, Japan underwent a recession that brought about a prolonged slump in consumer spending and capital investment. (Some estimates were that in 1994 only 65% of Japan's manufacturing capacity was being used.) At the same time, the U.S. economy emerged from its recession and began expanding rapidly. Under these circumstances, what would you predict would happen to the U.S. trade deficit with Japan?

10. It has been argued that with freer markets, Third World nations now are able to attract capital and technology from the advanced nations. As a result, they can achieve productivity close to western levels while paying low wages. Hence, the low-wage Third World nations will run huge trade surpluses, creating either large-scale unemployment or sharply falling wages in the advanced nations. Comment on this apocalyptic scenario.

PROBLEMS

1. How would each of the following transactions show up on the U.S. balance-of-payments accounts?

   a. Payment of $50 million in Social Security to U.S. citizens living in Costa Rica,

   b. Sale overseas of 125,000 Elvis Presley CDs,

   c. Tuition receipts of $3 billion received by American universities from foreign students,

   d. Payment of $1 million to U.S. consultants A.D. Little by a Mexican company,

   e. Sale of a $100 million Eurobond issue in London by IBM,

f. Investment of $25 million by Ford to build a parts plant in Argentina: and

g. Payment of $45 million in dividends to U.S. citizens from foreign companies.

2. Set up the double-entry accounts showing the appropriate debits and credits associated with the following transactions:

a. ConAgra, a U.S. agribusiness, exports $80 million of soybeans to China and receives payment in the form of a check drawn on a U.S. bank.

b. The U.S. government provides refugee assistance to Somalia in the form of corn valued at $1 million.

c. Dow Chemical invests $500 million in a chemical plant in Germany financed by issuing bonds in London.

d. General Motors pays $5 million in dividends to foreign residents, who choose to hold the dividends in the form of bank deposits in New York.

e. The Bank of Japan buys up $1 billion in the foreign exchange market to hold down the value of the yen and uses these dollars to buy U.S. Treasury bonds.

f. Cemex, a Mexican company, sells $2 million worth of cement to a Texas company and deposits the check in a bank in Dallas.

g. Colombian drug dealers receive $10 million in cash for the cocaine they ship to the U.S. market. The money is smuggled out of the United States and then invested in U.S. corporate bonds on behalf of a Cayman Islands bank.

3. During the year, Japan had a current-account surplus of $98 billion and a financial-account deficit, aside from the change in its foreign-exchange reserves, of $67 billion.

a. Assuming the preceding data are measured with precision, what can you conclude about the change in Japan's foreign exchange reserves during the year?

b. What is the gap between Japan's national expenditure and its national income?

c. What is the gap between Japan's savings and its domestic investment?

d. What was Japan's net foreign investment for the year?

e. Suppose the Japanese government's budget ran a $22 billion surplus during the year. What can you conclude about Japan's private savings-investment balance for the year?

4. The following transactions (expressed in U.S. $ billions) take place during a year. Calculate the U.S. merchandise-trade, current-account, financial-account, and official reserves balances.

a. The United States exports $300 of goods and receives payment in the form of foreign demand deposits abroad.

b. The United States imports $225 of goods and pays for them by drawing down its foreign demand deposits.

c. The United States pays $15 to foreigners in dividends drawn on U.S. demand deposits here.

d. American tourists spend $30 overseas using traveler's checks drawn on U.S. banks here.

e. Americans buy foreign stocks with $60, using foreign demand deposits held abroad.

f. The U.S. government sells $45 in gold for foreign demand deposits abroad.

g. In a currency support operation, the U.S. government uses its foreign demand deposits to purchase $8 from private foreigners in the United States.

5. During the Reagan era, 1981–1988, the U.S. current account moved from a tiny surplus to a large deficit. The following table provides U.S. macroeconomic data for that period.

a. Based on these data, to what extent would you attribute the changes in the U.S. current-account balance to a decline in the U.S. private savings-investment balance?

b. To what extent would you attribute the changes in the U.S. current-account balance to an increase in the U.S. government budget deficit?

c. Based on these data, what was the excess of national spending over national income during this period?

YEAR	1980	1981	1982	1983	1984	1985	1986	1987	1988
Private Savings	500	586	617	641	743	736	721	731	802
Private Investment	468	558	503	547	719	715	718	749	794
Government Budget Deficit	−35	−30	−109	−140	−109	−125	−147	−112	−98
Current-Account Balance	2	5	−11	−45	−100	−125	−151	−167	−129

INTERNET RESOURCES

www.bea.doc.gov Web site of the Bureau of Economic Analysis (BEA). Contains data and articles on U.S. international trade and capital flows.

http://www.oecd.org/ Website of the Organization for Economic Co-operation and Development. Contains news, analyses, and data on international finance and economics including interest rates and foreign exchange rates.

https://www.cia.gov/library/publications/the-world-factbook/index.html Website of CIA: The World Factbook. Contains demographic, social, political, and economic data for every country.

INTERNET EXERCISES

1. Which countries are the major customers for U.S. exports of goods and services? Which countries are the major exporters of goods and services to the United States?

2. Examine the U.S. balance of payments over the past year.

   a. What is the current-account balance, the financial-account balance, the capital-account balance, and the official reserves balance?

   b. How have these balances changed from the previous year? What economic factors might account for these changes?

3. Based on historical data from the BEA, what is the relationship between U.S. trade balances and U.S. economic growth?

4. What is the historical relationship between U.S. trade balances and the value of the U.S. dollar?

5. Select a country and analyze that country's balance of payments for 8 to 12 years, subject to availability of data. You can find such data by using the Google search engine (at www.google.com) and typing in the country name and "Balance of Payments data." For example, the site for Japanese balance of payments data is http://www.mof.go.jp/bpoffice/e1c004.htm and Canadian data can be found at http://www40.statcan.ca/l01/cst01/econ01a.htm. The analysis must include examinations (presentation of statistical data with discussion) of the trade balance, current-account balance, financial-account balance, basic balance, and overall balance. Your report should also address the following issues:

   a. What accounts for swings in these various balances over time?

   b. What is the relationship between shifts in the current-account balance and changes in savings and investment? Include an examination of government budget deficits and surpluses, explaining how they are related to the savings and investment and current-account balances.[8]

6. For the country selected in exercise 5, analyze the exchange rate against the dollar during the same period.

   a. Is there any observable relationship between the balance-of-payments accounts and the exchange rate?

   b. Provide a possible explanation for your observations in Part a above.

---

[8] Project suggested by Donald T. Buck.

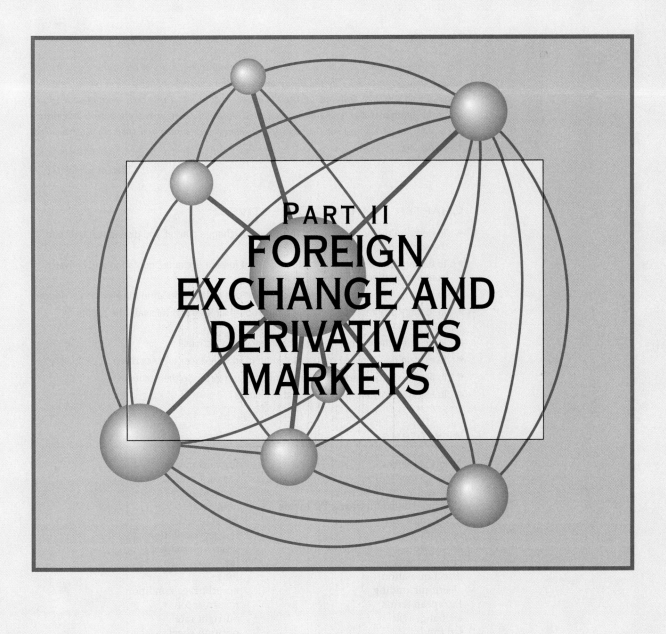

PART II
FOREIGN EXCHANGE AND DERIVATIVES MARKETS

THE FOREIGN EXCHANGE MARKET

The Spaniards coming into the West Indies had many commodities of the country which they needed, brought unto them by the inhabitants, to who when they offered them money, goodly pieces of gold coin, the Indians, taking the money, would put it into their mouths, and spit it out to the Spaniards again, signifying that they could not eat it, or make use of it, and therefore would not part with their commodities for money, unless they had such other commodities as would serve their use.

Edward Leigh (1671)

CHAPTER LEARNING OBJECTIVES

- To describe the organization of the foreign exchange market and distinguish between the spot and forward markets
- To distinguish between different methods of foreign exchange quotation and convert from one method of quotation to another
- To read and explain foreign currency quotations as they appear in the *Wall Street Journal*
- To identify profitable currency arbitrage opportunities and calculate the profits associated with these arbitrage opportunities
- To describe the mechanics of spot currency transactions
- To explain how forward contracts can be used to reduce currency risk
- To list the major users of forward contracts and describe their motives
- To calculate forward premiums and discounts

KEY TERMS

American terms	forward market
arbitrageurs	forward premium
bid—ask spread	forward price
Clearing House Interbank Payments System (CHIPS)	hedgers
	Herstatt risk
contract note	indirect quotation
cross rate	interbank market
currency arbitrage	liquidity
direct quotation	long
electronic trading	no-arbitrage condition
European terms	nostro account
exchange risk	outright rate
fed funds	position sheet
FedWire	settlement risk
foreign exchange brokers	short
foreign exchange market	Society for Worldwide Interbank
foreign exchange quotes	Financial Telecommunications
forward contract	(SWIFT)
forward discount	speculators

spot market
spot price
swap
swap rate

traders
triangular currency arbitrage
value date

The volume of international transactions has grown enormously over the past 50 years. Exports of goods and services by the United States now total more than 10% of gross domestic product. For both Canada and Great Britain, this figure exceeds 25%. Imports are about the same size. Similarly, annual capital flows involving hundreds of billions of dollars occur between the United States and other nations. International trade and investment of this magnitude would not be possible without the ability to buy and sell foreign currencies. Currencies must be bought and sold because the U.S. dollar is not the acceptable means of payment in most other countries. Investors, tourists, exporters, and importers must exchange dollars for foreign currencies, and vice versa.

The trading of currencies takes place in foreign exchange markets whose primary function is to facilitate international trade and investment. Knowledge of the operation and mechanics of these markets, therefore, is important for any fundamental understanding of international financial management. This chapter provides this information; it discusses the organization of the most important foreign exchange market—the interbank market—including the spot market in which currencies are traded for immediate delivery, and the forward market in which currencies are traded for future delivery; as well as examines the currency futures and options markets.

6.1 ORGANIZATION OF THE FOREIGN EXCHANGE MARKET

If there were a single international currency, there would be no need for a foreign exchange market. As it is, in any international transaction, at least one party is dealing in a foreign currency. The purpose of the **foreign exchange market** is to permit transfers of purchasing power denominated in one currency to another—that is, to trade one currency for another currency. For example, a Japanese exporter sells automobiles to a U.S. dealer for dollars, and a U.S. manufacturer sells machine tools to a Japanese company for yen. Ultimately, however, the U.S. company will likely be interested in receiving dollars, whereas the Japanese exporter will want yen. Similarly, an American investor in Swiss-franc-denominated bonds must convert dollars into francs, and Swiss purchasers of U.S. Treasury bills require dollars to complete these transactions. It would be inconvenient, to say the least, for individual buyers and sellers of foreign exchange to seek out one another, so a foreign exchange market has developed to act as an intermediary.

Most currency transactions are channeled through the worldwide **interbank market**, the wholesale market in which major banks trade with one another. This market, which accounts for about 95% of foreign exchange transactions, is normally referred to as *the* foreign exchange market. It is dominated by about 20 major banks. In the **spot market**, currencies are traded for immediate delivery, which is actually within two business days after the transaction has been concluded. In the **forward market**, contracts are made to buy or sell currencies for future delivery. Spot transactions account for about 35% of the market, with forward transactions accounting for another 12%. The remaining 53% of the market consists of **swap** transactions, which involve a package of a spot and a forward contract.[1]

The foreign exchange market is not a physical place; rather, it is an electronically linked network of banks, foreign exchange brokers, and dealers whose function is to

---

[1] These volume estimates appear in "Triennial Central Bank Survey of Foreign Exchange and Derivatives Market Activity 2004—Final Results," Bank for International Settlements, March 2005, p. 5. About 6% of transactions show up as "gaps in reporting." These missing transactions are just allocated proportionately to the spot, forward, and swap transactions.

bring together buyers and sellers of foreign exchange. The foreign exchange market is not confined to any one country but is dispersed throughout the leading financial centers of the world: London, New York, Paris, Zurich, Amsterdam, Tokyo, Hong Kong, Toronto, Frankfurt, Milan, and other cities.

Trading has historically been done by telephone, telex, or the SWIFT system. **SWIFT (Society for Worldwide Interbank Financial Telecommunications)**, an international bank-communications network, electronically links all brokers and traders. The SWIFT network connects more than 7,000 banks and broker-dealers in 192 countries and processes more than five million transactions a day, representing about $5 trillion in payments. Its mission is to quickly transmit standard forms to allow its member banks to automatically process data by computer. All types of customer and bank transfers are transmitted, as well as foreign exchange deals, bank account statements, and administrative messages. To use SWIFT, the corporate client must deal with domestic banks that are subscribers and with foreign banks that are highly automated. Like many other proprietary data networks, SWIFT is facing growing competition from Internet-based systems that allow both banks and nonfinancial companies to connect to a secure payments network.

Foreign exchange traders in each bank usually operate out of a separate foreign exchange trading room. Each trader has several telephones and is surrounded by terminals displaying up-to-the-minute information. It is a hectic existence, and many traders burn out by age 35. Most transactions are based on verbal communications; written confirmation occurs later. Hence, an informal code of moral conduct has evolved over time in which the foreign exchange dealers' word is their bond. Today, however, much of the telephone-based trading has been replaced by electronic brokering.

Although one might think that most foreign exchange trading is derived from export and import activities, this is not the case. In fact, trade in goods and services accounts for less than 5% of foreign exchange trading. More than 95% of foreign exchange trading relates to cross-border purchases and sales of assets, that is, to international capital flows.

Currency trading takes place 24 hours a day, but the volume varies depending on the number of potential counterparties available. Exhibit 6.1 indicates how participation levels in the global foreign exchange market vary by tracking electronic trading conversations per hour.

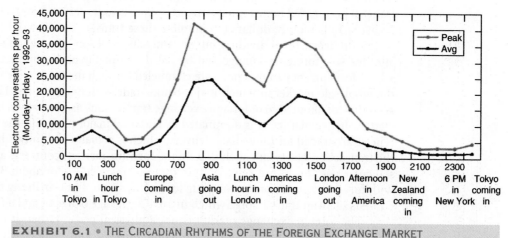

EXHIBIT 6.1 • THE CIRCADIAN RHYTHMS OF THE FOREIGN EXCHANGE MARKET

Note: Time (0100–2400) hours, Greenwich Mean Time.

Source: Reuters chart appears in Sam Y Cross, *"All About . . . the Foreign Exchange Market in the United States,"* Federal Reserve Bank of New York. *www.ny.frb.org/pihome/addpub.*

EXHIBIT 6.2 • LEADING FOREIGN EXCHANGE TRADERS IN 2007

Source: EuroMoney Magazine. FX poll 2007: Winners and Losers in 2007.

6.1.1 The Participants

The major participants in the foreign exchange market are the large commercial banks; foreign exchange brokers in the interbank market; commercial customers, primarily multinational corporations; and central banks, which intervene in the market from time to time to smooth exchange rate fluctuations or to maintain target exchange rates. Central bank intervention involving buying or selling in the market is often indistinguishable from the foreign exchange dealings of commercial banks or of other private participants.

Only the head or regional offices of the major commercial and investment banks are actually market makers—that is, they actively deal in foreign exchange for their own accounts. These banks stand ready to buy or sell any of the major currencies on a more or less continuous basis. Exhibit 6.2 lists some of the major financial institutions that are market makers and their estimated market shares.

A large fraction of the interbank transactions in the United States is conducted through **foreign exchange brokers**, specialists in matching net supplier and demander banks. These brokers receive a small commission on all trades (traditionally, 1/32 of 1% in the U.S. market, which translates into $312.50 on a $1 million trade). Some brokers tend to specialize in certain currencies, but they all handle major currencies such as the pound sterling, Canadian dollar, euro, Swiss franc, and yen. Brokers supply information (at which rates various banks will buy or sell a currency); they provide anonymity to the participants until a rate is agreed to (because knowing the identity of the other party may give dealers an insight into whether that party needs or has a surplus of a particular currency); and they help banks minimize their contacts with other traders (one call to a broker may substitute for half a dozen calls to traders at other banks). As in the stock market, the role of human brokers has declined as electronic brokers have significantly increased their share of the foreign exchange business.

Commercial and central bank customers buy and sell foreign exchange through their banks. However, most small banks and local offices of major banks do not deal directly in the interbank market. Rather, they typically will have a credit line with a large bank or with their home office. Thus, transactions with local banks will involve an extra step. The customer deals with a local bank that in turn deals with its head office or a major bank. The various linkages between banks and their customers are

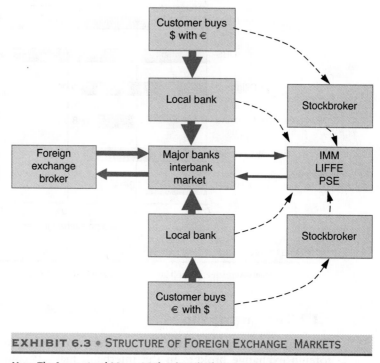

EXHIBIT 6.3 ● STRUCTURE OF FOREIGN EXCHANGE MARKETS

Note: The International Money Market (IMM) Chicago trades foreign exchange futures and euro futures options. The London International Financial Futures Exchange (LIFFE) trades foreign exchange futures. The Philadelphia Stock Exchange (PSE) trades foreign currency options.

Source: Federal Reserve Bank of St. Louis, *Review,* March 1984, p. 9, revised.

depicted in Exhibit 6.3. Note that the diagram includes linkages with currency futures and options markets, which we will examine in the next chapter.

The major participants in the forward market can be categorized as arbitrageurs, traders, hedgers, and speculators. **Arbitrageurs** seek to risk-free profits by taking advantage of differences in interest rates among countries. They use forward contracts to eliminate the exchange risk involved in transferring their funds from one nation to another.

Traders use forward contracts to eliminate or cover the risk of loss on export or import orders that are denominated in foreign currencies. More generally, a forward-covering transaction is related to a specific payment or receipt expected at a specified point in time.

Hedgers, mostly multinational firms, engage in forward contracts to protect the home currency value of various foreign currency-denominated assets and liabilities on their balance sheets that are not to be realized over the life of the contracts.

Arbitrageurs, traders, and hedgers seek to reduce (or eliminate, if possible) their exchange risks by "locking in" the exchange rate on future trade or financial operations.

In contrast to these three types of forward market participants, **speculators** actively expose themselves to currency risk by buying or selling currencies forward in order to profit from exchange rate fluctuations. Their degree of participation does not depend on their business transactions in other currencies; instead, it is based on prevailing forward rates and their expectations for spot exchange rates in the future.

The Clearing System Technology has standardized and sped up the international transfers of funds, which is at the heart of clearing, or settling, foreign exchange transactions. In the United States, where all foreign exchange transactions involving dollars are cleared, electronic funds transfers take place through the **Clearing House Interbank Payments System (CHIPS)**. A computerized network developed by the New York Clearing House Association for transfer of international dollar payments, CHIPS links about 150 depository institutions that have offices or affiliates in New York City. Currently, CHIPS handles about 105,000 interbank transfers daily valued at $350 billion. The transfers represent about 90% of all interbank transfers relating to international dollar payments.

The New York Fed (Federal Reserve Bank) has established a settlement account for member banks into which debit settlement payments are sent and from which credit settlement payments are disbursed. Transfers between member banks are netted out and settled at the close of each business day by sending or receiving **FedWire** transfers of **fed funds** through the settlement account. Fed funds are deposits held by member banks at Federal Reserve branches.

The FedWire system is operated by the Federal Reserve and is used for domestic money transfers. The system allows almost instant movement of balances between institutions that have accounts at the Federal Reserve Banks. A transfer takes place when an order to pay is transmitted from an originating office to a Federal Reserve Bank. The account of the paying bank is charged, and the receiving bank's account is credited with fed funds.

To illustrate the workings of CHIPS, suppose Fuji Bank has sold U.S.$15 million to Citibank in return for ¥1.5 billion to be paid in Tokyo. In order to complete its end of the transaction, Fuji Bank must transfer $15 million to Citibank. To do this, Fuji Bank enters the transaction into its CHIPS terminal, providing the identifying codes for the sending and receiving banks. The message—the equivalent of an electronic check—is then stored in the CHIPS central computer.

As soon as Fuji Bank approves and releases the "stored" transaction, the message is transmitted from the CHIPS computer to Citibank. The CHIPS computer also makes a permanent record of the transaction and makes appropriate debits and credits in the CHIPS accounts of Fuji Bank and Citibank, as both banks are members of CHIPS. Immediately after the closing of the CHIPS network at 4:30 P.M. (eastern time), the CHIPS computer produces a settlement report showing the net debit or credit position of each member bank.

Member banks with debit positions have until 5:45 P.M. (eastern time) to transfer their debit amounts through FedWire to the CHIPS settlement account on the books of the New York Fed. The Clearing House then transfers those fed funds via FedWire out of the settlement account to those member banks with net creditor positions. The process usually is completed by 6:00 P.M. (eastern time).

Electronic Trading   A major structural change in the foreign exchange market occurred in April 1992 when Reuters, the news company that supplies the foreign exchange market with the screen quotations used in telephone trading, introduced a new service that added automatic execution to the process, thereby creating a genuine screen-based market. Other quote vendors, such as EBS, Telerate, and Quotron, introduced their own automatic systems. These **electronic trading** systems offer automated matching. Traders enter buy and sell orders directly into their terminals on an anonymous basis, and these prices are visible to all market participants. Another trader, anywhere in the world, can execute a trade by simply hitting two buttons.

The introduction of automated trading has reduced the cost of trading, partly by eliminating foreign exchange brokers and partly by reducing the number of transactions traders had to engage in to obtain information on market prices. The new systems replicate the order matching and the anonymity that brokers offer, and do it more cheaply. For example, small banks can now deal directly with each other instead of having to channel trades through larger ones. At the same time, automated systems threaten the oligopoly of information that has underpinned the profits of those who now do most foreign exchange business. These new systems gather and publish information on the prices and quantities of currencies as they are actually traded, thereby revealing details of currency trades that until now the traders have profitably kept to themselves. Such comparisons are facilitated by new Internet-based foreign exchange systems designed to help users reduce costs by allowing them to compare rates offered by a range of banks. The largest such system, FXall, teams some of the biggest participants in the foreign exchange market—including J.P. Morgan Chase, Citigroup, Goldman Sachs, CSFB, UBS Warburg, Morgan Stanley, and Bank of America—to offer a range of foreign exchange services over the Internet.

The key to the widespread use of computerized foreign-currency trading systems is **liquidity**, as measured by the difference between the rates at which dealers can buy and sell currencies. Liquidity, in turn, requires reaching a critical mass of users. If enough dealers are putting their prices into the system, then users have greater assurance that the system will provide them with the best prices available. That critical mass has been achieved. By 2000, 85 to 95% of interbank trading in the major currencies was conducted using electronic brokers.[2]

6.1.2 Size

The foreign exchange market is by far the largest financial market in the world. A survey of the world's central banks by the Bank for International Settlements (BIS) placed the average foreign exchange trading volume in 2004 at $1.9 trillion daily, or $475 trillion a year.[3] This figure compares with an average daily trading volume of about $7 billion on the New York Stock Exchange. Indeed, the New York Stock Exchange's biggest day, Black Monday (October 19, 1987), was only $21 billion, or 1.1% of the daily foreign exchange volume. As another benchmark, the U.S. gross domestic product (GDP) was under $12 trillion in 2004. However, after peaking in 1998, foreign currency trading volumes fell, largely because the replacement of 12 European currencies with the euro, combined with the rise of electronic trading, greatly reduced the number of currency transactions. This trend reversed itself after 2001 for a variety of reasons, including investors' growing interest in foreign exchange as an asset class alternative to equity and fixed income, the more active role of asset managers, and the growing importance of hedge funds.

According to data from the 2004 triennial survey by the BIS, London is by far the world's largest currency trading market, with daily turnover in 2004 estimated at $753 billion, more than that of the next two markets—New York, at $461 billion, and Tokyo, at $199 billion—combined.[4] It is expected that the next central bank survey in 2007 would show that the daily volume of trading was about $3 trillion.[5] Exhibit 6.4a shows that the eight biggest financial centers have seen trading volume rise by an average of 57% since the last BIS survey was conducted in 2001, a sharp turnaround from the average decrease of 20% between 1998 and 2001. Despite its decline between 1998 and 2001, foreign exchange trading has historically outpaced the growth of international trade and the world's output of goods and services. The explosive growth in currency trading since 1973—daily volume was estimated at $10 billion in 1973 (see Exhibit 6.4b)—has been attributed to the growing integration of the world's economies and financial markets, as well as a growing desire among companies and financial institutions to manage their

---

[2] See Bank for International Settlements, *71st Annual Report*, p. 99.

[3] Survey results appear in "Triennial Central Bank Survey of Foreign Exchange and Derivatives Market Activity 2004–Final Results," Bank for International Settlements, March 2005, p. 1.

[4] "Triennial Central Bank Survey: Foreign Exchange and Derivatives Market Activity in 2001," *op cit.*

[5] Gordon Platt, "Trading Up," *Global Finance*, 21 (January), 2007, p 16.

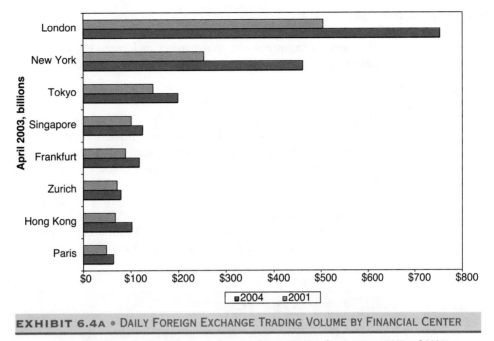

EXHIBIT 6.4A • DAILY FOREIGN EXCHANGE TRADING VOLUME BY FINANCIAL CENTER

Source: Triennial Central Bank survey: Foreign exchange and Derivatives Market Activity in 2001 and 2004.

currency risk exposure more actively. Dollar/DM trades used to be the most common, but with the replacement of the DM and 12 other currencies with the euro, dollar/euro trades have the biggest market share (28%) with dollar/yen trades at 17% and dollar/sterling trades at 14%.

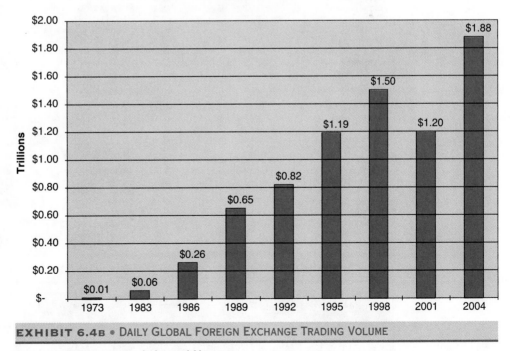

EXHIBIT 6.4B • DAILY GLOBAL FOREIGN EXCHANGE TRADING VOLUME

Note: Every 3 years, 2004 was the last available year

Source: Bank for International Settlement Surveys.

6.2 THE SPOT MARKET

This section examines the spot market in foreign exchange. It covers spot quotations, transaction costs, and the mechanics of spot transactions.

6.2.1 Spot Quotations

Almost all major newspapers print a daily list of exchange rates. For major currencies, up to four different **foreign exchange quotes** (prices) are displayed. One is the **spot price**. The others might include the 30-day, 90-day, and 180-day **forward prices**. These quotes are for trades among dealers in the interbank market. When interbank trades involve dollars (about 60% of such trades do), these rates will be expressed in either **American terms** (numbers of U.S. dollars per unit of foreign currency) or **European terms** (number of foreign currency units per U.S. dollar). In the *Wall Street Journal*, quotes in American and European terms are listed side by side (see Exhibit 6.5). For example, on May 22, 2007, the American quote for the Swiss franc was SFr 1 = $0.8132 (also expressed as $0.8132/SFr),

Currencies
May 22, 2007

U.S.-dollar foreign-exchange rates in late New York trading

Country/currency	Tues in US$	Tues per US$	US$ vs. YTD chg (%)	Country/currency	Tues in US$	Tues per US$	US$ vs. YTD chg (%)
Americas				**Europe**			
Argentina peso*	.3249	3.0779	0.6	Czech Rep. koruna**	.04767	20.978	0.7
Brazil real	.5133	1.9482	-8.8	Denmark krone	.1805	5.5402	-1.9
Canada dollar	.9207	1.0861	-6.9	Euro area euro	1.3450	.7435	-1.8
1-mos forward	.9216	1.0851	-6.9	Hungary forint	.005423	184.40	-3.2
3-mos forward	.9231	1.0833	-6.8	Malta lira	3.1331	.3192	-1.8
6-mos forward	.9250	1.0811	-6.8	Norway krone	.1654	6.0459	-3.0
Chile peso	.001902	525.76	-1.2	Poland zloty	.3554	2.8137	-3.1
Colombia peso	.0005114	1955.42	-12.7	Russia ruble‡	.03863	25.887	-1.7
Ecuador US dollar	1	1	unch	Slovak Rep koruna	.03985	25.094	-3.9
Mexico peso*	.0927	10.7898	-0.1	Sweden krona	.1463	6.8353	-0.1
Peru new sol	.3160	3.165	-1.0	Switzerland franc	.8132	1.2297	0.9
Uruguay peso†	.04190	23.87	-2.1	1-mos forward	.8154	1.2264	0.9
Venezuela bolivar	.000466	2145.92	unch	3-mos forward	.8192	1.2207	1.0
Asia-Pacific				6-mos forward	.8248	1.2124	1.0
				Turkey lira**	.7524	1.3290	-6.1
Australian dollar	.8193	1.2206	-3.6	UK pound	1.9750	.5063	-0.9
China yuan	.1306	7.6545	-2.0	1-mos forward	1.9746	.5064	-0.8
Hong Kong dollar	.1278	7.8240	0.6	3-mos forward	1.9733	.5068	-0.7
India rupee	.02485	40.241	-8.8	6-mos forward	1.9706	.5075	-0.6
Indonesia rupiah	.0001152	8681	-3.5	**Middle East/Africa**			
Japan yen	.008225	121.58	2.2				
1-mos forward	.008260	121.07	2.2	Bahrain dollar	2.6525	.3770	unch
3-mos forward*	.008324	120.13	2.2	Egypt pound*	.1757	5.6925	-0.3
6-mos forward	.008421	118.75	2.1	Israel shekel	.2520	3.9683	-5.9
Malaysia ringgit§	.2952	3.3875	-4.0	Jordan dinar	1.4112	.7086	-0.1
New Zealand dollar	.7263	1.3768	-3.0	Kuwait dinar	3.4715	.2881	-0.3
Pakistan rupee	.01647	60.717	-0.1	Lebanon pound	.0006612	1512.40	unch
Philippines peso	.0217	46.062	-6.1	Saudi Arabia riyal	.2666	3.7509	unch
Singapore dollar	.6533	1.5307	-0.2	South Africa rand	.1419	7.0472	0.8
South Korea won	.0010749	930.32	unch	UAE dirham	.2723	3.6724	unch
Taiwan dollar	.02994	33.400	2.5				
Thailand baht	.03065	32.626	-8.0	SDR††	1.5129	.6610	-0.6

*Floating rate †Financial §Government rate ‡Russian Central Bank rate **Rebased as of Jan 1, 2005 ††Special Drawing Rights (SDR) from the International Monetary Fund; based on exchange rates for U.S., British and Japanese currencies.
Note: Based on trading among banks of $1 million and more, as quoted at 4 p.m. ET by Reuters.

EXHIBIT 6.5 • FOREIGN EXCHANGE RATES WEDNESDAY, MAY 22, 2007

Source: The Wall Street Journal, May 23, 2007.

and the European quote was $1 = SFr 1.2297 (or SFr 1.2297/$). Nowadays, in trades involving dollars, all except U.K. and Irish exchange rates are expressed in European terms.

In their dealings with nonbank customers, banks in most countries use a system of **direct quotation**. A direct exchange rate quote gives the home currency price of a certain quantity of the foreign currency quoted (usually 100 units, but only one unit in the case of the U.S. dollar or the pound sterling). For example, the price of foreign currency is expressed in Swiss francs (SFr) in Switzerland and in euros in Germany. Thus, in Switzerland the euro might be quoted at SFr 1.65, whereas in Germany the Swiss franc would be quoted at €0.61.

There are exceptions to this rule, though. Banks in Great Britain quote the value of the pound sterling (£) in terms of the foreign currency, for example, £1 = $1.9721. This method of **indirect quotation** is also used in the United States for domestic purposes and for the Canadian dollar. In their foreign exchange activities abroad, however, U.S. banks adhere to the European method of direct quotation.

American and European terms and direct and indirect quotes are related as follows:

American terms	*European terms*
U.S. dollar price per unit of foreign currency	Foreign currency units per dollar
(for example, $0.008242/¥)	(for example, ¥121.35/$)
A direct quote in the United States	A direct quote outside the United States
An indirect quote outside the United States	An indirect quote in the United States

Banks do not normally charge a commission on their currency transactions, but they profit from the spread between the buying and selling rates on both spot and forward transactions. Quotes are always given in pairs because a dealer usually does not know whether a prospective customer is in the market to buy or to sell a foreign currency. The first rate is the buy, or bid, price; the second is the sell, or ask, or offer, rate. Suppose the pound sterling is quoted at $1.9719–28. This quote means that banks are willing to buy pounds at $1.9719 and sell them at $1.9728. If you are a customer of the bank, you can expect to sell pounds to the bank at the bid rate of $1.9719 and buy pounds from the bank at the ask rate of $1.9728. The dealer will profit from the spread of $0.0009 ($1.9728—$1.9719) between the bid and ask rates.

In practice, because time is money, dealers do not quote the full rate to each other; instead, they quote only the last two digits of the decimal. Thus, sterling would be quoted at 19–28 in the above example. Any dealer who is not sufficiently up-to-date to know the preceding numbers will not remain in business for long.

Note that when American terms are converted to European terms or direct quotations are converted to indirect quotations, bid and ask quotes are reversed; that is, the reciprocal of the American (direct) bid becomes the European (indirect) ask, and the reciprocal of the American (direct) ask becomes the European (indirect) bid. So, in the previous example, the reciprocal of the American bid of $1.9719/£ becomes the European ask of £0.5071/$, and the reciprocal of the American ask of $1.9728/£ equals the European bid of £0.5069/$, resulting in a direct quote for the dollar in London of £0.5069–71. Note, too, that the banks will always buy low and sell high.

Transaction Costs The **bid–ask spread**—that is, the spread between bid and ask rates for a currency—is based on the breadth and depth of the market for that currency as well as on the currency's volatility. The spread repays traders for the costs they incur in currency dealing—including earning a profit on the capital tied up in their business—and compensates them for the risks they bear. It is usually stated as a percentage cost of transacting in the foreign exchange market, which is computed as follows:

$$\text{Percent spread} = \frac{\text{Ask price} - \text{Bid price}}{\text{Ask price}} \times 100$$

For example, with pound sterling quoted at \$1.9719–28, the percentage spread equals 0.046%:

$$\text{Percent spread} = \frac{1.9728 - 1.9719}{1.9728} \times 100 = 0.046\%$$

For widely traded currencies, such as the pound, euro, Swiss franc, and yen, the spread used to be on the order of 0.05%–0.08%.[6] However, the advent of sophisticated electronic trading systems has pushed the spreads on trades of \$1 million or more to a tiny 0.02%.[7] Less heavily traded currencies, and currencies having greater volatility, have higher spreads. In response to their higher spreads and volatility (which increases the opportunity for profit when trading for the bank's own account), the large banks have expanded their trading in emerging market currencies, such as the Czech koruna, Russian ruble, Turkish lira, and Zambian kwacha. Although these currencies currently account for less than 5% of the global foreign exchange market, the forecast is for a rapid growth, in line with growing investment in emerging markets.

Mean forward currency bid–ask spreads are larger than spot spreads, but they are still small in absolute terms, ranging from 0.09% to 0.15% for actively traded currencies. There is a growing forward market for emerging currencies, but because of the thinness of this market and its lack of liquidity, the bid–ask spreads are much higher.

The quotes found in the financial press are not those that individuals or firms would get at a local bank. Unless otherwise specified, these quotes are for transactions in the interbank market exceeding \$1 million. (The standard transaction amount in the interbank market is now about \$10 million.) But competition ensures that individual customers receive rates that reflect, even if they do not necessarily equal, interbank quotations. For example, a trader may believe that he or she can trade a little more favorably than the market rates indicate—that is, buy from a customer at a slightly lower rate or sell at a somewhat higher rate than the market rate. Thus, if the current spot rate for the Swiss franc is \$0.7967–72, the bank may quote a customer a rate of \$0.7964–75. However, a bank that is temporarily short in a currency may be willing to pay a slightly more favorable rate; or if the bank has overbought a currency, it may be willing to sell that currency at a somewhat lower rate.

For these reasons, many corporations will shop around at several banks for quotes before committing themselves to a transaction. On large transactions, customers also may get a rate break inasmuch as it ordinarily does not take much more effort to process a large order than a small order.

The market for traveler's checks and smaller currency exchanges, such as might be made by a traveler going abroad, is quite separate from the interbank market. The spread on these smaller exchanges is much wider than that in the interbank market, reflecting the higher average costs banks incur on such transactions. As a result, individuals and firms involved in smaller retail transactions generally pay a higher price when buying and receive a lower price when selling foreign currency than those quoted in newspapers.

---

[6] Data on mean spot and forward bid–ask spreads appear in Hendrik Bessembinder, "Bid–Ask Spreads in the Interbank Foreign Exchange Markets," *Journal of Financial Economics*, June 1994, pp. 317–348.

[7] Zuckerman, "UBS Cleans Up in Currency-Trading Corner," *op cit.*

Cross Rates Because most currencies are quoted against the dollar, it may be necessary to work out the **cross rates** for currencies other than the dollar. For example, if the euro is selling for $1.35 and the buying rate for the Swiss franc is $0.81, then the €/SFr cross rate is €1 = SFr 1.67. A somewhat more complicated cross-rate calculation would be the following. Suppose that the European quotes for the Japanese yen and the South Korean won are as follows:

Japanese yen:	¥121.35/U.S.$
South Korean won:	W931.88/U.S.$

In this case, the cross rate of yen per won can be calculated by dividing the rate for the yen by the rate for the won, as follows:

$$\frac{\text{Japanese yen/U.S. dollar}}{\text{Korean won/U.S. dollar}} = \frac{¥121.35/\text{U.S.\$}}{\text{W}931.88/\text{U.S.\$}} = ¥0.13022/\text{W}$$

Exhibit 6.6 contains cross rates for major currencies on May 29, 2007.

For Late New York Trading May 29, 2007

	Dollar	Euro	Pound	SFranc	Peso	Yen	CdnDlr
Canada	1.0735	1.444	2.1262	0.8762	0.0993	0.0088	....
Japan	121.65	163.64	240.95	99.294	11.252	....	113.32
Mexico	10.812	14.543	21.414	8.8247	....	0.0889	10.071
Switzerland	1.2252	1.648	2.4266	....	0.1133	0.0101	1.1413
U.K.	0.5049	0.6791	....	0.4121	0.0467	0.0042	0.4703
Euro	0.7434	....	1.4725	0.6068	0.0688	0.0061	0.6925
U.S.	....	1.3451	1.9806	0.8162	0.0925	0.0082	0.9315

Source: The Wall Street Journal Online.

EXHIBIT 6.6 • KEY CURRENCY CROSS RATES

 ILLUSTRATION   *Calculating the Direct Quote for the British Pound in Zurich*

Suppose sterling is quoted at $1.9719–36, and the Swiss franc is quoted at $0.8130–47. What is the direct quote for the pound in Zurich?

Solution. The bid rate for the pound in Zurich can be found by realizing that selling pounds for SFr is equivalent to combining two transactions: (1) selling pounds for dollars at the bid rate of $1.9719 and (2) converting those dollars into SFr 1.9719/0.8147 = SFr 2.4204 per pound at the ask rate of $0.8147. Similarly, the franc cost of buying one pound (the ask rate) can be found by first buying $1.9736 (the ask rate for £1) with SFr and then using those dollars to buy one pound. Because buying dollars for francs is equivalent to selling francs for dollars (at the bid rate of $0.8130), it will take SFr 1.9736/0.8130 = SFr 2.4276 to acquire the $1.9736 needed to buy one pound. Thus, the direct quotes for the pound in Zurich are SFr 2.420–27.

Note that in calculating the cross rates you should always assume that you have to sell a currency at the lower (or bid) rate and buy it at the higher (or ask) rate, giving you the worst possible rate. This method of quotation is how banks make money in foreign exchange.

I L L U S T R A T I O N   *Calculating the Direct Quote for the Brazilian Real in Bangkok*

Suppose that the Brazilian *real* is quoted at R 1.9681–1.9751/U.S.$ and the Thai baht is quoted at B 32.4397–9397. What is the direct quote for the *real* in Bangkok?

Solution. Analogous to the prior example, the direct bid rate for the *real* in Bangkok can be found by recognizing that selling reais (plural of *real*) in exchange for baht is equivalent to combining two transactions: (1) selling the *real* for dollars (which is the same as buying dollars with reais) at the ask rate of R 1.9751/U.S.$ and (2) selling those dollars for baht at the bid rate of B 32.4397/U.S.$. These transactions result in the bid cross rate for the *real* being the bid rate for the baht divided by the ask rate for the *real*:

$$\text{Bid cross rate for the real} = \frac{\text{Bid rate for Thai baht/U.S.\$}}{\text{Ask rate for Brazilian real/U.S.\$}} = \frac{32.4397}{1.9751} = \text{B } 16.4243/\text{R}$$

Similarly, the baht cost of buying the *real* (the ask cross rate) can be found by first buying dollars for Thai baht at the ask rate of B 32.9397/U.S.$ and then selling those dollars to buy Brazilian reais at the bid rate of R 1.9681/U.S.$. Combining these transactions yields the ask cross rate for the *real* being the ask rate for the baht divided by the bid rate for the *real*:

$$\text{Ask cross rate for the real} = \frac{\text{Ask rate for Thai baht/U.S.\$}}{\text{Bid rate for Brazilian real/U.S.\$}} = \frac{32.9397}{1.9681} = \text{B } 16.7368/\text{R}$$

Thus, the direct quotes for the *real* in Bangkok are B 16.4243–7368.

Currency Arbitrage   Until recently, the pervasive practice among bank dealers was to quote all currencies against the U.S. dollar when trading among themselves. Now, however, a growing percentage of currency trades does not involve the dollar. For example, Swiss banks may quote the euro against the Swiss franc, and German banks may quote pounds sterling in terms of euros. Exchange traders remain continually alert to the possibility of taking advantage, through **currency arbitrage** transactions, of exchange rate inconsistencies in different money centers. These transactions involve buying a currency in one market and selling it in another. Such activities tend to keep exchange rates uniform in the various markets.

Currency arbitrage transactions also explain why such profitable opportunities are fleeting. In the process of taking advantage of an arbitrage opportunity, the buying and selling of currencies tend to move rates in a manner that eliminates the profit opportunity in the future. When profitable arbitrage opportunities disappear, we say that the **no-arbitrage condition** holds. If this condition is violated on an ongoing basis, we would wind up with a money machine, as shown in the following example.

Suppose the pound sterling is bid at $1.9724 in New York and the euro is offered at $1.3450 in Frankfurt. At the same time, London banks are offering pounds sterling at €1.4655. An astute trader would sell dollars for euros in Frankfurt, use the euros to acquire pounds sterling in London, and sell the pounds in New York.

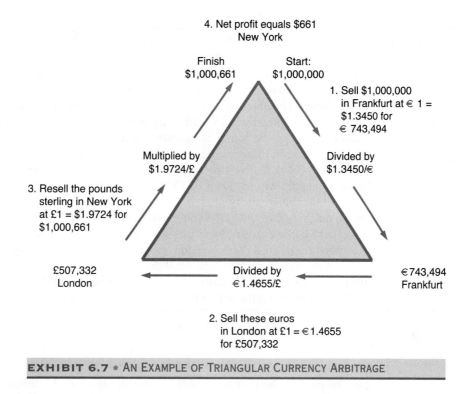

<EXHIBIT 6.7 • AN EXAMPLE OF TRIANGULAR CURRENCY ARBITRAGE>

Specifically, if the trader begins in New York with $1 million, he could acquire €743,494.42 for $1 million in Frankfurt (1,000,000/1.3450), sell these euros for £507,331.57 in London (743,494.42/1.4655), and resell the pounds in New York for $1,000,660.79 (507,331.57 × 1.9724). Thus, a few minutes' work would yield a profit of $660.79. In effect, by arbitraging through the euro, the trader would be able to acquire sterling at $1.9711 in London ($1.3450 × 1.4655) and sell it at $1.9724 in New York. This sequence of transactions, known as **triangular currency arbitrage**, is depicted in Exhibit 6.7.

In the preceding example, the arbitrage transactions would tend to cause the euro to appreciate vis-à-vis the dollar in Frankfurt and to depreciate against the pound sterling in London; at the same time, sterling would tend to fall in New York against the dollar. Acting simultaneously, these currency changes will quickly eliminate profits from this set of transactions, thereby enforcing the no-arbitrage condition. Otherwise, a money machine would exist, opening up the prospect of unlimited risk-free profits. Such profits would quickly attract other traders, whose combined buying and selling activities would bring exchange rates back into equilibrium almost instantaneously.

Opportunities for profitable currency arbitrage have been greatly reduced in recent years, given the extensive network of people—aided by high-speed, computerized information systems—who are continually collecting, comparing, and acting on currency quotes in all financial markets. The practice of quoting rates against the dollar makes currency arbitrage even simpler. The result of this activity is that rates for a specific currency tend to be the same everywhere, with only minimal deviations due to transaction costs.

ILLUSTRATION *Calculating the Direct Quote for the Euro in New York*

If the direct quote for the dollar is € 0.75 in Frankfurt, and transaction costs are 0.4%, what are the minimum and maximum possible direct quotes for the euro in New York?

Solution. The object here is to find the *no-arbitrage* range of euro quotes—that is, the widest bid–ask spread within which any potential arbitrage profits are eaten up by transaction costs. It can be found as follows. Begin with an arbitrageur who converts $1 into euros in Frankfurt. The arbitrageur would receive €0.75 × 0.996, after paying transaction costs of 0.4%. Converting these euros into dollars in New York at a direct quote of e, the arbitrageur would keep 0.75 × 0.996 × e × 0.996. The no-arbitrage condition requires that this quantity must be less than or equal to $1 (otherwise there would be a money machine), or $e \le 1/[0.75(0.996)^2] = \$1.3441$. Alternatively, an arbitrageur who converted $1 into euros in New York at a rate of e, and took those euros to Frankfurt and exchanged them for dollars, would wind up—after paying transaction costs in both New York and Frankfurt—with $(1/e) \times 0.996 \times 1/0.75 \times 0.996$. Because the no-arbitrage condition requires that this quantity must not exceed $1, $(0.996)^2 \times (1/0.75e) \le 1$, or $e \ge \$1.3227$. Combining these two inequalities yields $\$1.3227 \le e \le \$1.3441$.

Settlement Date The **value date** for spot transactions, the date on which the monies must be paid to the parties involved, is set as the second working day after the date on which the transaction is concluded. Thus, a spot deal entered into on Thursday in Paris will not be settled until the following Monday (French banks are closed on Saturdays and Sundays). It is possible, although unusual, to get one-day or even same-day value, but the rates will be adjusted to reflect interest differentials on the currencies involved.

MINI-CASE *Arbitraging Currency Cross Rates*

Your friendly foreign exchange trader has given you the following currency cross rates. The quotes are expressed as units of the currency represented in the left-hand column per unit of currency shown in the top row. Consider the dollar rates to be the quotes off which the cross rates are set.

Currency	SFr	DKr	£	¥	U.S.$
SFr	–	.2202–08	2.4246–57	0.0101–06	1.2250–56
DKr	4.5270–8	–	10.9781–91	0.0458–62	5.5675–85
£	.4122–35	.0910–20	–	.0042–46	.5070–82
¥	98.6532–44	21.779–807	239.240–54	–	121.330–38

QUESTIONS

1. Do any triangular arbitrage opportunities exist among these currencies? Assume that any deviations from the theoretical cross rates of 5 points or less are due to transaction costs.

2. How much profit could be made from a $5 million transaction associated with each arbitrage opportunity?

Exchange Risk Bankers also act as market makers, as well as agents, by taking positions in foreign currencies, thereby exposing themselves to **exchange risk**. The immediate adjustment of quotes as traders receive and interpret new political and economic information is the source of both exchange losses and gains by banks active in the foreign exchange market. For instance, suppose a trader quotes a rate of £1:$1.9712 for £500,000, and it is accepted. The bank will receive $985,600 in return for the £500,000. If the bank does not have an offsetting transaction, it may decide within a few minutes to cover its exposed position in the interbank market. If during this brief delay, news of a lower-than-expected British trade deficit reaches the market, the trader may be unable to purchase pounds at a rate lower than $1.9801. Because the bank would have to pay $990,050 to acquire £500,000 at this new rate, the result is a $4,450 ($990,050 − $985,600) exchange loss on a relatively small transaction within just a few minutes. Equally possible, of course, is a gain if the dollar strengthens against the pound.

Clearly, as a trader becomes more and more uncertain about the rate at which she can offset a given currency contract with other dealers or customers, the trader will demand a greater profit to bear this added risk. This expectation translates into a wider bid-ask spread. For example, during a period of volatility in the exchange rate between the Swiss franc and U.S. dollar, a trader will probably quote a customer a bid for francs that is distinctly lower than the last observed bid in the interbank market; the trader will attempt to reduce the risk of buying francs at a price higher than that at which she can eventually resell them. Similarly, the trader may quote a price for the sale of francs that is above the current asking price.

6.2.2 The Mechanics of Spot Transactions

The simplest way to explain the process of actually settling transactions in the spot market is to work through an example. Suppose a U.S. importer requires HK$1 million to pay his Hong Kong supplier. After receiving and accepting a verbal quote from the trader of a U.S. bank, the importer will be asked to specify two accounts: (1) the account in a U.S. bank that he wants debited for the equivalent dollar amount at the agreed exchange rate, say, U.S.$0.1280 per Hong Kong dollar, and (2) the Hong Kong supplier's account that is to be credited by HK$1 million.

On completion of the verbal agreement, the trader will forward to the settlement section of her bank a dealing slip containing the relevant information. That same day, a **contract note**, which includes the amount of the foreign currency (HK$1 million), the dollar equivalent at the agreed rate ($128,000 = 0.1280 × 1,000,000), and confirmation of the payment instructions, will be sent to the importer. The settlement section will then cable the bank's correspondent (or branch) in Hong Kong, requesting transfer of HK$1 million from its **nostro account**—working balances maintained with the correspondent to facilitate delivery and receipt of currencies—to the account specified by the importer. On the value date, the U.S. bank will debit the importer's account, and the exporter will have his account credited by the Hong Kong correspondent.

At the time of the initial agreement, the trader provides a clerk with the pertinent details of the transaction. The clerk, in turn, constantly updates a **position sheet** that shows the bank's position by currency, as well as by maturities of forward contracts. A number of the major international banks have fully computerized this process to ensure accurate and instantaneous information on individual transactions and on the bank's cumulative currency exposure at any time. The head trader will monitor this information for evidence of possible fraud or excessive exposure in a given currency.

As spot transactions are normally settled two working days later, a bank is never certain until one or two days after the deal is concluded whether the payment due the bank has actually been made. To keep this credit risk in bounds, most banks will transact large amounts only with prime names (other banks or corporate customers).

A different type of credit risk is **settlement risk**, also known as **Herstatt risk**. Herstatt risk, named after a German bank that went bankrupt after losing a fortune speculating on foreign currencies, is the risk that a bank will deliver currency on one side of a foreign exchange deal only to find that its counterparty has not sent any money in return. This risk arises because of the way foreign currency transactions are settled. Settlement requires a cash transfer from one bank's account to another at the central banks of the currencies involved. However, because those banks may be in different time zones, there may be a delay. In the case of Herstatt, German regulators closed the bank after it had received Deutsche marks in Frankfurt but before it had delivered dollars to its counterparty banks (because the New York market had not yet opened).

Because central banks have been slow to deal with this problem, some banks have begun to pool their trades in a particular currency, canceling out offsetting ones and settling the balance at the end of the day. In early 1996, 17 of the world's biggest banks went further and announced plans for a global clearing bank that would operate 24 hours a day. If and when this proposal is implemented, banks would trade through the clearing bank, which would settle both sides of foreign exchange trades simultaneously, as long as the banks' accounts had sufficient funds.

6.3 THE FORWARD MARKET

Forward exchange operations carry the same credit risk as spot transactions but for longer periods of time; however, there are significant exchange risks involved.

A **forward contract** between a bank and a customer (which could be another bank) calls for delivery, at a fixed future date, of a specified amount of one currency against dollar payment; the exchange rate is fixed at the time the contract is entered into. Although the euro is the most widely traded currency at present, active forward markets exist for the pound sterling, the Canadian dollar, the Japanese yen, and the Swiss franc. In general, forward markets for the currencies of less-developed countries (LDCs) are either limited or nonexistent.

In a typical forward transaction, for example, a U.S. company buys textiles from England with payment of £1 million due in 90 days. Thus, the importer is **short** pounds—that is, it owes pounds for future delivery. Suppose the spot price of the pound is $1.97. During the next 90 days, however, the pound might rise against the dollar, raising the dollar cost of the textiles. The importer can guard against this exchange risk by immediately negotiating a 90-day forward contract with a bank at a price of, say, £1 = $1.98. According to the forward contract, in 90 days the bank will give the importer £1 million (which it will use to pay for its textile order), and the importer will give the bank $1.98 million, which is the dollar equivalent of £1 million at the forward rate of $1.98.

In technical terms, the importer is offsetting a short position in pounds by going **long** in the forward market—that is, by buying pounds for future delivery. In effect, use of the forward contract enables the importer to convert a short underlying position in pounds to a zero net exposed position, with the forward contract receipt of £1 million canceling out the account payable of £1 million and leaving the importer with a net liability of $1,980,000:

Importer's T-Account

Forward contract receipt	£1,000,000	Account payable	£1,000,000
		Forward contract payment	$1,980,000

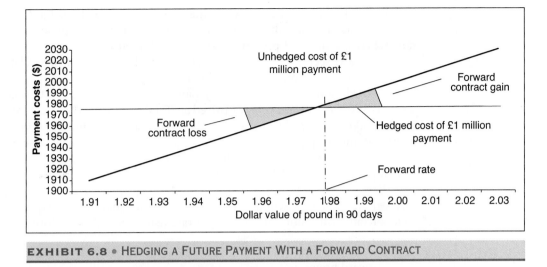

EXHIBIT 6.8 • HEDGING A FUTURE PAYMENT WITH A FORWARD CONTRACT

According to this T-account, the forward contract allows the importer to convert an unknown dollar cost ($1,000,000 \times e_1$, where e_1 is the unknown spot exchange rate—$/£—in 90 days) into a known dollar cost ($1,980,000), thereby eliminating all exchange risk on this transaction.

Exhibit 6.8 plots the importer's dollar cost of the textile shipment with and without the use of a forward contract. It also shows the gain or loss on the forward contract as a function of the contracted forward price and the spot price of the pound when the contract matures.

The gains and losses from long and short forward positions are related to the difference between the contracted forward price and the spot price of the underlying currency at the time the contract matures. In the case of the textile order, the importer is committed to buy pounds at $1.98 apiece. If the spot rate in 90 days is less than $1.98, the importer will suffer an implicit loss on the forward contract because the importer is buying pounds for more than the prevailing value. However, if the spot rate in 90 days exceeds $1.98, the importer will enjoy an implicit profit because the contract obliges the bank to sell the pounds at a price less than current value.

Three points are worth noting. First, the gain or loss on the forward contract is unrelated to the current spot rate of $1.97. Second, the forward contract gain or loss exactly offsets the change in the dollar cost of the textile order that is associated with movements in the pound's value. For example, if the spot price of the pound in 90 days is $2.02, the importer's cost of delivery is $2.02 million. However, the forward contract has a gain of $40,000, or $1,000,000 \times (2.02 - 1.98)$. The net cost of the textile order when covered with a forward contract is $1.98 million, no matter what happens to the spot exchange rate in 90 days. (Chapter 9 elaborates on the use of forward contracts to manage exchange risk.) Third, the forward contract is not an option contract. Both parties must perform the agreed behavior, unlike the situation with an option in which the buyer can choose whether to exercise the contract or allow it to expire. The bank must deliver the pounds, and the importer must buy them at the prearranged price. Options are discussed in Chapter 7.

6.3.1 Forward Quotations

Forward rates can be expressed in two ways. Commercial customers are usually quoted the actual price, otherwise known as the **outright rate**. In the interbank market, however, dealers quote the forward rate only as a discount from, or a premium on, the spot rate.

This forward differential is known as the **swap rate**. As explained in Chapter 4, a foreign currency is at a **forward discount** if the forward rate expressed in dollars is below the spot rate, whereas a **forward premium** exists if the forward rate is above the spot rate. As we see in the next section, the forward premium or discount is closely related to the difference in interest rates on the two currencies.

According to Exhibit 6.5, spot Japanese yen on May 22, 2007, sold at $0.008225, whereas 180-day forward yen was priced at $0.008421. Based on these rates, the swap rate for the 180-day forward yen was quoted as a 196-point premium (0.008421 − 0.008225), where a point, or "pip," refers to the last digit quoted. Similarly, because the 90-day British pound was quoted at $1.9733 while the spot pound was $1.9750, the 90-day forward British pound sold at a 17-point discount.

Based on Equation 4.1 from Chapter 4, which is repeated here as Equation 6.1, the forward premium or discount on a foreign currency may also be expressed as an annualized percentage deviation from the spot rate using the following formula:

$$\text{Forward premium or discount on foreign currency} = \frac{\text{Forward rate} - \text{Spot rate}}{\text{Spot rate}} \times \frac{360}{\text{Forward contract number of days}} \quad (6.1)$$

where the exchange rate is stated in domestic currency units per unit of foreign currency.

Thus, on May 22, 2007, the 180-day forward Japanese yen was selling at a 4.77% annualized premium:

$$\text{Forward premium annualized} = \frac{0.008421 - 0.008225}{0.008225} \times \frac{360}{180} = 0.0477$$

The 90-day British pound was selling at a 0.34% annualized discount:

$$\text{Forward discount annualized} = \frac{1.9733 - 1.9750}{1.9750} \times \frac{360}{90} = -0.0034$$

A swap rate can be converted into an outright rate by adding the premium (in points) to, or subtracting the discount (in points) from the spot rate. Although the swap rates do not carry plus or minus signs, you can determine whether the forward rate is at a discount or a premium using the following rule: When the forward bid in points is smaller than the ask rate in points, the forward rate is at a premium and the points should be added to the spot price to compute the outright quote. Conversely, if the bid in points exceeds the ask rate in points, the forward rate is at a discount and the points must be subtracted from the spot price to get the outright quotes.[8]

Suppose the following quotes are received for spot, 30-day, 90-day, and 180-day Swiss francs (SFr) and pounds sterling:

Spot	*30-day*	*90-day*	*180-day*
£:$2.0015–30	19–17	26–22	42–35
SFr:$0.6963–68	4–6	9–14	25–38

---

[8] This rule is based on two factors: (1) The buying rate, be it for spot or forward delivery, is always less than the selling price; and (2) the forward bid–ask spread always exceeds the spot bid–ask spread. In other words, you can always assume that the bank will be buying low and selling high and that bid–ask spreads widen with the maturity of the contract.

Bearing in mind the practice of quoting only the last two digits, a dealer would quote sterling at 15–30, 19–17, 26–22, and 42–35 and Swiss francs at 63–68, 4–6, 9–14, and 25–38. The outright rates are shown in the following chart.

	£			SFr		
Maturity	Bid	Ask	Spread (%)	Bid	Ask	Spread (%)
Spot	$2.0015	$2.0030	0.075	$0.6963	$0.6968	0.072
30-day	1.9996	2.0013	0.085	0.6967	0.6974	0.100
90-day	1.9989	2.0008	0.095	0.6972	0.6982	0.143
180-day	1.9973	1.9995	0.110	0.6988	0.7006	0.257

Thus, the Swiss franc is selling at a premium against the dollar, and the pound is selling at a discount. Note the slightly wider percentage spread between outright bid and ask on the Swiss franc compared with the spread on the pound. This difference is due to the broader market in pounds. Note too the widening of spreads by maturity for both currencies. This widening is caused by the greater uncertainty surrounding future exchange rates.

Exchange Risk   Spreads in the forward market are a function of both the breadth of the market (volume of transactions) in a given currency and the risks associated with forward contracts. The risks, in turn, are based on the variability of future spot rates. Even if the spot market is stable, there is no guarantee that future rates will remain invariant. This uncertainty will be reflected in the forward market. Furthermore, because beliefs about distant exchange rates are typically less secure than those about nearer-term rates, uncertainty will increase with lengthening maturities of forward contracts. Dealers will quote wider spreads on longer-term forward contracts to compensate themselves for the risk of being unable to reverse their positions profitably. Moreover, the greater unpredictability of future spot rates may reduce the number of market participants. This increased thinness will further widen the bid–ask spread because it magnifies the dealer's risk in taking even a temporary position in the forward market.

Cross Rates   Forward cross rates are figured in much the same way as spot cross rates. For instance, suppose a customer wants to sell 30-day forward euros against yen delivery. The market rates (expressed in European terms of foreign currency units per dollar) are as follows:

€:$ spot	0.81070–0.81103
30-day forward	0.81170–0.81243
¥:$ spot	107.490–107.541
30-day forward	107.347–107.442

Based on these rates, the forward cross rate for yen in terms of euros is found as follows: Forward euros are sold for dollars—that is, dollars are bought at the euro forward selling price of €0.81243 = $1—and the dollars to be received are simultaneously sold for 30-day forward yen at a rate of ¥107.347. Thus, €0.81243 = ¥107.347, or the forward buying rate for yen is €0.81243/107.347 = €0.0075683. Similarly, the forward selling rate for yen against euros (euros received per yen sold forward) is €0.81170/107.442 = €0.0075548. The spot buying rate for yen is €0.81103/107.490 = €0.0075452. Hence, based on its ask price, the yen is trading at an annualized 3.67% premium against the euro in the 30-day forward market:

$$\text{Forward premium annualized} = \frac{0.0075683 - 0.0075452}{0.007452} \times \frac{360}{30} = 3.67\%$$

ILLUSTRATION *Arbitraging Between Currencies and Interest Rates*

On checking the Reuters screen, you see the following exchange rate and interest rate quotes:

Currency	90-day Interest Rates	Spot Rates	90-Day Forward Rates
Pound	7 7/16–5/16%	¥240.9696–9912/£	¥224.5731–8692/£
Yen	2 3/8–1/4%		

a. Can you find an arbitrage opportunity?

Solution. There are two alternatives: (1) Borrow yen at 2 3/8%/4, convert the yen into pounds at the spot ask rate of ¥240.9912/£, invest the pounds at 7 5/16%/4, and sell the expected proceeds forward for yen at the forward bid rate of ¥224.5731/£; or (2) borrow pounds at 7 7/16%/4, convert the pounds into yen at the spot bid rate of ¥240.9696/£, invest the yen at 2 1/4%/4, and sell the proceeds forward for pounds at the forward ask rate of ¥224.8692/£. The first alternative will yield a loss of ¥5.70 per ¥100 borrowed, indicating that this is not a profitable arbitrage opportunity:

$$(100/240.9912) \times (1.0183) \times 224.5731 - 100 \times 1.0059 = -5.70$$

Switching to alternative 2, the return per £100 borrowed is £5.90, indicating that this is a very profitable arbitrage opportunity:

$$100 \times 240.9696 \times 1.0056/224.8692 - 100 \times 1.0186 = 5.90$$

b. What steps must you take to capitalize on it?

Solution. The steps to be taken have already been outlined in the answer to Part (a)

c. What is the profit per £1,000,000 arbitraged?

Solution. Based on the answer to Part (a), the profit is £590,000 (5.90 × 10,000).

6.3.2 Forward Contract Maturities

Forward contracts are normally available for 30-day, 60-day, 90-day, 180-day, or 360-day delivery. Banks will also tailor forward contracts for odd maturities (e.g., 77 days) to meet their customers' needs. Longer-term forward contracts can usually be arranged for widely traded currencies, such as the pound sterling, euro, or Japanese yen; however, the bid–ask spread tends to widen for longer maturities. As with spot rates, these spreads have widened for almost all currencies since the early 1970s, probably because of the greater turbulence in foreign exchange markets. For widely traded currencies, the 90-day bid–ask spread can vary from 0.1% to 1%.

Currency swap transactions, discussed in Chapter 8, are a means of converting long-term obligations in one currency into long-term obligations in another currency. As such, we will see that swaps act as substitutes for long-dated forward contracts.

6.4 SUMMARY AND CONCLUSIONS

In this chapter, we saw that the primary function of the foreign exchange market is to transfer purchasing power denominated in one currency to another and thereby facilitate international trade and investment. The foreign exchange market consists of two tiers: the interbank market, in which major banks trade with each other; and the retail market, in which banks deal with their commercial customers.

In the spot market, currencies are traded for settlement within two business days after the transaction has been concluded. In the forward market, contracts are made to buy or sell currencies for future delivery. Spot and forward quotations are given either in American terms, the dollar price of a foreign currency, or in European terms, the foreign currency price of a dollar. Quotations can also be expressed on a direct basis, the home currency price of another currency; or an indirect basis, the foreign currency price of the home currency.

The major participants in the forward market are categorized as arbitrageurs, traders, hedgers, and speculators. Forward rates can be stated on an outright basis or as a discount from, or a premium on, the spot rate. This forward differential is known as the swap rate. Because most currencies are quoted against the dollar, the exchange rate between two nondollar currencies, known as a cross rate, must be calculated on the basis of their direct quotes against the dollar.

QUESTIONS

1. Answer the following questions using the data in Exhibit 6.5.

   a. How many Swiss francs can you get for one dollar?

   b. How many dollars can you get for one Swiss franc?

   c. What is the 3-month forward rate for the Swiss franc?

   d. Is the Swiss franc selling at a forward premium or discount?

   e. What is the 90-day forward discount or premium on the Swiss franc?

2. What risks confront dealers in the foreign exchange market? How can they cope with those risks?

3. Suppose a currency increases in volatility. What is likely to happen to its bid–ask spread? Why?

4. Who are the principal users of the forward market? What are their motives?

5. How does a company pay for the foreign exchange services of a commercial bank?

PROBLEMS

1. The \$/€ exchange rate is € 1 = \$1.35, and the €/SFr exchange rate is SFr 1 = €0.61. What is the SFr/\$ exchange rate?

2. Suppose the direct quote for sterling in New York is 1.9880–85.

   a. How much would £500,000 cost in New York?

   b. What is the direct quote for dollars in London?

3. Using the data in Exhibit 6.5, calculate the 30-day, 90-day, and 180-day forward premiums for the Canadian dollar.

4. An investor wishes to buy euros spot (at \$1.3480) and sell euros forward for 180 days (at \$1.3526).

   a. What is the swap rate on euros?

   b. What is the forward premium or discount on 180-day euros?

5. Suppose Credit Suisse quotes spot and 90-day forward rates on the Swiss franc of \$0.7957–60, 8–13.

   a. What are the outright 90-day forward rates that Credit Suisse is quoting?

   b. What is the forward discount or premium associated with buying 90-day Swiss francs?

   c. Compute the percentage bid–ask spreads on spot and forward Swiss francs.

6. Suppose Dow Chemical receives quotes of \$0.008242–45 for the yen and \$0.03023–27 for the Taiwan dollar (NT\$).

   a. How many U.S. dollars will Dow Chemical receive from the sale of ¥50 million?

   b. What is the U.S. dollar cost to Dow Chemical of buying ¥1 billion?

   c. How many NT\$ will Dow Chemical receive for U.S.\$500,000?

   d. How many yen will Dow Chemical receive for NT\$200 million?

   e. What is the yen cost to Dow Chemical of buying NT\$80 million?

7. Suppose the euro is quoted at 0.6786–98 in London and the pound sterling is quoted at 1.4724–70 in Frankfurt.

   a. Is there a profitable arbitrage situation? Describe it.

   b. Compute the percentage bid–ask spreads on the pound and euro.

8. As a foreign exchange trader at Sumitomo Bank, you have a customer who would like spot and 30-day forward yen quotes on Australian dollars. Current market rates are as follows:

Spot	30-day
¥121.37–85/U.S.$1	15–13
A$1.1878–98/U.S.$1	20–26

   a. What bid and ask yen cross rates would you quote on spot Australian dollars?

   b. What outright yen cross rates would you quote on 30-day forward Australian dollars?

   c. What is the forward premium or discount on buying 30-day Australian dollars against yen delivery?

9. Suppose Air France receives the following indirect quotes in New York: €0.92–3 and £0.63–4. Given these quotes, what range of £/€ bid and ask quotes in Paris will permit arbitrage?

10. On checking the Telerate screen, you see the following exchange rate and interest rate quotes:

Currency	90-day interest rates (annualized)	Spot rates	90-day forward rates
Dollar	4.99%–5.03%		
Swiss franc	3.14%–3.19%	$0.8132–44	$0.8226–32

   a. Can you find an arbitrage opportunity?

   b. What steps must you take to capitalize on it?

   c. What is the profit per $1 million arbitraged?

BIBLIOGRAPHY

Bessembinder, H. "Bid–Ask Spreads in the Interbank Foreign Exchange Markets," *Journal of Financial Economics*, June 1994, pp. 317–348.

Fama, E. "Forward and Spot Exchange Rates," *Journal of Monetary Economics* 14, 1984, pp. 319–338.

Glassman, D. "Exchange Rate Risk and Transactions Costs: Evidence from Bid–Ask Spreads," *Journal of International Money and Finance*, December 1987, pp. 479–491.

Kubarych, R. M. *Foreign Exchange Markets in the United States.* New York: Federal Reserve Bank of New York, 1983.

Strongin, S. "International Credit Market Connections," *Economic Perspectives*, July/August 1990, pp. 2–10.

INTERNET RESOURCES

www.imf.org/external/fin.htm IMF Web page that contains exchange rate quotes for selected currencies.

www.ny.frb.org/markets/fxrates/noon.cfm Web page of the Federal Reserve Bank of New York that lists daily noon foreign exchange rates.

www.oanda.com Contains a wide variety of current and historical exchange rate data along with stories relating to foreign exchange and links to the world's central banks.

www.ny.frb.org/education/addpub/usfxm/ Lists of online publications by the Federal Reserve Bank of New York that offer detailed information about the foreign exchange market in the United States.

www.bis.org/ Contains the BIS Annual Report, statistics on derivatives, external debt, foreign exchange market activity, and so on.

http://www.bloomberg.com/index.html?Intro = intro3 Web site for Bloomberg. Contains a wide variety of data on financial markets worldwide, including foreign exchange and interest rate data.

http://online.wsj.com/public/us Website of the *Wall Street Journal*, prominent business newspaper in the U.S. Contains domestic and international business news.

http://www.euromoney.com/ Website of the *Euromoney* magazine. Contains economic and financial articles and studies in the EU area.

http://research.stlouisfed.org/ Website of the Federal Reserve Bank of St. Louis. Contains current and historical foreign exchange rate data.

INTERNET EXERCISES

1. Find the latest quotes for the euro, pound, and yen. By how much did these currencies rise or fall against the dollar in the last day?

2. Have emerging market currencies generally risen or fallen in the past day? You can use the Emerging Markets Companion for these data or the IMF Web site.

3. What was the volume of forward contracts traded in the past year? You can use data from the BIS Annual Report to answer this question.

4. Find the currency cross rates provided by Bloomberg for the euro/pound and euro/yen. Using these rates, calculate what the pound/yen cross rate should be. Compare your calculated pound/yen cross rate to the one reported by Bloomberg. Are the two cross rates the same?

CURRENCY FUTURES AND OPTIONS MARKETS

When I dip into the future far as human eye could see; Saw the vision of the world and all the wonder that would be.

Lord Alfred Tennyson (1842)

CHAPTER LEARNING OBJECTIVES

- To explain what currency futures and options contracts are and to describe the organization of the markets in which these contracts are traded
- To distinguish between currency forward and futures contracts
- To distinguish between currency futures and options contracts
- To describe the advantages and disadvantages of futures contracts relative to forward contracts
- To explain how currency futures and options contracts can be used to manage currency risk and to speculate on future currency movements
- To identify the basic factors that determine the value of a currency option
- To read and interpret the prices of currency futures and options contracts as they appear in the *Wall Street Journal*

KEY TERMS

American option	futures option
at-the-money	implied volatility
bear spread	initial margin
break-even price	initial performance bond
bull spread	International Monetary Market (IMM)
call option	in-the-money
Chicago Mercantile Exchange (CME)	intrinsic value
currency futures	knockout option
currency option	listed option
currency spread	maintenance margin
derivatives	maintenance performance bond
European option	margin call
exchanged-traded option	marking to market
exercise price	offsetting trade
expiration date	open interest
futures contract	out-of-the-money

over-the-counter (OTC) currency option
outstrike
OTC market
performance bond
performance bond call
Philadelphia Stock Exchange (PHLX)
put option

put-call option interest rate parity
retail market
round trip
strike price
time value
United Currency Options Market (UCOM)
wholesale market

Foreign currency futures and options contracts are examples of the new breed of financial instrument known as derivatives. Financial **derivatives** are contracts that derive their value from some underlying asset (such as a stock, bond, or currency), reference rate (such as a 90-day treasury bill rate), or index (such as the S&P 500 stock index). Popular derivatives include swaps, forwards, futures, and options. Chapter 6 discussed forward contracts, and Chapter 8 discusses swaps. This chapter describes the nature and valuation of currency futures and options contracts and shows how they can be used to manage foreign exchange risk or take speculative positions on currency movements. It also shows how to read the prices of these contracts as they appear in the financial press.

7.1 FUTURES CONTRACTS

The **Chicago Mercantile Exchange (CME)** provides an outlet for currency speculators and for those looking to reduce their currency risks. Trade takes place in **currency futures**, which are contracts for specific quantities of given currencies; the exchange rate is fixed at the time the contract is entered into, and the delivery date is set by the board of directors of the **International Monetary Market (IMM)**. These contracts are patterned after those for grain and commodity futures contracts, which have been traded on Chicago's exchanges for over 100 years.

Currency futures contracts are currently available for the Australian dollar, Brazilian real, British pound, Canadian dollar, Czech koruna, euro, Hungarian forint, Japanese yen, Mexican peso, New Zealand dollar, Norwegian krone, Polish zloty, Russian ruble, South African rand, Swedish krona, and Swiss franc. The CME is continually experimenting with new contracts. Those that meet the minimum volume requirements are added, and those that do not are dropped. For example, the CME recently added a number of cross-rate contracts, such as EC/JY and AD/SF cross-rate contracts, while dropping contracts in the Dutch guilder (before it was replaced by the euro). By taking the U.S. dollar out of the equation, cross-rate futures allow one to hedge directly the currency risk that arises in dealing with nondollar currencies. The number of contracts outstanding at any one time is called the **open interest**.

Private individuals are encouraged, rather than discouraged, to participate in the market. Contract sizes are standardized by amount of foreign currency, for example, £62,500, C$100,000, and SFr 125,000. Exhibit 7.1 shows contract specifications for some of the currencies traded. Leverage is high; margin requirements average less than 2% of the value of the futures contract. The leverage assures that investors' fortunes will be decided by tiny swings in exchange rates.

The contracts have minimum price moves, which generally translate into about $10–$12 per contract. At the same time, most exchanges set daily price limits on their contracts that restrict the maximum daily price move. When these limits are reached, additional margin requirements are imposed and trading may be halted for a short time.

Instead of using the bid–ask spreads found in the interbank market, traders charge commissions. Though commissions will vary, a **round trip**—that is, one buy and one

	Australian Dollar	British Pound	Canadian Dollar	Euro FX	Japanese Yen	Swiss Franc
Contract size	A$100,000	£62,500	C$100,000	€125,000	¥12,500,000	SFr 125,000
Symbol	AD	BP	CD	EC	JY	SF
Performance Bond						
Initial	$1,148	$1,688	$1,148	$2,295	$2,700	$1,485
Maintenance	$850	$1,250	$850	$1,700	$2,000	$1,100
Minimum price change	$0.0001 (1 pt.)	$0.0001 (1 pt.)	$0.0001 (1 pt.)	$0.0001 (1 pt.)	$0.000001 (1 pt.)	$0.0001 (1 pt.)
Value of 1 point	$10.00	$6.25	$10.00	$12.50	$12.50	$12.50
Months traded	March, June, September, December					
Trading hours	7:20 A.M. – 2:00 P.M. (Central time)					
Last day of trading	The second business day immediately preceding the third Wednesday of the delivery month					

*As of May, 2007

Source: Data collected from Chicago Mercantile Exchange's web site at www.cme.com.

EXHIBIT 7.1 ● CONTRACT SPECIFICATIONS FOR FOREIGN CURRENCY FUTURES*

sell—costs as little as $15. This cost works out to be less than 0.02% of the value of a sterling contract. The low cost, along with the high degree of leverage, has provided a major inducement for speculators to participate in the market. Other market participants include importers and exporters, companies with foreign currency assets and liabilities, and bankers.

Although volume in the futures market is still small compared with that in the forward market, it can be viewed as an expanding part of a growing foreign exchange market. As we will see shortly, the different segments of this market are linked by arbitrage.

The CME is still the dominant trader, but other exchanges also trade futures contracts. The most important of these competitors include the London International Financial Futures Exchange (LIFFE), the Chicago Board of Trade (CBOT), the New York Mercantile Exchange, the Philadelphia Stock Exchange (PHLX), the Singapore International Monetary Exchange (SIMEX), Deutsche Termin Borse (DTB) in Frankfurt, the Hong Kong Futures Exchange (HKFE), the Marché à Termes des Instruments Financiers (MATIF) in Paris, and the Tokyo International Financial Futures Exchange (TIFFE).

A notable feature of the CME and other futures markets is that deals are struck by brokers face to face on a trading floor rather than over the telephone. There are other, more important distinctions between the futures and forward markets.

7.1.1 Forward Contract versus Futures Contract

One way to understand futures contracts is to compare them with forward contracts. **Futures contracts** are standardized contracts that trade on organized futures markets for specific delivery dates only. In the case of the CME, the most actively traded currency futures contracts are for March, June, September, and December delivery. Contracts expire two business days before the third Wednesday of the delivery month. Contract sizes and maturities are standardized, so all participants in the market are familiar with the types of contracts available, a situation that facilitates trading. Forward contracts, on the other hand, are private deals between two individuals who can sign any type of contract they agree on. For example, two individuals may sign a forward contract for €70,000 in 20 months to be paid in Swiss francs. However, CME contracts trade only in round lots of €125,000 priced in U.S. dollars and with a limited range of maturities available. With only a few standardized contracts traded, the trading volume in available contracts is higher, leading to superior liquidity, smaller price fluctuations, and lower transaction costs.

Once a trade is confirmed, the exchange's clearing house, backed by its members' capital, becomes the legal counterparty to both the buyer and seller of the futures contract. The exchange members, in effect, guarantee both sides of a contract, largely eliminating the default risks of trading. Members of the futures exchange support their guarantee through margin requirements, marking contracts to market daily (explained later), and maintaining a guarantee fund in the event a member defaults. In contrast, a forward contract is a private deal between two parties and is subject to the risk that either side may default on the terms of the agreement.

The contract specifications in Exhibit 7.1 show the margin requirements (now called performance bonds by the CME). The **initial performance bond** (previously referred to as the **initial margin**) shows how much money must be in the account balance when the contract is entered into. This amount is $1,688 in the case of the pound. A **performance bond call** (formerly referred to as a **margin call**) is issued if—because of losses on the futures contract—the balance in the account falls below the **maintenance performance bond** (formerly referred to as the **maintenance margin**), which is $1,250 for the pound. At that time, enough new money must be added to the account balance to bring it up to the initial performance bond. For example, suppose you start with an initial balance of $1,838 ($150 in excess of the initial performance bond of $1,688) in your account on a pound futures contract and your contract losses, say, $680 in value. It is now $1,158, which is $92 below the maintenance performance bond of $1,250. Hence, you must add $1,688 to your account to meet the initial performance bond requirement ($1,838 − $1,158 + $530 = $1,688).

The CME periodically revises its performance bond requirements in line with changing currency volatilities using a computerized risk management program called SPAN, which stands for Standard Portfolio Analysis of Risk. Note also that the performance bond requirements set by the CME are minimums; brokers often require higher performance bonds on more volatile currency contracts.

Profits and losses of futures contracts are paid over every day at the end of trading, a practice called **marking to market**. This daily-settlement feature can best be illustrated with an example. On Tuesday morning, an investor takes a long position in a euro futures contract that matures on Thursday afternoon. The agreed price is $1.3400 for €125,000. To begin, the investor must deposit into his account an initial performance bond of $2,295. At the close of trading on Tuesday, the futures price has risen to $1.345. Because of daily settlement, three things occur. First, the investor receives his cash profit of $625 (125,000 × 0.005). Second, the existing futures contract with a price of $1.34 is canceled. Third, the investor receives a new futures contract with the prevailing price of $1.345. Thus, the value of the futures contracts is set to zero at the end of each trading day.

At Wednesday close, the price has declined to $1.333. The investor must pay the $1,500 loss (125,000 × 0.012) to the other side of the contract and trade in the old contract for a new one with a price of $1.333. At Thursday close, the price drops to $1.33, and the contract matures. The investor pays his $375 loss to the other side and takes delivery of the euros, paying the prevailing price of $1.33. The investor has had a net loss on the contract of $1,250 ($625 − $1,500 − $375) before paying his commission. Exhibit 7.2 details the daily settlement process.

Daily settlement reduces the default risk of futures contracts relative to forward contracts. Every day, futures investors must pay over any losses or receive any gains from the day's price movements. These gains or losses are generally added to or subtracted from the investor's account. An insolvent investor with an unprofitable position would be forced into default after only one day's trading rather than being allowed to build up huge

Time	Action	Cash Flow
Tuesday morning	Investor buys Euro futures contract that matures in two days. Price is $1.34.	None
Tuesday close	Futures price rises to $1.345. Position is marked to market.	Investor receives $125,000 \times (1.345 - 1.34) = \$625$
Wednesday close	Futures price drops to $1.333. Position is marked to market.	Investor pays $125,000 \times (1.345 - 1.333) = \$1,500$
Thursday close	Futures price drops to $1.33 (1) Contract is marked to market. (2) Investor takes delivery of Euro 125,000.	(1) Investor pays $125,000 \times (1.333 - 1.33) = \$375$ (2) Investor pays $125,000 \times 1.33 = \$166,250$ Net loss on the futures contract = $1,250

EXHIBIT 7.2 • An Example of Daily Settlement With A Futures Contract

losses that lead to one large default at the time the contract matures (as could occur with a forward contract). For example, if an investor decided to keep his contract in force, rather than closing it out on Wednesday, he would have had a performance bond call because his account would have fallen below the maintenance performance bond of $1,700. His performance bond call would be for $875 ($2,295 + $625 − $1,500 + $875 = $2,295) at the close of Wednesday trading in order to meet his $2,295 initial performance bond; that is, the investor would have had to add $875 to his account to maintain his futures contract.

Futures contracts can also be closed out with an **offsetting trade**. For example, if a company's long position in euro futures has proved to be profitable, it need not literally take delivery of the euros when the contract matures. Rather, the company can sell futures contracts on a like amount of euros just prior to the maturity of the long position. The two positions cancel on the books of the futures exchange, and the company receives its profit in dollars. Exhibit 7.3 summarizes these and other differences between forward and futures contracts.

ILLUSTRATION *Computing Gains, Losses, and Performance Bond Calls on a Futures Contract*

On Monday morning, you short one CME yen futures contract containing ¥12,500,000 at a price of $0.008233. Suppose the broker requires a performance bond of $4,590 and a maintenance performance bond of $3,400. The settlement prices for Monday through Thursday are $0.008342, $0.008381, $0.008175, and $0.008169, respectively. On Friday, you close out the contract at a price of $0.008194. Calculate the daily cash flows on your account. Describe any performance bond calls on your account. What is your cash balance with your broker as of the close of business on Friday? Assume that you begin with an initial balance of $4,590 and that your round-trip commission was $27.
Solution:

Time	Action	Cash Flow on Contract
Monday morning	Sell one CME yen futures contract. Price is $0.008233.	None.
Monday close	Futures price rises to $0.008342. Contract is marked-to-market.	You pay out $12,500,000 \times (0.008233 - 0.008342) = -\$1,362.50$
Tuesday close	Futures price rises to $0.008381. Contract is marked-to-market.	You pay out an additional $12,500,000 \times (0.008342 - 0.008381) = -\$487.50$

Wednesday close	Futures price falls to $0.008175. Contract is marked-to-market.	You receive $12,500,000 \times (0.008381 - 0.008175) = +\$2,575.00$
Thursday close	Futures price falls to $0.008169. Contract is marked-to-market.	You receive an additional $12,500,000 \times (0.008175 - 0.008169) = +\$75.00$
Friday	You close out your contract at a futures price of $0.008194.	You pay out $12,500,000 \times (0.008169 - 0.008194) = -\$312.50$ You pay out a round-trip commission = $-\$27.00$

| | | **Net gain on the futures contract** $\quad$ $\$460.50$ |

Your performance bond calls and cash balances as of the close of each day were as follows:

Monday	With a loss of $1,362.50, your account balance falls to $3,227.50 ($4,590 – $1,362.50). You must add $172.50 ($3,400 – $3,227.50) to your account to meet the maintenance performance bond of $3,400.
Tuesday	With an additional loss of $487.50, your balance falls to $2,912.50 (3,400 – $487.50). You must add $487.50 to the balance to meet the maintenance performance bond of $3,400.
Wednesday	With a gain of $2,575, your balance rises to $5,975.
Thursday	With a gain of $75, your account balance rises further to $6,050.
Friday	With a loss of $312.50, your account balance falls to $5,737.50. After subtracting the round-trip commission of $27, your account balance ends at $5,710.50.

Advantages and Disadvantages of Futures Contracts   The smaller size of a futures contract and the freedom to liquidate the contract at any time before its maturity in a well-organized futures market differentiate the futures contract from the forward contract. These features of the futures contract attract many users. On the contrary, the limited number of currencies traded, the limited delivery dates, and the rigid contractual amounts of currencies to be delivered are disadvantages of the futures contract to many commercial users. Only by chance will contracts conform exactly to corporate requirements. The contracts are of value mainly to those commercial customers who have a fairly stable and continuous stream of payments or receipts in the traded foreign currencies.

Arbitrage Between the Futures and Forward Markets   Arbitrageurs play an important role on the CME. They translate CME futures rates into interbank forward rates and, by realizing profit opportunities, keep CME futures rates in line with bank forward rates.

ILLUSTRATION   *Forward-Futures Arbitrage*

Suppose the interbank forward bid for June 18 on pounds sterling is $1.9727 at the same time that the price of CME sterling futures for delivery on June 18 is $1.9715. How could the dealer use arbitrage to profit from this situation?

Solution. The dealer would simultaneously buy the June sterling futures contract for $123,218.75 (62,500 × $1.9715) and sell an equivalent amount of sterling forward, worth $123,293.75 (62,500 × $1.9727), for June delivery. Upon settlement, the dealer would earn a profit of $75. Alternatively, if the markets come back together before June 18, the dealer can unwind his position (by simultaneously buying £62,500 forward and selling a futures contract, both for delivery on June 18) and earn the same $75 profit. Although the amount of profit on this transaction is tiny, it becomes $7,500 if 100 futures contracts are traded.

1 **Trading:**
   Forward contracts are traded by telephone or telex.
   Futures contracts are traded in a competitive arena.

2 **Regulation:**
   The forward market is self-regulating.
   The IMM is regulated by the Commodity Futures Trading Commission.

3 **Frequency of delivery:**
   More than 90% of all forward contracts are settled by actual delivery.
   Less than 1% of the IMM futures contracts are settled by delivery.

4 **Size of contract:**
   Forward contracts are individually tailored and tend to be much larger than the standardized contracts on the futures market.
   Future contracts are standardized in terms of currency amount.

5 **Delivery date:**
   Banks offer forward contracts for delivery on any date.
   IMM futures contracts are available for delivery on only a few specified dates a year.

6 **Settlement:**
   Forward contract settlement occurs on the agreed rate between the bank and the customer.
   Futures contract settlements are made daily via the Exchange's Clearing House; gains on position value may be withdrawn and losses are collected daily. The practice is known as marking to market.

7 **Quotes:**
   Forward prices generally are quoted in European terms (units of local currency per USD).
   Futures contracts are quoted in American terms (dollars per one foreign currency unit).

8 **Transaction costs:**
   Costs of forward contracts are based on bid–ask spread.
   Futures contracts entail brokerage fees for buy and sell orders.

9 **Margins:**
   Margins are not required in the forward market.
   Margins are required of all participants in the futures market.

10 **Credit risk:**
   The credit risk is borne by each party to a forward contract. Credit limits must therefore be set for each customer.
   The Exchange's Clearing Housing becomes the opposite side of each futures contract, thereby reducing credit risk substantially.

EXHIBIT 7.3 • BASIC DIFFERENCES BETWEEN FORWARD AND FUTURES CONTRACTS

Such arbitrage transactions as described in the "Forward-Futures Arbitrage" illustration will bid up the futures price and bid down the forward price until an approximate equality is restored. The word *approximate* is used because there is a difference between the two contracts. Unlike the forward contract, where gains or losses are not realized until maturity, marking to market means that day-to-day futures contract gains (or losses) will have to be invested (or borrowed) at uncertain future interest rates. However, a study of actual rates for the British pound, Canadian dollar, Deutsche mark, Swiss franc, and Japanese yen found that forward and futures prices do not differ significantly.[1]

7.2 CURRENCY OPTIONS

Whatever advantages the forward or the futures contract might hold for its purchaser, the two contracts have a common disadvantage: Although they protect the holder against the risk of adverse movements in exchange rates, they also eliminate the possibility of gaining a windfall profit from favorable movements. This disadvantage was apparently one of the considerations that led some commercial banks to offer **currency options** to their customers. Exchange-traded currency options were first offered in 1983 by the **Philadelphia Stock Exchange (PHLX)**, where they are now traded on the **United Currency Options Market (UCOM)**. Currency options are one of the fastest growing segments of the global foreign exchange market, accounting for more than 9% of daily trading volume in 2004.

In principle, an *option* is a financial instrument that gives the holder the right, but not the obligation, to sell (put) or buy (call) another financial instrument at a set price and expiration date. The seller of the put option or call option must fulfill the contract if the buyer so desires it. Because the option not to buy or sell has value, the buyer must pay the seller of the option some premium for this privilege. As applied to foreign currencies, **call options** give the customer the right to purchase—and **put options** give the right to sell—the contracted currencies at the **expiration date**. Note that because a foreign exchange transaction has two sides, a call (put) option on a foreign currency can be considered a foreign currency put (call) option on the domestic currency. For example, the right to buy euros against dollar payment is equivalent to the right to sell dollars for euro payment. An **American option** can be exercised at any time up to the expiration date; a **European option** can be exercised only at maturity.

An option that would be profitable to exercise at the current exchange rate is said to be **in-the-money**. Conversely, an **out-of-the-money** option is one that would not be profitable to exercise at the current exchange rate. The price at which the option is exercised is called the **exercise price** or **strike price**. An option whose exercise price is the same as the spot exchange rate is termed **at-the-money**. That is,

Option Description	*Strike Price Relative to Spot Rate*	*Effect of Immediate Exercise*
In-the-money	Strike price < spot rate	Profit
At-the-money	Strike price = spot rate	Indifference
Out-of-the-money	Strike price > spot rate	Loss

7.2.1 Market Structure

Options are purchased and traded either on an organized exchange (such as the United Currency Options Market of the PHLX) or in the **over-the-counter (OTC) market**. **Exchange-traded options** or **listed options** are standardized contracts with predetermined exercise prices, and standard expiration months (March, June, September, and December plus two near-term months). **United Currency Options Market (UCOM)** options are available in six currencies—the Australian dollar, British pound, Canadian dollar, euro, Japanese yen, and Swiss franc—and are traded in standard contracts half the size of the CME futures contracts. The euro contracts have replaced contracts in the Deutsche mark

---

[1] Bradford Cornell and Marc Reinganum, "Forward and Futures Prices: Evidence from the Foreign Exchange Markets," *Journal of Finance*, December 1981, pp. 1035–1045.

and French franc. Contract specifications are shown in Exhibit 7.4. The PHLX trades only European-style standardized currency options. Its margin requirements change over time.

The PHLX also offers customized currency options, which allow users to customize various aspects of a currency option, including choice of exercise price, expiration date (up to 2 years out), and premium quotation as either units of currency or percent of underlying

	Australian Dollar	British Pound	Canadian Dollar	Euro	Japanese Yen	Swiss Franc
TICKER SYMBOLS (American/European)	XAD/CAD	XBP/CBP	XCD/CCD	XEU/ECU* XEB/ECB**	XJY/CJY	XSF/CSF
Half-point Strike (*three near-term months only*)	XAZ/CAZ	n.a./n.a.	XCD/CCD	n.a./n.a.	XJZ/CJZ	XSZ/CSZ
Alternate symbols	XAY/CAY	XBX/CBX XBY/CBY	XCV/CCV	XEV/ECY	XJJ/CJJ XJV/CJV	XSY/CSY
CONTRACT SIZE	50,000	31,250	50,000	62,500	6,250,000	62,500
BASE CURRENCY	USD	USD	USD	USD	USD	USD
UNDERLYING CURRENCY	AUD	GBP	CAD	EUR	JPY	CHF
EXERCISE PRICE INTERVALS						
Three nearest months	1¢	1¢	.5¢	1¢	.005¢	.5¢
6, 9, and 12 Months	1¢	2¢	.5¢	1¢	.01¢	1¢
PREMIUM QUOTATIONS	Cents per unit	Cents per unit	Cents per unit	Cents per unit	Hundredths of a cent per unit	Cents per unit
MINIMUM PREMIUM CHANGE	$.(00)01 per unit = $5.00	$.(00)01 per unit = $3.125	$.(00)01 per unit = $5.00	$.(00)01 per unit = $6.25	$.(0000)01 per unit = $6.25	$.(00)01 per unit = $6.25
MARGIN	USD	USD	USD	USD	USD	USD

Expiration months

   March, June, September, and December + two near-term months

Expiration date/Llast trading day

   Providing it is a business day, otherwise the day immediately prior:

   Friday before the third Wednesday of expiring month

Expiration settlement date

   Third Thursday of expiring month, except for March, June, September, and December expirations which are the third Wednesday.

Exercise style

   American and European

Trading hours

   2:30 a.m. to 2:30 p.m. Philadelphia time, Monday through Friday.

Issuer and guarantor

   The options clearing corporation (OCC)

* Even Strike Prices (i.e., 100, 102)

** Odd Stike Prices (i.e., 99, 101)

Source: Philadelphia Stock Exchange. http://www.phlx.com/products/currency/standard.html

EXHIBIT 7.4 • CONTRACT SPECIFICATIONS FOR PHLX STANDARDIZED CURRENCY OPTIONS CONTRACTS

value. Customized currency options can be traded on any combination of the six currencies for which standardized options are available, along with the Mexican peso and the U.S. dollar.[2] The contract size is the same as that for standardized contracts in the underlying currency. Other organized options exchanges are located in Amsterdam (European Options Exchange), Chicago (CME), and Montreal (Montreal Stock Exchange).

Over-the-counter (OTC) *options* are contracts whose specifications are generally negotiated as to the amount, exercise price and rights, underlying instrument, and expiration. **OTC currency options** are traded by commercial and investment banks in virtually all financial centers. OTC activity is concentrated in London and New York, and it centers on the major currencies, most often involving U.S. dollars against pounds sterling, euros, Swiss francs, Japanese yen, and Canadian dollars. Branches of foreign banks in the major financial centers are generally willing to write options against the currency of their home country. For example, Australian banks in London write options on the Australian dollar. Generally, OTC options are traded in round lots, commonly $5 million–$10 million in New York and $2 million–$3 million in London. The average maturity of OTC options ranges from 2 to 6 months, and very few options are written for more than one year. American options are most common, but European options are popular in Switzerland and Germany because of familiarity.

The OTC options market consists of two sectors: (1) a **retail market** composed of nonbank customers who purchase from banks what amounts to customized insurance against adverse exchange rate movements and (2) a **wholesale market** among commercial banks, investment banks, and specialized trading firms; this market may include interbank OTC trading or trading on the organized exchanges. The interbank market in currency options is analogous to the interbank markets in spot and forward exchange. Banks use the wholesale market to hedge, or "reinsure," the risks undertaken in trading with customers and to take speculative positions in options.

Most retail customers for OTC options are either corporations active in international trade or financial institutions with multicurrency asset portfolios. These customers could purchase foreign exchange puts or calls on organized exchanges, but they generally turn to the banks for options in order to find precisely the terms that match their needs. Contracts are generally tailored with regard to amount, strike price, expiration date, and currency.

The existence of OTC currency options predates exchange-traded options by many years, but trading in OTC options grew rapidly at the same time that PHLX trading began. The acceleration in the growth of options trading in both markets appears to spring from the desire by companies to manage foreign currency risks more effectively and, in particular, from an increased willingness to pay a fee to transfer such risks to another party. Most commentators suggest that corporate demand has increased because the greater volatility of exchange rates has increasingly exposed firms to risks from developments that are difficult to predict and beyond their control.

The growth of listed options, especially for "wholesale" purposes, apparently is putting pressure on the OTC markets for greater standardization in interbank trading. In some instances, OTC foreign currency options are traded for expiration on the third Wednesday of March, June, September, and December, to coincide with expiration dates on the U.S. exchanges.

Although the buyer of an option can lose only the premium paid for the option, the seller's risk of loss is potentially unlimited. Because of this asymmetry between income and risk, few retail customers are willing to write options. For this reason, the market

---

[2] The Australian dollar may be matched only against the U.S. dollar.

structure is distinctly asymmetrical when compared with the ordinary market for spot and forward foreign exchange, where there is a balance between customers who are purchasing or selling currency and where the interbank market likewise has a reasonable balance.

7.2.2 Using Currency Options

To see how currency options might be used, consider a U.S. importer with a €125,000 payment to make to a German exporter in 60 days. The importer could purchase a European call option to have the euros delivered to him at a specified exchange rate (the strike price) on the due date. Suppose the option premium is $0.02 per euro and the exercise price is $1.34. The importer has paid $2,500 for a €1.34 call option, which gives him the right to buy €125,000 at a price of $1.34 per euro at the end of 60 days. If at the time the importer's payment falls due the value of the euro has risen to, say, $1.40, the option would be in-the-money. In this case, the importer exercises his call option and purchases euros for $1.34. The importer would earn a profit of $7,500 (125,000 × 0.06), which would more than cover the $2,500 cost of the option. If the rate has declined below the contracted rate to, say, $1.30, the €134 option would be out-of-the-money. Consequently, the importer would let the option expire and purchase the euros in the spot market. Despite losing the $2,500 option premium, the importer would still be $2500 better off than if he had locked in a rate of $1.34 with a forward or futures contract.

Exhibit 7.5 illustrates the importer's gains or losses on the call option. At a spot rate on expiration of $1.34 or lower, the option will not be exercised, resulting in a loss of the $2,500 option premium. Between $1.34 and $1.36, the option will be exercised, but the gain is insufficient to cover the premium. The *break-even price* at which the gain on the option just equals the option premium is $1.37. Above $1.36 per euro, the option is sufficiently deep in-the-money to cover the option premium and yield a potentially unlimited net profit.

Because this is a zero-sum game, the profit from selling a call, shown in Exhibit 7.6, is the mirror image of the profit from buying the call. For example, if the spot rate at expiration is above $1.36/€, the call option writer is exposed to potentially unlimited losses. Why would an option writer accept such risks? For one thing, the option writer may already be long euros, effectively hedging much of the risk. Alternatively, the writer might be willing to take a risk in the hope of profiting from the option premium because of a belief that the euro will depreciate over the life of the contract. If the spot rate at expiration is $1.34 or less, the option ends out-of-the-money and the call option writer gets to keep the full $2,500 premium. For spot rates between $1.34 and $1.36, the option writer still earns a profit, albeit a diminishing one.

In contrast to the call option, a put option at the same terms (exercise price of $1.34 and put premium of $0.02 per euro) would be in-the-money at a spot price of $1.31 and out-of-the-money at $1.35. Exhibit 7.7 illustrates the profits available on this euro put option. If the spot price falls to, say, $1.28, the holder of a put option will deliver €125,000 worth $160,000 (1.28 × 125,000) and receive $167,500 (1.34 × 125,000). The option holder's profit, net of the $2,500 option premium, is $5,000. As the spot price falls further, the value of the put option rises. At the extreme, if the spot rate falls to zero, the buyer's profit on the contract will reach $165,000 (1.34 × 125,000 − 2,500). Below a spot rate of $1.30, the gain on the put option will more than cover the $2,500 option premium. Between $1.32—the breakeven price for the put option—and $1.34, the holder would exercise the option, but the gain would be less than the option premium. At spot prices above $1.34, the holder would not exercise the option and so would lose the $2,500 premium. Both the put and the call options will be at-the-money if the spot rate in 60 days is $1.34, and the call or put option buyer will lose the $2,500 option premium.

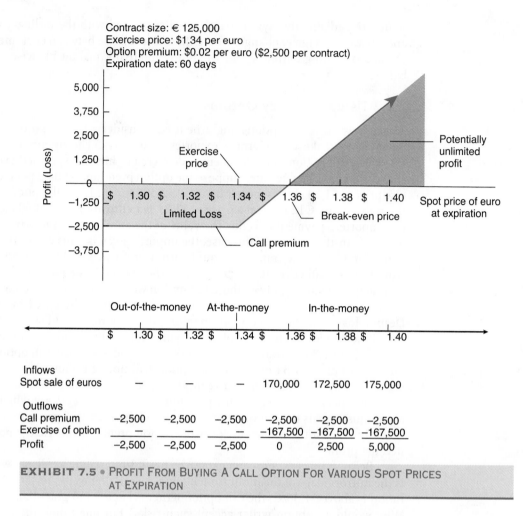

Contract size: € 125,000
Exercise price: $1.34 per euro
Option premium: $0.02 per euro ($2,500 per contract)
Expiration date: 60 days

	$ 1.30	$ 1.32	$ 1.34	$ 1.36	$ 1.38	$ 1.40
	Out-of-the-money		At-the-money		In-the-money	
Inflows						
Spot sale of euros	—	—	—	170,000	172,500	175,000
Outflows						
Call premium	–2,500	–2,500	–2,500	–2,500	–2,500	–2,500
Exercise of option	—	—	—	–167,500	–167,500	–167,500
Profit	–2,500	–2,500	–2,500	0	2,500	5,000

EXHIBIT 7.5 • PROFIT FROM BUYING A CALL OPTION FOR VARIOUS SPOT PRICES AT EXPIRATION

As in the case of the call option, the writer of the put option will have a payoff profile that is the mirror image of that for the buyer. As shown in Exhibit 7.8, if the spot rate at expiration is $1.34 or higher, the option writer gets to keep the full $2,500 premium. As the spot rate falls below $1.34, the option writer earns a decreasing profit down to $1.32. For spot rates below $1.32/€, the option writer is exposed to increasing losses, up to a maximum potential loss of $165,000. The writer of the put option will accept these risks in the hope of profiting from the put premium. These risks may be minimal if the put option writer is already short euro.

ILLUSTRATION   *Speculating with a Japanese Yen Call Option*

In March, a speculator who is gambling that the yen will appreciate against the dollar pays $680 to buy a yen June 81 call option. This option gives the speculator the right to buy ¥6,250,000 in June at an exchange rate of ¥1 = $0.0081 (the 81 in the contract description is expressed in hundredths of a cent). By the expiration date in June, the yen spot price has risen to $0.0083. What is the investor's net return on the contract?

Solution. Because the call option is in-the-money by 0.02 cents, the investor will realize a gain of $1,250 ($0.0002 × 6,250,000) on the option contract. This amount less the $680 paid for the option produces a gain of $570 on the contract.

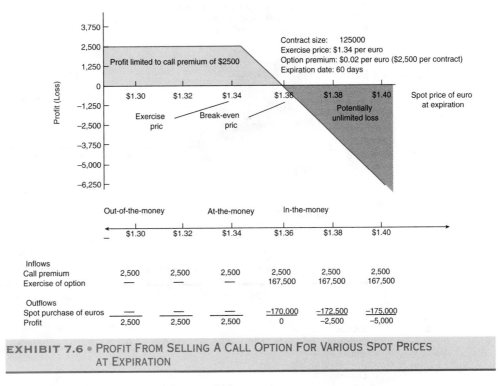

EXHIBIT 7.6 • PROFIT FROM SELLING A CALL OPTION FOR VARIOUS SPOT PRICES AT EXPIRATION

Typical users of currency options might be financial firms holding large investments overseas where sizable unrealized gains have occurred because of exchange rate changes and where these gains are thought likely to be partially or fully reversed. Limited use of currency options has also been made by firms that have a foreign currency inflow or outflow that is possibly forthcoming but not definitely. In such cases, where future foreign currency cash flows are contingent on an event such as acceptance of a bid, long call or put positions can be safer hedges than either futures or forwards.

For example, assume that a U.S. investor makes a firm bid in pound sterling to buy a piece of real estate in London. If the firm wishes to hedge the dollar cost of the bid, it can buy pounds forward so that if the pound sterling appreciates, the gain on the forward contract will offset the increased dollar cost of the prospective investment. But if the bid is eventually rejected, and if the pound has fallen in the interim, losses from the forward position will have no offset. If no forward cover is taken and the pound appreciates, the real estate will cost more than expected.

Currency call options can provide a better hedge in such a case. Purchased-pound call options would provide protection against a rising pound; and yet, if the bid were rejected and the pound had fallen, the uncovered hedge loss would be limited to the premium paid for the calls. Note that a U.S. company in the opposite position, such as one bidding to supply goods or services priced in pounds to a British project, whose receipt of future pound cash inflows is contingent on acceptance of its bid, would use a long pound put position to provide the safest hedge.

Currency options also can be used by pure speculators, those without an underlying foreign currency transaction to protect against. The presence of speculators in the options markets adds to the breadth and depth of these markets, thereby making them more liquid and lowering transactions costs and risk.

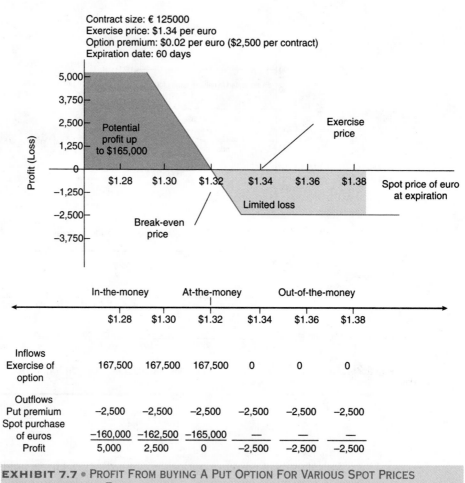

Contract size: € 125000
Exercise price: $1.34 per euro
Option premium: $0.02 per euro ($2,500 per contract)
Expiration date: 60 days

	In-the-money		At-the-money	Out-of-the-money		
	$1.28	$1.30	$1.32	$1.34	$1.36	$1.38
Inflows						
Exercise of option	167,500	167,500	167,500	0	0	0
Outflows						
Put premium	−2,500	−2,500	−2,500	−2,500	−2,500	−2,500
Spot purchase of euros	−160,000	−162,500	−165,000	—	—	—
Profit	5,000	2,500	0	−2,500	−2,500	−2,500

EXHIBIT 7.7 ● PROFIT FROM BUYING A PUT OPTION FOR VARIOUS SPOT PRICES AT EXPIRATION

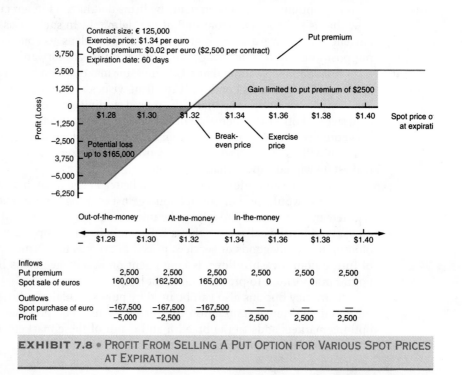

Contract size: € 125,000
Exercise price: $1.34 per euro
Option premium: $0.02 per euro ($2,500 per contract)
Expiration date: 60 days

	Out-of-the-money		At-the-money	In-the-money		
	$1.28	$1.30	$1.32	$1.34	$1.36	$1.38	$1.40
Inflows						
Put premium	2,500	2,500	2,500	2,500	2,500	2,500
Spot sale of euros	160,000	162,500	165,000	0	0	0
Outflows						
Spot purchase of euro	−167,500	−167,500	−167,500	—	—	—
Profit	−5,000	−2,500	0	2,500	2,500	2,500

EXHIBIT 7.8 ● PROFIT FROM SELLING A PUT OPTION FOR VARIOUS SPOT PRICES AT EXPIRATION

Currency Spread   A **currency spread** allows speculators to bet on the direction of a currency but at a lower cost than buying a put or a call option alone. It involves buying an option at one strike price and selling a similar option at a different strike price. The currency spread limits the holder's downside risk on the currency bet but at the cost of limiting the position's upside potential. As shown in Exhibit 7.9a, a spread designed to bet on a currency's appreciation, also called a **bull spread**, would involve buying a call at one strike price and selling another call at a higher strike price. The net premium paid for this position is positive because the former call will be higher priced than the latter (with a lower strike, the option is less out-of-the-money), but it will be less than the cost of buying the former option alone. At the same time, the upside is limited by the strike price of the latter option. Exhibit 7.9b shows the payoff profile of a currency spread designed to bet on a currency's decline. This spread, also called a **bear spread**, involves buying a put at one strike price and selling another put at a lower strike price.

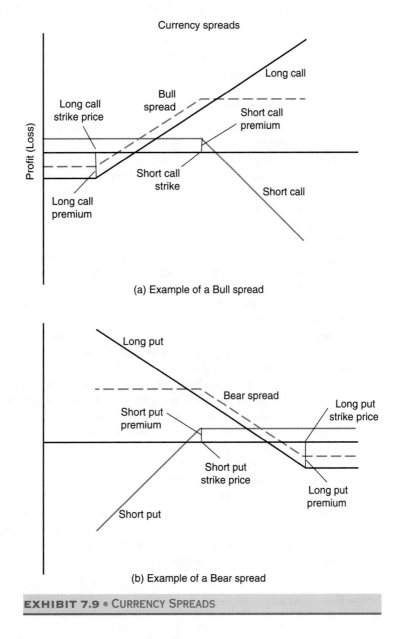

(a) Example of a Bull spread

(b) Example of a Bear spread

EXHIBIT 7.9 • CURRENCY SPREADS

Knockout Options   Another way to bet on currency movements at a lower cost than buying a call or a put alone is to use knockout options. A **knockout option** is similar to a standard option except that it is canceled—that is, knocked out—if the exchange rate crosses, even briefly, a pre-defined level called the **outstrike**. If the exchange rate breaches this barrier, the holder cannot exercise this option, even if it ends up in-the-money. Knockout options, also known as *barrier options*, are less expensive than standard currency options precisely because of this risk of early cancellation.

There are different types of knockout options. For example, a *down-and-out call* will have a positive payoff to the option holder if the underlying currency strengthens but is canceled if it weakens sufficiently to hit the outstrike. Conversely, a *down-and-out put* has a positive payoff if the currency weakens but will be canceled if it weakens beyond the outstrike. In addition to lowering cost (albeit at the expense of less protection), down-and-out options are useful when a company believes that if the foreign currency declines below a certain level, it is unlikely to rebound to the point that it will cause the company losses. *Up-and-out options* are canceled if the underlying currency strengthens beyond the outstrike. In contrast to the previous knockout options, *down-and-in* and *up-and-in options* come into existence if, and only if, the currency crosses a preset barrier. The pricing of these options is extremely complex.

7.2.3 Option Pricing and Valuation

From a theoretical standpoint, the value of an option comprises two components: intrinsic value and time value. The **intrinsic value** of the option is the amount by which the option is in-the-money, or $S - X$, where S is the current spot price and X the exercise price. In other words, the intrinsic value equals the immediate exercise value of the option. Thus, the further into the money an option is, the more valuable it is. An out-of-the-money option has no intrinsic value. For example, the intrinsic value of a call option on Swiss francs with an exercise price of $0.77 and a spot rate of $0.80 would be $0.03 per franc. The intrinsic value of the option for spot rates that are less than the exercise price is zero. Any excess of the option value over its intrinsic value is called the **time value** of the contract. An option will generally sell for at least its intrinsic value. The more out-of-the-money an option is, the lower the option price. These features are shown in Exhibit 7.10.

During the time remaining before an option expires, the exchange rate can move so as to make exercising the option profitable or more profitable. That is, an out-of-the-money option can move into the money, or one already in-the-money can become more so. The chance that an option will become profitable or more profitable is always greater than zero. Consequently, the time value of an option is always positive for an out-of-the-money option and is usually positive for an in-the-money option. Moreover, the more time that remains until an option expires, the higher the time value tends to be. For example, an option with 6 months remaining until expiration will tend to have a higher price than an option with the same strike price but with only 3 months until expiration. As the option approaches its maturity, the time value declines to zero.

The value of an American option always exceeds its intrinsic value because the time value is always positive up to the expiration date. For example, if $S > X$, then $C(X) > S - X$, where $C(X)$ is the dollar price of an American call option on one unit of foreign currency. However, the case is more ambiguous for a European option because increasing the time to maturity may not increase its value, given that it can be exercised only on the maturity date.[3] That is, a European currency option may be in-the-money before expiration, yet it may be out-of-the-money by the maturity date.

---

[3] For a technical discussion of foreign currency option pricing, see Mark B. Garman and Steven W. Kohlhagen, "Foreign Currency Option Values," *Journal of International Money and Finance* December 1983, pp. 231–237.

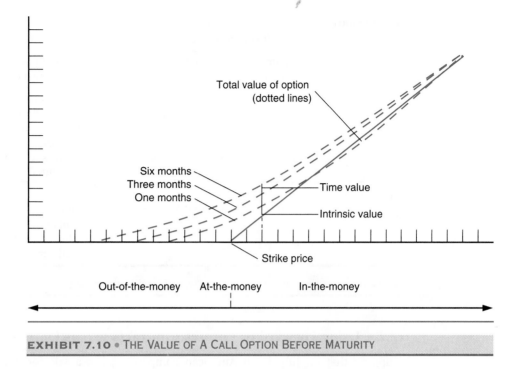

Total value of option
(dotted lines)

Six months
Three months
One months

Time value

Intrinsic value

Strike price

Out-of-the-money   At-the-money   In-the-money

EXHIBIT 7.10 • THE VALUE OF A CALL OPTION BEFORE MATURITY

Before expiration, an out-of-the-money option has only time value, but an in-the-money option has both time value and intrinsic value. At expiration, an option can have only intrinsic value. The time value of a currency option reflects the probability that its intrinsic value will increase before expiration; this probability depends, among other things, on the volatility of the exchange rate. An increase in currency volatility increases the chance of an extremely high or low exchange rate at the time the option expires. The chance of a very high exchange rate benefits the call owner. The chance of a very low exchange rate, however, is irrelevant; the option will be worthless for any exchange rate less than the striking price, whether the exchange rate is "low" or "very low." Inasmuch as the effect of increased volatility is beneficial, the value of the call option is higher. Put options similarly benefit from increased volatility in the exchange rate.

Another aspect of time value involves interest rates. In general, options have a present intrinsic value, determined by the exercise price and price of the underlying asset. Because the option is a claim on a specified amount of an asset over a period of time into the future, that claim must have a return in line with market interest rates on comparable instruments. Therefore, a rise in the interest rate will cause call values to rise and put values to fall.

Pricing foreign currency options is more complex because it requires consideration of both domestic and foreign interest rates. A foreign currency is normally at a forward premium or discount vis-à-vis the domestic currency. As we saw in Chapter 4, this forward premium or discount is determined by relative interest rates. Consequently, for foreign currency options, call values rise and put values fall when the domestic interest rate increases or the foreign interest rate decreases.

The flip side of a more valuable put or call option is a higher option premium. Hence, options become more expensive when exchange rate volatility rises. Similarly, when the domestic-foreign interest differential increases, call options become more expensive and put options less expensive. These elements of option valuation are summarized in Exhibit 7.11.

Price Equals the Sum of	Intrinsic Value	Time Value
	The amount by which the option is in-the-money	The amount by which the price of the contract exceeds its intrinsic value.
Call option	$= S - X$, where S is the current spot price and X the exercise price Intrinsic value is zero if $S - X < 0$	Positively affected by an increase in: ● time to expiration (usually) ● volatility ● domestic—foreign interest rate differential
Put option	$= X - S$ Intrinsic value is zero if $X - S < 0$	Positively affected by an increase in: ● time to expiration (usually) ● volatility ● domestic—foreign interest rate differential

EXHIBIT 7.11 ● CURRENCY OPTION PRICING AND VALUATION

7.2.4 Using Forward or Futures Contracts versus Options Contracts

Suppose that on July 1, an American company makes a sale for which it will receive €125,000 on September 1. The firm will want to convert those euros into dollars, so it is exposed to the risk that the euro will fall below its current spot rate of $1.3425 in the meantime. The firm can protect itself against a declining euro by selling its expected euro receipts forward (using a futures contract at a futures rate of $1.3456) or by buying a euro put option.

Exhibit 7.12 shows possible results for each choice, using options with strike prices just above and just below the spot exchange of July 1 ($1.33 and $1.35). The example assumes a euro decline to $1.3125 and the consequent price adjustments of associated futures and options contracts. The put quotes are the option premiums per euro. Thus, the dollar premium associated with a particular quote equals the quote multiplied by the number of euros covered by the put options. For example, the quote of $0.0046 for a September put option with a strike price of 1.33 represents a premium for covering the exporter's €125,000 transaction equal to $0.0046 × 125,000 = $575.

In the example just described, a decision to remain unhedged would yield a loss of 125,000 × (1.3425 − 1.3125), or $3,750. The outcomes of the various hedge possibilities are shown in Exhibit 7.13.

Exhibit 7.13 demonstrates the following two differences between the futures and options hedging strategies:

1. The futures hedge offers the closest offset to the loss due to the decline of the euro.
2. The purchase of the in-the-money put option (the 1.35 strike price) offers greater protection (but at a higher premium) than the out-of-the-money put (the 1.33 strike price).

	July 1	September 1
Spot	$1.3425	$1.3125
September futures	$1.3456	$1.3150
September 1.33 put	$0.0046	$0.0212
September 1.35 put	$0.0138	$0.0402

EXHIBIT 7.12 ● DECLINING EXCHANGE RATE SCENARIO

Result of selling futures

$(1.3456 - 1.3150) \times 125,000 = \$3,825$ profit

Results of buying put options

1.33 output: $(0.0212 - 0.0046) \times 125,000 = \$2,075$ profit

1.35 output: $(0.0402 - 0.0138) \times 125,000 = \$3,300$ profit

---

EXHIBIT 7.13 • HEDGING ALTERNATIVES: OFFSETTING A $3,750 LOSS DUE TO A DECLINING EURO

Note that the September futures price is unequal to the spot rate on September 1 because settlement is not until later in the month. As the euro declines in value, the company will suffer a larger loss on its euro receivables, to be offset by a further increase in the value of the put and futures contracts.

Although the company wants to protect against the possibility of a euro depreciation, what would happen if the euro appreciated? To answer this question, so as to assess fully the options and futures hedge strategies, assume the hypothetical conditions in Exhibit 7.14.

In this scenario, the rise in the euro would increase the value of the unhedged position by $125,000 \times (1.3761 - 1.3425)$, or $4,200. This gain would be offset by losses on the futures or options contracts, as shown in Exhibit 7.15.

We can see that the futures hedge again provides the closest offset. Because these hedges generate losses, however, the company would be better served under this scenario by the smallest offset. With rapidly rising exchange rates, the company would benefit most from hedging with a long put position as opposed to a futures contract; conversely, with rapidly falling exchange rates, the company would benefit most from hedging with a futures contract.

7.2.5 Futures Options

In January 1984, the CME introduced a market in options on DM (now replaced by euro) futures contracts. Since then, the **futures option** market has grown to include options on futures in the Australian dollar, Brazilian real, British pound, Canadian dollar, euro, Japanese yen, Mexican peso, New Zealand dollar, Russian ruble, South African rand, and Swiss franc as well. Trading involves purchases and sales of puts and calls on a contract calling for delivery of a standard CME futures contract in the currency rather than the currency itself. When such a contract is exercised, the holder receives a short or long position in the underlying currency futures contract that is marked-to-market, providing the

	July 1	*September 1*
Spot	$1.3425	$1.3761
September futures	$1.3456	$1.3796
September 1.33 put	$0.0046	$0.0001
September 1.35 put	$0.0138	$0.0001

EXHIBIT 7.14 • RISING EXCHANGE RATE SCENARIO

Result of selling futures

$(1.3456 - 1.3796) \times 125,000 = \$4,250$ loss

Result of buying put options

133 put: $(0.0046 - 0.0001) \times 125,000 = \$562.5$ loss

135 put: $(0.0138 - 0.0001) \times 125,000 = \$1,712.50$ loss

---

EXHIBIT 7.15 • HEDGING ALTERNATIVES: OFFSETTING A $4,200 GAIN DUE TO A RISING EURO

---

holder with a cash gain. (If there were a loss on the futures contract, the option would not be exercised.) Specifically,

- If a call futures option contract is exercised, the holder receives a long position in the underlying futures contract plus an amount of cash equal to the current futures price minus the strike price.

- If a put futures option is exercised, the holder receives a short position in the futures contract plus an amount of cash equal to the strike price minus the current futures price.

The seller of these options has the opposite position to the holder after exercise: a cash outflow plus a short futures position on a call and a long futures position on a put option.

ILLUSTRATION   *Exercising a Pound Call Futures Option Contract*

An investor is holding a pound call futures option contract for June delivery (representing £62,500) at a strike price of $1.9565. The current price of a pound futures contract due in June is $1.9663. What will the investor receive if she exercises her futures option?

Solution. The investor will receive a long position in the June futures contract established at a price of $1.9565 and the option writer has a short position in the same futures contract. These positions are immediately marked to market, triggering a cash payment to the investor from the option writer of $62,500(\$1.9663 - \$1.9565) = \$612.50$. If the investor desires, he or she can immediately close out her long futures position at no cost, leaving her with the $612.50 payoff.

ILLUSTRATION   *Exercising a Swiss Franc Put Futures Option Contract*

An investor is holding one Swiss franc March put futures option contract (representing SFr 125,000) at a strike price of $0.8132. The current price of a Swiss franc futures contract for March delivery is $0.7950. What will the investor receive if he or she exercises futures option?

Solution. The investor will receive a short position in the March futures contract established at a price of $0.8132, and the option writer has a long position in the same futures contract. These positions are immediately marked to market and the investor will receive a cash payment from the option writer of $125,000(\$0.8132 - 0.7950) = \$2,275$. If the investor desires, he or she can immediately close out her short futures position at no cost, leaving her with the $2,275 payoff.

A futures option contract has this advantage over a futures contract: With a futures contract, the holder must deliver one currency against the other or reverse the contract, regardless of whether this move is profitable. In contrast, with the futures option contract, the holder is protected against an adverse move in the exchange rate but may allow the option to expire unexercised if using the spot market would be more profitable.

7.3 READING CURRENCY FUTURES AND OPTIONS PRICES

Futures and exchange-listed options prices appear daily in the financial press. Exhibit 7.16 shows prices for May 29, 2007 as displayed in the *Wall Street Journal* on the following day. Futures prices on the CME are listed for seven currencies, with two contracts quoted for each currency: June 2007 and September 2007. Included are the opening and last settlement (settle) prices, the change from the previous trading day, the range for the day, and the number of contracts outstanding (open interest). For example, the September euro futures contract opened at $1.3498 per euro and closed at $1.3501, down $0.0001 per euro relative to its previous closing price of $1.3502. Futures prices are shown in Exhibit 7.16a.

Exhibit 7.16b shows the CME options on CME futures contracts. To interpret the numbers in this column, consider the September euro call options. These are rights to buy the September euro futures contract at specified prices—the strike prices. For example, the call option with a strike price of 13300 means that you can purchase an option to buy a September euro futures contract, up to the September settlement date, for $1.3300 per euro. This option will cost $0.0272 per euro, or $3,400, plus brokerage commission, for a €125,000 contract. The price is high because the option is in-the-money. In contrast, the September futures option with a strike price of 13600, which is out-of-the-money, costs only $0.0109 per euro, or $1,362.50 for one contract. These option prices indicate that the market expects the dollar price of the euro to exceed $1.3300 but is less confident it will rise much beyond $1.3600 by September.

As we have just seen, a futures call option allows you to buy the relevant futures contract, which is settled at maturity. On the contrary, the Philadelphia call options contract is an option to buy foreign exchange spot, which is settled when the call option is exercised; the buyer receives foreign currency immediately.

Exhibit 7.17 summarizes how to read price quotations for futures and options on futures using a euro illustration.

7.4 SUMMARY AND CONCLUSIONS

In this chapter, we examined the currency futures and options markets and looked at some of the institutional characteristics and mechanics of these markets. We saw that currency futures and options offer alternative hedging (and speculative) mechanisms for companies and individuals. Like forward contracts, futures contracts must be settled at maturity. By contrast, currency options give the owner the right but not the obligation to buy (call option) or sell (put option) the contracted currency. An American option can be exercised at any time upto the expiration date; a European option can be exercised only at maturity.

Futures contracts are standardized contracts that trade on organized exchanges. Forward contracts, however, are custom-tailored contracts, typically entered into

Japanese Yen (CME)-¥12,500,000; $ per 100¥

	Open	High	Low	Settle	Chg	LIFETIME High	Low	Open Int
7-Jun	0.8237	0.8274	0.823	0.8249	0.001	0.9655	0.0001	286,091
7-Sep	0.833	0.8369	0.8327	0.8345	0.001	0.9457	0.0001	11,155
7-Dec	0.8436	0.8444	0.8422	0.8437	0.001	0.925	0.8422	5,787

Est vol 96,755; vol Fri 99,274; open int, 315,053, −2,630

Canadian dollar (CME)-CAD 100,000; $ per CAD

	Open	High	Low	Settle	Chg	LIFETIME High	Low	Open Int
7-Jun	0.927	0.9342	0.9234	0.9323	0.006	0.9342	0.8452	172,267
7-Sep	0.9298	0.9363	0.9257	0.9344	0.0059	0.9363	0.8476	4,465
7-Dec	0.9311	0.938	0.9284	0.9362	0.0059	0.938	0.8498	1,982
8-Jun	0.9368	0.9393	0.9313	0.9387	0.0059	0.9393	0.8542	230
8-Sep	0.934	0.94	0.9322	0.9396	0.0059	0.94	0.8699	27

Est vol 63,559; vol Fri 40,773; open int, 179,365, +5,400

British pound (CME)-£62,500; $ per £

	Open	High	Low	Settle	Chg	LIFETIME High	Low	Open Int
7-Jun	1.9836	1.9897	1.9788	1.9798	−0.0045	2.0128	1.7426	132,874
7-Sep	1.9791	1.9875	1.9769	1.9777	−0.0045	2.01	1.8408	1,391
7-Dec	1.9765	1.9821	1.9745	1.9744	−0.0045	2.0055	1.8546	175

Est vol 99,275; vol Fri 60,000; open int, 134,459, −1,724

Swiss franc (CME)-CHF 125,000; $ per CHF

	Open	High	Low	Settle	Chg	LIFETIME High	Low	Open Int
7-Jun	0.8161	0.8211	0.8138	0.818	0.0019	0.8624	0.7926	98,437
7-Sep	0.8228	0.8267	0.8197	0.8238	0.0019	0.8604	0.8101	997

Est vol 65,710; vol Fri 35,490; open int, 99,487, −1,935

Australian dollar (CME)-AUD 100,000; $ per AUD

	Open	High	Low	Settle	Chg	LIFETIME High	Low	Open Int
7-Jun	0.8178	0.8208	0.8158	0.8181	0.0001	0.8378	0.7033	99,899
7-Sep	0.815	0.8188	0.814	0.8161	0.0001	0.8346	0.7364	1,924
7-Dec	0.8152	0.8153	0.8136	0.8139	0.0001	0.8304	0.7342	423

Est vol 32,156; vol Fri 27,190; open int, 102,255, +1,033

Mexican Peso (CME)-MXN 500,000; $ per 10MXN

	Open	High	Low	Settle	Chg	LIFETIME High	LIFETIME Low	Open Int
7-Jun	0.9275	0.9275	0.9225	0.9235	−0.00225	0.93	0.86825	112,584
7-Sep	0.92075	0.92125	0.9175	0.91825	−0.00225	0.92475	0.88	1,481

Est vol 17,891; vol Fri 43,482; open int, 136,631, +3,982

Euro (CME)-€125,000; $ per €

	Open	High	Low	Settle	Chg	LIFETIME High	LIFETIME Low	Open Int
7-Jun	1.346	1.3531	1.343	1.3461	−0.0001	1.3715	1.219	207,987
7-Sep	1.3498	1.3571	1.3472	1.3501	−0.0001	1.3749	1.229	3,228
7-Dec	1.352	1.3599	1.3519	1.353	−0.0001	1.3777	1.272	648

Est vol 205,666; vol Fri 129,127; open int, 211,982, +2,731

EXHIBIT 7.16A • Foreign Currency Futures Contracts. May 29, 2007

Japanese Yen (CME)

12,500,000 yen, cents per 100 yen

Strike Price	Calls Jun	Calls Jul	Calls Sep	Puts Jun	Puts Jul	Puts Sep
825	36	126	167	37	31	73
830	19	95	139	70	50	95
835	10	69	115	111	74	120
840	6	50	95	157	105	149
845	4	36	79	205	140	183
850	3	26	65	254	180	218
855	2.5	20	54	303	224	256
860	2	15	45	353	269	297
865	1.5	11	38	402	315	339
870	1	9	32	452	–	383
875	1	7	27	501	–	427
Volume		Calls		464	Puts	302
Open Interest		Calls		61,049	Puts	40,431

British Pound (CME)

62,500 pounds, cents per pound

Strike Price	Calls Jun	Calls Jul	Calls Sep	Puts Jun	Puts Jul	Puts Sep
1900	798	7.5	805	0.01	5	36
1910	698	7.06	4.1	1	7	47
1920	598	586	631	1	12	61

(Continued)

British Pound (CME) (Continued)

Strike Price	Calls Jun	Jul	Sep	Puts Jun	Jul	Sep
1930	499	493	549	2	18	78
1940	400	404	472	3	29	100
1950	304	322	400	6	46	126
1960	213	247	333	15	71	158
1970	133	183	272	35	106	196
1980	65	128	218	67	151	241
1990	30	88	178	132	210	299
2000	13	58	143	215	280	363
2010	5	39	115	307	360	434
2020	2	26	91	404	–	5.9
Volume			Calls	1,707	Puts	747
Open Interest			Calls	15,731	Puts	14,871

Canadian Dollar (CME)

100,000 dollars, cents per dollar

Strike Price	Calls Jun	Jul	Sep	Puts Jun	Jul	Sep
885	473	494	498	0.5	1	8
890	423	445	451	1	2	11
895	373	396	405	0.02	3	15
900	323	347	361	0.5	4.5	21
905	274	300	319	1	7	28
910	225	254	278	2	11	37
915	177	210	240	4	17	48
920	130	168	205	7	25	63
925	87	132	172	14	38	79
930	54	99	142	31	55	99
935	30	74	119	57	80	–
Volume			Calls	3,875	Puts	1,716
Open Interest			Calls	19,458	Puts	25,364

Swiss Franc (CME)

125,000 francs, cents per franc

Strike Price	Calls Jun	Jul	Sep	Puts Jun	Jul	Sep
820	27	83	122	47	45	84
825	13	57	96	83	69	108
830	6	38	75	126	100	136
835	2.5	25	57	172	136	168
840	1	16	43	221	–	203
845	0.01	0.1	32	2.7	221	–
850	0.01	6	23	320	–	–
855	0.01	4	18	–	–	–
860	1	2.5	14	–	–	–
865	–	–	0.11	–	–	–

870	1.5	1	9	–	–	–
875	1	–	7	–	–	–
880	0.5	–	5	–	–	–
Volume		Calls		145	Puts	126
Open Interest		Calls		4,572	Puts	3,230

Euro (CME)

125,000 Euros, cents per Euro

Strike Price	Calls Jun	Jul	Sep	Puts Jun	Jul	Sep
12800	6.61	7.01	7.04	0.015	0.005	0.08
12850	6.11	6.51	–	0.005	0.01	0.1
12900	5.61	6.01	6.08	0.01	0.015	0.13
12950	5.11	5.51	–	0.005	0.02	0.16
13000	4.61	5.02	5.17	0.005	0.03	0.21
13050	4.11	4.53	4.72	0.005	0.04	0.26
13100	3.61	4.05	4.29	0.005	0.06	0.33
13150	3.12	3.57	3.88	0.01	0.08	0.41
13200	2.62	3.12	3.47	0.015	0.12	0.5
13250	2.13	2.68	3.09	0.025	0.18	0.61
13300	1.66	2.26	2.72	0.05	0.26	0.74
13350	1.22	1.87	2.39	0.11	0.37	0.9
13400	0.84	1.51	2.08	0.23	0.51	1.08
13450	0.53	1.19	1.79	0.42	0.68	1.29
13500	0.3	0.92	1.53	0.69	0.91	1.52
13550	0.16	0.69	1.29	1.05	1.18	1.77
13600	0.08	0.5	1.09	1.47	1.48	2.07
13650	0.04	0.36	0.91	1.93	1.84	2.38
13700	0.025	0.25	0.76	2.41	2.23	2.72
13750	0.015	0.18	0.63	2.9	2.66	3.09
13800	0.01	0.12	0.52	3.4	3.1	–
13850	0.005	0.08	0.42	3.89	–	–
13900	0.01	0.06	0.34	4.39	–	–
13950	0.01	0.045	0.28	–	–	–
14000	0.005	0.035	0.22	5.39	–	5.16
14050	0.005	0.025	0.18	–	–	–
14100	0.01	0.02	0.14	6.39	4.18	–
14150	0.005	0.015	0.12	–	–	–
14200	0.005	0.01	0.1	7.39	–	–
14250	0.005	0.005	0.08	–	–	–
14300	0.015	0.005	0.06	–	–	–
14350	0.01	0.005	0.05	–	–	–
14400	0.005	0.005	0.04	–	–	8.99
Volume		Calls		3,004	Puts	2,117
Open Interest		Calls		73,802	Puts	82,169

Source: WSJ online.

EXHIBIT 16(B) • FOREIGN CURRENCY FUTURES OPTIONS. MAY 29, 2007

Trading activity can be monitored daily in the business pages of most major newspapers. The following displays illustrate the way these prices are shown.
Futures

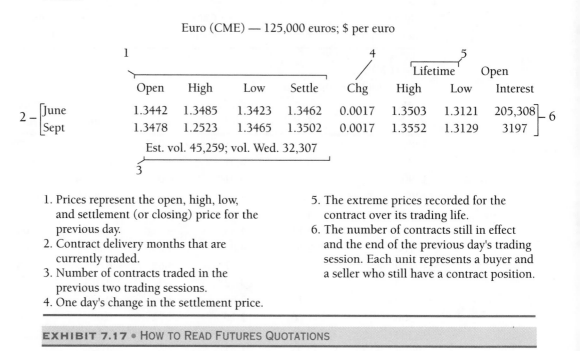

Euro (CME) — 125,000 euros; $ per euro

	Open	High	Low	Settle	Chg	Lifetime High	Low	Open Interest
June	1.3442	1.3485	1.3423	1.3462	0.0017	1.3503	1.3121	205,308
Sept	1.3478	1.2523	1.3465	1.3502	0.0017	1.3552	1.3129	3197

Est. vol. 45,259; vol. Wed. 32,307

1. Prices represent the open, high, low, and settlement (or closing) price for the previous day.
2. Contract delivery months that are currently traded.
3. Number of contracts traded in the previous two trading sessions.
4. One day's change in the settlement price.

5. The extreme prices recorded for the contract over its trading life.
6. The number of contracts still in effect and the end of the previous day's trading session. Each unit represents a buyer and a seller who still have a contract position.

EXHIBIT 7.17 • HOW TO READ FUTURES QUOTATIONS

between a bank and its customers. Options contracts are sold both on organized exchanges and in the OTC market. Like forward contracts, OTC options are contracts whose specifications are generally negotiated as to the terms and conditions between a bank and its customers.

QUESTIONS

1. On April 1, the spot price of the British pound was $1.96 and the price of the June futures contract was $1.95. During April the pound appreciated, so that by May 1 it was selling for $2.01. What do you think happened to the price of the June pound futures contract during April? Explain.

2. What are the basic differences between forward and futures contracts? Between futures and options contracts?

3. A forward market already existed, so why was it necessary to establish currency futures and currency options contracts?

4. Suppose that Texas Instruments (TI) must pay a French supplier €10 million in 90 days.

   a. Explain how TI can use currency futures to hedge its exchange risk. How many futures contracts will TI need to fully protect itself?

   b. Explain how TI can use currency options to hedge its exchange risk. How many options contracts will TI need to fully protect itself?

   c. Discuss the advantages and disadvantages of using currency futures versus currency options to hedge TI's exchange risk.

5. Suppose that Bechtel Group wants to hedge a bid on a Japanese construction project. But because the yen exposure is contingent on acceptance of its bid, Bechtel decides to buy a put option for the ¥15 billion bid amount rather than sell it forward. In order to reduce its hedging cost, however, Bechtel simultaneously sells a call option for ¥15 billion with the same strike price. Bechtel reasons that it wants to protect its downside risk on the contract and is willing to sacrifice the upside potential in order to collect the call premium. Comment on Bechtel's hedging strategy.

PROBLEMS

1. On Monday morning, an investor takes a long position in a pound futures contract that matures on Wednesday afternoon. The agreed price is $1.95 for £62,500. At the close of trading on Monday, the futures price has risen to $1.96. At Tuesday close, the price rises further to $1.98. At Wednesday close, the price falls to $1.955, and the contract matures. The investor takes delivery of the pounds at the prevailing price of $1.955. Detail the daily settlement process (see Exhibit 7.3). What will be the investor's profit (loss)?

2. Suppose that the forward ask price for March 20 on euros is $1.3327 at the same time that the price of CME euro futures for delivery on March 20 is $1.3345. How could an arbitrageur profit from this situation? What will be the arbitrageur's profit per futures contract (contract size is €125,000)?

3. Suppose that Dell buys a Swiss franc futures contract (contract size is SFr 125,000) at a price of $0.83. If the spot rate for the Swiss franc at the date of settlement is SFr 1 = $0.8250, what is Dell's gain or loss on this contract?

4. On January 10, Volkswagen (VW) agrees to import auto parts worth $7 million from the United States. The parts will be delivered on March 4 and are payable immediately in dollars. VW decides to hedge its dollar position by entering into CME futures contracts. The spot rate is $1.3447/€, and the March futures price is $1.3502/€.

   a. Calculate the number of futures contracts that VW must buy to offset its dollar exchange risk on the parts contract.

   b. On March 4, the spot rate turns out to be $1.3452/€, while the March futures price is $1.3468/€. Calculate VW's net euro gain or loss on its futures position. Compare this figure with VW's gain or loss on its unhedged position.

5. Citigroup sells a call option on euros (contract size is €500,000) at a premium of $0.04 per euro. If the exercise price is $1.34 and the spot price of the euro at date of expiration is $1.36, what is Citigroup's profit (loss) on the call option?

6. Suppose you buy three June PHLX euro call options with a 90 strike price at a price of 2.3 (¢/€).

   a. What would be your total dollar cost for these calls, ignoring broker fees?

   b. After holding these calls for 60 days, you sell them for 3.8 (¢/€). What is your net profit on the contracts, assuming that brokerage fees on both entry and exit were $5 per contract and that your opportunity cost was 8% per annum on the money tied up in the premium?

7. A trader executes a "bear spread" on the Japanese yen consisting of a long PHLX 103 March put and a short PHLX 101 March put.

   a. If the price of the 103 put is 2.81 (100th of ¢/¥), while the price of the 101 put is 1.6 (100th of ¢/¥), what is the net cost of the bear spread?

   b. What is the maximum amount the trader can make on the bear spread in the event the yen depreciates against the dollar?

   c. Redo your answers to Parts (a) and (b) assuming the trader executes a "bull spread" consisting of a long PHLX 97 March call priced at 1.96 (100th of ¢/¥) and a short PHLX 103 March call priced at 3.91 (100th of ¢/¥). What is the trader's maximum profit? Maximum loss?

8. Apex Corporation must pay its Japanese supplier ¥125 million in 3 months. It is thinking of buying 20 yen call options (contract size is ¥6.25 million) at a strike price of $0.00800 in order to protect against the risk of a rising yen. The premium is 0.015 cents per yen. Alternatively, Apex could buy 10 three-month yen futures contracts (contract size is ¥12.5 million) at a price of $0.007940/¥. The current spot rate is ¥1 = $0.007823. Apex's treasurer believes that the most likely value for the yen in 90 days is $0.007900, but the yen could go as high as $0.008400 or as low as $0.007500.

   a. Diagram Apex's gains and losses on the call option position and the futures position within its range of expected prices (see Exhibit 7.4). Ignore transaction costs and margins.

   b. Calculate what Apex would gain or lose on the option and futures positions if the yen settled at its most likely value.

   c. What is Apex's break-even future spot price on the option contract? On the futures contract?

   d. Calculate and diagram the corresponding profit and loss and break-even positions on the futures and options contracts for the sellers of these contracts.

BIBLIOGRAPHY

Bates, D. S. "Jumps and Stochastic Volatility: Exchange Rate Processes Implicit in PHLX Deutschemark Options," Wharton School Working Paper, 1993.

Black, F. and Myron Scholes, "The Pricing of Options and Corporate Liabilities," *Journal of Political Economy*, May–June 1973, pp. 637–659.

Bodurtha, J. N., Jr. and G. R. Courtadon, "Tests of an American Option Pricing Model on the Foreign Currency Options Market," *Journal of Financial and Quantitative Analysis*, June 1987, pp. 153–167.

Chicago Mercantile Exchange. *Using Currency Futures and Options*. Chicago: CME, 1987.

Cornell, B. and M. Reinganum, "Forward and Futures Prices: Evidence from the Foreign Exchange Markets," *Journal of Finance*, December 1981, pp. 1035–1045.

Garman, M. B. and Steven W. Kohlhagen, "Foreign Currency Option Values," *Journal of International Money and Finance*, December 1983, pp. 231–237.

Jorion, P. "On Jump Processes in the Foreign Exchange and Stock Markets," *Review of Financial Studies* 1, No. 4 (1988): 427–445.

Shastri, K. and K. Wethyavivorn, "The Valuation of Currency Options for Alternate Stochastic Processes," *Journal of Financial Research*, Winter 1987, pp. 283–293.

INTERNET RESOURCES

www.ny.frb.org/markets/impliedvolatility.html Web page of the Federal Reserve Bank of New York that lists implied volatilities for foreign currency options.

www.bis.org/ Web page of the Bank for International Settlements that lists downloadable publications such as BIS Annual Report, statistics on derivatives, external debt, foreign exchange market activity, and so on.

www.cme.com Web site of the Chicago Mercantile Exchange (CME). Contains information and quotes on currency futures and options contracts.

www.phlx.com Web site of the Philadelphia Stock Exchange (PHLX). Contains information and quotes on currency options contracts.

http://online.wsj.com/public/us Website of the *Wall Street Journal* prominent business newspaper in the U.S. Contains domestic and international business news.

INTERNET EXERCISES

1. What currency futures contracts are currently being traded on the CME?
2. Have currency futures prices generally risen or fallen in the past day?
3. What currency options contracts are currently traded on the PHLX?
4. What are the implied volatilities of the euro and the yen over the past week and month? Are implied volatilities generally higher or lower for longer maturity contracts?

SWAPS AND INTEREST RATE DERIVATIVES

Man is not the creature of circumstances, circumstances are the creatures of men.

Benjamin Disraeli (1826)

CHAPTER LEARNING OBJECTIVES

- To describe interest rate and currency swaps and explain how they can be used to reduce financing costs and risk
- To calculate the appropriate payments and receipts associated with a given interest rate or currency swap
- To identify the factors that underlie the economic benefits of swaps
- To describe the use of forward forwards, forward rate agreements, and Eurodollar futures to lock in interest rates on future loans and deposits and hedge interest rate risk

KEY TERMS

all-in cost
basis swap
currency swap
dual currency bond
Eurobond
Eurocurrency
Eurodollar futures
exchange of principals
fixed rate
floating rate

forward forward
forward rate agreement
interest rate/currency swap
interest rate swap
London Interbank Offered Rate
  (LIBOR)
notional principal
right of offset
step-down coupon note
swap

This chapter examines several currency and interest rate derivatives that multinational corporations can use to fund their foreign investments and manage their interest rate risk. These derivatives include interest rate, currency, and interest rate/currency swaps, interest rate forward and futures contracts, and structured notes. Each of them presents opportunities to the multinational firm to reduce financing costs and/or risk.

8.1 INTEREST RATE AND CURRENCY SWAPS

Corporate financial managers can use **swaps** to arrange complex, innovative financings that reduce borrowing costs and increase control over interest rate risk and foreign currency exposure. For example, General Electric points out in its 2006 Annual Report (p. 102) that it uses swaps to hedge risk:

> *We conduct our business activities in diverse markets around the world, including in countries where obtaining local funding is sometimes inefficient. The nature of our activities exposes us to changes in interest rates and currency exchange rates. . . We use interest rate swaps, currency derivatives and commodity derivatives to reduce the variability of expected future cash flows associated with variable rate borrowings and commercial purchase and sales transactions, including commodities. We use interest rate swaps, currency swaps and interest rate and currency forwards to hedge the fair value effects of interest rate and currency exchange rate changes on local and non-functional currency denominated fixed-rate borrowings and certain types of fixed-rate assets. We use currency swaps and forwards to protect our net investments in global operations conducted in non-U.S. dollar currencies.*

As a result of deregulation and integration of national capital markets and extreme interest rate and currency volatility, the relatively new swaps market has experienced explosive growth, with the Bank for International Settlements (BIS) estimating outstanding interest rate and currency swaps as of June 30, 2004 of $145.2 trillion.[1] Few Eurobonds are issued without at least one swap behind them to give the borrower cheaper or in some way more desirable funds.

This section discusses the structure and mechanics of the two basic types of swaps—interest rate swaps and currency swaps—and shows how swaps can be used to achieve diverse goals. Swaps have had a major impact on the treasury function, permitting firms to tap new capital markets and to take further advantage of innovative products without an increase in risk. Through the swap, they can trade a perceived risk in one market or currency for a liability in another. The swap has led to a refinement of risk management techniques, which in turn has facilitated corporate involvement in international capital markets.

8.1.1 Interest Rate Swaps

An **interest rate swap** is an agreement between two parties to exchange U.S. dollar interest payments for a specific maturity on an agreed notional amount. The term *notional* refers to the theoretical principal underlying the swap. Thus, the **notional principal** is simply a reference amount against which the interest is calculated. No principal ever

---

[1] "Triennial Central Bank Survey of Foreign Exchange and Derivatives Market Activity 2004—Final Results," Bank for International Settlements, March 2005, p. 22.

changes hands. Maturities range from less than a year to more than 15 years; however, most transactions fall within a 2-year to 10-year period. The two main types are coupon swaps and basis swaps. In a **coupon swap**, one party pays a *fixed rate* calculated at the time of trade as a spread to a particular treasury bond, and the other side pays a *floating rate* that resets periodically throughout the life of the deal against a designated index. In a **basis swap**, two parties exchange floating interest payments based on different reference rates. Using this relatively straightforward mechanism, interest rate swaps transform debt issues, assets, liabilities, or any cash flow from type to type and—with some variation in the transaction structure—from currency to currency.

The most important reference rate in swap and other financial transactions is the **London Interbank Offered Rate (LIBOR)**. LIBOR is the average interest rate offered by a specific group of multinational banks in London (selected by the British Bankers Association for their degree of expertise and scale of activities) for U.S. dollar deposits of a stated maturity and is used as a base index for setting rates of many floating rate financial instruments, especially in the Eurocurrency and Eurobond markets. A **Eurocurrency** is a dollar or other freely convertible currency deposited in a bank outside its country of origin. For example, a dollar on deposit in London is a Eurodollar. A **Eurobond** is a bond sold outside the country in whose currency it is denominated. So, for example, a dollar bond sold in Paris by IBM would be a Eurobond. Eurobonds can carry either fixed rates or floating rates. **Fixed-rate** bonds have a fixed coupon, whereas **floating-rate** issues have variable coupons that are reset at fixed intervals, usually every 3 to 6 months. The new coupon is set at a fixed margin above a mutually agreed reference rate such as LIBOR.

The Classic Swap Transaction   Counterparties A and B both require $100 million for a 5-year period. To reduce their financing risks, Counterparty A would like to borrow at a fixed rate, whereas Counterparty B would prefer to borrow at a floating rate. Suppose that A is a company with a BBB rating and B is a AAA-rated bank. Although A has good access to banks or other sources of floating-rate funds for its operations, it has difficulty raising fixed-rate funds from bond issues in the capital markets at a price it finds attractive. By contrast, B can borrow at the finest rates in either market. The cost to each party of accessing either the fixed-rate or the floating-rate market for a new 5-year debt issue is as follows:

Borrower	Fixed-Rate Available	Floating-Rate Available
Counterparty A: BBB-rated	8.5%	6-month LIBOR + 0.5%
Counterparty B: AAA-rated	7.0%	6-month LIBOR
Difference	1.5%	0.5%

It is obvious that there is an anomaly between the two markets: One judges that the difference in credit quality between a AAA-rated firm and a BBB-rated firm is worth 150 basis points; the other determines that this difference is worth only 50 basis points (a basis point equals 0.01%). Through an interest rate swap, both parties can take advantage of the 100 basis-point spread differential.

To begin, Counterparty A will take out a $100 million, 5-year floating-rate Eurodollar loan from a syndicate of banks at an interest rate of LIBOR plus 50 basis points. At the same time, Counterparty B will issue a $100 million, five-year Eurobond carrying a fixed rate of 7%. A and B then will enter into the following interest rate swaps with BigBank. Counterparty A agrees that it will pay BigBank 7.35% for 5 years, with payments calculated by multiplying that rate by the $100 million notional principal amount.

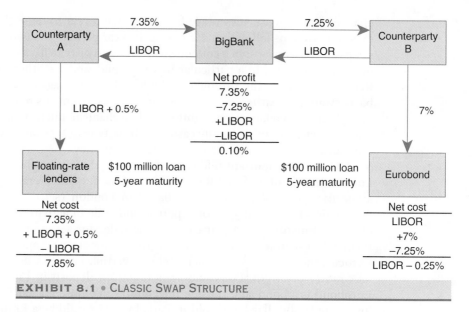

EXHIBIT 8.1 • CLASSIC SWAP STRUCTURE

In return, BigBank agrees to pay Counterparty A 6-month LIBOR (LIBOR6) over 5 years, with reset dates matching the reset dates on its floating-rate loan. Through the swap, A has managed to turn a floating-rate loan into a fixed-rate loan costing 7.85%.

In a similar fashion, Counterparty B enters into a swap with BigBank whereby it agrees to pay LIBOR6 to BigBank on a notional principal amount of $100 million for 5 years in exchange for receiving payments of 7.25%. Thus, B has swapped a fixed-rate loan for a floating-rate loan carrying an effective cost of LIBOR6 minus 25 basis points.

Why would BigBank or any financial intermediary enter into such transactions? The reason BigBank is willing to enter into such contracts is more evident when you look at the transaction in its entirety. This classic swap structure is shown in Exhibit 8.1.

As a financial intermediary, BigBank puts together both transactions. The risks net out, and BigBank is left with a spread of 10 basis points:

Receive (from A)	7.35%
Pay (to B)	(7.25%)
Receive (from B)	LIBOR6
Pay (to A)	(LIBOR6)
Net	10 basis points

BigBank thus receives compensation equal to $100,000 annually for the next 5 years on the $100 million swap transaction.

Cost Savings Associated with Swaps   The example just discussed shows the risk-reducing potential of interest rate swaps. Swaps also may be used to reduce costs. Their ability to do so depends on a difference in perceived credit quality across financial markets. In essence, interest rate swaps exploit the comparative advantages, if they exist, enjoyed by different borrowers in different markets, thereby increasing the options available to both borrower and investor.

Returning to the previous example, we can see that there is a spread differential of 100 basis points between the cost of fixed- and floating-rate borrowing for A and B that the interest rate swap has permitted the parties to share among themselves as follows:

Party	Normal Funding Cost (%)	Cost After Swap (%)	Difference (%)
Counterparty A	8.50	7.85	0.65
Counterparty B	LIBOR	LIBOR − 0.25	0.25
BigBank	–	–	<u>0.10</u>
		Total	1.00

In this example, A lowers its fixed-rate costs by 65 basis points, B lowers its floating-rate costs by 25 basis points, and BigBank receives 10 basis points for arranging the transaction and bearing the credit risk of the counterparties.

You might expect that the process of financial arbitrage would soon eliminate any such cost savings opportunities associated with a mispricing of credit quality. Despite this efficient markets view, many players in the swaps market believe that such anomalies in perceived credit risk continue to exist. The explosive growth in the swaps market supports this belief. It may also indicate the presence of other factors, such as differences in information and risk aversion of lenders across markets, which are more likely to persist.

ILLUSTRATION   *Payments on a 2-Year Fixed-for-Floating Interest Rate Swap*

Suppose that on December 31, 2008 IBM issues a 2-year, floating-rate bond in the amount of $100 million on which it pays LIBOR6 − 0.5% semiannually, with the first payment due on June 30, 2009. Because IBM would prefer fixed-rate payments, it enters into a swap with Citibank as the intermediary on December 31, 2008. Under the swap contract, IBM agrees to pay Citibank an annual rate of 8% and will receive LIBOR6. All payments are made on a semiannual basis. In effect, IBM has used a swap to convert its floating-rate debt into a fixed-rate bond yielding 7.5%.

To see how the payments on the swap are computed, suppose that LIBOR6 on December 31, 2008 is 7%. On June 30, 2009, IBM will owe Citibank $4 million (0.5 × 0.08 × $100 million) and will receive in return $3.5 million (0.5 × 0.07 × $100 million). Net, IBM will pay Citibank $0.5 million. IBM will also pay its bondholders $3.25 million (0.5 × (0.07 − 0.005) × $100 million). Combining the swap and the bond payments, IBM will pay out $3.75 million, which converts into a coupon rate of 7.5% paid semiannually. On subsequent reset periods, payments will vary with LIBOR6 (see Exhibit 8.2 for possible payments).

Period Ending	LIBOR6	Fixed-Rate Payment to Citibank	Floating-Rate Payment from Citibank	Net Payment to Citibank	Payment to Bondholders	Net Payment by IBM
June 2009	7%	$4,000,000	$3,500,000	$500,000	$3,250,000	$3,750,000
December 2009	6%	$4,000,000	$3,000,000	$1,000,000	$2,750,000	$3,750,000
June 2010	8%	$4,000,000	$4,000,000	$0	$3,750,000	$3,750,000
December 2010	9%	$4,000,000	$4,500,000	−$500,000	$4,250,000	$3,750,000

EXHIBIT 8.2 • SWAP PAYMENT OVER THE 2-YEAR LIFE OF IBM'S SWAP

8.1.2 Currency Swaps

Swap contracts can also be arranged across currencies. Such contracts are known as currency swaps and can help manage both interest rate and exchange rate risk. Many financial institutions count the arranging of swaps, both domestic and foreign currency, as an important line of business.

Technically, a **currency swap** is an exchange of debt-service obligations denominated in one currency for the service on an agreed principal amount of debt denominated in another currency. By swapping their future cash-flow obligations, the counterparties are able to replace cash flows denominated in one currency with cash flows in a more desired currency. In this way, company A, which has borrowed, say, Japanese yen at a fixed interest rate, can transform its yen debt into a fully hedged dollar liability by exchanging cash flows with counterparty B. As illustrated in Exhibit 8.3, the two loans that comprise the currency swap have parallel interest and principal repayment schedules. At each payment date, company A will pay a fixed interest rate in dollars and receive a fixed rate in yen. The counterparties also exchange principal amounts at the start and the end of the swap arrangement (denoted as time *T* in the diagram).

In effect, a U.S. firm engaged in a currency swap has borrowed foreign currency and converted its proceeds into dollars, while simultaneously arranging for a counterparty to make the requisite foreign currency payment in each period. In return, the firm pays an agreed amount of dollars to the counterparty. Given the fixed nature of the periodic exchanges of currencies, the currency swap is equivalent to a package of forward contracts. For example, in the dollar:yen swap just discussed, firm A has contracted to sell fixed amounts of dollars forward for fixed amounts of yen on a series of future dates.

The counterparties to a currency swap will be concerned about their **all-in cost**—that is, the effective interest rate on the money they have raised. This interest rate is calculated as the discount rate that equates the present value of the future interest and principal payments to the net proceeds received by the issuer.

Currency swaps contain the **right of offset**, which gives each party the right to offset any nonpayment of principal or interest with a comparable nonpayment. Absent a right of offset, default by one party would not release the other from making its contractually obligated payments. Moreover, because a currency swap is not a loan, it does not appear as a liability on the parties' balance sheets.

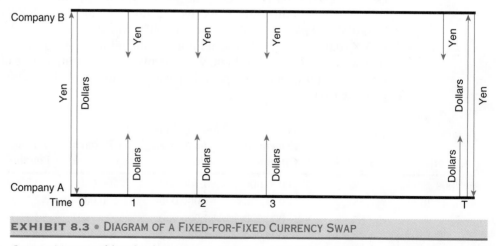

EXHIBIT 8.3 • D IAGRAM OF A F IXED-FOR-F IXED C URRENCY S WAP

Company A issues yen debt and exchanges the yen principal amount for dollars with Company B, which has issued dollar debt. At each subsequent interest date, A pays dollar interest to B and receives yen interest from B. A uses the yen it receives from B to service its yen debt. At maturity, there is a final interest exchange and an exchange of principal amounts.

Although the structure of currency swaps differs from interest rate swaps in a variety of ways, the major difference is that with a currency swap, there is always an exchange of principal amounts at maturity at a predetermined exchange rate. Thus, the swap contract behaves like a long-dated forward foreign exchange contract, where the forward rate is the current spot rate.

That there is always an exchange of principal amounts at maturity can be explained as follows. Assume that the prevailing coupon rate is 8% in one currency and 5% in the other currency. What would persuade an investor to pay 8% and receive 300 basis points less? The answer lies in the spot and long-term forward exchange rates and how currency swaps adjust to compensate for the differentials. According to interest rate parity theory, forward rates are a direct function of the interest rate differential for the two currencies involved. As a result, a currency with a lower interest rate has a correspondingly higher forward exchange value. It follows that future exchange of currencies at the present spot exchange rate would offset the current difference in interest rates. This **exchange of principals** is what occurs in every currency swap at maturity based on the original amounts of each currency and, by implication, is done at the original spot exchange rate.

In the classic currency swap, the counterparties exchange fixed-rate payments in one currency for fixed-rate payments in another currency. The hypothetical example of a swap between Dow and Michelin illustrates the structure of a fixed-for-fixed currency swap.

ILLUSTRATION   *Dow Chemical Swaps Fixed-for-Fixed with Michelin*

Suppose that Dow Chemical is looking to hedge some of its euro exposure by borrowing in euros. At the same time, French tire manufacturer Michelin is seeking dollars to finance additional investment in the U.S. market. Both want the equivalent of $200 million in fixed-rate financing for 10 years. Dow can issue dollar-denominated debt at a coupon rate of 7.5% or euro-denominated debt at a coupon rate of 8.25%. Equivalent rates for Michelin are 7.7 in dollars and 8.1% in euros. Given that both companies have similar credit ratings, it is clear that the best way for them to borrow in the other's currency is to issue debt in their own currencies and then swap the proceeds and future debt-service payments.

Assuming a current spot rate of €0.75/$, Michelin would issue €150 million in 8.1% debt and Dow Chemical would float a bond issue of $200 million at 7.5%. The coupon payments on these bond issues are €12,150,000 (0.081 × €150 million) and $15,000,000 (0.075 × $200 million), respectively, giving rise to the following debt-service payments:

Year	Michelin	Dow Chemical
1–10	€12,150,000	$15,000,000
10	€150,000,000	$200,000,000

After swapping the proceeds at time 0 (now), Dow Chemical winds up with €150 million in euro debt and Michelin has $200 million in dollar debt to service. In subsequent years, they would exchange coupon payments and the principal amounts at repayment. The cash inflows and outflows for both parties are summarized in Exhibit 8.4. The net result is that the swap enables Dow to borrow fixed-rate euros indirectly at 8.1%, saving 15 basis points relative to its 8.25% cost of borrowing euros directly, and Michelin can borrow dollars at 7.5%, saving 20 basis points relative to its direct cost of 7.7%.

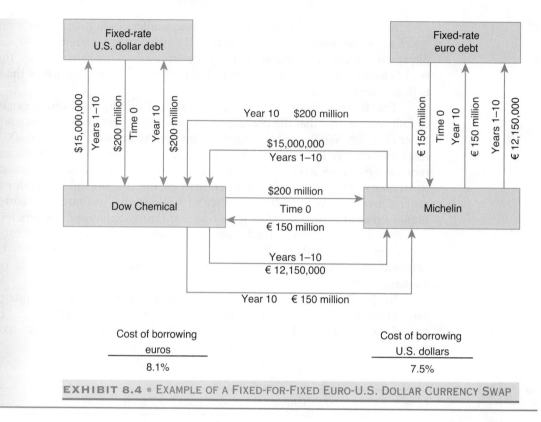

EXHIBIT 8.4 ● EXAMPLE OF A FIXED-FOR-FIXED EURO–U.S. DOLLAR CURRENCY SWAP

Interest Rate/Currency Swaps   Although the currency swap market began with fixed-for-fixed swaps, most such swaps today are interest rate/currency swaps. As its name implies, an **interest rate/currency swap** combines the features of both a currency swap and an interest rate swap. This swap is designed to convert a liability in one currency with a stipulated type of interest payment into one denominated in another currency with a different type of interest payment. The most common form of interest rate/currency swap converts a fixed-rate liability in one currency into a floating-rate liability in a second currency. We can use the previous example of Dow Chemical and Michelin to illustrate the mechanics of a fixed-for-floating currency swap.

ILLUSTRATION   *Dow Chemical Swaps Fixed-for-Floating with Michelin*

Suppose that Dow Chemical decides to borrow floating-rate euros instead of fixed-rate euros, whereas Michelin maintains its preference for fixed-rate dollars. Assume that Dow Chemical can borrow floating-rate euros directly at LIBOR + 0.35%, versus a cost to Michelin of borrowing floating-rate euros of LIBOR + 0.125%. As before, given Dow's cost of borrowing dollars of 7.5%, versus Michelin's cost of 7.7%, the best way for them to achieve their currency and interest rate objectives is to issue debt in their own currencies and then swap the proceeds and future debt-service payments.

Exhibit 8.5 summarizes the cash inflows and outflows for both parties. The net result of the swap is that Dow Chemical can borrow euros indirectly at a floating rate of

LIBOR + 0.125%, saving 22.5 basis points relative to its cost of borrowing floating-rate euros directly. Michelin's cost of borrowing fixed-rate dollars remains at 7.5%, a savings of 20 basis points.

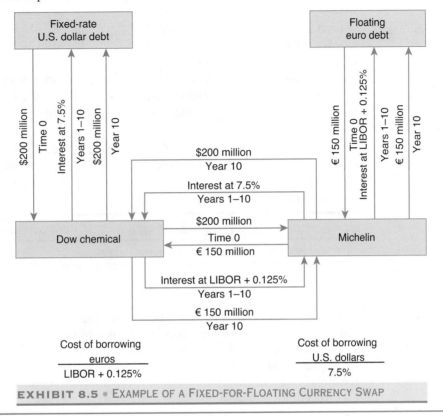

EXHIBIT 8.5 • EXAMPLE OF A FIXED-FOR-FLOATING CURRENCY SWAP

The two examples of Dow Chemical and Michelin have them dealing directly with one another. In practice, they would use a financial intermediary, such as a commercial bank or an investment bank, as either a broker or a dealer to arrange the swap. As a broker, the intermediary simply brings the counterparties together for a fee. In contrast, if the intermediary acts as a dealer, it not only arranges the swap, but it also guarantees the swap payments that each party is supposed to receive. Because the dealer guarantees the parties to the swap arrangement against default risk, both parties will be concerned with the dealer's credit rating. Financial intermediaries in the swap market must have high credit ratings because most intermediaries these days act as dealers. However, actual interest rate/currency swaps tend to be more complicated than the plain-vanilla Dow Chemical/Michelin swap.

Dual Currency Bond Swaps   Another variant on the currency swap theme is a currency swap involving a **dual currency bond**—one that has the issue's proceeds and interest payments stated in foreign currency and the principal repayment stated in dollars. The following is an example of a dual currency bond swap. On October 1, 1985, the Federal National Mortgage Association (FNMA, or Fannie Mae) agreed to issue 10-year, 8% coupon debentures in the amount of ¥50 billion (with net proceeds of ¥49,687,500,000) and to swap these yen for just over $209 million (an implied swap rate of ¥237.5479/$1). In return, Fannie Mae agreed to pay interest averaging about $21 million annually and to redeem these bonds at the end of 10 years at a cost of

Payment Date	Payment on Dual Currency Debenture	Dollar Payment Under Swap	Exchange Rate (Yen/Dollar)
October 1, 1985	−¥49,687,500,000*	−$209,468,314**	¥237.378
October 1, 1986	¥4,000,000,000	$18,811,800	¥212.633
October 1, 1987	¥4,000,000,000	$19,124,381	¥209.157
October 1, 1988	¥4,000,000,000	$19,464,370	¥205.504
October 1, 1989	¥4,000,000,000	$19,854,506	¥201.466
October 1, 1990	¥4,000,000,000	$20,304,259	¥197.003
October 1, 1991	¥4,000,000,000	$20,942,375	¥191.000
October 1, 1992	¥4,000,000,000	$21,499,712	¥186.049
October 1, 1993	¥4,000,000,000	$22,116,872	¥180.857
October 1, 1994	¥4,000,000,000	$22,718,882	¥176.065
October 1, 1995	¥4,000,000,000	$23,665,096	¥169.025
October 1, 1996	$240,400,000	$240,400,000	¥207.987

EXHIBIT 8.6 • Cash Flows Associated with Yen Debenture Currency Swap

* This figure is the ¥ 50 billion face amount net of issue expenses.
** Net proceeds received after reimbursing underwriters for expenses of $150,000.
Source: Exchanges Rates from www.oanda.com

$240,400,000. Exhibit 8.6 shows the detailed yen and dollar cash flows associated with this currency swap. The net effect of this swap was to give Fannie Mae an all-in dollar cost of 10.67% annually. In other words, regardless of what happened to the yen: dollar exchange rate in the future, Fannie Mae's dollar cost on its yen bond issue would remain at 10.67%. The 10.67% figure is the interest rate that just equates the dollar figures in column 2 to zero.

Let us illustrate the mechanics of this swap. Note that at the end of the first year, Fannie Mae is obligated to pay its bondholders ¥ 4 billion in interest (an 8% coupon payment on a ¥ 50 billion face value debenture). To satisfy this obligation, Fannie Mae pays $18,811,795 to Nomura, which in turn makes the ¥ 4 billion interest payment. As column 3 of Exhibit 8.6 shows, Fannie Mae has effectively contracted with Nomura to buy ¥ 4 billion forward for delivery in 1 year at a forward rate of ¥ 212.6325.

Similarly, Fannie Mae satisfies its remaining yen obligations (shown in column 1) by paying a series of dollar amounts (shown in column 2) to Nomura, which in turn makes the required yen payments. The exchange of fixed dollar payments in the future for fixed yen payments in the future is equivalent to a sequence of forward contracts entered into at the forward exchange rates shown in column 3. Since the actual spot rate at the time the swap was entered into (August 29, 1985) was about ¥ 240/$1, the implicit forward rates on these forward contracts reveal that the yen was selling at a forward premium relative to the dollar; that is, it cost fewer yen to buy a dollar in the forward market than in the spot market. The reason the yen was selling at a forward premium was the same as Fannie Mae was borrowing yen at an interest rate below the interest rate on dollars.

Since this particular issue was a dual currency bond, with the issue's proceeds and interest payments stated in yen and the principal repayment stated in dollars, the final payment is stated in dollars only. However, it should be noted that by agreeing to a principal repayment of $240,400,000, instead of ¥ 50 billion, Fannie Mae actually was entering into the equivalent of a long-dated forward contract at an implicit forward rate of ¥ 207.9867/$1 (¥ 50 billion/$240,400,000).

8.1.3 Economic Advantages of Swaps

Swaps provide a real economic benefit to both parties only if a barrier exists to prevent arbitrage from functioning fully. Such impediments may include legal restrictions on spot and forward foreign exchange transactions, different perceptions by investors of risk and creditworthiness of the two parties, appeal or acceptability of one borrower to a certain class of investor, tax differentials, and so forth.[2]

Swaps also allow firms who are parties to the contracts to lower their cost of foreign exchange risk management by arbitraging their relative access to different currency markets. A borrower whose paper is much in demand in one currency can obtain a cost saving in another currency sector by raising money in the former and swapping the funds into the latter currency. A U.S. corporation, for example, may want to secure fixed-rate funds in euros in order to reduce its euro exposure, but it may be hampered in doing so because it is relatively unknown in the German financial market. In contrast, a German company that is well established in its own country, but is relatively unknown in the U.S. financial market, may desire floating-rate dollar financing.

In this case, a bank intermediary familiar with the funding needs and "comparative advantages" in borrowing of both parties may arrange a currency swap. The U.S. company borrows floating-rate dollars, and the German company borrows fixed-rate euros. The two companies then swap both principal and interest payments. When the term of the swap matures, say, in 5 years, the principal amounts revert to the original holder. Both parties receive a cost saving, because they initially borrow in the market where they have a comparative advantage and then swap for their preferred liability. In general currency, swaps allow the parties to the contract to arbitrage their relative access to different currency markets. A borrower whose paper is much in demand in one currency can obtain a cost saving in another currency sector by raising money in the former and swapping the funds into the latter currency.

Currency swaps are, therefore, often used to provide long-term financing in foreign currencies. This function is important because in many foreign countries long-term capital and forward foreign exchange markets are notably absent or not well developed. Swaps are one vehicle that provides liquidity to these markets.

In effect, swaps allow the transacting parties to engage in some form of tax, regulatory-system, or financial-market arbitrage. If the world capital market were fully integrated, the incentive to swap would be reduced because fewer arbitrage opportunities would exist. However, even in the United States, where financial markets function freely, interest rate swaps are very popular and are credited with cost savings.

8.2 INTEREST RATE FORWARDS AND FUTURES

In addition to swaps, companies can use a variety of forward and futures contracts to manage their interest rate expense and risk. These contracts include forward forwards, forward rate agreements, and Eurodollar futures. All of them allow companies to lock in interest rates on future loans and deposits.

8.2.1 Forward Forwards

A **forward forward** is a contract that fixes an interest rate today on a future loan or deposit. The contract specifies the interest rate, the principal amount of the future deposit or loan, and the start and ending dates of the future interest rate period.

---

[2] This explanation is provided in Clifford W. Smith, Jr., Charles W. Smithson, and Lee M. Wakeman, "The Evolving Market for Swaps," *Midland Corporate Finance Journal*, Winter 1986, pp. 20–32.

ILLUSTRATION   *Telecom Argentina Fixes a Future Loan Rate*

Suppose that Telecom Argentina needs to borrow $10 million in 6 months for a 3-month period. It could wait 6 months and borrow the money at the then-current interest rate. Rather than risk a significant rise in interest rates over the next 6 months, however, Telecom Argentina decides to enter into a forward forward with Daiwa Bank that fixes this rate at 8.4% per annum. This contract guarantees that 6 months from today, Daiwa Bank will lend Telecom Argentina $10 million for a 3-month period at a rate of 2.1% (8.4%/4). In return, 9 months from today, Telecom Argentina will repay Daiwa the principal plus interest on the loan, or $10,210,000 ($10 million × 1.021).

The forward forward rate on a loan can be found through arbitrage. For example, suppose that a company wishes to lock in a 6-month rate on a $1 million Eurodollar deposit to be placed in 3 months. It can buy a forward forward or it can create its own. To illustrate this process, suppose that the company can borrow or lend at LIBOR. Then the company can derive a 3-month forward rate on LIBOR6 by simultaneously borrowing the present value of $1 million for 3 months and lending that same amount of money for 9 months. If 3-month LIBOR (LIBOR3) is 6.7%, the company will borrow $1,000,000/(1 + 0.067/4) = $983,526 today and lend that same amount for 9 months. If 9-month LIBOR (LIBOR9) is 6.95%, at the end of 9 months the company will receive $983,526 × (1 + 0.0695 × 3/4) = $1,034,792. The cash flows on these transactions are

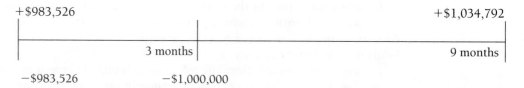

+$983,526   +$1,034,792

| | |
| 3 months | 9 months |

−$983,526   −$1,000,000

Notice that the borrowing and lending transactions are structured so that the only net cash flows are the cash outlay of $1 million in 3 months and the receipt of $1,034,792 in 9 months. These transactions are equivalent to investing $1,000,000 in 3 months and receiving back $1,034,792 in 9 months. The interest receipt of $34,792, or 3.479% for 6 months, is equivalent to a rate of 6.958% per annum.

The process of arbitrage will ensure that the actual forward rate for LIBOR6 in 3 months will almost exactly equal the "homemade" forward forward rate.

8.2.2 Forward Rate Agreement

In recent years, forward forwards have been largely displaced by the forward rate agreement. A **forward rate agreement** (FRA) is a cash-settled, over-the-counter forward contract that allows a company to fix an interest rate to be applied to a specified future interest period on a notional principal amount. It is analogous to a forward foreign currency contract but instead of exchanging currencies, the parties to an FRA agree to exchange interest payments. As of June 30, 2004, the estimated notional amount of FRAs outstanding was $14.4 trillion.[3]

The formula used to calculate the interest payment on a LIBOR-based FRA is

$$\text{Interest payment} = \text{notional principal} \times \frac{(\text{LIBOR} - \text{forward rate})\left(\frac{\text{days}}{360}\right)}{1 + \text{LIBOR} \times \left(\frac{\text{days}}{360}\right)} \qquad (8.1)$$

---

[3] "Triennial Central Bank Survey of Foreign Exchange and Derivatives Market Activity 2004—Final Results," Bank for International Settlements, March 2005, p. 22.

where *days* refers to the number of days in the future interest period. The discount reflects the fact that the FRA payment occurs at the start of the loan period, whereas the interest expense on a loan is not paid until the loan's maturity. To equate the two, the differential interest expense must be discounted back to its present value using the actual interest rate. The example of Unilever shows how a borrower can use an FRA to lock in the interest rate applicable for a future loan.

ILLUSTRATION *Unilever Uses an FRA to Fix the Interest Rate on a Future Loan*

Suppose that Unilever needs to borrow $50 million in 2 months for a 6-month period. To lock in the rate on this loan, Unilever buys a "2 × 6" FRA on LIBOR at 6.5% from Bankers Trust for a notional principal of $50 million. This means that Bankers Trust has entered into a 2-month forward contract on 6-month LIBOR. Two months from now, if LIBOR6 exceeds 6.5%, Bankers Trust will pay Unilever the difference in interest expense. If LIBOR6 is less than 6.5%, Unilever will pay Bankers Trust the difference.

Assume that in 2 months LIBOR6 is 7.2%. Because this rate exceeds 6.5%, and assuming 182 days in the 6-month period, Unilever will receive from Bankers Trust a payment determined by Equation 8.1 of

$$\text{Interest payment} = \$50{,}000{,}000 \times \frac{(0.072 - 0.065)\left(\frac{182}{360}\right)}{1 + 0.072 \times \left(\frac{182}{360}\right)} = \$170{,}730$$

In addition to fixing future borrowing rates, FRAs can also be used to fix future deposit rates. Specifically, by selling an FRA, a company can lock in the interest rate applicable for a future deposit.

8.2.3 Eurodollar Futures

A **Eurodollar future** is a cash-settled futures contract on a 3-month, $1 million Eurodollar deposit that pays LIBOR. These contracts are traded on the Chicago Mercantile Exchange (CME), the London International Financial Futures Exchange (LIFFE), and the Singapore International Monetary Exchange (SIMEX). Eurodollar futures contracts are traded for March, June, September, and December delivery. Contracts are traded out to 3 years, with a high degree of liquidity out to 2 years.

Eurodollar futures act like FRAs in that they help lock in a future interest rate and are settled in cash. However, unlike FRAs, they are marked to market daily. (As in currency futures, this means that gains and losses are settled in cash each day.) The price of a Eurodollar futures contract is quoted as an index number equal to 100 minus the annualized forward interest rate. For example, suppose the current futures price is 91.68. This price implies that the contracted-for LIBOR3 rate is 8.32%, that is, 100 minus 91.68. The value of this contract at inception is found by use of the following formula:

$$\text{Initial value of Eurodollar futures contract} = \$1{,}000{,}000 \left[1 - 0.0832\left(\frac{90}{360}\right)\right]$$
$$= \$979{,}200$$

The interest rate is divided by four to convert it into a quarterly rate. At maturity, the cash settlement price is determined by subtracting LIBOR3 on that date from 100. Whether the contract gained or lost money depends on whether cash LIBOR3 at settlement is greater or less than 8.32%. If LIBOR3 at settlement is 7.54%, the Eurodollar future on that date is valued at $981,150:

$$\text{Settlement value of Eurodollar futures contract} = \$1{,}000{,}000 \left[1 - 0.0754\left(\frac{90}{360}\right)\right]$$
$$= \$981{,}150$$

At this price, the buyer has earned $1,950 ($981,150 − $979,200) on the contract. As can be seen from the formula for valuing the futures contract, each basis point change in the forward rate translates into $25 for each contract ($1 million × 0.0001/4), with increases in the forward rate reducing the contract's value and decreases raising its value. For example, if the forward rate rose three basis points, a long position in the contract would lose $75. This arithmetic suggests that borrowers looking to lock in a future cost of funds would *sell* futures contracts because increases in future interest rates would be offset by gains on the short position in the futures contracts. Conversely, investors seeking to lock in a forward interest rate would *buy* futures contracts, because declines in future rates would be offset by gains on the long position in the futures contracts.

ILLUSTRATION   *Using a Futures Contract to Hedge a Forward Borrowing Rate*

In late June, a corporate treasurer projects that a shortfall in cash flow will require a $10 million bank loan on September 16. The contractual loan rate will be LIBOR3 + 1%. LIBOR3 is currently at 5.63%. The treasurer can use the September Eurodollar futures, which are currently trading at 94.18, to lock in the forward borrowing rate. This price implies a forward Eurodollar rate of 5.82% (100 − 94.18). By selling 10 September Eurodollar futures contract, the corporate treasurer ensures a borrowing rate of 6.82% for the 3-month period beginning September 16. This rate reflects the bank's 1% spread above the rate locked in through the futures contract.

A lengthier explanation of what is going on is as follows. In June, 10 September Eurodollar contracts will be worth $9,854,500:

$$\text{Initial value of 10 Eurodollar futures contracts} =$$
$$\$10,000,0000 \left[1 - 0.0582 \left(\frac{90}{360} \right) \right] = \$9,854,500$$

Suppose that in September, LIBOR3 is 6%. At that rate, these 10 contracts will be closed out in September at a value of $9,850,000:

$$\text{Settlement value of 10 Eurodollar futures contracts} =$$
$$\$10,000,0000 \left[1 - 0.06 \left(\frac{90}{360} \right) \right] = \$9,850,000$$

The difference in values results in a $4,500 gain on the 10 contracts ($9,854,500 − $9,850,000). At the same time, in September, the company will borrow $10 million for 3 months, paying LIBOR3 + 1%, or 7%. In December, the company has to pay interest on its debt of $175,000 ($10 million × 0.07/4). This interest payment is offset by the $4,500 gain on the 10 Eurodollar contracts, resulting in a net interest cost of $170,500, which is equivalent to an interest rate of 6.82% (4 × 170,500/10,000,000).[4]

8.3 SUMMARY AND CONCLUSIONS

Multinational corporations can use creative financing to achieve various objectives, such as lowering their cost of funds, cutting taxes, and reducing political risk. This chapter focused on two such techniques, interest rate and currency swaps and interest rate forward and futures contracts.

---

[4] The fact that $4,500 is received in September and $175,000 is paid in December does not change matters. If $4,500 is invested at the company's opportunity cost of 7% for those 3 months, the $175,000 would be offset by $4,578.75 in earnings ($4,500 × 1.0175). That would result in an effective interest of $170,421.25, or a 6.82% rate annualized.

Interest and currency swaps involve a financial transaction in which two counter-parties agree to exchange streams of payments over time. In an interest rate swap, no actual principal is exchanged either initially or at maturity, but interest payment streams are exchanged according to predetermined rules and are based on an underlying notional amount. The two main types are coupon swaps (or fixed rate to floating rate) and basis swaps (from floating rate against one reference rate to floating rate with another reference rate).

Currency swap refers to a transaction in which two counterparties exchange specific amounts of two currencies at the outset and repay over time according to a predetermined rule that reflects both interest payments and amortization of principal. A cross-currency interest rate swap involves swapping fixed-rate flows in one currency to floating-rate flows in another.

Interest forward and futures contracts enable companies to manage their interest rate expense and risk. These contracts include forward forwards, forward rate agreements, and Eurodollar futures. All of them allow companies to lock in interest rates on future loans and deposits. A forward forward is a contract that fixes an interest rate today on a future loan or deposit. The contract specifies the interest rate, the principal amount of the future deposit or loan, and the start and ending dates of the future interest rate period.

A forward rate agreement is a cash-settled, over-the-counter forward contract that allows a company to fix an interest rate to be applied to a specified future interest period on a notional principal amount. Eurodollar futures, which are based on a 3-month, $1 million Eurodollar deposit that pays LIBOR, act like FRAs as they help lock in a future interest rate and are settled in cash. However, unlike FRAs they are marked to market daily. Eurodollar futures contracts are traded on several U.S. and overseas exchanges.

QUESTIONS

1. What is an interest rate swap? What is the difference between a basis swap and a coupon swap?

2. What is a currency swap?

3. Comment on the following statement. "In order for one party to a swap to benefit, the other party must lose."

4. The Swiss Central Bank bans the use of Swiss francs for Eurobond issues. Explain how currency swaps can be used to enable foreign borrowers who want to raise Swiss francs through a bond issue outside of Switzerland to get around this ban.

5. Explain how IBM can use a forward rate agreement to lock in the cost of a 1-year $25 million loan to be taken out in 6 months. Alternatively, explain how IBM can lock in the interest rate on this loan by using Eurodollar futures contracts. What is the major difference between using the FRA and the futures contract to hedge IBM's interest rate risk?

PROBLEMS

1. Dell Inc. would like to borrow pounds, and Virgin Airlines wants to borrow dollars. Because Dell is better known in the United States, it can borrow on its own dollars at 7% and pounds at 9%, whereas Virgin can on its own borrow dollars at 8% and pounds at 8.5%.

   a. Suppose Dell wants to borrow £10 million for 2 years, Virgin wants to borrow $16 million for 2 years, and the current ($/£) exchange rate is $1.60. What swap transaction would accomplish this objective? Assume the counterparties would exchange principal and interest payments with no rate adjustments.

   b. What savings are realized by Dell and Virgin?

   c. Suppose, that Dell can borrow dollars at 7% and pounds at 9%, whereas Virgin can borrow dollars at 8.75% and pounds at 9.5%. What range of interest rates would make this swap attractive to both parties?

   d. Based on the scenario in Part (c), suppose Dell borrows dollars at 7% and Virgin borrows pounds at 9.5%. If the parties swap their currency proceeds, with Dell paying 8.75% to Virgin for pounds and Virgin paying 7.75% to Dell for dollars, what are the cost savings to each party?

2. In May 1988, Walt Disney Productions sold to Japanese investors a 20-year stream of projected yen royalties from Tokyo Disneyland. The present value of that stream of royalties, discounted at 6% (the return required by the Japanese investors), was ¥93 billion. Disney took the yen proceeds from the sale, converted them to dollars, and invested the dollars in bonds yielding 10%. According to Disney's chief financial officer, Gary Wilson, "In effect, we got money at a 6% discount rate, reinvested it at 10%, and hedged our royalty stream against yen fluctuations—all in one transaction."

   a. At the time of the sale, the exchange rate was ¥124 = $1. What dollar amount did Disney realize from the sale of its yen proceeds?

   b. Demonstrate the equivalence between Walt Disney's transaction and a currency swap. (*Hint*: A diagram would help.)

   c. Comment on Gary Wilson's statement. Did Disney achieve the equivalent of a free lunch through its transaction?

3. Suppose that IBM would like to borrow fixed-rate yen, whereas Korea Development Bank (KDB) would like to borrow floating-rate dollars. IBM can borrow fixed-rate yen at 4.5% or floating-rate dollars at LIBOR + 0.25%. KDB can borrow fixed-rate yen at 4.9% or floating-rate dollars at LIBOR + 0.8%.

   a. What is the range of possible cost savings that IBM can realize through an interest rate/currency swap with KDB?

   b. Assuming a notional principal equivalent to $125 million and a current exchange rate of ¥105/$, what do these possible cost savings translate into in yen terms?

   c. Redo Parts (a) and (b) assuming that the parties use Bank of America, which charges a fee of 8 basis points to arrange the swap.

4. At time *t*, 3M borrows ¥12.8 billion at an interest rate of 1.2%, paid semiannually, for a period of 2 years. It then enters into a 2-year yen/dollar swap with Bankers Trust (BT) on a notional principal amount of $100 million (¥12.8 billion at the current spot rate). Every 6 months, 3M pays BT U.S. dollar LIBOR6, while BT makes payments to 3M of 1.3% annually in yen. At maturity, BT and 3M reverse the notional principals. Assume that LIBOR6 (annualized) and the ¥/$ exchange rate evolve as follows.

Time (months)	LIBOR6	¥/$ (spot)	Net $ receipt (1)/ payment (2)
t	5.7%	128	
t + 6	5.4%	132	
t + 12	5.3%	137	
t + 18	5.9%	131	
t + 24	5.8%	123	

   a. Calculate the *net* dollar amount that 3M pays to BT ("−") or receives from BT ("+") in each 6-month period.

   b. What is the all-in dollar cost of 3M's loan?

   c. Suppose 3M decides at *t* + 18 to use a six-month forward contract to hedge the *t* + 24 receipt of yen from BT. Six-month interest rates (annualized) at *t* + 18 are 5.9% in dollars and 2.1% in yen. With this hedge in place, what fixed dollar amount would 3M have paid (received) at time *t* + 24? How does this amount compare to the *t* + 24 net payment computed in Part (a)?

   d. Does it make sense for 3M to hedge its receipt of yen from BT? Explain.

5. Suppose LIBOR3 is 7.93% and LIBOR6 is 8.11%. What is the forward forward rate for a LIBOR3 deposit to be placed in 3 months?

6. Suppose that Skandinaviska Ensilden Banken (SEB), the Swedish bank, funds itself with 3-month Eurodollar time deposits at LIBOR. Assume that Alfa Laval comes to SEB seeking a 1-year, fixed-rate loan of $10 million, with interest to be paid quarterly. At the time of the loan disbursement, SEB raises 3-month funds at 5.75% but has to roll over this funding in three successive quarters. If it does not lock in a funding rate and interest rates rise, the loan could prove to be unprofitable. The three quarterly refunding dates fall shortly before the next three Eurodollar futures-contract expirations in March, June, and September.

   a. At the time the loan is made, the price of each contract is 94.12, 93.95, and 93.80. Show how SEB can use Eurodollar futures contracts to lock in its cost of funds for the year. What is SEB's hedged cost of funds for the year?

   b. Suppose that the settlement prices of the March, June, and September contracts are, respectively, 92.98, 92.80, and 92.66. What would have been SEB's unhedged cost of funding the loan to Alfa Laval?

BIBLIOGRAPHY

Smith, C. W., Jr., C. W. Smithson, and L. M. Wakeman, "The Evolving Market for Swaps," *Midland Corporate Finance* *Journal*, Winter 1986, pp. 20–32.

INTERNET RESOURCES

www.bis.org Web page of the Bank for International Settlements (BIS) that lists downloadable publications such as the BIS Annual Report, statistics on derivatives, external debt, foreign exchange market activity, and so on.

www.isda.org Web site of the International Swaps and Derivatives Association (ISDA). Provides information and data on swaps and other derivatives.

http://www.oanda.com/ Contains current and historical foreign exchange rate data for all currencies.

INTERNET EXERCISES

1. What were the volumes of interest and currency swaps during the past year? How do these figures compare to those from the previous year?
2. What risk factors associated with swaps does the ISDA discuss on its Web site?

PART III
FOREIGN EXCHANGE RISK MANAGEMENT

MEASURING AND MANAGING TRANSLATION AND TRANSACTION EXPOSURE

The stream of time sweeps away errors, and leaves the truth for the inheritance of humanity.

George Brandes

CHAPTER LEARNING OBJECTIVES

- To define translation and transaction exposure and distinguish between the two
- To describe the four principal currency translation methods available and to calculate translation exposure using these different methods
- To describe and apply the current (FASB-52) currency translation method prescribed by the Financial Accounting Standards Board
- To identify the basic hedging strategy and techniques used by firms to manage their currency transaction and translation risks
- To explain how a forward market hedge works
- To explain how a money-market hedge works
- To describe how foreign currency contract prices should be set to factor in exchange rate change expectations
- To describe how currency risk-sharing arrangements work
- To explain when foreign currency options are the preferred hedging technique
- To describe the costs associated with using the different hedging techniques
- To describe and assess the economic soundness of the various corporate hedging objectives
- To explain the advantages and disadvantages of centralizing foreign exchange risk management

KEY TERMS

accounting exposure	exposure netting
balance-sheet exposure	Financial Accounting Standards Board
cross-hedge	foreign exchange risk
currency call option	forward market hedge
currency collar	functional currency
currency options	funds adjustment
currency put option	hard currency
currency risk sharing	hedging
current exchange rate	historical exchange rate
current/noncurrent method	hyperinflationary country
current rate method	monetary/nonmonetary method
cylinder	money-market hedge
economic exposure	neutral zone

operating exposure
opportunity cost
price adjustment clauses
range forward
reporting currency
risk shifting
soft currency

Statement of Financial Accounting Standards
    No. 52 (FASB 52)
Statement of Financial Accounting Standards
    No. 133 (FASB 133)
temporal method
transaction exposure
translation exposure

Consider the case of Dell Inc., which operates assembly plants for its computers in several locations within the U.S. as well as in Ireland, Malaysia, China, and Brazil; operates offices and call centers in several other countries; and markets its products in over 100 countries. Dell may manufacture a product in Ireland for sale in, say, Denmark and obtain payments in Danish krone. Given foreign exchange fluctuations, Dell would like to ensure that its foreign profits are not eroded by currency fluctuations. Also, at the end of the year, when Dell consolidates its financial statements for the year at its headquarters in the U.S., it wants to ensure that currency fluctuations do not adversely impact its financial performance. The problems faced by Dell in accounting for its transactions as well as fiscal performance are mainly due to the foreign currency fluctuations that occur during the transaction as well as by the end of the fiscal year. Such problems and the risks thereof are common to all multinationals.

Foreign currency fluctuations are one of the key sources of risk in multinational operations. The pressure to monitor and manage foreign currency risks has led many companies to develop sophisticated computer-based systems to keep track of their foreign exchange exposure and aid in managing that exposure. The general concept of *exposure* refers to the degree to which a company is affected by exchange rate changes. This impact can be measured in several ways. As so often happens, economists tend to favor one approach to measuring foreign exchange exposure, while accountants favor an alternative approach. This chapter deals with the measurement and management of accounting exposure, including both translation and transaction exposure. Management of accounting exposure centers around the concept of hedging. **Hedging** a particular currency exposure means establishing an offsetting currency position so that whatever is lost or gained on the original currency exposure is exactly offset by a corresponding foreign exchange gain or loss on the currency hedge. Regardless of what happens to the future exchange rate, therefore, hedging locks in a dollar (home currency) value for the currency exposure. In this way, hedging can protect a firm from **foreign exchange risk**, which is the risk of valuation changes resulting from unforeseen currency movements.

9.1 ALTERNATIVE MEASURES OF FOREIGN EXCHANGE EXPOSURE

The three basic types of exposure are translation exposure, transaction exposure, and operating exposure. Transaction exposure and operating exposure combine to form economic exposure. Exhibit 9.1 illustrates and contrasts translation, transaction, and operating exposure. As can be seen, these exposures cannot always be neatly separated but instead overlap to some extent.

9.1.1 Translation Exposure

Translation exposure, also known as **accounting exposure**, arises from the need, for purposes of reporting and consolidation, to convert the financial statements of foreign operations from the local currencies (LC) involved to the home currency (HC). If exchange rates have changed since the previous reporting period, this *translation*, or restatement, of those

Translation Exposure	**Operating Exposure**
Changes in income statement items and the book value of balance sheet assets and liabilities that are caused by an exchange rate change. The resulting exchange gains and losses are determined by accounting rules and are paper only. The measurement of accounting exposure is retrospective in nature as it is based on activities that occurred in the past.	Changes in the amount of future operating cash flows caused by an exchange rate change. The resulting exchange gains or losses are determined by changes in the firm's future competitive position and are real. The measurement of operating exposure is prospective in nature as it is based on future activities.
Impacts: Balance sheet assets and liabilities and income statement items that already exist.	Impacts: Revenues and costs associated with future sales.

Exchange rate
change occurs

Transaction Exposure

Changes in the value of outstanding foreign-currency–denominated contracts (i.e., contracts that give rise to future foreign currency cash flows) that are brought about by an exchange rate change. The resulting exchange gains and losses are determined by the nature of the contracts already entered into and are real. The measurement of transaction exposure mixes the retrospective and prospective, because it is based on activities that occurred in the past but will be settled in the future. Contracts already on the balance sheet are part of the accounting exposure, whereas contracts not yet on the balance sheet are part of the operating exposure.

Impacts: Contracts already entered into, but . . . to be settled at a later date.

EXHIBIT 9.1 • COMPARISON OF TRANSLATION, TRANSACTION, AND OPERATING EXPOSURE

assets, liabilities, revenues, expenses, gains, and losses that are denominated in foreign currencies will result in foreign exchange gains or losses. The possible extent of these gains or losses is measured by the translation exposure figures. The rules that govern translation are devised by an accounting association such as the **Financial Accounting Standards Board** (FASB) in the United States, the parent firm's government, or the firm itself. Appendix 8A discusses **Statement of Financial Accounting Standards No. 52 (FASB 52)—** the present currency translation method prescribed by the FASB.

9.1.2 Transaction Exposure

Transaction exposure results from transactions that give rise to known, contractually binding future foreign-currency-denominated cash inflows or outflows. As exchange rates change between now and when these transactions settle, so does the value of their associated foreign currency cash flows, leading to currency gains and losses. Examples of transaction exposure for a U.S. company would be the account receivable associated with a sale denominated in euros or the obligation to repay a Japanese yen debt. Although transaction exposure is rightly part of economic exposure, it is usually lumped under accounting exposure. In reality, transaction exposure overlaps with both accounting and operating exposure. Some elements of transaction exposure, such as foreign-currency-denominated accounts receivable and debts, are included in a firm's accounting exposure because they already appear on the firm's balance sheet. Other elements of transaction exposure, such as foreign currency sales contracts that have been entered into but where the goods have not yet been delivered (and so receivables have not yet been created), do not appear on the firm's current financial statements and instead are part of the firm's operating exposure.

9.1.3 Operating Exposure

Operating exposure measures the extent to which currency fluctuations can alter a company's future operating cash flows, that is, its future revenues and costs. Any company whose revenues or costs are affected by currency changes has operating exposure, even if it is a purely domestic corporation and has all its cash flows denominated in home currency.

The two cash-flow exposures—operating exposure and transaction exposure—combine to equal a company's economic exposure. In technical terms, **economic exposure** is the extent to which the value of the firm, as measured by the present value of its expected cash flows, will change when exchange rates change.

9.2 ALTERNATIVE CURRENCY TRANSLATION METHODS

Companies with international operations will have foreign-currency-denominated assets and liabilities, revenues, and expenses. However, because home-country investors and the entire financial community are interested in home currency (HC) values, the foreign currency balance sheet accounts and income statement must be assigned HC values. In particular, the financial statements of an MNC's overseas subsidiaries must be translated from local currency (LC) to home currency before consolidation with the parent's financial statements.

If currency values change, foreign exchange translation gains or losses may result. Assets and liabilities that are translated at the current (postchange) exchange rate are considered to be exposed; those translated at a historical (prechange) exchange rate will maintain their historic HC values and, hence, are regarded as not exposed. *Translation exposure* is simply the difference between exposed assets and exposed liabilities. The controversies among accountants center on which assets and liabilities are exposed and on when accounting-derived foreign exchange gains and losses should be recognized (reported on the income statement). A crucial point to realize in putting these controversies in perspective is that such gains or losses are of an accounting nature—that is, no cash flows are necessarily involved.

Four principal translation methods are available: the current/noncurrent method, the monetary/nonmonetary method, the temporal method, and the current rate method. In practice, there are also variations of each method.

9.2.1 Current/Noncurrent Method

At one time, the **current/noncurrent method**, whose underlying theoretical basis is maturity, was used by almost all U.S. multinationals. With this method, all the foreign subsidiary's current assets and liabilities are translated into home currency at the **current exchange rate**. Each noncurrent asset or liability is translated at its **historical exchange rate**—that is, at the rate in effect at the time the asset was acquired or the liability was incurred. Hence, a foreign subsidiary with positive local currency working capital will give rise to a translation loss (gain) from a devaluation (revaluation) with the current/noncurrent method, and vice versa if working capital is negative.

The income statement is translated at the average exchange rate of the period, except for those revenues and expense items associated with noncurrent assets or liabilities. The latter items, such as depreciation expense, are translated at the same rates as the corresponding balance sheet items. Thus, it is possible to see different revenue and expense items with similar maturities being translated at different rates.

9.2.2 Monetary/Nonmonetary Method

The **monetary/nonmonetary method** differentiates between *monetary* assets and liabilities—that is, those items that represent a claim to receive, or an obligation to pay, a fixed amount of foreign currency units—and *nonmonetary*, or physical, assets and liabilities. Monetary items (for example, cash, accounts payable and receivable, and long-term debt) are translated at the current rate; nonmonetary items (for example, inventory, fixed assets, and long-term investments) are translated at historical rates.

Income statement items are translated at the average exchange rate during the period, except for revenue and expense items related to nonmonetary assets and liabilities. The latter items, primarily depreciation expense and cost of goods sold, are translated at the same rate as the corresponding balance sheet items. As a result, the cost of goods sold may be translated at a rate different from that used to translate sales.

9.2.3 Temporal Method

The **temporal method** appears to be a modified version of the monetary/nonmonetary method. The only difference is that under the monetary/nonmonetary method, inventory is always translated at the historical rate. Under the temporal method, inventory is normally translated at the historical rate, but it can be translated at the current rate if the inventory is shown on the balance sheet at market values. Despite the similarities, the theoretical bases of the two methods are different. The choice of exchange rate for translation is based on the type of asset or liability in the monetary/nonmonetary method; in the temporal method, it is based on the underlying approach to evaluating cost (historical versus market). Under a historical cost accounting system, as the United States now has, most accounting theoreticians probably would argue that the temporal method is the appropriate method for translation.

Income statement items normally are translated at an average rate for the reporting period. However, cost of goods sold and depreciation and amortization charges related to balance sheet items carried at past prices are translated at historical rates.

9.2.4 Current Rate Method

The **current rate method** is the simplest: All balance sheet and income items are translated at the current rate. This method is widely employed by British companies. With some variation, it is the method mandated by the current U.S. translation standard FASB 52. Under the current rate method, if a firm's foreign-currency-denominated assets exceed its foreign-currency-denominated liabilities, a devaluation must result in a loss and a revaluation must result in a gain.

Exhibit 9.2 applies the four methods to a hypothetical balance sheet that is affected by both a 25% devaluation and a 37.5% revaluation. Depending on the method chosen, the translation results for the LC devaluation can range from a loss of $205,000 to a gain of $215,000; LC revaluation results can vary from a gain of $615,000 to a loss of $645,000. The assets and liabilities that are considered exposed under each method are the ones that change in dollar value. Note that the translation gains or losses for each method show up as the change in the equity account. For example, the LC devaluation combined with the current rate method results in a $205,000 reduction in the equity account ($1,025,000 − $820,000), which equals the translation loss for this method. Another way to calculate this loss is to take the net LC translation exposure, which equals exposed assets minus exposed liabilities (for the current rate method this figure is LC

	Local Currency	U.S. Dollars Prior to Exchange Rate Change (LC 4 = $1)	After Devaluation of Local Currency (LC 5 = $1)				After Revaluation of Local Currency			
			Monetary/ Non-monetary	Temporal	Current/ Non-current	Current Rates for All Assets and Liabilities	Monetary/ Non-monetary	Temporal	Current/ Non-current	Current Rates for All Assets and Liabilities
Assets										
Current assets										
Cash, marketable securities, and receivables	LC 2,600	650	520	520	520	520	1,040	1,040	1,040	1,040
Inventory (at market)	3,600	900	900	720	720	720	900	1,440	1,440	1,440
Prepaid expenses	200	50	50	50	40	40	50	50	80	80
Total current assets	6,400	1,600	1,470	1,290	1,280	1,280	1,990	2,530	2,560	2,560
Fixed assets less accumulated depreciation	3,600	900	900	900	900	720	900	900	900	1,440
Goodwill	1,000	250	250	250	250	200	250	250	250	400
Total assets	LC 11,000	2,750	2,620	2,440	2,430	2,200	3,140	3,680	3,710	4,400
Liabilities										
Current liabilities	3,400	850	680	680	680	680	1,360	1,360	1,360	1,360
Long-term debt	3,000	750	600	600	750	600	1,200	1,200	750	1,200
Deferred income taxes	500	125	100	100	125	100	200	200	125	200
Total liabilities	6,900	1,725	1,380	1,380	1,555	1,380	2,760	2,760	2,235	2,760
Capital stock	1,500	375	375	375	375	375	375	375	375	375
Retained earnings	2,600	650	865	685	500	445	5	545	1,100	1,265
Total equity	4,100	1,025	1,240	1,060	875	820	380	920	1,475	1,640
Total liabilities plus equity	LC 11,000	2,750	2,620	2,440	2,430	2,200	3,140	3,680	3,710	4,400
Translation gain (loss)	—	—	215	35	(150)	(205)	(645)	(105)	450	615

EXHIBIT 9.2 • Financial Statement Impact of Translation Alternatives (U.S. $ Thousands)

4,100,000, which, not coincidentally, equals its equity value) and multiply it by the $0.05 ($0.25 − $0.20) change in the exchange rate. This calculation yields a translation loss of $205,000 ($0.05 × 4,100,000), the same as calculated in Exhibit 9.2. Another way to calculate this loss is to multiply the net dollar translation exposure by the fractional change in the exchange rate, or $1,025,000 × 0.05/0.25 = $205,000. Either approach gives the correct answer.

9.3 TRANSACTION EXPOSURE

Companies often include transaction exposure as part of their accounting exposure, although as a cash-flow exposure it is rightly part of a company's economic exposure. As we have seen, *transaction exposure* stems from the possibility of incurring future exchange gains or losses on transactions already entered into and denominated in a foreign currency. For example, when IBM sells a mainframe computer to Royal Dutch Shell in England, it typically will not be paid until a later date. If that sale is priced in pounds, IBM has a pound transaction exposure.

A company's transaction exposure is measured currency by currency and equals the difference between contractually fixed future cash inflows and outflows in each currency. Some of these unsettled transactions, including foreign currency-denominated debt and accounts receivable, are already listed on the firm's balance sheet. However, other obligations, such as contracts for future sales or purchases, are not.

ILLUSTRATION *Computing Transaction Exposure for Boeing*

Suppose Boeing Airlines sells five 747s to Air India, India's national airline, in rupees. The rupee price is Rs 50 billion. To help reduce the impact on India's balance of payments, Boeing agrees to buy parts from various Indian companies worth Rs 22 billion.

a. If the spot rate is $0.0243/Rs, what is Boeing's net rupee transaction exposure?

Solution. Boeing's net rupee exposure equals its projected rupee inflows minus its projected rupee outflows, or Rs 50 billion − Rs 22 billion = Rs 28 billion. Converted into dollars at the spot rate of $0.0243/Rs, Boeing's transaction exposure equals $680.4 million.

b. If the rupee depreciates to $0.024255/Rs, what is Boeing's transaction loss?

Solution. Boeing will lose an amount equal to its rupee exposure multiplied by the change in the exchange rate, or 28 billion × (0.0243 − 0.02425) = $1.4 million. This loss can also be determined by multiplying Boeing's exposure in dollar terms by the fractional change in the exchange rate, or 680.4 million × (0.00005/0.0243) = $1.4 million.

Although translation and transaction exposures overlap, they are not synonymous. Some items included in translation exposure, such as inventories and fixed assets, are excluded from transaction exposure, whereas other items included in transaction exposure, such as contracts for future sales or purchases, are not included in translation exposure. Thus, it is possible for transaction exposure in a currency to be positive and translation exposure in that same currency to be negative and vice versa. For example, Sterling Ltd. has translation exposure of £120,000,000 (£1,000,000,000 − £880,000,000). At the same time, ignoring off-balance sheet items, it has transaction exposure of −£580,000,000 (by eliminating £700,000,000 in inventory and fixed assets from our calculations).

9.4 DESIGNING A HEDGING STRATEGY

Exposure to currency fluctuations can be managed by means of hedging. As mentioned earlier, hedging a particular currency exposure means establishing an offsetting currency position so as to lock in a dollar (home currency) value for the currency exposure and thereby eliminate the risk posed by currency fluctuations. A variety of hedging techniques are available for managing exposure, but before a firm uses them it must decide on which exposures to manage and how to manage them. Addressing these issues successfully requires an operational set of goals for those involved in exchange risk management. Failure to set out objectives can lead to possibly conflicting and costly actions on the part of employees. Although many firms do have objectives, their goals are often so vague and simplistic (for example, "eliminate all exposure" or "minimize reported foreign exchange losses") that they provide little realistic guidance to managers.[1] For example, should an employee told to eliminate all exposure do so by using forward contracts and currency options, or by borrowing in the local currency? And if hedging is not possible in a particular currency, should sales in that currency be forgone even if it means losing potential profits? The latter policy is likely to present a manager with the dilemma of choosing between the goals of increased profits and reduced exchange losses. Moreover, reducing translation exposure could increase transaction exposure and vice versa. What trade-offs, if any, should a manager be willing to make between these two types of exposure?

These and similar questions demonstrate the need for a coherent and effective strategy. The following elements are suggested for an effective exposure management strategy:[2]

1. Determine the types of exposure to be monitored;
2. Formulate corporate objectives and give guidance in resolving potential conflicts in objectives;
3. Ensure that these corporate objectives are consistent with maximizing shareholder value and can be implemented;
4. Clearly specify who is responsible for which exposures, and detail the criteria by which each manager is to be judged;
5. Make explicit any constraints on the use of exposure-management techniques, such as limitations on entering into forward contracts;
6. Identify the channels by which exchange rate considerations are incorporated into operating decisions that will affect the firm's exchange risk posture; and
7. Develop a system for monitoring and evaluating exchange risk management activities.

9.4.1 Objectives

The usefulness of a particular hedging strategy depends on both *acceptability* and *quality*. Acceptability refers to approval by those in the organization who will implement the strategy, and quality refers to the ability to provide better decisions. To be acceptable, a hedging strategy must be consistent with top management's values and overall corporate objectives. In turn, these values and objectives are strongly motivated by management's beliefs about financial markets and how its performance will be evaluated. The quality, or

---

[1] Dow Chemical stated in its 2006 Form 10-K Filing that the primary objective of its hedging activity is "to optimize the U.S. dollar value of the Company's assets, liabilities and future cash flows with respect to exchange rate fluctuations" (p. 75 of Form 10-K, December 31, 2006, available from the company website). While a laudable objective, it is difficult to determine what specific actions a manager should take to accomplish it.

[2] Most of these elements are suggested in Thomas G. Evans and William R. Folks, Jr., "Defining Objectives for Exposure Management," *Business International Money Report*, February 2, 1979, pp. 37–39.

1. **Minimize translation exposure.** This common goal necessitates a complete focus on protecting foreigncurrency-denominated assets and liabilities from changes in value due to exchange rate fluctuations. Given that translation and transaction exposures are not synonymous, reducing the former could cause an increase in the latter (and vice versa).

2. **Minimize quarter-to-quarter (or year-to-year) earnings fluctuations owing to exchange rate changes.** This goal requires a firm to consider both its translation exposure and its transaction exposure.

3. **Minimize transaction exposure.** This objective involves managing a subset of the firm's true cash-flow exposure.

4. **Minimize economic exposure.** To achieve this goal, a firm must ignore accounting earnings and concentrate on reducing cash-flow fluctuations stemming from currency fluctuations.

5. **Minimize foreign exchange risk management costs.** This goal requires a firm to balance off the benefits of hedging with its costs. It also assumes risk neutrality.

6. **Avoid surprises.** This objective involves preventing large foreign exchange losses.

EXHIBIT 9.3 ● VARIOUS OBJECTIVES FOR HEDGING

value to the shareholders, of a particular hedging strategy is, therefore, related to the congruence between those perceptions and the realities of the business environment. The most frequently occurring objectives, explicit and implicit, in management behavior are provided in Exhibit 9.3.[3]

The basic purpose of hedging is to reduce exchange risk, where exchange risk is defined as that element of cash-flow variability attributable to currency fluctuations (Objective 4 in Exhibit 9.3). To the extent that earnings fluctuations or large losses can adversely affect the company's perceptions in the minds of potential investors, customers, employees, and so on, there may be reason to pay attention to Objectives 2 and 6 as well. There are likely to be few, if any, advantages to devoting substantial resources to managing earnings fluctuations or accounting exposure more generally (Objectives 1 and 3). To begin, trying to manage accounting exposure is inconsistent with a large body of empirical evidence that investors have the uncanny ability to peer beyond the ephemeral and concentrate on the firm's true cash-flow-generating ability. In addition, whereas balance sheet gains and losses can be dampened by hedging, operating earnings will also fluctuate in line with the combined and offsetting effects of currency changes and inflation. Moreover, hedging costs themselves will vary unpredictably from one period to the next, leading to unpredictable earnings changes. Thus, it is impossible for firms to protect themselves from earnings fluctuations due to exchange rate changes except in the very short run.

In operational terms, hedging to reduce the variance of cash flows translates into the following exposure management goal: *to arrange a firm's financial affairs in such a way that however the exchange rate may move in the future, the effects on dollar returns are minimized.* This objective is not universally subscribed to, however. Instead, many firms follow a selective hedging policy designed to protect against anticipated currency movements. A selective hedging policy is especially prevalent among those firms that organize their treasury departments as profit centers. In such firms, the desire to reduce the expected costs of hedging (Objective 5), and thereby increase profits, often leads to taking higher risks by hedging only when a currency change is expected and going unhedged otherwise.

---

[3] See, for example, David B. Zenoff, "Applying Management Principles to Foreign Exchange Exposure," *Euromoney,* September 1978, pp. 123–130.

If financial markets are efficient, however, firms cannot hedge against *expected* exchange rate changes. Interest rates, forward rates, and sales-contract prices should already reflect currency changes that are anticipated, thereby offsetting the loss-reducing benefits of hedging with higher costs. In the case of Mexico, for instance, the one-year forward discount in the futures market was close to 100% just before the peso was floated in 1982. The unavoidable conclusion is that a firm can protect itself only against *unexpected* currency changes.

Moreover, there is always the possibility of bad timing. For example, big Japanese exporters such as Toyota and Honda have incurred billions of dollars in foreign exchange losses. One reason for these losses is that Japanese companies often try to predict where the dollar is going and hedge (or not hedge) accordingly. At the beginning of 1994, many thought that the dollar would continue to strengthen, and thus they failed to hedge their exposure. When the dollar plummeted instead, they lost billions. The lesson is that firms that try simultaneously to use hedging both to reduce risk and to beat the market may end up with more risk, not less.

ILLUSTRATION   *Malaysia Gets Mauled by the Currency Markets*

In January 1994, Bank Negara, Malaysia's central bank, declared war on "currency speculators" who were trying to profit from an anticipated rise in the Malaysian dollar. The timing of this declaration struck a nerve among currency traders because Bank Negara had itself long been a major speculator in the currency markets—a speculator whose boldness was matched only by its incompetence. During the 2-year period 1992–1993, Bank Negara had foreign exchange losses of M$14.7 billion (US$5.42 billion). It seems that even central banks are not immune to the consequences of market efficiency—and stupidity.

9.4.2 Costs and Benefits of Standard Hedging Techniques

Standard techniques for responding to anticipated currency changes are summarized in Exhibit 9.4. Such techniques, however, are vastly overrated in terms of their ability to minimize hedging costs.

Costs of Hedging   If a devaluation is unlikely, hedging may be a costly and inefficient way of doing business. If a devaluation is expected, the cost of using the techniques (like the cost of local borrowing) rises to reflect the anticipated devaluation. Just before the August 1982 peso devaluation, for example, every company in Mexico was trying to delay peso payments. Of course, this technique cannot produce a net gain because one company's payable is another company's receivable. As another example, if one company wants peso trade credit, another must offer it. Assuming that both the borrower and the lender are rational, a deal will not be struck until the interest cost rises to reflect the expected decline in the peso.

Even shifting funds from one country to another is not a costless means of hedging. The net effect of speeding up remittances while delaying receipt of intercompany receivables is to force a subsidiary in a devaluation-prone country to increase its local currency (LC) borrowings to finance the additional working capital requirements. The net cost of shifting funds, therefore, is the cost of the LC loan minus the profit generated from use of the funds—for example, prepaying a hard currency loan—with both adjusted for

Depreciation	Appreciation
• Sell local currency forward	• Buy local currency forward
• Buy a local currency put option	• Buy a local currency call option
• Reduce levels of local currency cash and marketable securities	• Increase levels of local currency cash and marketable securities
• Tighten credit (reduce local currency receivables)	• Relax local currency credit terms
• Delay collection of hard currency receivables	• Speed up collection of soft currency receivables
• Increase imports of hard currency goods	• Reduce imports of soft currency goods
• Borrow locally	• Reduce local borrowing
• Delay payment of accounts payable	• Speed up payment of accounts payable
• Speed up dividend and fee remittances to parent and other subsidiaries	• Delay dividend and fee remittances to parent and other subsidiaries
• Speed up payment of intersubsidiary accounts payable	• Delay payment of intersubsidiary accounts payable
• Delay collection of intersubsidiary accounts receivable	• Speed up collection of intersubsidiary accounts receivable
• Invoice exports in foreign currency and imports in local currency	• Invoice exports in local currency and imports in foreign currency

EXHIBIT 9.4 • BASIC HEDGING TECHNIQUES

expected exchange rate changes. As mentioned previously, loans in local currencies subject to devaluation fears carry higher interest rates that are likely to offset any gains from LC devaluation.

Reducing the level of cash holdings to lower exposure can adversely affect a subsidiary's operations, whereas selling LC-denominated marketable securities can entail an opportunity cost (the lower interest rate on hard currency securities). A firm with excess cash or marketable securities should reduce its holdings regardless of whether a devaluation is anticipated. After cash balances are at the minimum level, however, any further reductions will involve real costs that must be weighed against the expected benefits.

Invoicing exports in the foreign currency and imports in the local currency may cause the loss of valuable sales or may reduce a firm's ability to extract concessions on import prices. Similarly, tightening credit may reduce profits more than costs.

In summary, hedging exchange risk costs money and should be scrutinized like any other purchase of insurance. The costs of these hedging techniques are summarized in Exhibit 9.5.

Benefits of Hedging A company can benefit from the preceding techniques only to the extent that it can forecast future exchange rates more accurately than the general market. For example, if the company has a foreign currency cash inflow, it would hedge only if the forward rate exceeds its estimate of the future spot rate. Conversely, with a foreign currency cash outflow, it would hedge only if the forward rate was below its estimated future spot rate. In this way, it would apparently be following the profit-guaranteeing dictum of buy low-sell high. The key word, however, is *apparently* because attempting to profit from foreign exchange forecasting is speculating rather than hedging. The hedger is well advised to assume that the market knows as much as he or she does. Those who feel that they have superior information may choose to speculate, but this activity should not be confused with hedging.

Depreciation	*Costs*
• Sell local currency forward	• Transaction costs; difference between forward and future spot rates
• Buy a local currency put option	• Put option premium
• Reduce levels of local currency cash and marketable securities	• Operational problems; opportunity cost (loss of higher interest rates on LC securities)
• Tighten credit (reduce local currency receivables)	• Lost sales and profits
• Delay collection of hard currency receivables	• Cost of financing additional receivables
• Increase imports of hard currency goods	• Financing and holding costs
• Borrow locally	• Higher interest rates
• Delay payment of accounts payable	• Harm to credit reputation
• Speed up dividend and fee remittances to parent and other subsidiaries	• Borrowing cost if funds not available or loss of higher interest rates if LC securities must be sold
• Speed up payment of intersubsidiary accounts payable	• Opportunity cost of money
• Delay collection of intersubsidiary accounts receivable	• Opportunity cost of money
• Invoice exports in foreign currency and imports in local currency	• Lost export sales or lower price; premium price for imports

EXHIBIT 9.5 • COST OF THE BASIC HEDGING TECHNIQUES

ILLUSTRATION *Selective Hedging*

In March, 2007 Multinational Industries, Inc. (MII) assessed the September spot rate for sterling at the following rates:

$1.80/£ with probability 0.15

$1.85/£ with probability 0.20

$1.90/£ with probability 0.25

$1.95/£ with probability 0.20

$2.00/£ with probability 0.20

a. What is the expected spot rate for September?

Solution. The expected future spot rate is 1.80(0.15) + 1.85(0.2) + 1.90(0.25) + 1.95(0.20) + 2.00(0.20) = $1.905.

b. If the 6-month forward rate is $1.90, should the firm sell forward its £500,000 pound receivables due in September?

Solution. If MII sells its pound proceeds forward, it will lock in a value of $950,000 (1.90 × 500,000). Alternatively, if it decides to wait until September and sell its pound proceeds in the spot market, it expects to receive $952,500 (1.905 × 500,000). Based on these figures, if MII wants to maximize expected profits, it should retain its pound receivables and sell the proceeds in the spot market upon receipt.

c. What factors are likely to affect MII's hedging decision?

Solution. Risk aversion could lead MII to sell its receivables forward to hedge their dollar value. However, if MII has pound liabilities, they could provide a natural hedge and reduce (or eliminate) the amount necessary to hedge. The existence of a cheaper hedging alternative, such as borrowing pounds and converting them to dollars for the duration of the receivables, would also make undesirable the use of a forward contract. This latter situation assumes that interest rate parity is violated. The tax treatment of foreign exchange gains and losses on forward contracts could also affect the hedging decision.

Under some circumstances, a company may benefit at the expense of the local government without speculating. Such a circumstance would involve the judicious use of market imperfections or existing tax asymmetries, or both. In the case of an overvalued currency, such as the Mexican peso in 1982, if exchange controls are not imposed to prevent capital outflows and if hard currency can be acquired at the official exchange rate, then money can be moved out of the country via intercompany payments. For instance, a subsidiary can speed payments of intercompany accounts payable, make immediate purchases from other subsidiaries, or speed remittances to the parent. Unfortunately, governments are indeed aware of these tactics. During a currency crisis, when hard currency is scarce, the local government can be expected to block such transfers or at least make them more expensive.

Another often-cited reason for market imperfection is that individual investors may not have equal access to capital markets. For example, because forward exchange markets exist only for the major currencies, hedging often requires local borrowing in heavily regulated capital markets. As a legal citizen of many nations, the MNC normally has greater access to these markets.

Similarly, if forward contract losses are treated as a cost of doing business, whereas gains are taxed at a lower capital gains rate, the firm can engage in tax arbitrage. In the absence of financial market imperfections or tax asymmetries, however, the net expected value of hedging over time should be zero. Despite the questionable value to shareholders of hedging balance sheet exposure or even transaction exposure, however, managers often try to reduce these exposures, because they are evaluated, at least in part, on translation or transaction gains or losses.

In one area, however, companies can reduce their exchange risk at no cost. This costless hedging technique is known as exposure netting.

Exposure Netting   **Exposure netting** involves offsetting exposures in one currency with exposures in the same or another currency, where exchange rates are expected to move in a way such that losses (gains) on the first exposed position will be offset by gains (losses) on the second currency exposure. This portfolio approach to hedging recognizes that the total variability or risk of a currency exposure portfolio will be less than the sum of the individual variabilities of each currency exposure considered in isolation. The assumption underlying exposure netting is that the net gain or loss on the entire currency exposure portfolio is what matters, rather than the gain or loss on any individual monetary unit.

9.4.3 Centralization versus Decentralization

In the area of foreign exchange risk management, there are good arguments both for and against centralization. Favoring centralization is the reasonable assumption that local treasurers want to optimize their own financial and exposure positions, regardless of the overall corporate situation. An example is a multibillion-dollar U.S. consumer-goods firm that gives its affiliates a free hand in deciding on their hedging policies. The firm's local treasurers ignore the possibilities available to the corporation to trade off positive and negative currency exposure positions by consolidating exposure worldwide. If subsidiary A sells to subsidiary B in sterling, then from the corporate perspective, these sterling exposures net out on a consolidated translation basis (but only before tax). If A or B or both hedge their sterling positions, however, unnecessary hedging takes place, or a zero sterling exposure turns into a positive or negative position. Furthermore, in their dealings with external customers, some affiliates may wind up with a positive exposure and others with a negative exposure in the same currency. Through lack of knowledge or incentive, individual subsidiaries may undertake hedging actions that increase rather than decrease overall corporate exposure in a given currency.

A further benefit of centralized exposure management is the ability to take advantage, through exposure netting, of the portfolio effect discussed previously. Thus, centralization of exchange risk management should reduce the amount of hedging required to achieve a given level of safety.

After the company has decided on the maximum currency exposure it is willing to tolerate, it can then select the cheapest option(s) worldwide to hedge its remaining exposure. Tax effects can be crucial at this stage, in computing both the amounts to hedge and the costs involved, but only headquarters will have the required global perspective. Centralized management also is needed to take advantage of the before-tax hedging cost variations that are likely to exist among subsidiaries because of market imperfections.

All these arguments for centralization of currency risk management are powerful. Against the benefits must be weighed the loss of local knowledge and the lack of incentive for local managers to take advantage of particular situations that only they may be familiar with. Companies that decentralize the hedging decision may allow local units to manage their own exposures by engaging in forward contracts with a central unit at negotiated rates. The central unit, in turn, may or may not lay off these contracts in the marketplace.

9.4.4 Managing Risk Management

A number of highly publicized cases of derivatives-related losses have highlighted the potential dangers in the use of derivatives such as futures and options. Although these losses did not involve the use of currency derivatives, several lessons for risk management can be drawn from these cases, which include the bankruptcies of Orange County and Barings PLC and the huge losses taken at Metallgesellschaft, Kidder Peabody, Sumitomo, Daiwa, Allied Irish Banks, Union Bank of Switzerland, and Procter & Gamble. The most important lesson to be learned is that risk management failures have their origins in inadequate systems and controls rather than from any risk inherent in the use of derivatives themselves.[4] In every case of large losses, senior management did not fully understand the activities of those taking positions in derivatives and failed to monitor and supervise their activities adequately. Some specific lessons include the following.

First, segregate the duties of those trading derivatives from those supposed to monitor them. For example, Nicholas Leeson, the rogue trader who sank Barings, was in charge of trading and also kept his own books. When he took losses, he covered them up and doubled his bets. Similarly, the manager responsible for the profits generated by

---

[4] According to Anthony M. Santomero, president of the Federal Reserve Bank of Philadelphia, some bank managers have little knowledge of controls on their trading activities. For example, when he visited a major financial institution in New York, the CEO assured him that the bank had a highly sophisticated risk-management system already in place, the CFO said they had just implemented it, the head of trading said they were about to implement it, and the traders had never heard of it. See Anthony M. Santomero, "Processes and Progress in Risk Management," *Business Review*, Federal Reserve Bank of Philadelphia, Q1 2003, p. 3.

trading derivatives at UBS also oversaw the risks of his position. No one else at the bank was allowed to examine the risks his department was taking. And a rogue trader at Sumitomo, who lost $1.8 billion, oversaw the accounts that kept track of his dealings. Such conflicts of interest are a recipe for disaster. Second, derivatives positions should be limited to prevent the possibility of catastrophic losses, and they should be marked to market every day to avoid the possibility of losses going unrecognized and being allowed to accumulate. As in the cases of Barings and Sumitomo, traders who can roll over their positions at nonmarket prices tend to make bigger and riskier bets to recoup their losses.

Third, compensation arrangements should be designed to shift more of the risk onto the shoulders of those taking the risks. For example, deferring part of traders' salaries until their derivatives positions actually pay off would make them more cognizant of the risks they are taking. Fourth, one should pay attention to warning signs. For example, Barings was slow to respond to an audit showing significant discrepancies in Leeson's accounts. Similarly, Kidder Peabody's executives ignored a trader who was generating record profits while supposedly engaged in risk-free arbitrage. A related lesson is that there's no free lunch. Traders and others delivering high profits deserve special scrutiny by independent auditors. The auditors must pay particular attention to the valuation of *exotic derivatives*—specialized contracts not actively traded. Given the lack of ready market prices for exotics, it is easy for traders to overvalue their positions in exotics without independent oversight. Finally, those who value reward above risk will likely wind up with risk at the expense of reward.

ILLUSTRATION   *The Luck of the Irish Eludes Allied Irish Banks*

In February 2002, Allied Irish Banks announced that a rogue trader at its U.S. unit lost $750 million through unauthorized foreign-exchange trades. Allied said John Rusnak, a foreign-exchange dealer at its U.S. unit Allfirst tried to disguise huge losses through fictitious foreign-exchange trades over the past year. Traders in the foreign-exchange market believe that Mr. Rusnak bet on the wrong direction of the Japanese yen, which was the only currency that moved enough during that period to have enabled a trader to pile up such colossal losses. The foreign-exchange trades at issue were believed by the bank to have been hedged with currency options to reduce their risk. As it turned out, however, the options that Mr. Rusnak claimed to have bought were fictitious, leaving the bank with enormous "naked" (unhedged) foreign-exchange positions. As his losses piled up, he placed even larger foreign currency bets, which turned sour as well. Bank analysts said the episode raised serious issues about the risk-management controls in place at Allied and throughout the entire banking industry that are supposed to prevent the kinds of events that apparently hit Allied.

9.4.5 Accounting for Hedging and FASB 133

Companies have a greater incentive for systematizing their hedging practices since FASB issued its **Statement of Financial Accounting Standards No. 133 (FASB 133)** to establish accounting and reporting standards for derivative instruments and for hedging activities. Under FASB 133, a foreign currency derivative that qualifies as a foreign currency hedge gets special hedge accounting treatment that essentially matches gains or losses resulting from the changes in the value of the derivative with losses or gains in the value of the underlying transaction or asset, thereby removing these hedging gains and losses from current income. However, any change in the value of the derivative not offset by a change in the value of the hedged item is recorded to earnings in the current period. Foreign currency hedges include hedges of net investments in foreign operations, of forecasted foreign currency transactions, and of foreign-currency-denominated assets or liabilities.

Under FASB, an entity that elects to apply hedge accounting is required to formally document each hedging transaction from the outset, explain its risk management objective and strategy for undertaking the hedge, the nature of the risk being hedged, and establish the method it will use for assessing the effectiveness of the hedging derivative and its measurement approach for determining the ineffective aspect of the hedge.

Three points are worth noting.

> *Hedge designations are critical.* Each hedging relationship should fit into the company's risk management objectives and strategy, which must be documented.
>
> *Hedging must be effective.* To qualify for hedge accounting, an entity must demonstrate a hedging relationship to be highly effective in achieving offsetting changes in fair value or cash flows for the risk being hedged. "Highly effective" has been interpreted to mean a correlation ratio between 80% and 125% (this is the change in value of the derivative divided by the change in value of the hedged item).
>
> *Hedge ineffectiveness can lead to earnings volatility.* A foreign currency derivative that cannot be shown to be effective in hedging a specific foreign currency risk must be marked to market and any gain or loss on it included in current earnings, making reported earnings more volatile.

9.5 MANAGING TRANSLATION EXPOSURE

As noted earlier, translation exposure arises from the need to convert local currencies (LCs) involved to the home currency for reporting and consolidating financial statements. Firms have three available methods for managing their translation exposure: (1) adjusting fund flows, (2) entering into forward contracts, and (3) exposure netting. The basic hedging strategy for reducing translation exposure shown in Exhibit 9.6 uses these methods. Essentially, the strategy involves increasing **hard currency** (likely to appreciate) assets and decreasing **soft currency** (likely to depreciate) assets, while simultaneously decreasing hard currency liabilities and increasing soft currency liabilities. For example, if a devaluation appears likely, the basic hedging strategy will be executed as follows: Reduce the level of cash, tighten credit terms to decrease accounts receivable, increase LC borrowing, delay accounts payable, and sell the weak currency forward. An expected currency appreciation would trigger the opposite tactics.

Despite their prevalence among firms, these hedging activities are not automatically valuable. As discussed in the previous section, if the market already recognizes the likelihood of currency appreciation or depreciation, this recognition will be reflected in the costs of various hedging techniques. Only if the firm's anticipations differ from the

	Assets	*Liabilities*
Hard currencies (Likely to appreciate)	Increase	Decrease
Soft currencies (Likely to depreciate)	Decrease	Increase

EXHIBIT 9.6 • BASIC STRATEGY FOR HEDGING TRANSLATION EXPOSURE

market's and are also superior to the market's can hedging lead to reduced costs. Otherwise, the principal value of hedging would be to protect a firm from unforeseen currency fluctuations.

9.5.1 Funds Adjustment

Most techniques for hedging an impending local currency (LC) devaluation reduce LC assets or increase LC liabilities, thereby generating LC cash. If accounting exposure is to be reduced, these funds must be converted into hard currency assets. For example, a company will reduce its translation loss if, before an LC devaluation, it converts some of its LC cash holdings to the home currency. This conversion can be accomplished, either directly or indirectly, by means of funds adjustment techniques.

Funds adjustment involves altering either the amounts or the currencies (or both) of the planned cash flows of the parent or its subsidiaries to reduce the firm's local currency accounting exposure. If an LC devaluation is anticipated, direct funds-adjustment methods include pricing exports in hard currencies and imports in the local currency, investing in hard currency securities, and replacing hard currency borrowings with local currency loans. The indirect methods, which are elaborated upon in Chapter 16, include adjusting transfer prices on the sale of goods between affiliates; speeding up the payment of dividends, fees, and royalties; and adjusting the leads and lags of intersubsidiary accounts. The last method, which is the one most frequently used by multinationals, involves speeding up the payment of intersubsidiary accounts payable and delaying the collection of intersubsidiary accounts receivable. These hedging procedures for devaluations would be reversed for revaluations (see Exhibit 9.4).

Some of these techniques or tools may require considerable lead time and—as is the case with a transfer price—once they are introduced, they cannot easily be changed. In addition, techniques such as transfer price, fee and royalty, and dividend flow adjustments fall into the realm of corporate policy and are not usually under the treasurer's control, although this situation may be changing. It is, therefore, incumbent on the treasurer to educate other decision makers about the impact of these tools on the costs and management of corporate exposure.

Although entering forward contracts is the most popular coverage technique, the leading and lagging of payables and receivables is almost as important. For those countries in which a formal market in LC forward contracts does not exist, leading and lagging and LC borrowing are the most important techniques. The bulk of international business, however, is conducted in those few currencies for which forward markets do exist.

Forward contracts can reduce a firm's translation exposure by creating an offsetting asset or liability in the foreign currency. For example, suppose that IBM U.K. has translation exposure of £40 million (that is, sterling assets exceed sterling liabilities by that amount). IBM U.K. can eliminate its entire translation exposure by selling £40 million forward. Any loss (gain) on its translation exposure will then be offset by a corresponding gain (loss) on its forward contract. Note, however, that the gain (or loss) on the forward contract is of a cash-flow nature and is netted against an unrealized translation loss (or gain).

Selecting convenient (less risky) currencies for invoicing exports and imports and adjusting transfer prices are two techniques that are less frequently used, perhaps because of constraints on the use of those techniques. It is often difficult, for instance, to make a customer or supplier accept billing in a particular currency.

Exposure netting is an additional exchange-management technique that is available to multinational firms with positions in more than one foreign currency or with offsetting positions in the same currency. As defined earlier, this technique involves offsetting exposures in one currency with exposures in the same or another currency such that gains and losses on the two currency positions will offset each other.

9.5.2 Evaluating Alternative Hedging Mechanisms

Ordinarily, the selection of a funds-adjustment strategy cannot proceed by evaluating each possible technique separately without risking suboptimization; for example, whether a firm chooses to borrow locally is not independent of its decision to use or not use those funds to import additional hard currency inventory. However, where the level of forward contracts the financial manager can enter into is unrestricted, the following two-stage methodology allows the optimal level of forward transactions to be determined apart from the selection of what funds-adjustment techniques to use.[5] Moreover, this methodology is valid regardless of the manager's (or firm's) attitude toward risk.

Stage 1: Compute the profit associated with each funds-adjustment technique on a covered after-tax basis. Transactions that are profitable on a covered basis ought to be undertaken regardless of whether they increase or decrease the firm's accounting exposure. However, such activities should not be termed *hedging*; rather, they involve the use of *arbitrage* to exploit market distortions.

Stage 2: Any unwanted exposure resulting from the first stage can be corrected in the forward market. Stage 2 is the selection of an optimal level of forward transactions based on the firm's initial exposure, adjusted for the impact on exposure of decisions made in stage 1. Where the forward market is nonexistent, or where access to it is limited, the firm must determine both the techniques to use and their appropriate levels. In the latter case, a comparison of the net cost of a funds-adjustment technique with the anticipated currency depreciation will indicate whether the hedging transaction is profitable on an expected-value basis.

9.6 MANAGING TRANSACTION EXPOSURE

As we saw in Section 9.1, transaction exposure arises whenever a company is committed to a foreign-currency-denominated transaction. Since the transaction will result in a future foreign currency cash inflow or outflow, any change in the exchange rate between the time the transaction is entered into and the time it is settled in cash will lead to a change in the dollar (HC) amount of the cash inflow or outflow. Protective measures to guard against transaction exposure involve entering into foreign currency transactions whose cash flows exactly offset the cash flows of the transaction exposure.

These protective measures include using forward contracts, price adjustment clauses, currency options, and borrowing or lending in the foreign currency. Alternatively, the company could try to invoice all transactions in dollars and to avoid transaction exposure entirely. However, eliminating transaction exposure does not eliminate all foreign exchange risk. The firm still is subject to exchange risk on its future revenues and costs—its operating cash flows. For example, in its 2006 Annual Report (p. 47), IBM explained that its hedging program may not completely eliminate all the risks:

> *The company earned approximately 45 percent of its net income in currencies other than the U.S. dollar. The company also maintains hedging programs to limit the volatility of currency impacts on the company's financial results. These hedging programs limit the impact of currency changes on the company's financial results but do not eliminate them.*

We will now look at the various techniques for managing transaction exposure by examining the case of General Electric's euro exposure. Suppose that on January 1, GE is

---

[5] This methodology is presented in William R. Folks, Jr., "Decision Analysis for Exchange Risk Management," *Financial Management*, Winter 1972, pp. 101–112.

awarded a contract to supply turbine blades to Lufthansa, the German airline. On December 31, GE will receive payment of €10 million for these blades. The most direct way for GE to hedge this receivable is to sell a €10 million forward contract for delivery in one year. Alternatively, it can use a money-market hedge, which would involve borrowing €10 million for one year, converting it into dollars, and investing the proceeds in a security that matures on December 31. As we will see, if interest rate parity holds, the two methods will yield the same results. GE can also manage its transaction exposure through risk shifting, risk sharing, exposure netting, and currency options.

9.6.1 Forward Market Hedge

In a **forward market hedge**, a company that is long a foreign currency will sell the foreign currency forward, whereas a company that is short a foreign currency will buy the currency forward. In this way, the company can fix the dollar value of future foreign currency cash flow. For example, by selling forward the proceeds from its sale of turbine blades, GE can effectively transform the currency denomination of its €10 million receivable from euros to dollars, thereby eliminating all currency risk on the sale. For example, suppose the current spot price for the euro is $1.3382/€, and the one-year forward rate is $1.2800/€. Then, a forward sale of €10 million for delivery in one year will yield GE $12.8 million on December 31. Exhibit 9.7 shows the cash-flow consequences of combining the forward sale with the euro receivable, given three possible exchange rate scenarios.

Regardless of what happens to the future spot rate, Exhibit 9.7 demonstrates that GE still gets to collect $12.8 million on its turbine sale. Any exchange gain or loss on the forward contract will be offset by a corresponding exchange loss or gain on the receivable. The effects of this transaction also can be seen with the following simple T-account describing GE's position as of December 31:

December 31: GE T-Account (Millions)

Account receivable	€10.00	Forward contract payment	€10.00
Forward contract receipt	$12.8		

Without hedging, GE will have a €10 million asset whose value will fluctuate with the exchange rate. The forward contract creates an equal euro liability, offset by an asset worth $12.8 million dollars. The euro asset and liability cancel each other out, and GE is left with a $12.8 million asset.

This example illustrates another point as well: *Hedging with forward contracts eliminates the downside risk at the expense of forgoing the upside potential.*

The True Cost of Hedging   Exhibit 9.7 also shows that the true cost of hedging cannot be calculated in advance because it depends on the future spot rate, which is unknown at the time the forward contract is entered into. In the GE example, the actual cost of hedging can

Spot Exchange Rate	Value of Original Receivable (1)	+	Gain (Loss) on Foward Contract (2)	=	Total Cash Flow (3)
€1 = $1.3382	$13,382,000		($582,000)		$12,800,000
€1 = $1.2800	$12,800,000		$0		$12,800,000
€1 = $1.2500	$12,500,000		$300,000		$12,800,000

EXHIBIT 9.7 • POSSIBLE OUTCOMES OF FORWARD MARKET HEDGE AS OF DECEMBER 31

vary from +$582,000 to −$300,000; a plus (+) represents a cost, and a minus (−) represents a negative cost or a gain. In percentage terms, the cost varies from −2.24% to +4.35%.

This example points out the distinction between the traditional method of calculating the cost of a forward contract and the correct method, which measures its opportunity cost. Specifically, the cost of a forward contract is usually measured as its forward discount or premium:

$$\frac{f_1 - e_0}{e_0}$$

where e_0 is the current spot rate (dollar price) of the foreign currency and f_1 is the forward rate. In GE's case, this cost would equal 4.35%.

However, this approach is wrong because the relevant comparison must be between the dollars per unit of foreign currency received with hedging, f_1, and the dollars received in the absence of hedging, e_1, where e_1 is the future (unknown) spot rate on the date of settlement. That is, the real cost of hedging is an **opportunity cost**. In particular, if the forward contract had not been entered into, the future value of each unit of foreign currency would have been e_1 dollars. Thus, the true dollar cost of the forward contract per dollar's worth of foreign currency sold forward equals

$$\frac{f_1 - e_1}{e_0}$$

The expected cost (value) of a forward contract depends on whether or not a risk premium or other source of bias exists. Absent such bias, the expected cost of hedging via a forward contract will be zero. Otherwise, there would be an arbitrage opportunity. Suppose, for example, that management at GE believes that despite a one-year forward rate of $1.28, the euro will actually be worth about $1.3005 on December 31. Then GE could profit by buying (rather than selling) euros forward for one year at $1.28 and, on December 31, completing the contract by selling euros in the spot market at $1.3005. If GE is correct, it will earn $0.0205 (1.3005 − 1.2800) per euro sold forward. On a €10 million forward contract, this profit would amount to $205,000, a substantial reward for a few minutes of work.

The prospect of such rewards would not go unrecognized for long, which explains why, on average, the forward rate appears to be unbiased. Therefore, unless GE or any other company has some special information about the future spot rate that it has good reason to believe is not adequately reflected in the forward rate, it should accept the forward rate's predictive validity as a working hypothesis and avoid speculative activities. After the fact, of course, the actual cost of a forward contract will turn out to be positive or negative (unless the future spot rate equals the forward rate), but the sign cannot be predicted in advance.

On the other hand, the evidence presented in Chapter 4 points to the possibility of bias in the forward rate at any point in time. The nature of this apparent bias suggests that the selective use of forward contracts in hedging may reduce expected hedging costs; but beware of the peso problem—the possibility that historical returns may be unrepresentative of future returns. The specific cost-minimizing selective hedging policy to take advantage of this bias would depend on whether you are trying to hedge a long or a short position in a currency. The policy is as follows:

- If you are long a currency, hedge (by selling forward) if the currency is at a forward premium; if the currency is at a forward discount, do not hedge.

- If you are short a currency, hedge (by buying forward) if the currency is selling at a forward discount; if the currency is at a forward premium, do not hedge.

Spot Exchange Rate	Value of Original Receivable (1)	+	Gain (Loss) on Money Market Contract (2)	=	Total Cash Flow (3)
€1 = $1.3382	$13,382,000		($582,000)		$12,800,000
€1 = $1.2800	$12,800,000		$0		$12,800,000
€1 = $1.2500	$12,500,000		$300,000		$12,800,000

EXHIBIT 9.8 • POSSIBLE OUTCOMES OF MONEY MARKET HEDGE AS OF DECEMBER 31

As discussed in Section 9.4, however, this selective hedging policy does not come free; it may reduce expected costs but at the expense of higher risk. Absent other considerations, therefore, the impact on shareholder wealth of selective hedging via forward contracts should be minimal, with any expected gains likely to be offset by higher risk.

9.6.2 Money-Market Hedge

An alternative to a forward market hedge is to use a money-market hedge. A **money-market hedge** involves simultaneous borrowing and lending activities in two different currencies to lock in the dollar value of a future foreign currency cash flow. For example, suppose Euro and U.S. dollar interest rates are 15% and 10%, respectively. Using a money-market hedge, GE will borrow €(10/1.15) million = €8.70 million for one year, convert it into $11.64 million (at the rate of $1.3382 per euro) in the spot market, and invest it for one year. On December 31, GE will receive 1.10 × $11.64 million = $12.8 million from its dollar investment. GE will then use the proceeds of its euro receivable, collectible on that date, to repay the 1.15 × €8.70 million = €10 million it owes in principal and interest. As Exhibit 9.8 shows, the exchange gain or loss on the borrowing and lending transactions exactly offsets the dollar loss or gain on GE's euro receivable.

The gain or loss on the money-market hedge can be calculated simply by subtracting the cost of repaying the euro debt from the dollar value of the investment. For example, in the case of an end-of-year spot rate of $1.3382, the €10 million in principal and interest will cost $13.382 million to repay. The return on the dollar investment is only $12.8 million, leaving a loss on the money-market hedge of $582,000.

We can also view the effects of this transaction with the simple T-account used earlier:

December 31: GE T-Account (Millions)

Account receivable	€10.00	Loan repayment (including interest)	€10.00
Investment return (including interest)	$12.8		

As with the forward contract, the euro asset and liability (the loan repayment) cancel each other out, and GE is left with a $12.8 million asset (its investment).

The equality of the net cash flows from the forward market and money-market hedges is not coincidental. The interest rates and forward and spot rates were selected so that interest rate parity would hold. In effect, the simultaneous borrowing and lending transactions associated with a money-market hedge enable GE to create a "homemade" forward contract. The effective rate on this forward contract will equal the actual forward rate if interest rate parity holds. Otherwise, a covered interest arbitrage opportunity would exist.

In reality, there are transaction costs associated with hedging: the bid-ask spread on the forward contract and the difference between borrowing and lending rates. These transaction costs must be factored in when comparing a forward contract hedge with a money-market hedge. The key to making these comparisons, as shown in Chapter 7, is to ensure that the correct bid and ask and borrowing and lending rates are used.

ILLUSTRATION *Comparing Hedging Alternatives When There Are Transaction Costs*

PespsiCo would like to hedge its C$40 million payable to Alcan, a Canadian aluminum producer, which is due in 90 days. Suppose it faces the following exchange and interest rates.

Spot rate:	$0.9422–31/C$
Forward rate (90 days):	$0.9440–61/C$
Canadian dollar 90-day interest rate (annualized):	4.71%–4.64%
U.S. dollar 90-day interest rate (annualized):	5.50%–5.35%

Which hedging alternative would you recommend? Note that the first interest rate is the borrowing rate and the second one is the lending rate.

Solution. The hedged cost of the payable using the forward market is U.S.$37,844,000 (0.9461 × 40,000,000), remembering that PepsiCo must buy forward Canadian dollars at the ask rate. Alternatively, PepsiCo could use a money-market hedge. This hedge would entail the following steps:

1. Borrow U.S. dollars at 5.50% annualized for 90 days (the borrowing rate). The actual interest rate for 90 days will be 1.375% (5.50% × 90/360).
2. Convert the U.S. dollars into Canadian dollars at $0.9431 (the ask rate).
3. Invest the Canadian dollars for 90 days at 4.64% annualized for 90 days (the lending rate) and use the loan proceeds to pay Alcan. The actual interest rate for 90 days will be 1.16% (4.64% × 90/360).

Since PepsiCo needs C$40 million in 90 days and will earn interest equal to 1.16%, it must invest the present value of this sum or C$39,541,321 (40,000,000/1.0116). This sum is equivalent to U.S.$37,291,419.84 converted at the spot ask rate (39,541,321 × 0.9431). At a 90-day borrowing rate of 1.375%, PepsiCo must pay back principal plus interest in 90 days of U.S.$37,804,176.86 (37,291,419.84 × 1.01375). Thus, the hedged cost of the payable using the money-market hedge is $37,804,176.86.

Comparing the two hedged costs, we see that by using the money-market hedge instead of the forward market hedge, PepsiCo will save $39,823.14 (37,844,000 − 37,804,176.86). Other things being equal, therefore, this is the recommended hedge for PepsiCo.

ILLUSTRATION   *Plantronics Hedges Its Exposure*

Plantronics owes SKr 50 million, due in one year, for electrical equipment it recently bought from ABB 'Asea Brown Boveri'. At the current spot rate of $0.1480/SKr, this payable is $7.4 million. It wishes to hedge this payable but is undecided how to do it. The one-year forward rate is currently $0.1436. Plantronics' treasurer notes that the company has $10 million in a marketable U.S. dollar CD yielding 7% per annum. At the same time, SE Banken in Stockholm is offering a one-year time deposit rate of 10.5%.

a. What is the low-cost hedging alternative for Plantronics? What is the cost?

Solution. Plantronics can use the forward market to lock in a cost for its payable of $7.18 million. Alternatively, Plantronics can use a money market hedge to lock in a lower dollar cost of $7,165,611 for its payable. Thus, the money market hedge is the low-cost hedge. To compute this cost, note that Plantronics must invest SKr 45,248,869 today at 10.5% to have SKr 50 million in one year (45,248,869 × 0.105 = 50 million). This amount is equivalent to $6,696,833 at the current spot rate of SKr $0.1480/SKr. The opportunity cost to Plantronics of taking this amount from its CD today and converting it into SKr is $7,165,611, which is the future value of $6,696,833 invested at 7%.

b. Suppose interest rate parity held. What would the one-year forward rate be?

Solution. Interest rate parity holds when the dollar return on investing dollars equals the dollar return on investing SKr, or $1.07 = (1/0.1480) \times 1.105 \times f_1$, where f_1 is the equilibrium 1-year forward rate. The solution to this equation is $f_1 = \$0.1433/SKr$. Because the actual 1-year forward rate exceeds this number, interest rate parity does not hold and a forward hedge is more expensive than a money-market hedge.

9.6.3 Risk Shifting

General Electric can avoid its transaction exposure altogether if Lufthansa allows it to price the sale of turbine blades in dollars. Dollar invoicing, however, does not eliminate currency risk; it simply shifts that risk from GE to Lufthansa, which now has dollar exposure. Lufthansa may or may not be better able, or more willing, to bear it. Despite the fact that this form of **risk shifting** is a zero-sum game, it is common in international business. Firms typically attempt to invoice exports in strong currencies and imports in weak currencies.

Is it possible to gain from risk shifting? Not if one is dealing with informed customers or suppliers. To see why, consider the GE-Lufthansa deal. If Lufthansa is willing to be invoiced in dollars for the turbine blades, that must be because Lufthansa calculates that its euro equivalent cost will be no higher than the €10 million price it was originally prepared to pay. Since Lufthansa does not have to pay for the turbine blades until December 31, its cost will be based on the spot price of the dollars as of that date. By buying dollars forward at the one-year forward rate of $1.28/€, Lufthansa can convert a dollar price of P into a euro cost of $P/1.28$ Thus, the maximum dollar price P_M that Lufthansa should be willing to pay for the turbine blades is the solution to

$$\frac{P_M}{1.28} = €10 \text{ million}$$

or

$$P_M = \$12.8 \text{ million}$$

Considering that GE can guarantee itself $12.8 million by pricing in euros and selling the resulting €10 million forward, it will not accept a lower dollar price. The bottom line is that both Lufthansa and General Electric will be indifferent between a U.S. dollar price and a euro price only if the two prices are equal at the forward exchange rate. Therefore, because the euro price arrived at through arm's-length negotiations is €10 million, the dollar price that is equally acceptable to Lufthansa and GE can only be $12.8 million. Otherwise, one or both of the parties involved in the negotiations has ignored the possibility of currency changes. Such naiveté is unlikely to exist for long in the highly competitive world of international business.

9.6.4 Pricing Decisions

Notwithstanding the view just expressed, top management sometimes has failed to take anticipated exchange rate changes into account when making operating decisions, leaving financial management with the essentially impossible task, through purely financial operations, of recovering a loss already incurred at the time of the initial transaction. To illustrate this type of error, suppose that GE has priced Lufthansa's order of turbine blades at $13.382 million and then, because Lufthansa demands to be quoted a price in euro, converts the dollar price to a euro quote of €10 million, using the spot rate of $1.3382/€.

In reality, the quote is worth $12.8 million—even though it is booked at $13.382 million—because that is the risk-free price that GE can guarantee for itself by using the forward market. If GE management wanted to sell the blades for $13.382 million, it should have set a euro price equal to €13.382 million/1.28 = €10.455 million. Thus, GE lost $580,000,000 the moment it signed the contract (assuming that Lufthansa would have agreed to the higher price rather than turn to another supplier). This loss is not an exchange loss; it is a loss due to management inattentiveness.

The general rule on credit sales overseas is to convert between the foreign currency price and the dollar price by using the forward rate, not the spot rate. If the dollar price is high enough, the exporter should follow through with the sale. Similarly, if the dollar price on a foreign currency-denominated import is low enough, the importer should follow through on the purchase. All this rule does is to recognize that a euro (or any other foreign currency) tomorrow is not the same as a euro today. This rule is the international analogue to the insight that a dollar tomorrow is not the same as a dollar today. In the case of a sequence of payments to be received at several points in time, the foreign currency price should be a weighted average of the forward rates for delivery on those dates.

ILLUSTRATION   *Weyerhaeuser Quotes a Euro Price for Its Lumber*

Weyerhaeuser is asked to quote a price in euros for lumber sales to a French company. The lumber will be shipped and paid for in four equal quarterly installments. Weyerhaeuser requires a minimum price of $1 million to accept this contract. If P_F is the euro price contracted for, then Weyerhaeuser will receive $0.25P_F$ every three months, beginning 90 days from now. Suppose the spot and forward rates for the euro are as follows:

Spot	90-Day	180-Day	270-Day	360-Day
$1.345	$1.33	$1.325	$1.32	$1.315

On the basis of these forward rates, the certainty-equivalent dollar value of this euro revenue is $0.25P_F(1.33 + 1.325 + 1.32 + 1.315)$, or $0.25P_F(5.29) = \$1.3225P_F$. In order for

Weyerhaeuser to realize $1 million from this sale, the minimum euro price must be the solution to

$$\$1.3225 P_F = \$1,000,000$$

or

$$P_F = €756,143.67$$

At any lower euro price, Weyerhaeuser cannot be assured of receiving the $1 million it demands for this sale. Note that the spot rate did not enter into any of these calculations.

9.6.5 Exposure Netting

As defined in Section 9.4, *exposure netting* involves offsetting exposures in one currency with exposures in the same or another currency, where exchange rates are expected to move in such a way that losses (gains) on the first exposed position should be offset by gains (losses) on the second currency exposure. Although simple conceptually, implementation of exposure netting can be more involved. It is easy to see, for example, that a €1 million receivable and €1 million payable cancel each other out, with no net (before-tax) exposure. Dow Chemical explained this basic form of exposure netting in its 2006 Form 10-K filing when it stated that "Assets and liabilities denominated in the same currency are netted and only the net exposure is hedged." It may be less obvious that such exposure netting can also be accomplished by using positions in different currencies. However, companies practice multicurrency exposure netting all the time.

In practice, exposure netting involves one of the following three possibilities:

1. A firm can offset a long position in a currency with a short position in that same currency.
2. If the exchange rate movements of two currencies are positively correlated (for example, the Swiss franc and euro), then the firm can offset a long position in one currency with a short position in the other.
3. If the currency movements are negatively correlated, then short (or long) positions can be used to offset each other.

ILLUSTRATION   *Using Exposure Netting to Manage Transaction Exposure*

Suppose that Apex Computers has the following transaction exposures:

Apex T-Account (Millions)

Marketable securities	€2.4	Accounts payable	Mex$15.4
Accounts receivable	SFr 6.2	Bank loan	SFr 14.8
		Tax liability	€1.1

On a net basis, before taking currency correlations into account, Apex's transaction exposures, now converted into dollar terms, are:

Apex T-Account (Millions)

Euro (1.3)	$1.75	Swiss franc (8.6)	$6.88
		Mexican peso (15.4)	$1.4

Given the historical positive correlation between the euro and Swiss franc, Apex decides to net out its euro long position from its franc short position, leaving it with a net short position in the Swiss franc of $5.18 million ($1.7 million − $6.88 million). Last, Apex takes into account the historical negative correlation between the Mexican peso and the Swiss franc and offsets these two short positions. The result is a net short position in Swiss francs of $3.78 million ($5.18 million − $1.4 million). By hedging only this residual transaction exposure, Apex can dramatically reduce the volume of its hedging transactions. The latter exposure netting—offsetting euro, Swiss franc, and Mexican peso exposures with each other—depends on the strength of the correlations among these currencies. Specifically, Apex's offsetting its exposures on a dollar-for-dollar basis will be fully effective and appropriate only if the correlations are +1 for the €/SFr currency pair and −1 for the SFr/Mex$ currency pair.

9.6.6 Currency Risk Sharing

In addition to, or instead of, a traditional hedge, GE and Lufthansa can agree to share the currency risks associated with their turbine blade contract. **Currency risk sharing** can be implemented by developing a customized hedge contract embedded in the underlying trade transaction. This hedge contract typically takes the form of a **price adjustment clause**, whereby a base price is adjusted to reflect certain exchange rate changes. For example, the base price could be set at €10 million, but the parties would share the currency risk beyond a neutral zone. The **neutral zone** represents the currency range in which risk is not shared.

Suppose the neutral zone is specified as a band of exchange rates: $1.30 − 1.36/€, with a base rate of $1.33/€. This means that the exchange rate can fall as far as $1.30/€ or rise as high as $1.36/€ without reopening the contract. Within the neutral zone, Lufthansa must pay GE the dollar equivalent of €10 million at the base rate of $1.33, or $13.3 million. Thus, Lufthansa's cost within the neutral zone can vary from €9.779 million to €10.231 million (13.3 million/1.36 to 13.3 million/1.30). However, if the euro depreciates from $1.33 to, say, $1.22, the actual rate will have moved $0.08 beyond the lower boundary of the neutral zone ($1.30/€). This amount is shared equally. Thus, the exchange rate actually used in settling the transaction is $1.29/€ ($1.33 − 0.08/2). The new price of the turbine blades becomes €10 million × 1.29, or $12.9 million. Lufthansa's cost rises to €10.57 million (12,900,000/1.22). In the absence of a risk-sharing agreement, the contract value to GE would have been $12.2 million. Of course, if the euro appreciates beyond the upper bound to, say, $1.44, GE does not get the full benefit of the euro's rise in value. Instead, the new contract exchange rate becomes $1.37 (1.33 + 0.08/2). GE collects €10 million × 1.37, or $13.7 million, and Lufthansa pays a price of €9.51 million (13,700,000/1.44).

Exhibit 9.9 compares the currency risk protection features of the currency risk-sharing arrangement with that of a traditional forward contract (at a forward rate of $1.28) and a no-hedge alternative. Within the neutral zone, the dollar value of GE's contract under the risk-sharing agreement stays at $10 million. This situation is equivalent to Lufthansa selling GE a forward contract at the current spot rate of $1.33. Beyond the neutral zone, the contract's dollar value rises or falls only half as much under the risk-sharing agreement as under the no-hedge alternative. The value of the hedged contract remains the same, regardless of the exchange rate.

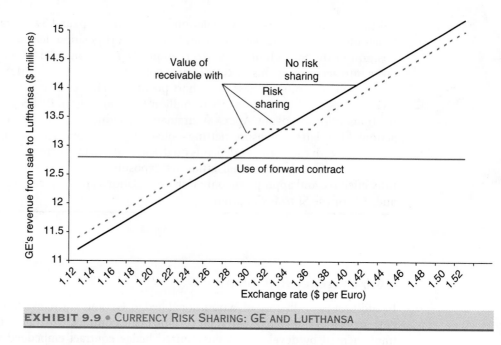

EXHIBIT 9.9 • CURRENCY RISK SHARING: GE AND LUFTHANSA

MINI-CASE   *Chrysler Shares Its Currency Risk with Mitsubishi*

In 1983, Chrysler entered into a contract with Mitsubishi Motors Corporation for V6 engines. This contract, which became the major element of Chrysler's foreign currency exposure, stipulated that for exchange rates from ¥240 to ¥220 to the dollar, Mitsubishi would absorb the entire cost of an exchange rate change. Within the range ¥220/$ to ¥190/$, Chrysler and Mitsubishi split the cost of exchange rate shifts evenly. In the range from ¥190/$ to ¥130/$, Chrysler bore 75% of the costs of exchange rate shifts; below ¥130/$, Chrysler had to absorb the entire cost. Assume that the exchange rate at the time of the contract was ¥240/$ and that the price of a V6 engine was contractually set at ¥270,000.

QUESTIONS

1. Show how the dollar cost to Chrysler of an engine changed over the range ¥240/$ to ¥100/$.

2. Show how Mitsubishi's yen revenue per engine changed over the range ¥240/$ to ¥100/$.

3. Suppose at the time of a new engine shipment, the exchange rate was ¥150/$. What was the dollar cost to Chrysler per engine? What was Mitsubishi's yen revenue per engine?

9.6.7 Currency Collars

Suppose that GE is prepared to take some but not all of the risk associated with its Euro receivable. In this case, it could buy a **currency collar**, which is a contract that provides protection against currency moves outside an agreed on range. For example, suppose that GE is willing to accept variations in the value of its euro receivable associated with fluctuations in the euro in the range of $1.28 to $1.38. Beyond that point, however, it wants protection. With a currency collar, also known as a **range forward**, GE will convert its euro receivable at the following range forward rate, RF, which depends on the actual future spot rate, e_1:

$$\text{If } e_1 < \$1.28, \text{ then } RF = \$1.28$$

$$\text{If } \$1.28 \leq e_1 \leq \$1.38, \text{ then } RF = e_1$$

$$\text{If } e_1 > \$1.38, \text{ then } RF = \$1.38$$

In effect, GE is agreeing to convert its euro proceeds at the future spot rate if that rate falls within the range $1.28–$1.38 and at the boundary rates beyond that range. Specifically, if the future spot rate exceeds $1.38, then it will convert the euro proceeds at $1.38, giving the bank a profit on the range forward. Alternatively, if the future spot rate falls below $1.28, then GE will convert the proceeds at $1.28 and the bank suffers a loss.

Exhibit 9.10 shows that with the range forward, GE has effectively collared its exchange risk (hence the term, currency collar). Exhibit 9.10a shows the payoff profile of the euro receivable; Exhibit 9.10b shows the payoff profile for the currency collar; and Exhibit 9.10c shows the payoff profile for GE's receivable hedged with the collar. With the collar, GE is guaranteed a minimum cash flow of 10 million × $1.28, or $12.8 million. Its maximum cash flow with the collar is $13.8 million, which it receives for any exchange rate beyond $1.38. For exchange rates within the range, it receives 10 million × (actual spot rate).

Why would GE accept a contract that limits its upside potential? In order to lower its cost of hedging its downside risk. The cost saving can be seen by recognizing that a currency collar can be created by simultaneously buying an out-of-the-money put option and selling an out-of-the-money call option of the same size. In effect, the purchase of the put option is financed by the sale of the call option. By selling off the upside potential with the call option, GE can reduce the cost of hedging its downside risk with the put option. The payoff profile of the combined put purchase and call sale, also known as a **cylinder**, is shown in Exhibit 9.11. By adjusting the strike prices such that the put premium just equals the call premium, you can always create a cylinder with a zero net cost, in which case you have a range forward. In this exhibit, it is assumed that the put premium at a strike price of $1.28 just equals the call premium at a strike price of $1.38.

9.6.8 Cross-Hedging

Hedging with futures is very similar to hedging with forward contracts. However, a firm that wants to manage its exchange risk with futures may find that the exact futures contract it requires is unavailable. In this case, it may be able to **cross-hedge** its exposure by using futures contracts on another currency that is correlated with the one of interest.

The idea behind cross-hedging is as follows: If we cannot find a futures/forward contract on the currency in which we have an exposure, we will hedge our exposure via a futures/forward contract on a related currency. Lacking a model or theory to tell us the exact relationship between the exchange rates of the two related currencies, we estimate the relationship by examining the historical association between these rates. The resulting regression coefficient tells us the sign and approximate size of the futures/forward position we should take in the related currency. However, the cross-hedge is only as good as the stability and economic significance of the correlation between the two currencies. A key output of the regression equation, such as the one

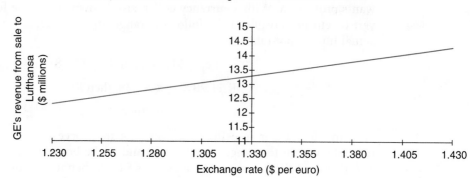

a. Payoff Profile of GE's unhedged receivable from Lufthansa

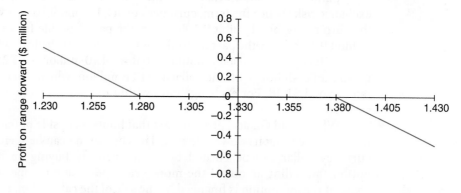

b. Payoff profile of range forward

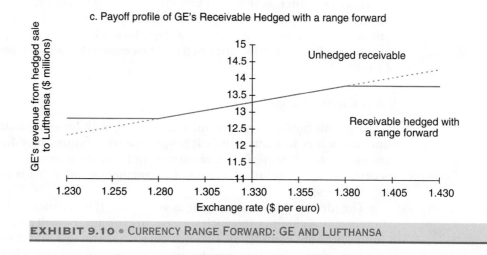

c. Payoff profile of GE's Receivable Hedged with a range forward

EXHIBIT 9.10 • CURRENCY RANGE FORWARD: GE AND LUFTHANSA

between the Danish krone and euro, is the R^2, which measures the fraction of variation in the exposed currency that is explained by variation in the hedging currency. In general, the greater the R^2 of the regression of one exchange rate on the other, the better the cross-hedge will be.

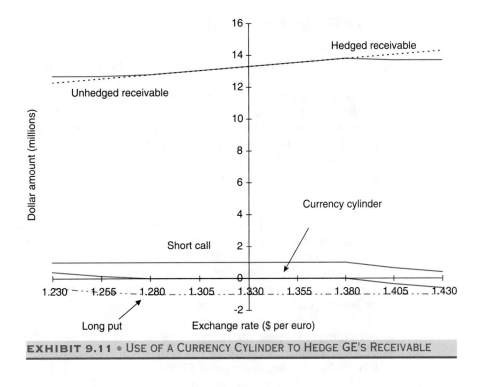

EXHIBIT 9.11 • USE OF A CURRENCY CYLINDER TO HEDGE GE'S RECEIVABLE

ILLUSTRATION   *Hedging a Danish Krone Exposure Using Euro Futures*

An exporter with a receivable denominated in Danish krone will not find krone futures available. Although an exact matching futures contract is unavailable, the firm may be able to find something that comes close. The exporter can cross-hedge his Danish krone position with euro futures, as the dollar values of those currencies tend to move in unison.

Suppose it is October 15 and our exporter expects to collect a DK 5 million receivable on December 15. The exporter can always sell the Danish kroner on the spot market at that time but is concerned about a possible fall in the krone's value between now and then. The exporter's treasurer has tracked the spot prices of the Danish krone and euro from the *Wall Street Journal* every day for the past three months and has estimated the following regression relationship using this information:

$$\Delta DK/\$ = 0.8(\Delta€/\$)$$

where $\Delta = e_t - e_{t-1}$ and e_t is the spot rate for day t (that is, Δ is the change in the exchange rate). In addition, the R^2 of the regression is 0.91, meaning that 91% of the variation in the Danish krone is explained by movements in the euro. With an R^2 this high, the exporter can confidently use euro futures contracts to cross-hedge the Danish krone.

According to this relationship, a 1¢ change in the value of the euro leads to a 0.8¢ change in the value of the DK. To cross-hedge the forthcoming receipt of DK, 0.8 units of euro futures must be sold for every unit of DK to be sold on December 15. With a Danish krone exposure of DK 5 million, the exporter must sell euro futures contracts in the amount of €4 million (0.8 × 5 million). With a euro futures contract size of €125,000, this euro amount translates into 32 contracts (4 million/125,000). The example illustrates the idea that the euro futures can be used to effectively offset the risk posed by the DK receivable.

9.6.9 Foreign Currency Options

Thus far, we have examined how firms can hedge known foreign currency transaction exposures. Yet, in many circumstances, the firm is uncertain whether the hedged foreign currency cash inflow or outflow will materialize. For example, the previous assumption was that GE learned on January 1 that it had won a contract to supply turbine blades to Lufthansa. But suppose that, although GE's bid on the contract was submitted on January 1, the announcement of the winning bid would not be until April 1. During the three-month period from January 1 to April 1, GE does not know if it will receive a payment of €10 million on December 31. This uncertainty has important consequences for the appropriate hedging strategy.

GE would like to guarantee that the exchange rate does not move against it between the time it bids and the time it gets paid, should it win the contract. The danger of not hedging is that its bid will be selected and the euro will decline in value, possibly wiping out GE's anticipated profit margin. For example, if the forward rate on April 1 for delivery on December 31 falls to €1 = $1.215, the value of the contract will drop from $12.8 million to $12.15 million, for a loss in value of $650,000.

The apparent solution is for GE to sell the anticipated €10 million receivable forward on January 1. However, if GE does that and loses the bid on the contract, it still has to sell the currency that it will have to get by buying on the open market, perhaps at a big loss. For example, suppose the forward rate on April 1 for December 31 delivery has risen to $1.35. To eliminate all currency risk on its original forward contract, GE would have to buy €10 million forward at a price of $1.356. The result would be a loss of $700,000 [(1.28 − 1.35) × 10 million] on the forward contract entered into on January 1 at a rate of $1.28.

Using Options to Hedge Bids   Until recently, GE, or any company that bid on a contract denominated in a foreign currency and was not assured of success, would be unable to resolve its foreign exchange risk dilemma. The advent of **currency options** has changed all that. Specifically, the solution to managing its currency risk in this case is for GE, at the time of its bid, to purchase an option to sell €10 million on December 31. For example, suppose that on January 1, GE can buy for $100,000 the right to sell Citigroup €10 million on December 31 at a price of $1.28/€. If it enters into this put option contract with Citigroup, GE will guarantee itself a minimum price ($12.8 million) should its bid be selected, while simultaneously ensuring that if it lost the bid, its loss would be limited to the price paid for the option contract (the premium of $100,000). Should the spot price of the euro on December 31 exceed $1.28, GE would let its option contract expire unexercised and convert the €10 million at the prevailing spot rate.

Instead of a straight put option, GE could use a futures put option. This would entail GE buying a put option on a December futures contract with the option expiring in April. If the put were in-the-money on April 1, GE would exercise it and receive a short position in a euro futures contract plus a cash amount equal to the strike price minus the December futures price as of April 1. Assuming it had won the bid, GE would hold on to the December futures contract. If it had lost the bid, GE would pocket the cash and immediately close out its short futures position at no cost.

As we saw in Chapter 7, two types of options are available to manage exchange risk. A **currency put option**, such as the one appropriate to GE's situation, gives the buyer the right, but not the obligation, to sell a specified number of foreign currency units to the option seller at a fixed dollar price, up to the option's expiration date. Alternatively, a **currency call option** is the right, but not the obligation, to buy the foreign currency at a specified dollar price, up to the expiration date.

A call option is valuable, for example, when a firm has offered to buy a foreign asset, such as another firm, at a fixed foreign currency price but is uncertain whether its bid will be accepted. By buying a call option on the foreign currency, the firm can lock in a maximum dollar price for its tender offer, while limiting its downside risk to the call premium in the event its bid is rejected.

ILLUSTRATION   *Air Products Loses Twice*

In May 2000, Air Products & Chemicals Inc. announced a $300 million after-tax charge. The bulk of this charge came about from currency losses associated with the acquisition of British pounds to be used in a failed attempt to buy BOC Group PLC. After Air Products bought the pounds, the currency fell in value. According to the *Wall Street Journal* (May 11, 2000, p. A4), "While it would have had losses from the hedge even if it were to have acquired BOC, it would have effectively paid less as well, because of the currency's decline." Purchase of a call option on pounds sterling instead of its outright currency purchase would have protected Air Products from the currency losses on its failed acquisition.

Using Options to Hedge Other Currency Risks   Currency options are a valuable risk-management tool in other situations as well. Conventional transaction-exposure management says you wait until your sales are booked or your orders are placed before hedging them. If a company does that, however, it faces potential losses from exchange rate movements because the foreign currency price does not necessarily adjust right away to changes in the value of the dollar. As a matter of policy, to avoid confusing customers and sales-people, most companies do not change their price list every time the exchange rate changes. Unless and until the foreign currency price changes, the unhedged company may suffer a decrease in its profit margin. Because of the uncertainty of anticipated sales or purchases, however, forward contracts are an imperfect tool to hedge the exposure.

For example, a company that commits to a foreign currency price list for, say, 3 months has a foreign currency exposure that depends on the unknown volume of sales at those prices during this period. Thus, the company does not know what volume of forward contracts to enter into to protect its profit margin on these sales. For the price of the premium, currency put options allow the company to insure its profit margin against adverse movements in the foreign currency while guaranteeing fixed prices to foreign customers. Without options, the firm might be forced to raise its foreign currency prices sooner than the competitive situation warranted.

ILLUSTRATION   *Hewlett-Packard Uses Currency Options to Protect Its Profit Margins*

Hewlett-Packard (H-P), the California-based computer firm, uses currency options to protect its dollar profit margins on products made in the United States but sold in Europe. The firm needs to be able to lower LC prices if the dollar weakens and hold LC prices steady for about 3 months (the price adjustment period) if the dollar strengthens.

Suppose H-P sells anticipated euro sales forward at €0.75/$ to lock in a dollar value for those sales. If 1 month later the dollar weakens to €0.65/$, H-P faces tremendous competitive pressure to lower its euro prices. H-P would be locked into a loss on the forward contracts that would not be offset by a gain on its sales because it had to cut euro prices. With euro put options, H-P would just let them expire, and it would lose only the put premium. Conversely, options help H-P delay LC price increases when the dollar strengthens until it can raise them without suffering a competitive disadvantage. The reduced profit margin on local sales is offset by the gain on the put option.

Currency options also can be used to hedge exposure to shifts in a competitor's currency. Companies competing with firms from other nations may find their products at a price disadvantage if a major competitor's currency weakens, allowing the competitor to reduce its prices. Thus, the company will be exposed to fluctuations in the competitor's currency even if it has no sales in that currency. For example, a Swiss engine manufacturer selling in Germany will be placed at a competitive disadvantage if dollar depreciation allows its principal competitor, located in the United States, to sell at a lower price in Germany. Purchasing out-of-the-money put options on the dollar and selling them for a profit if they move into the money (which will happen if the dollar depreciates enough) will allow the Swiss firm to partly compensate for its lost competitiveness. The exposure is not contractually set, so forward contracts are again not as useful as options in this situation.

Options versus Forward Contracts   The ideal use of forward contracts is when the exposure has a straight risk-reward profile: Forward contract gains or losses are exactly offset by losses or gains on the underlying transaction. If the transaction exposure is uncertain, however, because the volume or the foreign currency prices of the items being bought or sold are unknown, a forward contract will not match it. By contrast, currency options are a good hedging tool in situations in which the quantity of foreign exchange to be received or paid out is uncertain.

ILLUSTRATION   *How Cadbury Schweppes Uses Currency Options*

Cadbury Schweppes, the British candy manufacturer, uses currency options to hedge uncertain payables. The price of its key product input, cocoa, is quoted in sterling but is really a dollar-based product. That is, as the value of the dollar changes, the sterling price of cocoa changes as well. The objective of the company's foreign exchange strategy is to eliminate the currency element in the decision to purchase the commodity, thus leaving the company's buyers able to concentrate on fundamentals. However, this task is complicated by the fact that the company's projections of its future purchases are highly uncertain.

As a result, Cadbury Schweppes has turned to currency options. After netting its total exposure, the company covers with forward contracts a base number of exposed, known payables. It covers the remaining uncertain portion with options. The options act as an insurance policy.

A company could use currency options to hedge its exposure in lieu of forward contracts. However, each type of hedging instrument is more advantageous in some situations, and it makes sense to match the instrument to the specific situation. The three general rules to follow when choosing between currency options and forward contracts for hedging purposes are summarized as follows:

1. When the quantity of a foreign currency cash outflow is known, buy the currency forward; when the quantity is unknown, buy a call option on the currency.

2. When the quantity of a foreign currency cash inflow is known, sell the currency forward; when the quantity is unknown, buy a put option on the currency.

3. When the quantity of a foreign currency cash flow is partially known and partially uncertain, use a forward contract to hedge the known portion and an option to hedge the maximum value of the uncertain remainder.[6]

---

[6] For elaboration, see Ian H. Giddy, "The Foreign Exchange Option as a Hedging Tool," *Midland Corporate Finance Journal,* Fall 1983, pp. 32–42.

These rules presume that the financial manager's objective is to reduce risk and not to speculate on the direction or volatility of future currency movements. They also presume that both forward and options contracts are fairly priced. In an efficient market, the expected value or cost of either of these contracts should be zero. Any other result would introduce the possibility of arbitrage profits. The presence of such profits would attract arbitrageurs as surely as bees are attracted to honey. Their subsequent attempts to profit from inappropriate prices would return these prices to their equilibrium values.

MINI-CASE   *Help DKNY Cover Up Its Mexican Peso Transaction Exposure*

DKNY, the apparel design firm, owes Mex$7 million in 30 days for a recent shipment of textiles from Mexico. DKNY's treasurer is considering hedging the company's peso exposure on this shipment and is looking for some help in figuring out what his or her different hedging options might cost and which option is preferable. You call up your favorite foreign exchange trader and receive the following interest rate and exchange rate quotes:

Spot rate:	Mex$10.93/$
Forward rate (30 days):	Mex$11.03/$
30-day put option on dollars at Mex$10.83/$:	1% premium
30-day call option on dollars at Mex$11.03/$:	3% premium
U.S. dollar 30-day interest rate (annualized):	7.5%
Peso 30-day interest rate (annualized):	15%

Based on these quotes, the treasurer presents you with a series of questions that she would like you to address.

QUESTIONS

1. What hedging options are available to DKNY?
2. What is the hedged cost of DKNY's payable using a forward market hedge?
3. What is the hedged cost of DKNY's payable using a money market hedge?
4. What is the hedged cost of DKNY's payable using a put option?
5. At what exchange rate is the cost of the put option just equal to the cost of the forward market hedge? To the cost of the money market hedge?
6. How can DKNY construct a currency collar? What is the net premium paid for the currency collar? Using this currency collar, what is the net dollar cost of the payable if the spot rate in 30 days is Mex$10.75/$? Mex$11.03/$? Mex$11.25/$?
7. What is the preferred alternative?
8. Suppose that DKNY expects the 30-day spot rate to be Mex$11.25/$. Should it hedge this payable? What other factors should go into DKNY's hedging decision?

9.7 SUMMARY AND CONCLUSIONS

In this chapter, we examined the concept of exposure to exchange rate changes from the perspective of the accountant. The accountant's concern is the appropriate way to translate foreign currency-denominated items on financial statements to their home currency values. If currency values change, translation gains or losses may result. We surveyed the four principal translation methods available: the current/noncurrent method, the monetary/nonmonetary method, the temporal method, and the current rate method. In addition, we analyzed the present translation method mandated by the Financial Accounting Standards Board, FASB-52.

Regardless of the translation method selected, measuring accounting exposure is conceptually the same. It involves determining which foreign-currency-denominated assets and liabilities will be translated at the current (postchange) exchange rate and which will be translated at the historical (prechange) exchange rate. The former items are considered to be exposed, whereas the latter items are regarded as not exposed. Translation exposure is simply the difference between exposed assets and exposed liabilities.

Hedging this exposure is a complicated and difficult task. As a first step, the firm must specify an operational set of goals for those involved in exchange risk management. Failure to do so can lead to possibly conflicting and costly actions on the part of employees. We saw that the hedging objective that is most consistent with the overarching objective of maximizing shareholder value is to reduce exchange risk, where exchange risk is defined as that element of cash-flow variability attributable to currency fluctuations. This objective translates into the following exposure management goal: to arrange a firm's financial affairs in such a way that however the exchange rate may move in the future, the effects on dollar returns are minimized.

We saw that firms normally cope with anticipated currency changes by engaging in forward contracts, borrowing locally, and adjusting their pricing and credit policies. However, there is reason to question the value of much of this activity. In fact, in normal circumstances hedging cannot provide protection against expected exchange rate changes.

A number of empirical studies indicate that on average the forward rate appears to be an unbiased estimate of the future spot rate. On the other hand, the evidence also points to the possibility of bias in the forward rate at any point in time. However, trying to take advantage of this apparent bias via selective hedging is likely to expose the company to increased risk. Furthermore, according to the international Fisher effect, in the absence of government controls, interest rate differentials among countries should equal anticipated currency devaluations or revaluations. Empirical research substantiates the notion that over time, gains or losses on debt in hard currencies tend to be offset by low interest rates; in soft currencies, they will be offset by higher interest rates unless, of course, there are barriers that preclude equalization of real interest rates. Again, to the extent that bias exists in the interest rate differential because of a risk premium or other factor, the risk associated with selective hedging is likely to offset any expected gains.

The other hedging methods, which involve factoring anticipated exchange rate changes into pricing and credit decisions, can be profitable only at the expense of others. Thus, to consistently gain by these trade-term adjustments, it is necessary to deal continuously with less-knowledgeable people. Certainly, however, a policy predicated on the continued existence of naive firms is unlikely to be viable for very long in the highly competitive and well-informed world of international business. The real value to a firm of factoring currency change expectations into its pricing and credit decisions is to prevent others from profiting at its expense.

The basic value of hedging, therefore, is to protect a company against unexpected exchange rate changes; however, by definition, these changes are unpredictable and, consequently, impossible to profit from. To the extent that a government does not permit interest or forward rates to fully adjust to market expectations, a firm with access to these financial instruments can expect, on average, to gain from currency changes. Nevertheless, the very nature of these imperfections severely restricts a company's ability to engage in such profitable financial operations.

QUESTIONS

1. What is translation exposure? Transaction exposure?

2. What are the basic translation methods? How do they differ?

3. What factors affect a company's translation exposure? What can the company do to affect its degree of translation exposure?

4. What alternative hedging transactions are available to a company seeking to hedge the translation exposure of its German subsidiary? How would the appropriate hedge change if the German affiliate's functional currency were the U.S. dollar?

5. In order to eliminate all risk on its exports to Japan, a company decides to hedge both its actual and anticipated sales there. To what risk is the company exposing itself? How could this risk be managed?

6. Instead of its previous policy of always hedging its foreign currency receivables, Sun Microsystems has decided to hedge only when it believes the dollar will strengthen. Otherwise, it will go uncovered. Comment on this new policy.

7. Your bank is working with an American client who wishes to hedge its long exposure in the Malaysian ringgit. Suppose it is possible to invest in ringgit but not borrow in that currency. However, you can both borrow and lend in U.S. dollars.

   a. Assuming there is no forward market in ringgit, can you create a homemade forward contract that would allow your client to hedge its ringgit exposure?

   b. Several of your Malaysian clients are interested in selling their U.S. dollar export earnings forward for ringgit. Can you accommodate them by creating a forward contract?

8. Eastman Kodak gives its traders bonuses if their selective hedging strategies are less expensive than the cost of hedging all their transaction exposure on a continuous basis. What problems can you foresee from this bonus plan?

9. Many managers prefer to use options to hedge their exposure, because it allows them the possibility of capitalizing on favorable movements in the exchange rate. In contrast, a company using forward contracts avoids the downside but also loses the upside potential. Comment on this strategy.

10. In January 1988, Arco bought a 24.3% stake in the British oil firm Britoil PLC. It intended to buy a further $1 billion worth of Britoil stock if Britoil was agreeable. However, Arco was uncertain whether Britoil, which had expressed a strong desire to remain independent, would accept its bid. To guard against the possibility of a pound appreciation in the interim, Arco decided to convert $1 billion into pounds and place them on deposit in London, pending the outcome of its discussions with Britoil's management. What exchange risk did Arco face, and did it choose the best way to protect itself from that risk?

11. Sumitomo Chemical of Japan has one week in which to negotiate a contract to supply products to a U.S. company at a dollar price that will remain fixed for one year. What advice would you give Sumitomo?

12. U.S. Farm-Raised Fish Trading Co., a catfish concern in Jackson, Mississippi, tells its Japanese customers that it wants to be paid in dollars. According to its director of export marketing, this simple strategy eliminates all its currency risk. Is he right? Why?

13. The Montreal Expos are a major-league baseball team located in Montreal, Canada. What currency risk is faced by the Expos, and how can this exchange risk be managed?

14. GE recently had to put together a $50 million bid, denominated in Swiss francs, to upgrade a Swiss power plant. If it won, GE expected to pay subcontractors and suppliers in five currencies. The payment schedule for the contract stretched over a five-year period.

    a. How should GE establish the Swiss franc price of its $50 million bid?

    b. What exposure does GE face on this bid? How can it hedge that exposure?

15. Dell Inc. produces its computers in Asia with components largely imported from the United States and sells its products in various Asian nations in local currencies.

    a. What is the likely impact on Dell's Asian profits of a strengthened dollar? Explain.

    b. What hedging technique(s) can Dell employ to lock in a desired currency conversion rate for its Asian sales during the next year?

    c. Suppose Dell wishes to lock in a specific conversion rate but does not want to foreclose the possibility of profiting from future currency moves. What hedging technique would be most likely to achieve this objective?

    d. What are the limits of Dell's hedging approach?

PROBLEMS

1. Suppose that at the start and at the end of the year, Bell U.K., the British subsidiary of Bell U.S., has current assets of £1 million, fixed assets of £2 million, and current liabilities of £1 million. It has no long-term liabilities.

   a. What is Bell U.K.'s translation exposure under the current/noncurrent, monetary/nonmonetary, temporal, and current rate methods?

   b. Assuming the pound is the functional currency, if the pound depreciates during the year from $1.95 to $1.75, what will be the FASB-52 translation gain (loss) to be included in the equity account of Bell's U.S. parent?

   c. Redo Part (b) assuming the dollar is the functional currency. Included in current assets is inventory of £0.5 million. The historical exchange rates for inventory and fixed assets are $1.90 and $2.00, respectively. If the dollar is the functional currency, where does Bell U.K.'s translation gain or loss show up on Bell U.S.'s financial statements?

2. Rolls-Royce, the British jet engine manufacturer, sells engines to U.S. airlines and buys parts from U.S. companies. Suppose it has accounts receivable of $1.5 billion and accounts payable of $740 million. It also has borrowed $600 million. The current spot rate is $1.9528/£.

   a. What is Rolls-Royce's dollar transaction exposure in dollar terms? In pound terms?

   b. Suppose the pound appreciates to $2.064/£. What is Rolls-Royce's gain or loss, in pound terms, on its dollar transaction exposure?

3. Zapata Auto Parts, the Mexican affiliate of American Diversified, Inc., had the following balance sheet on January 1:

Assets (Mex$ millions)		Liabilities (Mex$ millions)	
Cash, marketable securities	Mex$1	Current liabilities	Mex$47
Accounts receivable	50	Long-term debt	12
Inventory	32	Equity	135
Net fixed assets	111		
Total assets	Mex$194	Liabilities plus equity	Mex$194

The exchange rate on January 1 was Mex$10.5 = $1.

   a. What is Zapata's FASB-52 peso translation exposure on January 1?

   b. Suppose the exchange rate on December 31 is Mex$12. What will be Zapata's translation loss for the year?

   c. Zapata can borrow an additional Mex$15 million. What will happen to its translation exposure if it uses the funds to pay a dividend to its parent? If it uses the funds to increase its cash position?

4. Walt Disney expects to receive a Mex$16 million theatrical fee from Mexico in 90 days. The current spot rate is $0.0915/Mex$, and the 90-day forward rate is $0.0903/Mex$.

   a. What is Disney's peso transaction exposure associated with this fee?

   b. If the spot rate expected in 90 days is $0.0908, what is the expected U.S. dollar value of the fee?

   c. What is the hedged dollar value of the fee?

   d. What factors will influence the hedging decision?

5. A foreign exchange trader assesses the euro exchange rate three months hence as follows:

   $1.31 with probability 0.25
   $1.33 with probability 0.50
   $1.35 with probability 0.25

   The 90-day forward rate is $1.32.

   a. Will the trader buy or sell euros forward against the dollar if she is concerned solely with expected values? In what volume?

   b. In reality, what is likely to limit the trader's speculative activities?

   c. Suppose the trader revises his or her probability assessment as follows:

   $1.29 with probability 0.33
   $1.33 with probability 0.33
   $1.37 with probability 0.33

   If the forward rate remains at $1.32, will this new assessment affect the trader's decision? Explain.

6. An investment manager hedges a portfolio of Bunds (German government bonds) with a 6-month forward contract. The current spot rate is €0.75/$, and the 180-day forward rate is €0.72/$. At the end of the 6-month period, the Bunds have risen in value by 3.75% (in euro terms), and the spot rate is now €0.66/$.

   a. If the Bunds earn interest at the annual rate of 5%, paid semiannually, what is the investment manager's total dollar return on the hedged Bunds?

   b. What would the return on the Bunds have been without hedging?

   c. What was the true cost of the forward contract?

7. Magnetronics, Inc., a U.S. company, owes its Taiwanese supplier NT$205 million in 3 months. The company wishes to hedge its NT$ payable. The current spot rate is NT$1 = U.S.$0.03987, and the 3-month forward rate is NT$1 = U.S.$0.04051. Magnetronics can also borrow or lend U.S. dollars at an annualized interest rate of 12% and Taiwanese dollars at an annualized interest rate of 8%.

a. What is the U.S. dollar accounting entry for this payable?

b. What is the minimum U.S. dollar cost that Magnetronics can lock in for this payable? Describe the procedure it would use to get this price.

c. At what forward rate would interest rate parity hold given the interest rates?

8. Cooper Inc., a U.S. firm, has just invested £500,000 in a note that will come due in 90 days yielding 9.5% annualized. The current spot value of the pound is $1.9612, and the 90-day forward rate is $1.9467.

a. What is the hedged dollar value of this note at maturity?

b. What is the annualized dollar yield on the hedged note?

c. Cooper anticipates that the value of the pound in 90 days will be $1.9550. Should it hedge? Why or why not?

d. Suppose that Cooper has a payable of £980,000 coming due in 180 days. Should this affect its decision of whether to hedge its sterling note? How and why?

9. American Airlines is trying to decide how to go about hedging SFr 70 million in ticket sales receivable in 180 days. Suppose it faces the following exchange and interest rates.

Spot rate:	$0.6433–42/SFr
Forward rate (180 days):	$0.6578–99/SFr
Swiss Franc 180-day interest rate (annualized):	4.01%–3.97%
U.S. dollar 180-day interest rate (annualized):	8.01%–7.98%

a. What is the hedged value of American Airlines's ticket sales using a forward market hedge?

b. What is the hedged value of the airline's ticket sales using a money-market hedge? Assume the first interest rate is the rate at which money can be borrowed and the second one the rate at which it can be lent.

c. Which hedge is less expensive?

d. Is there an arbitrage opportunity here?

e. Suppose the expected spot rate in 180 days is $0.67/SFr, with a most likely range of $0.64–$0.70/SFr. Should American Airlines hedge? What factors should enter into its decision?

10. Madison Inc. imports olive oil from Chilean firms, and the invoices are always denominated in pesos (Ch$). It currently has a payable in the amount of Ch$250 million that it would like to hedge. Unfortunately, there are no peso futures contracts available and Madison is having difficulty arranging a peso forward contract. Its treasurer, who recently received her MBA, suggests using the Brazilian *real* (R) to cross-hedge the peso exposure. She recently ran the following regression of the change in the exchange rate for the peso against the change in the *real* exchange rate:

$$\Delta Ch\$/US\$ = 1.6(\Delta R/US\$)$$

a. There is an active market in the forward *real*. To cross-hedge Madison's peso exposure, should the treasurer buy or sell the *real* forward?

b. What is the risk-minimizing amount of reais that the treasurer would have to buy or sell forward to hedge Madison's peso exposure?

BIBLIOGRAPHY

Bishop, M. "A Survey of Corporate Risk Management," *The Economist*, February 10, 1996, Special Section.

Cornell, B. and A. C. Shapiro, "Managing Foreign Exchange Risks," *Midland Corporate Finance Journal*, Fall 1983, pp. 16–31.

Dufey, G. and S. L. Srinivasulu, "The Case for Corporate Management of Foreign Exchange Risk," *Financial Management*, Summer 1984, pp. 54–62.

Evans, T. G. and W. R. Folks, Jr. "Defining Objectives for Exposure Management," *Business International Money Report*, February 2, 1979, pp. 37–39.

Folks, W. R., Jr. "Decision Analysis for Exchange Risk Management," *Financial Management*, Winter 1972, pp. 101–112.

Froot, K. D. Scharfstein, and J. Stein, "A Framework for Risk Management," *Harvard Business Review*, November 1994, pp. 91–102.

Giddy, I. H. "The Foreign Exchange Option as a Hedging Tool," *Midland Corporate Finance Journal*, Fall 1983, pp. 32–42.

Goeltz, R. K. *Managing Liquid Funds on an International Scope*. New York: Joseph E. Seagram and Sons, 1971.

Shapiro, A. C. and D. P. Rutenberg. "Managing Exchange Risks in a Floating World." *Financial Management*, Summer 1976, pp. 48–58.

Srinivasulu, S. and E. Massura, "Sharing Currency Risks in Long-Term Contracts," *Business International Money Reports*, February 23, 1987, pp. 57–59.

Statement of Financial Accounting Standards No. 52. Stamford, Conn.: Financial Accounting Standards Board, December 1981.

Zenoff, D. B. "Applying Management Principles to Foreign Exchange Exposure." *Euromoney*, September 1978, pp. 123–130.

INTERNET RESOURCES

www.fasb.org Web site of the Financial Accounting Standards Board. Provides information on FASB 52 and other FASB pronouncements on currency translation and hedge accounting.

www.florin.com/v4/valore4.html Web site that contains material discussing currency risk management.

www.reportgallery.com Web site that contains links to annual reports of over 2,200 companies, many of which are multinationals.

INTERNET EXERCISES

1. Go to General Electric's home page (www.ge.com) and find its latest annual report. What is GE's accumulated translation adjustment? Does GE use any functional currencies other than the dollar? What was GE's reported currency translation gain or loss during the year? What exchange rates (year-end or average) did GE use to translate its asset and liability accounts and revenue and expense items?

2. What are the latest FASB pronouncements dealing with currency translations?

3. Review the annual reports on the Web sites of three of the multinational companies listed in www.reportgallery.com.

   a. What types of currency exposure are these companies hedging?

   b. What hedging techniques are they using?

   c. What hedging strategy (if any) appears to underlie their hedging activities?

APPENDIX 9A

STATEMENT OF FINANCIAL ACCOUNTING STANDARDS 52

The current translation standard, Statement of Financial Accounting Standards No. 52 (FASB 52), was adopted in 1981.[7] According to FASB 52, firms must use the current rate method to translate foreign currency-denominated assets and liabilities into dollars. All foreign currency revenue and expense items on the income statement must be translated at either the exchange rate in effect on the date these items are recognized or at an appropriately weighted average exchange rate for the period. The most important aspect of this standard is that most FASB 52 translation gains and losses bypass the income statement and are accumulated in a separate equity account on the parent's balance sheet. This account is usually called something like "cumulative translation adjustment."

FASB 52 differentiates between the functional currency and the reporting currency. An affiliate's **functional currency** is the currency of the primary economic environment in which the affiliate generates and expends cash. If the enterprise's operations are relatively self-contained and integrated within a particular country, the functional currency will generally be the currency of that country. An example of this case would be an English affiliate that both manufactures and sells most of its output in England. Alternatively, if the foreign affiliate's operations are a direct and integral component or extension of the parent company's operations, the functional currency will be the U.S. dollar. An example of this would be a Hong Kong assembly plant for radios that sources the components in the United States and sells

---

[7] The previous translation standard, Statement of Financial Accounting Standards No. 8 (or FASB 8), was based on the temporal method. Its principal virtue was its consistency with generally accepted accounting practice that requires balance sheet items to be valued (translated) according to their underlying measurement basis (that is, current or historical). Almost immediately upon its adoption, however, controversy ensued over FASB 8. A major source of corporate dissatisfaction with FASB 8 was the ruling that all reserves for currency losses be disallowed. Before FASB 8, many companies established a reserve and were able to defer unrealized translation gains and losses by adding them to, or charging them against, the reserve. In that way, corporations generally were able to cushion the impact of sharp changes in currency values on reported earnings. With FASB 8, however, fluctuating values of pesos, pounds, yen, Canadian dollars, and other foreign currencies often had far more impact on profit-and-loss statements than did the sales and profit margins of multinational manufacturers' product lines.

Foreign Unit	Local Currency Indicators	Dollar Indicators
Cash flows	Primarily in the local currency; do not directly affect parent company cash flows	Direct impact on parent company; cash flow available for remittance
Sales prices	Not responsive to exchange rate changes in the short run; determined more by local conditions	Determined more by worldwide competition; affected in the short run by exchange rate changes
Sales markets	Active local market for entity's products	Products sold primarily in the United States; sales contracts denominated in dollars
Expenses	Labor, materials, and other costs denominated primarily in local currency	Inputs primarily from sources in the United States or otherwise denominated in dollars
Financing	Primarily in local currency; operations generate sufficient funds to service these debts	Primarily from the parent company or otherwise denominated in dollars; operations don't generate sufficient dollars to service its dollar debts
Intercompany transactions	Few intracorporate transactions; little connection between local and parent's operations	High volume of intracorporate transactions; extensive interrelationship between local and parent's operations

EXHIBIT 9A.1 • FACTORS INDICATING THE APPROPRIATE FUNCTIONAL CURRENCY

the assembled radios in the United States. It is also possible that the functional currency is neither the local currency nor the dollar but, rather, a third currency. However, in the remainder of this chapter, we will assume that if the functional currency is not the local currency, then it is the U.S. dollar.

Guidelines for selecting the appropriate functional currency are presented in Exhibit 9A.1. There is sufficient ambiguity to give companies some leeway in selecting the functional currency. However, in the case of **a hyperinflationary country**, defined as one that has cumulative inflation of approximately 100% or more over a three-year period, the functional currency must be the dollar.

Companies will usually explain in the notes to their annual report how they accounted for foreign currency translation. A typical statement is that found in Dow Chemical's 2006 Form 10-K Filing (p.61):

> *The local currency has been primarily used as the functional currency throughout the world. Translation gains and losses of those operations that use local currency as the functional currency, and the effects of exchange rate changes on transactions designated as hedges of net foreign investments, are included in "Accumulated other comprehensive income (loss)." ("AOCI") Where the U.S. dollar is used as the functional currency, foreign currency gains and losses are reflected in income.*

The **reporting currency** is the currency in which the parent firm prepares its own financial statements—that is, U.S. dollars for a U.S. firm. FASB 52 requires that the financial statements of a foreign unit first be stated in the functional currency, using generally accepted accounting principles of the United States. At each balance sheet date, any assets and liabilities denominated in a currency other than the functional currency of the recording entity must be adjusted to reflect the current exchange rate on that date. Transaction gains and losses that result from adjusting assets and liabilities denominated in a currency other than the functional currency, or from settling such items, generally must appear on the foreign unit's income statement. The only exceptions to the general requirement to include transaction gains and losses in income as they arise are listed as follows:

1. Gains and losses attributable to a foreign currency transaction that is designated as an economic hedge of a net investment in a foreign entity must be included in the separate component of shareholders' equity in which adjustments arising from translating foreign currency financial statements are accumulated. An example of such a transaction would be a euro borrowing by a U.S. parent. The transaction would be designated as a hedge of the parent's net investment in its German subsidiary.

2. Gains and losses attributable to intercompany foreign currency transactions that are of a long-term investment nature must be included in the separate component of shareholders' equity. The parties to the transaction in this case are accounted for by the equity method in the reporting entity's financial statements.

3. Gains and losses attributable to foreign currency transactions that hedge identifiable foreign currency commitments are to be deferred and included in the measurement of the basis of the related foreign transactions.

The requirements regarding translation of transactions apply both to transactions entered into by a U.S. company and denominated in a currency other than the U.S. dollar and to transactions entered into by a foreign affiliate of a U.S. company and denominated in a currency other than its functional currency. Thus, for example, if a German subsidiary of a U.S. company owed $270,000 and the euro declined from $1.35 to $1.25, the euro amount of the liability would increase from €200,000 (270,000/1.35) to €216,000 (270,000/1.25), for a loss of €16,000. If the subsidiary's functional currency is the euro, the €16,000 loss must be translated into dollars at the average exchange rate for the period (say, $1.30), and the resulting amount ($20,800) must be included as a transaction loss in the U.S. company's consolidated statement of income. This loss results even though the liability is denominated in the parent company's reporting currency, because the subsidiary's functional currency is the euro, and its financial statements must be measured in terms of that currency. Similarly, under FASB 52, if the subsidiary's functional currency is the U.S. dollar, no gain or loss will arise on the $270,000 liability.

After all financial statements have been converted into the functional currency, the functional currency statements are then translated into dollars, with translation gains and losses flowing directly into the parent's foreign exchange equity account.

If the functional currency is the dollar, the unit's local currency financial statements must be remeasured in dollars. The objective of the remeasurement process is to produce the same results that would have been reported if the accounting records had been kept in dollars rather than the local currency. Translation of the local currency accounts into dollars takes place according to the temporal method; thus, the resulting translation gains and losses *must* be included in the income statement.

A large majority of firms have opted for the local currency as the functional currency for most of their subsidiaries. The major exceptions are those subsidiaries operating in Latin American and other highly inflationary countries; they must use the dollar as their functional currency.

APPLICATION OF FASB 52

Sterling Ltd., the British subsidiary of a U.S. company, started business and acquired fixed assets at the beginning of a year when the exchange rate for the pound sterling was £1 = $2.00. The average exchange rate for the period was $1.90, the rate at the end of the period was $1.80, and the historical rate for inventory was $1.95. Refer to Exhibits 9A.2 and 9A.3 for the discussion that follows.

During the year, Sterling Ltd. has income after tax of £20 million, which goes into retained earnings—that is, no dividends are paid. Thus, retained earnings rise from 0 to £20 million. Exhibit 9A.2 shows how the income statement

| | | Pound Sterling | | U.S. Dollar | |
	Pound Sterling	Rates Used	U.S. Dollars	Rates Used	U.S. Dollars
Revenue	£ 120	$1.90	228	$1.90	228
Cost of goods sold	(50)	1.90	(95)	1.95	(98)
Depreciation	(20)	1.90	(38)	2.00	(40)
Other expenses, net	(10)	1.90	(19)	1.90	(19)
Foreign exchange gain	—		—		108
Income before taxes	40		76		179
Income after taxes	(20)	1.90	(38)		(38)
Net income	£ 20		38		141
Ratios					
Net income to revenue	0.17		0.17		0.62
Gross profit to revenue	0.58		0.58		0.57
Debt to equity	7.33		7.33		4.07

EXHIBIT 9A.2 • TRANSLATION OF STERLING LTD.'S INCOME STATEMENT UNDER FASB-52 (MILLIONS)

would be translated into dollars under two alternatives: (1) The functional currency is the pound sterling, and (2) the functional currency is the U.S. dollar.

If the functional currency is the pound sterling, Sterling Ltd. will have a translation loss of $12 million, which bypasses the income statement (because the functional currency is identical to the local currency) and appears on the balance sheet as a separate item called *cumulative translation adjustment* under the stockholders' equity account. The translation loss is calculated as the number that reconciles the equity account with the remaining translated accounts to balance assets with liabilities and equity. Exhibit 9A.3 shows the balance sheet translations for Sterling Ltd. under the two alternative functional currencies.

Similarly, if the dollar is the functional currency, the foreign exchange translation gain of $108 million, which appears on Sterling Ltd.'s income statement (because the functional currency differs from the local currency), is calculated as the difference between translated income before currency gains ($33 million) and the retained earnings figure ($141 million). This amount just balances Sterling Ltd.'s books.

Two comments are appropriate here.

1. Fluctuations in reported earnings in the preceding example are reduced significantly under FASB 52 when the local currency is the functional currency, as compared with the case when the U.S. dollar is the functional currency.
2. Key financial ratios and relationships such as net income-to-revenue, gross profit, and debt-to-equity are the same when translated into dollars under FASB 52, using the local currency as the functional currency, as they are in the local currency financial statements. These ratios and relationships are significantly different if the dollar is used as the functional currency. The ratios appear at the bottom of Exhibit 9A.2.

| | | Functional Currency | | | |
| | | Pound Sterling | | U.S. Dollar | |
	Pound Sterling	Rates Used	U.S. Dollars	Rates Used	U.S. Dollars
Assets					
Cash	£ 100	1.80	180	1.80	180
Receivables	200	1.80	360	1.80	360
Inventory	300	1.80	540	1.95	585
Fixed assets, net	400	1.80	720	2.00	800
Total Assets	£ 1,000		1,800		1,925
Liabilities					
Current liabilities	180	1.80	324	1.80	324
Long-term debt	700	1.80	1,260	1.80	1,260
Stockholders' equity					
Common stock	100	2.00	200	2.00	200
Retained earnings	20		28		141
Cumulative translation adjustment	—		(12)		—
Total liabilities plus equity	1,000		1,800		1,925

EXHIBIT 9A.3 • TRANSLATION OF STERLING LTD.'S BALANCE SHEET UNDER FASB-52 (MILLIONS)

MEASURING AND MANAGING ECONOMIC EXPOSURE

Let's face it. If you've got 75% of your assets in the U.S. and 50% of your sales outside it, and the dollar's strong, you've got problems.

Donald V. Fites
Executive Vice President
Caterpillar Inc.

CHAPTER LEARNING OBJECTIVES

- To define economic exposure and exchange risk and distinguish between the two
- To define operating exposure and distinguish between it and transaction exposure
- To identify the basic factors that determine the foreign exchange risk faced by a particular company or project
- To calculate economic exposure given a particular exchange rate change and specific cost and revenue scenarios
- To describe the marketing, production, and financial strategies that are appropriate for coping with the economic consequences of exchange rate changes
- To explain how companies can develop contingency plans to cope with exchange risk and the consequences of their ability to rapidly respond to currency changes
- To identify the role of the financial executive in facilitating the operation of an integrated exchange risk management program

KEY TERMS

competitive exposure	price elasticity of demand
currency of denomination	pricing flexibility
currency of determination	pricing strategy
differentiated products	product cycles
economic exposure	product innovation
exchange risk	production shifting
flow-back effect	product sourcing
market selection	product strategy
operating exposure	real exchange rate
outsourcing	transaction exposure
plant location	

Chapter 9 focused on the accounting effects of currency changes. As we saw in that chapter, the adoption of FASB 52 has helped to moderate the wild swings in the translated earnings of overseas subsidiaries. Nevertheless, the problem of coping with volatile currencies remains essentially unchanged. Fluctuations in exchange rates will continue to have "real" effects on the cash profitability of foreign subsidiaries—complicating overseas selling, pricing, buying, and plant-location decisions.

This chapter develops an appropriate definition of foreign exchange risk. It discusses the *economic*, as distinguished from the accounting, consequences of currency changes on a firm's value and shows how economic exposure can be measured. This chapter also discusses the marketing, production, and financial management strategies that are appropriate for coping with the economic consequences of exchange rate changes.

10.1 FOREIGN EXCHANGE RISK AND ECONOMIC EXPOSURE

The most important aspect of foreign exchange risk management is to incorporate currency change expectations into *all* basic corporate decisions. In performing this task, the firm must know what is at risk. However, there is a major discrepancy between accounting practice and economic reality in terms of measuring *exposure*, which is the degree to which a company is affected by exchange rate changes.

As we saw in Chapter 9, those who use an accounting definition of exposure, whether FASB 52 or some other method, divide the balance sheet's assets and liabilities into those accounts that will be affected by exchange rate changes and those that will not. In contrast, economic theory focuses on the impact of an exchange rate change on future cash flows. That is, **economic exposure** is based on the extent to which the value of the firm—as measured by the present value of its expected future cash flows—will change when exchange rates change.

Exchange risk, in turn, is defined as the variability in the firm's value that is caused by uncertain exchange rate changes. Thus, exchange risk is viewed as the possibility that currency fluctuations can alter the expected amounts or variability of the firm's future cash flows.

Economic exposure can be separated into two components: transaction exposure and operating exposure. We saw that **transaction exposure** stems from exchange gains or losses on foreign currency-denominated contractual obligations. Although transaction exposure is often included under accounting exposure, as it was in Chapter 9, it is more properly a cash-flow exposure and, hence, part of economic exposure. However, even if the company prices all contracts in dollars or otherwise hedges its transaction exposure, the residual exposure—longer-term operating exposure—still remains.

Operating exposure arises because currency fluctuations can alter a company's future revenues and costs—that is, its operating cash flows. Consequently, measuring a firm's operating exposure requires a longer-term perspective, viewing the firm as an ongoing concern with operations whose cost and price competitiveness could be affected by exchange rate changes.

Thus, the firm faces operating exposure the moment it invests in servicing a market subject to foreign competition or in sourcing goods or inputs abroad. This investment includes new-product development, a distribution network, foreign supply contracts, or production facilities. Transaction exposure arises later on and only if the company's commitments lead it to engage in foreign-currency-denominated sales or purchases. Exhibit 10.1 shows the time pattern of economic exposure.

Non-contractual	Quasi-Contractual		Contractual
Investment in new product development, distribution facilities, brand name, marketing, foreign production capacity, foreign supplier relationship	Quote a foreign currency price, receive a foreign currency price quote	Ship product/bill customers in foreign currency, receive bill for supplies in foreign currency	Collect foreign currency receivables, pay foreign currency liabilities

EXHIBIT 10.1 • THE TIME PATTERN OF ECONOMIC EXPOSURE

ILLUSTRATION *American Filmmakers Suffer When the Euro Slumps*

According to a recent story in the *Wall Street Journal* (May 19, 2000, p. B1), "The euro's plunge against the dollar is casting a pall over this year's Cannes Film Festival, forcing European distributors to curtail their purchases of American films and triggering concessions by U.S. producers of a sort once unheard of in this glitzy resort." The euro's decline by 24% against the dollar is a problem for European distributors, because the international movie business is priced almost exclusively in dollars; it is a problem for U.S. producers because Europe is such a big market for American films. Before a film goes into production, a studio will usually "presell" the foreign rights to distributors and use these presale revenues to finance the film's production. The presale of rights to continental European distribution often accounts for about a third of a film's budget. The rise in the value of the dollar has hurt the prices that U.S. producers can get for these rights. At the same time, the higher euro prices for these rights has caused European distributors to seek better financing terms, such as stretching out payment for their acquired rights. Although some U.S. producers have talked about switching to pricing their rights in euros, the problem of a fallen euro would still remain: If the euro price is set at a level that yields the same dollar price, European distributors will face the same higher cost; if it is set at the same euro price as in the past, the U.S. producer will receive fewer dollars.

ILLUSTRATION *European Manufacturers Suffer When the Euro Soars*

At the beginning of 2002, the euro was about $0.86. By mid-2007, it had soared to $1.33, a rise of over 54%. European manufacturers suffered a profit squeeze on their exports as well as on goods competing against American imports. Consider, for example, the problems facing Head NV, the Dutch sporting-goods maker. The immediate impact of euro appreciation is to make dollar sales less valuable when converted into euros. For example, a tennis racket it might sell in the United States for $50 brought back €58.14 when the euro was at $0.86 (50/0.86) but would translate into only €37.59 at an exchange rate of $1.33 (50/1.33). With Head's costs set in euros, the result of euro appreciation is severe margin pressure on its U.S. exports. If Head decides to raise its dollar prices to improve its euro profit margin, it will lose export sales. European companies also face greater competitive pressure in their home markets as well as in third-country markets from U.S. companies selling in those markets. The reason: Given the large jump in the euro's value, U.S. exporters can offer foreign customers lower prices expressed in euros, while still maintaining or improving their dollar profit margins.

10.1.1 Real Exchange Rate Changes and Exchange Risk

The exchange rate changes that give rise to operating exposure are **real exchange rate changes**. As presented in Chapter 4, the **real exchange rate** is defined as the nominal exchange rate (for example, the number of dollars per franc) adjusted for changes in the relative purchasing power of each currency since some base period. Specifically,

$$e'_t = e_t \times \frac{(1 + i_{f,t})}{(1 + i_{h,t})} \qquad (10.1)$$

where

e'_t = the real exchange rate (home currency per one unit of foreign currency) at time t

e_t = the nominal exchange rate (home currency per one unit of foreign currency) at time t

$i_{f,t}$ = the amount of foreign inflation between times 0 and t

$i_{h,t}$ = the amount of domestic inflation between times 0 and t

Given that the base period nominal rate, e_0, is also the real base period exchange rate, the change in the real exchange rate can be computed as follows:

$$\frac{e'_t - e_0}{e_0} \qquad (10.2)$$

For example, suppose the Danish krone has devalued by 5% during the year. At the same time, Danish and U.S. inflation rates were 3% and 2%, respectively. Then, according to Equation 10.1, if e_0 is the exchange rate (dollar value of the krone) at the beginning of the year, the real exchange rate for the krone at year's end is

$$0.95e_0 \times \frac{1.03}{1.02} = 0.96e_0$$

Applying Equation 10.2, we can see that the real value of the krone has declined by 4% during the year:

$$\frac{0.96\overline{e}_0 - e_0}{e_0} = -4\%$$

In effect the krone's 5% nominal devaluation more than offset the 1% inflation differential between Denmark and the United States, leading to a 4% decline in the real value of the krone.

10.1.2 Importance of the Real Exchange Rate

The distinction between the nominal exchange rate and the real exchange rate is important because of their vastly different implications for exchange risk. A dramatic change in the nominal exchange rate accompanied by an equal change in the price level should have no effects on the relative competitive positions of domestic firms and their foreign competitors and, therefore, will not alter real cash flows. Alternatively, if the real exchange rate changes, it will cause relative price changes—changes in the ratio of domestic goods' prices to prices of foreign goods. In terms of currency changes affecting relative competitiveness, therefore, the focus must be not on nominal exchange rate changes, but instead on changes in the purchasing power of one currency relative to another. Put another way, it is impossible to assess the effects of an exchange rate change without simultaneously considering the impact on cash flows of the underlying relative rates of inflation associated with each currency.

10.1.3 Inflation and Exchange Risk

Let us begin by holding relative prices constant and looking only at the effects of general inflation. This condition means that if the inflation rate is 10%, the price of every good in the economy rises by 10%. In addition, we will initially assume that all goods are traded in a competitive world market without transaction costs, tariffs, or taxes of any kind. Given these conditions, economic theory tells us that the law of one price must prevail. That is, the price of any good, measured in a common currency, must be equal in all countries.

If the law of one price holds and if there is no variation in the relative prices of goods or services, then the rate of change in the exchange rate must equal the difference between the inflation rates in the two countries. The implications of a constant real exchange rate—that is, the purchasing power parity (PPP) holds—are worth exploring further. To begin with PPP does not imply exchange rate changes will necessarily be small or easy to forecast. If a country for example, Russia, has high and unpredictable inflation, then its exchange rate will also fluctuate randomly.

Nonetheless, without relative price changes, a multinational company faces no real operating exchange risk. As long as the firm avoids contracts fixed in foreign currency terms, its foreign cash flows will vary with the foreign rate of inflation. Because the exchange rate also depends on the difference between the foreign and the domestic rates of inflation, the movement of the exchange rate exactly cancels the change in the foreign price level, leaving real dollar cash flows unaffected.

ILLUSTRATION *Calculating the Effects of Exchange Rate Changes and Inflation on Apex Philippines*

Apex Philippines, the Philippines subsidiary of Apex Company, produces and sells medical imaging devices in the Philippines. At the current peso exchange rate of P 1 = $0.02, the devices cost P 40,000 ($800) to produce and sell for P 100,000 ($2,000). The profit margin of P 60,000 provides a dollar margin of $1200. Suppose that Philippine inflation during the year is 20%, and the U.S. inflation rate is zero. All prices and costs are assumed to move in line with inflation. If we assume that PPP holds, the peso will devalue to $0.0167 [0.02 × (1/1.2)]. The real value of the peso stays at $0.02 [0.0167 × (1.2/1.0)], so Apex Philippines's dollar profit margin will remain at $1200. These effects are shown in Exhibit 10.2.

Price Level	Philippines	United States
Beginning of year	100	100
End of year	120	100

Exchange Rate	Beginning of Year	End of Year
Nominal rate	P1 = $0.02	P1 = $0.0167
Real Rate	P1 = $0.02	P1 = $0.0167 × 1.2/1
		= $0.02

| | Beginning of Year | | End of Year | |
Profit Impact	Pesos	U.S. Dollars	Pesos	U.S. Dollars
Price*	P100,000	$2,000	P120,000	$2,000
Cost of production*	40,000	800	48,000	800
Profit margin	P60,000	$1,200	P72,000	$1,200

* Peso prices and costs are assumed to increase at the 20% rate of Philippine inflation.

EXHIBIT 10.2 • THE EFFECTS OF NOMINAL EXCHANGE RATE CHANGES AND INFLATION ON APEX PHILIPPINES

Of course, the conclusion in the Apex Philippines illustration does not hold if the firm enters into contracts fixed in terms of the foreign currency. Examples of such contracts are debt with fixed interest rates, long-term leases, labor contracts, and rent. However, if the real exchange rate remains constant, the risk introduced by entering into fixed price contracts is not exchange risk; it is inflation risk. For instance, a Mexican firm with fixed-rate debt in pesos faces the same risk as the subsidiary of an American firm with peso debt. If the rate of inflation declines, the real interest cost of the debt rises, and the real cash flow of both companies falls. The solution to the problem of inflation risk is to avoid writing contracts fixed in nominal terms in countries with unpredictable inflation. If the contracts are indexed and if the real exchange rate remains constant, exchange risk is eliminated.

10.1.4 Competitive Effects of Real Exchange Rate Changes

In general, a decline in the real value of a nation's currency makes its exports and import-competing goods more competitive. Conversely, an appreciating currency hurts the nation's exporters and those producers competing with imports.

When the real value of the dollar began rising against other currencies during the early 1980s, U.S. exporters found themselves facing the unpleasant choice of either keeping dollar prices constant and losing sales volume (because foreign currency prices rose in line with the appreciating dollar), or setting prices in the foreign currency to maintain market share, with a corresponding erosion in dollar revenues and profit margins. At the same time, the dollar cost of American labor remained the same or rose in line with U.S. inflation. The combination of lower dollar revenues and unchanged or higher dollar costs resulted in severe hardship for those U.S. companies selling abroad. Similarly, U.S. manufacturers competing domestically with imports whose dollar prices were declining saw both their profit margins and sales volumes reduced. In a great reversal of fortune, Japanese firms then had to cope with a yen that appreciated by more than 150% in real terms between 1985 and 1995.

ILLUSTRATION *Yen Appreciation Harms Japanese TV Producers*

For most of 1985, the yen traded at about ¥240 = $1. By 1995, the yen's value had risen to about ¥90 = $1, without a commensurate increase in U.S. inflation. This rise had a highly negative impact on Japanese television manufacturers. If it cost, say, ¥100,000 to build a color TV set in Japan, ship it to the United States, and earn a normal profit, that TV set could be sold in 1985 for about $417 (100,000/240). However, in 1995, the price would have had to be about $1,111 (100,000/90) for Japanese firms to break even, presenting them with the following dilemma. Because other U.S. prices had not risen much, as Japanese firms raised their dollar price to compensate for yen appreciation, Americans would buy fewer Japanese color TVs, and yen revenues would fall. If Japanese TV producers decided to keep their price constant at $417 to preserve market share in the United States, they would have to cut their yen price to about ¥37,530 (417 × 90). In general, whether they held the line on yen prices or cut them, real yen appreciation was bad news for Japanese TV manufacturers. Subsequent yen depreciation eased the pressure on Japanese companies.

Alternatively, Industrias Penoles, the Mexican firm that is the world's largest refiner of newly mined silver, increased its dollar profits by more than 200% after the real devaluation of the Mexican peso relative to the U.S. dollar in 1982. Similarly, when the peso plunged in 1995, the company saw its profits rise again. The reason for the firm's success is that its costs, which are in pesos, declined in dollar terms, and the dollar value of its revenues, which are derived from exports, held steady.

In summary, the economic impact of a currency change on a firm depends on whether the exchange rate change is fully offset by the difference in inflation rates or whether (because of price controls, a shift in monetary policy, or some other reason) the real exchange rate and, hence, relative prices, change. It is these relative price changes that ultimately determine a firm's long-run exposure.

A less obvious point is that a firm may face more exchange risk if nominal exchange rates do *not* change. Consider, for example, a Brazilian shoe manufacturer producing for export to the United States and Europe. If the Brazilian *real's* exchange rate remains fixed in the face of Brazil's typically high rate of inflation, then both the *real's* real exchange rate and the manufacturer's dollar costs of production will rise. Therefore, unless the *real* devalues, the Brazilian exporter will be placed at a competitive disadvantage vis-à-vis producers located in countries with less rapidly rising costs, such as Taiwan and South Korea.

Suppose, for example, that the Brazilian firm sells a pair of shoes in the U.S. market for $10. Its profit margin is $6, or R12, because the shoes cost $4 to produce at the current exchange rate of R1 = $0.50. If Brazilian inflation is 100% but the nominal exchange rate remains constant, it will cost the manufacturer $8 to produce the same pair of shoes by the end of the year. Assuming there is no U.S. inflation, the firm's profit margin will drop to $2. The basic problem is the 100% real appreciation of the *real* (0.50 × 2/1). This situation is shown in Exhibit 10.3 as Scenario 1.

In order to preserve its dollar profit margin (but not its inflation-adjusted *real* margin), the firm will have to raise its price to $14. (Why?[1]) But if it does that, it will be placed at a competitive disadvantage. By contrast, Scenario 2 shows that if the *real* devalues by 50%, to $0.25, the real exchange rate will remain constant at $0.50 ($.2501 × 2/1), the Brazilian firm's competitive situation will be unchanged, and its profit margin will stay at $6. Its inflation-adjusted *real* profit margin also remains the same. Note that with 100% inflation, today's R12 profit margin must rise to R24 by year end, which it does, to stay constant in inflation-adjusted *real* terms.

---

[1] If the price is raised to $14, the profit margin is $6 ($14 − $8). However, at an exchange rate of R1 = $0.50, the *real* margin is still R12. With 100% inflation, the inflation-adjusted value of this margin is equivalent to only half of today's margin of R12 (R2 at year end has the purchasing power of R1 today).

Price Level	Brazil	United States
Beginning of year	100	100
End of year	200	100

Scenario 1	Beginning of Year	End of Year
Nominal rate	R1 = $0.50	R2 = $0.50
Real rate	R1 = $0.50	R2 = $0.50 × 2/1 = $1

| Profit Impact | Beginning of Year | | End of Year | |
	Reais*	U.S. Dollars	Reais	U.S. Dollars
Price	20.00	10.00	20.00	10.00
Cost of production	8.00	4.00	16.00	8.00
Profit margin	12.00	6.00	4.00	2.00

Scenario 2	Beginning of Year	End of Year
Nominal rate	R1 = $0.50	R2 = $0.25
Real rate	R1 = $0.50	R2 = $0.25 × 2/1 = $0.50

| Profit Impact | Beginning of Year | | End of Year | |
	Reais	U.S. Dollars	Reais	U.S. Dollars
Price	20.00	10.00	40.00	10.00
Cost of production	8.00	4.00	16.00	4.00
Profit margin	12.00	6.00	24.00	6.00

* Reais is the plural of Brazilian real.

EXHIBIT 10.3 • THE EFFECTS OF REAL EXCHANGE RATE CHANGES ON THE BRAZILLIAN SHOE MANUFACTURER

ILLUSTRATION　*Chile Mismanages Its Exchange Rate*

A particularly dramatic illustration of the unfortunate effects of a fixed nominal exchange rate combined with high domestic inflation is provided by Chile. As part of its plan to bring down the inflation, the Chilean government fixed the exchange rate in the middle of 1979 at 39 pesos to the U.S. dollar. Over the next two and a half years, the Chilean price level rose 60%, but U.S. prices rose by only about 30%. Thus, by early 1982, the Chilean peso had appreciated in real terms by approximately 23% (1.6/1.3 − 1) against the U.S. dollar. These data are summarized in Exhibit 10.4.

An 18% "corrective" devaluation was enacted in June 1982. Overall, the peso fell by 90% over the next 12 months. However, the artificially high peso had already done its double damage to the Chilean economy: It made Chile's manufactured products more expensive abroad, pricing many of them out of international trade; and it made imports cheaper, undercutting Chilean domestic industries. The effects of the overvalued peso were devastating. Banks became insolvent, factories and copper smelters were thrown

Price Level		Chile	United States
1979		100	100
1982		160	300
Nominal exchange rate	1979	Ps. 1 = $0.02564	
	1982	Ps. 1 = $0.02564	
Real exchange rate	1979	Ps. 1 = $0.02564	
	1982	Ps. 1 = $0.02564 $\times \dfrac{1.60}{1.30}$	
		= $0.03156	
Increase in real value of the chilean peso		$\dfrac{0.03156 - 0.02564}{1.30}$ = 23.1%	

Result: economic devastation

—Loss of export markets

—Loss of domestic markets to imports

—Massive unemployment

—Numerous bankruptcies

—Numerous bank failures

EXHIBIT 10.4 • NOMINAL AND REAL EXCHANGE RATES FOR CHILE, 1979–1982

into bankruptcy, copper mines were closed, construction projects were shut down, and farms were put on the auction block. Unemployment approached 25%, and some areas of Chile resembled industrial graveyards.

The implosion of the Chilean peso did have a silver lining: Chilean companies became dynamic exporters, which today sell chopsticks and salmon to Japan, wine to Europe, and machinery to the United States. It also sped the acceptance of free market economic policies that have given Chile one of the strongest growth rates in the world.

The Chilean example illustrates a critical point: *An increase in the real value of a currency acts as a tax on exports and a subsidy on imports.* Hence, firms that export or that compete with imports are hurt by an appreciating home currency. Conversely, such firms benefit from home-currency depreciation. These general principles identify a company's economic exposure.

10.2 THE ECONOMIC CONSEQUENCES OF EXCHANGE RATE CHANGES

We now examine more closely the specifics of a firm's economic exposure. Solely for the purpose of exposition, the discussion of exposure is divided into its component parts: transaction exposure and real operating exposure.

10.2.1 Transaction Exposure

Transaction exposure arises out of the various types of transactions that require settlement in a foreign currency. Examples are cross-border trade, borrowing and lending in foreign currencies, and the local purchasing and sales activities of foreign subsidiaries. Strictly speaking, of course, the items already on a firm's balance sheet, such as loans and receivables, capture some of these transactions. However, a detailed transaction exposure report must also contain a number of off-balance-sheet items as well, including future sales and purchases, lease payments, forward contracts, loan repayments, and other contractual or anticipated foreign currency receipts and disbursements.

In terms of measuring economic exposure, however, a transaction exposure report, no matter how detailed, has a fundamental flaw: the assumption that local currency cost and revenue streams remain constant following an exchange rate change.

That assumption does not permit an evaluation of the typical adjustments that consumers and firms can be expected to undertake under conditions of currency change. Hence, attempting to measure the likely exchange gain or loss by simply multiplying the projected predevaluation (prerevaluation) local currency cash flows by the forecast devaluation (revaluation) percentage will lead to misleading results. Given the close relationship between nominal exchange rate changes and inflation as expressed in PPP, measuring exposure to a currency change without reference to the accompanying inflation is also a misguided task.

We will now take a closer look at the typical demand and cost effects that result from a real exchange rate change and show how these effects combine to determine a firm's true operating exposure. In general, an appreciating real exchange rate can be expected to have the opposite effects. The dollar is assumed to be the home currency (HC).

10.2.2 Operating Exposure

A real exchange rate change affects a number of aspects of the firm's operations. With respect to dollar (HC) appreciation, the key issue for a domestic firm is its degree of **pricing flexibility**—that is, can the firm maintain its dollar margins both at home and abroad? Can the company maintain its dollar price on domestic sales in the face of lower-priced foreign imports? In the case of foreign sales, can the firm raise its foreign currency selling price sufficiently to preserve its dollar profit margin?

The answers to these questions depend largely on the **price elasticity of demand**. The less price elastic the demand the more price flexibility a company will have to respond to exchange rate changes. Price elasticity, in turn, depends on the degree of competition and the location of key competitors. The more **differentiated** (distinct) a company's products are, the less competition it will face and the greater its ability will be to maintain its domestic currency prices, both at home and abroad. Examples here are IBM and DaimlerChrysler (producer of Mercedes-Benz cars), both of which sell highly differentiated products whose demand has been relatively insensitive to price (at least historically, but competition is changing that). Similarly, if most competitors are based in the home country, then all will face the same change in their cost structure from home currency appreciation, and all can raise their foreign currency prices without putting any of them at a competitive disadvantage relative to their domestic competitors. Examples of this situation are in the precision instrumentation and high-end telecommunications industries, in which virtually all the important players are U.S.-based companies.

Conversely, the less differentiated a company's products are and the more internationally diversified its competitors (for example, the low-priced end of the auto industry) are, the greater the price elasticity of demand for its products will be and the less pricing flexibility it will have. These companies face the greatest amount of exchange risk. For example, in the wake of the Asian currency crisis, Chinese exporters suffered from intense price competition by Asian producers whose currencies had fallen by 40% or more against the yuan. The main culprit was the nature of products they were producing—commodity-type products such as polyester fibers, steel, textiles, and ships that sell almost exclusively on the basis of price. On the other hand, when the yuan fell against other Asian currencies during 2003 (because it was tied to a falling dollar), Chinese manufacturers benefited greatly while other Asian manufacturers were hurt.[2]

ILLUSTRATION *Product Differentiation and Susceptibility to Exchange Risk of the U.S. Apparel and Textile Industries*

The U.S. textile and apparel industries are highly competitive, with each composed of many small manufacturers. In addition, nearly every country has a textile industry, and apparel industries are also common to most countries.

Despite these similarities, the textile industry exists in a more competitive environment than the apparel industry because textile products are more standardized than apparel products. Buyers of textiles can easily switch from a firm that sells a standard good at a higher price to one that sells virtually the same good at a lower price. Because they are more differentiated, the products of competing apparel firms are viewed as more distinct and are less sensitive than textile goods to changes in prices. Thus, even though both textile and apparel firms operate in highly competitive environment, apparel firms—with their greater degree of pricing flexibility—are less subject to exchange risk than are textile firms.

To cope with their currency risk, American textile manufacturers have slashed their production costs while concentrating on sophisticated textile materials such as industrial fabrics and on goods such as sheets and towels that require little direct labor and are less price sensitive.

American producers are also competing by developing a service edge in the domestic market, which enables them to differentiate even commodity products. For example, the industry developed a computerized inventory management and ordering program, called Quick Response, which provides close coordination among textile mills, apparel manufacturers, and retailers. The system cuts in half the time between a fabric order and delivery of the garment to a retailer and gives all the parties better information for planning, thereby placing foreign manufacturers at a competitive disadvantage. In response, Japanese companies, and even some Korean ones, are looking to set up U.S. factories.

MINI-CASE *Euro Appreciation Hurts Southern European Exports*

Southern European countries (e.g., Spain, Greece, Italy, and Portugal) traditionally export low-tech manufactured items such as textiles, toys, and footwear that are in direct competition with inexpensive goods from China. The steady strengthening of the euro from 2002 through 2007 made exports from these countries more expensive and less competitive, costing them global market share. Unfortunately, the strong euro also comes at the same time as relatively high inflation in southern Europe, especially Spain, Greece, and Portugal. By 2007, the euro's appreciation had driven many exporters in those countries to shift production to China and other countries with lower labor costs and weaker currencies.

---

[2] A falling dollar means that Asian exporters to the United States must either raise their dollar prices to maintain margins or accept lower revenues when converted into their home currencies. An added problem is that the costs of their Chinese competitors are denominated in yuan and the yuan is falling against other Asian currencies in line with the dollar's decline. At the same time, a yuan tied to the dollar means that U.S. manufacturers competing with Chinese firms get less of a boost from a falling dollar.

QUESTIONS

1. Why are southern European countries particularly vulnerable to a strong euro?

2. How does the relatively high inflation rate in southern Europe add to the problems created by a strong euro?

3. In contrast to southern Europe, northern Europe, especially Germany, exports more complex and branded manufactured items, such as automobiles, machine tools, and specialty chemicals. Would you expect German exports to be more or less sensitive to pricing pressures from a strong euro than southern European exports? Explain.

4. It turns out that Italian companies exporting food products such as Parma ham and Parmigiano cheese have not seen a drop in exports, nor have high-fashion exporters such as Armani and Valentino despite the strong euro. Explain

Another important determinant of a company's susceptibility to exchange risk is its ability to shift production and the sourcing of inputs among countries. The greater a company's flexibility to substitute between home-country and foreign-country inputs or production, the less exchange risk the company will face. Other things being equal, firms with worldwide production systems can cope with currency changes by increasing production in a nation whose currency has undergone a real devaluation and decreasing production in a nation whose currency has revalued in real terms.

With respect to an MNC's foreign operations, the determinants of its economic exposure will be similar to those just mentioned. A foreign subsidiary selling goods or services in its local market will generally be unable to raise its local currency (LC) selling price to the full extent of an LC devaluation, causing it to register a decline in its postdevaluation dollar revenues. However, because an LC devaluation will also reduce import competition, the more import competition the subsidiary was facing prior to the devaluation, the smaller its dollar revenue decline will be.

The harmful effects of LC devaluation will be mitigated somewhat since the devaluation should lower the subsidiary's dollar production costs, particularly those attributable to local inputs. However, the higher the import content of local inputs, the less dollar production costs will decline. Inputs used in the export or import-competing sectors will decline less in dollar price than other domestic inputs.

An MNC using its foreign subsidiary as an export platform will benefit from an LC devaluation since its export revenues should stay about the same, whereas its dollar costs will decline. The net result will be a jump in dollar profits for the MNC.

The major conclusion is that the sector of the economy in which a firm operates (export, import-competing, or purely domestic), the sources of the firm's inputs (imports, domestic traded or nontraded goods), and fluctuations in the real exchange rate are far more important in delineating the firm's true economic exposure than is any accounting definition. The economic effects are summarized in Exhibit 10.5.

A surprising implication of this analysis is that domestic facilities that supply foreign markets normally entail much greater exchange risk than do foreign facilities that supply local markets. The explanation is that material and labor used in a domestic plant are paid for in the home currency, whereas the products are sold in a foreign currency. For example, take a Japanese company such as Nissan Motors that builds a plant to produce cars for export, primarily to the United States. The company will incur an exchange risk from the point at which it invests in facilities to supply a foreign market (the United States) because its yen expenses will be matched with dollar revenues rather than yen revenues. The point seems obvious; however, all too frequently, firms neglect those effects when analyzing a proposed foreign investment.

Cash-Flow Categories	Relevant Economic Factors	Devaluation Impact	Revaluation Impact
Revenue		**Parent-Currency revenue impact**	**Parent-Currency revenue impact**
Export sales	Price-sensitive demand	Increase (+ +)	Decrease (− −)
	Price-insensitive demand	Slight increase (+)	Slight decrease (−)
Local sales	Weak prior import competition	Sharp decline(− −)	Increase (+ +)
	Strong prior import competition	Decrease (−) (less than devaluation %)	Slight increase (+)
Costs		**Parent-Currency cost impact**	**Parent-Currency cost impact**
Domestic inputs	Low import content	Decrease (− −)	Increase (+ +)
	High import content/ inputs used in export or import-competing sectors	Slight decrease (−)	Slight increase (+)
Imported inputs	Small local market	Remain the same (0)	Remain the same (0)
	Large local market	Slight decrease (−)	Slight increase (+)
Depreciation		**Cash-Flow Impact**	**Cash-Flow impact**
Fixed assets	No asset valuation adjustment	Decrease by devaluation % (− −)	Increase by revaluation % (+ +)
	Asset valuation adjustment	Decrease (−)	Increase (+)

Note: To interpret the above chart, and taking the impact of a devaluation on local demands as an example, it is assumed that if import competition is weak, local prices will climb slightly, if at all; in such a case, there would be a sharp contraction in parent-company revenue. If imports generate strong competition, local-currency prices are expected to increase, although not to the full extent of the devaluation; in this instance, only a moderate decline in parent-company revenue would be registered.

Source: Alan C. Shapiro, "Developing a Profitable Exposure Management System," reprinted from p. 188 of the June 17, 1977, issue of *Business International Money Report*, with the permission of the Economist Intelligence Unit, NA, Incorporated.

EXHIBIT 10.5 ● CHARACTERISTIC ECONOMIC EFFECTS OF EXCHANGE RATE CHANGES ON MMCs

Similarly, a facility producing solely for the domestic market and using only domestic sources of inputs can be strongly affected by currency changes, even though its accounting exposure is zero. Consider, for example, a Ford factory in Detroit that produces cars for sale only in the United States and uses only U.S. labor and materials. Because it buys and sells only in dollars, this factory has no accounting exposure. However, because its cars are subject to competition from foreign imports, this plant will be hurt by appreciation of the dollar. Conversely, a dollar decline will enhance its competitive position and boost its profits.

 M I N I - C A S E   *How Rising Gold Prices Hurt Harmony*

The notion of gold as a store of value has flourished since September 11, 2001. On that horrible day, the price of gold stood at $288 an ounce. Three years later, it was around $420 an ounce. Harmony, a South African mining company, should have flourished as well from the jump in the price of gold. However, the rising value of the South African rand has stolen much of that gain. On the day the Twin Towers fell, the dollar bought 8.62 rand. Three years later, it bought only R6.35. Gold is priced in dollars but South African miners are paid in rand and their wages have risen rapidly as well. Harmony has felt the pain. When gold was at its dollar low in April–June 2001 (2001:Q2) of $252, Harmony made a profit of $20 an ounce. In 2004:Q2, with gold at $390, Harmony lost about $50 an ounce.

QUESTIONS

1. How much rand revenue per ounce was Harmony generating on September 11, 2001? Three years later?

2. Compare Harmony's earnings per ounce in rand terms during 2001:Q2 with the same figure in 2004:Q2.

3. The average exchange rate during 2001:Q2 was R8.04/$; in 2004:Q2, it was R6.60/$. By how much would Harmony have to reduce its rand costs per ounce in 2004:Q2 in order to make the same rand profit per ounce it was earning in 2001:Q2?

10.3 IDENTIFYING ECONOMIC EXPOSURE

At this point, it makes sense to illustrate some of the concepts just discussed by examining several firms to see in what ways they may be susceptible to exchange risk. The companies are Aspen Skiing Company, Petróleos Mexicanos, and Toyota Motor Company.

10.3.1 Aspen Skiing Company

Aspen Skiing Company owns and operates ski resorts in the Colorado Rockies, catering primarily to Americans. It buys all its supplies in dollars and uses only American labor and materials. All guests pay in dollars. Because it buys and sells only in dollars, by U.S. standards it has no accounting exposure. Yet, Aspen Skiing Company does face economic exposure because changes in the value of the dollar affect its competitive position. For example, the strong dollar in the early 1980s adversely affected the company because it led to bargains abroad that offered stiff competition for domestic resorts, including the Rocky Mountain ski areas.

Despite record snowfalls in the Rockies during the early 1980s, many Americans decided to ski in the European Alps instead. Although airfare to the Alps cost much more than a flight to Colorado, the difference between expenses on the ground made a European ski holiday less expensive. For example, in January 1984, American Express offered a basic one-week ski package in Aspen for $439 per person, including double-occupancy lodging, lift ticket, and free rental car or bus transfer from Denver.[3] Throw in round-trip airfare between New York and Denver of $300 and the trip's cost totaled $739.

At the same time, skiers could spend a week in Chamonix in the French Alps for $234, including lodging, lift ticket, breakfast, and a bus transfer from Geneva, Switzerland. Adding in round-trip airfare from New York of $579 brought the trip's cost to $813. The Alpine vacation became less expensive than the one in the Rockies when the cost of meals was included: an estimated $50 a day in Aspen versus $30 a day in Chamonix.

In effect, Aspen Skiing Company is operating in a global market for skiing or, more broadly, vacation services. As the dollar appreciates in real terms, both foreigners and Americans find less-expensive skiing and vacation alternatives outside the United States. In addition, even if California and other West Coast skiers find that high transportation costs continue to make it more expensive to ski in Europe than in the Rockies, they are not restricted to the American Rockies. They have the choice of skiing in the Canadian Rockies, where the skiing is fine and their dollars go further.

---

[3] Report in the *Wall Street Journal,* January 17, 1984, p. 1.

Conversely, a depreciating dollar makes Aspen Skiing Company more competitive and should increase its revenues and profits. In either event, the use of American products and labor means that its costs will not be significantly affected by exchange rate fluctuations.

10.3.2 Petróleos Mexicanos

Petróleos Mexicanos, or Pemex, is the Mexican national oil company. It is the largest company in Mexico and ranks as one of the biggest non-U.S. industrial companies. Most of its sales are overseas. Suppose Pemex borrows U.S. dollars. If the peso devalues, is Pemex a better or worse credit risk?

The instinctive response of most people is that devaluation of the peso makes Pemex a poorer credit risk. This response is wrong. Consider Pemex's revenues. Assume that it exports all its oil. Because oil is priced in dollars, Pemex's dollar revenues will remain the same following peso devaluation. Its dollar costs, however, will change. Most of its operating costs are denominated in pesos. These costs include labor, local supplies, services, and materials.

Although the peso amount of these costs may go up somewhat, they will not rise to the extent of the devaluation of the peso. Hence, the dollar amount of peso costs will decline. Pemex also uses a variety of sophisticated equipment and services to aid in oil exploration, drilling, and production. Because these inputs are generally from foreign sources, their dollar costs are likely to be unaffected by peso devaluation. Inasmuch as some costs will fall in dollar terms and other costs will stay the same, the overall effect of peso devaluation is a decline in Pemex's dollar costs.

Since its dollar revenue will stay the same while the dollar amount of its costs will fall, the net effect on Pemex of a peso devaluation is to increase its dollar cash flow. Hence, it becomes a better credit risk in terms of its ability to service dollar debt.

Might this conclusion be reversed if it turns out that Pemex sells much of its oil domestically? Surprisingly, the answer is no if we add the further condition that the Mexican government does not impose oil price controls. Suppose the price of oil is $20 a barrel. If the initial peso exchange rate is U.S.$0.16/Mex$, that means that the price of oil in Mexico must be Mex$125 (20/0.16) a barrel. Otherwise, there would be an arbitrage opportunity because oil transportation costs are a small fraction of the price of oil. If the peso now devalues to $0.08, the price of oil must rise to Mex$250. Consider what would happen if the price stayed at Mex$125. The dollar equivalent price would now be $10. But why would Pemex sell oil in Mexico for $10 a barrel when it could sell the same oil outside Mexico for $20 a barrel? It would not do so unless there were price controls in Mexico and the government prohibited foreign sales. Hence, in the absence of government intervention, the peso price of oil must rise to Mex$250 and Pemex's dollar profits will rise whether it exports all or part of its oil.

This situation points out the important distinction between the currency of denomination and the currency of determination. The **currency of denomination** is the currency in which prices are stated. For example, oil prices in Mexico are stated in pesos. However, although the currency of denomination for oil sales in Mexico is the peso, the peso price itself is determined by the dollar price of oil. That is, as the peso:dollar exchange rate changes, the peso price of oil changes to equate the dollar equivalent price of oil in Mexico with the dollar price of oil in the world market. Thus, the **currency of determination** for Pemex's domestic oil sales is the U.S. dollar.

10.3.3 Toyota Motor Company

Toyota is the largest Japanese auto company and the fourth largest non-U.S. industrial firm in the world. Over half of its sales are overseas, primarily in the United States. If the yen appreciates, Toyota has the choice of keeping its yen price constant or its dollar price constant. If Toyota holds its yen price constant, the dollar price of its auto exports will

1 Where is the company selling?
  Domestic versus foreign sales breakdown

2 Who are the company's key competitors?
  Domestic versus foreign companies

3 How sensitive is demand to price?
  Price-sensitive demand versus price-insensitive demand

4 Where is the company producing?
  Domestic production versus foreign production

5 Where are the company's inputs coming from?
  Domestic inputs versus foreign inputs

6 How are the company's inputs or outputs priced?
  Priced in a world market or in a domestic market; the currency of determination as opposed
to the currency of denomination

EXHIBIT 10.6 ● KEY QUESTIONS TO ASK THAT HELP IDENTIFY EXCHANGE RISK

rise and sales volume will decline. However, if Toyota decides to maintain its U.S. market share, it must hold its dollar price constant. In either case, its yen revenues will fall.

If Toyota decides to focus on the Japanese market, it will face the **flow-back effect**, as previously exported products flow back into Japan. Flow-back occurs because other Japanese firms, finding that a high yen makes it difficult to export their cars, emphasize Japanese sales as well. The result is increased domestic competition and lower profit margins on domestic sales.

Toyota's yen production costs will also be affected by yen appreciation. Steel, copper, aluminum, oil (from which plastics are made), and other materials that go into making a car are all imported. As the yen appreciates, the yen cost of these imported materials will decline. Yen costs of labor and domestic services, products, and equipment will likely stay the same. The net effect of lower yen costs for some inputs and constant yen costs for other inputs is a reduction in overall yen costs of production.

The net effect on profits of lower yen revenues and lower yen costs is an empirical question. This question can be answered by examining the profit consequences of yen appreciation. Here, the answer is unambiguous: Yen appreciation hurts Toyota; the reduction in its revenues more than offsets the reduction in its costs.

These three examples illustrate a progression of ideas. Aspen Skiing Company's revenues were affected by exchange rate changes, but its costs were largely unaffected. By contrast, Pemex's costs, but not its revenues, were affected by exchange rate changes. Toyota had both its costs and its revenues affected by exchange rate changes. The process of examining these companies includes a systematic approach to identifying a company's exposure to exchange risk. Exhibit 10.6 summarizes this approach by presenting a series of questions that underlie the analysis of economic exposure.

10.4 CALCULATING ECONOMIC EXPOSURE

We will now work through a hypothetical, though comprehensive, example illustrating all the various aspects of exposure that have been discussed so far. This example emphasizes the quantitative, rather than qualitative, determination of economic exposure. It shows how critical the underlying assumptions are.

Spectrum Manufacturing AB is the wholly owned Swedish affiliate of a U.S. multinational industrial plastics firm. It manufactures patented sheet plastic in Sweden, with 60% of its output currently being sold in Sweden and the remaining 40% exported to other European countries. Spectrum uses only Swedish labor in its manufacturing

	Units (hundred thousands)	Unit price (SKr)	Total	
Domestic sales	6	20	(SKr) 12,000,000	
Export sales	4	20	8,000,000	
Total revenue				20,000,000
Total operating expenditures				10,800,000
Overhead expenses				3,500,000
Interest on krona debt @ 10%				300,000
Depreciation				900,000
Net profit before tax			(SKr)	4,500,000
Income tax @ 40%				1,800,000
Profit after tax			(SKr)	2,700,000
Add back depreciation				900,000
Net cash flow in kronor			(SKr)	3,600,000
Net cash flow in dollars (Skr 4 = $1)				$ 900,000

EXHIBIT 10.7 • SUMMARY OF PROJECTED OPERATIONS FOR SPECTRUM MANUFACTURING AB: BASE CASE

process, but it uses both local and foreign sources of raw material. The effective Swedish tax rate on corporate profits is 40%, and the annual depreciation charge on plant and equipment, in Swedish kronor (SKr), is SKr 900,000. In addition, Spectrum AB has outstanding SKr 3 million in debt, with interest payable at 10% annually.

Exhibit 10.7 presents Spectrum's projected sales, costs, after-tax income, and cash flow for the coming year, based on the current exchange rate of SKr 4 = $1. All sales are invoiced in kronor (singular, krona).

10.4.1 Spectrum's Accounting Exposure

Exhibit 10.8 shows Spectrum's balance sheet before and after an exchange rate change. To contrast the economic and accounting approaches to measuring exposure, assume that the Swedish krona devalues by 20%, from SKr 4 = $1 to SKr 5 = $1. The third column of Exhibit 10.8 shows that under the current rate method mandated by FASB 52, Spectrum will have a translation loss of $935,000. Use of the monetary/nonmonetary method leads to a much smaller reported loss of $300,000.

10.4.2 Spectrum's Economic Exposure

On the basis of current information, it is impossible to determine the precise economic impact of the krona devaluation. Therefore, three different scenarios have been constructed, with varying degrees of plausibility, and Spectrum's economic exposure has been calculated under each scenario. The three scenarios are

1. All variables remain the same.
2. Krona sales prices and all costs rise; volume remains the same.
3. There are partial increases in prices, costs, and volume.

Scenario 1: All Variables Remain the Same. If all prices remain the same (in kronor) and sales volume doesn't change, then Spectrum's krona cash flow will stay at SKr 3,600,000.

	Kronor	U.S. Dollars Before Krona Devaluation (SKr 4 = $1)	U.S. Dollars after Krona Devaluation (SKr 5 = $1)	
			Current rate	Monetary/ Nonmonetary
Assets				
Cash	SKr 1,000,000	$ 250,000	200,000	200,000
Accounts receivable	5,000,000	$ 1,250,000	1,000,000	1,000,000
Inventory	2,700,000	$ 675,000	540,000	675,000
Net fixed assets	10,000,000	$ 2,500,000	2,000,000	2,500,000
Total assets	SKr 18,700,000	$ 4,675,000	3,740,000	4,375,000
Liabilities				
Accounts payable	2,000,000	$ 500,000	400,000	400,000
Long-term debt	3,000,000	$ 750,000	600,000	600,000
Equity	13,700,000	$ 3,425,000	2,740,000	3,375,000
Total liabilities plus equity	SKr 18,700,000	$ 4,675,000	3,740,000	4,375,000
Translation gain (loss)			(935,000)	(300,000)

EXHIBIT 10.8 • IMPACT OF KRONA DEVALUATION ON SPECTRUM AB'S FINANCIAL STATEMENT UNDER FASB-52

At the new exchange rate, this amount will equal $720,000 (3,600,000/5). Then the net loss in dollar operating cash flow in year 1 can be calculated as follows:

First-year cash flow (SKr 4 = $1)	$900,000
First-year cash flow (SKr 5 = $1)	720,000
Net loss from devaluation	$180,000

Moreover, this loss will continue until relative prices adjust. Part of this loss, how-ever, will be offset by the $150,000 gain that will be realized when the SKr 3 million loan is repaid (3 million × 0.05).[4] If a three-year adjustment process is assumed and the krona loan is repaid at the end of year 3, then the present value of the economic loss from operations associated with the krona devaluation, using a 15% discount rate, equals $312,420:

Year	Postdevaluation Cash Flow (1)	−	Predevaluation Cash Flow (2)	=	Change in Cash Flow (3)	×	15% Present Value Factor (4)	=	Present Value (5)
1	$720,000		$900,000		−$180,000		0.870		−$156,600
2	720,000		900,000		− 180,000		0.756		− 136,080
3	870,000*		900,000		− 30,000		0.658		− 19,740
							Net Loss		−$312,420

*Includes a gain of $150,000 on loan repayment.

This loss is due primarily to the inability to raise the sales price. The resulting con-stant krona profit margin translates into a 20% reduction in dollar profits. The economic

---

[4] No Swedish taxes will be owed on this gain because SKr 3 million were borrowed and SKr 3 million were repaid.

	Units (Hundred Thousands)	Unit Price (SKr)	Total	
Domestic sales	6	25.00	(SKr) 15,000,000	
Export sales	4	25.00	10,000,000	
Total revenue				25,000,000
Total operating expenditures				13,500,000
Overhead expenses				4,375,000
Interest on krona debt @ 10%				300,000
Depreciation				900,000
Net profit before tax			(SKr)	5,925,000
Income tax @ 40%				2,370,000
Profit after tax			(SKr)	3,555,000
Add back depreciation				900,000
Net cash flow in kronor			(SKr)	4,455,000
Net cash flow in dollars (SKr 5 = $1)				$891,000

EXHIBIT 10.9 • SUMMARY OF PROJECTED OPERATIONS FOR SPECTRUM MANUFACTURING AB: SCENARIO 2

loss of $312,420 contrasts with the accounting recognition of a $935,000 foreign exchange loss. In reality, of course, the prices, costs, volume, and input mix are unlikely to remain fixed. The discussion will now focus on the economic effects of some of these potential adjustments. *Scenario 2: Krona Sales Prices and All Costs Rise; Volume Remains the Same.* It is assumed here that all costs and prices increase in proportion to the krona devaluation, but unit volume remains the same. However, the operating cash flow in kronor does not rise to the same extent because depreciation, which is based on historical cost, remains at SKr 900,000. As a potential offset, interest payments also hold steady at SKr 300,000. Working through the numbers in Exhibit 10.9 gives us an operating cash flow of $891,000.

The $9,000 reduction in cash flow equals the decreased dollar value of the SKr 900,000 depreciation tax shield less the decreased dollar cost of paying the SKr 300,000 in interest. Before devaluation, the depreciation tax shield was worth (900,000 × 0.4)/4 dollars, or $90,000. After devaluation, the dollar value of the tax shield declines to (900,000 × 0.4)/5 dollars = $72,000, or a loss of $18,000 in cash flow. Similarly, the dollar cost of paying SKr 300,000 in interest declines by $15,000 to $60,000 (from $75,000). After tax, this decrease in interest expense equals $9,000. Adding the two figures (−$18,000 + $9,000) yields a net loss of $9,000 annually in operating cash flow. The net economic gain over the coming three years, relative to predevaluation expectations, is $78,150.

Year	Postdevaluation Cash Flow (1)	−	Predevaluation Cash Flow (2)	=	Change in Cash Flow (3)	×	15% Present Value Factor (4)	=	Present Value (5)
1	$ 891,000		$900,000		−$9,000		0.870		− $7,830
2	891,000		900,000		− 9,000		0.756		− 6,800
3	1,041,000*		900,000		+141,000		0.658		92,780
							Net Gain		$78,150

*Includes a gain of $150,000 on loan repayment.

	Units (Hundred Thousands)	Unit price (SKr)	Total	
Domestic sales	7.2	22	(SKr) 15,840,000	
Export sales	4.6	24	11,040,000	
Total revenue				26,880,000
Total operating expenditures				14,906,000
Overhead expenses				3,850,000
Interest on krona debt @ 10%				300,000
Depreciation				900,000
Net profit before tax			(SKr)	6,924,000
Income tax @ 40%				2,769,000
Profit after tax			(SKr)	4,155,000
Add back depreciation				900,000
Net cash flow in kronor			(SKr)	5,055,000
Net cash flow in dollars (SKr 5 = $1)			$	1,011,00

EXHIBIT 10.10 • SUMMARY OF PROJECTED OPERATIONS FOR SPECTRUM MANUFACTURING AB: SCENARIO 3

All of this gain in economic value comes from the gain on repayment of the krona loan. *Scenario 3: Partial Increases in Prices, Costs, and Volume.* In the most realistic situation, all variables will adjust somewhat. It is assumed here that the sales price at home rises by 10% to SKr 22 and the export price rises to SKr 24, still providing a competitive advantage in dollar terms over foreign products. The result is a 20% increase in domestic sales and a 15% increase in export sales.

Local input prices are assumed to go up, but the dollar price of imported material stays at its predevaluation level. As a result of the change in relative cost, some substitutions are made between domestic and imported goods. The result is an increase in SKr unit cost of approximately 17%. Overhead expenses rise by only 10% because some components of this account, such as rent and local taxes, are fixed in value. The net result of all these adjustments is an operating cash flow of $1,011,000, which is a gain of $111,000 over the predevaluation level of $900,000. The calculations are shown in Exhibit 10.10.

Over the next three years, cash flows and the firm's economic value will change as follows:

Year	Postdevaluation Cash Flow (1)	−	Predevaluation Cash Flow (2)	=	Change in Cash Flow (3)	×	15% Present Value Factor (4)	=	Present Value (5)
1	$1,011,000		$900,000		$111,000		0.870		$ 96,570
2	1,011,000		900,000		111,000		0.756		83,920
3	1,161,000*		900,000		261,000		0.658		171,740
							Net Gain		$352,230

*Includes a gain of $150,000 on loan repayment.

Thus, under this scenario, the economic value of the firm will increase by $352,230. This gain reflects the increase in operating cash flow combined with the gain on loan repayment.

	Forecast Change in Cash Flows		
Year	*Scenario 1*	*Scenario 2*	*Scenario 3*
1	–$ 180,000	–$ 9,000	$ 111,000
2	–$ 180,000	–$ 9,000	$ 111,000
3	–$ 30,000*	$141,000*	$ 261,000*
Change in present value (15% discount factor)	–$ 312,420	$ 78,150	$ 352,230

*Includes a gain of $150,000 on loan repayment.

EXHIBIT 10.11 • SUMMARY OF ECONOMIC EXPOSURE IMPACT OF KRONA DEVALUATION ON SPECTRUM MANUFACTURING AB

Case Analysis   The three preceding scenarios demonstrate the sensitivity of a firm's economic exposure to assumptions concerning its price elasticity of demand, its ability to adjust its mix of inputs as relative costs change, its pricing flexibility, subsequent local inflation, and its use of local currency financing. Perhaps most important of all, this example makes clear the lack of any necessary relationship between accounting-derived measures of exchange gains or losses and the true impact of currency changes on a firm's economic value. The economic effects of this devaluation under the three alternative scenarios are summarized in Exhibit 10.11.

10.5 AN OPERATIONAL MEASURE OF EXCHANGE RISK

The preceding example demonstrates that determining a firm's true economic exposure is a daunting task, requiring a singular ability to forecast the amounts and exchange rate sensitivities of future cash flows. Most firms that follow the economic approach to managing exposure, therefore, must settle for a measure of their economic exposure and the resulting exchange risk that often is supported by nothing more substantial than intuition.

This section presents a workable approach for determining a firm's true economic exposure and susceptibility to exchange risk. The approach avoids the problem of using seat-of-the-pants estimates in performing the necessary calculations.[5] The technique is straightforward to apply, and it requires only historical data from the firm's actual operations or, in the case of a *de novo* venture, data from a comparable business.

This approach is based on the following operational definition of the exchange risk faced by a parent or one of its foreign affiliates: *A company faces exchange risk to the extent that variations in the dollar value of the unit's cash flows are correlated with variations in the nominal exchange rate.* This correlation is precisely what a *regression analysis* seeks to establish. A simple and straightforward way to implement this definition, therefore, is to regress the changes in actual cash flows from past periods, converted into their dollar values, on changes in the average exchange rate during the corresponding period. Specifically, this involves running the following regression[6]:

$$\Delta CF_t = a + \beta \Delta EXCH_t + u_t \tag{10.3}$$

---

[5] This section is based on C. Kent Garner and Alan C. Shapiro, "A Practical Method of Assessing Foreign Exchange Risk," *Midland Corporate Finance Journal,* Fall 1984, pp. 6–17.

[6] The application of the regression approach to measuring exposure to currency risk is illustrated in Garner and Shapiro, "A Practical Method of Assessing Foreign Exchange Risk," and in Michael Adler and Bernard Dumas, "Exposure to Currency Risk: Definition and Measurement," *Financial Management,* Summer 1984, pp. 41–50. We use changes, rather than levels, of the variables in the regression because the variables are nonstationary. In addition, such a regression may include lagged values of $\Delta EXCH_t$ given that sales and costs often respond with a lag to exchange rate changes.

where

$\Delta CF_t = CF_t - CF_{t-1}$, and CF_t equals the dollar value of total affiliate (parent) cash flows in period t

$\Delta EXCH_t = EXCH_t - EXCH_{t-1}$, and $EXCH_t$ equals the average nominal exchange rate (dollar value of one unit of the foreign currency) during period t

u = a random error term with mean 0

The output from a regression such as Equation 10.3 includes three key parameters: (1) the foreign exchange beta (β) coefficient, which measures the sensitivity of dollar cash flows to exchange rate changes; (2) the t-statistic, which measures the statistical significance of the beta coefficient; and (3) the R^2, which measures the fraction of cash flow variability explained by variation in the exchange rate. The higher the beta coefficient the greater the impact of a given exchange rate change on the dollar value of cash flows. Conversely, the lower the beta coefficient, the less exposed the firm is to exchange rate changes. A larger t-statistic means a higher level of confidence in the value of the beta coefficient.

However, even if a firm has a large and statistically significant beta coefficient and thus faces real exchange risk, this situation does not necessarily mean that currency fluctuations are an important determinant of overall firm risk. What really matters is the percentage of total corporate cash-flow variability that is due to these currency fluctuations. Thus, the most important parameter, in terms of its impact on the firm's exposure management policy, is the regression's R^2. For example, if exchange rate changes explain only 1% of total cash-flow variability, the firm should not devote much in the way of resources to foreign exchange risk management, even if the beta coefficient is large and statistically significant.

10.5.1 Limitations

The validity of this method clearly depends on the sensitivity of future cash flows to exchange rate changes being similar to their historical sensitivity. In the absence of additional information, this assumption seems to be reasonable. However, the firm may have reasons to modify the implementation of this method. For example, the nominal foreign currency tax shield provided by a foreign affiliate's depreciation is fully exposed to the effects of currency fluctuations. If the amount of depreciation in the future is expected to differ significantly from its historical values, then the depreciation tax shield should be removed from the cash flows used in the regression analysis and treated separately. Similarly, if the firm has recently entered into a large purchase or sales contract fixed in terms of the foreign currency, it might decide to consider the resulting transaction exposure apart from its operating exposure.

10.6 MANAGING OPERATING EXPOSURE

The basic message of this section is straightforward: Because currency risk affects all facets of a company's operations, it should not be the concern of financial managers alone. Operating managers, in particular, should develop marketing and production initiatives that help to ensure profitability over the long run. They should also devise anticipatory or proactive, rather than reactive, strategic alternatives in order to gain competitive leverage internationally.

The focus on the real (economic) effects of currency changes and how to cope with the associated risks suggests that a sensible strategy for exchange risk management is one that is designed to protect the dollar (HC) earning power of the company as a whole. But whereas firms can easily hedge transaction exposures, **competitive exposures**—those arising from competition with firms based in other currencies—are longer-term and cannot be dealt with solely through financial hedging techniques. Rather, they require making the longer-term operating adjustments described in Section 10.6.1.

10.6.1 Marketing Management of Exchange Risk

The design of a firm's marketing strategy under conditions of home currency (HC) fluctuation presents considerable opportunity for gaining competitive leverage. Thus, one of the international marketing manager's tasks should be to identify the likely effects of a currency change and then act on them by adjusting pricing and product policies.

Market Selection   Major strategic considerations for an exporter are the markets in which to sell—that is, **market selection**—and the relative marketing support to devote to each market. As a result of the strong dollar during the early 1980s, for example, some discouraged U.S. firms pulled out of markets that foreign competition made unprofitable. From the perspective of foreign companies, however, the strong U.S. dollar was a golden opportunity to gain market share at the expense of their U.S. rivals. Japanese and European companies also used their dollar cost advantage to carve out market share against American competitors in third markets. The subsequent drop in the dollar helped U.S. firms turn the tables on their foreign competitors, both at home and abroad.

Pricing Strategy   The key issue that must be addressed when developing a **pricing strategy** in the face of currency volatility is whether to emphasize market share or profit margin. Following dollar depreciation, for example, U.S. exports will gain a competitive price advantage on the world market. A U.S. exporter now has the option of raising its dollar price and boosting its profit margins or keeping its dollar price constant and expanding its market share. The decision is influenced by such factors as whether this change is likely to persist, economies of scale, the cost structure of expanding output, consumer price sensitivity, and the likelihood of attracting competition if high unit profitability is obvious.

The greater the *price elasticity of demand*—the change in demand for a given change in price—the greater the incentive to hold down price and thereby expand sales and revenues. Similarly, if significant *economies of scale* exist, it generally will be worthwhile to hold down price, expand demand, and thereby lower unit production costs. The reverse is true if economies of scale are nonexistent or if price elasticity is low.

ILLUSTRATION   *A.T. Cross Marks Down Its Pen Prices*

In February 1993, following a 10% decline in the dollar (from ¥123 to ¥111), A.T. Cross cut the yen prices of its pens by 20%. For example, a 10-carat gold Cross pen was marked down to ¥8,000 from ¥10,000. Suppose that the manufacturing and shipping costs of this Cross pen were $25 and distribution costs were ¥2,000, giving Cross a pre-exchange rate change contribution margin of $40 (¥10,000/123 − $25 − ¥2,000/123). Assuming these costs stay the same, how much additional volume must Cross generate in order to maintain its dollar profits on this pen?

Solution: The contribution margin given the new exchange rate and the price change equals $29 (¥8,000/111 − $25 − ¥2,000/111). In order to maintain dollar profits on this pen at their previous level, unit sales must rise by 38% (40/29). A sales increase of this magnitude implies a price elasticity of demand of 1.9 (38/20).

Turning now to domestic pricing after a fall in the home currency, a domestic firm facing strong import competition may have much greater latitude in pricing. It then has the choice of potentially raising prices consistent with import price increases or of holding prices constant in order to improve market share. Again, the strategy depends on such variables as economies of scale and the price elasticity of demand. For example, the sharp rise in the value of the yen and Deutsche mark during the 1990s led the German and Japanese automakers to raise their dollar prices and allowed Ford and General Motors to raise their prices on competing models. The price increases by the U.S. auto manufacturers, which were less than the sharp rise in import prices, improved their profit margins and kept U.S. cars competitive with their foreign rivals.

The competitive situation is reversed following appreciation of the dollar, which is equivalent to a foreign currency (FC) depreciation. In this case, a U.S. firm selling overseas should consider opportunities to increase the FC prices of its products. The problem, of course, is that local producers now will have a competitive cost advantage, limiting an exporter's ability to recoup dollar profits by raising FC selling prices.

At best, therefore, an exporter will be able to raise its product prices by the extent of the FC depreciation. For example, suppose Avon is selling cosmetics in England priced at £2.00 when the exchange rate is $1.80/£. This gives Avon revenue of $3.60 per unit. If the pound declines to $1.50/£, Avon's unit revenue will fall to $3.00, unless it can raise its selling price to £2.40 (2.40 × 1.50 = $3.60). At worst, in an extremely competitive situation, the exporter will have to absorb a reduction in HC revenues equal to the percentage decline in the value of the foreign currency. For example, if Avon cannot raise its pound price, its new dollar price of $3.00 represents a 16.7% drop in dollar revenue, the same percentage decline as the fall in the pound's value [(1.80 − 1.50)/1.80]. In the most likely case, FC prices can be raised somewhat, and the exporter will make up the difference through a lower profit margin on its foreign sales.

In deciding whether to raise prices following a foreign currency depreciation, companies must consider not just sales that will be lost today but also the likelihood of losing future sales as well. For example, foreign capital goods manufacturers used the period when they had a price advantage to build strong U.S. distribution and service networks. U.S. firms that had not previously bought foreign-made equipment became loyal customers. When the dollar fell, foreign firms opened U.S. plants to supply their distribution systems and hold onto their customers.

The same is true in many other markets as well: *A customer who is lost may be lost forever.* For example, a customer who is satisfied with a foreign automobile may stick with that brand for a long time.

MINI-CASE *Check the Euro and Ship the Boxes!*

In 2001, Kim Reynolds, president of Markel Corp., located in Plymouth Meeting, Pennsylvania, had to take a 40% pay cut to offset the effects of a skyrocketing dollar. Markel, which makes Teflon-based tubing and insulated wire used in the automotive, appliance, and water-purification industries, has developed a four-part strategy to cope with currency volatility: (1) Charge customers relatively stable prices in their own currencies to build overseas market share, while absorbing currency gains or losses; (2) use forward contracts to lock in dollar revenues for the next several months; (3) improve efficiency to survive when the dollar appreciates; and (4) pray. Mr. Reynolds believes his policy of keeping prices set in foreign currencies, mainly the euro, has helped Markel capture 70% of the world market for high-performance, Teflon-coated cable-control liners. However, it also means that Markel signs multiyear contracts denominated in euros. When he thinks the dollar will rise, Markel's CFO, James Hoban, might hedge the company's entire expected euro revenue stream for the next several months with a forward contract. If he thinks the dollar will fall, he will hedge perhaps 50% and take a chance that he will make more dollars by remaining exposed. Mr. Hoban sometimes guesses wrong, as when he sold euros forward assuming—incorrectly—that the euro would continue falling. To make matters worse, Markel entered a multiyear contract with a German firm in 1998 and set the sales price assuming that the euro would be at $ 1.18 for the next several years. In fact, the euro sank like a rock and Markel had over $625,000 in currency losses in 2001 and 2002 combined. One of Markel's responses was to buy new equipment that cut production down-time and waste material. By 2003, most of Markel's contracts outstanding were written assuming that the euro would be valued between 90 cents and 95 cents. The jump in the euro's dollar value thus created a currency windfall for Markel. To lock in his dollar costs and reduce his currency risk, Mr. Reynolds demands that his Japanese supplier of raw materials sign multiyear dollar contracts.

QUESTIONS

1. Why does a rise in the dollar hurt Markel? How does a falling dollar help Markel?

2. What does Markel do to hedge its currency risk? Can Markel use hedging to completely eliminate its currency risk?

3. Comment on Markel's policy of selective hedging. Are there any speculative elements involved in such a policy? Would you recommend Markel continue to follow a policy of selective hedging? Why or why not?

4. What are the basic elements of Market's pricing policy? Does this pricing policy reduce its currency risk? Explain.

5. Does locking in Markel's dollar costs of raw materials through multiyear dollar contracts automatically reduce the company's currency exposure?

Product Strategy   Companies often respond to exchange risk by altering their **product strategy**, which deals with such areas as new-product introduction, product line decisions, and product innovation. One way to cope with exchange rate fluctuations is to change the timing of the introduction of new products. For example, because of the competitive price advantage, the period after a home currency depreciation may be the ideal time to develop a brand franchise.

Exchange rate fluctuations also affect product line decisions. Following home currency devaluation, a firm will potentially be able to expand its product line and cover a wider spectrum of consumers both at home and abroad. Conversely, home currency appreciation may force a firm to reorient its product line and target it to a higher-income, more quality-conscious, less price-sensitive constituency. Volkswagen, for example, achieved its export prominence on the basis of low-priced, stripped-down, low-maintenance cars. The appreciation of the Deutsche mark in the early 1970s, however, effectively ended Volkswagen's ability to compete primarily on the basis of price. The company lost over $310 million in 1974 alone attempting to maintain its market share by lowering DM prices. To compete in the long run, Volkswagen was forced to revise its product line and sell relatively high-priced cars to middle-income consumers, from an extended product line, on the basis of quality and styling rather than cost.

The equivalent strategy for firms selling to the industrial rather than consumer market and confronting a strong home currency is **product innovation**, financed by an expanded research and development (R&D) budget. For example, Japanese exporters responded to the rising yen by shifting production from commodity-type goods to more sophisticated, high-value products. Demand for such goods, which embody advanced technology, high-quality standards, and other nonprice features, is less sensitive to price increases caused by yen appreciation.

ILLUSTRATION   *Automatic Feed Survives Through Ingenuity*

The strong dollar of the late 1990s and early 2000s set off a small revolution in factories across America. Consider Automatic Feed Co. Located in Napoleon, Ohio, it makes machinery used in auto plants. To cope with the strong dollar, it undertook the most extensive product redesign in its 52-year history. Its aim was to neutralize the cost advantages its foreign competitors enjoyed because of their weak home currencies. The company redesigned its machines to make them easier and less expensive to build and also modernized its production system to reduce the costs of manufacturing. By 2002, the production overhaul and redesign efforts had cut production costs by 20%. At the same time, Automatic Feed developed new software that allows customers to track such things as the productivity of a particular machine on a manufacturing line and to pinpoint exactly where a problem is when a line breaks down. By quickly flagging the source of a problem and displaying a digital rendering of it on a computer monitor, the software saves time and cost for customers. This ingenious software reduces the price elasticity of demand for the company's offerings, thereby making it less subject to currency risk.

Companies can also differentiate their product offerings by adding service features that customers value. For this to be a viable strategy, the premium customers are prepared to pay for this differentiation must exceed the cost of adding these service features.

ILLUSTRATION   *Fresco Group Is Squeezed by Dollarization*

It is 2005, and while the rest of the world tries to cope with a weak dollar, Fresco Group, a clothing manufacturer in El Salvador, is worried that the dollar is too strong. Fresco's concerns stem from El Salvador's decision in 2001 to adopt the U.S. dollar as its official currency. Although dollarization has brought price stability to El Salvador, it has also made it clothing manufacturing industry less competitive. The reason is that its Central American neighbors, Honduras and Nicaragua, regularly devalue their currencies against the U.S. dollar to gain a competitive edge over U.S. manufacturers. As a result, labor costs for Fresco Group are more than twice as much as in Nicaragua and about 40% higher than in Honduras. Transportation costs in El Salvador are also higher.

Fresco Group has responded to its high labor costs by transforming its business. In 2001, Fresco simply sewed together orders of jeans, underwear, and T-shirts for U.S. customers who transported the finished goods to the United States. Now, Fresco creates designs, procures materials, and manufactures higher-priced garments based on a single sketch. Its logistics team includes shipping and customs specialists who can speed delivery of finished goods directly to U.S. warehouses and retail stores in half the time it takes Asian rivals. By significantly improving both its ability to produce finished products and its customer response time, Fresco Group has managed to move into higher-end niche markets where currency problems matter less and to increase its revenue by an average of 30% for every piece of clothing its sells.

10.6.2 Production Management of Exchange Risk

Sometimes exchange rates move so much that pricing or other marketing strategies cannot save the product. This was the case for U.S. firms in the early 1980s and for Japanese firms in the early 1990s. Firms facing this situation must either drop uncompetitive products or cut their costs.

Product sourcing and **plant location** are the principal variables that companies manipulate to manage competitive risks that cannot be dealt with through marketing changes alone. Consider, for example, the possible responses of U.S. firms to a strong dollar. The basic strategy would involve shifting the firm's manufacturing base overseas, but this can be accomplished in more than one way.

Input Mix   Outright additions to facilities overseas naturally accomplish a manufacturing shift. A more flexible solution is to change the *input mix* by purchasing more components overseas. Following the rise of the dollar in the early 1980s, most U.S. companies increased their global sourcing. For example, Caterpillar responded to the soaring U.S. dollar and a tenacious competitor, Japan's Komatsu, by "shopping the world" for components. More than 50% of the pistons that Caterpillar uses in the United States now come from abroad, mainly from a Brazilian company. Some work previously done by Caterpillar's Milwaukee plant was moved in 1984 to a subsidiary in Mexico. Caterpillar also stopped most U.S. production of lift trucks and began importing a new line, complete with Cat's yellow paint and logo, from South Korea's Daewoo.

ILLUSTRATION   *Japanese Automakers Outsource to Cope with a Rising Yen*

Japanese automakers have protected themselves against the rising yen by purchasing a significant percentage of intermediate components from independent suppliers. This practice, called **outsourcing**, gives them the flexibility to shift purchases of intermediate inputs toward suppliers with costs least affected by exchange rate changes. Some of these inputs come from South Korea and Taiwan, nations whose currencies have been closely linked to the U.S. dollar. Thus, even if such intermediate goods are not priced in dollars, their yen-equivalent prices tend to decline with the dollar and, thereby, lessen the impact of a falling dollar on the cost of Japanese cars sold in the United States.

Outsourcing in countries whose currencies are linked to the currency of the export market also creates competitive pressures on domestic suppliers of the same intermediate goods. To cope in such an environment, domestic suppliers must themselves have flexible arrangements with their own input suppliers. In many cases, these smaller firms can survive because they have greater ability to recontract their costs than do the larger firms specializing in assembly and distribution. When the suppliers are faced with the reality of an exchange rate change that reduces the competitive price of their outputs, they are able to recontract with their own inputs (typically by lowering wages) to reduce costs sufficiently to remain economically viable.

Shifting Production Among Plants   Multinational firms with worldwide production systems can allocate production among their several plants in line with the changing dollar costs of production, increasing production in a nation whose currency has devalued and decreasing production in a country where there has been a revaluation. Contrary to conventional wisdom, therefore, multinational firms may well be subject to less exchange risk than an exporter, given the MNC's greater ability to adjust its production (and marketing) operations on a global basis, in line with changing relative production costs.

A good example of this flexibility is provided by Westinghouse Electric Corporation of Pittsburgh, Pennsylvania. Westinghouse can quote its customers prices from numerous foreign affiliates: gas turbines from Canada, generators from Spain, circuit breakers and robotics from Britain, and electrical equipment from Brazil. Its sourcing decisions take into account both the effect of currency values and the subsidized export financing available from foreign governments.

The theoretical ability to shift production is more limited in reality, depending on many factors, not the least of which is the power of the local labor unions involved. However, the innovative nature of the typical MNC means a continued generation of new products. The sourcing of those new products among the firm's various plants can certainly be done with an eye to the costs involved.

A strategy of **production shifting** presupposes that the MNC has already created a portfolio of plants worldwide. For example, as part of its global sourcing strategy, Caterpillar now has dual sources, domestic and foreign, for some products. These sources allow Caterpillar to "load" the plant that offers the best economies of production, given exchange rates at any moment. But multiple plants also create manufacturing redundancies and impede cost cutting.

The cost of multiple sourcing is especially great where there are economies of scale that would ordinarily dictate the establishment of only one or two plants to service the global market. But most firms have found that in a world of uncertainty, significant benefits may be derived from production diversification. In fact, having redundant capacity is the equivalent of buying an option to execute volume shifts fairly easily. As in the case of currency options, the value of such a real option increases with the volatility of the exchange rate. Hence, despite the higher unit costs associated with smaller plants and excess capacity, currency risk may provide one more reason for the use of multiple production facilities. Indeed, 63% of foreign exchange managers surveyed cited having locations "to increase flexibility by shifting plant loading when exchange rates changed" as a factor in international siting.[7]

The auto industry illustrates the potential value of maintaining a globally balanced distribution of production facilities in the face of fluctuating exchange rates. For Japanese and Swedish auto manufacturers, which historically located all their factories domestically, it has been feast or famine. When the home currency appreciates, as in the 1970s or the late 1980s and early 1990s, the firms' exports suffer from a lack of cost competitiveness. On the other hand, a real depreciation of the home currency, as in the early 1980s, is a time of high profits.

By contrast, Ford and General Motors, with their worldwide manufacturing facilities, have substantial leeway in reallocating various stages of production among their several plants in line with relative production and transportation costs. For example, Ford can shift production among the United States, Spain, Germany, Great Britain, Brazil, and Mexico.

Plant Location   A firm without foreign facilities that is exporting to a competitive market whose currency has devalued may find that sourcing components abroad is insufficient to maintain unit profitability. Despite its previous hesitancy, the firm may have to locate new plants abroad. For example, the economic response by the Japanese to the strong yen was to build new plants in the United States as opposed to expanding plants in Japan. Similarly, German automakers such as BMW and Mercedes-Benz have built plants in the United States to shield themselves from currency fluctuations.

---

[7] Donald B. Lessard, "Survey on Corporate Responses to Volatile Exchange Rates," MIT Sloan School of Management Working Paper, 1990.

Third-country plant locations are also a viable alternative in many cases, depending especially on the labor intensity of production or the projections for further monetary realignments. Many Japanese firms, for example, have shifted production offshore—to Taiwan, South Korea, Singapore, and other developing nations, as well as to the United States—in order to cope with the high yen. Japanese automakers have been particularly aggressive in making these shifts. Moving production offshore can be a mixed blessing, however. Although it makes companies less vulnerable to a strong yen, it means less of a payoff if the yen declines. For example, when the yen began to weaken in 1995, Japanese manufacturers with foreign production facilities found they could not take full advantage of the yen's fall.

Raising Productivity   Many U.S. companies assaulted by foreign competition made prodigious efforts to improve their productivity—closing inefficient plants, automating heavily, and negotiating wage and benefit cutbacks and work-rule concessions with unions. Many of them also began programs to heighten productivity and improve product quality through employee motivation. These cost cuts stood U.S. firms in good stead as they tried to use the weaker dollar that began in 2002 to gain back market share lost to foreign competitors.

Another way to improve productivity and lower one's cost structure is to revise product offerings. This is the route now being taken by the Japanese. Despite their vaunted super-lean production systems, many Japanese firms, in an attempt to gain market share, have created too much product variety and offered too many options to customers. The result is that parts makers and assembly plants have to accommodate very small and very rare orders too frequently. This variety requires too much design work, too much capital investment for small-volume parts, too many parts inventories, and constant equipment setups and changeovers. By slashing variety to the 20% or so of models and product variations that account for 80% of sales and profits and by reducing unique parts by 30% to 50% for new models, Japanese companies are finding that they can dramatically reduce costs without sacrificing much in the way of market share.

ILLUSTRATION   *Nissan Reverses Course*

In 1993, Nissan renounced a decade-long quest to build cars in ever more sizes, colors, and functions to cater to every conceivable consumer whim. That effort had spun out of control. For the 1993 model lineup alone, Nissan offered 437 different kinds of dashboard meters, 110 types of radiators, 1,200 types of floor carpets, and more than 300 varieties of ashtrays. Its Laurel model alone had 87 variations of steering wheels and 62 varieties of wiring harnesses (which link up electrical components in a car). To assemble these vehicles, Nissan used more than 6,000 different fasteners.

The payoff from this product proliferation was pathetic. Nissan engineers discovered that 70 of the 87 types of steering wheels accounted for just 5% of the Laurel's sales. Overall, 50% of Nissan's model variations contributed only about 5% of total sales.

Nissan ordered its designers to reduce the number of unique parts in its vehicles by 40%. Model variations, which had ballooned to more than 2,200, were rolled back by 50%. The goal of this reformation was to reduce annual production costs by at least ¥200 billion ($2 billion at an exchange rate of ¥100/$ 1). These production cost savings helped Nissan to maintain its profitability as it cut its prices in the United States to remain competitive in the face of a surging yen.

10.6.3 Planning for Exchange Rate Changes

The marketing and production strategies advocated thus far assume knowledge of exchange rate changes. Even if currency changes are unpredictable, however, contingency plans can be made. This planning involves developing several plausible currency scenarios (see Section 11.4), analyzing the effects of each scenario on the firm's competitive position, and deciding on strategies to deal with these possibilities.

When a currency change actually occurs, the firm is able to quickly adjust its marketing and production strategies in line with the plan. Given the substantial costs of gathering and processing information, a firm should focus on scenarios that have a high probability of occurrence and that also would have a strong impact on the firm.

ILLUSTRATION *Kodak Plans for Currency Changes*

Historically, Eastman Kodak focused its exchange risk management efforts on hedging near-term transactions. It now looks at exchange rate movements from a strategic perspective. Kodak's moment of truth came in the early 1980s when the strong dollar enabled overseas rivals such as Fuji Photo Film of Japan to cut prices and make significant inroads into its market share. This episode convinced Kodak that it had been defining its currency risk too narrowly. It appointed a new foreign exchange planning director, David Fiedler, at the end of 1985. According to Mr. Fiedler, "We were finding a lot of things that didn't fit our definition [of exposure] very well, and yet would have a real economic impact on the corporation."[8] To make sure such risks no longer go unrecognized, Mr. Fiedler now spends about 25% of his time briefing Kodak's operating managers on foreign exchange planning, advising them on everything from sourcing alternatives to market pricing. Kodak's new approach figured in a 1988 decision against putting in a factory in Mexico. Kodak decided to locate the plant elsewhere because of its assessment of the peso's relative strength. In the past, currency risk would have been ignored in such project assessments. According to Kodak's chief financial officer, before their reassessment of the company's foreign exchange risk management policy, its financial officers "would do essentially nothing to assess the possible exchange impact until it got to the point of signing contracts for equipment."[9]

The ability to plan for volatile exchange rates has fundamental implications for exchange risk management because there is no longer such a thing as the "natural" or "equilibrium" rate. Rather, there is a sequence of equilibrium rates, each of which has its own implications for corporate strategy. Success in such an environment, where change is the only constant, depends on a company's ability to react to change within a shorter time horizon than ever before. To cope, companies must develop competitive options such as outsourcing, flexible manufacturing systems, a global network of production facilities, and shorter product cycles.

In a volatile world, these investments in flexibility are likely to yield high returns. For example, flexible manufacturing systems permit faster production response times to shifting market demand. Similarly, foreign facilities, even if they are uneconomical at the moment, can pay off by enabling companies to shift production in response to changing exchange rates or other relative cost shocks.

---

[8] Quoted in Christopher J. Chipello, "The Market Watcher," *Wall Street Journal,* September 23, 1988, p. 14.
[9] Quoted in Chipello, "The Market Watcher."

The greatest boost to competitiveness comes from compressing the time it takes to bring new and improved products to market. The edge a company gets from shorter **product cycles** is dramatic: Not only can it charge a premium price for its exclusive products, but it can also incorporate more up-to-date technology in its goods and respond faster to emerging market niches and changes in taste.

With better planning and more competitive options, corporations can now change their strategies substantially before the impact of any currency change can make itself felt. As a result, the adjustment period following a large exchange rate change has been compressed dramatically. The 100% appreciation of the Japanese yen against the dollar from 1985 to 1988, for example, sparked some changes in Japanese corporate strategy that have proven to be long-lasting: increased production in the United States and East Asia to cope with the high yen and to protect their foreign markets from any trade backlash; purchase of more parts overseas to take advantage of lower costs; upscaling to reduce the price sensitivity of their products and broaden their markets; massive cost-reduction programs in their Japanese plants, with a long-term impact on production technology; and an increase in joint ventures between competitors.

ILLUSTRATION   *Toshiba Copes with a Rising Yen by Cutting Costs*

By 1988, Toshiba's cost cutting reduced its cost-to-sales ratio to where it was before the yen began rising. The company shifted production of low-tech products to developing nations and moved domestic production to high-value-added products. At a VCR (videocassette recorder) plant outside of Tokyo, it halved the number of assembly-line workers by minimizing inventories and simplifying operations. Other cost-reducing international activities included production of color picture tubes with Westinghouse in the United States, photocopier production in a joint venture with Rhone-Poulenc in France, assembly of VCRs in Tennessee, production of similar VCRs in Germany, and establishment of a new plant in California for assembling and testing telephones and medical electronics equipment. Overall, Toshiba is estimated to have saved ¥115 billion—¥53 billion by redesigning products, ¥ 47 billion in parts cutbacks and lower raw material costs, and ¥15 billion in greater operating efficiency. Similarly, by 1989, with the dollar around ¥125, Fujitsu Fanuc, a robot maker, had streamlined itself so thoroughly and differentiated its products so effectively that it estimated it could break even with only a fifth of its plant in use and a dollar down to ¥70.

In the early 2000s, Japanese companies once again faced a rising yen (¥107/$ by 2005). And once again they are coping, by restructuring to become more efficient, focusing on higher-end products, and shifting production of lower-end products to China. For example, Ricoh, the Japanese copier company, has cut the cost of its liquid-crystal operation panels from ¥12,000 in 1994 to ¥8,000 in 2004, while making them more sophisticated. Ricoh is also monitoring sales in real time to adjust production volume every week, thereby reducing its stock of copiers that will be outdated when a new version supersedes it; previously, it adjusted production every month. Similar measures by other Japanese companies have ensured they can profit even if the dollar buys less than ¥100.

10.6.4 Financial Management of Exchange Risk

The one attribute that all the strategic marketing and production adjustments have in common is that accomplishing them in a cost-effective manner takes time. The role of financial management in this process is to structure the firm's liabilities in such a way that during the time the strategic operational adjustments are under way, the reduction in asset earnings is matched by a corresponding decrease in the cost of servicing these liabilities.

One possibility is to finance the portion of a firm's assets used to create export profits so that any shortfall in operating cash flows caused by an exchange rate change is offset by a reduction in debt-servicing expenses. For example, a firm that has developed a sizable export market should hold a portion of its liabilities in that country's currency. The portion to be held in the foreign currency depends on the size of the loss in profitability associated with a given currency change. No more-definite recommendations are possible because the currency effects will vary from one company to another.

Volkswagen is a case in point. To hedge its operating exposure, the company should have used dollar financing in proportion to its net dollar cash flow from U.S. sales. This strategy would have cushioned the impact of the DM revaluation that almost brought Volkswagen to its knees. For the longer term, however, it could manage its competitive exposure only by developing new products with lower price elasticities of demand and by establishing production facilities in lower-cost nations. Evidently, both DaimlerChrysler and Porsche have learned Volkswagen's lesson as to the importance of hedging, as shown in "DaimlerChrysler Hedges Its Operating Exposure" and "Porsche Revs Up Its Results."

ILLUSTRATION *DaimlerChrysler Hedges Its Operating Exposure*

In August 2003, DaimlerChrysler AG acknowledged that over half its second-quarter operating profit was generated by foreign-exchange hedging transactions. In July, the automaker had reported quarterly operating profit of €641 million, beating analyst expectations. At the time, the company said that currency trading activities to reduce the effect of the euro's rise against the dollar had had a positive effect but did not provide details. The August admission that €350 million of its operating profit came from currency trades indicated that the company made more money on foreign exchange than it did from selling cars. Analysts said that these hedging gains explained how DaimlerChrysler managed to hold its profit margins despite a brutal price war in North America and the euro's rise against the dollar, yen, and other currencies. Analysts said DaimlerChrysler deserved credit for managing the effects of the dollar's decline but that it was a worrying sign if 50% of your operating profit is coming from currency trading.

MINI-CASE *Porsche Revs Up Its Results*

The strong euro dented the profits of most European automakers in 2004 but Porsche found a way to turbo-charge its profits, despite the fact that Porsche has greater exposure to currency risk than most of its peers. Unlike Mercedes or BMW, both of which have U.S. plants, Porsche makes its cars entirely in Europe but generates 40% to 45% of its sales revenue in the United States. For Porsche, therefore, the inability to cope with a strong euro by switching production from domestic to foreign plants places an extra burden on financial hedging. Porsche's use of hedging explains its profits in the face of a weak dollar. According to the *Wall Street Journal,* "Goldman Sachs, for one, estimates that as much as 75% of the company's pretax profits—or up to €800 million ($1.07 billion) of the €1.1 billion Porsche reported for the fiscal year that ended July 31 [2004]—came from skillfully executing currency options."[10] In fact, Porsche bought put options on the dollar enabling it to sell dollars for euros at a low price for the euro. Although, hedging is

---

[10] Stephen Power, "Porsche Powers Profit With Currency Plays," the *Wall Street Journal,* December 8, 2004, C3.

usually done to smooth out short-term earnings, in Porsche's case, hedging is used strategically on a long-term basis. Specifically, as of 2004, Porsche claims to be fully hedged through July 31,2007 and was looking to extend its protection well beyond that date.[11] Presumably, Porsche is accounting for the length of time it will take to make the necessary strategic adjustments to adapt to the difficult competitive position a strong euro has put it in.

QUESTIONS

1. Why does Porsche face more operating exposure than Mercedes or BMW?

2. Is Porsche really fully hedged through July 31, 2007? Suppose that gains on all its outstanding options were included in reported earnings for its fiscal year ended July 31, 2004.

3. Why would analysts be nervous if upto 75% of Porsche's pretax profit for fiscal year 2004 came from gains on foreign currency options?

The implementation of a hedging policy is likely to be quite difficult in practice, if only because the specific cash-flow effects of a given currency change are hard to predict. Trained personnel are required to implement and monitor an active hedging program. Consequently, hedging should be undertaken only when the effects of anticipated exchange rate changes are expected to be significant.

A highly simplified example can illustrate the application of the financing rule developed previously, namely, that the liability structure of the combined MNC—parent and subsidiaries—should be set up in such a way that any change in the inflow on assets due to a currency change should be matched by a corresponding change in the outflow on the liabilities used to fund those assets. Consider the effect of a local currency (LC) change on the subsidiary depicted in Exhibit 10.12. In the absence of any exchange rate changes, the subsidiary is forecast to have an operating profit of $800,000. If a predicted 20% devaluation of the local currency from LC 1 = $0.25 to LC 1 = $0.20 occurs, the subsidiary's LC profitability is expected to rise to LC 3.85 million from LC 3.2 million because of price increases. However, this LC profit rise still entails a loss of $30,000, despite a reduction in the dollar cost of production.

Suppose the subsidiary requires assets equaling LC 20 million, or $5 million at the current exchange rate. It can finance these assets by borrowing dollars at 8% and converting them into their local currency equivalent, or it can use LC funds at 10%. How can the parent structure its subsidiary's financing in such a way that a 20% devaluation will reduce the cost of servicing the subsidiary's liabilities by $30,000 and thus balance operating losses with a decrease in cash outflows?

Actually, a simple procedure is readily available. If S is the dollar outflow on local debt service, then it is necessary that $0.2S$, the dollar gain on devaluation, equal $30,000, the operating loss on devaluation. Hence, $S = \$150,000$, or LC 600,000 at the current exchange rate. At a local currency interest rate of 10%, that debt-service amount corresponds to a debt of LC 6 million. The remaining LC 14 million can be provided by borrowing $3.5 million. Exhibit 10.13 illustrates the offsetting cash effects associated with such a financial structure.

This example would certainly become more complex if the effects of taxes, depreciation, and working capital were included. Although the execution becomes more difficult, a rough equivalence between operating losses (gains) and debt-service gains (losses)

---

[11] *Op cit.*

	Units (Hundred Thousands)	Unit Price (LC)	Total	
LC 1 = $0.25				
Domestic sales	4	20	8,000,000	
Export sales	4	20	8,000,000	
Total revenue				16,000,000
Local labor (h)	8	10	8,000,000	
Local material	8	3	2,400,000	
Imported material	6	4	2,400,000	
Total expenditures				12,800,000
Net cash flow from operations in LC			LC	3,200,000
Net cash flow from operations in U.S.$				$800,000
LC 1= $0.20				
Domestic sales	3	24	7,200,000	
Export sales	5	24	12,000,000	
Total revenue				19,200,000
Local labor (h)	8	12	9,600,000	
Local material	10	3.5	3,500,000	
Imported material	4.5	5	2,250,000	
Total expenditures				15,350,000
Net cash flow from operations in LC			LC	3,850,000
Net cash flow from operations in U.S.$				$770,000

EXHIBIT 10.12 • STATEMENT OF PROJECTED CASH FLOW

can still be achieved as long as all cash flows are accounted for. The inclusion of other foreign operations just requires the aggregation of the cash-flow effects over all affiliates because the MNC's total exchange risk is based on the sum of Hie changes of the profit contributions of each individual subsidiary. As mentioned earlier, this approach concentrates exclusively on risk reduction rather than on cost reduction. Where financial market imperfections are significant, a firm might consider exposing itself to more exchange risk in order to lower its expected financing costs.

	LC 1 = $0.25		LC 1 = $0.20	
Year	Local Currency	Dollars	Local Currency	Dollars
Operating cash flows	LC 3,200,000	$800,000	LC $3,850,000	$770,000
Debt service requirements:				
Local currency debt	600,000	150,000	600,000	120,000
Dollar debt	1,120,000	280,000	1,400,000	280,000
Total debt service outflow	1,720,000	430,000	2,000,000	400,000
Net cash flow	LC 1,480,000	$370,000	LC 1,850,000	$370,000

EXHIBIT 10.13 • EFFECT OF FINANCIAL STRUCTURE ON NET CASH FLOW

An important contributing factor to the magnitude of the collapse of the South Korean won was the currency mismatch faced by Korean companies and banks. Specifically, Korean banks lent huge amounts of won to the Korean *chaebol,* or conglomerates. The banks, in turn, financed their loans by borrowing dollars, yen, and other foreign currencies. The chaebol also borrowed large amounts of foreign currencies and invested the proceeds in giant industrial projects both at home and abroad. Considering how highly leveraged the chaebol were already, with debt-to-equity ratios on the order of 10:1, everything had to go right in order for them to be able to service their debts. When the won lost 40% of its value against the dollar during 1997, the chaebol had difficulty servicing their debts and many of them became insolvent. To the extent the Korean banks continued to receive won interest and debt repayments from the chaebol, devaluation of the won meant that the banks' won cash flows were insufficient to service their foreign debts. Similarly, although the chaebol's overseas projects were expected to generate foreign exchange to service their dollar debts, these projects turned out to be ill-conceived money losers. With both banks and chaebol scrambling to come up with dollars to service their foreign debts, the won was put under additional pressure and fell further, exacerbating the problems faced by Korean borrowers. In the last three months of 1997, eight out of the 30 largest chaebol went bankrupt.

In August 2003, Empresa Brasileira de Aeronautica SA (Embraer) of Brazil, the world's fourth-largest aircraft maker, reported that its net income had fallen by 87% for the second quarter, despite recent multibillion orders from JetBlue and US Airways, due to Brazil's stronger currency and foreign-exchange hedging losses. Embraer President Mauricio Botelho said that the company was "strongly hit by two factors beyond our control." He pointed out that the Brazilian *real* had appreciated by about 18% against the dollar during the quarter and that this had adversely affected Embraer. Embraer said that the appreciation raised its cost of goods sold, as well as its operating costs such as research and development and SG&A expenses. At the same time, nearly all of Embraer's revenue comes from exports. Its primary competitor in the regional jet market, Embraer's specialty, is Canada's Bombardier; to a lesser extent, Boeing and Airbus are also competitors. However, the biggest impact of the rising *real* came from $85 million in losses on currency swaps that Embraer used to convert its dollar-denominated liabilities into reais as a hedge. Embraer also lost money when Brazil's main export-credit agency, BNDES, delayed paying for $397 million in outstanding receivables. By the time BNDES made the payment, the *real*'s strength meant that Embraer received fewer reais. In addition, BNDES had still not paid for $211 million of receivables for jets already delivered. Payments in reais are made at the spot rate in fact at the time of the payment.

QUESTIONS

1. What factors affect Embraer's operating exposure? Why did the *real*'s appreciation reduce Embraer's operatmg profits?

2. Did Embraer decrease or increase its currency risk by hedging its dollar liabilities? Explain.

3. How can Embraer use financial hedging to reduce its currency risk?

4. Suppose that Embraer's $608 million in dollar receivables mentioned above were outstanding at the beginning of the second quarter and that payment for $397 million was not received until the end of the quarter. The remaining $211 million was still outstanding at the end of the quarter. With an 18% *real* appreciation during the quarter, how much of a dollar loss would Embraer take on these receivables? In performing this calculation, consider that Embraer must first translate its dollar receivables into reais and then convert any loss measured in reais back into dollars.

ILLUSTRATION   *Avon Is Calling in Asia*

The currency turmoil in Asia in 1997 was unexpected, but Avon Products was prepared to deal with it. An examination of what Avon did before the crisis and how it responded afterward illustrates many of the principles of managing operating exposure. It also provides insights into the role of financial officers as key members of strategic management teams.

Avon has a long history of international operations. As a general rule, Avon tries to hedge its currency risk by buying almost all its raw materials and making nearly all its products in the markets in which they are sold. For example, Avon Asia-Pacific has factories that make cosmetics in its largest markets—China, Indonesia, the Philippines, and Japan—and contracts out production in six other Asian countries. It further hedged its currency risk by financing its local operations with local currency loans. Altogether, the 10 Asian countries in which Avon operated accounted for $751 million of its $4.8 billion in revenue in 1996.

When the crisis began in Thailand in July 1997, Avon's executives did not anticipate that Thailand's problems would spread but as a precaution decided to further reduce currency risk by having the Asian units remit earnings weekly instead of monthly. By late August, however, the currency markets got nervous after the remarks of Malaysia's Prime Minister Mahathir Mohamad, who complained that Asia's economic crisis was provoked by an international cabal of Jewish financiers intent on derailing the region's growth. The head of Avon's Asia-Pacific region, Jose Ferriera, Jr., also considered the possibility that other Asian countries would have to allow their currencies to depreciate to maintain their export competitiveness. In response, Avon decided to sell about $50 million worth of five Asian currencies forward against the dollar for periods of up to 15 months.

Having done what it could financially, Avon then turned to its operating strategy. Anticipating tough times ahead, Avon Asia-Pacific decided to redirect its marketing budget to hire more salespeople in Asia to bring in more customers rather than offering incentives to the existing sales force to get their current, cash-strapped customers to spend more money. Mr. Ferriera also urged his country managers to step up their purchase of local materials wherever possible and not allow local vendors to pass on all of their cost increases. At the same time, Avon began planning to compete more aggressively against disadvantaged competitors who have to import their products and raw materials. Finally, Avon began to analyze the incremental profits it could realize by using its Asian factories to supply more of the noncosmetic products sold in the United States. Avon Asia-Pacific was helped by a team of Latin American executives who traveled to Asia to share their experiences of how they had managed to cope in similar circumstances of currency turmoil in their countries. For example, during the Mexican crisis of 1994–1995, prices were raised slowly on price-sensitive brands aimed at low- and middle-income customers. Avon Mexico raised prices on premium brands much faster, since those brands were less price sensitive and competed with imports whose prices had doubled with the peso devaluation.

In all of these deliberations and decisions, Avon Treasurer Dennis Ling was a full and active participant. For example, he helped the head of Avon's jewelry business renegotiate the terms of its contract with a Korean company that supplies jewelry for sale in the United States. The result was a substantial price discount based on the won's steep decline against the dollar. According to Mr. Ling, "Part of my job is to help our managers of operations understand and take advantage of the impact of currencies on their business."[12]

MINI-CASE *Laker Airways Crashes and Burns*

The crash of Sir Freddie Laker's Skytrain had little to do with the failure of its navigational equipment or its landing gear; indeed, it can largely be attributed to misguided management decisions. Laker's management erred in selecting the financing mode for the acquisition of the aircraft fleet that would accommodate the booming transatlantic business spearheaded by Sir Freddie's sound concept of a "no-frill, low-fare, stand-by" air travel package.

In 1981, Laker was a highly leveraged firm with a debt of more than $400 million. The debt resulted from the financing provided by the U.S. Eximbank and the U.S. aircraft manufacturer McDonnell Douglas. As most major airlines do, Laker Airways incurred three major categories of cost: (1) fuel, typically paid for in U.S. dollars (even though the United Kingdom is more than self-sufficient in oil); (2) operating costs incurred in sterling (administrative expenses and salaries), but with a nonnegligible dollar cost component (advertising and booking in the United States); and (3) financing costs from the purchase of U.S.-made aircraft, denominated in dollars. Revenues accruing from the sale of transatlantic airfare were about evenly divided between sterling and dollars. The dollar fares, however, were based on the assumption of a rate of $2.25 to the pound. The imbalance in the currency denomination of cash flows, with dollar-denominated cash outflows far exceeding dollar-denominated cash inflows, left Laker vulnerable to a sterling depreciation below the budgeted exchange rate of £1 = $2.25. Indeed, the dramatic plunge of the exchange rate to £1 = $1.60 over the 1981–1982 period brought Laker Airways to default.

QUESTIONS

1. What were the key components of Laker Airways' operating exposure?
2. What options did it have to hedge its operating exposure?
3. Could Laker have hedged its "natural" dollar liability exposure?
4. Should Laker have financed its purchase of DC 10 aircraft by borrowing sterling from a British bank rather than using the dollar-denominated financing supplied by McDonnell Douglas and the Eximbank? Consider the fact that Eximbank, a U.S. government agency, subsidized this financing in order to promote U.S. exports.

---

[12] Fred R. Bleakky, "How U.S. Firm Copes with Asian Crisis," *Wall Street Journal,* December 26, 1997, p. A2.

10.7 SUMMARY AND CONCLUSIONS

In this chapter, we examined the concept of exposure to exchange rate changes from the perspective of the economist. We saw that the accounting profession's focus on the balance-sheet impact of currency changes has led accountants to ignore the more important effect that these changes may cause on future cash flows. We also saw that to measure exposure properly, we must focus on inflation-adjusted, or real, exchange rates instead of on nominal, or actual, exchange rates. Therefore, economic exposure has been defined as the extent to which the value of a firm is affected by currency fluctuations, inclusive of price-level changes. Thus, any accounting measure that focuses on the firm's past activities and decisions, as reflected in its current balance-sheet accounts, is likely to be misleading.

Although exchange risk is conceptually easy to identify, it is difficult in practice to determine what the actual economic impact of a currency change will be. For a given firm, this impact depends on a great number of variables including the location of its major markets and competitors, supply and demand elasticities, substitutability of inputs, and offsetting inflation.

Finally, we concluded that since currency risk affects all facets of a company's operations, it should not be the concern of financial managers alone. Operating managers, in particular, should develop marketing and production initiatives that help to ensure profitability in the long run. They should also devise anticipatory or proactive, rather than reactive, strategic alternatives to gain competitive leverage internationally.

The key to effective exposure management is to integrate currency considerations into the general management process. One approach that many MNCs use to develop the necessary coordination among executives responsible for different aspects of exchange risk management is to establish a committee for managing foreign currency exposure. Besides financial executives, such committees should, and often do, include the senior officers of the company such as the vice president-international, top marketing and production executives, the director of corporate planning, and the chief executive officer. This arrangement is desirable because top executives are exposed to the problems of exchange risk management, so they can incorporate currency expectations into their own decisions.

In this kind of integrated exchange risk program, the role of the financial executive is fourfold: (1) to provide local operating management with forecasts of inflation and exchange rates, (2) to identify and highlight the risks of competitive exposure, (3) to structure evaluation criteria so that operating managers are not rewarded or penalized for the effects of unanticipated currency changes, and (4) to estimate and hedge whatever operating exposure remains after the appropriate marketing and production strategies have been put in place.

QUESTIONS

1. a. Define exposure, differentiating between accounting and economic exposure. What role does inflation play?

   b. Describe at least three circumstances under which economic exposure is likely to exist.

   c. Of what relevance are the international Fisher effect and purchasing power parity to your answers to Parts (a) and (b)?

   d. What is exchange risk, as distinct from exposure?

   e. Under what circumstances might multinational firms be less subject to exchange risk than purely domestic firms in the same industry?

2. The sharp decline of the U.S. dollar between 1985 and 1995 significantly improved the profitability of U.S. firms both at home and abroad.

   a. In what sense was this profit improvement a false prosperity?

   b. How would you incorporate the decline in the dollar in evaluating management performance? In making investment decisions?

   c. Comment on the following statement: "The sharp appreciation of the U.S. dollar during the early 1980s might have been the best thing that ever happened to American industry."

3. What marketing and production techniques can firms initiate to cope with exchange risk?

4. What is the role of finance in protecting against exchange risk?

5. E & J Gallo is the largest vintner in the United States. It gets its grapes in California (some of which it grows itself) and sells its wines throughout the United States. Does Gallo face currency risk? Why and how?

6. DaimlerChrysler's Chrysler division exports vans from the United States to Europe in competition with the Japanese. Similarly, Compaq exports computers to Europe. However, all of Compaq's biggest competitors are American companies—IBM, Hewlett-Packard, and Tandem. Assuming all else is equal, which of these companies—Chrysler or Compaq–is likely to benefit more from a weak dollar? Explain.

7. Suppose, the Singapore dollar rose by 9% in real terms against the U.S. dollar. What would be the likely impact of the strong Singapore dollar on U.S. electronics manufacturers using Singapore as an export platform? Consider the following: on average, materials and components—85% of which are purchased abroad—account for about 60% of product costs; labor accounts for an additional 15%; and other operating costs account for the remaining 25%.

8. Di Giorgio International, a subsidiary of California-based Di Giorgio Corporation, processes fruit juices and packages condiments in Turnhout, Belgium. It buys Brazilian orange concentrate in dollars, German apples in marks, Italian peaches in lire, and cartons in Dutch guilders. At the same time, it exports 85% of its production. Assess Di Giorgio International's currency risk and determine how it can structure its financing to reduce this risk.

9. A U.S. company needs to borrow $ 100 million for a period of 7 years. It can issue dollar debt at 7% or yen debt at 3%.

   a. Suppose the company is a multinational firm with sales in the United States and inputs purchased in Japan. How should this affect its financing choice?

   b. Suppose the company is a multinational firm with sales in Japan and inputs that are determined primarily in dollars. How should this affect its financing choice?

10. Huaneng Power International is a large Chinese company that runs coal-fired power plants in five provinces and in Shanghai. It has a close to $1.2 billion in U.S. dollar debt whose proceeds it has used to purchase equipment abroad.

   a. What currency risks does Huaneng face?

   b. Do its lenders face any currency risks? Explain.

PROBLEMS

1. Hilton International is considering investing in a new Swiss hotel. The required initial investment is $1.5 million (or SFr 1.875 million at the current exchange rate of $0.80 = SFr 1). Profits for the first 10 years will be reinvested, at which time Hilton will sell out to its partner. Based on projected earnings, Hilton's share of this hotel will be worth SFr 3.88 million in 10 years.

   a. What factors are relevant in evaluating this investment?

   b. How will fluctuations in the value of the Swiss franc affect this investment?

   c. How would you forecast the $:SFr exchange rate 10 years ahead?

2. A proposed foreign investment involves a plant with its entire output of 1 million units per annum to be exported. With a selling price of $10 per unit, the yearly revenue from this investment equals $10 million. At the present rate of exchange, dollar costs of local production equal $6 per unit. A 10% devaluation is expected to lower unit costs by $0.30, while a 15% devaluation will reduce these costs by an additional $0.15. Suppose a devaluation of either 10% or 15% is likely, with respective probabilities of 0.4 and 0.2 (the probability of no currency change is 0.4). Depreciation at the current exchange rate equals $1 million annually, and the local tax rate is 40%.

   a. What will annual dollar cash flows be if no devaluation occurs?

   b. Given the currency scenario described above, what is the expected value of annual after-tax dollar cash flows assuming no repatriation of profits to the United States?

3. Mucho Macho is the leading beer in Patagonia, with a 65% share of the market. Because of trade barriers, it faces essentially no import competition. Exports account for less than 2% of sales. Although some of its raw material is bought overseas, the large majority of the value added is provided by locally supplied goods and services. Over the past 5 years, Patagonian prices have risen by 300%, and U.S. prices have risen by about 10%. During this time period, the value of the Patagonian peso has dropped from P 1 = $1.00 to P 1 = $0.50.

   a. What has happened to the real value of the peso over the past 5 years? Has it gone up or down? A little or a lot?

   b. What has the high inflation over the past 5 years likely done to Mucho Macho's peso profits? Has it moved profits up or down? A lot or a little? Explain.

   c. Based on your answer to Part (a) what has been the likely effect of the change in the peso's real value on Mucho Macho's peso profits converted into dollars? Have dollar-equivalent profits gone up or down? A lot or a little? Explain.

d. Mucho Macho has applied for a dollar loan to finance its expansion. Were you to look solely at its past financial statements in judging its creditworthiness, what would be your likely response to Mucho Macho's dollar loan request?

e. What foreign exchange risk would such a dollar loan face? Explain.

4. In 1990, GE acquired Tungsram Ltd., a Hungarian lightbulb manufacturer. Hungary's inflation rate was 28% in 1990 and 35% in 1991, while the forint (Hungary's currency) was devalued by 5% and 15%, respectively, during those years. Corresponding inflation for the United States was 6.1% in 1990 and 3.1% in 1991.

a. What happened to GE's Hungarian operation's competitiveness during 1990 and 1991? Explain.

b. In early 1992, GE announced that it would cut back its capital investment in Tungsram. What might have been the purpose of GE's publicly announced cutback?

5. In 1985, Japan Airlines (JAL) bought $3 billion of foreign exchange contracts at ¥180/$1 over 11 years to hedge its purchases of U.S. aircraft. By 1994, with the yen at about ¥100/$1, JAL had incurred over $1 billion in cumulative foreign exchange losses on that deal.

a. What was the likely economic rationale behind JAL's hedges?

b. Did JAL's forward contracts constitute an economic hedge? That is, is it likely that JAL's losses on its forward contracts were offset by currency gains on its operations?

6. Nissan produces a car that sells in Japan for ¥1.8 million. On September 1, the beginning of the model year, the exchange rate is ¥150:$1. Consequently, Nissan sets the U.S. sticker price at $12,000. By October 1, the exchange rate has dropped to ¥125:$1. Nissan is upset because it now receives only $12,000 × 125 = ¥1.5 million per U.S. sale.

a. What scenarios are consistent with the U.S. dollar's depreciation?

b. What alternatives are open to Nissan to improve its situation?

c. How should Nissan respond to this situation?

d. Suppose that on November 1, the U.S. Federal Reserve intervenes to rescue the dollar, and the exchange rate adjusts to ¥220:$1 by the following July. What problems and/or opportunities does this situation present for Nissan and for General Motors?

7. Chemex, a U.S. maker of specialty chemicals, exports 40% of its $600 million in annual sales: 5% goes to Canada and 7% each to Japan, Britain, Germany, France, and Italy. It incurs all its costs in U.S. dollars, while most of its export sales are priced in the local currency.

a. How is Chemex affected by exchange rate changes?

b. Distinguish between Chemex's transaction exposure and its operating exposure.

c. How can Chemex protect itself against transaction exposure?

d. What financial, marketing, and production techniques can Chemex use to protect itself against operating exposure?

e. Can Chemex eliminate its operating exposure by hedging its position every time it makes a foreign sale or by pricing all foreign sales in dollars? Why or why not?

8. During 1993, the Japanese yen appreciated by 11% against the dollar. In response to the lower cost of the main imported ingredients—beef, cheese, potatoes, and wheat for burger buns—McDonald's Japanese affiliate reduced the price on certain set menus. For example, a cheeseburger, soda, and a small order of french fries were marked down to ¥ 410 from ¥530. Suppose the higher yen lowered the cost of ingredients for this meal by ¥30.

a. How much of a volume increase is necessary to justify the price cut from ¥530 to ¥ 410? Assume that the previous profit margin (contribution to overhead) for this meal was ¥220. What is the implied price elasticity of demand associated with this necessary rise in demand?

b. Suppose sales volume of this meal rises by 60%. What will be the percentage change in McDonald's dollar profit from this meal?

c. What other reasons might McDonald's have had for cutting price besides raising its profits?

9. In 1990, a Japanese investor paid $100 million for an office building in downtown Los Angeles. At the time, the exchange rate was ¥145/$. When the investor went to sell the building 5 years later, in early 1995, the exchange rate was ¥85/$ and the building's value had collapsed to $50 million.

a. What exchange risk did the Japanese investor face at the time of his purchase?

b. How could the investor have hedged his risk?

c. Suppose the investor financed the building with a 10% down payment in yen and a 90% dollar loan accumulating interest at the rate of 8% per annum. Since this is a zero-coupon loan, the interest on it (along with the principal) is not due and payable until the building is sold. How much has the investor lost in yen terms? In dollar terms?

d. Suppose the investor financed the building with a 10% down payment in yen and a 90% yen loan accumulating interest at the rate of 3% per annum.

Since this is a zero-coupon loan, the interest on it (along with the principal) is not due and payable until the building is sold. How much has the investor lost in yen terms? In dollar terms?

10. Over the past year, China has experienced an inflation rate of about 22%, in contrast to U.S. inflation of about 3%. At the same time, the exchange rate has gone from Y8.7/U.S.$l to Y8.3/U.S.$l.

a. What has happened to the real value of the yuan over the past year? Has it gone up or down? A little or a lot?

b. What are the likely effects of the change in the yuan's real value on the dollar profits of a multinational company like Procter & Gamble that sells almost exclusively in the local market? What can it do to cope with these effects?

c. What are the likely effects of the change in the yuan's real value on the dollar profits of a textile manufacturer that exports most of its output to the United States? What can it do to cope with these effects?

BIBLIOGRAPHY

Adler, M. and B. Dumas, "Exposure to Currency Risk: Definition and Measurement." *Financial Management*, Summer 1984, pp. 41–50.

Ankrom, R. K. "Top Level Approach to the Foreign Exchange Problem," *Harvard Business Review*, July–August 1974, pp. 79–90.

Cornell, B. and A. C. Shapiro, "Managing Foreign Exchange Risks," *Midland Corporate Finance Journal*, Fall 1983, pp. 16–31.

Eaker, M. R. "The Numeraire Problem and Foreign Exchange Risk," *Journal of Finance*, May 1981, pp. 419–426.

Garner, C. K. and A. C. Shapiro, "A Practical Method of Assessing Foreign Exchange Risk," *Midland Corporate Finance Journal*, Fall 1984, pp. 6–17.

Giddy, I. H. "Exchange Risk: Whose View?" *Financial Management*, Summer 1977, pp. 23–33.

Lessard, D. R. and J. B. Lightstone, "Volatile Exchange Rates Can Put Operations at Risk," *Harvard Business Review*, July–August 1986, pp. 107–114.

Shapiro, A. C. "Exchange Rate Changes, Inflation, and the Value of the Multinational Corporation," *Journal of Finance*, May 1975, pp. 485–502.

— and T. S. Robertson, "Managing Foreign Exchange Risks: The Role of Marketing Strategy," Working Paper, The Wharton School, University of Pennsylvania, 1976.

INTERNET RESOURCES

www.reportgallery.com Web site that contains links to annual reports of over 2,200 companies, many of which are multinationals.

http://online.wsi.com/public/us Website of the *Wall Street Journal*, prominent business newspaper in the U.S. Contains domestic and international business news and exchange rates.

INTERNET EXERCISES

Review the annual reports of three MNCs found at www.reportgallery.com.

1. Is it obvious from their annual reports whether these companies are hedging their economic, transaction, or translation exposure?

2. Which currencies have these companies borrowed in besides the U.S. dollar? Do these foreign currency borrowings offset any obvious economic exposures they have in those currencies (e.g., because they have a subsidiary located in that country)?

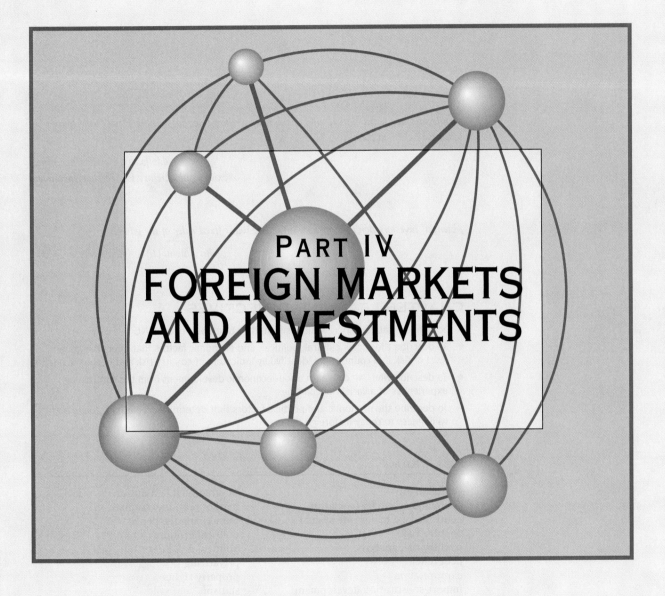

PART IV
FOREIGN MARKETS AND INVESTMENTS

COUNTRY RISK ANALYSIS

People say they want clarification of the rules of the game, but I think it isn't very clear what isn't clear to them.

Adolfo Hegewisch Fernandez,
Mexico's Subsecretary for Foreign Investment

Potential investors don't want flexibility, they want fixed rules of the game.

John Gavin, U.S. Ambassador to Mexico

CHAPTER LEARNING OBJECTIVES

- To define what country risk means from the standpoint of an MNC
- To describe the social, cultural, political, and economic factors that affect the general level of risk in a country and identify key indicators of country risk and economic health
- To describe what we can learn about economic development from the contrasting experiences of a variety of countries
- To describe the economic and political factors that determine a country's ability and willingness to repay its foreign debts

KEY TERMS

capital flight	international banking crisis of 1982
command economy (socialism)	market economy (capitalism)
controlled exchange rate system	monetizing the deficit
country risk	political economy
country risk analysis	political risk
debt relief	privatizing
expropriation	property rights
import-substitution development	statism
strategy	terms-of-trade risk

Multinational firms must constantly assess the business environments of the countries they are already operating in as well as the ones they are considering investing in. Similarly, private and public investors alike are interested in determining which countries offer the best prospects for sound investments. This is the realm of **country risk analysis**, the assessment of the potential risks and rewards associated with making investments and doing business in a country. Ultimately, we are interested in whether sensible economic policies are likely to be pursued because countries adopting such policies will generally have good business environments in which enterprise can flourish. However, because political considerations often lead countries to pursue economic policies that are detrimental to business and to their own economic health, the focus of country risk analysis cannot be exclusively economic in nature. By necessity, it must also study the political factors that give rise to particular economic policies. This is the subject matter of **political economy**—the interaction of politics and economics. Such interactions occur on a continuous basis and affect not just monetary and fiscal (tax and spending) policies but also a host of other policies that affect the business environment, such as currency or trade controls, changes in labor laws, regulatory restrictions, and requirements for additional local production.

By extension, the international economic environment is heavily dependent on the policies that individual nations pursue. Given the close linkage between a country's economic policies and the degree of exchange risk, inflation risk, and interest rate risk that multinational companies and investors face, it is vital in studying and attempting to forecast those risks to understand their causes. Simply put, no one can intelligently assess a country's risk profile without comprehending its economic and political policies and how those policies are likely to affect the country's prospects for economic growth. Similarly, attempts to forecast exchange rates, inflation rates, or interest rates are helped immensely by a deeper understanding of how those economic parameters are affected by national policies.

The purpose of this chapter is to provide a framework that can facilitate a formal assessment of **country risk** and its implications for corporate decision making. Both international banks and nonbank multinationals analyze country risk, but from different perspectives. Nonbank MNCs analyze country risk in order to determine the investment climate in various countries, whereas banks are interested in the country's ability to service its foreign debts. Country risk assessments may be used in investment analyses to screen out countries that are excessively risky or to monitor countries in which the firm is currently doing business to determine whether new policies are called for. Banks analyze country risk to determine which countries to lend to, the currencies in which to denominate their loans, and the interest rates to demand on these loans.

The chapter begins with a discussion of political risk and then moves to an analysis of the economic and political factors underlying country risk. The third section focuses on country risk from the perspective of an international bank.

11.1 MEASURING POLITICAL RISK

Although **expropriation**[1] is the most obvious and extreme form of **political risk**, there are other significant political risks, including currency or trade controls, changes in tax or labor laws, regulatory restrictions, and requirements for additional local production. The common denominator of such risks is not hard to identify: government intervention into the workings of the economy that affects, for good or ill, the value of the firm. Although

---

[1] The terms *expropriation* and *nationalization* are used interchangeably in this book and refer specifically to the takeover of foreign property, with or without compensation.

the consequences usually are adverse, changes in the political environment can provide opportunities as well. The imposition of quotas on autos from Japan, for example, was undoubtedly beneficial to U.S. automobile manufacturers.

ILLUSTRATION   *Overseas Risks Faced by Convergys*

The following discussion of the types of risks that multinational corporations are subject to is contained in the 2006 annual report of Convergys Corporation, an Ohio-based company that provides services globally in customer care, billing, and human resources.

Expansion of our existing international operations and entry into additional countries will require management attention and financial resources. In addition, there are cartain risks inherent in conducting business internationally including: exposure to currency fluctuations, longer payment cycles, greater difficulties in complying with a variety of foreign laws, changes in legal or regulatory requirements, difficulties in staffing and managing foreign operations, political instability, civil disturbances, terrorist attacks and potentially adverse tax consequences. To the extent that we are adversely affected by these risks, our business could be adversely affected and our revenues and/or earnings could be reduced.

Despite the near-universal recognition among multinational corporations, political scientists, and economists of the existence of political risk, no unanimity has yet been reached about what constitutes that risk and how to measure it. The two basic approaches to viewing political risk are from a country-specific and a firm-specific perspective. The first perspective depends on *country risk analysis*, whereas the second depends on a more micro approach. This chapter focuses on macro indicators. Chapter 14 will discuss political risk from the perspective of an individual firm. Appendix 11A in this chapter provides details on managing political risk.

A number of commercial and academic political risk forecasting models are available today. Some prominent ones include the Business Environment Risk Intelligence (BERI), Political Risk Services (PRS), Control Risks' Country Risk Forecasts, Deutsche Bank Eurasia Group Stability Index as well as ratings provided by Economist Intelligence Unit (EIU), *Euromoney*, *Institutional Investor*, Standard & Poor's Rating Group, and Moody's Investors Services. These models normally supply country risk indices that attempt to quantify the level of political risk in each nation. Most of these indices rely on some measure(s) of the stability of the local political regime.

11.1.1 Political Stability

Measures of political stability may include the frequency of changes of government, the level of violence in the country (e.g. violent deaths per 100,000 population), the number of armed insurrections, the extent of conflicts with other states, and so on. The basic function of these stability indicators is to determine how long the current regime will be in power and whether that regime also will be willing and able to enforce its foreign investment guarantees. For example, the Deutsche Bank Eurasia Group Stability Index measures risk according to long-term conditions that affect stability (structural scores) and temporal assessment on impacts of policies, events and developments each month.[2] Most companies believe that greater political stability means a safer investment environment.

---

[2] Ian Bremmer, "Managing Risk in an Unstable World," *Harvard Business Review, June, 2005*, pp. 51–60.

A basic problem in many developing countries is that the local actors have all the external trappings of genuine nation-states—United Nations—endorsed borders, armies, foreign ministries, flags, currencies, national airlines—but they are nothing of the kind. They lack social cohesion, political legitimacy, and the institutional infrastructures necessary for economic growth.

ILLUSTRATION   *Threats to the Nation-State*

From Canada to the former Czechoslovakia, from India to Ireland, and from South Africa to the former Soviet Union, political movements centered around ethnicity, national identity, and religion are reemerging to contest some of the most fundamental premises of the modern nation-state. In the process, they are reintroducing ancient sources of conflict so deeply submerged by the Cold War that they seemed almost to have vanished from history's equation.

The implications of this resurgence of national, ethnic, and religious passions are profound.

- A host of modern nation, states, from Afghanistan to Canada to Lebanon to Indonesia and Iraq, are beginning to crumble, while others such as Yugoslavia, Czechoslovakia, and Somalia have already disintegrated, because the concept of the *melting pot*, the idea that diverse and even historically hostile peoples could readily be assimilated under larger political umbrellas in the name of modernization and progress, has failed them. Even in the strongest nations, including the United States, the task of such assimilation has proved difficult and the prognosis is for even greater tension in the years ahead.

- After 70 years on the road to nowhere, the Soviet Union finally arrived in 1991. Now, turmoil in the states making up the former Soviet Union and parts of China threaten to blow apart the last remnants of an imperial age that began more than 500 years ago. The turbulent dismantling of 19th-century European empires after World War II may be matched by new waves of disintegration within the former Soviet and Chinese Communist empires, with incalculable consequences for the rest of the world. Stretching from the Gulf of Finland to the mountains of Tibet and beyond, the sheer scale of the potential instability would tax the world's capacity to respond. Ethnic unrest could spill into neighboring countries, old border disputes could reignite, and, if the central governments tried to impose order with force, civil wars could erupt within two of the world's largest nuclear powers.

- Around the world, fundamentalist religious movements have entered the political arena in a direct challenge to one of the basic principles of the modern age: that governments and other civic institutions should be predominantly secular and religion confined to the private lives of individuals and groups. Since the end of the Middle Ages, when religion dominated not just government but every aspect of society, the pervasive trend in the past 500 years has been to separate church and state. Now, in many parts of the world, powerful movements— reacting against the secular quality of modern public culture and the tendency of traditional values to be swept aside in periods of rapid change—are insisting on a return to God-centered government. One consequence of this trend is to make dealings between states and groups more volatile. As the United States learned with the terrorist attacks on September 11, the war against the Taliban and al-Qaeda terror network in Afghanistan, Iraq, and elsewhere, the Arab–Israeli conflict, the Iranian revolution, and the Persian Gulf war, disputes are far harder to manage when governments or groups root their positions in religious principle.

Paradoxically, at the same time that many states and societies are becoming more fragmented over religion, ethnicity, and national culture, their people nourish hopes of achieving economic progress by allying themselves to one or another of the new trade blocs—Europe, North America, Pacific Rim—now taking shape. Yet in many cases such dreams will not materialize. Civil strife and dogmatic politics hold little allure for foreign investors; bankers lend money to people whose first priority is money, not religion or ethnic identity. The challenge for business is to create profitable opportunities in a world that is simultaneously globalizing and localizing.

11.1.2 Economic Factors

Other frequently used indicators of political risk include economic factors such as inflation, balance-of-payments deficits or surpluses, and the per capita GDP growth rate. The intention behind these measures is to determine whether the economy is in good shape or requires a quick fix, such as expropriation to increase government revenues or currency inconvertibility to improve the balance of payments. In general, the better a country's economic outlook, the less likely it is to face political and social turmoil that will inevitably harm foreign companies.

11.1.3 Subjective Factors

More subjective measures of political risk are based on a general perception of the country's attitude toward private enterprise: whether private enterprise is considered a necessary evil to be eliminated as soon as possible or whether it is actively welcomed. The attitude toward multinationals is particularly relevant and may differ from the feeling regarding local private ownership. Consider, for example, the former Soviet Union and other Eastern European countries that actively sought products, technology, and even joint ventures with Western firms while refusing to tolerate (until recently) domestic free enterprise. In general, most countries probably view foreign direct investment (FDI) in terms of a cost/benefit trade-off and are not either for or against it in principle.

An index that tries to incorporate all these economic, social, and political factors into an overall measure of the business climate, including the political environment, is the Profit Opportunity Recommendation (POR) rating as developed by Business Environment Risk Intelligence (BERI), shown in Exhibit 11.1. The scores of countries listed on the POR scale are based on an aggregation of the subjective assessments of a panel of experts.

Political Risk and Uncertain Property Rights Models such as POR are useful insofar as they provide an indication of the general level of political risk in a country. From an economic standpoint, political risk refers to uncertainty over **property rights**. If the government can expropriate either legal title to property or the stream of income it generates, then political risk exists. Political risk also exists if property owners may be constrained in the way they use their property. This definition of political risk encompasses government actions ranging from outright expropriation to a change in the tax law that alters the government's share of corporate income to laws that change the rights of private companies to compete against state-owned companies. Each action affects corporate cash flows and hence the value of the firm.

Low Risk (70–100)	POR Combined Score	High Risk (40–54)	POR Combined Score
1 Switzerland	82	26 Czech Republic	49
2 Singapore	79	27 Italy	49
3 Netherlands	75	28 South Africa	49
4 Japan	74	29 Kazakhstan	48
5 Norway	73	30 Thailand	48
6 Taiwan (R.O.C.)	72	31 India	47
7 Germany	71	32 Russia	47
		33 Egypt	45
		34 Hungary	45
Moderate Risk (55–69)		35 Poland	45
8 Austria	69	36 Argentina	44
9 Belgium	67	37 Brazil	44
10 Sweden	66	38 Philippines	44
11 United States	66	39 Iran	43
12 Finland	65	40 Ukraine	43
13 Canada	63	41 Vietnam	43
14 Ireland	63	42 Greece	42
15 Denmark	62	43 Venezuela	42
16 France	62	44 Colombia	41
17 China (P.R.C.)	61	45 Indonesia	41
18 United Kingdom	61	46 Mexico	41
19 Malaysia	60	47 Peru	41
20 Spain	59	48 Turkey	40
21 Australia	58		
22 Korea (South)	58	**Prohibitive Risk (0–39)**	
23 Chile	56	49 Pakistan	39
24 Portugal	55	50 Romania	38
25 Saudi Arabia	55		

Source: Business Environment Risk Intelligence, by permission.

EXHIBIT 11.1 ● PROFIT OPPORTUNITY RECOMMENDATION RANKINGS, MARCH 2007

ILLUSTRATION *Property Rights in China*

Despite attracting record amounts of FDI, China's record on the protection of property rights is quite poor. In 1992, McDonald's opened a very large restaurant with a (seating capacity of 700) in the Wangujing shopping district of Beijing, only two blocks away from Tiananmen Square. McDonald's had signed a 20-year lease with Beijing's municipal government; however, two years later it received an eviction notice. The municipal government now favored the proposal by Li Ka-shing, a Hong Kong businessman, to build a commercial, residential and office complex in the space occupied by McDonald's. A Chinese official stated: "The land belongs to the state; so the government has the power to use the land for projects." But that was not all; Ll Ka-shing was extremely close to the Chinese leadership and had also donated a building for the central government's office in Hong Kong. Needless to say, even though McDonald's lease was protected by Chinese law, McDonald's lost the case in court.

There could be several reasons for why property rights protection in China is low. For one, China's Communist past, especially the revolutionary ideology of Mao Zedong's China (1949–1976) wherein private property was denounced, may still have cultural ramifications. Moreover, despite several laws and regulations that relate to economic activities and property rights, the Constitution was written by the Chinese Communist Party and does not give an inviolable status to private property as it does to "socialist public property." Also, the Constitution does not give citizens rights to enter into business or protect the property rights of citizens from state appropriation.

Also, as the McDonald's case shows, business transactions are still governed primarily by personal connections and informal networks, commonly known as *guanxi* (pronounced "gwan-shee"). Those with connections find it easy to do business in China, while others relying primarily on legal systems stand a greater risk of losing their investments since the legal system is neither impartial nor independent of the government.

Source: Shaomin Li, "Why is Property Right Protection Lacking in China? An Institutional Explanation," *California Management Review*, 46 (Spring), 2004, pp. 100–115.

ILLUSTRATION *Mr. Yampel Gets Trampled in Ukraine*

In August 2000, Jacob Yampel had just won a Ukrainian court decision in his battle to regain a 50% stake in a pharmaceutical factory. This stake had been taken from him by the plant's managers through a complicated series of transactions involving share dilution, transfer of plant assets to a new private company, doctored documents, and a bankruptcy declaration of the original joint venture. Unfortunately for Mr. Yampel, the losing side then enlisted the aid of the Ukrainian President. In a televised broadcast, President Leonid Kuchma said, "I often say . . . we must obey laws. But there is something higher than the law: the country's national interest. And this means the interests of our people, not of someone else." Twelve days later, Ukraine's High Arbitration Court overturned Mr. Yampel's victory on a technicality.

An official at the U.S. Embassy called the timing of the unfavorable court decision "suspicious" and said it was "likely to raise questions in the minds of investors about their ability to obtain a fair hearing . . . particularly if they have disputes with prominent domestic producers."[3]

Mr. Yampel's plight is not that uncommon in Ukraine, a large, underdeveloped market that holds lucrative opportunities along with big risks. Although the government hopes to attract foreign investors by combining economic reforms with privatization, Ukrainian leaders have sent potential investors mixed messages about their attitude toward foreign business. In addition to Mr. Yampel's company, a number of U.S. firms have complained to the U.S. Congress about their treatment in Ukraine. Their grievances range from commercial disputes with government agencies or companies to bureaucratic interference to improper handling by the judicial system of their disputes with Ukrainian firms. The "orange revolution" in December 2004, which replaced Ukraine's corrupt government with opposition leader Viktor Yushchenko and his record of commitment to democracy and the rule of law, has inspired new hope of economic reform and a less risky business environment.

---

[3] Tom Warner, "Lessons for Foreign Investors in Ukraine," *Wall Street Journal*, August 16, 2000, A18.

The key questions that companies should ask in assessing the degree of political risk they face in a country, particularly one undergoing a political and economic transition, are as follows:

- Has economic reform become institutionalized, thereby minimizing the chance of abrupt policy changes that would adversely affect an investment's value?

- Are the regulatory and legal systems predictable and fair? Constant rule changes involving foreign ownership, taxes, currency controls, trade, or contract law raise investment risk.

- Is the government reasonably competent, maintaining the value of its currency and preserving political stability?

ILLUSTRATION *Political Risk in Venezuela*

According to the *Wall Street Journal* (December 31, 1980, p. 10), when Venezuela's oil income quadrupled in 1973, a high government official declared, "Now we have so much money that we won't need any new foreign investment." President Carlos Perez calculated that the country was rich enough to buy machinery from abroad and set up factories without any foreign participation. He overlooked the fact that Venezuela did not have enough skilled technicians to run and maintain sophisticated equipment. Despite an orgy of buying foreign-made machinery, economic growth stalled as companies were left with equipment they could not operate.

By 1980, President Luis Herrera, who succeeded Perez, recognized the mistake and invited foreigners back. But once shunned, foreigners did not rush back, particularly because the Herrera administration sent out such mixed signals that investors could not be certain how sincere the welcome was or how long it would last.

Consider the uncertainty faced by a foreign investor trying to decipher government policy from the following statements. On the one hand, the Superintendent of Foreign Investment insisted that the government had had "a change of heart" and declared that the country needed "new capital and new technology in manufacturing, agro-industry, and construction of low-cost housing." On the other hand, the head of the powerful Venezuelan Investment Fund, which invests much of the country's oil income, was downright hostile to foreign investors. He said, "Foreign investment is generally unfavorable to Venezuela. Foreign investors think Venezuela is one big grab bag, where they can come and pick out whatever goodies they want." Still another official, the president of the Foreign Trade Institute, said, "It is a grave error to think that foreign investment can contribute to the transfer of technology, capital formation, the development of managerial capacity, and equilibrium in the balance of payments."

The collapse of oil prices brought the return of Carlos Perez as a free-market reformer, who instituted needed economic changes in Venezuela. However, the Venezuelan government failed to pursue political reforms in tandem with economic reforms, and the economic reforms themselves worsened the existing economic inequality and undermined President Perez's hold on power. After Perez was forced out of office on corruption charges in 1994, his successor, President Rafael Caldera, spent more than 10% of the nation's GDP to bail out weak banks (financed by running the central bank's printing presses overtime), stopped all privatization, appointed the country's best known Marxist economist to the board of the central bank, imposed price and currency controls, and spoke out strongly against the private sector. The result was high inflation and a massive outflow of capital, prompting an 87% devaluation of the Venezuelan bolivar.

In 1998, Hugo Chavez, a military officer whose rise to power began with a bloody attempted military coup in 1992, swept into power based on the promise of a "Bolivarian revolution" to attack poverty. Instead of battling poverty, however, Chavez, an open admirer of Fidel Castro and Saddam Hussein, has spent much of his time fighting a growing list of political opponents. First businesses turned against him, then unions, and then the media. In 2001, without consulting Congress, Chavez issued 49 "revolutionary" decrees that gave him near-total control of the economy. A fierce foe of capitalism ("I have said it already, I am convinced that the way to build a new and better world is not capitalism. Capitalism leads us straight to hell.") with a deep antipathy toward property rights (his administration pledged to seize about 3.4% of the area of Venezuela in 2005 to give to poor farmers), Chavez has seen his alternative path to socialism lead to further misery and poverty for the Venezuelan masses. In his first six years in office (1998–2004), Venezuela's per capita income declined by 47% (see Exhibit 11.2) even as the country's oil revenues zoomed from high oil prices. Moreover, despite the imposition of exchange controls, by April 2005, the Venezuelan bolivar had declined in value by 73%.

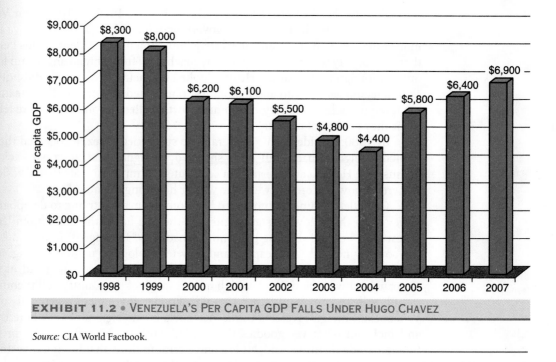

EXHIBIT 11.2 ● VENEZUELA'S PER CAPITA GDP FALLS UNDER HUGO CHAVEZ

Source: CIA World Factbook.

Capital Flight   A useful indicator of the degree of political risk is the seriousness of capital flight. **Capital flight** refers to the export of savings by a nation's citizens because of fears about the safety of their capital. By its nature, capital flight is difficult to measure accurately because it is not directly observed in most cases. Nevertheless, one can usually infer the capital outflows, using balance-of-payments figures, particularly the entry labeled "errors and omissions." The World Bank methodology estimates capital flight as "the sum of gross capital inflows and the current account deficit, less increases in foreign reserves."[4] These estimates indicate that capital flight represents an enormous outflow of funds from developing countries.

---

[4] World Bank, *World Development Report*. New York: Oxford University Press, 1985, at p. 64.

ILLUSTRATION   *Capital Flight From Latin America*

Between 1974 and 1982, Argentina borrowed $32.6 billion. Estimates of the level of capital flight from Argentina over the same period range from $15 billion to more than $27 billion.[5] These estimates would mean that capital flight amounted to between half and four-fifths of the entire inflow of foreign capital to Argentina. For Venezuela, the inflow was $27 billion over the same period, with capital flight estimated at between $12 billion and $22 billion. The inflow for Mexico was $79 billion between 1979 and 1984; the out-flow has been estimated at between $26 billion and $54 billion for the same period. Other debtor countries, such as Nigeria and the Philippines, have also had large capital out-flows. As conditions in many of these countries worsened, capital flight continued. As of the end of 1988, just prior to the end of the Latin American debt crisis, Morgan Guaranty estimated that Latin Americans held $243 billion in assets abroad, far exceeding the amount of loans to the region held by U.S. banks. And this excludes assets taken abroad before 1977. Exhibit 11.3 shows the breakdown of the $243 billion figure by country.

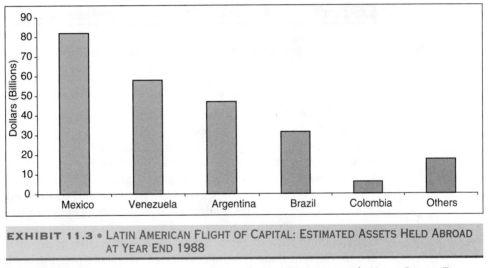

EXHIBIT 11.3 • LATIN AMERICAN FLIGHT OF CAPITAL: ESTIMATED ASSETS HELD ABROAD AT YEAR END 1988

Matt Mottett, "Cripling Export," *Wall Street Journal*, September 25, 1989. Citing report by Morgan Guaranty Trust.

Capital flight occurs for several reasons, most of which have to do with inappropriate economic policies. These reasons include government regulations, controls, and taxes that lower the return on domestic investments. In countries where inflation is high and domestic inflation hedging is difficult or impossible, investors may hedge by shifting their savings to foreign currencies deemed less likely to depreciate. They may also make the shift when domestic interest rates are artificially held down by their governments or when they expect a devaluation of an overvalued currency. Yet another reason for capital flight could be increases in a country's external debt. Such an increase may signal the probability of a fiscal crises and therefore, induce capital flight.[6]

India is one case where capital flight was unusually large when the economy was still shackled by a socialist ideology combined with a large amount of external debt. As

---

[5] These figures come from Steven Plaut, "Capital Flight and LDC Debt," *FRBSF Weekly Letter*, Federal Reserve Bank of San Francisco, January 8, 1988.

[6] Donald R. Lessard, "Comment," in Donald R. Lessard and John Williamson, ed. *Capital Flight and Third World Debt*. Washington D.C.: Institute for International Economics, 1987, pp. 97–100.

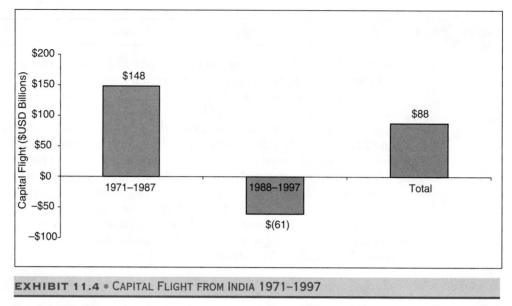

EXHIBIT 11.4 • CAPITAL FLIGHT FROM INDIA 1971–1997

Note: In 1997 Dollars.
Source: Niranjan Chipalkatti and Meenakshi Rishi, "External Debt and Capital Flight in the Indian Economy," *Oxford Development Studies*, Vol. 29, No. 1, 2001.

the Indian economy engaged in liberalization and started attracting non-debt inflows such as FDI, capital flight was reversed (see Exhibit 11.4)[7].

Perhaps the most powerful motive for capital flight is political risk. In unstable political regimes, and in some stable ones, wealth is not secure from government seizure, especially when changes in regime occur. Savings may be shifted overseas to protect them. For example, the citizens of Hong Kong, which was turned over to Communist China on July 1, 1997, responded to the anticipated change in regime by sending large sums of money abroad in advance.

Common sense dictates that if a nation's own citizens do not trust the government, then investment there is unsafe. After all, residents presumably have a better feel for conditions and government intentions than do outsiders. Thus, when analyzing investment or lending opportunities, multinational firms and international banks must bear in mind the apparent unwillingness of the nation's citizens to invest and lend in their own country.

What is needed to halt capital flight are tough-minded economic policies—the kind of policies that make investors want to put their money to work instead of taking it out. As we shall see in the next section, these policies include cutting budget deficits and taxes, removing barriers to investment by foreigners, selling off state-owned enterprises, allowing for freer trade, and avoiding currency overvaluations that virtually invite people to ship their money elsewhere before the official exchange rate falls.

Starting around 1990, such policies began to be employed in much of Latin America, with predictable results. As seen in Exhibit 11.5, beginning in 1990, capital flight was reversed, with private capital flooding back into Latin America. These capital inflows helped fuel an extraordinary performance of the Latin American stock markets.

---

[7] Niranjan Chipalkatti and Meenakshi Rishi, "External Debt and Capital Flight in the Indian Economy," *Oxford Development Studies*, 29 (1), 2001, pp. 31–44.

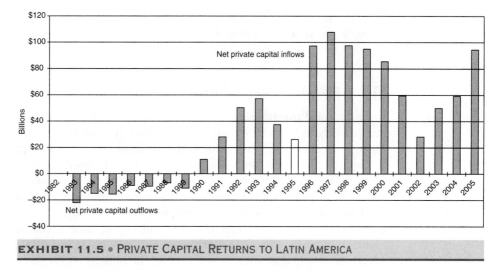

EXHIBIT 11.5 • PRIVATE CAPITAL RETURNS TO LATIN AMERICA

Source: Bank for International Settlement, Inter-American Development Bank, Institute for Internatonal Finance, and World Bank.

11.2 ECONOMIC AND POLITICAL FACTORS UNDERLYING COUNTRY RISK

We now examine in more detail some of the economic and political factors that contribute to the general level of risk in the country as a whole, termed **country risk**. The primary focus here is on how well the country is doing economically. As noted earlier, the better a nation's economic performance, the lower the likelihood that its government will take actions that adversely affect the value of companies operating there.

Although many of the examples used in this section involve less-developed countries (LDCs), country risk is not confined to them. The same considerations affect developed countries as well. As we have already seen in Chapters 2 and 3, for example, Western European nations are currently confronting economic stagnation and business risk stemming from over-regulated economies, inflexible labor markets, and overly expansive and expensive social welfare states. Similarly, companies operating in the United States face systemic litigation risks and arbitrary changes in employment and environmental laws. Meanwhile, Japan is stuck with a rigid and highly regulated business system that puts too much power in the hands of the state and makes it difficult to adapt to a changed environment. Moreover, Japan has a banking system that refuses to tackle a problem of almost biblical proportions, with an estimated $1.23 trillion in bad bank loans (in contrast, the U.S. savings and loan fiasco cost about $150 billion to resolve); and a government that—fearing higher unemployment and temporary economic pain if the problem is forcefully addressed—has, until recently, gone along with this game of let's pretend that all is well. The failure to put insolvent borrowers out of their misery left the Japanese economy loaded down with crippled companies too weak to do anything except pile up more bad debts. The result has been almost 15 years of recession and economic stagnation, with politicians unwilling to induce the Japanese to take the bitter medicine needed to get their economy going again. The appointment in 2002 of a tough new bank regulator, who forced Japanese banks to write off bad loans, has helped the ailing banking system to recover. Even more significantly, the victory in September 2005 of Prime Minister Junichiro Koizumi's plan to privatize Japan's huge postal savings and life insurance system generated widespread optimism that serious structural reform will commence and that the Japanese economy has finally turned the corner.

The bottom line is that no country offers a perfect business environment. Rather, countries are better or worse than average for doing business. We now examine key factors that determine the economic performance of a country and its degree of risk.

11.2.1 Fiscal Irresponsibility

To begin, fiscal irresponsibility, excessive government spending, is one sign of a country that is likely to be risky because it will probably have an insatiable appetite for money. Thus, one country risk indicator is the government deficit as a percentage of GDP. The higher this figure, the more the government is promising to its citizens relative to the resources it is extracting in payment.[8] This gap lowers the possibility that the government can meet its promises without resorting to expropriations of property, raising taxes, or printing money. These actions, in turn, will adversely affect the nation's economic health. Expropriation will cause capital flight and dry up new investment; raising taxes will adversely affect incentives to work, save, and take risks; and printing money to finance a government deficit, known as **monetizing the deficit**, will result in monetary instability, high inflation, high interest rates, and currency depreciation.

ILLUSTRATION   *Japan as Number One in Fiscal Irresponsibility*

Even apparently stable countries are not immune to fiscal irresponsibility. For example, since 1992 Japan has attempted to kick-start its long-suffering economy by running huge budget deficits, the traditional Keynesian remedy for an economic downturn. Aside from giving Japan the highest debt-to-GDP ratio in the developed world (see Exhibit 11.6a), the end result has been a Japanese economy mired in a seemingly endless recession—and a clear repudiation of Keynesian economics (Exhibit 11.6b shows that after deficit spending totaling some $1.03 trillion over the 10-year period 1992–2001, Japan's GDP grew an average of 0.9% annually during this period—with four recessions thrown in for good measure—in contrast to average annual growth of 4.1% during the preceding 10-year period).[9] Only when Japan began to refocus its antirecessionary efforts away from fiscal stimulus and toward structural reforms—privatization and deregulation of its economy along with continuing to clean up its bad bank loan problem and allowing insolvent companies to go bankrupt—did the Japanese economy appear to recover from its "lost decade" and start to grow again.[10]

---

[8] An increasingly important driver of government deficits and high taxes worldwide is state-run pension and retiree health care plans, such as Social Security and Medicare in the United States. Most of these plans are funded on a pay-as-you-go basis in which the payroll taxes of current workers are paid directly in benefits to current retirees; there are no savings to draw on. That leaves them vulnerable to a declining workforce and an increasing number of dependents, which is the situation in most developed nations today. And it will only get worse. As populations age and there are fewer workers to pay taxes for each person drawing pension and medical benefits, these plans will run ever-larger deficits. The political will to deal with these deficits by cutting benefits or raising taxes sharply is often lacking owing to the voting power of the elderly and the resistance of the young.

[9] Another apparent side effect of Japan's recent experience is to have silenced the numerous Japanologists who were exhorting the United States to emulate Japanese economic policies. Although Japan began growing again in 2003–2004, largely owing to expanding trade with China and other Asian nations, an expansionary monetary policy by the Bank of Japan, and the start of corporate restructuring by large Japanese firms, the Japanese economy still has major structural problems and stalled once again in early 2005.

[10] Many observers have pointed to Japan's hostility toward competition in many aspects of its economic life as being a key roadblock to its recovery. In inefficient sectors such as construction and distribution, for example, losers continue to be propped up by government policy instead of being allowed to fail. Similarly, farming, health care, and education largely exclude private companies, thereby depriving Japan of the innovation that has driven its export-oriented industries and hobbling its economic growth. Not surprisingly, the lack of competition in its domestic economy makes Japan one of the highest-cost nations in the world.

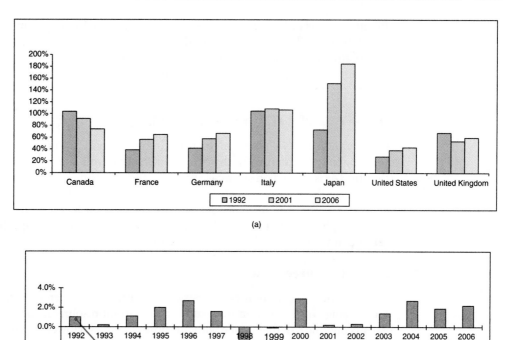

EXHIBIT 11.6 • **(A)** GROSS GOVERNMENT DEBT AS A PERCENTAGE OF GDP: 1992, 2001 AND 2006; AND **(B)** JAPANESE ECONOMIC PERFORMANCE: 1992–2007

Source: International Monetary Fund.

11.2.2 Monetary Instability

As we saw in Chapter 4, according to modern monetary theory, inflation is the logical outcome of an expansion of the money supply in excess of real output growth. Large and unpredictable changes in the money supply lead to high and volatile inflation. Rapid expansion in the money supply is typically traceable to large government deficits that the central bank monetizes.

11.2.3 Controlled Exchange Rate System

The economic problems presented by a fiscally and monetarily irresponsible government are compounded by having a **controlled exchange rate system**, where currency controls are used to fix the exchange rate. A controlled rate system goes hand in hand with an overvalued local currency, which is the equivalent of taxing exports and subsidizing imports. The risk of tighter currency controls and the ever-present threat of a devaluation encourage capital flight. Similarly, multinational firms will try to repatriate their local affiliates' profits rather than reinvest them. A controlled rate system also leaves the economy with little flexibility to respond to changing relative prices and wealth positions, exacerbating any unfavorable trend in the nation's *terms of trade*, the weighted average of the nation's export prices relative to its import prices—that is, the exchange rate between exports and imports.

11.2.4 Wasteful Government Spending

Another indicator of potential increased country risk is the amount of unproductive spending in the economy. To the extent that capital from abroad is used to subsidize consumption or is wasted on showcase projects, the government will have less wealth to draw on to repay the nation's foreign debts and is more likely to resort to exchange controls, higher taxes, and the like. In addition, funds diverted to the purchase of assets abroad (capital flight) will not add to the economy's dollar-generating capacity unless investors feel safe in repatriating their overseas earnings.

11.2.5 Resource Base

The resource base of a country consists of its natural, human, and financial resources. Other things being equal, a nation with substantial natural resources, such as oil or copper, is a better economic risk than is one without those resources. However, typically, all is not equal. Hence, nations such as South Korea and Taiwan turn out to be better risks than resource-rich Argentina and Brazil. The reason has to do with the quality of human resources and the degree to which these resources are allowed to be put to their most efficient use.

A nation with highly skilled and productive workers, a large pool of scientists and engineers, and ample management talent will have many of the essential ingredients needed to pursue a course of steady growth and development. Three additional factors are necessary: (1) a stable political system that encourages hard work and risk taking by allowing entrepreneurs to reap the rewards (and bear the losses) from their activities, (2) a flexible labor market that permits workers to be allocated to those jobs in which they will be the most productive, and (3) a free-market system that ensures that the prices people respond to correctly signal the relative desirability of engaging in different activities. In this way, the nation's human and natural resources will be put to their most efficient uses. The evidence by now is overwhelming that free markets bring wealth and that endless state meddling brings waste. The reason is simple: Unlike a government-controlled economy, free markets do not tolerate and perpetuate mistakes.

11.2.6 Country Risk and Adjustment to External Shocks

Recent history shows that the impact of external shocks is likely to vary from nation to nation; some countries deal successfully with these shocks, while others succumb to them. The evidence suggests that domestic policies play a critical role in determining how effectively a particular nation will deal with external shocks. Asian nations, for example, successfully coped with falling commodity prices, rising interest and exchange rates during the 1980s, because their policies promoted timely internal and external adjustment, as is manifest in their relatively low inflation rates and small current-account deficits.

The opposite happened in Latin America, where most countries accepted the then-prevalent ideology that growth is best promoted by an **import-substitution development strategy** characterized by extensive state ownership, controls, and policies to encourage import substitution. Many of these countries took over failing private businesses, nationalized the banks, protected domestic companies against imports, ran up large foreign debts, and heavily regulated the private sector. Whereas the "East Asian Tigers"—Hong Kong, South Korea, Taiwan, and Singapore—tested their ability to imitate and innovate in the international marketplace, Latin American producers were content with the exploitation of the internal market, charging prices that were typically several times the international price for their goods. The lack of foreign competition has contributed to long-term inefficiency among Latin American manufacturers.

In addition, by raising the cost of imported materials and products used by the export sector, the Latin American import-substitution development strategies worsened their international competitive position, leaving the share of exports in GDP far below that of other LDCs. Moreover, state expenditures on massive capital projects diverted resources from the private sector and exports. Much of the investment went to inefficient state enterprises, leading to wasted resources and large debts.

The decline in commodity prices and the simultaneous rise in real interest rates in the early 1980s should have led to reduced domestic consumption. However, fearing that spending cuts would threaten social stability, Latin American governments delayed cutting back on projects and social expenditures. The difference between consumption and production was made up by borrowing overseas, thereby enabling their societies to temporarily enjoy artificially high standards of living.

Latin American governments also tried to stimulate their economies by increasing state spending, fueled by high rates of monetary expansion. This response exacerbated their difficulties because the resulting high rates of inflation combined with their fixed exchange rates to boost real exchange rates substantially and resulted in higher imports and lower exports. Moreover, the overvalued exchange rates, interest rate controls, and political uncertainties triggered massive capital flight from the region, estimated at up to $100 billion during the 2-year period of 1981 and 1982. The result was larger balance-of-payments deficits that necessitated more foreign borrowing and higher debt-service requirements. Moreover, in an attempt to control inflation, the Latin American governments imposed price controls and interest rate controls. These controls led to further capital flight and price rigidity. Distorted prices gave the wrong signals to the residents, sending consumption soaring and production plummeting.

11.2.7 Market-Oriented versus Statist Policies

The great economic lesson of the ill-fated, post—World War II experiment in Communism is that markets work and command economies do not. The truly extraordinary difference in the economic results of these two systems—contrast the disparate experiences of East Germany and West Germany; North Korea and South Korea; and Hong Kong, Taiwan, and China under Mao—stems directly from their diametrically opposite means of organizing economic activity. In a **market economy**, also known as **capitalism**, economic decisions are made by individual decision makers based on prices—of goods, services, capital, labor, land, and other resources. In a **command economy**, often termed **socialism**, people at the top decide what is to be produced, how it is to be produced, and where it is to be produced, and then command others to follow the central plan.

Why Capitalism Works   The core distinction between a market economy and a command economy, and the one that accounts for the huge disparity in their performances, is the different ways in which they harness information and incentives. Given that resources are scarce, economic decisions involve a series of trade-offs. In order to make these trade-offs successfully, command economies demand that all the fragments of knowledge existing in different minds be brought together in the mind of the central planner, an impossible informational requirement. Markets work because economic decisions are made by those who have the information necessary to determine the trade-offs that must be made and the suitability of those trade-offs, given their own unique skills, circumstances, and preferences combined with market prices that signal the relative values and costs placed on those activities by society. Equally important, in a market economy, people have the incentives to efficiently act on that information.

Statist Policies Constrain Growth Most countries today have a mixture of market and command economies. Pure command economies are rare nowadays—only Cuba and North Korea remain—and markets tend to predominate in the production and distribution of goods and services around the world. However, many nations follow *statist* policies in which markets are combined with heavy government intervention in their economies through various regulations and tax and spending policies. In addition, so-called critical industries, such as air transportation, mining, telecommunications, aerospace, oil, and power generation are typically owned or controlled by the state. As a result, economic power is often heavily centralized in the state, usually with harmful consequences for wealth creation.

The centralization of economic power in much of the Third World turned the state into a huge patronage machine and spawned a swollen and corrupt bureaucracy to administer the all-encompassing rules and regulations. Avaricious elites, accountable to no one, used the labyrinthine controls and regulations to enrich themselves and further the interests of their own ethnic groups or professional class at the expense of national economic health and well-being.

Why Statist Policies Persist Many of these countries are finally rejecting their earlier statist policies and trying to stimulate the private sector and individual initiative. The experience in countries that are reforming their economies, including the former Soviet Union, China, and India, as well as much of Latin America illustrates that it is far easier to regulate and extend the state's reach than to deregulate and retrench. When the state becomes heavily involved in the economy, many special interests from the state bureaucracy, business, labor, and consumer groups come to rely on state benefits. Of course, they actively oppose reforms that curtail their subsidies.

The process of reform is greatly complicated by egalitarian ideologies that deprecate private success while justifying public privilege and by the pervasiveness of the state, which distorts the reward pattern and makes it easier to get rich by politics rather than by industry, by connections rather than by performance. These ideologies tend to take investment and the provision of productive capacity for granted (they like capital but dislike capitalists), while being generally more concerned with redistributing the benefits and mitigating the costs of economic progress than with protecting its foundations.

The message is clear. In evaluating a nation's riskiness, it is not sufficient to identify factors—such as real interest shocks or world recession—that would systematically affect the economies of all foreign countries to one extent or another. It is necessary also to determine the susceptibility of the various nations to these shocks. This determination requires a focus on the financial policies and development strategies pursued by the different nations.

ILLUSTRATION   *Can Russia Shake Off Its Past?*

Commenting on the St. Petersburg Economic Forum that was held in June 2007 and attended by 6000 delegates, including over 100 CEOs of global companies, the *Financial Times* noted: "In Russia today, the rule of law remains erratic, the courts are corrupt, and property ownership can seldom be guaranteed. Moreover, in an autocratic society—even if its politely called a "managed democracy"—decision-making is much less predictable than in an open democratic society. Anyone who does business in Russia must do so with their eyes open. They must recognise that politics, as much as economics, dictates the commercial climate. It is whom you know, as much as what you know, that is the key to success. That means the risks are greater, but so are the rewards."[11] Further, the same article stated: "Of course Russia has changed, beyond all recognition, from the dreadful old world of state controls and five-year plans. But it has yet to decide what sort of capitalism it is going to adopt. Anyone doing business there would do well to remember the words of Vladimir Illyich Lenin: 'A capitalist is someone who sells you the rope with which you hang him.' They have not been entirely forgotten in Moscow."

11.2.8 Key Indicators of Country Risk and Economic Health

Based on the preceding discussion, some of the common characteristics of high country risk are:

- A large government deficit relative to GDP
- A high rate of money expansion, especially if it is combined with a relatively fixed exchange rate
- Substantial government expenditures yielding low rates of return
- Price controls, interest rate ceilings, trade restrictions, rigid labor laws, and other government-imposed barriers to the smooth adjustment of the economy to changing relative prices
- High tax rates that destroy incentives to work, save, and invest
- Vast state-owned firms run for the benefit of their managers and workers
- A citizenry that demands, and a political system that accepts, government responsibility for maintaining and expanding the nation's standard of living through public-sector spending and regulations (the less stable the political system, the more important this factor will likely be)
- Pervasive corruption that acts as a large tax on legitimate business activity, holds back development, discourages foreign investment, breeds distrust of capitalism, and weakens the basic fabric of society
- The absence of basic institutions of government—a well-functioning legal system, reliable regulation of financial markets and institutions, and an honest civil service

Alternatively, positive indicators of a nation's long-run economic health include the following:

- *A structure of incentives that rewards risk taking in productive ventures*: People have clearly demonstrated that they respond rationally to the incentives they face, given the information and resources available to them. This statement is true whether we are talking about shopkeepers in Nairobi or bankers in New York. A necessary precondition for productive investment to take place is secure legal rights to own and sell at least some forms of property. If property is not secure, people have an incentive to consume their resources immediately or transfer them overseas, lest they be taken away. Low taxes are also important because they encourage productive efforts and promote savings and investment.

---

[11] *Financial Times*, "Russian Realities: Investors Cannot Ignore the Importance of Politics," June 13, 2007, p.

- *A legal structure that stimulates the development of free markets*: Wealth creation is made easier by stable rules governing society and fair and predictable application of laws administered by an independent judicial system free of corruption. Such a legal structure, which replaces official whim with the rule of law, combined with a system of property rights and properly enforceable contracts, facilitates the development of free markets. The resulting market price signals are most likely to contain the data and provide the incentives that are essential to making efficient use of the nation's resources. Free markets, however, do more than increase economic efficiency. By quickly rewarding success and penalizing failure, they also encourage successful innovation and economic growth. Conversely, the lack of a rule of law and a well-defined commercial code, as in Russia, and the persistence of corruption, as in much of Africa and Latin America, hampers the development of a market economy by making it difficult to enforce contracts and forcing businesses to pay protection money to thugs, bureaucrats, or politicians.

- *Minimal regulations and economic distortions*: Complex regulations are costly to implement and waste management time and other resources. Moreover, reduced government intervention in the economy lowers the incidence of corruption. After all, why bribe civil servants if their ability to grant economic favors is minimal? Instead, the way to succeed in an unregulated economy is to provide superior goods and services to the market.

- *Clear incentives to save and invest*: In general, when there are such incentives—that is, the economic rules of the game are straightforward and stable, property rights are secure, taxes on investment returns are low, and there is political stability—a nation's chances of developing are maximized.

- *An open economy*: Free trade not only increases competition and permits the realization of comparative advantage, it also constrains government policies and makes them conform more closely to those policies conducive to raising living standards and rapid economic growth. An open economy strengthens the rule of law as well, because it must compete for investment capital by demonstrating that it protects property rights.

- *Stable macroeconomic policies*: Macroeconomic stability, largely promoted by a stable monetary policy, reduces economic risk and leads to lower inflation and lower real interest rates. The resulting increase in the willingness of people to save and entrepreneurs to invest in the domestic economy stimulates economic growth.

The sorry economic state of Eastern Europe dramatically illustrates the consequences of pursuing policies that are the exact opposite of those recommended. Thus, the ability of the Eastern European countries to share in the prosperity of the Western world depends critically on reversing the policies they followed under Communist rule.

Similarly, investors assessing the prospects for Western nations would also do well to recognize the benefits of markets and incentives. Government economic intervention in the form of subsidies and regulations is appealing to many, but governments make poor venture capitalists and for a simple reason: Industries not yet born do not have lobbyists, whereas old and established ones have lots of them. The net result is that the bulk of subsidies go to those industries resisting change. For example, Germany spends more on subsidies for powerful smokestack industries such as shipbuilding and coal mining than to support basic research. Until recently, it also sheltered the state-owned telecommunications monopoly, Deutsche Telekom, and its suppliers, such as Siemens, from most foreign competition;[12] government sheltering in turn dampens innovation across a range of

---

[12] The German telecommunications industry was deregulated in 1998. However, Deutsche Telekom is still majority-owned by the German government.

industries. When government does invest in high-tech industries, it usually botches the job. Examples are legion, including the tens of billions of wasted tax dollars spent to develop European software, semiconductor, computer, and aerospace industries.

Market-Oriented Policies Work   Realism demands that nations, especially those in the Third World and Eastern Europe, come to terms with their need to rely more on self-help. The most successful economies, such as Hong Kong, South Korea, and Taiwan, demonstrate the importance of aligning domestic incentives with world market conditions. As a result of their market-oriented policies, Asian nations have had remarkable economic success over the past three decades as reflected in their strong economic growth and rising standards of living. Their recent problems just reinforce the importance of such policies: When Asian nations substituted the visible hand of state intervention for the invisible hand of the market in allocating capital, they helped create the financial crisis that rocked Asia in 1997. The evidence indicates that the more distorted the prior economic policies the more severe the crisis, with Indonesia, South Korea, Thailand, and Malaysia being hit much harder than Hong Kong, Taiwan, and Singapore.

Like it or not, nations must make their way in an increasingly competitive world economy that puts a premium on self-help and has little time for the inefficiency and pretension of **statism**—that is, the substitution of state-owned or state-guided enterprises for the private sector—as the road to economic success. Statism destroys initiative and leads to economic stagnation. Free enterprise is the road to prosperity.

The recognition that countries cannot realize the benefits of capitalism without the institutions of capitalism is dawning in even the most socialist countries of Europe, Asia, and Latin America. For example, in 1989, Vietnamese families were given the right to work their own land and sell their output at market prices. Within a year, rice production rose so dramatically that Vietnam went from the edge of famine to the world's third-largest rice exporter.

Market-oriented reform of Eastern European and LDC economic policies lies at the heart of any credible undertaking to secure these nations' economic and financial rehabilitation. The first and most critical step is to cut government spending. In practical terms, cutting government spending means reducing the bloated public sectors that permeate most Latin American and Communist countries.

Market-Oriented Reform in Latin America   Reform of the public sector probably went the furthest in Latin America, where, shocked by the severe miseries of the 1980s (known in Latin America as the *Lost Decade*), many of these countries abandoned the statism, populism, and protectionism that have crippled their economies since colonial times. Chile and Colombia have embarked on fairly comprehensive reform programs, emphasizing free markets and sound money, and, despite some backsliding and significant problems with corruption, Mexico has made surprisingly good headway (see Exhibit 11.7 for a summary of the changes in Mexico's economic policies). Argentina also undertook radical reform of its economy, highlighted by **privatizing**—returning to the private sector from the public sector—major activities and galvanizing the private sector by deregulation and the elimination of protectionism. Unfortunately, Latin America's reforms of the 1990s failed to bring the promised hope and opportunity. Instead, "Countries replaced inflation with new taxes on the poor, high tariffs with regional trading blocs, and, especially, state monopolies with government-sanctioned private monopolies. Moreover, the courts were subjected to the whims of those in power, widening the divide between official institutions and ordinary people."[13]

---

[13] Alvaro Vargas Llosa, "The Return of Latin America's Left," *New York Times*, March 22, 2005, http://www.independent.org/newsroom/article.asp?id=1483.

Old Mexican Model	New Mexican Model
Large budget deficits	Fiscal restraint
Rapid expension of money supply	Monetary discipline
Nationalization	Privatization
Restricted foreign direct investment	Attract foreign direct investment
High tax rates	Tax reform
Import substitution	Trade liberalization
Controlled Currency	End currency controls
Price and interest rate controls	Prices and interest rates set by market
Government-dominated economy	Reduced size and scope of government

EXHIBIT 11.7 • MEXICO'S ECONOMIC POLICIES: THEN AND NOW

The resulting disappointment brought leftist governments to power in several countries, including Argentina, Brazil, and Venezuela, with predictable results. After the failure of the interventionist model in the 1960s and '70s, which floundered in the big crisis of 1982–83, a series of free-market reforms, including monetary and fiscal restraint and privatization, was initiated that stabilized the situation, writes *Sabino* in his latest op-ed. "But the reforms—partial as they were, and always limited in their intention and objectives—could not furnish the rapid growth many citizens desired, or reduce the social inequalities that in reality had dragged on for several centuries."

After dismantling their government-favored monopolies, the next big challenge for those countries that are trying to move forward is to revamp the entire civil service, including police, regulatory agencies, judiciaries, and all the other institutions necessary for the smooth functioning of a market economy. Most importantly, they must end the legal favoritism so prevalent in the region's judicial systems. The United States offers a persuasive example of how well-constructed institutions permit enterprising people of diverse cultures to flourish together.

ILLUSTRATION   *The Potential Gains from Privatization*

A recent study points to the potential gains from privatization.[14] Government-owned entities in India own about 43% of the country's capital stock and account for about 15% of nonagricultural employment. However, according to Exhibit 11.8, the labor (capital) productivity of public sector entities relative to that of their private sector competitors varies from 11% for labor (20% for capital) to 50% (88%) and averages just 26% (63%). Two factors largely account for these stark differences: (1) Public sector companies experience little pressure to perform better and (2) the government subsidies they receive means they can survive despite their extraordinary inefficiency. Privatizing these government entities would boost productivity, save on subsidies, and give their customers better products and services at lower prices.

---

[14] Amadeo M. Di Lodovico, William W. Lewis, Vincent Palmade, and Shirish Sankhe, "India—From Emerging to Surging," *The McKinsey Quarterly* 4 (2001): 1–5.

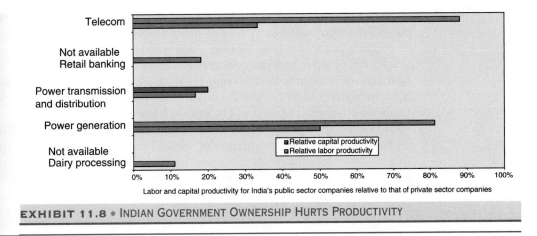

Labor and capital productivity for India's public sector companies relative to that of private sector companies

EXHIBIT 11.8 • INDIAN GOVERNMENT OWNERSHIP HURTS PRODUCTIVITY

Obstacles to Economic Reform   Yet in the best of circumstances, structural reform meets formidable political obstacles: labor unions facing job and benefit losses, bureaucrats fearful of diminished power and influence (not to mention their jobs), and local industrialists concerned about increased competition and reduced profitability. All are well aware that the benefits of restructuring are diffuse and materialize only gradually, while they must bear the costs immediately. Many are also trapped by a culture that sanctifies the state and distrusts the market's ability to bring about fair or wise results. This distrust reflects an ideology that equates inequality with inequity and is unwilling to accept the fact that the prospect of large rewards for some is the fuel that drives the economic engine of growth.

Despite these obstacles, reducing state subsidies on consumer goods and to inefficient industries, privatizing bloated state enterprises to boost productivity and force customer responsiveness, removing trade barriers and price controls, and freeing interest rates and the exchange rate to move to market levels are probably the most straightforward and workable solutions to economic stagnation. These actions, if implemented, can increase output (by making the economy more efficient) and reduce consumption, therefore increasing the quantity of goods available for export. They will also discourage capital flight and stimulate domestic savings and investment.

The simple truth is that a nation's success is not a function of the way its government harnesses resources, manages workers, or distributes wealth. Rather, economic success depends on the ability and willingness of a nation's people to work hard and take risks in the hopes of a better life. From this perspective, the state's best strategy is to provide basic stability, and little else, thereby permitting the humble to rise and the great to fall.

11.3 COUNTRY RISK ANALYSIS IN INTERNATIONAL BANKING

This section explores country risk from a bank's standpoint, the possibility that borrowers in a country will be unable or unwilling to service or repay their debts to foreign lenders in a timely manner. Countries that default will lose access, at least temporarily, to the international financial markets. For many borrowers, this penalty is severe enough that they do not voluntarily default on their bank loans. Thus, countries will sometimes go to extraordinary lengths to continue servicing their debts. Bank country risk analysis can, therefore, focus largely on the ability to repay rather than willingness to repay. Consequently, the essence of country risk analysis at commercial banks is an assessment of factors that affect the likelihood that a country, such as Mexico, will be able to generate sufficient dollars to repay foreign debts as these debts come due.

These factors are both economic and political and are very similar to those we have already examined in analyzing country risk from an MNC's perspective. Among economic factors often pointed to are the country's resource base and its external financial position. Most important, however, are the quality and effectiveness of a country's economic and financial management policies. The evidence from those countries that have defaulted on their international debts is that all too often the underlying causes of country risk are homegrown, with massive corruption, bloated bureaucracies, and government intervention in the economy leading to inefficient and uncompetitive industries and huge amounts of capital squandered on money-losing ventures. In addition, poor macroeconomic policies have made their own contribution to economic instability. Many of these countries have large budget deficits that they monetized, leading to high rates of inflation, overvalued currencies, and periodic devaluations. The deficits stem from too many promises that cannot be met from available resources and high tax rates that result in tax evasion, low revenue collections, and further corruption.

Political factors that underlie country risk include the degree of political stability of a country and the extent to which a foreign entity, such as the United States, is willing to implicitly stand behind the country's external obligations. Lending to a private-sector borrower also exposes a bank to commercial risks, in addition to country risk. Because these commercial risks are generally similar to those encountered in domestic lending, they are not treated separately.

11.3.1 Country Risk and the Terms of Trade

What ultimately determines a nation's ability to repay foreign loans is that nation's ability to generate U.S. dollars and other hard currencies. This ability, in turn, is based on the nation's terms of trade. Most economists would agree that these terms of trade are largely independent of the nominal exchange rate, unless the observed exchange rate has been affected by government intervention in the foreign exchange market.

In general, if its terms of trade increase, a nation will be a better credit risk. Alternatively, if its terms of trade decrease, a nation will be a poorer credit risk. This **terms-of-trade risk**, however, can be exacerbated by political decisions. When a nation's terms of trade improve, foreign goods become relatively less expensive, the nation's standard of living rises, and consumers and businesses become more dependent on imports. However, because there is a large element of unpredictability to relative price changes, shifts in the terms of trade also will be unpredictable. When the nation's terms of trade decline, as must inevitably happen when prices fluctuate randomly, the government will face political pressure to maintain the nation's standard of living.

As we saw in Section 11.2, a typical response is for the government to fix the exchange rate at its former (and now overvalued) level—that is, to subsidize the price of dollars. Loans made when the terms of trade improved are now doubly risky: first, because the terms of trade have declined and, second, because the government is maintaining an *overvalued currency*, further reducing the nation's net inflow of dollars. The deterioration in the trade balance usually results in added government borrowing. Capital flight exacerbates this problem, as residents recognize their country's deteriorating economic situation.

To summarize, a terms-of-trade risk can be exacerbated if the government tries to avoid the necessary drop in the standard of living when the terms of trade decline by maintaining the old and now-overvalued exchange rate. In reality, of course, this element of country risk is a political risk. The government is attempting by political means to hold off the necessary economic adjustments to the country's changed wealth position.

A key issue, therefore, in assessing country risk is the speed with which a country adjusts to its new wealth position. In other words, how fast will the necessary austerity policy be implemented? The speed of adjustment will be determined in part by the government's perception of the costs and benefits associated with austerity versus default.

11.3.2 The Government's Cost/Benefit Calculus

The cost of austerity is determined primarily by the nation's external debts relative to its wealth, as measured by its gross domestic product. The lower this ratio, the lower the relative amount of consumption that must be sacrificed to meet a nation's foreign debts.

The cost of default is the likelihood of being cut off from international credit. This possibility brings with it its own form of austerity. Most nations will follow this path only as a last resort, preferring to stall to buy time in the hope that something will happen in the interim. That something could be a bailout by the IMF, the Bank for International Settlements, the Federal Reserve, or some other major central bank. The bailout decision is largely a political decision. It depends on the willingness of citizens of another nation, usually the United States, to tax themselves on behalf of the country involved.[15] This willingness is a function of two factors: (1) the nation's geopolitical importance to the United States and (2) the probability that the necessary economic adjustments will result in an unacceptable political turmoil.

The more a nation's terms of trade fluctuate and the less stable its political system, the greater the odds the government will face a situation that will tempt it to hold off on the necessary adjustments. Terms-of-trade variability probably will be inversely correlated with the degree of product diversification in the nation's trade flows. With limited diversification—for example, dependence on the export of one or two primary products or on imports heavily weighted toward a few commodities—the nation's terms of trade are likely to be highly variable. This characterizes the situation facing many Third World countries. It also describes, in part, the situation of those OECD (Organisation for Economic Cooperation and Development) nations heavily dependent on oil imports.

11.3.3 Lessons from Successful Economic Reform

The experiences of Mexico, Chile, and Argentina—countries that appear to have successfully implemented economic reform programs—show that they all met the following criteria:[16]

- A head of state who demonstrates strong will and political leadership
- A viable and comprehensive economic plan that is implemented in a proper sequence
- A motivated and competent economic team working in harmony
- Belief in the plan from the head of state, the cabinet, and other senior officials
- An integrated program to sell the plan to all levels of society through the media

These criteria are applicable not only to Latin America but to all LDCs anywhere in the world. Even with the best of intentions, however, economic reform is painful and difficult to make stick unless all levels of society are convinced that instituting free-market policies will bring the long-term benefits of sustained growth.

---

[15] See Tamir Agmon and J. K. Dietrich, "International Lending and Income Redistribution: An Alternative View of Country Risk," *Journal of Banking and Finance*, December 1983, pp. 483–495, for a discussion of this point.

[16] These criteria appear in William R. Rhodes, "Third World Debt: The Disaster That Didn't Happen," *The Economist*, September 12, 1992, pp. 21–23.

11.4 SUMMARY AND CONCLUSIONS

From the standpoint of a multinational corporation, country risk analysis is the assessment of factors that influence the likelihood that a country will have a healthy investment climate. A favorable business environment depends on the existence of a stable political and economic system in which entrepreneurship is encouraged and free markets predominate. Under such a system, resources are most likely to be allocated to their highest-valued uses, and people will have the greatest incentive to take risks in productive ventures. To fully achieve these desirable outcomes requires the institutions of a free society: limited government, rule of law fostered by an independent judiciary, protection of private property, free markets, and free speech.

Several costly lessons have led to a new emphasis on country risk analysis in international banking as well. From the bank's standpoint, country risk—the credit risk on loans to a nation—is largely determined by the real cost of repaying the loan versus the real wealth that the country has to draw on. These parameters, in turn, depend on the variability of the nation's terms of trade and the government's willingness to allow the nation's standard of living to adjust rapidly to changing economic fortunes.

The experience of those countries that have made it through the international debt crisis suggests that others in a similar situation can get out only if they institute broad systemic reforms. Their problems are caused by governments spending too much money to meet promises they should not make. They create public-sector jobs for people to do things they should not do and subsidize companies to produce high-priced goods and services. These countries need less government and fewer bureaucratic rules. Debt forgiveness or further capital inflows would only tempt these nations to postpone economic adjustment further.

QUESTIONS

1. What are some indicators of country risk? Of country economic health?

2. What can we learn about economic development and political risk from the contrasting experiences of East and West Germany, North and South Korea, and China and Taiwan, Hong Kong, and Singapore?

3. What role do property rights and the price system play in national development and economic efficiency?

4. What indicators would you look for in assessing the political riskiness of an investment in Eastern Europe?

5. Exhibit 6.6 describes some economic changes that have been instituted by Mexico in recent years.
   a. What are the likely consequences of those changes?
   b. Who are the winners and the losers from these economic changes?

PROBLEMS

1. Comment on the following statement discussing Mexico's recent privatization: "Mexican state companies are owned in the name of the people but are run and now privatized to benefit Mexico's ruling class."

2. Between 1981 and 1987, FDI in the Third World plunged by more than 50%. The World Bank is concerned about this decline and wants to correct it by improving the investment climate in Third World countries. Its solution: Create a Multilateral Investment Guarantee Agency (MIGA) that will guarantee foreign investments against expropriation at rates to be subsidized by western governments.
   a. Assess the likely effects of MIGA on both the volume of western capital flows to Third World nations and the efficiency of international capital allocation.
   b. How will MIGA affect the probability of expropriation and respect for property rights in Third World countries?
   c. Is MIGA likely to improve the investment climate in Third World nations?

d. According to a senior World Bank official (*Wall Street Journal*, December 22, 1987, p. 20), "There is vastly more demand for political risk coverage than the sum total available." Is this a valid economic argument for setting up MIGA? Explain.

e. Assess the following argument made on behalf of MIGA by a State Department memo: "We should avoid penalizing a good project (by not providing subsidized insurance) for bad government policies over which they have limited influence . . . Restrictions on eligible countries (receiving insurance subsidies because of their doubtful investment policies) will decrease MIGA's volume of business and spread of risk, making it harder to be self-sustaining." (Quoted in the *Wall Street Journal*, December 22, 1987, p. 20.)

3. In the early 1990s, China decided that by 2000 it would boost its electricity-generating capacity by more than half. To do that, it is planning on foreigners' investing at least $20 billion of the roughly $100 billion tab. However, Beijing has informed investors that, contrary to their expectations, they will not be permitted to hold majority stakes in large power-plant or equipment-manufacturing ventures. In addition, Beijing has insisted on limiting the rate of return that foreign investors can earn on power projects. Moreover, this rate of return will be in local currency without official guarantees that the local currency can be converted into dollars, and it will not be permitted to rise with the rate of inflation. Beijing says that if foreign investors fail to invest in these projects, it will raise the necessary capital by issuing bonds overseas. However, these bonds will not carry the "full faith and credit of the Chinese government."

   a. What problems do you foresee for foreign investors in China's power industry?

   b. What options do potential foreign investors have to cope with these problems?

   c. How credible is the Chinese government's fallback position of issuing bonds overseas to raise capital in lieu of foreign direct investment?

4. You have been asked to head a special presidential commission on the Russian economy. Your first assignment is to assess the economic consequences of the following six policies and suggest alternative policies that may have more favorable consequences.

   a. Under the current Russian system, any profits realized by a state enterprise are turned over to the state to be used as the state sees fit. At the same time, shortfalls of money do not constrain enterprises from consuming resources. Instead, the state bank automatically advances needy enterprises credit, at a zero interest rate, to buy the inputs they need to fulfill the state plan and to make any necessary investments.

   b. The Russian fiscal deficit has risen to an estimated 13.1% of GDP. This deficit has been financed almost exclusively by printing rubles. At the same time, prices are controlled for most goods and services.

   c. Russian enterprises are allocated foreign exchange to buy goods and services necessary to accomplish the state plan. Any foreign exchange earned must be turned over to the state bank.

   d. In an effort to introduce a more market-oriented system, the government has allowed some Russian enterprises to set their own prices on goods and services. However, other features of the system have not been changed: Each enterprise is still held accountable for meeting a certain profit target; only one state enterprise can produce each type of good or service; and individuals are not permitted to compete against state enterprises.

   e. Given the disastrous state of agriculture, the Russian government has permitted some private plots on which anything grown can be sold at unregulated prices in open-air markets. Because of their success, the government has recently expanded this program, giving Russian farmers access to much more acreage. At the same time, a number of western nations are organizing massive food shipments to Russia to cope with the current food shortages.

   f. The United States and other western nations are considering instituting a Marshall Plan for Eastern Europe that would involve massive loans to Russia and other Eastern European nations in order to prop up the reform governments.

5. The president of Mexico has asked you to advise him on the likely economic consequences of the following five policies designed to improve Mexico's economic environment. Describe the consequences of each policy, and evaluate the extent to which these proposed policies will achieve their intended objective.

   a. Expand the money supply to drive down interest rates and stimulate economic activity.

   b. Increase the minimum wage to raise the incomes of poor workers.

   c. Impose import restrictions on most products to preserve the domestic market for local manufacturers and thereby increase national income.

   d. Raise corporate and personal tax rates from 50% to 70% to boost tax revenues and reduce the Mexican government deficit.

   e. Fix the nominal exchange rate at its current level in order to hold down the cost to Mexican consumers of imported necessities (assume that inflation is currently 100% annually in Mexico).

BIBLIOGRAPHY

Agmon, T. and J. K. Dietrich, "International Lending and Income Redistribution: An Alternative View of Country Risk," *Journal of Banking and Finance*, December 1983, pp. 483–495.

Carlos Sabino, "No stalgia for the left, "Independent Institute, May 15, 2006, http://www.independent.org/newsroom.

Kobrin, S. J. "Political Risk: A Review and Reconsideration," *Journal of International Business Studies*, Spring–Summer 1979, pp. 67–80.

Krueger, A. O. "Asian Trade and Growth Lessons," *American Economic Review*, May 1990, pp. 108–112.

Landes, D. S. "Why Are We So Rich and They So Poor?" *American Economic Review*, May 1990, pp. 1–13.

Lessard, D. R. and John Williamson, eds. *Capital Flight and Third World Debt*. Washington, D.C.: Institute for International Economics, 1987.

Plaut, S. "Capital Flight and LDC Debt," *FRBSF Weekly Letter*, Federal Reserve Bank of San Francisco, January 8, 1988.

Rhodes, W. R. "Third World Debt: The Disaster That Didn't Happen," *The Economist*, September 12, 1992, pp. 21–23.

Shapiro, A. C. "The Management of Political Risk," *Columbia Journal of World Business*, Fall 1981, pp. 45–56.

_____. "Risk in International Banking," *Journal of Financial and Quantitative Analysis*, December 1982, pp. 727–739.

_____. "Currency Risk and Country Risk in International Banking," *Journal of Finance*, July 1985, pp. 881–891.

INTERNET RESOURCES

www.moodys.com Web site of Moody's. Contains country risk ratings and analyses.

www.standardandpoors.com Web site of Standard & Poor's. Contains country risk ratings and analyses.

www.countryrisk.com Web site dedicated to the analysis of country risk. Provides editorials, reviews, bibliography, and links to prominent country risk analysis Web sites.

http://www.beri.com/ Web site of Business Environment Risk Intelligence (BERI). Contains analyses of business environment in various countries, as well as political and operational risks associated with specific countries.

https://www.cia.gov/library/publications/the-world-factbook/index.html Web site of CIA: The World Factbook. Contains demographic, social, political, and economic data for every country.

http://www.bis.org/ Web site of the Bank for International Settlements which contains information on international banking activities and links to central banks of the world.

http://www.imf.org/ Web site of the International Monetary Fund. Contains information and data on the IMF, SDRs and exchange rates, position of each country in the IMF, and lending arrangements with member nations.

INTERNET EXERCISES

1. What country risk factors do Moody's and Standard & Poor's emphasize?
2. Pick out a country (e.g., Argentina, China). What is the general assessment of your pick's country risk? Has it increased or decreased over the past year? What factors caused this change?

APPENDIX 11A

MANAGING POLITICAL RISK

After the firm has analyzed the political environment of a country, assessed its implications for corporate operations, and decided to invest there, it must then determine how to structure its investment to minimize political risk. The key point is that political risk is not independent of the firm's activities; the configuration of the firm's investments will, in large measure, determine its susceptibility to changing government policies.

PREINVESTMENT PLANNING

Given the recognition of political risk, an MNC can follow at least four separate, though not necessarily mutually exclusive, policies: (1) avoidance, (2) insurance, (3) negotiating the environment, and (4) structuring the investment.

Avoidance   The easiest way to manage political risk is to avoid it, and many firms do so by screening out investments in politically uncertain countries. However, inasmuch as all governments make decisions that influence the profitability of business, all investments, including those made in the United States, face some degree of political risk. For example, U.S. steel companies have had to cope with stricter environmental regulations requiring the expenditure of billions of dollars for new pollution control devices, and U.S. oil companies have been beleaguered by so-called windfall profit taxes, price controls, and mandatory allocations. Thus, political risk avoidance is impossible.

The real issue is the degree of political risk a company is willing to tolerate and the return required to bear it. A policy of staying away from countries considered to be politically unstable ignores the potentially high returns available and the extent to which a firm can control these risks. After all, companies are in business to take risks, provided these risks are recognized, intelligently managed, and provide compensation.

Insurance   An alternative to risk avoidance is insurance. Firms that insure assets in politically risky areas can concentrate on managing their businesses and forget about political risk, or so it appears. Most developed countries sell *political risk insurance* to cover the foreign assets of domestic companies. The coverage provided by the U.S. government through the **Overseas Private Investment Corporation** (OPIC) is typical. The OPIC program provides U.S. investors with insurance against loss due to the specific political risks of expropriation, currency inconvertibility, and political violence—that is, war, revolution, or insurrection. To qualify, the investment must be a new one or a substantial expansion of an existing facility and must be approved by the host government. Coverage is restricted to 90% of equity participation. For very large investments or for projects deemed especially risky, OPIC coverage may be limited to less than 90%. The only exception is institutional loans to unrelated third parties, which may be insured for the full amount of principal and interest.

Similar OPIC political risk protection is provided for leases. OPIC's insurance provides lessors with coverage against loss due to various political risks, including the inability to convert local currency received in lease payments into dollars.

OPIC also provides business income coverage (BIC), which protects a U.S. investor's income flow if political violence causes damage that interrupts operation of the foreign enterprise. For example, an overseas facility could be bombed and partially or totally destroyed. It may take weeks or months to rebuild the plant, but during the rebuilding process the company still must meet its interest and other contractual payments and pay skilled workers in order to retain their services pending reopening of the business. BIC allows a business to meet its continuing expenses and to make a normal profit during the period its operations are suspended. This is similar to the business interruption insurance available from private insurers for interruptions caused by nonpolitical events.

Two fundamental problems arise when one relies exclusively on insurance as a protection from political risk. First, there is an asymmetry involved. If an investment proves unprofitable, it is unlikely to be expropriated. Because business risk is not covered, any losses must be borne by the firm itself. On the other hand, if the investment proves successful and is then expropriated, the firm is compensated only for the value of its assets. This result is related to the second problem: Although the economic value of an investment is the present value of its future cash flows, only the capital investment in assets is covered by insurance. Thus, although insurance can provide partial protection from political risk, it falls far short of being a comprehensive solution.

Negotiating the Environment   In addition to insurance, therefore, some firms try to reach an understanding with the host government before undertaking the investment, defining rights and responsibilities of both parties. Also known as a **concession agreement**, such an understanding specifies precisely the rules under which the firm can operate locally.

In the past, these concession agreements were quite popular among firms investing in less-developed countries, especially in colonies of the home country. They often were negotiated with weak governments. In time, many of these countries became independent or their governments were overthrown. Invariably, the new rulers repudiated these old concession agreements, arguing that they were a form of exploitation.

Concession agreements still are being negotiated today, but they seem to carry little weight among Third World countries. Their high rate of obsolescence has led many firms to pursue a more active policy of political risk management.

Structuring the Investment   Once a firm has decided to invest in a country, it then can try to minimize its exposure to political risk by increasing the host government's cost of interfering with company operations. This action involves adjusting the operating policies (in the areas of production, logistics, exporting, and technology transfer) and the financial policies to closely link the value of the foreign project to the multinational firm's continued control. In effect, the MNC is trying to raise the cost to the host government of exercising its ever-present option to expropriate or otherwise reduce the local affiliate's value to its parent.[17]

One key element of such a strategy is keeping the local affiliate dependent on sister companies for markets or supplies or both. Chrysler, for example, managed to hold on to its Peruvian assembly plant even though other foreign property was being nationalized. Peru ruled out expropriation because of Chrysler's stranglehold on the supply of essential components. Only 50% of the auto and truck parts were manufactured in Peru. The remainder—including engines, transmissions, sheet metal, and most accessories—were supplied from Chrysler plants in Argentina, Brazil, and Detroit. In a similar instance of vertical integration, Ford's Brazilian engine plant generates substantial exports, but only to other units of Ford. Not surprisingly, the data reveal no expropriations of factories that sell more than 10% of their output to the parent company.[18]

Similarly, by concentrating R&D facilities and proprietary technology, or at least key components thereof, in the home country, a firm can raise the cost of nationalization. This strategy will be effective only if other multinationals with licensing agreements are not permitted to service the nationalized affiliate. Another element of this strategy is establishing a single, global trademark that cannot be legally duplicated by a government. In this way, an expropriated consumer-products company would sustain significant losses by being forced to operate without its recognized brand name.

Control of transportation including shipping, pipelines, and railroads has also been used at one time or another by the United Fruit Company and other multinationals to gain leverage over governments. Similarly, sourcing production in multiple plants reduces the government's ability to hurt the worldwide firm by seizing a single plant, and, thereby, it changes the balance of power between government and firm.

Another defensive ploy is to develop external financial stakeholders in the venture's success. This defense involves raising capital for a venture from the host and other governments, international financial institutions, and customers (with payment to be provided out of production) rather than employing funds supplied or guaranteed by the parent company. In addition to spreading risks, this strategy will elicit an international response to any expropriation move or other adverse action by a host government. A last approach, particularly for extractive projects, is to obtain unconditional host government guarantees for the amount of the investment that will enable creditors to initiate legal action in foreign courts against any commercial transactions between the host country and third parties if a subsequent government repudiates the nation's obligations. Such guarantees provide investors with potential sanctions against a foreign government, without having to rely on the uncertain support of their home governments.

OPERATING POLICIES

After the multinational has invested in a project, its ability to further influence its susceptibility to political risk is greatly diminished but not ended. It still has at least three different policies that it can pursue with varying chances of success: (1) changing the benefit/cost ratio of expropriation, (2) developing local stakeholders, and (3) adaptation.

Before examining these policies, it is better to recognize that the company can do nothing and hope that even though the local regime can take over an affiliate (with minor cost), it will choose not to do so. This wish is not necessarily in vain because it rests on the premise that the country needs foreign direct investment and will be unlikely to receive it if existing operations are expropriated without fair and full compensation. However, this strategy is essentially passive, resting on a belief that other multinationals will hurt the country (by withholding potential investments) if the country nationalizes local affiliates. Whether this passive approach will succeed is a function of how dependent the country is on foreign investment to realize its own development plans and the degree to which economic growth will be sacrificed for philosophical or political reasons.

ILLUSTRATION   *Beijing Jeep Company*

After the United States restored diplomatic relations with China in 1979, western businesses rushed in to take advantage of the world's largest undeveloped market. Among them was American Motors Corporation (AMC). In 1983, AMC and Beijing Automotive Works formed a joint venture

---

[17] Arvind Mahajan, "Pricing Expropriation Risk," *Financial Management*, Winter 1990, pp. 77–86, points out that when a multinational firm invests in a country, it is effectively writing a call option to the government on its property. The aim of political risk management is to reduce the value to the government of exercising this option.

[18] David Bradley, "Managing Against Expropriation," *Harvard Business Review*, July–August, 1977, pp. 75–83.

called the Beijing Jeep Company to build and sell jeeps in China.[19] The aim of Beijing Jeep was first to modernize the old Chinese jeep, the BJ212, and then to replace it with a "new, second-generation vehicle" for sale in China and overseas. Because it was one of the earliest attempts to combine Chinese and foreign forces in heavy manufacturing, Beijing Jeep became the flagship project other U.S. firms watched to assess the business environment in China. Hopes were high.

AMC viewed this as a golden opportunity: Build jeeps with cheap labor and sell them in China and the rest of the Far East. The Chinese government wanted to learn modern automotive technology and earn foreign exchange. Most important, the People's Liberation Army wanted a convertible-top, four-door jeep, so that Chinese soldiers could jump in and out and open fire from inside the car.

That the army had none of these military vehicles when they entered Tienanmen Square in 1989 has to do with the fact that this jeep could not be made from any of AMC's existing jeeps. However, in signing the initial contracts, the two sides glossed over this critical point. They also ignored the realities of China's economy. For managers and workers, productivity was much lower than anybody at AMC had ever imagined. Equipment maintenance was minimal. Aside from windshield solvents, spare-tire covers, and a few other minor parts, no parts could be manufactured in China. The joint venture, therefore, had little choice but to turn the new Beijing jeep into the Cherokee Jeep, using parts kits imported from the United States. The Chinese were angry and humiliated not to be able to manufacture any major jeep components locally.

They got even angrier when Beijing Jeep tried to force its Chinese buyers to pay half of the Cherokee's $19,000 sticker price in U.S. dollars. With foreign exchange in short supply, the Chinese government ordered its state agencies, the only potential customers, not to buy any more Cherokees and refused to pay the $2 million that various agencies owed on 200 Cherokees already purchased.

The joint venture would have collapsed right then had Beijing Jeep not been such an important symbol of the government's modernization program. After deciding it could not let the venture fail, China's leadership arranged a bailout. The Chinese abandoned their hopes of making a new military jeep, and AMC gained the right to convert renminbi (the Chinese currency) into dollars at the official (and vastly overvalued) exchange rate. With this right, AMC realized it could make more money by replacing the Cherokee with the old, and much cheaper to build, BJ212s. The BJ212s were sold in China for renminbi, and these profits were converted into dollars.

It was the ultimate irony: An American company that originally expected to make huge profits by introducing modern technology to China and by selling its superior products to the Chinese found itself surviving, indeed thriving, by selling the Chinese established Chinese products. AMC succeeded because its venture attracted enough attention to turn the future of Beijing Jeep into a test of China's open-door policy.

A more active strategy is based on the premise that expropriation is basically a rational process—that governments generally seize property when the economic benefits outweigh the costs. This premise suggests two maneuvers characteristic of active political risk management: Increase the benefits to the government if it does not nationalize a firm's affiliate, and increase the costs if it does.

Changing the Benefit/Cost Ratio   If the government's objectives in an expropriation are rational—that is, based on the belief that economic benefits will more than compensate for the costs—the multinational firm can initiate a number of programs to reduce the perceived advantages of local ownership and thereby diminish the incentive to expel foreigners. These steps include establishing local R&D facilities, developing export markets for the affiliate's output, training local workers and managers, expanding production facilities, and manufacturing a wider range of products locally as substitutes for imports. Many of the foregoing actions lower the cost of expropriation and, consequently, reduce the penalty for the government. A delicate balance must be observed.

Realistically, however, it appears that those countries most likely to expropriation view the benefits—real, imagined, or both—of local ownership as more important than the cost of replacing the foreign investor. Although the value

---

[19] This example is adapted from Jim Mann, *Beijing Jeep: The Short, Unhappy Romance of American Business in China* (New York: Simon and Schuster, 1989).

of a subsidiary to the local economy can be important, its worth may not be sufficient to protect it from political risk. Thus, one aspect of a protective strategy must be to engage in actions that raise the cost of expropriation by increasing the negative sanctions it would involve. These actions include control over export markets, transportation, technology, trademarks and brand names, and components manufactured in other nations. Some of these tactics may not be available once the investment has been made, but others still may be implemented. However, an exclusive focus on providing negative sanctions may well be self-defeating by exacerbating the feelings of dependence and loss of control that often lead to expropriation in the first place. Where expropriation appears inevitable, with negative sanctions only buying more time, it may be more productive to prepare for negotiations to establish a future contractual-based relationship.

Developing Local Stakeholders   A more positive strategy is to cultivate local individuals and groups who have a stake in the affiliate's continued existence as a unit of the parent MNC. Potential stakeholders include consumers, suppliers, the subsidiary's local employees, local bankers, and joint venture partners.

Consumers worried about a change in product quality or suppliers concerned about a disruption in their production schedules (or even a switch to other suppliers) brought about by a government takeover may have an incentive to protest. Similarly, well-treated local employees may lobby against expropriation.[20] Local borrowing could help give local bankers a stake in the health of the MNC's operations if any government action threatened the affiliate's cash flows and thereby jeopardized loan repayments.

Having local private investors as partners seems to provide protection. One study found that joint ventures with local partners have historically suffered only a 0.2% rate of nationalization, presumably because this arrangement establishes a powerful local voice with a vested interest in opposing government seizure.[21]

The shield provided by local investors may be of limited value to the MNC, however. The partners will be deemed to be tainted by association with the multinational. A government probably would not be deterred from expropriation or enacting discriminatory laws because of the existence of local shareholders. Moreover, the action can be directed solely against the foreign investor, and the local partners can be the genesis of a move to expropriate the venture to enable them to acquire the whole of a business at a low or no cost.

Adaptation   Today, some firms are trying a more radical approach to political risk management. Their policy entails adapting to the inevitability of potential expropriation and trying to earn profits on the firm's resources by entering into licensing and management agreements. For example, oil companies whose properties were nationalized by the Venezuelan government received management contracts to continue their exploration, refining, and marketing operations. These firms have recognized that it is not necessary to own or control an asset such as an oil well to earn profits. This form of arrangement may be more common in the future as countries develop greater management abilities and decide to purchase from foreign firms only those skills that remain in short supply at home. Firms that are unable to surrender control of their foreign operations because these operations are integrated into a worldwide production-planning system or some other form of global strategy are also the least likely to be troubled by the threat of property seizure, as was pointed out in the aforementioned Chrysler example.

---

[20] French workers at U.S.-owned plants, satisfied with their employers' treatment of them, generally stayed on the job during the May 1968 student-worker riots in France, even though most French firms were struck.

[21] Bradley, "Managing Against Expropriation," pp. 75–83.

INTERNATIONAL FINANCING AND NATIONAL CAPITAL MARKETS

Money, like wine, must always be scarce with those who have neither wherewithal to buy it nor credit to borrow it.

Adam Smith (1776)

CHAPTER LEARNING OBJECTIVES

- To describe trends and differences in corporate financing patterns around the world
- To define securitization and explain the forces that underlie it and how it has affected the financing policies of MNCs
- To explain why bank lending is on the decline worldwide and how banks have responded to their loss of market share
- To explain what is meant by the globalization of financial markets and identify the factors that have affected the process of globalization
- To describe the external medium- and long-term financing options available to the multinational corporation
- To identify the functions and consequences of financial markets
- To describe the links between national and international capital markets
- To describe the Eurocurrency and Eurobond markets and explain why they exist
- To describe the characteristics and pricing of Eurocurrency loans, Eurobonds, Euronotes, and Euro-commercial paper
- To explain the links between the Euromarkets and their domestic counterparts
- To explain why firms may choose to raise capital overseas

KEY TERMS

all-in cost
Asiacurrency (Asiadollar) market
basis points
capital productivity
convertible bonds
corporate governance
covenants
dragon bond
drawdown
entrepôt
equity-related bonds
equity warrants
Eurobank
Eurobond
Eurobond market

Euro-commercial paper (Euro-CP)
Eurocurrency
Eurocurrency market
Eurodollar
Euro-medium term note (Euro-MTN)
Euronote
Financial deregulation
financial innovation
financial intermediaries
fixed-rate issue
floating-rate note (FRN)
foreign bank market
foreign bond market
foreign equity market
global bond issue

global shares
globalization of financial markets
international financial markets
inverse floater
investment banker
keiretsu
London interbank bid rate (LIBID)
London interbank offered rate (LIBOR)
note issuance facility (NIF)
privately placed bonds
project finance
publicly issued bonds

regulatory arbitrage
revolving underwriting facility (RUF)
Rule 144A
Samurai bond
securitization
Shogun bond
swap
underwriting
universal banking
Yankee bond
Yankee stock issue

The growing internationalization of capital markets and the increased sophistication of companies means that the search for capital no longer stops at the water's edge. This is true particularly for multinational corporations. A distinctive feature of the financial strategy of MNCs is the wide range of external sources of funds that they use on an ongoing basis. General Motors packages car loans as securities and sells them in Europe and Japan. British Telecommunications offers stock in London, New York, and Tokyo, whereas Beneficial Corporation issues Euroyen notes that may not be sold in either the United States or Japan. Swiss Bank Corporation—aided by Italian, Belgian, Canadian, and German banks, as well as other Swiss banks—helps RJR Nabisco sell Swiss franc bonds in Europe and then swap the proceeds back into U.S. dollars.

This chapter also explores the MNC's external medium- and long-term financing alternatives. These sources include both national and international capital markets, along with specialized sources of capital such as project finance. The international capital markets include the Eurocurrency and Eurobond markets, which are increasingly important sources of funds for MNCs. We begin by discussing trends in corporate financing patterns.

12.1 CORPORATE SOURCES AND USES OF FUNDS

Firms have three general sources of funds available: internally generated cash, short-term external funds, and long-term external funds. External finance can come from investors or lenders. Investors give a company money by buying the securities it issues in the financial markets. These securities, which are generally *negotiable* (tradable), usually take the form of publicly issued debt or equity. Debt is the preferred alternative: Regardless of the country studied, debt accounts for the overwhelming share of external funds. By contrast, new stock issues play a relatively small and declining role in financing investment. Regardless of whether debt or equity is offered to the public, the issuer will likely turn to a financing specialist, the **investment banker**, to assist in designing and marketing the issue. The latter function usually requires purchasing, or **underwriting**, the securities and then distributing them. Investment bankers are compensated by the *spread* between the price at which they buy the security and the price at which they can resell it to the public.

The main alternative to issuing public debt securities directly in the open market is to obtain a loan from a specialized financial intermediary that issues securities (or deposits) of its own in the market. These alternative debt instruments usually are commercial bank loans for short-term and medium-term credit or privately placed bonds for longer-term credit. Unlike **publicly issued bonds**, **privately placed bonds** are sold directly to only a limited number of sophisticated investors, usually life insurance companies and pension funds. Moreover, privately placed bonds are generally nonnegotiable and have complex, customized loan agreements called **covenants**. The restrictions in the covenants range from limits on dividend payments to prohibitions on asset sales and new debt issues. They provide a series of checkpoints that permit the lender to review actions by the borrower that have the potential to impair the lender's position. These agreements have to be regularly renegotiated before maturity. As a result, privately placed bonds are much more like loans than like publicly issued and traded securities.

12.1.1 Financial Markets versus Financial Intermediaries

Sources of external finance differ widely from country to country. German, French, and Japanese companies rely heavily on bank borrowing, whereas U.S. and British industry raise much more money directly from financial markets by the sale of securities. In all these countries, however, bank borrowing is on the decline. Corporate borrowing is increasingly taking the form of negotiable securities issued in the public capital markets rather than the form of nonmarketable loans provided by financial intermediaries.

This process, termed **securitization**, is most pronounced among Japanese companies. Securitization largely reflects a reduction in the cost of using financial markets when the cost of bank borrowing has risen. Until recently, various regulatory restrictions enabled banks to attract low-cost funds from depositors. With **financial deregulation**, which began in the United States in 1981 and in Japan in 1986 and is still ongoing, banks now must compete for funds with a wide range of institutions at market rates. In addition, regulatory demands for a stronger capital base have forced U.S. banks to use more equity financing, raising their cost of funds. Inevitably, these changes have pushed up the price of bank loans. Any top-flight company now can get money more cheaply by issuing commercial paper than it can from its banks. As a result, banks have a smaller share of the market for short-term business credit. Japanese companies also are finding that issuing bonds and leasing equipment are cheaper sources of medium-term and long-term money as well.

At the same time, the cost of accessing the public markets is coming down, especially for smaller and less well-known companies. Historically, these companies found it more economical to obtain loans from banks or to place private bond issues with life insurance companies. These *private placements* have proved cheaper because banks and life insurance companies specialize in credit analysis and assume a large amount of a borrower's debt. Consequently, they could realize important cost savings in several functions, such as gathering information about the condition of debtor firms, monitoring their actions, and renegotiating loan agreements.

Recent technological improvements in such areas as data manipulation and telecommunications have greatly reduced the costs of obtaining and processing information about the conditions that affect the creditworthiness of potential borrowers. Any analyst now has computerized access to a wealth of economic and financial information at a relatively low cost, along with programs to store and manipulate this information. Thus, investors are now more likely to find it cost-effective to lend directly to companies rather than indirectly through **financial intermediaries**, such as commercial banks.

12.1.2 Financial Systems and Corporate Governance

Despite the apparent convergence of financial systems, there are still some notable differences among countries in terms of **corporate governance**, which refers to the means whereby companies are controlled. The United States and United Kingdom are often viewed as prototypes of a market-oriented financial system (frequently referred to as the Anglo-Saxon or AS model), whereas Germany, France, and Japan are generally regarded as typical representatives of bank-centered finance (the Continental European and Japanese or CEJ type of financial system). In AS countries, institutional investors (pension funds, mutual funds, university and other nonprofit endowments, and insurance companies) make up an important part of the financial system. In CEJ countries, banks dominate the picture. Equity finance is important in AS countries and institutional shareholders exert a great deal of corporate control. The accepted objective is to maximize shareholder value, and boosting the return on capital employed is stressed. The emphasis on shareholder value has recently been endorsed by an international advisory panel to the Organisation for Economic Cooperation and Development (OECD). According to the head of the panel, the Asian economic crisis can be traced to weak corporate governance: "Nobody was watching [Asian] management; they were growing for the sake of growth with no concern for shareholder value."[1] The crisis could most likely have been avoided, he said, had American-style corporate governance been in place.[2]

In CEJ countries, bank finance is prominent, share ownership and control are concentrated in banks and other firms, and corporate decision making is heavily influenced by close personal relationships between corporate leaders who sit on each other's boards of directors. Individual shareholders have little voice, resulting in much less concern for shareholder value and relatively low returns on capital. However, in all countries, competitive pressures and the threat of hostile takeovers of underperforming companies are forcing greater managerial accountability and an increased focus on shareholder value.

The difference in financial systems has real consequences for financial structures. For example, as already noted, large Japanese companies employ a high degree of leverage, particularly compared with U.S. companies. The ability to take on such large amounts of debt stems in part from the vast mutual-aid networks that most large Japanese firms can tap. These are the fabled **keiretsu**, the large industrial groupings, often with a major bank at the center, that form the backbone of corporate Japan. Keiretsu ties constitute a complex web of tradition, cross-shareholdings, trading relationships, management, cooperative projects, and information swapping. The keiretsu offer financial backing, management advice, and favorable contracts to their members and provide a safety net when corporate relatives get into trouble.

Partly because of the difference in industrial structures in the two countries, U.S. and Japanese firms relate to the banking system in a different way. Almost all big Japanese companies have one main bank—usually the bank around which the keiretsu is formed—that is their primary source of long-term loans. The main bank will have access to information about the company and have a say in its management that in most other countries would be unacceptable. Moreover, Japanese banks, unlike their U.S. counterparts, can hold industrial shares, so the main bank often holds a sizable amount of the equity of its borrowers. For example, until recently, Japanese banks owned almost 40% of the outstanding stock of Japanese manufacturing companies. Thus, for Japanese companies, the strong relation with one main bank—along with close ties with the other members of their keiretsu—is their main method of minimizing the risk of financial distress.[3]

The same is true of Germany, where so-called **universal banking** is practiced; German commercial banks not only perform investment banking activities but also take major equity positions in companies. As both stockholder and creditor, German banks can reduce the conflicts between the two classes of investors, leading to lower costs and

---

[1] Quoted in Robert L. Simison, "Firms Worldwide Should Adopt Ideas of U.S. Management, Panel Tells OECD," *Wall Street Journal,* April 2, 1998, p. A4.

[2] Rene Stulz argues ("The Limits of Financial Globalization," Ohio State University Working paper, January 2004) that the benefits of financial globalization are limited in those nations where weak corporate governance and weak property rights lead to significant agency problems. These agency problems arise because rulers of sovereign states and corporate insiders can pursue their own interests at the expense of outside investors.

[3] For a detailed analysis of the governance structure of the keiretsu, see Steven N. Kaplan and Bernadette A. Minton, "Appointments of Outsiders to Japanese Boards: Determinants and Implications for Managers," *Journal of Financial Economics,* October 1994, pp. 225–258; Erik Berglif and Enrico Perotti, "The Governance Structure of the Japanese Financial Keiretsu," *Journal of Financial Economics,* October 1994, pp. 259–284.

speedier action in "workouts" of financial problems. The resulting increase in organizational efficiency should mean less risk for German companies in taking on large amounts of debt. In the United States, where corporate bank relations are less intimate, companies rely primarily on equity as a shock absorber. However, these cross-shareholdings have also created a highly stable corporate structure that sheltered German companies from competition and aggressive shareholders and resulted in underperforming operations.

The price that Japanese and German companies pay for their heavy reliance on bank debt is less freedom of action. As the cost of accessing the capital markets directly has dropped, the main-bank relationship has gradually eroded in Japan and Germany, and Japanese and German companies have looked more to the equity market as their cushion against financial distress. In turning to the capital markets, German and Japanese firms are now confronting the same market pressures that U.S. companies have long faced. The result is a new shareholder-oriented management approach in many German and Japanese companies. With money being harder to come by, equity capital is forced to earn its keep. The result will be fewer poor investments and a greater focus on profits and shareholder value rather than on size and market share.

12.1.3 Globalization of Financial Markets

The same advances in communications and technology that have lowered the cost of accessing financial markets directly, together with financial deregulation abroad—the lifting of regulatory structures that inhibit competition and protect domestic markets—have blurred the distinction between domestic and foreign financial markets. As the necessary electronic technology has been developed and transaction costs have plummeted, the world has become one vast, interconnected market. Markets for U.S. government securities and certain stocks, foreign exchange trading, interbank borrowing and lending, to cite a few examples, operate continuously round the clock and around the world and in enormous size. The **globalization of financial markets** has brought about an unprecedented degree of competition among key financial centers and financial institutions that has further reduced the costs of issuing new securities.

Growing competition also has led to increasing deregulation of financial markets worldwide. Deregulation is hastened by the process of **regulatory arbitrage**, whereby the users of capital markets issue and trade securities in financial centers with the lowest regulatory standards and, hence, the lowest costs. In order to win back business, financial centers around the world are throwing off obsolete and costly regulations. For example, concerned that Tokyo had fallen behind London and New York as a global finance center, the Japanese government has developed a "Big Bang" financial reform program. This program would break down regulatory barriers between Japanese banks, insurance companies, and brokerage houses, and would also create opportunities in Japan for foreign financial companies by cutting red tape and barriers to the market. Deregulation, in Japan and elsewhere, is little more than an acknowledgment that the rules do not, and cannot, work.

Financial deregulation also has been motivated by the growing recognition in nations with bank-centered financial systems that such systems are not providing adequately for the credit needs of the small and medium-sized firms that are the engines of growth and innovation. It has not escaped the notice of governments worldwide that the corporate success stories of the past 20 years—companies like Microsoft, Dell, Cisco, Amazon.com, 3Com, Yahoo!, Oracle, and Amgen—have come predominantly from the United States. Germany and Japan can boast of few Netscapes, AOLs, Iomegas, Suns, Compaqs, or Genentechs. By deregulating their financial markets, policymakers hope that their countries will emulate the results of the U.S. system of corporate finance.

The combination of freer markets with widely available information has laid the foundation for global growth. Fund raising is global now as well, with a growing amount of money being raised on the international capital markets. According to BIS figures, the amount of money raised on the international capital markets has grown rapidly, rising to over $3.6 trillion in 2004. Treasurers are no longer confined to domestic markets as their source of funding and are now quick to exploit any attractive opportunity that occurs anywhere in the world.

Whereas competition drives the international financial system, innovation is its fuel. **Financial innovation** segments, transfers, and diversifies risk. It also enables companies to tap previously inaccessible markets and permits investors and issuers alike to take advantage of tax loopholes. More generally, financial innovation presents opportunities for value creation. To the extent that a firm can design a security that appeals to a special niche in the capital market, it can attract funds at a cost that is less than the market's required return on securities of comparable risk. However, such a rewarding situation is likely to be temporary because the demand for a security that fits a particular niche in the market is not unlimited. On the other hand, the supply of securities designed to tap that niche is likely to increase dramatically once the niche is recognized. Even though financial innovation may not be a sustainable form of value creation, it nonetheless can enable the initial issuers to raise money at a below-market rate.

ILLUSTRATION   *The Swedish Export Credit Corporation Innovates*

The Swedish Export Credit Corporation (SEK) borrows about $2 billion annually. To reduce its funding costs, SEK relies heavily on financial innovation. For example, SEK issued a straight bond, stripped it down to its two components—an annuity consisting of the interest payments and a zero-coupon bond consisting of the principal repayment at maturity—and sold the pieces to different investors. The annuity cash flow was tailored to meet the demands of a Japanese insurance company that was looking for an interest-only security, whereas the zero-coupon portion appealed to European investors who desired earnings taxed as capital gains rather than interest income. By unbundling the bond issue into separate parts that appealed to distinct groups of investors, SEK created a financial transaction whose parts were worth more than the whole.

Financial innovation has dramatically increased international capital mobility. As in the domestic case, cross-border financial transfers can take place through international securitization or international financial intermediation. The hypothetical case depicted in Exhibit 12.1 illustrates the distinction between these two mechanisms for international fund flows. A Belgian corporation with surplus funds seeks an investment outlet, and a Japanese corporation requires additional funds. International securitization might involve the Japanese firm issuing new bonds and selling them directly to the Belgian firm.

Alternatively, the Belgian firm's surplus funds could be transferred to the Japanese firm through international financial intermediation. This intermediation could involve three (or more) stages. First, the Belgian firm deposits its funds with a local Belgian bank. Second, the Belgian bank redeposits the money with an international money center bank in London that turns around and lends those funds to a Japanese bank. Third, the Japanese bank lends those funds to the Japanese corporation.

Whether international fund flows take place through financial intermediation or securitization depends on the relative costs and risks of the two mechanisms. The key determinant here is the cost of gathering information on foreign firms. As these costs continue to come down, international securitization should become increasingly more cost-effective.

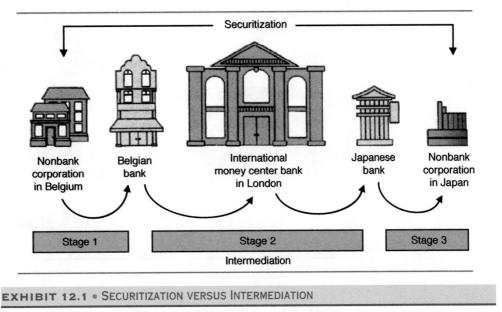

EXHIBIT 12.1 • SECURITIZATION VERSUS INTERMEDIATION

Source: Anthony Saunders, "The Eurocurrency Interbank Market: Potential for International Crises?" Reprinted from *Business Review,* January/February 1988, p. 19. Used with permission of Federal Reserve Bank of Philadelphia.

12.2 NATIONAL CAPITAL MARKETS AS INTERNATIONAL FINANCIAL CENTERS

The principal functions of a financial market and its intermediaries are to mobilize savings (which involves gathering current purchasing power in the form of money from savers and transferring it to borrowers in exchange for the promise of greater future purchasing power) and to allocate those funds among potential users on the basis of expected risk-adjusted returns. Financial markets also facilitate both the transfer of risk (from companies to investors) and the reduction of risk (by investors holding a diversified portfolio of financial assets). Subsequent to the investment of savings, financial markets help to monitor managers (by gathering information on their performance) and exert corporate control (through the threat of hostile takeovers for underperforming firms and bankruptcy for insolvent ones). Financial markets also supply *liquidity* to investors by enabling them to sell their investments before maturity, thereby encouraging investment in worthwhile longer-term projects.

The consequences of well-functioning financial markets are as follows. More and better projects get financed (because of higher savings, a more realistic scrutiny of investment opportunities, and the lower cost of capital associated with risk diversification and increased liquidity); managers are compelled to run companies in accordance with the interests of investors (through active monitoring and the threat of bankruptcy or a hostile takeover for underperformers and by linking managerial compensation to stock prices); the rate of innovation is higher (by identifying and funding those entrepreneurs with the best chances of successfully initiating new goods and production processes); and individuals are able to select their preferred time pattern of consumption (saving consists of individuals deferring consumption in some periods so as to increase their consumption in later periods) and their preferred risk-return trade-off. The result is stronger economic growth and greater consumer satisfaction. These factors are summarized in Exhibit 12.2.

Financial markets work best when property rights are secure, contracts are easily enforceable, meaningful accounting information is available, and borrowers and investors

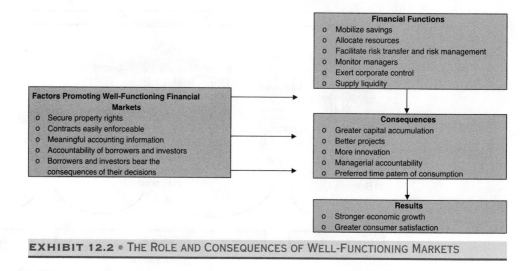

EXHIBIT 12.2 • THE ROLE AND CONSEQUENCES OF WELL-FUNCTIONING MARKETS

are accountable for their decisions and bear the economic consequences of their behavior. In the absence of these conditions, markets cannot allocate capital efficiently and economic growth suffers.

The financial disaster in Asia points out the dangers of allocating capital by cronyism and bureaucratic dictate rather than through a rational process governed by realistic estimates of prospective risks and rewards. This command-and-control capitalism produced dysfunctional financial sectors that squandered hundreds of billions of dollars of hard-earned savings on unproductive investments and grandiose projects and begot corruption without end. The banking calamity in Japan bears continuing witness to the problems that can arise when the fundamental elements of openness and accountability are not just absent from a financial system but contrary to official policy.

ILLUSTRATION *Japanese Regulators Press Shinsei Bank to Make Bad Loans*

Even as the Japanese government has pledged to clean up its ravaged banking industry, Japanese regulators have pressured Shinsei Bank Ltd., the first Japanese bank bought by foreigners, to continue lending to some of its shakiest customers. In meetings with Shinsei executives, top officials of Japan's Financial Services Agency (FSA) directed Shinsei to loosen its credit policy and be more lenient to ailing borrowers. Shinsei was formed in March 2000 when a U.S. investor group, Ripplewood Holdings, acquired the failed Long Term Credit Bank of Japan Ltd. (LTCB).

LTCB failed because it was unable, and unwilling, to follow the basic prescription for revitalizing a collapsing bank: Write off bad loans and cut credit to hopeless companies. That failure, and the difficulties faced by Shinsei, point up the clash between two visions of finance—a competitive, rational American one and Japan's longstanding system of entangled preferences and noneconomic motives. These conflicting visions are best expressed by the former head of LTCB, who said, "Perhaps the American way might be more efficient in a narrow economic sense, but it risked sacrificing the values that were most precious in Japan; ideas of harmony, respect and consensus." As Japan's property and stock markets collapsed during the 1990s, and bad loans proliferated, the Ministry of Finance quietly told banks to understate their bad debts and keep their borrowers on financial life support. LTCB followed this advice and kept growing, even showing profits by adopting ever more lenient loan classifications. Eventually, after several rescue plans fell through, LTCB was sold to Ripplewood.

Shinsei has stirred controversy since it opened under new management, because it told its corporate borrowers that if loans did not meet new standards for profitability the borrowers had to repay them, pay higher interest, or offer collateral. Even more shocking to Japanese sensibilities, Shinsei has refused to help bail out delinquent borrowers and has cut off credit to risky customers. Such practices, standard among western banks, are a novelty in Japan and have resulted in a spate of newspaper and magazine articles criticizing Shinsei for being tight-fisted. Foreign investors are closely watching Shinsei as a test case of whether Japan will allow modern lending practices in its clubby banking world. Arm-twisting of bankers by politicians and regulators to support deadbeat borrowers is a major reason why Japan's banks have been crippled by bad loans for over a decade. Although Shinsei agreed to some of the FSA's changes to its lending policy, the bank said it would not make concessions that compromise its financial health.

Conversely, a healthy dose of market discipline and the stringent credit standards it enforces can work wonders for an economy. A study by the McKinsey Global Institute examined **capital productivity**—the ratio of output (goods and services) to the input of physical capital (plant and equipment)—in Germany, Japan, and the United States.[4] Overall, U.S. capital productivity exceeded that of Japan and Germany by about 50%. As a result, the United States can simultaneously save less, consume more, and grow faster. This economic hat trick can be traced directly to activist shareholders demanding management accountability and paying for performance; tough disclosure rules and financial transparency in corporate accounts that allow investors to make informed decisions; rigorous credit analysis that helps screen out bad risks; and a willingness to inflict pain on imprudent lenders, cut off capital to less competitive companies, and allow inefficient companies to fail. Although many politicians and others claim that U.S. financial markets have hindered U.S. productivity by forcing American companies to be short-term oriented, the McKinsey report suggests exactly the opposite that the focus of U.S. financial markets on financial performance, reinforced by strong corporate governance (the Enron and WorldCom scandals notwithstanding), leads directly to improved business performance. In the process of rewarding success and penalizing failure, financial virtue creates its own reward.

Good corporate governance also adds value for its practitioners. Another McKinsey study found that over 80% of potential investors would be willing to pay more for the shares of a well-governed company than for those of a poorly governed company with comparable financial performance. The actual premium investors say they would be willing to pay for a well-governed company differs by country: an 18% premium for a well-governed U.S. or U.K. company; a 20% premium for a well-governed German or Japanese company; a 22% premium for a well-governed Italian company; and a 27% premium for one in Venezuela or Indonesia.[5]

[4] McKinsey Global Institute, *Capital Productivity*, Washington, D.C., June 1996. This report is summarized in Raj Agrawal, Stephen Findley, Sean Greene, Kathryn Huang, Aly Jeddy, William W. Lewis, and Markus Petry, "Capital Productivity: Why the U.S. Leads and Why It Matters," *The McKinsey Quarterly*, 1996, No. 3, pp. 38–55.

[5] *Investor Opinion Survey on Corporate Governance*, McKinsey & Company, June 2000. For the purpose of the country surveys, a well-governed company is defined as having a majority of outside directors on the board with no management ties; holding formal evaluations of directors; and being responsive to investor requests for information on governance issues. In addition, directors hold significant stockholdings in the company, and a large proportion of directors' pay is in the form of stock options.

MINI-CASE   *Beijing Tries to Overhaul Banks Through IPOs*

China's banks are estimated to hold $500–$700 billion in bad loans, or about half the nation's annual GDP. This lending disaster makes China the home of the world's largest potential banking crisis. Faulty corporate governance is at the heart of this ticking time bomb. A history of low pay, lax supervision, and politicized lending has resulted in loans being made that were doomed from the outset. Beyond the ever-present corruption that plagues the banking system, the biggest problem is the role that Communist Party officials continue to play in lending decisions. Being government owned, China's banks report to party bosses rather than to independent boards of directors or to shareholders. The result is a lack of accountability and transparency. Moreover, as tools for government-directed lending, China's banks have little expertise in assessing risk or pricing capital.

State-owned enterprises (SOEs), which tend to be far less efficient than foreign-funded enterprises, account for over 50% of outstanding bank credit. This figure reflects the fact that banks in China traditionally were required to finance the operations of SOEs, regardless of their profitability or risk. Owing to various obstacles, such as barriers to laying off workers, SOEs find it difficult to reduce their costs. At the same time, because they employ millions of workers, banks face enormous pressure to continue lending to SOEs.

Although the government is unlikely to permit the banking sector to collapse, a healthy banking industry is critical to achieve Beijing's goal of maintaining strong, but more efficient, economic growth. One answer that Beijing has come up with to reform the banking sector is to have its largest state-owned banks launch initial public offerings (IPOs). Beijing's main goal in listing these banks is not to raise cash but rather to subject them to the discipline and scrutiny of financial markets and international regulators that accompany a public listing. According to Fred Hu of Goldman Sachs in Hong Kong, "Given all the political interference, it is very hard to run the banks on a commercial basis. The first step is to change their ownership, and IPOs are a way to achieve that."[6] Similarly, Beijing has made overseas listings a key component of state-owned industrial enterprise reform because they provide companies with pressure from public shareholders to pursue profits and wean themselves from government handouts.

QUESTIONS

1. Would you expect loans to SOEs to be safer or riskier than other Chinese bank loans? Explain.

2. How can IPOs improve the sorry performance of Chinese banks?

3. What difficulties will China face in preparing their state-owned banks for IPOs?

4. What other steps can the Chinese government take to improve the performance of their banks?

5. How would a more efficient banking system benefit China?

6. What is the downside of introducing market forces into China's banking system?

---

[6] Kathy Chen and Karby Leggett, "China Plans IPO for State Banks as Part of Overhaul," *Wall Street Journal*, October 22, 2003, A18.

12.2.1 International Financial Markets

Not surprisingly, most of the major financial markets attract both investors and fund raisers from abroad. That is, these markets are also **international financial markets**, where foreigners can both borrow and lend money. International financial markets can develop anywhere, provided that local regulations permit the market and that the potential users are attracted to it. The most important international financial centers are London, Tokyo, and New York. All the other major industrial countries have important domestic financial markets as well, but only some, such as Germany and, recently, France, are also important international financial centers. On the other hand, some countries that have relatively unimportant domestic financial markets are important world financial centers. The markets of those countries, which include Switzerland, Luxembourg, Singapore, Hong Kong, the Bahamas, and Bahrain, serve as financial **entrepôts**, or channels through which foreign funds pass. That is, these markets serve as financial intermediaries between nonresident suppliers of funds and nonresident users of funds.

Political stability and minimal government intervention are prerequisites for becoming and remaining an important international financial center, especially an entrepôt center. Historically, London's preeminence as an entrepôt for international finance comes from its being a lightly regulated offshore market in a world of financial rigidities. That is why it became home to the Euromarkets about 40 years ago. As financial markets deregulate, London's strength has shifted to its central location (including its central time zone) and financial infrastructure—its access to information by dint of its position astride huge international capital flows, its pool of financial talent, its well-developed legal system, and its telecommunications links. Even more important, financial firms need to be near big investors, and there is more money under management in London than anywhere else in Europe.

12.2.2 Foreign Access to Domestic Markets

Despite the increasing liberalization of financial markets, governments are usually unwilling to rely completely on the market to perform the functions of gathering and allocating funds. Foreigners in particular are often hampered in their ability to gain access to domestic capital markets because of government-imposed or government-suggested restrictions relating to the maturities and amounts of money that they can raise. They are also hampered by the government-legislated extra costs, such as special taxes (for example, the U.S. interest equalization tax, or IET, in effect from 1963 to 1974), which they must bear on those funds that they can raise. Nonetheless, the financial markets of many countries are open wide enough to permit foreigners to borrow or invest.

As a citizen of many nations, the multinational firm has greater leeway in tapping a variety of local money markets than does a purely domestic firm, but it, too, is often the target of restrictive legislation aimed at reserving local capital for indigenous companies or the local government. The capital that can be raised is frequently limited to local uses through the imposition of exchange controls. As we have seen previously, however, multinationals are potentially capable of transferring funds, even in the presence of currency controls, by using a variety of financial channels. To the extent, therefore, that local credits substitute for parent- or affiliate-supplied financing, the additional monies are available for removal.

The Foreign Bond Market   The **foreign bond market** is an important part of the international financial markets. It is simply that portion of the domestic bond market that represents issues floated by foreign companies or governments. As such, foreign bonds are subject to local laws and must be denominated in the local currency. At times, these issues face additional restrictions as well. For example, foreign bonds floated in Switzerland,

Germany, and the Netherlands are subject to a queuing system, where they must wait for their turn in line.

The United States and Switzerland contain the most important foreign bond markets. (Dollar-denominated foreign bonds sold in the United States are called **Yankee bonds**.) Major foreign bond markets are also located in Japan and Luxembourg. (Yen bonds sold in Japan by a non-Japanese borrower are called **Samurai bonds**, in contrast to **Shogun bonds**, which are foreign currency bonds issued within Japan by Japanese corporations.)

In recent years, more of these foreign bond offerings have consisted of global bond issues. A **global bond** issue is an offering, usually denominated in dollars, that is registered in several national jurisdictions and marketed to investors around the world. A typical global issue is Philip Morris's $1 billion 8-year bond offering sold in 1997. The benefits of these global offerings are that issuing companies become better known overseas, broaden their investor base, and often save on financing costs.

Foreign bond issues, like their purely domestic counterpart, come in three primary flavors: fixed-rate issues, floating-rate notes (FRNs), and equity-related issues. **Fixed-rate issues** are similar to their domestic counterparts, with a fixed coupon, set maturity date, and full repayment of the principal amount at maturity. **Floating-rate notes** have variable coupons that are reset at fixed intervals, usually every 3 to 6 months. The new coupon is set at a fixed margin above a mutually agreed reference rate such as the treasury bill rate or the commercial paper rate.

Equity-related bonds combine features of the underlying bond and common stock. The two principal types of equity-related bonds are convertible bonds and bonds with equity warrants. **Convertible bonds** are fixed-rate bonds that are convertible into a given number of shares before maturity. **Equity warrants** give their holder the right to buy a specified number of shares of common stock at a specified price during a designated time period. The relative amount of foreign bonds issued in the three different categories varies from year to year depending on market conditions.

After the economic crisis in Asia, Asian corporations scrambled for new equity to recapitalize and shore up balance sheets overloaded with debt and unsupported by much remaining equity at the new exchange rates. The preferred method of providing new equity or its equivalent was through convertible bonds and preferred shares. Both give fresh money coming into a troubled company a higher claim on assets under liquidation than would straight equity, while at the same time providing a significant upside opportunity for investors who thought the markets had overreacted. The benefit for struggling companies is that convertibles reduce debt-service charges because they carry lower interest rates than the debt they replace. In addition, upon conversion (if it occurs), the debt becomes equity.

The Foreign Bank Market   The **foreign bank market** represents that portion of domestic bank loans supplied to foreigners for use abroad. As in the case of foreign bond issues, governments often restrict the amounts of bank funds destined for foreign purposes. Foreign banks, particularly Japanese banks, have become an important funding source for U.S. corporations.

One indication of the importance of foreign banks is the fact that very few of the world's 25 largest banks ranked by assets are American. This can be attributed primarily to prohibitions on interstate banking in the United States. However, it should be noted that size is not everything. In terms of market capitalization, which reflects current and anticipated profitability, U.S. banks fare much better than banks from other countries.

The Foreign Equity Market   The idea of placing stock in foreign markets has long attracted corporate finance managers. One attraction of the **foreign equity market** is the diversification of equity funding risk: A pool of funds from a diversified shareholder base insulates a company from the vagaries of a single national market. Some issues are too large to be taken up only by investors in the national stock market. For large companies located in small countries, foreign sales may be a necessity. When KLM, the Dutch airline, issued 50 million shares to raise $304 million, it placed 7 million shares in Europe, 7 million in the United States, and 1 million in Japan. According to a spokesman for the company, "The domestic market is too small for such an operation."[7]

Selling stock overseas also can increase the potential demand for the company's shares, and hence its price, by attracting new shareholders. An international stock offering can also spread the firm's name in local markets, an advantage for a firm that wants to project an international presence. In the words of a London investment banker, "If you are a company with a brand name, it's a way of making your product known and your presence known in the financial markets, which can have a knock-off effect on your overall business. A marketing exercise is done; it's just like selling soap."[8] According to Apple Computer's investor relations manager, Apple listed its shares on the Tokyo exchange and the Frankfurt exchange "to raise the profile of Apple in those countries to help us sell computers. In Japan, being listed there gets us more interest from the business press."[9] Recent empirical research supports the hypothesis that raising equity globally is associated with significant benefits.[10]

To capture some of these potential benefits, many companies have sold stock issues overseas. Many foreign companies have decided to sell their IPOs in the United States because they "get a better price, a shareholder base that understands their business, and they can get publicity in a major market for their products."[11]

ILLUSTRATION   *Daimler-Benz Becomes a Yankee*

In 1993, Daimler-Benz (now DaimlerChrysler), the industrial conglomerate that makes the Mercedes-Benz, became the first German company to list its shares on the New York Stock Exchange. To qualify for the listing, Daimler-Benz had to provide an onerous, by German standards, level of financial disclosure and undertake a costly revision of its accounting practices to conform to U.S. generally accepted accounting principles (GAAP). The difference between GAAP and German accounting rules is apparent in Daimler-Benz's published results for fiscal 1994. Although Daimler showed a profit of $636 million under German rules, it reported a loss of $748 million after conforming to GAAP and eliminating the impact of drawing down hidden reserves (which is allowed in Germany). Daimler-Benz undertook the arduous task of revising its financial statements because the company wanted access to the large and liquid pool of capital represented by the U.S. market. Daimler also felt that the positive image of its Mercedes cars would help it raise capital at a lower price from wealthy Americans. During the 6 weeks between the announcement of its plans for a New York Stock Exchange (NYSE) listing and actually receiving the listing, Daimler-Benz's shares rose more than 30%, in contrast to an 11% rise for the German stock market overall.

---

[7] "International Equities: The New Game in Town," *Business International Money Report*, September 29, 1987, p. 306.

[8] "International Equities: The New Game in Town."

[9] Quoted in Kathleen Doler, "More U.S. Firms See Foreign Shareholdings as a Plus," *Investors Business Daily*, February 17, 1994, p. A4.

[10] See Vihang R. Errunza and Darius P. Miller, "Valuation Effects of Seasoned Global Equity Offerings," *Journal of Banking and Finance*, 27 (2003), pp. 1611–1623.

[11] Quoted in Michael R. Sesit, "Foreign Firms Flock to U.S. for IPOs," *Wall Street Journal*, June 23, 1995, p. C1.

Similarly, it is not just large foreign companies that have issued stock in the United States. The existence of numerous U.S. investment analysts, entrepreneurs, and investors familiar with the nature and needs of emerging firms meant that many medium-sized European firms found it easier and quicker to do IPOs on the Nasdaq exchange in the United States than to raise capital in their underdeveloped domestic capital markets.

Most major stock exchanges permit sales of foreign issues provided they satisfy all the listing requirements of the local market. Despite a downturn in foreign listings since 2000, some of the major stock markets, including the German, British, and U.S. exchanges, still list large numbers of foreign stocks. Although many foreign companies are listed on the NYSE, even more would be were it not for the Securities and Exchange Commission's (SEC) demand that they first conform to tougher U.S. accounting and disclosure practices. The SEC, however, is under pressure to relax its stand by both foreign companies and the NYSE, the latter because it worries about falling behind in the race to list large non-U.S. companies. Nonetheless, in 1997, one out of every four new listings on the NYSE was a foreign company, and such listings almost quadrupled between 1992 and 2000 to 400. However, the number of foreign company listings on U.S. stock exchanges declined by 8% in 2005 as compared to 2001. Moreover, in 2005, only one of the 25 largest IPOs was listed on the U.S. stock exchange. Observers charge that the stricter requirements of the Sarbanes-Oxley Act have dissuaded foreign companies from listing on the U.S. stock exchange.[12]

An important new avenue for foreign equity (and debt) issuers, ranging from France's Rhone-Poulenc to Korea's Pohang Iron & Steel, to gain access to the U.S. market was opened up in 1990 when the SEC adopted **Rule 144A**, which allows qualified institutional investors to trade in unregistered private placements, making them a closer substitute for public issues. This rule greatly increases the liquidity of the private placement market and makes it more attractive to foreign companies, who are frequently deterred from entering the U.S. market by the SEC's stringent disclosure and reporting requirements. An advantage of a private placement is that its total cost could be half of a public offering's cost. It also takes less time to do a private placement. However, pricing for private placements is not as competitive and the issuing company has limited ongoing access to U.S. securities markets compared to a public offering.

The desire to build a global shareholder base also has been inducing many American companies, which until the late 1980s issued stock almost exclusively in the United States, to sell part of their issues overseas. For example, in May 1992, General Motors raised $2.1 billion by selling 40 million shares in the United States, 6 million in Britain, 4.5 million in Europe, and 4.5 million in the Far East. Exhibit 12.3 shows the announcement of that issue. As usual, the benefits of expanded ownership must be traded off against the added costs of inducing more investors to become shareholders.

As mentioned above, since 2000, the trend toward listing on overseas exchanges has reversed, particularly for large multinationals. For example, in 2005, IBM announced it would delist from the Tokyo Stock Exchange, following its departure from exchanges in Vienna, Frankfurt, and Zurich. Other U.S. companies that have announced foreign delistings include Pepsico, Apple, and Procter & Gamble.

The primary reason for foreign delistings is that investors prefer to trade shares in the market in which they get the best price—which is usually the stocks' home market. Companies pay annual fees to list on foreign markets, so they have an incentive to delist when trading is light overseas. In London, foreign share listings dropped to 351 in 2004 from 419 in 2002, but rebounded further to 642 by January 2007. Over the same period of time, the number of foreign stock listings on the NYSE dropped to 460 from 473. Till

---

[12] Jeffrey Marshall, "Are Foreign Issuers Shunning the U.S.?" *Financial Executive*, 22 (October), 2006, pp. 25–28.

All of these Securities have been sold. This announcement appears as a matter of record only.

$2,145,000,000

GM

General Motors Corporation
$1⅔ Par Value Common Stock

55,000,000 Shares

Global Coordinator
MORGAN STANLEY & CO.
Incorporated

40,000,000 Shares

MORGAN STANLEY & CO
Incorporated

The portion of the offering has been offered in the United States by the undersigned.

THE FIRST BOSTON CORPORATION

LEHMAN BROTHERS

MERRILL LYNCH & CO.

J.P. MORGAN SECURITIES INC.

PAINEWEBBER INCORPORATED

SMITH BARNEY, HARRIS UPHAM & CO.
Incorporated

DEAN WITTER REYNOLDS INC.

6,000,000 Shares

MORGAN STANLEY INTERNATIONAL

This portion of the offering has been offered in the United Kingdom by the undersigned.

CAZENOVE & CO.

S. G. WARBURG SECURITIES

4,500,000 Shares

MORGAN STANLEY INTERNATIONAL

This portion of the offering has been offered in the Asia Pacific region by the undersigned.

DAIWA EUROPE LIMITED

NOMURA INTERNATIONAL

4,500,000 Shares

MORGAN STANLEY INTERNATIONAL

This portion of the offering has been offered elsewhere internationally by the undersigned.

DEUTSCHE BANK
Aktiengesellschaft

UBS PHILLIPS & DREW SECURITIES LIMITED

May 21, 1992

EXHIBIT 12.3 • GENERAL MOTORS' GLOBAL EQUITY ISSUE

Source: Reprinted with permission both General Motors Corporation.

February 2007, 451 foreign companies were listed on the NYSE and 324 foreign companies were listed on the Nasdaq. On the Tokyo Stock Exchange, the number of foreign company listings stood at 28 in mid-2006, down from 125 in 1990.

Many companies continue to list shares in multiple countries because it gives individual investors greater access to shares in their own currency. For example, IBM still lists its shares on the London Stock Exchange and Euronext in Paris. Some have also argued that there is evidence of a "cross-listing premium"—or additional valuation as compared to a stay-at-home value—especially when the United States is home to one of the exchanges where the stock is listed. This phenomenon supposedly arises because investors place greater trust in a company that had undergone the detailed scrutiny of U.S. regulators. However, for many companies, the costs of multiple country listings outweigh the benefits. For example, almost two-thirds of the foreign companies listing on the Nasdaq through IPOs in 2004 chose not to list elsewhere. Simply put, both companies and investors are becoming increasingly selective in where they do business. Companies are searching the world's stock exchanges for those markets where they can access new shareholders at the lowest cost while investors are looking for the best prices and lowest transaction costs on their trades.

The rise of electronic exchanges and the growing desire of investors and companies to move beyond national borders for trading shares and raising capital—and to do so more cheaply—has put pressure on national stock exchanges to internationalize. National exchanges are consolidating (Euronext is an integrated exchange that combines the Paris Bourse, the Amsterdam Exchange, the Brussels Exchange, and the Lisbon Exchange), merging (or attempting to; the London Stock Exchange and the German Börse announced a merger in May 2000 that later fell apart), or entering into alliances (Nasdaq has formed affiliations with stock exchanges in Japan, Hong Kong, and Canada and the NYSE is exploring links with exchanges in Japan and France) in an attempt to capture more business or just to survive. The ultimate aim is to create a global stock market in which the shares of the world's largest companies can be traded 24 hours a day cheaply and efficiently. Such a market should bring greater liquidity and lower costs.

One outcome of the increasing globalization of stock markets is the global share. **Global shares** are ordinary shares of a non-U.S. company listed and traded in the same form on any market in the world. They are tracked in a single global registry, and trade in the home currency of each market. Cross-border clearing and settlement occurs electronically, as the leading international clearing and settlement organizations are setting up one global system of securities processing and settlement.

12.2.3 Globalization of Financial Markets Has Its Downside

The army of investors searching worldwide for the highest risk-adjusted returns wields a two-edged sword: It is likely to reward sound economic policies, and it is swift to abandon countries whose economic fundamentals are questionable. As a result, countries such as Italy, Spain, Sweden, and Mexico with large public sector or trade deficits or rapid money-supply growth have earned harsh treatment from financial markets. By demanding bigger premiums for the risk of holding these nations' currencies, the markets force *de facto* devaluations of their currencies, thereby serving to punish the profligate and reward the virtuous. In the eyes of many international economists, markets have replaced the International Monetary Fund as the disciplinary force for the global economy.

A devaluation raises the cost of imports for a country, boosts its interest rates (to lure investors back), and forces the government to take steps to address the monetary, budget, or trade problems that led to the capital flight and devaluation in the first place. Of course, changing the policies that created these problems can impose significant costs on favored political constituents, which is why these problems were not addressed earlier. For example, Japanese bureaucrats and politicians have long acted as if market forces exist only to be tamed or subverted. After a decade of Japanese economic stagnation, however, foreign investors pushed the stock and currency markets to levels so low that they threatened the existence of major Japanese banks and other corporations. The fear of further adverse financial market reaction has created a sense of crisis in Japan and pushed the nation's notoriously stodgy government to finally offer concrete plans to clean up its bankrupt financial sector and deregulate the economy.

Blaming financial markets for the political and economic disruptions caused by these policy changes misses the point. Financial markets are in the business of gathering and processing information from millions of savers and borrowers around the world in order to perform their real function, which is to price capital and allocate it to its most productive uses. In performing this function, markets reflect the perceptions of risk and reward of its participants. However, they do not create the underlying reality that caused those perceptions.

The long-run risk to the global economy caused by the abrupt shifts in capital flows and attendant waves of devaluations is that some politicians will seek to reimpose controls on capital and trade flows, particularly if the politicians manage to convince themselves that the markets are behaving in an irresponsible fashion. Such controls—whatever their motivation—would reverse the trend toward freer trade and capital markets and make the world worse off.

12.3 THE EUROCURRENCY MARKET

A **Eurocurrency** is a dollar or other freely convertible currency deposited in a bank outside its country of origin. Thus, U.S. dollars on deposit in London become **Eurodollars**. These deposits can be placed in a foreign bank or in the foreign branch of a domestic U.S. bank.[13] The **Eurocurrency market** then consists of those banks—called **Eurobanks**—that accept deposits and make loans in foreign currencies. Note that the prefix *Euro* as used here has nothing to do with the currency known as the euro.

The Eurobond and Eurocurrency markets are often confused with each other, but there is a fundamental distinction between the two. In the **Eurobond market**, **Eurobonds**, which are bonds sold outside the countries in whose currencies they are denominated, are issued directly by the final borrowers. The Eurocurrency market enables investors to hold short-term claims on commercial banks, which then act as intermediaries to transform these deposits into long-term claims on final borrowers. However, banks do play an important role in placing Eurobonds with the final investors.

The dominant Eurocurrency remains the U.S. dollar, but the importance of the Eurodollar waxes and wanes with the strength of the U.S. dollar. With dollar weakness in the latter parts of both the 1970s and 1980s, other currencies, particularly the Deutsche mark and the Swiss franc, increased in importance. Dollar strength in the 1990s again boosted the relative importance of the Eurodollar. The euro has now become an important currency for denominating Eurocurrency loans and Eurobonds.

12.3.1 Modern Origins

The origin of the post–World War II Eurodollar market is often traced to the fear of Soviet Bloc countries that their dollar deposits in U.S. banks might be attached by U.S. citizens with claims against Communist governments. Therefore, they left their dollar balances with banks in France and England.

Whatever its postwar beginnings, the Eurocurrency market has thrived for one reason: government regulation. By operating in Eurocurrencies, banks and suppliers of funds are able to avoid certain regulatory costs and restrictions that would otherwise be imposed. These costs and restrictions include:

- Reserve requirements that lower a bank's earning asset base (that is, a smaller percentage of deposits can be lent out).
- Special charges and taxes levied on domestic banking transactions, such as the requirement to pay Federal Deposit Insurance Corporation fees.
- Requirements to lend money to certain borrowers at concessionary rates, thereby lowering the return on the bank's assets.
- Interest rate ceilings on deposits or loans that inhibit the ability to compete for funds and lower the return on loans.
- Rules or regulations that restrict competition among banks.

Although many of the most burdensome regulations and costs have been eased or abolished, the Eurocurrency market still exists. It will continue to exist as long as there are profitable opportunities to engage in offshore financial transactions. These opportunities persist because of continuing government regulations and taxes that raise costs and lower returns on domestic transactions. Because of the ongoing erosion of domestic

---

[13] The term "foreign" is relative to the operating unit's location, not to its nationality.

regulations, however, these cost and return differentials are much less significant today than they were in the past. As a consequence, the domestic money market and Eurocurrency market are now tightly integrated for most of the major currencies, effectively creating a single worldwide money market for each participating currency.

12.3.2 Eurodollar Creation

The creation of Eurodollars can be illustrated by using a series of T-accounts to trace the movement of dollars into and through the Eurodollar market.

First, suppose that Leksell AB, a Swedish firm, sells medical diagnostic equipment worth $1 million to a U.S. hospital. It receives a check payable in dollars drawn on Citibank in New York. Initially, Leksell AB deposits this check in its Citibank checking account for dollar-working-capital purposes. This transaction would be represented on the firm's and Citibank's accounts as follows:

Citibank		Leksell AB	
	Demand deposit due Leksell AB +$1M	Demand deposit in Citibank +$1M	

In order to earn a higher rate of interest on the $1 million account (U.S. banks cannot pay interest on corporate checking accounts), Leksell decides to place the funds in a time deposit with Barclays Bank in London. This transaction is recorded as follows:

Citibank		Barclays	
	Demand deposit due Leksell AB −$1M	Demand deposit in Citibank +$1M	Time deposit owed Leksell +$1M
	Demand deposit due Barclays +$1M		

Leksell AB	
Demand deposit in Citibank −$1M	
Demand deposit in Barclays +$1M	

One million Eurodollars have just been created by substituting a dollar account in a London bank for a dollar account held in New York. Notice that no dollars have left New York, although ownership of the U.S. deposit has shifted from a foreign corporation to a foreign bank.

Barclays could leave those funds idle in its account in New York, but the opportunity cost would be too great. If it cannot immediately lend those funds to a government or commercial borrower, Barclays will place the $1 million in the London interbank market. This involves lending the funds to another bank active in the Eurodollar market. We saw in Chapter 9 that the interest rate at which such interbank loans are made is called the **London interbank offered rate (LIBOR)**. In this case, however, Barclays chooses to lend these funds to Ronningen SA, a Norwegian importer of fine wines. The loan is recorded as follows:

Citibank		Barclays	
Demand deposit due Barclays $-\$1M$	Demand deposit in Citibank $-\$1M$	Time deposit owed Leksell $+\$1M$	
Demand deposit due Ronningen SA` $+\$1M$	Loan to Ronningen SA $+\$1M$		

Ronningen SA	
Demand deposit in Citibank $+\$1M$	Eurodollar loan from Barclays $+\$1M$

We can see from this example that the Eurocurrency market involves a chain of deposits and a chain of borrowers and lenders, not buyers and sellers. One does not buy or sell Eurocurrencies. Ordinarily, an owner of dollars will place them in a time-deposit or demand-deposit account in a U.S. bank, and the owner of a pound deposit will keep it in an account with a British bank. Until the dollar (or pound) deposit is withdrawn, control over its use resides with the U.S. (or British) bank. In fact, the majority of Eurocurrency transactions involve transferring control of deposits from one Eurobank to another Eurobank. Loans to non-Eurobanks account for fewer than half of all Eurocurrency loans. The net market size (subtracting off inter-Eurobank liabilities) is much smaller than the gross market size.

The example and data presented indicate that Eurocurrency operations differ from the structure of domestic banking operations in two ways:

1. There is a *chain of ownership* between the original dollar depositor and the U.S. bank.
2. There is a *changing control over the deposit* and the use to which the money is put.

Despite the chain of transactions, the total amount of foreign dollar deposits in the United States remains the same. Moreover, on the most fundamental level—taking in deposits and allocating funds—the Eurocurrency market operates much as does any other financial market, except for the absence of government regulations on loans that can be made and interest rates that can be charged. Section 12.3.3 now examines some of the particular characteristics of Eurocurrency lending.

12.3.3 Eurocurrency Loans

The most important characteristic of the Eurocurrency market is that loans are made on a floating-rate basis. Interest rates on loans to governments and their agencies, corporations, and nonprime banks are set at a fixed margin above LIBOR for the given period and currency chosen. At the end of each period, the interest for the next period is calculated at the same fixed margin over the new LIBOR. For example, if the margin is 75 **basis points** (100 basis points equal 1%) and the current LIBOR is 6%, then the borrower is charged 6.75% for the upcoming period. The reset period normally chosen is 6 months, but shorter periods such as 1 month or 3 months are possible. The LIBOR used corresponds to the maturity of the reset period (for example, 6-month LIBOR, or LIBOR6, for a 6-month reset period).

Terms   The *margin*, or spread between the lending bank's cost of funds and the interest charged the borrower, varies a good deal among borrowers and is based on the borrower's perceived riskiness. Typically, such spreads have ranged from as little as 15 basis points (0.15%) to more than 3%, with the median being somewhere between 1% and 2%.

The *maturity* of a loan can vary from approximately 3 to 10 years. Maturities have tended to lengthen over time, from a norm of about 5 years originally to a norm of 8 to 10 years these days for prime borrowers. Lenders in this market are almost exclusively banks. In any single loan, there normally will be a number of participating banks that form a syndicate. The bank originating the loan usually will manage the syndicate. This bank, in turn, may invite one or two other banks to co-manage the loan. The managers charge the borrower a once-and-for-all syndication fee of 0.25% to 2% of the loan value, depending on the size and type of the loan. Part of this fee is kept by the managers, and the rest is divided up among all the participating banks (including the managing banks) according to the amount of funds each bank supplies.

The **drawdown**—the period over which the borrower may take the loan—and the repayment period vary in accordance with the borrower's needs. A commitment fee of about 0.5% per annum is paid on the unused balance, and prepayments in advance of the agreed schedule are permitted but are sometimes subject to a penalty fee. Borrowers in the Eurocurrency market are concerned about the effective interest rate on the money they have raised. This rate compares the interest rate paid to the net loan proceeds received by the borrower. Its computation is shown in the following example.

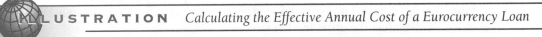

ILLUSTRATION *Calculating the Effective Annual Cost of a Eurocurrency Loan*

San Miguel, the Filipino beer brewer, has arranged a €250 million, 5-year, euro-denominated Eurocurrency (Euroeuro) loan with a syndicate of banks led by Credit Suisse and Deutsche Bank. With an up-front syndication fee of 2.0%, net proceeds to San Miguel are

$$€250,000,000 - (0.02 \times €250,000,000) = €245,000,000$$

The interest rate is set at LIBOR + 1.75%, with LIBOR reset every 6 months. Assuming an initial LIBOR6 rate for euros of 5.5%, the first semiannual debt service payment is

$$\frac{0.055 + 0.0175}{2} \times €250,000,000 = €9,062,500$$

San Miguel's effective annual interest rate for the first six months is thus

$$\frac{€9,062,500}{€245,000,000} \times 2 \times 100 = 7.40\%$$

Every six months, this annualized cost will change with LIBOR6.

MINI-CASE *Siemens Negotiates a Eurocurrency Loan*

Siemens AG, the large German electronics company, is looking to raise $500 million for the next 5 years. Bank of America and Deutsche Bank have come up with competing bids for the mandate to syndicate a $500 million Eurodollar loan for Siemens. Their proposals are as follows:

	Principal	Maturity
Interest rate	Bank of America proposal	Deutsche Bank proposal
Reset period	$0.5 billion	$0.5 billion
Syndication fee	5 years	5 years
	LIBOR + 0.25%	LIBOR + 0.375%
	Every six months	Every six months
	1.125%	0.75%

QUESTIONS

1. What are the net proceeds to Siemens from each of these syndicated loan proposals?
2. Assuming that 6-month LIBOR is currently at 4.35%, what is the effective annual interest cost to Siemens for the first 6 months of each loan?
3. Which of these two loans would you select on the basis of cost, all else being equal?
4. What other factors might you consider in deciding between these two loan proposals?

Multicurrency Clauses   Borrowing can be done in many different currencies, although the dollar is still the dominant currency. Increasingly, Eurodollars have a multicurrency clause. This clause gives the borrower the right (subject to availability) to switch from one currency to another on any rollover (or reset) date. The multicurrency option enables the borrower to match currencies on cash inflows and outflows (a potentially valuable exposure management technique as we saw in Chapter 9). Equally important, the option allows a firm to take advantage of its own expectations regarding currency changes (if they differ from the market's expectations) and shop around for those funds with the lowest effective cost.

An example of a typical multicurrency loan is a $100 million, 10-year revolving credit arranged by the Dutch firm Thyssen Bornemisza NV with nine Dutch, German, U.S., and Swiss banks, led by Amsterdam-Rotterdam Bank. Rates are fixed at the company's discretion at 3-month, 6-month, or 12-month intervals. At each rollover date, the firm can choose from any freely available Eurocurrency except Eurosterling, but only four different Eurocurrencies may be outstanding at any one time.

12.3.4 Relationship Between Domestic and Eurocurrency Money Markets

The presence of arbitrage activities ensures a close relationship between interest rates in national and international (Eurocurrency) money markets. Interest rates in the U.S. and Eurodollar markets, for example, can differ only to the extent that additional costs, controls, or risks are associated with moving dollars between, say, New York and London. Otherwise, arbitrageurs would borrow in the low-cost market and lend in the high-return market, quickly eliminating any interest differential between the two.

Interest Differentials   Since the cost of shifting funds is relatively insignificant, we must look to currency controls or risk to explain any substantial differences between

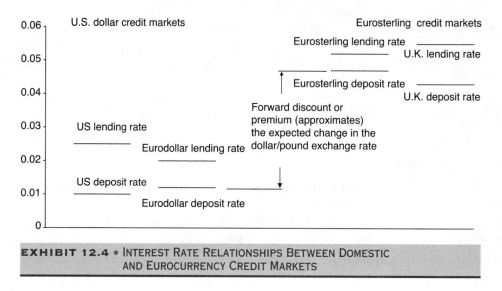

EXHIBIT 12.4 • INTEREST RATE RELATIONSHIPS BETWEEN DOMESTIC AND EUROCURRENCY CREDIT MARKETS

domestic and external rates. To the extent that exchange controls are effective, the national money market can be isolated or segmented from its international counterpart. In fact, the difference between internal and external interest rates can be taken as a measure of the effectiveness of the monetary authorities' exchange controls.

Interest differentials also can exist if there is a danger of future controls. The possibility that at some future time either the lender or borrower will not be able to transfer funds across a border, also known as sovereign risk, can help sustain persistent differences between domestic and external money market rates.

Eurocurrency Spreads In general, Eurocurrency spreads (a spread is the margin between lending and deposit rates) are narrower than in domestic money markets (see Exhibit 12.4). Lending rates can be lower because:

- The absence of the previously described regulatory expenses that raise costs and lower returns on domestic transactions.
- Most borrowers are well known, reducing the cost of information gathering and credit analysis.
- Eurocurrency lending is characterized by high volumes, allowing for lower margins; transactions costs are reduced because most of the loan arrangements are standardized and conducted by telephone or telex.
- Eurocurrency lending can and does take place out of tax-haven countries, providing for higher after-tax returns.

Eurocurrency deposit rates are higher than domestic rates for the following reasons:

- They must be higher to attract domestic deposits.
- Eurobanks can afford to pay higher rates based on their lower regulatory costs.
- Eurobanks are able to pay depositors higher interest rates because they are not subject to the interest rate ceilings that prevail in many countries.
- A larger percentage of deposits can be lent out.

Euromarket Trends   In recent years, the London interbank offered rate has started to fade as a benchmark for lending money in the Eurocurrency market, in much the same way that the prime rate is no longer the all-important benchmark in the U.S. bank loan market. Although Eurocurrency rates are still computed off LIBOR, a number of credit-worthy borrowers, including Denmark, Sweden, several major corporations, and some banks, are obtaining financing in the Euromarkets at interest rates well below LIBOR. For example, high-quality borrowers can borrow at the **London interbank bid** rate (**LIBID**), the rate paid by one bank to another for a deposit, which is about 12.5 basis points (1/8 of 1%) below LIBOR. The highest-quality borrowers, such as the World Bank, can raise funds at below LIBID.

This trend largely reflects the fact that the ability of banks to impose themselves as the credit yardstick by which all other international borrowers are measured has faltered. What the Euromarkets are saying in effect is that borrowers such as Denmark and the World Bank are considered better credit risks than are many banks.

Moreover, investor preferences for an alternative to bank Eurodollar certificates of deposit (whereby banks substitute their credit risk for their borrowers') have enabled investment banks to transform the usual bank-syndicated lending into securities offerings, such as FRNs. This preference for the ultimate borrower's credit risk, rather than the bank's credit risk, has led to rapid growth in the Eurobond market, particularly the floating-rate segment of the market.

12.4 EUROBONDS

Eurobonds are similar in many respects to the public debt sold in domestic capital markets, consisting largely of fixed-rate, floating-rate, and equity-related debt. Unlike domestic bond markets, however, the Eurobond market is almost entirely free of official regulation and is instead self-regulated by the Association of International Bond Dealers. The prefix *Euro* indicates that the bonds are sold outside the countries in whose currencies they are denominated. For example, the General Motors issue shown in Exhibit 12.5 is a Eurobond. You can tell that because the tombstone says, "These securities have not been registered under the United States Securities Act of 1933 and may not be offered or sold in the United States or to United States persons as part of the distribution."

Borrowers in the Eurobond market are typically well known and have impeccable credit ratings (for example, developed countries, international institutions, and large multinational corporations like GM). Even then the amounts raised in the Eurobond market have historically been far less than those in the Eurocurrency market. However, the Eurobond market has grown dramatically during the past 20 years, and its size now exceeds that of the Eurocurrency market.

12.4.1 Swaps

The major catalyst for growth in the Eurobond market in the last 20 years has been the emergence of the **swap** transactions discussed in Chapter 8. It is now estimated that 70% of Eurobond issues are "swap-driven." These swaps allow the parties to the contract to arbitrage their relative access to different currency markets or differences in perceived credit quality.

12.4.2 Links Between the Domestic and Eurobond Markets

The growing presence of sophisticated investors willing to arbitrage between the domestic dollar and Eurodollar bond markets—in part because the United States no longer imposes withholding taxes on foreign investors—has eliminated much of the interest

These securities have not been registered under the United States Securities Act of 1933 and may not be offered or sold in the United States to United States persons as part of the distribution.

General Motors Acceptance Corporation

(Incorporated in the State of New York, United States of America)

U.S.$200,000,000

7⅝ per cent. Notes due September 3, 1991

Swiss Bank Corporation International Limited

Credit Suisse First Boston Limited	Deutsche Bank Capital Markets Limited
Merrill Lynch Capital Markets	Morgan Stanley International
Nomura International Limited	Salomon Brothers International Limited

Union Bank of Switzerland (Securities) Limited

Algemene Bank Nederland N.V.	BankAmerica Capital Markets Group
Bankers Trust International Limited	Banque Bruxelles Lambert S.A.
Banque Générale du Luxembourg S.A.	Banque Nationale de Paris
Banque Paribas Capital Markets Limited	Commerzbank Aktiengesellschaft
Crédit Lyonnais	Creditanstalt-Bankverein
Daiwa Europe Limited	IBJ International Limited
Leu Securities Limited	The Nikko Securities Co., (Europe) Ltd.
Shearson Lehman Brothers International	Société Générale
Sumitomo Trust International Limited	Swiss Volksbank
S.G. Warburg Securities	Wood Gundy Inc.

Yamaichi International (Europe) Limited

EXHIBIT 12.5 • ANNOUNCEMENT OF A GMAC EUROBOND ISSUE

Source: Reprinted with permission of General Motors Acceptance Corporation.

disparity that once existed between Eurobonds and domestic bonds. Despite the closer alignment of the two markets, the Eurobond issuer may at any given time take advantage of Eurobond "windows" when a combination of domestic regulations, tax laws, and expectations of international investors enables the issuer to achieve a lower financing cost—often involving currency and interest swaps—than is available in domestic markets.[14] In addition to the possibility of reduced borrowing costs, the Eurobond issuer may diversify its investor base and funding sources by having access to the international Eurocapital markets of Western Europe, North America, and the Far East.

Placement   Issues are arranged through an underwriting group, often with a hundred or more underwriting banks involved for an issue as small as $25 million. A growing volume of Eurobonds is being placed privately because of the simplicity, speed, and privacy with which private placements can be arranged.

Currency Denomination   Historically, about 75% of Eurobonds have been dollar denominated. The most important nondollar currencies for Eurobond issues are the euro, the Japanese yen, and the pound sterling. The absence of Swiss franc Eurobonds is due to the Swiss Central Bank's ban on using the Swiss franc for Eurobond issues.

---

[14] The existence of such windows is documented by Yong-Cheol Kim and Rene M. Stulz, "The Eurobond Market and Corporate Financial Policy: A Test of the Clientele Hypothesis," *Journal of Financial Economics* 22, (1988): 189–205; and Yong-Cheol Kim and Rene M. Stulz, "Is There a Global Market for Convertible Bonds?" *Journal of Business* 65 (1992): 75–91.

Interest Rates on Fixed-Rate Eurobonds   Fixed-rate Eurobonds ordinarily pay their coupons once a year, in contrast to bonds issued in the U.S. market, where interest is normally paid on a semiannual basis. Issuers, of course, are interested in their **all-in cost**—that is, the effective interest rate on the money they have raised. This interest rate is calculated as the discount rate that equates the present value of the future interest and principal payments to the net proceeds received by the issuer. In other words, it is the *internal rate of return* on the bond. To compare a Eurobond issue with a U.S. domestic issue, therefore, the all-in cost of funds on an annual basis must be converted to a semiannual basis or vice versa.

The annual yield can be converted to a semiannual rate by use of the following formula:

$$\text{Semiannual yield} = (1 + \text{Annual yield})^{\frac{1}{2}} - 1 \qquad (12.1)$$

Alternatively, a semiannual yield can be annualized by rearranging the terms in Equation 12.1 as follows:

$$\text{Annual yield} = (1 + \text{Semiannual yield})^2 - 1 \qquad (12.2)$$

For example, suppose that Procter & Gamble plans to issue a 5-year bond with a face value of $100 million. Its investment banker estimates that a Eurobond issue would have to bear a 7.5% coupon and that fees and other expenses will total $738,000, providing net proceeds to P&G of $99,262,000. Exhibit 12.6a shows the cash flows associated with the Eurobond issue. The all-in cost of this issue, which is an annual rate, is shown as 7.68% (rounded to the nearest basis point). The computation was done using an Excel spreadsheet. To ensure that we have the correct all-in cost of funds, the third column shows that the present values of the cash flows, using a discount rate of 7.68%, sum to P&G's net proceeds of $99,262,000.

Alternatively, its investment banker tells Procter & Gamble that it can issue a $100 million 5-year bond in the U.S. market with a coupon of 7.4%. With estimated issuance costs of $974,000, P&G will receive net proceeds of $99,026,000. Exhibit 12.6b shows the cash flows associated with this issue and its all-in cost of 3.82%. Notice that the cash flows are semiannual, as is the all-in cost. The third column performs the same check on the present value of these cash flows to ensure that we have the correct all-in cost.

According to Equation 12.1, the equivalent semiannual all-in cost for the Eurobond issue is $(1.0768)^{1/2} - 1 = 3.77\%$. These figures reveal that the all-in cost of the Eurobond is lower, making it the preferred issue assuming that other terms and conditions on the bonds are the same.

We could have converted the U.S. bond yield to its annual equivalent using Equation 12.2 and then compared that figure to the Eurobond yield of 7.68%. This computation would have yielded an annualized all-in cost of the U.S. bond issue equal to $(1.0382)^2 - 1 = 7.78\%$. As before, the decision is to go with the Eurobond issue because its all-in cost is 10 basis points lower.

Interest Rates on Floating-Rate Eurobonds   The interest rates on floating-rate Eurobonds or FRNs are normally set in the same way as on Eurocurrency loans—as a fixed spread over a reference rate, usually LIBOR. The reset period is usually three months or six months, and the maturity of LIBOR corresponds to the reset period (for example, LIBOR6 for a 6-month reset period). So, for example, if LIBOR3 on a reset date is 6.35%, an FRN that pays 50 basis points over LIBOR3 will bear an interest rate of 6.85% for the next three months.

Unlike the previous example, some FRNs have coupons that move opposite to the reference rate. As we saw in Chapter 8, such notes are known as **inverse floaters**. An example would be a bond that pays 12% − LIBOR6. If LIBOR6 is, say, 7% on the reset

a. Calculation of Eurobond all-in cost

Year	Cash flows	Present value at 7.68%
0[1]	99,626,000	99,262,000
1[2]	(7,500,000)	(6,964,868)
2	(7,500,000)	(6,467,919)
3	(7,500,000)	(6,006,427)
4	(7,500,000)	(5,577,864)
5[3]	(107,500,000)	(74,244,921)

Internal rate of return	7.68%	Sum	0

Note: [1] Proceeds of $100 million net of $738,000 in expenses.
[2] Coupon of 7.5% applied to $100 million principal.
[3] Repayment of $100 million principal plus last interest payment.

b. Calculation of U.S. dollar bond all-in cost

Year	Cash flows	Present value at 3.82%
0[1]	99,026,000	99,026,000
1[2]	(3,700,000)	(3,563,895)
2	(3,700,000)	(3,432,796)
3	(3,700,000)	(3,306,520)
4	(3,700,000)	(3,184,889)
5	(3,700,000)	(3,067,732)
6	(3,700,000)	(2,954,885)
7	(3,700,000)	(2,846,189)
8	(3,700,000)	(2,741,491)
9	(3,700,000)	(2,640,644)
10[3]	(103,700,000)	(71,286,961)

Internal rate of return	3.82%	Sum	0

Note: [1] Proceeds of $100 million net of $974,000 in expenses.
[2] Semiannual coupon of 3.7% (7.4% annual) applied to $100 million principal.
[3] Repayment of $100 million principal plus last interest payment.

EXHIBIT 12.6 • COMPARISON OF ALL-IN COSTS OF A EUROBOND ISSUE AND A U.S. DOLLAR BOND ISSUE

date, the FRN's interest rate would be 5% (12% − 7%) for the coming 6-month period. The risk to the issuer is that LIBOR will decline. Conversely, the investor's return suffers if LIBOR rises. There is a floor on the coupon at zero, meaning that the interest rate on an inverse floater is never negative.

Eurobond Retirement   Sinking funds or purchase funds are usually required if a Eurobond is of more than 7 years' maturity. A *sinking fund* requires the borrower to retire a fixed amount of bonds yearly after a specific number of years. By contrast, a *purchase fund* often starts in the first year, and bonds are retired only if the market price is below the issue price. The purpose of these funds is to support the market price of the bonds, as well as reduce bondholder risk by assuring that not all the firm's debt will come due at once.

Most Eurobond issues carry *call provisions*, giving the borrower the option of retiring the bonds before maturity should interest rates decline sufficiently in the future. As with domestic bonds, Eurobonds with call provisions require both a call premium and higher interest rates relative to bonds without call provisions.

Ratings As noted earlier, Eurobond issuers are typically large multinational companies, government agencies, state-owned enterprises, or international organizations, all with familiar names and impeccable credit reputations. For this reason, in the past most Eurobonds carried no credit ratings, particularly because rating agencies charge a fee. But as the market has expanded to include newer issuers who are less well-known and with lesser credit reputations, investors have demanded ratings to better assess an issuer's credit risk. The majority of Eurobond ratings are provided by Moody's and Standard & Poor's, the dominant U.S. rating agencies. Euroratings is another agency that specializes in the Euromarkets, particularly in the dollar-denominated debt of non-U.S. issuers.

Eurobond issues are rated according to their relative degree of default risk. Note that interest rate changes or currency movements can make even default-free Eurobonds very risky. Bond raters, however, stick to just credit risk. Their focus is on the issuer's ability to generate sufficient quantities of the currency in which their debt is denominated. This element is particularly important for borrowers issuing foreign-currency-denominated debt (for example, the government of Mexico issuing debt denominated in U.S. dollars).

12.4.3 Rationale for Existence of Eurobond Market

The Eurobond market survives and thrives because, unlike any other major capital market, it remains largely unregulated and untaxed. Thus, big borrowers, such as Exxon, IBM, and Sears Roebuck, can raise money more quickly and more flexibly than they can at home. And because the interest investors receive is tax free, these companies have historically been able to borrow below the rate at which the U.S. treasury could borrow.

The tax-free aspect of Eurobonds is related to the notice in the tombstone for the GMAC Eurobond issue that it may not be offered to the U.S. public. U.S. tax law requires that for interest and principal to be payable in the United States, bonds must be in registered form. Eurobonds, however, are issued in bearer form, meaning they are unregistered, with no record to identify the owners. (Money can be considered to be a zero-coupon bearer bond.) This feature allows investors to collect interest in complete anonymity and, thereby, evade taxes. Although U.S. law discourages the sale of such bonds to U.S. citizens or residents, bonds issued in bearer form are common overseas.[15] As expected, investors are willing to accept lower yields on bearer bonds than on non-bearer bonds of similar risk.

Highly rated U.S. firms have long taken advantage of this opportunity to reduce their cost of funds by selling overseas Eurobonds in bearer form. Often, corporations could borrow abroad below the cost at which the U.S. government could borrow at home. Exxon's issue of zero-coupon Eurobonds shows how companies were able to exploit the arbitrage possibilities inherent in such a situation. Zero-coupon bonds pay no interest until maturity. Instead, they are sold at a deep discount from their par value.

---

[15] Americans can buy Eurobonds, but not until 40 days after they have been issued, which cuts down on availability because many Eurobond issues are bought and stashed away.

ILLUSTRATION *Exxon Engages in International Tax Arbitrage*

In the fall of 1984, Exxon sold $1.8 billion principal amount of zero-coupon Eurobonds due November 2004 at an annual compounded yield of 11.65%, realizing net proceeds of about $199 million:

$$\text{Bond value} = \$1,800,000,000/(1.1165)^{20}$$
$$= \$199,000,000$$

It then used part of the proceeds to buy $1.8 billion principal amount of U.S. treasury bonds maturing in November 2004 from which the coupons had been removed and sold separately. The yield on these "stripped" Treasurys, which are effectively zero-coupon treasury bonds, was around 12.20%.[16] At this yield, it would have cost Exxon $180 million to purchase the $1.8 billion in stripped Treasury bonds:

$$\text{Bond value} = \$1,800,000,000/(1.1220)^{20}$$
$$= \$180,000,000$$

At this price, Exxon earned the difference of about $19 million.

A peculiar quirk in Japanese law is largely responsible for the big difference in yield between zero-coupon Eurobonds and stripped Treasurys: Japanese investors, who were the principal buyers of the Eurobonds, did not have to pay tax on a zero-coupon bond's accrued interest if they sold the bond prior to maturity. Because of this tax advantage, they were willing to pay a premium price for zeros (relative to coupon-bearing bonds). Although in principle the Japanese would have preferred to purchase the higher-yielding (and safer) stripped U.S. treasury bonds, they are prohibited by Japanese law from doing so. The threatened taxation of the accrued interest on zeros in Japan has eliminated this arbitrage opportunity.

The Eurobond market, like the Eurocurrency market, exists because it enables borrowers and lenders alike to avoid a variety of monetary authority regulations and controls, as well as providing them with an opportunity to escape the payment of some taxes. As long as governments attempt to regulate domestic financial markets but allow a (relatively) free flow of capital among countries, the external financial markets will survive.

Recent years have seen a reduction in some of these regulatory costs. For example, the United States began permitting well-known companies-precisely the ones that would otherwise have used the Eurobond market–to bypass complex securities laws when issuing new securities by using the *shelf registration* procedure. By lowering the cost of issuing bonds in the United States and dramatically speeding up the issuing process, shelf registration improved the competitive position of the U.S. capital market relative to the Eurobond market. More recently, the SEC's adoption of Rule 144A now enables companies to issue bonds simultaneously in Europe and the United States, further blurring the distinction between the U.S. bond market and its Eurobond equivalent. Other nations, such as Japan and England, are also deregulating their financial markets.

With financial market deregulation in the United States and elsewhere, the Eurobond market lost some of the cost advantage that lured corporate borrowers in the

---

[16] This case is discussed at greater length in John D. Finnerty, "Zero Coupon Bond Arbitrage: An Illustration of the Regulatory Dialectic at Work," *Financial Management*, Winter 1985, pp. 13–17.

past. Nonetheless, as long as Eurobond issuance entails low regulatory and registration costs relative to domestic bond issuance, the Eurobond market will continue to attract investors and borrowers from all over the world. Part of the lower registration costs stems from the less-stringent disclosure requirements in the Eurobond market, particularly as compared to the U.S. market. Even after the advent of shelf registration and Rule 144A, SEC disclosure requirements still are considered to be costly, time consuming, and burdensome by both U.S. and non-U.S. issuers.

Despite several forecasts of imminent death, the Eurobond market has survived, largely because its participants are so fleet of foot. As demand for one type of bond declines, quick-witted investment bankers seem to find other opportunities to create value for their customers. When the demand for fixed-rate Eurobonds fell, the Eurobond market led the boom in floating-rate note issues. When the FRN market collapsed in 1986, this business was replaced by issues of Japanese corporate bonds with equity warrants attached. In return for what is in effect a long-dated call option on the issuer's stock, the investor accepts a lower interest rate on the Eurobond to which the equity warrant is attached.

Demand for such issues soared as investors used the warrants to play Japan's rising stock market. In turn, Japanese companies found the Eurobond market easier and cheaper to use than the regulated domestic-yen market. However, the Tokyo stock market's plunge in 1990 triggered a steep decline in the Japanese equity-warrant issue market and in the Eurobond market overall. The equity-related Eurobond issue market has still not regained its former prominence.

The financial infrastructure in place in London should ensure the Eurobond market's survival. However, tax harmonization, financial deregulation, and the widespread loosening of capital controls mean that issuers have less incentive to borrow money offshore and are returning to their domestic markets to raise capital. If these trends persist, the Eurobond market may never regain its preeminence. However, it can still preserve its basic role as the nimblest intermediary for international capital flows between domestic markets.

12.4.4 Eurobonds versus Eurocurrency Loans

Both Eurocurrency and Eurobond financing have their advantages and disadvantages. Although many of these factors are reflected in the relative borrowing costs, not all factors are so reflected. For a given firm, therefore, and for a specific set of circumstances, one method of financing may be preferred to the other. The differences are categorized in five ways.

1. *Cost of borrowing*: Eurobonds are issued in both fixed-rate and floating-rate forms. Fixed-rate bonds are an attractive exposure-management tool because known long-term currency inflows can be offset with known long-term outflows in the same currency. In contrast, the interest rate on a Eurocurrency loan is variable, making Eurocurrency loans better hedges for noncontractual currency exposures. The variable interest rate benefits borrowers when rates decline, but it hurts them when rates rise. Arbitrage between Eurobonds and Eurocurrencies, however, should not provide an automatic cost advantage to one or the other form of borrowing.

2. *Maturity*: Although the period of borrowing in the Eurocurrency market has tended to lengthen over time, Eurobonds still have longer maturities.

3. *Size of issue*: Historically, the amount of loanable funds available at any one time has been much greater in the interbank market than in the bond market. Now, however, the volume of Eurobond offerings exceeds global bank lending. In many instances, borrowers have discovered that the Eurobond market can easily accommodate financings of a size and at a price not previously thought possible.

Moreover, although in the past the flotation costs of a Eurocurrency loan have been much lower than those on a Eurobond (about 0.5% of the total loan amount versus about 2.25% of the face value of a Eurobond issue), competition has worked to lower Eurobond floatation costs.

4. *Flexibility*: In the case of a Eurobond issue, the funds must be drawn down in one sum on a fixed date and repaid according to a fixed schedule unless the borrower pays an often substantial prepayment penalty. By contrast, the drawdown in a floating-rate loan can be staggered to suit the borrower's needs with a fee of about 0.5% per annum paid on the unused portion (normally much cheaper than drawing down and redepositing) and can be prepaid in whole or in part at any time, often without penalty. Moreover, a Eurocurrency loan with a multicurrency clause enables the borrower to switch currencies on any rollover date, whereas switching the denomination of a Eurobond from currency A to currency B would require a costly combined refunding and reissuing operation. A much cheaper and comparable alternative, however, would be to sell forward for currency B an amount of currency A equal to the value of the Eurobond issue still outstanding. There is a rapidly growing market in such currency swaps that enable the proceeds from bonds issued in one currency to be converted into money in another currency.

5. *Speed*: Internationally known borrowers can raise funds in the Eurocurrency market very quickly, often within 2 to 3 weeks of first request. A Eurobond financing generally takes more time to put together, although here again the difference is becoming less significant.

12.4.5 Euronotes

Eurobanks have responded to the competition from the Eurobond market by creating a new instrument: the **note issuance facility** (NIF). The NIF, which is a low-cost substitute for syndicated credits, allows borrowers to issue their own short-term **Euronotes**, which are then placed or distributed by the financial institutions providing the NIF. NIFs, sometimes also called *short-term note issuance facilities* (SNIFs), have some features of the U.S. commercial paper market and some features of U.S. commercial lines of credit. Like commercial paper, notes under NIFs are unsecured short-term debt generally issued by large corporations with excellent credit ratings. Indeed, notes issued under NIFs are sometimes referred to as Euro-commercial paper or Euro-CP. Typically, however, the name Euro-CP is reserved for those Euronotes that are not underwritten (see Section 12.5, "Euro-Commercial Paper"). Like loan commitments in the United States, NIFs generally include multiple pricing components for various contract features, including a market-based interest rate and one or more fees known as participation, facility, and underwriting fees. Participation fees are paid when the contract is formalized and are generally about 10 basis points times the facility size. Other fees are paid annually and sometimes are based on the full size of the facility, sometimes on the unused portions.

Many NIFs include underwriting services as part of the arrangements. When they are included, the arrangement generally takes the form of a **revolving underwriting facility** (RUF). The RUF gives borrowers long-term continuous access to short-term money underwritten by banks at a fixed margin.

NIFs are more flexible than floating-rate notes and usually cheaper than syndicated loans. Banks eager to beef up their earnings without fattening their loan portfolios (which would then require them to add expensive equity capital) made NIFs an important new segment of the Euromarket. As in the case of floating-rate notes, the popularity of NIFs benefits from the market's preference for lending to high-grade borrowers through securities rather than bank loans.

The pricing of the Euronotes issued under NIFs depends on two conventions. First, instead of carrying a coupon rate, Euronotes are sold at a discount from their face value. The return to the investor is the difference between the purchase price of the security and its face value. Second, the yield is usually quoted on a discount basis from its face value.

Securitization is rearing its head in the Euronote market too. A growing number of firms are now bypassing financial intermediaries and issuing **Euro-medium term notes (Euro-MTNs)** directly to the market. The Euro-MTN, which grew out of the medium-term notes issued in the U.S. market, is one of the most important developments in the Euromarkets in the past decade.

The three basic reasons for the success of the Euro-MTN market—speed, cost, and flexibility—ensure its continued growth and survival. Like their U.S. counterpart, Euro-MTNs are offered continuously rather than all at once like a bond issue. Euro-MTNs give issuers the flexibility to take advantage of changes in the shape and level of the yield curve and of the specific needs of investors with respect to amount, maturity, currency, and interest rate form (fixed or floating). They can be issued in maturities of as much as 30 years, although most are under five years, and in an ever-increasing range of currencies (including the Polish zloty, Czech koruna, Indonesian rupiah, and South African rand, in addition to the standards, such as the dollar, yen, euro, sterling, and Swiss franc). Unlike conventional underwritten debt securities, a program of medium-term notes can be offered in small amounts; in different maturities, currencies, seniority, and security; and on a daily basis, depending on the issuer's needs and the investors' appetites. By contrast, it is not customary to issue underwritten securities in batches of less than $50 million. In this way, Euro-MTNs bridge the maturity gap between Euro-CP and the longer-term international bond. However, with more Euro-MTNs being issued with maturities of less than one year, this has cut into the Euro-CP market.

The risk to the borrower of issuing Euro-MTNs rather than taking out a fixed-term Eurocurrency loan or Eurobond is that it might not be able to roll over its existing notes or place additional notes when necessary. This risk can be mitigated by extending the maturity of the MTNs issued or by issuing the notes under a revolving credit commitment, such as the NIFs discussed earlier. In the event that market conditions at the time of any note issue are unfavorable and there is insufficient investor demand, the syndicate of banks underwriting the NIF provides the necessary funds by guaranteeing to purchase the notes or make advances in lieu of this, on pre-agreed terms. At maturity, the issuer repays the notes by either issuing new notes or drawing on other resources.

12.5 EURO-COMMERCIAL PAPER

Another innovation in nonbank short-term credits that bears a strong resemblance to commercial paper is the nonunderwritten short-term Euronote, often called **Euro-commercial paper (Euro-CP, for short)**. There are some differences between U.S. commercial paper and Euro-CP, however. For one thing, the average maturity of Euro-CP is about twice as long as the average maturity of U.S. CP. Also, Euro-CP is actively traded in a secondary market, but most U.S. CP is held to maturity by the original investors. Central banks, commercial banks, and corporations are important parts of the investor base for particular segments of the Euro-CP market; the most important holders of U.S. CP are money-market funds, which are not very important in the Euro-CP market. In addition, the distribution of U.S. issuers in the Euro-CP market is of significantly lower quality than the distribution of U.S. issuers in the U.S.-CP market. An explanation of this finding may lie in the importance of banks as buyers of less-than-prime paper in the Euro-CP market.

Although still dwarfed by the U.S. CP market, the Euro-CP market has grown rapidly since its founding in 1985, reaching $360 billion in March 2004.

The Euro-CP market has one advantage, however: flexibility. Unlike its U.S. counterpart, Euro-CP is multidenominational, allowing issuers to borrow in a range of currencies. For example, AT&T's $1 billion program allowed it to issue CP in several currencies, including dollars, Swedish kronor, and euros. Although historically Euro-CP was mostly denominated in dollars, nondollar issues now account for over two-thirds of all issues.

Aside from the obvious benefit of allowing overseas subsidiaries to borrow in their local currencies, a multicurrency Euro-CP program also allows considerable scope for swap arbitrage. By combining a commercial paper issue with a cross-currency swap (see Chapter 8), borrowers are able to achieve significant interest savings. About 40% of all Euro-CP issues are now swapped. The development of computer technology that permits both the dealer and the issuer easier access to swap arbitrage opportunities and investor demand presages more growth ahead for swap-driven Euro-CP programs.

12.6 THE ASIACURRENCY MARKET

Although dwarfed by its European counterpart, the **Asiacurrency** (or **Asiadollar**) **market** has been growing rapidly in terms of both size and range of services provided. Located in Singapore, because of the lack of restrictive financial controls and taxes there, the Asiadollar market was founded in 1968 as a satellite market to channel to and from the Eurodollar market the large pool of offshore funds, mainly U.S. dollars, circulating in Asia. Its primary economic functions these days are to channel investment dollars to a number of rapidly growing Southeast Asian countries and to provide deposit facilities for those investors with excess funds. As with all such investments, credit analysis is critical. The following example shows what could happen when lenders become too aggressive.

ILLUSTRATION   *Steady Safe Isn't*

On January 12, 1998, the Asian financial crisis claimed another victim when Peregrine Investments Holdings Ltd., Hong Kong's premier investment bank and the largest Asian investment bank outside Japan, announced it would file for liquidation. Its collapse was triggered by the failure of a single large loan to an entrepreneur in Indonesia, where the dramatic decline of the rupiah brought a wave of loan defaults and bankruptcies and ultimately brought down President Suharto's authoritarian government. According to news reports, Peregrine lent $260 million—in the form of an unsecured bridge loan (a temporary loan to be repaid from the expected proceeds of a bond issue)—to a local taxicab operator named Yopie Widjara. Widjara, who reportedly enlisted President Suharto's eldest daughter as an equity investor, planned to create a system of car ferries linking the islands of Indonesia's sprawling archipelago. Peregrine's loan, which represented a third of its capital, was to be repaid through the sale of dollar-denominated bonds issued by Widjara's company, Steady Safe.

Peregrine's troubles started when the value of Asian currencies began falling during the summer of 1997, and it was unable to sell the Steady Safe bonds it had underwritten. Then the Indonesian government lifted trading curbs on the rupiah and the bottom fell out of the currency. From Rp 2,400:$1 in July 1997, the rupiah exchange rate fell to more than Rp 8,000:$1 in January 1998. With the rupiah cost of servicing its debt rising by more than 200%, Steady Safe was unable (or unwilling—it is not clear what happened to the $260 million it borrowed) to repay its dollar-denominated bridge loan, and Peregrine collapsed.

The Asiabond counterpart to the Asiadollar market is the dragon bond. A **dragon bond** is debt denominated in a foreign currency, usually dollars, but launched, priced, and traded in Asia. The first dragon bond was issued in November 1991 by the Asian Development Bank. After growing rapidly in the early 1990s, however, the bond portion of the non-Japanese Asiabond market has slumped despite the existence of plentiful Asian savers and borrowers. The market's fundamental problem is that Asian borrowers with a good international credit rating can raise money for longer, and less, in Europe or the United States.

12.7 Project Finance

A frequently used mechanism for financing large-scale, long-term capital investments is **project finance**. Some examples of project finance transactions include the $16 billion Channel Tunnel, or Chunnel, connecting France and England; the $5 billion Iridium global satellite project; and a $4 billion Venezuelan oil and gas refinery known as SINCOR.[17] Most project financings take the form of nonrecourse loans secured solely by the project and its cash flows. This mechanism helps shield the parent company from any financial obligations and risks associated with borrowings by the project. The ownership vehicle for a project is a single-purpose corporation that is legally independent of its sponsors.

This financial structure is consistent with the nature and purpose of project financing. Project financing can be defined as "the raising of funds to finance an economically separable capital investment project in which the providers of the funds look primarily to the cash flow from the project as the source of funds to service their loans and provide the return of and a return on their equity investment in the project."[18]

This definition highlights several key attributes of project financing. First, it focuses on the economically separable nature of investment projects suitable for project financing, such as power plants or pipelines. Second, because projects are set up as legally independent entities, nonrecourse lenders have resort only to project assets and cash flows; they have no recourse to the sponsors. Third, unlike the case for financial instruments such as mortgage-backed securities, the underlying assets in project finance are large, illiquid industrial assets. Finally, although not specified in the definition, projects have a finite life, at the end of which all debt and equity investors are repaid.

The projects' sponsors benefit from project finance by shielding themselves from the large risks they would otherwise have to bear. But project finance is not a free lunch. Because lenders rightly perceive that they cannot look to the parent to honor its projects' debts, they factor this greater degree of credit risk into the price at which they are willing to lend to these projects. The result is that the cost of project financing exceeds the parent's cost of borrowing. It is also expensive to arrange. Nonetheless, its widespread use indicates that project finance has net benefits to its sponsors.

Project financing is likely to create value through its ability to resolve certain agency problems, reduce taxes and the costs of financial distress, and facilitate risk management.[19] For example, the relatively transparent nature of project finance, which stems from its single-purpose corporate structure and the fact that project assets are tangible (in contrast to, say, the value of an Internet strategy), improves credit risk analysis. The credit analyst need assess only the risk of the project, not the riskiness of the sponsor(s) as well.

---

[17] These examples are given in "An Overview of the Project Finance Market."

[18] John D. Finnerty, *Project Finance: Asset-Based Financial Engineering* (New York: John Wiley & Sons, 1996).

[19] For a discussion and illustration of these advantages, see Benjamin C. Esty, "Petrozuata: A Case Study of the Effective Use of Project Finance," *Journal of Applied Corporate Finance*, Fall 1999, pp. 26–42.

In addition, the project is insulated from problems that its sponsors may have: Its credit-worthiness depends solely on the project's cash flows (which are dedicated to debt-service payments) and not on investment and other decisions made by the parent's management that might dissipate these cash flows. At the same time, the sponsor is relieved of the prospect of financial distress if the project goes bankrupt. The use of project finance may also help reduce corporate taxes by allowing the sponsors to take advantage of special tax holidays, tax rate reductions, and reduced royalty payments. Finally, project finance permits the allocation of specific risks and returns to those best able to bear those risks and influence the outcomes on which the returns depend. This careful alignment of risks and returns improves incentives and increases the likelihood that the project will be operated with maximum efficiency.

12.8 SUMMARY AND CONCLUSIONS

Although there are significant differences among countries in their methods and sources of finance, corporate practice appears to be converging. Most significantly, more firms are bypassing financial intermediaries, mainly commercial banks, and are going directly to the financial markets for funds. The convergence of corporate financing practice largely reflects the globalization of financial markets, that is, the inextricable linkage, through arbitrage, of financial markets worldwide. In line with this trend, firms are finding that it pays to seek capital on a global basis rather than restricting their search to any one nation or capital market. These global sources include national capital markets, financial intermediaries, and project financing.

Competition among companies for capital is also forcing them to be more investor-friendly. The result is a trend toward more financial transparency and improved corporate governance with a greater focus on the rights of shareholders rather than managers. We saw that the growth of the international capital markets, specifically the Eurocurrency and Eurobond markets, is largely a response to the restrictions, regulations, and costs that governments impose on domestic financial transactions. At the same time, capital flows between the international capital markets and domestic markets have linked domestic markets in a manner that increasingly makes such government intervention irrelevant. A principal means whereby markets are linked is the use of interest rate and currency swaps, whereby two counterparties agree to exchange streams of payments over time in order to convert from one interest rate structure and/or currency to another.

As Eurobonds became a viable alternative to Eurocurrency loans, banks responded by creating note issuance facilities under which borrowers were able to issue their own Euronotes. Nonunderwritten short-term Euronotes, often termed Euro-commercial paper, is another important financial innovation in the Euromarkets. The Asiacurrency and Asiabond markets are the Asian counterparts to the Euromarkets and are located in Singapore.

QUESTIONS

1. What are some basic differences between the financing patterns of U.S. and Japanese firms? What might account for some of these differences?

2. What is securitization? What forces underlie it, and how has it affected the financing policies of multinational corporations?

3. Why is bank lending on the decline worldwide? How have banks responded to their loss of market share?

4. a. What is meant by the globalization of financial markets?

   b. How has technology affected the process of globalization?

c. How has globalization affected government regulation of national capital markets?

5. Many financial commentators believe that bond owners and traders today have an enormous collective influence over a nation's economic policies. Explain why this might be correct.

6. Why are large multinational corporations located in small countries such as Sweden, Holland, and Switzerland interested in developing a global investor base?

7. Why are many U.S. multinationals seeking to improve their visibility with foreign investors, even going so far as to list their shares on foreign stock exchanges?

8. List some reasons why a U.S.-based corporation might issue debt denominated in a foreign currency.

9. In an attempt to regain business lost to foreign markets, Swiss authorities abolished stamp duties on transactions between foreigners as well as on new bond issues by foreign borrowers. However, transactions involving Swiss citizens will still incur a 0.15% tax, and bond issues by Swiss borrowers were also made more expensive. What are the likely consequences of these changes for Swiss financial markets?

10. What is the difference between a Eurocurrency loan and a Eurobond?

11. What is the difference between a foreign bond and a Eurobond?

12. What is the basic reason for the existence of the Eurodollar market? What factors have accounted for its growth over time?

13. Why have Eurobonds traditionally yielded less than comparable domestic issues?

PROBLEMS

1. A European company issues common shares that pay taxable dividends and bearer shares that pay an identical dividend but offer an opportunity to evade taxes: Bearer shares come with a large supply of coupons that can be redeemed anonymously at banks for the current value of the dividend.

   a. Suppose taxable dividends are taxed at the rate of 10%. What is the ratio between market prices of taxable and bearer shares? If a new issue is planned, should taxable or bearer shares be sold?

   b. Suppose, in addition, that it costs 10% of proceeds to issue a taxable dividend, whereas it costs 20% of the proceeds to issue bearer stocks because of the expense of distribution and coupon printing. What type of share will the company prefer to issue?

   c. Suppose now that individuals pay 10% taxes on dividends, and corporations pay no taxes, but bear an administrative cost of 10% of the value of any bearer dividends. Can you determine the relative market prices for the two types of shares?

2. Suppose that the current 180-day interbank Eurodollar rate is 9% (all rates are stated on an annualized basis). If next period's rate is 9.5%, what will a Eurocurrency loan priced at LIBOR plus 1% cost?

3. Citibank offers to syndicate a Eurodollar credit for the government of Poland with the following terms:

Principal	U.S.$1 billion
Maturity	7 years
Interest rate	LIBOR + 1.5%, reset every 6 months
Syndication fee	1.75%

   a. What are the net proceeds to Poland from this syndicated loan?

   b. Assuming that 6-month LIBOR is currently at 6.35%, what is the effective annual interest cost to Poland for the first 6 months of this loan?

4. IBM wishes to raise $1 billion and is trying to decide between a domestic dollar bond issue and a Eurobond issue. The U.S. bond can be issued at a coupon of 6.75%, paid semiannually, with underwriting and other expenses totaling 0.95% of the issue size. The Eurobond would cost only 0.55% to issue but would bear an annual coupon of 6.88%. Both issues would mature in 10 years.

   a. Assuming all else is equal, which is the least expensive issue for IBM?

   b. What other factors might IBM want to consider before deciding which bond to issue?

BIBLIOGRAPHY

Agrawal, R., S. Findley, S. Greene, K. Huang, A. Jeddy, W. W. Lewis, and M. Petry, "Capital Productivity: Why the U.S. Leads and Why It Matters," *The McKinsey Quarterly*, 1996, No. 3, pp. 38–55.

Alexander, G. J., C. S. Eun, and S. Janakiramanan, "International Listings and Stock Returns: Some Empirical Evidence," *Journal of Financial and Quantitative Analysis*, June 1988, pp. 135–151.

Berglöf, E. and E. Perotti, "The Governance Structure of the Japanese Financial Keiretsu," *Journal of Financial Economics*, October 1994, pp. 259–284.

Business International Corporation. *Financing Foreign Operations*, various issues.

Dufey, G. and I. H. Giddy. *The International Money Market.* Englewood Cliffs, N.J.: Prentice-Hall, 1978.

Finnerty, J. D. "Zero Coupon Bond Arbitrage: An Illustration of the Regulatory Dialectic at Work," *Financial Management*, Winter 1985, pp. 13–17.

Grabbe, O. J. *International Financial Markets*. 3rd ed. Englewood Cliffs, N.J.: Prentice-Hall, 1995.

Kaplan, S. N. and B. A. Minton, "Appointments of Outsiders to Japanese Boards: Determinants and Implications for Managers," *Journal of Financial Economics*, October 1994, pp. 225–258.

Kim, Y.-C. and R. M. Stulz, "The Eurobond Market and Corporate Financial Policy: A Test of the Clientele Hypothesis," *Journal of Financial Economics* 22, 1988, pp. 189–205.

_____. "Is There a Global Market for Convertible Bonds?"*Journal of Business* 65, 1992, pp. 75–91.

Logue, D. E and A. K. Sundaram, "Valuation Effects of Foreign Company Listings on U.S. Exchanges," *Journal of International Business Studies*, 1996, pp. 67–88.

Merton, R. C. "A Simple Model of Capital Market Equilibrium with Incomplete Information," *Journal of Finance*, July 1987, pp. 483–510.

Solnik, B. H. *International Investments*, 4th ed. Reading, Mass.: Addison-Wesley, 1996.

INTERNET RESOURCES

http://www.oecd.org/document/36/0,2340,en_2825_495635_1962020_1_1_1_1,00.html Web site for *Financial Market Trends*. This publication provides an up-to-date analysis of developments and trends in international and national capital markets. Each issue includes highlights of recent developments in financial markets; analysis of policy issues affecting financial markets; overviews of new statistical information from OECD countries in areas such as international direct investment, overall bank profitability, institutional investment, and privatization; and statistics and charts dealing with international financial markets.

http://www2.standardandpoors.com/portal/site/sp/en/us/page.my_homepage Web site of Standard & Poor's. Contains information on various project financings and other international financings, along with country risk ratings.

www.bis.org The BIS Web site that contains extensive information on the amounts and types of funds raised in the international banking and capital markets, including the Eurocurrency and Eurobond markets and the international equity markets.

http://ppi.worldbank.org/index.aspx The World Bank Group's Private Participation in Infrastructure (PPI) Project Database has data on more than 3,300 projects in 150 low- and middle-income countries. The database is the leading source of PPI trends in the developing world, covering projects in the energy, telecommunications, transport, and water and sewerage sectors.

INTERNET EXERCISES

1. What is the breakdown of currencies in which international borrowing has taken place in the past year?

2. How much money has been raised in the past year in the international bond market? Eurocurrency market? International equity market?

3. How much money has been raised in the past year in the Eurocurrency market? Eurobond market? Euronote market? Euro-commercial market?

4. What were the currency denominations of the past year's borrowings in the Euromarkets?

CHAPTER 13

INTERNATIONAL PORTFOLIO INVESTMENT

Capital now flows at the speed of light across national borders and into markets once deemed impregnable.

Citicorp Annual Report (1991)

CHAPTER LEARNING OBJECTIVES

- To describe the risks and advantages of international investing
- To explain how international investing can allow investors to achieve a better risk-return trade-off than by investing solely in U.S. securities
- To identify the barriers to investing overseas
- To describe the various ways in which U.S. investors can diversify into foreign securities
- To explain why investing in foreign stocks and bonds provides a better risk-return trade-off than investing in either foreign stocks or bonds only
- To calculate the currency risk associated with investing in securities issued in different markets and denominated in various currencies
- To calculate the return associated with investing in securities issued in different markets and denominated in various currencies

KEY TERMS

American Depository Receipt (ADR)
American Depository Share (ADS)
efficient frontier
emerging markets
foreign market beta
global depository receipt (GDR)
global fund
home bias
IFC Emerging Markets Index
international asset allocation
international diversification
international fund

international investing
liquidity
Morgan Stanley Capital International Europe, Australia, Far East (EAFE) Index
Morgan Stanley Capital International World Index
regional fund
risk-return trade-off
single-country fund
total dollar return

There was a time when investors treated national boundaries as impregnable barriers, limiting their reach and financial options to predominantly domestic and regional markets. Times have changed. Just as companies and consumers are going global, so are increasing numbers of investors. American investors are buying foreign stocks and bonds, and foreign investors are purchasing U.S. securities. This chapter examines the nature and consequences of international portfolio investing. Although the focus is on international investing from an American perspective, the lessons drawn are applicable to investors from around the world.

13.1 THE RISKS AND BENEFITS OF INTERNATIONAL EQUITY INVESTING

Although you take risks when you invest in any stock, **international investing** has some special risks. These risks are spelled out in a publication put out by the U.S. Securities and Exchange Commission (SEC).[1] Here is what the SEC has to say about these risks, which it divides into seven different categories:

1. *Changes in currency exchange rate*: When the exchange rate between the foreign currency of an international investment and the U.S. dollar changes, it can increase or reduce your investment return. How does this work? Foreign companies trade and pay dividends in the currency of their local market. When you receive dividends or sell your international investment, you will need to convert the cash you receive into U.S. dollars. During a period when the foreign currency is strong compared to the U.S. dollar, this strength increases your returns because your foreign earnings translate into more dollars. If the currency weakens compared to the U.S. dollar, this reduces your returns because your earnings translate into fewer dollars. In addition to exchange rates, you should be aware that some countries may impose foreign currency controls that restrict or delay you from moving currency out of a country.

2. *Dramatic changes in market value*: Foreign markets, like all markets, can experience dramatic changes in market value. One way to reduce the impact of these price changes is to invest for the long term and try to ride out sharp upswings and downturns in the market. Individual investors frequently lose money when they try to "time" the market in the United States and are even less likely to succeed in a foreign market. When you "time" the market you have to make two astute decisions: deciding when to get out before prices fall and when to get back in before prices rise again.

3. *Political, economic, and social events*: It is difficult for investors to understand all the political, economic, and social factors that influence foreign markets. These factors provide diversification, but they also contribute to the risk of international investing.

4. *Lack of liquidity*: Foreign markets may have lower trading volumes and fewer listed companies. They may only be open a few hours a day. Some countries restrict the amount or type of stocks that foreign investors may purchase. You may have to pay premium prices to buy a foreign security and have difficulty finding a buyer when you want to sell.

5. *Less information*: Many foreign companies do not provide investors with the same type of information as U.S. public companies. It may be difficult to locate up-to-date information, and the information the company publishes may not be in English.

---

[1] "International Investing: Get the Facts," Securities and Exchange Commission, http://www.sec.gov/pdf/ininvest.pdf.

6. *Reliance on foreign legal remedies*: If you have a problem with your investment, you may not be able to sue the company in the United States. Even if you sue successfully in a U.S. court, you may not be able to collect on a U.S. judgment against a foreign company. You may have to rely on whatever legal remedies are available in the company's home country.

7. *Different market operations*: Foreign markets often operate differently from the major U.S. trading markets. For example, there may be different periods for clearance and settlement of securities transactions. Some foreign markets may not report stock trades as quickly as U.S. markets. Rules providing for the safekeeping of shares held by custodian banks or depositories may not be as well developed in some foreign markets, with the risk that your shares may not be protected if the custodian has credit problems or fails.

Despite these risks, international investing offers several less-obvious advantages. First, an international focus offers far more opportunity than a domestic focus. More than half of the world's stock market capitalization is in non-U.S. companies, and this fraction generally has increased over time. In fact, if you want to invest in certain products with huge global markets, you will find that most of the big, highly profitable manufacturers are overseas. For example, in the 1990s, videotape recorders were the world's best-selling consumer electronics product, and 95% of them were made in Japan. Also, more than 80% of all cars, 85% of all stereo systems, and 99% of all 35mm cameras are made abroad. The Japanese dominance of these and other consumer-product markets helps explain why by 1989 Japan's market capitalization actually exceeded that of the United States. The 67% plunge in the Tokyo Stock Exchange between 1990 and 2000 and the dramatic rise in the U.S. stock market during the same period once again gave the U.S. stock market—at about four times Japan's capitalization—the dominant share of the world's stock market capitalization. Japan's market capitalization has now fallen to third place, behind that of Great Britain.

13.1.1 International Diversification

The expanded universe of securities available internationally suggests the possibility of achieving a better **risk-return trade-off** than by investing solely in U.S. securities. That is, expanding the universe of assets available for investment should lead to higher returns for the same level of risk or less risk for the same level of expected return. This relation follows from the basic rule of portfolio diversification: *The broader the diversification, the more stable the returns and the more diffuse the risks.*

Prudent investors know that diversifying across industries leads to a lower level of risk for a given level of expected return. For example, a fully diversified U.S. portfolio is only about 27% as risky as a typical individual stock. Put another way, about 73% of the risk associated with investing in the average stock can be eliminated in a fully diversified U.S. portfolio. Ultimately, though, the advantages of such diversification are limited because all companies in a country are more or less subject to the same cyclical economic fluctuations. Through **international diversification**—that is, by diversifying across nations whose economic cycles are not perfectly in phase—investors should be able to reduce still further the variability of their returns. In other words, risk that is systematic in the context of the U.S. economy may be unsystematic in the context of the global economy. For example, an oil price shock that hurts the U.S. economy helps the economies of oil-exporting nations, and vice versa. Thus, just as movements in different stocks partially offset one another in an all-U.S. portfolio, so also do movements in U.S. and non-U.S. stock portfolios cancel each other out somewhat.

The possibility of achieving a better risk-return tradeoff by investing internationally is supported by Exhibit 13.1, which shows the annualized returns and standard deviations

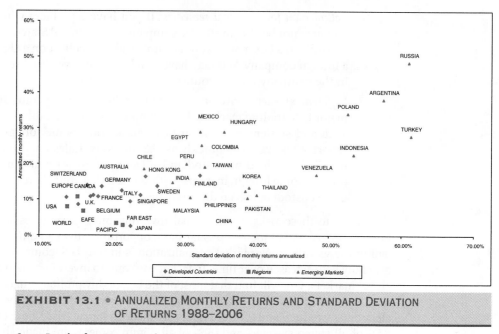

EXHIBIT 13.1 • ANNUALIZED MONTHLY RETURNS AND STANDARD DEVIATION OF RETURNS 1988–2006

Source: Raw data from Morgan Stanley Captial International, http://www.mscibarra.com

of returns for a variety of developed and emerging stock markets over the 19-year period 1988–2006.[2] The exhibit illustrates four points:

1. Historically, national stock markets have wide differences in returns and risk (as measured by the standard deviation of annual returns).

2. **Emerging markets** (shown as circles)—a term that encompasses all of South and Central America; all of the Far East with the exception of Japan, Hong Kong, Singapore, Australia, and New Zealand; all of Africa; and parts of Southern Europe, as well as Eastern Europe and countries of the former Soviet Union—have generally had higher risk and return than the developed markets (shown as diamonds).

3. The **Morgan Stanley Capital International Europe, Australia, Far East (EAFE) Index** (which reflects all major stock markets outside of North America, 20 altogether) has had lower risk than most of its individual country components. The relatively low return for the EAFE Index reflects the dismal performance since 1989 of the Japanese stock market, which is a key component of the index.

4. The **Morgan Stanley Capital International World Index**, which combines the EAFE nations with North America, has lower risk than any of its component countries except for the United States.

Empirical research bears out the significant benefits from international equity diversification suggested by Exhibit 13.1. Evidence suggests that national factors have a strong impact on security returns relative to that of any common world factor.[3] Also, returns from the different national equity markets have relatively low correlations with one another. Differences in industrial structure and currency movements account for very little of the

---

[2] The standard deviations used in this chapter are all monthly standard deviations annualized (multiplied by 12). They are significantly larger than annual standard deviations calculated using yearly data because monthly returns are more volatile than yearly returns. Monthly ups and downs often cancel each other out.

[3] Bruno H. Solnik, "Why Not Diversify Internationally Rather Than Domestically?" *Financial Analysts Journal*, July–August 1974, pp. 48–54; and Donald R. Lessard, "World, Country, and Industry Relationships in Equity Returns: Implications for Risk Reduction Through International Diversification," *Financial Analysts Journal*, January–February 1976, pp. 32–38.

Country	Correlation with U.S. Market	Standard Deviation of Returns[1] (%)	Market Risk (Beta) from U.S.Perspective	Correlation with World Index	Market Risk (Beta) from World Perspective
USA	1.00	15.16	1.00	0.86	0.92
Australia	0.49	23.75	0.77	0.58	0.97
Austria	0.19	20.50	0.25	0.35	0.50
Belgium	0.45	18.91	0.56	0.62	0.83
Canada	0.72	18.94	0.90	0.73	0.98
Denmark	0.39	18.61	0.48	0.54	0.71
Finland	0.40	29.94	0.79	0.52	1.09
France	0.50	22.20	0.73	0.67	1.04
Germany	0.46	21.07	0.64	0.64	0.94
Hong Kong	0.35	36.58	0.84	0.45	1.15
Ireland	0.55	19.51	0.71	0.69	0.95
Italy	0.29	25.06	0.48	0.48	0.84
Japan	0.30	22.09	0.44	0.66	1.03
Netherlands	0.61	18.06	0.73	0.76	0.97
New Zealand	0.32	25.86	0.55	0.43	0.79
Norway	0.47	26.08	0.80	0.55	1.00
Singapore	0.48	29.08	0.92	0.55	1.12
Spain	0.39	22.11	0.56	0.56	0.87
Sweden	0.50	23.42	0.76	0.63	1.03
Switzerland	0.51	18.28	0.62	0.68	0.88
United Kingdom	0.53	22.36	0.78	0.69	1.09
EAFE	0.55	16.43	0.59	0.89	1.02
Europe	0.62	16.48	0.67	0.83	0.96
Far East	0.34	21.42	0.48	0.69	1.05
Pacific	0.37	20.50	0.50	0.73	1.05
The World Index	0.86	14.21	0.80	1.00	1.00

[1] Monthly standard deviation annualized.

Source: Raw data from Morgan Stanley Capital International, http://www.mscibarra.com

EXHIBIT 13.2 ● HOW FOREIGN MARKETS WERE CORRELATED WITH U.S. MARKET AND WORLD INDEX, 1970–2006

low correlation between national stock market returns.[4] The more likely explanation for the low degree of international return correlation is that local monetary and fiscal policies, differences in institutional and legal regimes, and regional economic shocks induce large country-specific variation in returns.

Correlations and the Gains from Diversification
Exhibit 13.2 contains some data on correlations between the U.S. and non-U.S. stock markets. **Foreign market betas**, which are a measure of market risk derived from the capital asset pricing model,[5]

---

[4] Steven L. Heston and K. Geert Rouwenhorst, "Does Industrial Structure Explain the Benefits of International Diversification?" *Journal of Financial Economics*, August 1994, pp. 3–27; and Pierre Ruiz and Bruno Solnik, "Domestic and Global Factors in Individual Stock Returns," HEC School of Management Working Paper, November 2000.

[5] Detailed discussion of the capital asset pricing model appears in Chapter 14.

are calculated relative to the U.S. market in the same way as individual asset betas are calculated:

$$\frac{\text{Foreign market}}{\text{beta}} = \frac{\text{Correlation with}}{\text{U.S. market}} \times \frac{\text{Standard deviation of foreign market}}{\text{Standard deviation of U.S. market}}$$

For example, the Canadian market beta is $0.72 \times 18.94/15.16 = 0.90$. Market risk is also calculated from a world perspective, where the correlations are calculated relative to the world index. Notice that the betas calculated relative to the world index are higher than the betas calculated relative to the U.S. market for all but the U.S. market.

Measured for the 37-year period 1970–2000, foreign markets in developed (EAFE) countries were correlated with the U.S. market from a high of 0.72 for Canada to a low of 0.19 for Austria. The relatively high correlation for Canada reveals that this market tracked the U.S. market's ups and downs. Austria's low correlation, on the other hand, indicates that the Austrian and U.S. markets have tended to move largely independently of each other.

Notice also that the investment risks associated with these different markets can be quite different; the Hong Kong market shows the highest level and the Dutch market the lowest. Indeed, all the markets had a higher level of risk, as measured by the standard deviation of returns, than the U.S. market. Yet the internationally diversified Morgan Stanley Capital International World Index had the lowest level of risk—lower even than the U.S. market. The reason is that much of the risk associated with markets in individual countries is unsystematic and so can be eliminated by diversification, as indicated by the relatively low betas of these markets.

These results imply that international diversification may significantly reduce the risk of portfolio returns. In fact, the standard deviation of an internationally diversified portfolio appears to be as little as 11.7% of that of individual securities. In addition, as shown in Exhibit 13.3, the benefits from international diversification are significantly greater than those that can be achieved solely by adding more domestic stocks to a portfolio. Specifically, an internationally diversified portfolio according to Exhibit 13.3 is less

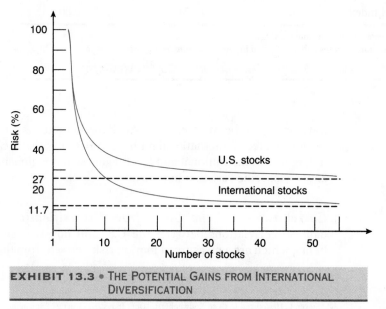

EXHIBIT 13.3 • THE POTENTIAL GAINS FROM INTERNATIONAL DIVERSIFICATION

Source: Bruno H. Solnik, "Why Not Diversify Internationally Rather Than Domestically?" Reprinted with permission from Financial Analysts Federation, Charlettesville, VA. All rights reserved. *Financial Analysts Journal,* July–August 1974.

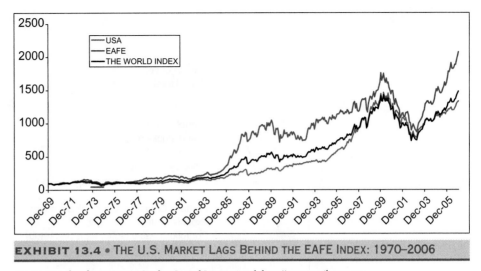

EXHIBIT 13.4 • THE U.S. MARKET LAGS BEHIND THE EAFE INDEX: 1970–2006

Source: Raw data from Morgan Stanley Capital International, http://www.mscibarra.com

than half as risky as a fully diversified U.S. portfolio. However, the data from Exhibit 13.2 indicate that the risk reduction associated with an internationally diversified portfolio is now about 10%.

Moreover, as shown in Exhibit 13.4, historically the EAFE Index outpaced the U.S. market. However, the strong bull market in the United States since 1982, combined with the collapse of the Japanese market since 1989, brought the U.S. index close to the EAFE Index. After 2000, however, the U.S. index once again started lagging behind the EAFE Index. Overall, in the 37 years till May 2007, the U.S. portion on the Morgan Stanley Capital International's world stock index was up 1,461.9%, and the cumulative return for the EAFE Index was 2,194.8%. These are extraordinary returns and unlikely to be repeated. Even more astounding, from 1949 to 1990, the Japanese market soared to an incredible 25,000%. Even with the recent plunge in the Tokyo Stock Exchange, an investor in the Japanese stock market would still be way ahead. Taking a longer-term perspective, it should be noted that the EAFE Index outpaced the U.S. market 22 times during the 40-year period 1961–2000, indicating the advantages of international diversification. Moreover, anyone thinking of investing solely in the U.S. market because of its outstanding performance during the 1990s might consider the fact that Japanese investors likely felt justified in keeping their money at home when the Nikkei index hit a record high of 38,916 on December 31, 1989. In April 2003, it dived to under 7,900, about 20% of its peak value. Thereafter, it regained and in May 2007, it stood at 17,875.

The obvious conclusion is that international diversification pushes out the **efficient frontier**—the set of portfolios that has the smallest possible standard deviation for its level of expected return and has the maximum expected return for a given level of risk—allowing investors simultaneously to reduce their risk and increase their expected return.[6] Exhibit 13.5 illustrates the effect of international diversification on the efficient frontier.

One way to estimate the benefits of international diversification is to consider the expected return and standard deviation of return for a portfolio consisting of a fraction α invested in U.S. stocks and the remaining fraction, $1 - \alpha$, invested in foreign stocks. Define r_{us} and r_{rw} to be the expected returns on the U.S. and rest-of-world stock portfolios, respectively. Similarly, let σ_{us} and σ_{rw} be the standard deviations of the U.S. and rest-of-world

[6] Although calculation of the efficient frontier usually entails the use of historical data, the efficient frontier itself is forward looking, that is, it seeks to describe the *future* risks and returns associated with different investment portfolios.

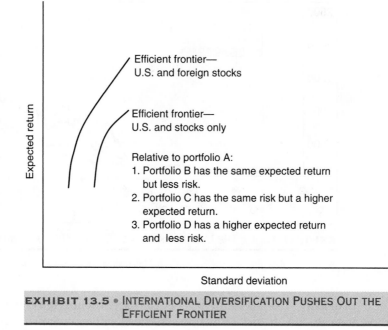

EXHIBIT 13.5 • INTERNATIONAL DIVERSIFICATION PUSHES OUT THE EFFICIENT FRONTIER

portfolios. The expected return on this internationally diversified portfolio, r_p, can be calculated as

$$r_p = \alpha r_{us} + (1 - \alpha)r_{rw} \qquad (13.1)$$

To calculate the standard deviation of this portfolio, it helps to know that the general formula for the standard deviation of a two-asset portfolio with weights w_1 and w_2 ($w_1 + w_2 = 1$) is

$$\text{Portfolio standard deviation} = [w_1^2\sigma_1^2 + w_2^2\sigma_2^2 + 2w_1w_2\rho_{12}\sigma_1\sigma_2]^{1/2} \qquad (13.2)$$

where σ_1^2 and σ_2^2 are the respective variances of the two assets, σ_1 and σ_2 are their standard deviations, and ρ_{12} is their correlation. We can apply Equation 13.2 to our internationally diversified portfolio by treating the domestic and foreign portfolios as separate assets. This operation yields a portfolio standard deviation σ_p equal to

$$\sigma_p = [\alpha^2\sigma_{us}^2 + (1 - \alpha)^2\sigma_{rw}^2 + 2\alpha(1 - \alpha)\sigma_{us}\sigma_{rw}\rho_{us,rw}]^{1/2} \qquad (13.3)$$

where $\rho_{us,rw}$ is the correlation between the returns on the U.S. and foreign stock portfolios.

To see the benefits of international diversification, assume that the portfolio is equally invested in U.S. and foreign stocks, where the EAFE Index represents the foreign stock portfolio. Using data from Exhibit 13.2, we see that $\sigma_{us} = 15.16\%$, $\sigma_{rw} = 16.43\%$, and $\rho_{us,rw} = 0.50$. According to Equation 13.3, these figures imply that the standard deviation of the internationally diversified portfolio is

$$\begin{aligned}
\sigma_p &= [0.5^2(15.16)^2 + 0.5^2(16.43)^2 + 0.5^2 \times 2 \times 15.16 \times 16.43 \times 0.50]^{1/2} \\
&= (187.212)^{1/2} \\
&= 13.68\%
\end{aligned}$$

Here the risk of the internationally diversified portfolio is about 10% below the risk of the U.S. portfolio.

Recent Correlations   The benefits of diversification depend on relatively low correlations among assets. It is often assumed that, as their underlying economies become more

	1977–2006	*1977–1986*	*1987–1996*	*1997–2006*
Australia	0.47	0.34	0.50	0.62
Austria	0.19	0.09	0.16	0.34
Belgium	0.44	0.27	0.55	0.54
Canada	0.72	0.66	0.75	0.77
Denmark	0.41	0.26	0.34	0.62
Finland	0.40	−0.18	0.30	0.64
France	0.51	0.37	0.53	0.72
Germany	0.48	0.24	0.41	0.74
Hong Kong	0.39	0.13	0.55	0.55
Ireland	0.55	n/a	0.45	0.64
Italy	0.32	0.23	0.22	0.56
Japan	0.29	0.16	0.26	0.46
Netherlands	0.63	0.51	0.66	0.71
New Zealand	0.32	0.04	0.37	0.46
Norway	0.49	0.36	0.56	0.57
Pacific	0.35	0.21	0.32	0.55
Singapore	0.49	0.28	0.62	0.57
Spain	0.44	0.15	0.51	0.68
Sweden	0.51	0.32	0.48	0.69
Switzerland	0.49	0.38	0.52	0.60
United Kingdom	0.56	0.39	0.65	0.75
EAFE	0.53	0.36	0.48	0.78
Europe	0.63	0.45	0.66	0.78
Far East	0.32	0.18	0.30	0.51
The World Index	0.84	0.83	0.74	0.95

Source: Raw data from Morgan Stanley Capital International, http://www.mscibarra.com

EXHIBIT 13.6 • CORRELATION OF MONTHLY RETURNS WITH THE U.S. MARKET; DEVELOPED COUNTRY MARKETS

closely integrated and cross-border financial flows accelerate, national capital markets will become more highly correlated, significantly reducing the benefits of international diversification. Indeed, the correlations between the U.S. and non-U.S. stock markets are generally higher today than they were during the 1970s. As Exhibit 13.6 shows, this pattern has persisted. Using 10-year periods—1977–1986, say, versus 1997–2006—correlations are almost uniformly higher in more recent periods. As can be seen in Exhibit 13.7, the increase in correlations has continued, with the correlation between the EAFE Index and the U.S. market climbing from about +0.4 in the mid-1990s to roughly +0.84 in 2006.

In addition to the higher correlations over time, the U.S. market outperformed the Japanese and European markets during the 1990s and reduced the expected return on the EAFE Index relative to the U.S. market. However, the U.S. market has underperformed as compared to the Japanese and European markets as well as the EAFE Index from September 2005 onwards.

Research points to another problematic aspect of international investing as well: When markets are the most volatile and investors most seek safety, global diversification is of limited value.[7] In particular, Exhibit 13.8 shows that the correlations among markets appear to increase when market volatility is at its highest. This effect suggests that the

---

[7] See Patrick Odier and Bruno Solnik, "Lessons for International Asset Allocation," *Financial Analysts Journal*, March-April 1993, pp. 63–77.

EXHIBIT 13.7 • CORRELATION OF US AND EAFE RETURNS

Source: Raw data from Morgan Stanley Capital International, http://www.mscibarra.com

higher correlations seen in the latter half of the 1990s could reflect the impact of the Asian crisis, with its high degree of volatility. Even worse, the markets appear to move in synchrony only when they are falling, not when they are rising. In other words, only bear markets seem to be contagious, not bull markets. For example, immediately following the World Trade Center and Pentagon terrorist attacks on September 11, 2001, stock markets worldwide plunged in unison. In general, correlations between U.S. and foreign stocks increase during down markets, such as from 2000 to 2002, thereby providing little, if any, scope for diversification when they are most needed.

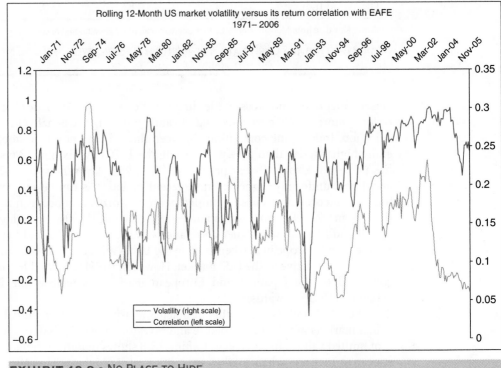

EXHIBIT 13.8 • NO PLACE TO HIDE

Source: Raw data from Morgan Stanley Capital International, http://www.mscibarra.com

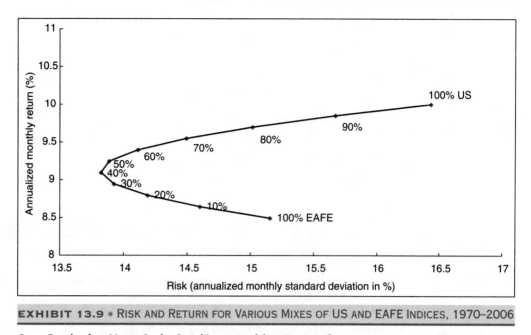

EXHIBIT 13.9 • RISK AND RETURN FOR VARIOUS MIXES OF US AND EAFE INDICES, 1970–2006

Source: Raw data from Morgan Stanley Capital International, http://www.mscibarra.com

Taken together, these changes have diminished the risk-return benefits of international investing. Nonetheless, these benefits still exist, particularly for those who have patience to invest for the long term. Exhibit 13.9 calculates the standard deviations and annualized returns of different mixes of the U.S. (MSCI) Index and the EAFE Index using quarterly data for the 37-year period 1970–2006. Shifting from a portfolio invested 100% in the EAFE Index to one that contains up to 60% invested in the U.S. Index reduces risk and at the same time increases return. As the percentage invested in the U.S. Index is increased past 60%, both portfolio risk and return rise. However, the change in return is minimal.

13.1.2 Investing in Emerging Markets

We have already seen in Exhibit 13.1 some of the high risks and rewards historically associated with investing in emerging markets. So it should perhaps come as no surprise that it is often these countries, with volatile economic and political prospects, which offer the greatest degree of diversification and the highest expected returns.[8] Exhibit 13.10 shows how some of these "emerging markets" performed over the 17-year period ending December 31, 2006. As can be seen, historically no other stock markets so lavishly rewarded investors—and none penalized them so heavily either. Gains of 30% to 40% a year were not unusual, and neither were returns of close to zero. The low returns for the Asian markets reflect the effects of the Asian currency crisis.

In response to the high potential returns, since 1989 private capital flows to emerging stock markets expanded from less than $10 billion a year to between $60 billion and $80 billion a year by the mid-1990s. These flows have contracted in recent years because of the perceptions of increased risk associated with investments in emerging markets. Indeed, as can be seen in Exhibit 13.10, the high returns possible in emerging markets are matched by some breathtaking risks. To begin with, these are small markets, representing in the aggregate less than 10% of the world's stock market capitalization. Hence, they are subject to the usual volatility and lack of liquidity associated with small markets. Yet they face some unique risks

---

[8] See, for example, Vihang R. Errunza, "Gains from Portfolio Diversification into Less Developed Countries," *Journal of International Business Studies*, Fall–Winter 1977, pp. 83–99; and Warren Bailey and René M. Stulz, "Benefits of International Diversification: The Case of Pacific Basin Stock Markets," *Journal of Portfolio Management*, Summer 1990, pp. 57–62.

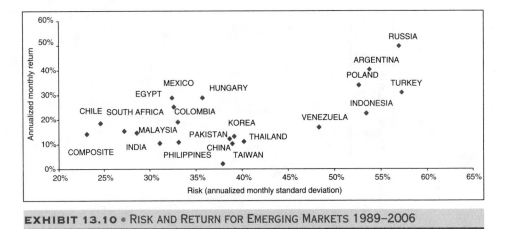

EXHIBIT 13.10 • RISK AND RETURN FOR EMERGING MARKETS 1989–2006

Source: Raw data from Morgan Stanley Capital International, http://www.mscibarra.com

as well: relatively unstable governments, the risk of nationalization of businesses, less protection of property rights, and the threat of abrupt price movements. For example, in February 1990, when the newly elected Brazilian president froze most personal bank accounts, the São Paulo exchange plummeted by 70% in just a few days. Similarly, Taiwan's market rose more than 1,000% from January 1987 to its peak in February 1990. It then gave back most of these gains, falling nearly 80% by October 1990. The Indian stock market also has taken a roller-coaster ride. In the euphoria that accompanied the liberalization of the Indian economy, the Bombay stock index rose 458% between June 1991 and April 1992. It then fell 30% in April and May after disclosure of a scandal in which a broker cheated financial institutions out of at least half a billion dollars to play the market. The more recent debacle in the Asian stock markets will remain fresh in the minds of investors for some time to come.

Despite their high investment risks, emerging markets can reduce portfolio risk because of their low correlations with returns elsewhere. That is, most of their high total risk is unsystematic in nature. For example, Exhibit 13.11 shows how some emerging markets were correlated with the U.S. market for the same six-year periods shown in Exhibit 13.6. For the six-year period 2001–2006, these correlations ranged from a high of 0.74 for Chile and Israel to a low of 0.13 for Pakistan. As the composite indices show, these correlations have generally risen in recent years. Nonetheless, these correlations are still relatively low, particularly as compared to the developed countries. Moreover, although not shown here, these emerging markets also have a low correlation with the MSCI World Index. However, as Exhibit 13.12 shows, the correlation between the S&P 500 and the MSCI Emerging Markets Index has risen over time, reducing the benefits of diversification into emerging markets.

Despite the rising correlations over time, the potential for diversification benefits by means of investing in emerging markets remains. Exhibit 13.13 shows for the 18-year period 1989–2006 the risk and return of a global portfolio that combines in varying proportions the MSCI World Index with the **IFC Emerging Markets Index**, published by the International Finance Corporation.

We see that shifting from a portfolio invested 100% in the MSCI World Index to one that contains up to 10% invested in the IFC Emerging Markets Index reduces risk and at the same time increases expected return. Beyond that point, portfolio risk starts increasing as the higher volatility of the Emerging Markets Index more than offsets the benefits of diversification. Thus, even if one did not expect the emerging markets to outperform the developed country markets, risk reduction alone would dictate an investment of up to 10% in the emerging markets. Because the emerging markets outperformed the developed country markets during this period, a 10% investment in the IFC Index would have reduced the annualized standard deviation while increasing the annual return as well. However, the gains are small, reflecting the weak performance of the emerging markets in the latter part of the 1990s.

	1989–2006	*1989–1994*	*1995–2000*	*2001–2006*
Argentina	0.25	0.20	0.46	0.28
Chile	0.41	0.21	0.46	0.71
China	0.42	0.42	0.39	0.63
Colombia	0.17	−0.08	0.12	0.40
Egypt	0.20	N/A	0.25	0.20
Hungary	0.46	N/A	0.46	0.49
India	0.24	0.29	0.11	0.49
Indonesia	0.28	0.15	0.46	0.22
Israel	0.53	0.55	0.33	0.74
Jordan	0.08	0.17	0.16	0.06
Korea	0.36	0.19	0.32	0.69
Malaysia	0.32	0.39	0.35	0.31
Mexico	0.51	0.36	0.56	0.74
Pakistan	0.10	−0.16	0.15	0.13
Peru	0.23	0.29	0.26	0.29
Philippines	0.37	0.35	0.49	0.32
Poland	0.32	0.36	0.34	0.59
Russia	0.44	N/A	0.48	0.45
South Africa	0.43	0.19	0.50	0.48
Taiwan	0.31	0.14	0.41	0.54
Thailand	0.43	0.38	0.55	0.42
Turkey	0.26	−0.14	0.27	0.69
Venezuela	0.24	0.07	0.21	0.35
Emerging Eastern Europe	0.49	N/A	0.52	0.56
Emerging Far East	0.54	0.45	0.58	0.71
Emerging Latin America	0.50	0.31	0.58	0.76
Emerging Markets Composite	0.60	0.44	0.66	0.78

Source: Raw data from Morgan Stanley Capital International, http://www.mscibarra.com

EXHIBIT 13.11 • CORRELATION OF MONTHLY RETURNS WITH THE U.S. MARKET; EMERGING MARKETS

One caveat with regard to the data presented on the low correlations between U.S. and emerging-country stock market returns, which are based on monthly data, is that monthly return correlations have tended to understate the long-run interrelatedness of emerging markets and their developed-country counterparts. A recent study shows that correlations between developed and developing country markets are much higher when these correlations are computed using yearly data instead of monthly data.[9] In contrast, correlations between developed-nation markets do not vary significantly when computed using yearly instead of monthly data. These results suggest that, because of various impediments to capital mobility in emerging markets, events that immediately affected developed country returns tended to affect emerging market returns with a lag. As these impediments to capital mobility, including government restrictions on capital flows and a lack of liquidity, are reduced, the low monthly correlations between developed and developing markets are likely to rise in the future.

[9] John Mullin, "Emerging Equity Markets in the Global Economy," *Federal Reserve Bank of New York Quarterly Review*, Summer 1993, pp. 54–83.

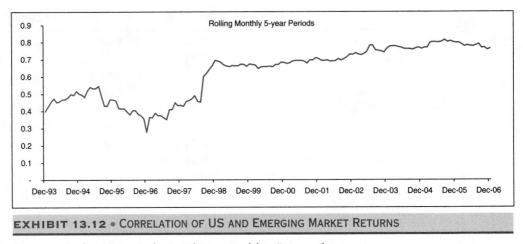

EXHIBIT 13.12 • CORRELATION OF US AND EMERGING MARKET RETURNS

Source: Raw data from Morgan Stanley Capital International, http://www.mscibarra.com

Questions also exist as to the returns that can reliably be expected from emerging market investments. A number of researchers have suggested that these high measured returns may owe more to selection and survivorship bias than to economic reality.[10] In particular, given the way in which the IFC database is constructed, emerging markets that fail to reach a certain threshold capitalization are not included in the emerging market series. We do not observe emerging markets that fail to survive or to achieve the minimum size. Because high-return emerging markets are far more likely to survive and to

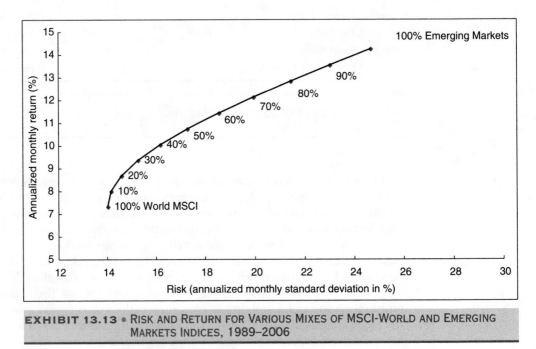

EXHIBIT 13.13 • RISK AND RETURN FOR VARIOUS MIXES OF MSCI-WORLD AND EMERGING
MARKETS INDICES, 1989–2006

Source: Raw data from Morgan Standley Capital International, http://www.mscibarra.com

[10] See, for example, Stephen J. Brown, William N. Goetzmann, and Stephen A. Ross, "Survival," *Journal of Finance*, 50, pp. 853–873; Campbell Harvey, "Predictable Risk and Returns in Emerging Markets," *Review of Financial Studies*, 8, pp. 773–816; and William N. Goetzmann and Philippe Jorion, "Re-emerging Markets," Yale School of Management Working Paper, July 1996.

ILLUSTRATION   *When Latin American Stocks Were Hotter Than Salsa*

A conversion to free-market economics in much of Latin America did wonders for those countries' stock markets in the early 1990s. Investors expected that tighter monetary policies, lower tax rates, significantly lower budget deficits, and the sale of money-losing state enterprises would go a long way to cure the sickly Latin economies. These expectations, in turn, helped stock markets to soar during the early 1990s in all the countries shown in Exhibit 13.14 except Brazil, the one country that has backslid on instituting serious market-oriented reforms. Overall, from 1984 through 1996, the six Latin American stock markets depicted in Exhibit 13.14 rose an average 2,300% in dollar terms, far exceeding the returns available in any other region of the world. It should be noted, however, that these gains reflect the markets' low starting points as much as the success of the economic reforms. Most Latin American markets took a tumble in 1994, led by the Mexican market, as interest rates rose in the United States and it became obvious that the payoffs from these economic changes would take more time to be realized and would be riskier than expected.

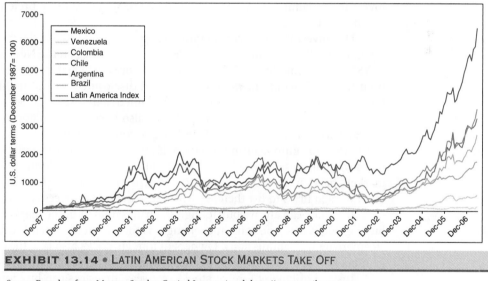

EXHIBIT 13.14 • LATIN AMERICAN STOCK MARKETS TAKE OFF

Source: Raw data from Morgan Stanley Capital International, http://www.mscibarra.com

reach the threshold, the IFC series is clearly biased against low-return markets. Similarly, emerging markets with historically low returns will enter the database if their recent returns are high, again biasing measured emerging-market returns. For example, a number of Latin American stock markets were in existence with low returns for many years before they entered the IFC database. These biases result in an overly optimistic picture of the future returns that can be expected from emerging-market investments.

13.1.3 Barriers to International Diversification

Despite the demonstrated benefits to international diversification, these benefits will be limited because of barriers to investing overseas. Such barriers do exist. They include legal, informational, and economic impediments that serve to segment national capital markets, deterring investors seeking to invest abroad. The lack of **liquidity**, the ability to buy and sell securities efficiently, is a major obstacle on some overseas exchanges. Other barriers include currency controls, specific tax regulations, relatively less-developed capital markets abroad, exchange risk, and the lack of readily accessible and comparable information on potential foreign security acquisitions. The lack of adequate information can significantly increase the perceived riskiness of foreign securities, giving investors an added incentive to keep their money at home.

Some of these barriers are apparently being eroded. Money invested abroad by both large institutions and individuals is growing dramatically. Despite the erosion in barriers to foreign investing and the consequent growth in the level of foreign investing, however, these investments still represent a relatively minor degree of international diversification. For example, in 1993, Americans held 94% of their equity investments in domestic stocks. The large proportion of stock held in domestic assets reflects what is known as **home bias**. While home bias among U.S. investors has somewhat declined, as much as 88% of the U.S. investor portfolio still consisted of domestic stocks in 2004.[11] Absent home bias, it has been estimated that the share of foreign stocks in the U.S. stock portfolio could have easily been larger than 41%. Home bias is also apparent in other countries, with domestic residents holding a disproportionate share of the nation's stock market wealth.[12]

Several explanations for the home bias in portfolio investments have been put forth,[13] notably the existence of political and currency risks and the natural tendency to invest in the familiar and avoid the unknown. Whether these preferences are rational is another issue.

U.S. investors can diversify into foreign securities in several ways. A small number of foreign firms, fewer than 100, have listed their securities on the New York Stock Exchange (NYSE) or the American Stock Exchange. Historically, a major barrier to foreign listing has been the NYSE requirements for substantial disclosure and audited financial statements. For firms wishing to sell securities in the United States, the U.S. Securities and Exchange Commission's (SEC) disclosure regulations also have been a major obstruction. However, the gap between acceptable NYSE and SEC accounting and disclosure standards and those acceptable to European multinationals has narrowed substantially over the years. Moreover, Japanese and European multinationals that raise funds in international capital markets have been forced to conform to stricter standards. This change may encourage other foreign firms to list their securities in order to gain access to the U.S. capital market.

Investors can always buy foreign securities in their home markets. One problem with buying stocks listed on foreign exchanges is that it can be expensive, primarily because of steep brokerage commissions. Owners of foreign stocks also face the complications of foreign tax laws and the nuisance of converting dividend payments into dollars.

Instead of buying foreign stocks overseas, investors can buy foreign equities traded in the United States in the form of **American Depository Receipts** (**ADRs**). An ADR is a negotiable certificate issued by a U.S. bank evidencing ownership of **American depository shares** (**ADSs**).[14] An ADS is a U.S. dollar-denominated security representing shares of stock in a foreign company that are held on deposit on behalf of the ADS owner by a custodian bank in the issuing company's home country. The ADS owner is entitled to the corporate and economic rights of the foreign shares, subject to the terms specified on the ADR certificate. The ADR ratio gives the number of foreign shares represented by one ADS. For example, a 1:5 ratio means that one ADS represents ownership of five foreign shares.

---

[11] Marcela Meirelles Aurélio, "Going Global: The Changing Pattern of U.S. Investment Abroad," *Economic Review: Federal Reserve Bank of Kansas City*, Third Quarter, 2007, pp. 5–32.

[12] The home bias has been documented by Kenneth R. French and James M. Poterba, "Investor Diversification and International Equity Markets," *American Economic Review, Papers and Proceedings*, 1991, pp. 222–226; Ian A. Cooper and Evi Kaplanis, "What Explains the Home Bias in Portfolio Investment," *Review of Financial Studies* 7, 1994, pp. 45–60; and Linda Tesar and Ingrid M. Werner, "Home Bias and High Turnover," *Journal of International Money and Finance* 14, 1995, pp. 467–493.

[13] See, for example, Jun-Koo Kang and René M. Stulz, "Why Is There a Home Bias? An Analysis of Foreign Portfolio Equity Ownership in Japan," *Journal of Financial Economics*, October 1997, pp. 3–28.

[14] Although they represent distinct concepts, the terms ADR and ADS are often used interchangeably.

ADRs provide U.S. investors with a convenient way to invest in and trade foreign shares in the United States. They are traded in the same way as shares in U.S. companies, on the New York Stock Exchange, the Nasdaq, and the American Stock Exchange. The investors in ADRs absorb the handling costs through transfer and handling charges. At the same time, they eliminate custodian safekeeping charges in the issuer's home country, reduce settlement delays, and facilitate prompt dividend payments. ADRs are estimated to save investors between 10 and 40 basis points annually as compared to the costs of investing in the underlying foreign shares directly.

Global depository receipts (GDRs) are similar to ADRs but differ in that they are generally traded on two or more markets outside the foreign issuer's home market. The GDR is generally structured as a combination of a Rule 144A ADR, which trades in the U.S. private placement market and can be sold only to Qualified Institutional Buyers, and a public offering outside the United States. A GDR program allows foreign companies to raise capital in two or more markets simultaneously and broaden their shareholder base.

By the end of 2006, 1,985 sponsored depository programs (both ADRs and GDRs) from 76 countries were available to investors.[15] The market value of these programs exceeded $1.2 trillion. The major US stock exchanges such as NYSE, NASDAQ, and AMEX remain the largest markets for depository receipts, accounting for 79% of depository receipt trading value worldwide.

An alternative to the ADR or GDR is the global registered share (GRS), or global share. Unlike ADRs, which are dollar-denominated certificates traded in the United States, a GRS is similar to an ordinary share with the added benefit that investors can trade it on any stock exchange in the world where it is registered and in the local currency. Global shares are a response to the perceived need for a single class of security to be traded among investors worldwide owing to the globalization of financial markets, the increased operations of multinational companies in multiple markets around the world, and the explosion in cross border merger and acquisition activity. However, before a global share can be launched, operators of the home country's clearing and settlement systems must work closely with their U.S. counterparts, as happened in Germany in 1998. Currently, there are only four global share issues, by DaimlerChrysler, Celanese, UBS, and Deutsche Bank.

M I N I - C A S E   *Deutsche Bank Lists as a Global Share*

In August 2001, as Deutsche Bank was preparing its hotly anticipated U.S. share offering, it was pursuing a strategy that only three other foreign companies had tried before: listing as a global registered share. A global share from Deutsche Bank, Europe's largest bank, was a victory for the New York Stock Exchange. The NYSE has been a big promoter of the concept since its chairman hailed the first one as "the moment when globalization came to the U.S. markets." That moment was in November 1998, when DaimlerChrysler began trading as a global share in the United States, Germany, Japan, and five other countries.

One argument in favor of global shares is that they are less expensive to trade than ADRs. Specifically, while ADRs have been a widely accepted way to trade non-North-American securities, fairly significant additional costs are associated with purchases and sales across markets. These costs arise from the need to convert ADRs to ordinary shares, and ordinary shares to ADRs with a cross border transaction. The depositary bank executes the conversion and charges a fee each way, as much as 5 cents per share. By comparison, the NYSE charges a flat $5 per trade, no matter how many shares change hands.

---

[15] Bank of New York, "Press Release: Depositary Receipt Trading Volume Increases Nearly 60%, Approaching Two Trillion Dollars in 2006, According to The Bank of New York Year-End Report," http://www.bankofny.com/htmlpages/npr_2007_2402.htm.

On the other hand, whereas the custodial bank that creates an ADR usually covers the listing costs, legal and other fees associated with global shares can run as much as $2 million. Moreover, a global share requires coordinating back-office systems and regulatory bodies. Creating such a global clearing and settlement system requires much more effort than issuing an ADR. However, as the world's markets edge closer to 24-hour trading, global shares will become increasingly convenient, as stock markets and clearing and settlement systems consolidate.

QUESTIONS

1. What are the pros and cons of Deutsche Bank listing on the NYSE as a global share instead of an ADR?

2. Are these pros and cons of a GRS issue likely to change over time? In which direction?

3. What changes would increase the desirability of issuing global shares?

The easiest approach to investing abroad is to buy shares in an internationally diversified mutual fund, of which a growing number are available. Four basic categories of mutual fund invest abroad:

1. **Global funds** can invest anywhere in the world, including the United States.

2. **International funds** invest only outside the United States.

3. **Regional funds** focus on specific geographical areas overseas, such as Asia or Europe.

4. **Single-country funds** invest in individual countries, such as Germany or Taiwan.

The greater diversification of the global and international funds reduces the risk for investors, but it also lessens the chances of a high return if one region (for example, Asia) or country (for example, Germany) suddenly gets hot. The problem with this approach is that forecasting returns is essentially impossible in an efficient market. This suggests that most investors would be better off buying an internationally diversified mutual fund. Of course, it is possible to construct one's own internationally diversified portfolio by buying shares in several different regional or country funds.

13.2 INTERNATIONAL BOND INVESTING

The benefits of international diversification extend to bond portfolios as well. G. Barnett and M. Rosenberg started with a portfolio fully invested in U.S. bonds and then replaced them, in increments of 10%, with a mixture of foreign bonds from seven markets.[16] They then calculated for the period 1973–1983 the risk and return of the 10 portfolios they created. Their conclusions were as follows:

1. As the proportion of U.S. bonds fell, the portfolio return rose. This result reflects the fact that foreign bonds outperformed U.S. bonds over this 10-year period.

2. As the proportion of U.S. bonds fell from 100% to 70%, the volatility of the portfolio fell. This fact reflects the low correlation between U.S. and foreign bond returns.

---

[16] G. Barnett and M. Rosenberg, "International Diversification in Bonds," *Prudential International Fixed Income Investment Strategy*, Second Quarter 1983.

3. By investing up to 60% of their funds in foreign bonds, U.S. investors could have raised their return substantially while not increasing risk above the level associated with holding only U.S. bonds.

Other studies examining different time periods and markets have similarly found that an internationally diversified bond portfolio delivers superior performance.

13.3 OPTIMAL INTERNATIONAL ASSET ALLOCATION

Clearly, both international stock diversification and international bond diversification pay off. Not surprisingly, expanding the investment set to include stock and bonds, both domestic and foreign, similarly pays off in terms of an improved risk-return trade-off.

The most detailed study to date of the advantages of international stock and bond diversification is by Bruno Solnik and Bernard Noetzlin.[17] They compared the performances of various investment strategies over the period 1970–1980. The right-hand curve in Exhibit 13.15 is the efficient frontier when investments are restricted to stocks only. The left-hand curve is the efficient frontier when investors can buy both stocks and bonds. All returns are calculated in U.S. dollars. The conclusions of their study were as follows:

1. International stock diversification yields a substantially better risk-return trade-off than does holding purely domestic stock.

2. International diversification combining stock and bond investments results in substantially less risk than international stock diversification alone.

3. A substantial improvement in the risk-return tradeoff can be realized by investing in internationally diversified stock and bond portfolios whose weights do not conform to relative market capitalizations. In other words, the various market indices used to measure world stock and bond portfolios (e.g., Capital International's EAFE Index and World Index) do not lie on the efficient frontier.

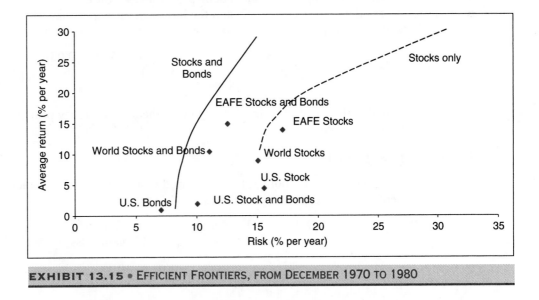

EXHIBIT 13.15 • EFFICIENT FRONTIERS, FROM DECEMBER 1970 TO 1980

[17] Bruno H. Solnik and Bernard Noetzlin, "Optimal International Asset Allocation," *Journal of Portfolio Management*, Fall 1982, pp. 11–21.

As indicated by Exhibit 13.15, optimal **international asset allocation** makes it possible to double or even triple the return from investing in an index fund without taking on more risk. Although Solnik and Noetzlin had the enormous advantage of hindsight in constructing their efficient frontier, they concluded that the opportunities for increased risk-adjusted returns are sizable and that the performance gap between optimal international asset allocations and passive investing in simple index funds is potentially quite large.

13.4 MEASURING THE TOTAL RETURN FROM FOREIGN PORTFOLIO INVESTING

This section shows how to measure the return associated with investing in securities issued in different markets and denominated in a variety of currencies. In general, the **total dollar return** on an investment can be divided into three separate elements: dividend/interest income, capital gains (losses), and currency gains (losses).

13.4.1 Bonds

The one-period total dollar return on a foreign bond investment $R_\$$ can be calculated as follows:

$$\begin{array}{ccc} \text{Dollar} \\ \text{return} \end{array} = \begin{array}{c} \text{Foreign currency} \\ \text{return} \end{array} \times \begin{array}{c} \text{Currency} \\ \text{gain (loss)} \end{array}$$

$$1 + R_\$ = \left[1 + \frac{B(1) - B(0) + C}{B(0)}\right](1 + g)$$

(13.4)

where $B(t)$ = foreign currency (FC) bond price at time t

C = foreign currency coupon income

g = percent change in dollar value of the foreign currency

For example, suppose the initial bond price is FC 95, the coupon income is FC 8, the end-of-period bond price is FC 97, and the local currency appreciates by 3% against the dollar during the period. Then, according to Equation 13.4, the total dollar return is 13.8%:

$$\begin{aligned} R_\$ &= [1 + (97 - 95 + 8)/95](1 + 0.03) - 1 \\ &= (1.105)(1.03) - 1 \\ &= 13.8\% \end{aligned}$$

Note that the currency gain applies both to the local currency principal and to the local currency return.

13.4.2 Stocks

Using the same terminology, the one-period total dollar return on a foreign stock investment $R_\$$ can be calculated as follows:

$$\begin{array}{ccc} \text{Dollar} \\ \text{return} \end{array} = \begin{array}{c} \text{Foreign currency} \\ \text{return} \end{array} \times \begin{array}{c} \text{Currency} \\ \text{gain (loss)} \end{array}$$

$$1 + R_\$ = \left[1 + \frac{P(1) - P(0) + DIV}{P(0)}\right](1 + g)$$

(13.5)

where $P(t)$ = foreign currency stock price at time t

DIV = foreign currency dividend income

For example, suppose the beginning stock price is FC 50, the dividend income is FC 1, the end-of-period stock price is FC 48, and the foreign currency depreciates by 5% against the dollar during the period. Then, according to Equation 13.5, the total dollar return is -6.9%:

$$R_\$ = \left[1 + \frac{(48 - 50 + 1)}{50}\right](1 - 0.05) - 1$$
$$= (0.98)(0.95) - 1$$
$$= -6.9\%$$

In this case, the investor suffered both a capital loss on the FC principal and a currency loss on the investment's dollar value.

13.5 MEASURING EXCHANGE RISK ON FOREIGN SECURITIES

We have just seen that the dollar return on a foreign security can be expressed as

$$\begin{array}{ccc} \text{Dollar} \\ \text{return} \end{array} = \begin{array}{c} \text{Foreign currency} \\ \text{return} \end{array} \times \begin{array}{c} \text{Currency} \\ \text{gain (loss)} \end{array}$$
$$1 + R_\$ = (1 + R_f)(1 + g) \tag{13.6}$$

where R_f is the foreign currency rate of return. Ignoring the cross-product term, $R_f g$, which should be quite small relative to the other terms (because R_f and g are usually much less than 1), we can approximate Equation 13.6 by Equation 13.7:

$$R_\$ = R_f + g \tag{13.7}$$

Equation 13.7 states that the dollar rate of return is approximately equal to the sum of the foreign currency return plus the change in the dollar value of the foreign currency. Foreign currency fluctuations introduce exchange risk. The prospect of exchange risk is one of the reasons that investors have a preference for home country securities.

Using Equation 13.7, we can see how exchange rate changes affect the risk of investing in a foreign security (or a foreign market index). Specifically, we can write the standard deviation of the dollar return, $\sigma_\$$, as

$$\sigma_\$ = [\sigma_f^2 + \sigma_g^2 + 2\sigma_f \sigma_g \rho_{f,g}]^{1/2} \tag{13.8}$$

where σ_f^2 = the variance (the standard deviation squared) of the foreign currency return
σ_g^2 = the variance of the change in the exchange rate
$\rho_{f,g}$ = the correlation between the foreign currency return and the exchange rate change

Equation 13.8 shows that the foreign exchange risk associated with a foreign security depends on both the standard deviation of the foreign exchange rate change and the correlation between the exchange rate change and the foreign currency return on the security.

For example, suppose that the standard deviation of the return on Matsushita, a Japanese firm, in terms of yen is 23% and the standard deviation of the rate of change in the dollar:yen exchange rate is 17%. In addition, the estimated correlation between the yen return on Matsushita and the rate of change in the exchange rate is 0.31. Then, according to Equation 13.8, the standard deviation of the dollar rate of return on investing in Matsushita stock is 32.56%:

$$\sigma_\$(\text{Matsushita}) = (0.23^2 + 0.17^2 + 2 \times .23 \times .17 \times .31)^{1/2} = 0.3256$$

Clearly, foreign exchange risk increases risk in this case. However, the foreign exchange risk is not additive; that is, the standard deviation of the dollar return—32.56%—is less than the sum of the individual standard deviations—23% + 17%, or 40%. It is conceivable that exchange risk could lower the risk of investing overseas. Lowering risk would require a sufficiently large negative correlation between the rate of exchange rate change and the foreign currency return.

13.4.1 Hedging Currency Risk

The existence of exchange risk leaves open the possibility of hedging to reduce it. Indeed, several studies have suggested that hedging currency risk can reduce the variability of returns on internationally diversified stock and bond portfolios while having little impact on or even enhancing expected returns.[18] These conclusions, however, rested mostly on data from the early 1980s. Later data called these conclusions into question. These data show that although during the period 1980–1985—when the dollar was rising—the risk-adjusted returns on hedged stock portfolios dominated those on unhedged portfolios, this result is reversed for the period 1986–1996, when the dollar was generally falling.[19] These reversals in the dominance of unhedged versus hedged efficient frontiers for international stock portfolios occurred because of changes over time in the standard deviations and correlation coefficients of national stock market returns expressed in dollars. That is, the covariance structure of national stock market returns and currency movements is unstable.

In contrast, the returns of hedged, internationally diversified, bond portfolios exhibited dramatically lower volatility than the returns of unhedged bond portfolios over both subperiods. Nonetheless, the case for hedging international bond portfolios is not decisive because the lower standard deviation of hedged bond returns is generally matched by lower returns. These results present investors with the familiar trade-off of risk versus return.

13.6 SUMMARY AND CONCLUSIONS

As the barriers to international capital flows come down and improved communications and data-processing technology provide low-cost information about foreign securities, investors are starting to realize the potential in international investing. We saw in this chapter that international stock and bond diversification can provide substantially higher returns with less risk than investment in a single market, particularly if the market in question is not the U.S. market. Even in a market as large as the United States, international investment offers a much broader range of opportunities than domestic investment alone. An investor restricted to the U.S. stock market, for example, is cut off, in effect, from more than half of the available investment opportunities.

Even though a passive international portfolio—one invested in an index fund based on market capitalization weights—improves risk-adjusted performance, an active strategy can do substantially better. The latter strategy bases the portfolio proportions of domestic and foreign investments on their expected returns and their correlations with the overall portfolio.

---

[18] See, for example, André F. Perold and Evan C. Schulman, "The Free Lunch in Currency Hedging: Implications for Investment Policy and Performance Standards," *Financial Analysts Journal*, May/June 1988, pp. 45–50; Mark R. Eaker and Dwight M. Grant, "Currency Risk Management in International Fixed-Income Portfolios," *Journal of Fixed Income*, December 1991, pp. 31–37; Jack Glen and Philippe Jorion, "Currency Hedging for International Portfolios," *Journal of Finance*, December 1993, pp. 1865–1886; and Richard M. Levich and Lee R. Thomas III, "Internationally Diversified Bond Portfolios: The Merits of Active Currency Management," NBER Working Paper No. 4340, April 1993.

[19] These results are contained in Peter A. Abken and Milind M. Shrikhande, "The Role of Currency Derivatives in Internationally Diversified Portfolios," *Federal Reserve Bank of Atlanta Economic Review*, Third Quarter 1997, pp. 34–59.

QUESTIONS

1. As seen in Exhibit 13.2, Hong Kong stocks are more than twice as volatile as U.S. stocks. Does that mean that risk-averse American investors should avoid Hong Kong equities? Explain.

2. What characteristics of foreign securities lead to diversification benefits for American investors?

3. Will increasing integration of national capital markets reduce the benefits of international diversifications?

4. Studies show that the correlations between domestic stocks are greater than the correlations between domestic and foreign stocks. Explain why this is likely to be the case. What implications does this fact have for international investing?

5. Who is likely to gain more from investing overseas, a resident of the United States or of Mexico? Explain.

6. Suppose that Mexican bonds are yielding more than 100% annually. Does this high yield make them suitable for American investors looking to raise the return on their portfolios? Explain.

7. According to one investment adviser, "I feel more comfortable investing in Western Europe or Canada. I would not invest in South America or other regions with a record of debt defaults and restructurings. The underwriters of large new issues of ADRs of companies from these areas assure us that things are different now. Maybe, but who can say that a government that has defaulted on debt won't change the rules again?" Comment on this statement.

8. As noted in the chapter, from 1949 to 1990, the Japanese market rose 25,000%.

   a. Given these returns, does it make sense for Japanese investors to diversify internationally?

   b. What arguments would you use to persuade a Japanese investor to invest overseas?

   c. Why might Japanese (and other) investors still prefer to invest in domestic securities despite the potential gains from international diversification?

9. Because ADRs are denominated in dollars and are traded in the United States, they present less foreign exchange risk to U.S. investors than do the underlying foreign shares of stock. Comment.

PROBLEMS

1. During the year, the price of British gilts (government bonds) went from £102 to £106, while paying a coupon of £9. At the same time, the exchange rate went from £1:$1.76 to £1:$1.62. What was the total dollar return, in percent, on gilts for the year?

2. Suppose during the first half of the year, Swiss government bonds yielded a local currency return of −1.6%. However, the Swiss franc rose by 8% against the dollar over this 6-month period. Corresponding figures for France were 1.8% and 2.6%. Which bond earned the higher U.S. dollar return? What was the return on the higher bond?

3. During the year, Toyota Motor Company shares went from ¥9,000 to ¥11,200, while paying a dividend of ¥60. At the same time, the exchange rate went from $1 = ¥145 to $1 = ¥120. What was the total dollar return, in percent, on Toyota stock for the year?

4. During 1989, the Mexican stock market climbed 112% in peso terms, whereas the peso depreciated by 28.6% against the U.S. dollar. What was the dollar return on the Mexican stock market during the year?

5. Suppose that the dollar is now worth €1.3472. If one-year German bunds are yielding 9.8% and one-year U.S. Treasury bonds are yielding 6.5%, at what end-of-year exchange rate will the dollar returns on the two bonds be equal? What amount of euro appreciation or depreciation does this equilibrating exchange rate represent?

6. a. In 1992, the Brazilian market rose by 1,117% in cruzeiro terms, while the cruzeiro fell by 91.4% in dollar terms. Meanwhile, the U.S. market rose by 8.5%. Which market did better?

   b. In 1993, the Brazilian market rose by 4,190% in cruzeiro terms, while the cruzeiro fell by 95.9% in dollar terms. Did the Brazilian market do better in dollar terms in 1992 or in 1993?

7. In 1990, Matsushita bought MCA Inc. for $6.1 billion. At the time of the purchase, the exchange rate was about ¥145/$. By the time that Matsushita sold an 80% stake in MCA to Seagram for $5.7 billion in 1995, the yen had appreciated to a rate of about ¥97/$.

   a. Ignoring the time value of money, what was Matsushita's dollar gain or loss on its investment in MCA?

   b. What was Matsushita's yen gain or loss on the sale?

   c. What did Matsushita's yen gain or loss translate into in terms of dollars? What accounts for the difference between this figure and your answer to Part (a)?

8. Suppose that the standard deviations of the British and U.S. stock markets have risen to 38% and 22%, respectively, and the correlation between the U.S. and British markets has risen to 0.67. What is the new beta of the British market from a U.S. perspective?

9. A portfolio manager is considering the benefits of increasing his diversification by investing overseas. She can purchase shares in individual country funds with the following characteristics:

	United States (%)	United Kingdom (%)	Spain (%)
Expected return	15	12	5
Standard deviation of return	10	9	4
Correlation with the United States	1.0	0.33	0.06

a. What are the expected return and standard deviation of return of a portfolio with 25% invested in the United Kingdom and 75% in the United States?

b. What are the expected return and standard deviation of return of a portfolio with 25% invested in Spain and 75% in the United States?

c. Calculate the expected return and standard deviation of return of a portfolio with 50% invested in the United States and 50% in the United Kingdom; with 50% invested in the United States and 50% invested in Spain.

d. Calculate the expected return and standard deviation of return of a portfolio with 25% invested in the United States and 75% in the United Kingdom; with 25% invested in the United States and 75% invested in Spain.

e. Plot these two sets of risk-return combinations (Parts (a) through (d)), as in Exhibit 13.5. Which leads to a better set of risk-return choices, Spain or the United Kingdom?

f. How can you achieve an even better risk-return combination?

10. Suppose that the standard deviation of the return on Nestlé, a Swiss firm, in terms of Swiss francs is 19% and the standard deviation of the rate of change in the dollar-franc exchange rate is 15%. In addition, the estimated correlation between the Swiss franc return on Nestlé and the rate of change in the exchange rate is 0.17. Given these figures, what is the standard deviation of the dollar rate of return on investing in Nestlé stock?

BIBLIOGRAPHY

Abken, P. A. and M. M. Shrikhande, "The Role of Currency Derivatives in Internationally Diversified Portfolios," *Federal Reserve Bank of Atlanta Economic Review,* Third Quarter 1997, pp. 34–59.

Bailey, W. and R. M. Stulz, "Benefits of International Diversification: The Case of Pacific Basin Stock Markets," *Journal of Portfolio Management,* Summer 1990, pp. 57–62.

Barnett, G. and M. Rosenberg, "International Diversification in Bonds," *Prudential International Fixed Income Investment Strategy,* Second Quarter 1983.

Errunza, V. R. "Gains from Portfolio Diversification into Less Developed Countries," *Journal of International Business Studies,* Fall-Winter 1977, pp. 83–99.

Heston, S. L. and K. G. Rouwenhorst, "Does Industrial Structure Explain the Benefits of International Diversification?" *Journal of Financial Economics,* August 1994, pp. 3–27.

Ibbotson, R. C., R. C. Car and A. W. Robinson, "International Equity and Bond Returns," *Financial Analysts Journal,* July–August 1982, pp. 61–83.

Kang, J.-K., and R. M. Stulz, "Why Is There a Home Bias? An Analysis of Foreign Portfolio Equity Ownership in Japan," *Journal of Financial Economics,* October 1997, pp. 3–28.

Lessard, D. R. "World, Country, and Industry Relationships in Equity Returns: Implications for Risk Reduction through International Diversification," *Financial Analysts Journal,* January–February 1976, pp. 32–38.

Odier, P. and B. Solnik, "Lessons for International Asset Allocation," *Financial Analysts Journal,* March–April 1993, pp. 63–77.

Solnik, B. H. *International Investments.* Reading, Mass.: Addison-Wesley, 1988.

_____. "Why Not Diversify Internationally Rather Than Domestically?" *Financial Analysts Journal,* July–August 1974, pp. 48–54.

Solnik, B. H. and B. Noetzlin, "Optimal International Asset Allocation," *Journal of Portfolio Management,* Fall 1982, pp. 11–21.

INTERNET RESOURCES

http://finance.yahoo.com Provides daily data on the performance of stock markets around the world as well as stories related to companies.

http://www.mscibarra.com/products/indices/stdindex/performance.jsp Web site of Morgan Stanley Capital International and Barra, Inc. Contains downloadable data on the performance of a number of country indices, several regional indices, and a world index. It also contains data on several fixed income indices. A number of the time series go back to 1970.

http://www.adr.com/index_sh.html Web site run by J.P. Morgan that contains detailed information and data on ADRs.

http://www.adrbny.com/home_dr.jsp Web page of the Bank of New York that contains a wealth of information on ADRs, including a complete listing of all ADRs and several regional ADR indexes along with an overall ADR index.

INTERNET EXERCISES

1. How has the MSCI World Index performed in dollar terms since the beginning of 2003? How has it performed in terms of the euro? What explains the difference in these returns?

2. What is the compound annual return on the Japanese stock market index since 2000 in yen terms? What is this same compound annual return expressed in dollar terms?

3. What was the return on the U.S. treasury bond index over the last year? How does this compare to the dollar return on U.K. gilts?

4. Compare the dollar return on U.S. treasury bonds to the hedged dollar return on Japanese government bonds. Which is higher? Why are they not the same?

5. These questions are based on the Bank of New York's ADR Web site.

    a. How many ADRs are currently trading in New York?

    b. How have Bank of New York's various ADR indexes performed so far this year?

CAPITAL BUDGETING FOR THE MULTINATIONAL CORPORATION

Nobody can really guarantee the future. The best we can do is size up the chances, calculate the risks involved, estimate our ability to deal with them, and then make our plans with confidence.

Henry Ford II

CHAPTER LEARNING OBJECTIVES

- To assess the profitability of foreign investments by identifying the incremental cash flows generated by these investments
- To explain the various ways in which incremental cash flow can differ from total project cash flow
- To identify the differences between foreign project and parent cash flows and describe a three-stage approach to account for these differences in a capital-budgeting analysis
- To describe the three main methods for incorporating political and economic risks into foreign investment analysis and determine the circumstances (if any) under which each of these methods is most appropriate
- To describe a two-step procedure for incorporating exchange rate changes and inflation into a foreign investment analysis
- To show how foreign project cash-flow adjustments can be carried out, especially in the case of political risk
- To determine the cost of capital for foreign investments and identify those circumstances under which that cost should be higher, lower, or the same as that for comparable domestic projects
- To compute the unlevered equity beta in order to calculate the all-equity cost of capital
- To identify and address the key issues involved in applying the capital asset pricing model to estimate the cost of capital for foreign projects
- To illustrate the impact of globalization on the cost of capital
- To calculate the effective dollar costs of foreign currency borrowing taking into account interest rates, exchange rate changes, and taxes
- To identify the relevant factors and trade-offs in establishing a company's worldwide capital structure
- To explain what growth options are, why they are of great importance to multinational firms, what factors affect their value, and how to incorporate them in a capital-budgeting analysis

KEY TERMS

adjusted present value (APV)	interest tax shield
all-equity beta	international portfolio diversification
all-equity rate	market risk premium
blocked funds	net present value (NPV)
cannibalization	opportunity cost
concession agreement	project beta
capital asset pricing model (CAPM)	sales creation
corporate international diversification	sovereign risk premium
cost of capital	systematic risk
cost of equity capital	target capital structure
depreciation tax shield	total corporate risk
domestic CAPM	true profitability
expropriation	value additivity principle
global CAPM	weighted average cost of capital
growth option	(WACC)
home bias	worldwide capital structure
incremental cash flows	

A central question for the multinational corporation is whether the required rate of return on foreign projects should be higher, lower, or the same as that for domestic projects. To answer this question, we must examine the issue of cost of capital for multinational firms, one of the most complex issues in international financial management. Yet it is an issue that must be addressed, because the foreign investment decision cannot be made properly without knowledge of the appropriate cost of capital.

In this chapter, we seek to determine the incremental cash flows and the cost-of-capital figure(s) that should be used in appraising the profitability of foreign investments. By definition, the **cost of capital** for a given investment is the minimum risk-adjusted return required by shareholders of the firm for undertaking that investment. As such, it is the basic measure of financial performance. Unless the investment generates sufficient funds to repay suppliers of capital, the firm's value will suffer. This return requirement is met only if the net present value of future project cash flows, using the project's cost of capital as the discount rate, is positive.

This chapter also examines the factors that are relevant in determining the appropriate mix of debt and equity financing for the parent and its affiliates. In selecting financial structures for its various units, the multinational corporation must consider the availability of different sources of funds and the relative cost and effects of these sources on the firm's operating risks. Multinational corporations evaluating foreign investments find their analyses complicated by a variety of problems that domestic firms rarely, if ever, encounter. This chapter examines several such problems, including differences between project and parent company cash flows, foreign tax regulations, expropriation, blocked funds, exchange rate changes and inflation, project-specific financing, and differences between the basic business risks of foreign and domestic projects. The purpose of this chapter is to develop a framework that allows measuring, and reducing to a common denominator, the effects of these complex factors on the desirability of the foreign investment opportunities under review. In this way, projects can be compared and evaluated on a uniform basis. The major principle behind methods proposed to cope with these complications is to maximize the use of available information while reducing arbitrary cash flow and cost of capital adjustments.

14.1 BASICS OF CAPITAL BUDGETING

Once a firm has compiled a list of prospective investments, it must then select from among them that combination of projects that maximizes the firm's value to its shareholders. This selection requires a set of rules and decision criteria that enable managers to determine, given an investment opportunity, whether to accept or reject it. The criterion of net present value is generally accepted as being the most appropriate one to use because its consistent application will lead the company to select the same investments the shareholders would make themselves, if they had the opportunity.

14.1.1 Net Present Value

The **net present value** (NPV) is defined as the present value of future cash flows discounted at the project's cost of capital minus the initial net cash outlay for the project. Projects with a positive NPV should be accepted; projects with a negative NPV should be rejected. If two projects are mutually exclusive, the one with the higher NPV should be accepted. The cost of capital is the expected rate of return on projects of similar risk. In this section, we take its value as given.

In mathematical terms, the formula for net present value is

$$NPV = -I_0 + \sum_{t=1}^{n} \frac{X_t}{(1 + k)^t} \tag{14.1}$$

where

I_0 = the initial cash investment

X_t = the net cash flow in period t

k = the project's cost of capital

n = the investment horizon

To illustrate the NPV method, consider a plant expansion project with the following stream of cash flows and their present values:

Year	Cash Flow	×	Present Value Factor (10%)	=	Present Value	Cumulative Present Value
0	−$4,000,000		1.00000		−$4,000,000	−$4,000,000
1	1,200,000		0.9091		1,091,000	−2,909,000
2	2,700,000		0.8264		2,231,000	−678,000
3	2,700,000		0.7513		2,029,000	1,351,000

Assuming a 10% cost of capital, the project is acceptable.

The most desirable property of the NPV criterion is that it evaluates investments in the same way as the company's shareholders do; the NPV method properly focuses on cash rather than on accounting profits and emphasizes the opportunity cost of the money invested. Thus, it is consistent with shareholder wealth maximization.

Another desirable property of the NPV criterion is that it obeys the **value additivity principle**. That is, the NPV of a set of independent projects is simply the sum of the NPVs of the individual projects. This property means that managers can consider each project on its own. It also means that when a firm undertakes several investments, its value increases by an amount equal to the sum of the NPVs of the accepted projects. Thus, if the firm invests in the previously described plant expansion, its value should increase by $1,351,000, the NPV of the project.

14.1.2 Incremental Cash Flows

The most important as well as the most difficult part of an investment analysis is to calculate the cash flows associated with the project: the cost of funding the project; the cash inflows during the life of the project; and the terminal, or ending, value of the project. Shareholders are interested in how many additional dollars they will receive in the future for the dollars they lay out today. Hence, what matters is not the project's total cash flow per period, but the **incremental cash flows** generated by the project.

The distinction between total and incremental cash flows is a crucial one. Incremental cash flow can differ from total cash flow for a variety of reasons. We now examine some of the reasons.

Cannibalization   When Gillette introduced its Fusion model of shaving razors and blades, some customers switched their purchases from the earlier models—Sensor and Mach3—to the new model. This example illustrates the phenomenon known as **cannibalization**, a new product taking sales away from the firm's existing products. Cannibalization also occurs when a firm builds a plant overseas and winds up substituting foreign production for parent company exports. To the extent that sales of a new product or plant just replace other corporate sales, the new project's estimated profits must be reduced by the earnings on the lost sales.

The previous examples notwithstanding, it is often difficult to assess the true magnitude of cannibalization because of the need to determine what would have happened to sales in the absence of the new product or plant. Consider Motorola's construction of a plant in Japan to supply chips to the Japanese market previously supplied via exports. In the past, Motorola got Japanese business whether or not it manufactured in Japan. But now Japan is a chip-making dynamo whose buyers no longer have to depend on U.S. suppliers. If Motorola had not invested in Japan, it might have lost export sales anyway. Instead of losing these sales to local production, however, it would have lost them to one of its rivals. The *incremental* effect of cannibalization—the relevant measure for capital-budgeting purposes—equals the lost profit on lost sales *that would not otherwise have been lost* had the new project not been undertaken. Those sales that would have been lost anyway should not be counted a casualty of cannibalization.

Sales Creation   Black & Decker, the U.S. power tool company, significantly expanded its exports to Europe after investing in European production facilities that gave it a strong local market position in several product lines. Similarly, GM's auto plants in Britain use parts made by its U.S. plants, parts that would not otherwise be sold if GM's British plants disappeared.

In both cases, an investment either created or was expected to create additional sales for existing products. Thus, **sales creation** is the opposite of cannibalization. In calculations of the project's cash flows, the additional sales and associated incremental cash flows should be attributed to the project.

Opportunity Cost   Suppose IBM decides to build a new office building in Sao Paulo on some land it bought 10 years ago. IBM must include the cost of the land in calculating the value of undertaking the project. Also, this cost must be based on the current market value of the land, not the price it paid 10 years ago.

This example demonstrates a more general rule. Project costs must include the true economic cost of any resource required for the project, regardless of whether the firm already owns the resource or has to go out and acquire it. This true cost is the **opportunity cost**, the maximum amount of cash the asset could generate for the firm should it be sold or put to some other productive use. It would be foolish for a firm that acquired oil at $30 a barrel and converted it into petrochemicals to sell them based on the acquisition price of $30 a barrel if the price of oil has risen to $60 per barrel. So, too, it would be foolish to value an asset used in a project at other than its opportunity cost, regardless of how much cash changes hands.

Transfer Pricing   By raising the price at which a proposed Ford plant in Dearborn, Michigan, will sell engines to its British subsidiary, Ford can increase the apparent profitability of the new plant but at the expense of its British affiliate. Similarly, if Matsushita lowers the price at which its Panasonic division buys microprocessors from its microelectronics division, the latter's new semiconductor plant will show a decline in profitability.

These examples demonstrate that the transfer prices at which goods and services are traded internally can significantly distort the profitability of a proposed investment. Wherever possible, the prices used to evaluate project inputs or outputs should be market prices. If no market exists for the product, then the firm must evaluate the project based on the cost savings or additional profits to the corporation of going ahead with the project. For example, when Atari decided to switch most of its production to Asia, its decision was based solely on the cost savings it expected to realize. This approach was the correct one to use because the stated revenues generated by the project were meaningless, an artifact of the transfer prices used in selling its output back to Atari in the United States.

Fees and Royalties   Often companies will charge projects for various items such as legal counsel, power, lighting, heat, rent, research and development, headquarters staff, management costs, and the like. These charges appear in the form of fees and royalties. They are costs to the project, but they are a benefit from the standpoint of the parent firm. From an economic standpoint, the project should be charged only for the additional expenditures that are attributable to the project; those overhead expenses that are unaffected by the project should not be included in estimates of project cash flows.

Getting the Base Case Right   In general, a project's incremental cash flows can be found only by subtracting worldwide corporate cash flows without the investment-the *base case*-from postinvestment corporate cash flows. To come up with a realistic base case, and thus a reasonable estimate of incremental cash flows, managers must ask the key question, "What will happen if we *don't* make this investment?" Failure to heed this question led General Motors during the 1970s to slight investment in small cars despite the Japanese challenge; small cars looked less profitable than GM's then current mix of cars. As a result, Toyota, Nissan, and other Japanese automakers were able to expand and eventually threaten GM's base business. Similarly, many American companies-such as Kodak and Zenith-that thought overseas expansion too risky or unattractive today find their domestic competitive positions eroding. They did not adequately consider the consequences of *not* building a strong global position.

The critical error made by these and other companies is to ignore competitor behavior and assume that the base case is the status quo. In a competitive world economy, however, the least likely future scenario is the status quo. A company that opts not to come out with a new product because it is afraid that the product will cannibalize its existing product line is most likely leaving a profitable niche for some other company to exploit. Sales will be lost anyway, but now they will be lost to a competitor. Similarly, a company that chooses not to invest in a new process technology, because it calculates that the higher quality is not worth the added cost, may discover that it is losing sales to competitors who have made the investment. In a competitive market, the rule is simple: *If you must be the victim of a cannibal, make sure the cannibal is a member of your family.*

Accounting for Intangible Benefits   Related to the choice of an incorrect base case is the problem of incorporating intangible benefits in the capital-budgeting process. Intangibles such as better quality, faster time to market, quicker and less error-prone order processing, and higher customer satisfaction can have a very tangible impact on corporate cash flows, even if they cannot be measured precisely. Similarly, many investments provide intangible benefits in the form of valuable learning experiences and a broader knowledge base. For example, investing in foreign markets can sharpen competitive skills: It exposes companies to tough foreign competition; it enables them to size up new products being developed overseas and figure out how to compete with them before these products show up in the home market; and it can aid in tracking emerging technologies to transfer back home. Adopting practices, products, and technologies discovered overseas can improve a company's competitive position worldwide.

ILLUSTRATION   *Intangible Benefits from Investing in Japan*

The prospect of investing in Japan scares many foreign companies. Real estate is prohibitively expensive. Customers are extraordinarily demanding. The government bureaucracy can seem impenetrable at times, and Japanese competitors fiercely protect their home market.

An investment in Japanese operations provides a variety of intangible benefits, however. More companies are realizing that to compete effectively elsewhere, they must first compete in the toughest market of all: Japan. What they learn in the process—from meeting the stringent standards of Japanese customers and battling a dozen relentless Japanese rivals—is invaluable and will possibly make the difference between survival and extinction. At the same time, operating in Japan helps a company such as IBM keep up the pressure on some of its most potent global competitors in their home market. A position in the Japanese market also gives a company an early look at new products and technologies originating in Japan, enabling it to quickly pick up and transfer back to the United States information on Japanese advances in manufacturing technology and product development. And monitoring changes in the Japanese market helps boost sales there as well.

Although the principle of incremental analysis is a simple one to state, its rigorous application is a complicated undertaking. However, this rule at least points in the right direction those executives responsible for estimating cash flows. Moreover, when estimation shortcuts or simplifications are made, it provides those responsible with some idea of what they are doing and how far they are straying from a thorough analysis.

14.2 DISCOUNT RATES FOR FOREIGN INVESTMENTS

One important component of Equation 14.1 is the project's cost of capital, which is the required rate of return for the project. The development of appropriate cost-of-capital measures for multinational firms is closely bound to how those measures will be used. Because they are to be used as discount rates to aid in the global resource allocation process, the rates must reflect the value to firms of engaging in specific activities. Thus, the emphasis here is on the cost of capital or required rate of return for a specific foreign project rather than for the firm as a whole. Unless the financial structures and commercial risks are similar for all projects engaged in, the use of a single overall cost of capital for project evaluation is incorrect. Different discount rates should be used to value projects that are expected to change the risk complexion of the firm.

14.2.1 The Cost of Equity Capital

The **cost of equity capital** for a firm is the minimum rate of return necessary to induce investors to buy or hold the firm's stock. This required return equals a basic yield covering the time value of money plus a premium for risk. Because owners of common stock have only a residual claim on corporate income, their risk is the greatest, and so too are the returns they demand.

Alternatively, the cost of equity capital is the rate used to capitalize total corporate cash flows. As such, it is just the weighted average of the required rates of return on the firm's individual activities. From this perspective, the corporation is a mutual fund of specified projects, selling a compound security to capital markets. According to the principle of value additivity, the value of this compound security equals the sum of the individual values of the projects.

Although the two definitions are equivalent, the latter view is preferred from a conceptual standpoint because it focuses on the most important feature of the cost of equity capital, namely, that this cost is not an attribute of the firm per se but is a function of the riskiness of the activities in which it engages. Thus, the cost of equity capital for the firm as a whole can be used to value the stream of future equity cash flows, that is, to set a price on equity shares in the firm. It cannot be used as a measure of the required return on equity investments in future projects unless these projects are of a similar nature to the average of those already being undertaken by the firm.

One approach to determining the project-specific required return on equity is based on modern capital market theory. According to this theory, an equilibrium relationship exists between an asset's required return and its associated risk, which can be represented by the **capital asset pricing model (CAPM)**:

where r_i = equilibrium expected return for asset i

r_f = rate of return on a risk-free asset, usually measured as the yield on a U.S. government treasury bill or treasury bond

$$r_i = r_f + \beta_i (r_m - r_f) \tag{14.2}$$

r_m = expected return on the market portfolio consisting of all risky assets

$\beta_i = \rho_{im} \sigma_i / \sigma_m$, where ρ_{im} equals the correlation between returns on security i and the market portfolio, σ_i is the standard deviation of returns on asset i, and σ_m is the standard deviation of returns on the market portfolio

The CAPM is based on the notion that intelligent, risk-averse shareholders will seek to diversify their risks, and, as a consequence, the only risk that will be rewarded with a risk premium will be systematic risk. As can be seen from Equation 14.2, the risk premium associated with a particular asset i is assumed to equal $\beta_i (r_m - r_f)$, where β_i is the systematic or nondiversifiable risk of the asset. The term $r_m - r_f$ is known as the **market risk premium**.

Where the returns and financial structure of an investment are expected to be similar to those of the firm's typical investment, the corporatewide cost of equity capital may serve as a reasonable proxy for the required return on equity of the project. In this case, estimates of the value of the **project beta**—the beta for the project taken on its own—can be found either by direct computation using the CAPM or through professional investment companies that keep track of company betas.

It should be emphasized again that using a company beta to estimate the required return on a project's equity capital is valid only for investments with financial characteristics typical of the "pool" of projects represented by the corporation. This cost-of-equity-capital estimate is useless in calculating project-specific required returns on equity when the characteristics of the project diverge from the corporate norm.

14.2.2 Estimating Discount Rates for Foreign Projects

The importance of the CAPM for the international firm is that the effect of a foreign project's risk on its cost of capital depends only on that project's systematic risk—that is the portion of return variability that cannot be eliminated through diversification. A project's systematic risk is measured by its beta coefficient and is the factor that determines the risk premium associated with the project. The definition of beta is shown here as Equation 14.3:

$$\beta_i = \frac{\rho_{im} \, \sigma_i}{\sigma_m} \tag{14.3}$$

where ρ_{im} equals the correlation between returns on project i and the market portfolio, σ_i is the standard deviation of returns on project i, and σ_m is the standard deviation of returns on the market portfolio. The correlation coefficient takes on values between -1 and $+1$. A positive correlation indicates that the project and market returns tend to move in the same direction; if the project and market are negatively correlated, their returns tend to move in opposite directions. A zero correlation means that the returns vary independently of each other.

The less positive or more negative the correlation between a foreign project's returns and returns on the market, the lower that project's systematic risk. However, we can see from Equation 14.3 that even if a foreign project's returns have a low correlation with market returns, the project can still have a high beta if the project risk, as measured by σ_i, is sufficiently high.

Evidence suggests that much of the economic and political risk faced by MNCs is unsystematic risk, which therefore can be eliminated through diversification on the level of the individual investor. Although these risks may be quite large, they should not affect the discount rate to be used in valuing foreign projects. In other words, the low correlation between project and market returns offsets the effects of a high degree of project risk.

On the other hand, much of the systematic or general market risk affecting a company, at least as measured using a domestic stock index such as the Standard & Poor's 500, is related to the cyclical nature of the national economy in which the company is domiciled. Consequently, the returns on a project located in a foreign country, whose economy is not perfectly synchronous with the home country's economy, should be less highly correlated with domestic market returns than the returns on a comparable domestic project. If this is the case, then the systematic risk of a foreign project actually could be lower than the systematic risk of its domestic counterpart.

Paradoxically, it is the less-developed countries (LDCs)—where political risks are greatest—that are likely to provide the largest diversification benefits. This is because the economies of LDCs are less closely tied to the economy of the United States or that of any other western nation. By contrast, the correlation among the economic cycles of developed countries is considerably stronger, so the diversification benefits from investing in industrialized countries, from the standpoint of a western investor, are proportionately less.

Yet the systematic risk of projects even in relatively isolated LDCs is unlikely to be far below the average for all projects because these countries are still tied into the world economy. The important point about projects in LDCs, then, is that their ratio of systematic to total risk generally is quite low; their systematic risk, though perhaps slightly lower, is probably not significantly less than that of similar projects located in industrialized countries (and could be somewhat more if their risk were sufficiently high to offset the effects of a low correlation with market returns).

Even if a nation's economy is not closely linked to the world economy, the systematic risk of a project located in that country might still be rather large. For example, a foreign copper-mining venture probably will face systematic risk very similar to that faced by an identical extractive project in the United States, whether the foreign project is located in Canada, Chile, or Zaire. The reason is that the major element of systematic risk in any extractive project is related to variations in the price of the mineral being extracted, which is set in a world market. The world market price, in turn, depends on worldwide demand, which itself is systematically related to the state of the world economy. By contrast, a market-oriented project in an LDC, whose risk depends largely on the evolution of the domestic market in that country, is likely to have a systematic risk that is small in both relative and absolute terms.

An example of the latter type of project would be a Ford plant in Brazil whose profitability is closely linked to the state of the Brazilian economy. The systematic risk of the project, therefore, largely depends on the correlation between the Brazilian economy and the U.S. economy. Although positive, this correlation is much less than 1.

Thus, **corporate international diversification** should prove beneficial to shareholders, particularly where there are barriers to **international portfolio diversification**. To the extent that multinational firms are uniquely able to supply low-cost international diversification, investors may be willing to accept a lower rate of return on shares of MNCs than on shares of single-country firms. By extension, the risk premium applied to foreign projects may be lower than the risk premium for domestic ones; that is, the required return on foreign projects may be less than the required return on comparable domestic projects. The net effect may be to enable MNCs to undertake overseas projects that would otherwise be unattractive.

However, if international portfolio diversification can be accomplished as easily and as cheaply by individual investors, then, although required rates of return on MNC securities would be lower to reflect the reduced covariability of MNC returns caused by international diversification, the discount rate would not be reduced further to reflect investors' willingness to pay a premium for the indirect diversification provided by the shares of MNCs. In fact, American investors actually undertake very little foreign portfolio investment. The lack of widespread international portfolio diversification has an important implication for estimating the beta coefficient.

14.2.3 Key Issues in Estimating Foreign Project Discount Rates

Although the CAPM is the model of choice for estimating the cost of capital for foreign projects, the type of information that is needed to estimate foreign subsidiary betas directly—a history of past subsidiary returns or future subsidiary returns relative to predicted market returns—does not exist. About the only practical way to get around this problem is to find publicly traded firms that share similar risk characteristics and use the average beta for the portfolio of corporate surrogates to proxy for the subsidiary's beta. This approach, however, introduces four additional questions for a U.S. multinational:

1. *Should the corporate proxies be U.S. or local (i.e., foreign) companies?* Although local companies should provide a better indication of risk, such companies may

not exist. By contrast, selecting U.S. proxies ensures that such proxies and their data exist, but their circumstances—and hence their betas—may be quite different from those facing the foreign subsidiaries. In addition, it is important to differentiate between the unsystematic risks faced by a foreign project-which individual investors can eliminate through diversification-and the systematic risks affecting that project, which may be small relative to the project's total risk.

2. *Is the relevant base portfolio against which the proxy betas are estimated the U.S. market portfolio, the local portfolio, or the world market portfolio?* Selecting the appropriate portfolio matters because a risk that is systematic in the context of the local market portfolio may well be diversifiable in the context of the U.S. or world portfolio. If this is the case, using the local market portfolio to calculate beta will result in a higher required return—and a less desirable project—than if beta were calculated using the U.S. or world market portfolio.

3. *Should the market risk premium be based on the U.S. market or the local market?* One argument in favor of using the local-market risk premium is that this is the risk premium demanded by investors on investments in that market. On the other hand, estimates of the local-market risk premium may be subject to a good deal of statistical error. Moreover, such estimates may be irrelevant to the extent that an MNC's investors are not the same as the investors in the local market and the two sets of investors measure risk differently.

4. *How, if at all, should country risk be incorporated in the cost of capital estimates?* One approach to incorporating country risk that has been widely adopted in recent years is to add a country risk premium to the discount rate estimated using the CAPM. These premiums are often computed from the yield spread on dollar-denominated local government bonds versus U.S. treasury bonds. However, such an approach may involve double counting of risks and be inconsistent with the theoretical foundations of the CAPM.

Let us now address these four questions and their related issues. As in any application of a theoretical model, the suggested answers are not precisely right but are instead based on a mix of theory, empirical evidence, and judgment.

14.2.4 Proxy Companies

Three alternatives for estimating proxy betas are proposed here. These alternatives are presented in the order of their desirability. Other approaches are also mentioned.[1]

Local Companies   As much as possible, the corporate proxies should be local companies. The returns on an MNC's local operations are likely to depend in large measure on the evolution of the local economy. Inevitably, therefore, the timing and magnitude of these returns will differ from those of the returns generated by comparable U.S. companies. This means that the degree of systematic risk for a foreign project, at least as measured from the perspective of an American investor, may well be lower than the systematic risk of comparable U.S. companies. Put differently, using U.S. companies and their returns to proxy for the returns of a foreign project will likely lead to an upward-biased estimate of the risk premium demanded by the MNC's investors.

---

[1] This section has benefited from a discussion with René Stulz.

ILLUSTRATION *Upward Bias in the Estimates of Beta by Using U.S. Proxy Companies*

Some indication of the upward bias in the estimate of beta imparted by using U.S. proxy companies to estimate the betas for foreign projects is provided by presenting the foreign market betas relative to the U.S. index for some foreign countries. The betas for the foreign markets from a U.S. perspective are calculated in the same way as individual asset betas are calculated:

$$\text{Foreign market beta} = \frac{\begin{array}{c}\text{Correlation with}\\ \text{U.S. market}\end{array} \times \begin{array}{c}\text{Standard deviation}\\ \text{of foreign market}\end{array}}{\text{Standard deviation of U.S. market}} \tag{14.4}$$

According to Equation 14.4, in conjunction with data from the 37-year period 1970–2006 as in Exhibit 13.2 in Chapter 13 the beta for the Australian market relative to the U.S. market was 0.77 (0.49 × 0.2375/0.1516). The corresponding betas for Hong Kong and Singapore were 0.85 and 0.94, respectively:

Country	Correlation with U.S. Market	Standard Deviation of Returns (%)	Beta from U.S. Perspective
Australia	0.49	23.75	0.77
Hong Kong	0.35	36.58	0.84
Singapore	0.48	29.08	0.92
United States	1.00	15.16	1.00

It is possible that some U.S. companies operating overseas have betas in the foreign markets in excess of 1.0, thereby raising their betas relative to the estimated foreign market betas. Nonetheless, this evidence does suggest the possibility that the average beta of U.S. proxy companies overstates the betas for foreign subsidiaries from a U.S. perspective.

Notice also that despite large investment risks associated with the Hong Kong and Singapore markets (standard deviations of 36.58% and 29.08%, respectively), risks that are about twice that of the U.S. market (a standard deviation of 15.16%), both markets had betas that were substantially lower than the U.S. market beta of 1.0. The reason is that much of the risk associated with markets in individual countries is unsystematic and so can be eliminated by diversification, as indicated by the relatively low betas of these markets.

Proxy Industry   If foreign proxies are not directly available, a second alternative is to find a proxy industry in the local market, that is, one whose U.S. industry beta is similar to that of the project's U.S. industry beta. One way to analyze the empirical validity of this approach is to check whether the betas of the two industries (the project's and the proxy's) are also similar in other national markets that contain both industries (e.g., Britain, Germany, and Japan).

Adjusted U.S. Industry Beta   The third alternative is to estimate the foreign project's beta by computing the U.S. industry beta for the project, β_{USPROXY}, multiplying it by the foreign market beta relative to the U.S. index. Specifically, suppose that β_{AUS} is the beta for the Australian market relative to the U.S. market. Then, under this proposed methodology, the beta for the Australian project, β_{AUSSUB}, would be estimated as

$$\beta_{\text{AUSSUB}} = \beta_{\text{USPROXY}} \times \beta_{\text{AUS}} \tag{14.5}$$

This approach is preferred only when the returns for a foreign project depend largely on the evolution of the local economy in which it operates.

Although these approaches to estimating foreign subsidiary betas involve a variety of assumptions, these assumptions appear to be no less plausible than the assumption that foreign operations are inherently riskier than comparable domestic operations and should be assessed an added risk premium.

14.2.5 The Relevant Base Portfolio

In employing the CAPM, the base portfolio against which the proxy betas are estimated can be the home portfolio or the global market portfolio. The resulting implementation of the CAPM depends on which base portfolio is selected. For a U.S. MNC evaluating a foreign investment opportunity, use of its home market portfolio would result in the following version of the CAPM:

$$r_i = r_f + \beta_{ius} (r_{us} - r_f) \tag{14.6}$$

where β_{ius} refers to the project beta when measured relative to the U.S. market (which is its home market) and r_{us} is the expected return on the U.S. market.

The **global capital asset pricing model** can be represented as

$$r_i = r_f + \beta_{ig}(r_g - r_f) \tag{14.7}$$

where β_{ig} refers to the project beta when measured relative to the global market and r_g is the expected return on the global market portfolio (which is measured by something like the Morgan Stanley Capital International, or MSCI, World Index). The foreign project beta using the **global CAPM** is computed as follows:

$$\beta_{ig} = \frac{\text{Correlation with} \atop \text{global market} \times \text{Standard deviation} \atop \text{of foreign project}}{\text{Standard deviation of global market}} \tag{14.8}$$

The appropriate market portfolio to use in measuring a foreign project's beta depends on one's view of world capital markets. More precisely, it depends on whether capital markets are globally integrated. If they are, then the world portfolio is the correct choice; if they are not, the correct choice is the home or domestic portfolio. The test of capital market integration depends on whether these assets are priced in a common context; that is, capital markets are integrated to the extent that security prices offer all investors worldwide the same trade-off between systematic risk and real expected return. Conversely, if capital markets are segmented from each other, then risk is priced in a domestic context.

The truth probably lies somewhere in between. Capital markets are now integrated to a great extent, and they can be expected to become ever more so with time. However, because of various government regulations and other market imperfections, that integration is not complete. Unfortunately, it is not currently within our power, if indeed it ever will be, to empirically determine the relevant market portfolio and, hence, the correct beta to use in project evaluation. (The problem of determining the appropriate market portfolio to use in estimating beta arises domestically as well as internationally.)

The Impact of Globalization on the Cost of Capital To the extent that a global CAPM is the appropriate model to use, it has important implications for companies. First, risk that is systematic in the context of the domestic economy may well be unsystematic in the context of the world economy. As long as the domestic economy is less than perfectly correlated with the world economy, the beta for a project that depends on the state of the local market will be less when measured against the global portfolio than when measured against the domestic portfolio. Other things being equal, the use of a global CAPM means a lower cost of capital for this company.

Another benefit of globally integrated markets is that investors are able to reduce some of the risk that they would otherwise have to bear in a segmented market. In particular, by diversifying across nations whose economic cycles are not perfectly in phase, a globally diversified portfolio will be less risky than a purely domestic portfolio. The reason is that risk which is systematic in the context of the U.S. economy may be unsystematic in the context of the global economy. For example, an oil price shock that hurts the U.S. economy helps the economies of oil-exporting nations, and vice versa. Thus, just as movements in different stocks partially offset one another in an all-U.S. portfolio, so also do movements in U.S. and non-U.S. stock portfolios cancel each other out somewhat.

The lower risk of a globally diversified portfolio translates into a lower risk premium if markets are globally integrated. To understand this result, consider a segmented national market in which domestic securities can only be held by local investors and local investors cannot buy foreign assets. These investors will bear more risk than if they were free to invest internationally. Hence, they will demand a higher rate of return for holding domestic securities than would a globally diversified investor who can diversify away the country-specific risk. Once the domestic market is integrated into a global market, the purely domestic risk on local stocks will be diversified away in the global portfolio. With investors holding domestic stocks now bearing less risk, they will demand a lower risk premium.

The lower risk premium can be seen by recognizing that if the global CAPM holds, the market risk premium for the domestic market portfolio will equal the domestic market beta relative to the global market portfolio, β_d multiplied by the global market risk premium. Given that β_d will usually be less than 1 and that the global market risk premium will be less than the domestic risk premium, the product of the two will also be smaller.

The evidence on asset pricing models is mixed, largely because of the statistical difficulty of testing any such model. While some evidence favors the use of global CAPM, a pragmatic recommendation is for U.S. MNCs to measure the betas of international operations against the U.S. market portfolio. This recommendation is based on the following two reasons:

1. It ensures comparability of foreign with domestic investments, which are evaluated using betas that are calculated relative to a U.S. market index.
2. The relatively minor amount of international diversification attempted (as yet) by American investors suggests that the relevant portfolio from their standpoint is the U.S. market portfolio.

This reasoning suggests that the required return on a foreign project may well be lower, and is unlikely to be higher, than the required return on a comparable domestic project. Thus, applying the same discount rate to an overseas project as to a similar domestic project probably will yield a conservative estimate of the relative systematic riskiness of the project.

Using the domestic cost of capital to evaluate overseas investments also is likely to understate the benefits that stem from the ability of foreign activities to reduce the firm's total risk. As we saw in Chapter 1, reducing total risk can increase a firm's cash flows. By confining itself to its domestic market, a firm will be sensitive to periodic downturns associated with the domestic business cycle and other industry-specific factors. By operating in a number of countries, the MNC can trade off negative swings in some countries against positive ones in others. This option is especially valuable for non-U.S. firms whose local markets are small relative to the efficient scale of operation.

For non-U.S. companies, especially those from smaller countries whose markets are open to foreign investors, it would probably make more sense to use the global CAPM. This model should be used for both domestic and foreign investments to ensure comparability across projects.

14.2.6 The Relevant Market Risk Premium

In line with the basic premise that multinationals should use a methodology that is as consistent as possible with the methodology used to calculate the cost of capital for U.S. investments, the recommended market risk premium to be used is the U.S. market risk premium. This is the appropriate market risk premium to use for several reasons. First, the U.S. market risk premium is the one likely to be demanded by a U.S. company's mostly American investors. A second reason for preferring the U.S. market risk premium is the earlier recommendation that the betas of foreign subsidiaries be estimated relative to the U.S. market. Using the U.S. market risk premium will ensure consistency between the measure of systematic risk and price per unit of this systematic risk. Finally, the quality, quantity, and time span of U.S. capital market data are by far the best in the world, increasing the statistical validity of the estimated market risk premium.

Conversely, no other country has a stock market data series of the same time span and quality as that of the United States. In addition, virtually all foreign countries have undergone dramatic economic and political changes since the end of the World War II—changes that inevitably will affect the required risk premium for those markets. To the extent that such regime changes have altered the market risk premium in foreign countries, estimates of these risk premiums based on historical data are less useful as forecasts of required risk premiums going forward.

The bottom line is that U.S. capital markets have the best data available on the required return that investors demand per unit of risk. Moreover, as national capital markets become increasingly integrated globally, the market price of risk becomes the same worldwide. Add to these points the fact that shareholders of U.S. firms are mostly American and a strong case can be made that the U.S. market risk premium is the appropriate price of risk for a foreign project.[2]

Even if the market price per unit of risk is the same worldwide, the market risk premium may differ across countries because market risk itself differs across countries, that is, some markets are more volatile than others. One way to account for these differences in market risk when valuing a project or a business in a foreign market is to start with the U.S. market risk premium and then adjust that risk premium for differences in risk on a market-by-market basis. The specific risk adjustment involves taking the U.S. market risk premium and multiplying it by the standard deviation of returns for the foreign market divided by the standard deviation of returns for the U.S. market:

$$MRP_f = MRP_{us} \times \frac{\sigma_f}{\sigma_{us}} \tag{14.9}$$

where σ_{us} is the standard deviation of returns on the U.S. market portfolio, σ_f is the standard deviation of returns for the foreign market portfolio, MRP_{us} is the U.S. market risk premium, and MRP_f is the market risk premium for the foreign market. In effect, the adjustment in Equation 14.9 takes the unit price of risk in the U.S. market and multiplies it by the number of units of market risk in the foreign market, where the standard deviation

---

[2] René M. Stulz ("Globalization, Corporate Finance, and the Cost of Capital," *Journal of Applied Corporate Finance*, Fall 1999, pp. 8–25) argues for the use of the global market risk premium, which be estimates at about two-thirds of the historical U.S. market risk premium based on the assumption that the standard deviation of an internationally diversified portfolio is about 20% lower than that of a diverstified portfolio invested only in U.S. stocks.

of returns represents the number of units of risk. For example, using 6% as the U.S. market risk premium, an annualized standard deviation of U.S. market returns of 18%, and 33% for Mexican market returns, the estimated market risk premium for Mexico would be 11.0% (6% × 33/18).

14.2.7 Recommendations

In summary, the recommended approach to estimating the cost of equity capital for the foreign subsidiary of a U.S. multinational is to find a proxy portfolio in the country in which that subsidiary operates and calculate its beta relative to the U.S. market. That beta should then be multiplied by the risk premium for the U.S. market. This estimated equity risk premium for the foreign subsidiary would then be added to the U.S. (home country) risk-free rate to compute a dollar (home currency) cost of equity capital.

An alternative, but problematic, approach used by many investment bankers these days is to estimate a **sovereign risk premium** for the foreign country (by taking the difference between the interest rate on U.S. dollar-denominated debt issued by the foreign government and the rate on U.S. government debt of the same maturity) and to add that figure to the estimated U.S. cost of equity capital. In particular, to the extent that the estimated sovereign risk premium measures risk (it may measure a liquidity premium), it is not systematic risk but rather default (or rescheduling) risk that is being measured. And default risk does not enter into the cost of equity capital. Of course, default risk is likely to be closely linked to political risk, but adjusting the cost of capital is not necessarily the best way to factor political risk into a foreign investment analysis. However, a better approach for dealing with political risk is to first identify its likely cash-flow consequences and then adjust projected cash flows to incorporate those consequences.

14.2.8 Weighted Average Cost of Capital for Foreign Projects

As commonly used, the required return on equity for a particular investment assumes that the financial structure and risk of the project is similar to that for the firm as a whole. This cost of equity capital, k_e, is then combined with the after-tax cost of debt, $k_d(1 - t)$, to yield a **weighted average cost of capital** (WACC) for the parent and the project, k_0, *computed as*

$$k_0 = (1 - L)k_e + Lk_d(1 - t) \tag{14.10}$$

where L is the parent's debt ratio (debt to total assets). This cost of capital is then used as the discount rate in evaluating the specific foreign investment. It should be stressed that k_e is the required return on the firm's stock given the particular debt ratio selected.

Two caveats in employing the weighted average cost of capital are appropriate here. First, the weights must be based on the proportion of the firm's capital structure accounted for by each source of capital using *market,* not *book,* values. Second, in calculating the WACC, the firm's historical debt–equity mix is not relevant. Rather, the weights

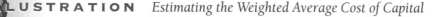

ILLUSTRATION   *Estimating the Weighted Average Cost of Capital*

Suppose a company is financed with 60% common stock and 40% debt, with respective after-tax costs of 14% and 6%. Based on the financing proportions and the after-tax costs of the various capital components and Equation 14.11, the WACC for this firm is calculated as 10.8% (0.6 × 0.14 + 0.4 × 0.06). If the net present value of a project's cash flows—discounted at the weighted average cost of capital—is positive, and assuming that the risk of the project is the same as that of the firm, the project should be undertaken; if it is negative, the investment should be rejected.

must be marginal weights that reflect the firm's **target capital structure**, that is, the proportions of debt and equity the firm plans to use in the future.

Both project risk and financial structure can vary from the corporate norm. For example, the project's capital structure can vary from the corporate norm because of its different debt capacity. It is necessary, therefore, to adjust the costs and weights of the different cost components to reflect their actual values. In particular, if the foreign project has a debt ratio of L', a cost of debt of k_d', and a cost of equity capital of k_e', the project's WACC will equal

$$k_0' = (1 - L')k_e' + L'k_d'(1 - t) \tag{14.11}$$

ILLUSTRATION   *Estimating a Foreign Project's Weighted Average Cost of Capital*

Consider the company in the previous illustration. It is now planning a new foreign investment whose debt capacity can only support a debt ratio of 0.30 instead of the 0.40 debt ratio for the parent. Given the project's high degree of risk, its cost of equity equals 16%, and its after-tax cost of debt is 8%. Based on these parameters, k_0' equals 13.6% (0.7 × 0.16 + 0.3 × 0.08). This rate contrasts with the parent's previously estimated cost of capital of 10.8%.

14.2.9 The Cost of Debt Capital

This section shows how to compute the dollar costs of foreign currency debt that would enter into the weighted average cost of capital calculation. These costs take into account the interest rate on the debt, any currency gains or losses, and the effects of taxes.

To illustrate, suppose that Alpha S.A., the French subsidiary of a U.S.-based multinational, borrows €10 million for one year at an interest rate of 7%. This euro loan is equivalent to a $1.34-million loan at the current exchange rate of $1.34/€. In one year, Alpha will have to repay the principal plus interest, or €10.7 million. If the end-of-year exchange rate is $1.30/€, Alpha's loan will cost $13,910,000 to repay (10,700,000 × 1.30). Although the euro interest rate is 7%, the dollar cost of the loan is 3.81%:

$$\$13,910,000/\$13,400,000 = 1.0381$$

The dollar cost is less than 7% because of the depreciation of the euro. It combines the effects of the euro interest rate and the percentage change in the dollar value of the euro.

In general, the dollar cost of borrowing local currency (LC) at an interest rate of r_L and a currency change of c is the sum of the dollar interest cost plus the percentage change in the exchange rate:

$$\begin{aligned}\text{Dollar cost} \\ \text{of LC loan}\end{aligned} = \text{Interest cost} + \text{Exchange rate change} \tag{14.12}$$
$$= r_L(1 + c) + c$$

The first term in Equation 14.12 is the dollar interest cost (paid at year end after an LC exchange rate change of c); the second term is the exchange gain or loss involved in repaying an LC loan valued at $1 at the beginning of the year with local currency worth $(1 + c)$ dollars at year end. The currency change c is computed as $c = (e_1 - e_0)/e_0$, where

e_0 and e_1 are the beginning and ending exchange rates (LC $1 = \$e$). For example, the change in the dollar value of the euro is calculated as $(1.30 - 1.34)/1.34 = -2.99\%$.

We can employ Equation 14.12 to compute the dollar cost of Alpha's euro loan as follows:

$$0.07(1 - 0.0299) - 0.0299 = 3.81\%$$

Taxes complicate the calculation of various loan costs. Suppose Alpha's effective tax rate is 40%. Then the after-tax cost of paying the €700,000 in interest is €700,000 × $(1 - 0.40)$, or €420,000. This figure translates into an after-tax interest expense of 4.2%. In dollar terms, the cost is even lower. Specifically, the net dollar cost of the loan equals the dollar cost of repaying the loan minus the dollar-equivalent value of the borrowed funds. Given that Alpha borrowed €10 million, the after-tax cost of repaying the principal plus interest is €10,420,000.[3] At the end-of-year exchange rate, this amount translates into $13,546,000. The net after-tax dollar cost of Alpha's loan then is $146,000 based on the difference between the $13.4 million value of its loan initially and the dollar cost of repaying the loan. This after-tax cost translates into an effective dollar interest rate of 1.09% ($146,000/$13,400,000).

In general, the after-tax dollar cost of borrowing in the local currency for a foreign affiliate equals the after-tax interest expense plus the change in the exchange rate, or

$$\text{After-tax dollar cost of LC loan} = \text{Interest cost} + \text{Exchange rate change}$$
$$= r_L(1 + c)(1 - t_a) + c \tag{14.13}$$

where t_a is the affiliate's marginal tax rate. The first term in Equation 14.13 is the after-tax dollar interest cost paid at year end after an LC currency change of c; the second is the exchange gain or loss in dollars of repaying a local currency loan valued at one dollar with local currency worth $(1 + c)$ dollars at the end of the year. The gain or loss has no tax effect for the affiliate because the same amount of local currency was borrowed and repaid.

14.2.10 Annual Exchange Rate Change

We can extend the preceding analysis to a multiyear LC loan. Suppose that the local currency is expected to change relative to the dollar at a steady rate of c per annum. That is, one dollar's worth of local currency today will be worth $(1 + c)^i$ dollars at the end of i years. Then, the interest expense in year i per dollar's worth of LC borrowed today equals $r_L(1 + c)^i$ while the principal repayment is $(1 + c)^n$.

$$-1 + \sum_{i=1}^{n} \frac{r_L(1 + c)^i}{(1 + r)^i} + \frac{(1 + c)^n}{(1 + r)^n} = 0 \tag{14.14}$$

The effective dollar interest rate is found as the solution r to Equation 14.14: In other words, the effective dollar yield, r, is the internal rate of return on the dollar-equivalent cash flows associated with the foreign currency-denominated bond per dollar of foreign currency financing. The effective yield, r, equals $r_L(1 + c) + c$. This is the same as the cost of a one-period LC loan that changes by an amount c during the period.

---

[3] Alpha borrowed €10 million and must repay €10.7 million. Given the tax deductibility of the interest expense, the after-tax cost of paying the €700,000 in interest is €700,000 × $(1 - 0.40)$, or €420,000.

Similarly, the after-tax dollar cost of an LC-denominated bond issued by a local affiliate can be found as the solution, r, to Equation 14.15:

$$-1 + \sum_{i=1}^{n} \frac{r_Z(1 + c)^i(1 - t_a)}{(1 + r)^i} + \frac{(1 + c)^n}{(1 + r)^n} = 0 \qquad (14.15)$$

The solution to Equation 14.15 is $r = r_L(1 + c)(1 - t_a) + c$, once again the same as in the single-period case.

For example, assume that $r_L = 6\%$, $t_a = 45\%$, and $c = 3\%$. Then the effective dollar cost of this LC loan equals $0.06 \times 1.03 \times 0.55 + 0.03$, or 6.4%. On a pretax basis, this cost would equal 9.18% ($0.06 \times 1.03 + 0.03$).

14.2.11 Using Sovereign Risk Spreads

Although the use of a sovereign risk premium was discouraged when computing the cost of equity capital, it is appropriate for estimating the cost of debt associated with a foreign project. This premium reflects the market's assessment of potential losses owing to various country risks noted above. These risks may not be perfectly correlated with the risks of a direct investment in that country, but they are probably representative of such risks. As such, the rate on dollar-denominated local government debt provides us with an objective estimate of the minimum return that investors demand for lending to a particular foreign country. Exhibit 14.1 presents sovereign spreads, expressed in basis points, for a group of developing countries in descending order. If the treasury bond yield was, say, 5.7% and the spread over U.S. treasuries in terms of basis points for Jamaica is 575, the dollar cost of debt for Jamaica would be 11.45% (5.7% + 5.75%).

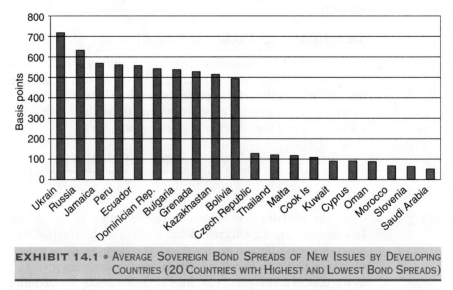

EXHIBIT 14.1 • AVERAGE SOVEREIGN BOND SPREADS OF NEW ISSUES BY DEVELOPING COUNTRIES (20 COUNTRIES WITH HIGHEST AND LOWEST BOND SPREADS)

Data source: "Exchange Rate Policy and Sovereign Bond Spreads in Developing Countries" Samir Jahjah and Vivian Zhanwei Yue. IMF Working Paper. November 2004. Original Data from J.P. Morgan EMBI Global composite index. Figure shows the average weekly stripped spreads from 12-31-1997 to 8-6-2003.

14.3 FOREIGN PROJECT APPRAISAL: THE CASE OF INTERNATIONAL DIESEL CORPORATION

This section illustrates how to deal with some of the complexities involved in foreign project analysis by considering the case of a U.S. firm with an investment opportunity in England. International Diesel Corporation (IDC-U.S.), a U.S.-based multinational firm, is trying to decide whether to establish a diesel manufacturing plant in the United Kingdom (IDC-U.K.). IDC-U.S. expects to significantly boost its European sales of small diesel engines (40–160 hp) from the 20,000 units it is currently exporting there. At the moment, IDC-U.S. is unable to increase exports because its domestic plants are producing to capacity. The 20,000 diesel engines it is currently shipping to Europe are the residual output that it is not selling domestically.

IDC-U.S. has made a strategic decision to significantly increase its presence and sales overseas. A logical first target of this international expansion is the European Community (EC). Market growth seems assured by recent large increases in fuel costs and the advent of Europe 1992 and European Monetary Union. IDC-U.S. executives believe that manufacturing in England will give the firm a key advantage with customers in England and throughout the rest of the EC.

England is the most likely production location because IDC-U.S. can acquire a 1.4-million-square-foot plant in Manchester from British Leyland (BL), which used it to assemble gasoline engines before its recent closing. As an inducement to locate in this vacant plant and thereby ease unemployment among autoworkers in Manchester, the National Enterprise Board (NEB) will provide a five-year loan of £5 million ($10 million) at 3% interest, with interest paid annually at the end of each year and the principal to be repaid in a lump sum at the end of the fifth year. Total acquisition, equipment, and retooling costs for this plant are estimated to equal $50 million.

Full-scale production can begin six months from the date of acquisition because IDC-U.S. is reasonably certain it can hire BL's plant manager and about 100 other former employees. In addition, conversion of the plant from producing gasoline engines to producing diesel engines should be relatively simple.

The parent will charge IDC-U.K. licensing and overhead allocation fees equal to 7% of sales in pounds sterling. In addition, IDC-U.S. will sell its British affiliate valves, piston rings, and other components that account for approximately 30% of the total amount of materials used in the manufacturing process. IDC-U.K. will be billed in dollars at the current market price for this material. The remaining components will be purchased locally. IDC-U.S. estimates that its all-equity nominal required rate of return for the project will equal 12%, based on an anticipated 3% U.S. rate of inflation and the business risks associated with this venture. The debt capacity of such a project is judged to be about 20%—that is, a debt-to-equity ratio for this project of about 1:4 is considered reasonable.

To simplify its investment analysis, IDC-U.S. uses a five-year capital-budgeting horizon and then calculates a terminal value for the remaining life of the project. If the project has a positive net present value for the first five years, there is no need to engage in costly and uncertain estimates of future cash flows. If the initial net present value is negative, then IDC-U.S. can calculate a breakeven terminal value at which the net present value will just be positive. This breakeven value is then used as a benchmark against which to measure projected cash flows beyond the first five years.

We now apply the three-stage investment analysis outlined in the preceding sections: (1) Estimate project cash flows; (2) forecast the amounts and timing of cash flows to the parent; and (3) add to, or subtract from, these parent cash flows the indirect benefits or costs that this project provides the remainder of the multinational firm.

14.3.1 Estimation of Project Cash Flows

A principal cash outflow associated with the project is the initial investment outlay, consisting of the plant purchase, equipment expenditures, and working-capital requirements. Other cash outflows include operating expenses, later additions to working capital as sales expand, and taxes paid on its net income.

IDC-U.K. has cash inflows from its sales in England and other EC countries. It also has cash inflows from three other sources:

1. The tax shield provided by depreciation and interest charges
2. Interest subsidies
3. The terminal value of its investment, net of any capital gains taxes owed upon liquidation

Recapture of working capital is not assumed until eventual liquidation because this working capital is necessary to maintain an ongoing operation after the fifth year.

Initial Investment Outlay   Total plant acquisition, conversion, and equipment costs for IDC-U.K. were previously estimated at $50 million. The plant and equipment will be depreciated on a straight-line basis over a five-year period, with a zero salvage value.

Of the $50 million in net plant and equipment costs, $10 million will be financed by NEB's loan of £5 million at 3%. The remaining $40 million will be supplied by the parent in the form of equity capital.

Working-capital requirements—comprising cash, accounts receivable, and inventory—are estimated at 30% of sales, but this amount will be partially offset by accounts payable to local firms, expected to average 10% of sales. Therefore, net investment in working capital will equal approximately 20% of sales. The transfer price on the material sold to IDC-U.K. by its parent includes a 25% contribution to IDC-U.S.'s profit and overhead. That is, the variable cost of production equals 75% of the transfer price. Lloyds Bank is providing an initial working-capital loan of £1.5 million ($3 million). All future working-capital needs will be financed out of internal cash flow. Exhibit 14.2 summarizes the initial investment.

Financing IDC-U.K   Based on the information just provided, IDC-U.K.'s initial balance sheet, in both pounds and dollars, is presented in Exhibit 14.3. The debt ratio (debt to total assets) for IDC-U.K. is 33:53, or 62%. Note that this debt ratio could vary from 25%, if the parent's total investment was in the form of equity, all the way up to 100%, if IDC-U.S. provided all of its $40 million investment for plant and equipment as debt. In other words, an affiliate's capital structure is not independent; rather, it depends on its parent's investment policies.

	£ (Millions)	*$ (Millions)*
Plant purchase and retooling expense	17.5	35
Equipment		
Supplied by parent (used)	2.5	5
Purchased in the United Kingdom	5	10
Working capital		
Bank financing	1.5	3
Total initial investment	£26.5	$53

EXHIBIT 14.2 • INITIAL INVESTMENT OUTLAY IN IDC-U.K. (£1 = $2)

	£ (Millions)	$ (Millions)
Assets		
Current Assets	1.5	3
Plant and equipment	25	50
Total assets	26.0	53
Liabilities		
Loan payable (to Lloyds)	1.5	3
Total current liabilities	1.5	3
Loan payable (to NEB)	5	10
Loan payable (to IDC-U.S.)	10	20
Total liabilities	16.5	33
Equity	10	20
Total liabilities plus equity	£26.5	53

EXHIBIT 14.3 • INITIAL BALANCE SHEET OF IDC-U.K. (£1 = $2)

The tax shield benefits of interest write-offs are represented separately. Assume that IDC-U.K. contributes $10.6 million to its parent's debt capacity (0.2 × $53 million), the dollar market rate of interest for IDC-U.K. is 8%, and the U.K. tax rate is 40%. This calculation translates into a cash flow in the first and subsequent years equal to $10,600,000 × 0.08 × 0.40, or $339,000. Discounted at 8%, this cash flow provides a benefit equal to $1.4 million over the next five years.

Interest Subsidies   Based on a 5% anticipated rate of inflation in England and on an expected annual 2% depreciation of the pound relative to the dollar, the market rate on the pound loan to IDC-U.K. would equal about 10%. Thus, the 3% interest rate on the loan by the NEB represents a 7% subsidy to IDC-U.K. The cash value of this subsidy equals £350,000 (£5,000,000 × 0.07, or approximately $700,000) annually for the next five years, with a present value of $2.7 million.[4]

Sales and Revenue Forecasts   At a profit-maximizing price of £250 per unit in the first year ($490 at the projected year 1 exchange rate), demand for diesel engines in England and the other EC countries is expected to increase by 10% annually, from 60,000 units in the first year to 88,000 units in the fifth year. It is assumed here that purchasing power parity (PPP) holds with no lag and that real prices remain constant in both absolute and relative terms. Hence, the sequences of nominal pound prices and exchange rates, reflecting anticipated annual rates of inflation equaling 5% and 3% for the pound and dollar, respectively, are

			Year			
	0	1	2	3	4	5
Price (pounds)	—	250	263	276	289	304
Exchange rate (dollars)	2.00	1.96	1.92	1.89	1.85	1.82

[4] The present value of this subsidy is found by discounting it at 10% and then converting the resulting pound present value into dollars at the current spot rate of $2/£. The appropriate discount rate is 10% because this is a pound loan. The exact present value of this subsidy is given by the difference between the present value of debt service on the 3% loan discounted at 10% and the face value of the loan.

It is also assumed here that purchasing power parity holds with respect to the euro and other currencies of the various EC countries to which IDC-U.K. exports. These exports account for about 60% of total IDC-U.K. sales. Disequilibrium conditions in the currency markets or relative price changes can be dealt with using an approach similar to that taken in the exposure measurement example of Spectrum Manufacturing AB in Chapter 10 (Section 10.4).

In the first year, although demand is at 60,000 units, IDC-U.K. can produce and supply the market with only 30,000 units (because of the 6-month start-up period). IDC-U.S. exports another 20,000 units to its British affiliate at a unit transfer price of £250, leading to no profit for IDC-U.K. Because these units would have been exported anyway, IDC-U.K. is not credited from a capital-budgeting standpoint with any profits on these sales. IDC-U.S. ceases its exports of finished products to England and the EC after the first year. From year 2 on, IDC-U.S. is counting on an expanding U.S. market to absorb the 20,000 units. Based on these assumptions, IDC-U.K.'s projected sales revenues are shown in Exhibit 14.4, line C.

In nominal terms, IDC-U.K.'s pound sales revenues are projected to rise at a rate of 15.5% annually, based on a combination of the 10% annual increase in unit demand and the 5% annual increase in unit price ($1.10 \times 1.05 = 1.155$). Dollar revenues will increase at about 13% annually, due to the anticipated 2% annual rate of pound depreciation.

Production Cost Estimates   Based on the assumptions that relative prices will remain constant and that purchasing power parity will hold continually, variable costs of production, stated in real terms, are expected to remain constant, whether denominated in pounds or in dollars. Hence, the pound prices of both labor and material sourced in England and components imported from the United States are assumed to increase by the rate of British inflation, or 5% annually. Unit variable costs in the first year are expected to equal £140, including £30 ($60) in components purchased from IDC-U.S.

In addition, the license fees and overhead allocations, which are set at 7% of sales, will rise at an annual rate of 15.5% because pound revenues are rising at that rate. With a full year of operation, initial overhead expenses would be expected to equal £1,100,000. Actual overhead expenses incurred, however, are only £600,000 because the plant does not begin operation until midyear. These expenses are partially fixed, so their rate of increase should be about 8% annually.

The plant and equipment, valued at £25 million, can be written off over 5 years, yielding an annual depreciation charge against an income of £5 million. The cash flow associated with this tax shield remains constant in nominal pound terms but declines in nominal dollar value by 2% annually. With a 3% rate of U.S. inflation, its real value is, therefore, reduced by 5% annually, the same as its loss in real pound terms.

Annual production costs for IDC-U.K. are estimated in Exhibit 14.4, lines D–I. It should be realized, of course, that some of these expenses, like depreciation, are a non-cash charge or, like licensing fees, a benefit to the overall corporation.

Total production costs rise less rapidly each year than the 15.5% annual increase in nominal revenue. This situation is due both to the fixed depreciation charge and to the semifixed nature of overhead expenses. Thus, the profit margin should increase over time.

Projected Net Income   Net income for years 1 through 5 is estimated on line L of Exhibit 14.4. The effective tax rate on corporate income faced by IDC-U.K. in England is estimated to be 40%. The £2.8 million loss in the first year is applied against income in years 2, 3, and 4, reducing corporate taxes owed against those years.

				Year			
	0	1	2	3	4	5	5+
A. Sales (units)		300000	66000	73000	80000	88000	
B. Price per unit (£)		250	263	276	289	304	
C. Sales revenue (£ millions)		7.5	17.3	20.1	23.2	26.7	
D. Variable cost per unit (£)		140	147	154	162	170	
E. Total Variable cost (£ in millions)		4.2	9.7	11.3	13	15	
F. Licensing fees and royalties (0.07 × line C, in £ millions)		0.5	1.2	1.4	1.6	1.9	
G. Overhead expenses (£ millions)		0.6*	1.2	1.3	1.4	1.5	
H. Depreciation (£ millions)		5	5	5	5	5	
I. Total expenses (E + F + G + H, in £ millions)		10.3	17.1	19	21	23.3	
J. Profit before tax (C − 1, in £ millions)		−2.8	0.2	1.2	2.2	3.4	
K. U.K. corporate income taxes @ 40% = 0.40 × J**		0	0	0	0.3	1.4	
L. Net profit after tax (J − K, in £ millions)		−2.8	0.2	1.2	1.9	2	
M. Terminal value for IDC-U.K. [2.7 × (L + H), for year 5, in £ millions]							19
N. Initial investment, including working capital (£ millions)	−26.5						
O. Working capital investment at 20% of revenue (0.2 × C, in £ millions)		1.5	3.5	4	4.6	5.3	
P. Required addition to working capital (line O for year t − line O for year t − 1; t = 2 , . . . ,5, in £ millions)	0		2	0.8	0.6	0.7	
Q. IDC-U.K. net cash flow (L + H + M + N − P, in £ millions)	−26.5	2.2	3.3	5.6	6.3	6.3	19
R. £ exchange rate ($)	2	1.96	1.92	1.89	1.85	1.82	1.82
S. IDC-U.K. cash flow (Q × R, in $ millions)	−53	4.3	6.3	10.6	11.6	11.5	34.5
T. Present value factor at 12%	1	0.8929	0.7972	0.7118	0.6355	0.5674	0.5674
U. Present value = S × T, in $ millions)	−53	3.8	5	7.5	7.4	6.5	19.6
V. Cumulative present value ($ millions)	−53	−49.2	−44.2	−36.7	−29.3	22.8	−3.2

* Represents overhead for less than one full year.
** Loss carryforward from year 1 of £2.8 million eliminates tax for years 2 and 3 and reduces tax for year 4.

EXHIBIT 14.4 • PRESENT VALUE OF IDC-U.K.: PROJECT VIEWPOINT

Additions to Working Capital   One of the major outlays for any new project is the investment in working capital. IDC-U.K. begins with an initial investment in working capital of £1.5 million ($3 million). Working-capital requirements are projected at a constant 20% of sales. Thus, the necessary investment in working capital will increase by 15.5% annually, the rate of increase in pound sales revenue. These calculations are shown on lines O and P of Exhibit 14.4.

Terminal Value   Calculating a terminal value is a complex undertaking, given the various possible ways to treat this issue. Three different approaches are pointed out here. One approach is to assume that the investment will be liquidated after the end of the planning horizon and to use this value. However, this approach just takes the question one step further: What would a prospective buyer be willing to pay for this project? The second approach is to estimate the market value of the project, assuming that it is the present value of remaining cash flows. Again, however, the value of the project to an outside buyer may differ from its value to the parent firm, owing to parent profits on sales to its affiliate, for instance. The third approach is to calculate a breakeven terminal value at which the project is just acceptable to the parent and then use that as a benchmark against which to judge the likelihood of the present value of future cash flows exceeding that value.

Most firms try to be quite conservative in estimating terminal values. IDC-U.K. calculates a terminal value based on the assumption that the market value of the project will be 2.7 times the net cash flow in year 5 (net income plus depreciation), or £19.0 million.

Estimated Project Present Value   We are now ready to estimate the net present value of IDC-U.K. from the viewpoint of the project. As shown in Exhibit 14.4, line V, the NPV of project cash flows equals −$3.2 million. Adding to this amount the $2.7 million value of interest subsidies and the $1.4 million present value of the tax shield on interest payments yields an overall positive project net present value of $0.9 million. The estimated value of the interest tax shield would be correspondingly greater if this analysis were to incorporate benefits derived over the full 10-year assumed life of the project, rather than including benefits from the first 5 years only. Over 10 years, the present value of the tax shield would equal $2.3 million, bringing the overall project net present value to $1.8 million. The latter approach is the conceptually correct one.

Despite the favorable net present value for IDC-U.K., it is unlikely a firm would undertake an investment that had a positive value only because of interest subsidies or the interest tax shield provided by the debt capacity of the project. However, this is exactly what most firms do if they accept a marginal project, using a weighted cost of capital. Based on the debt capacity of the project and its subsidized financing, IDC-U.K. would have a weighted cost of capital of approximately 10%. At this discount rate, IDC-U.K. would be marginally profitable.

It would be misleading, however, to conclude the analysis at this point without recognizing and accounting for differences between project and parent cash flows and their impact on the worth of investing in IDC-U.K. Ultimately, shareholders in IDC-U.S. will benefit from this investment only to the extent that it generates cash flows that are, or can be, transferred out of England. The value of this investment is now calculated from the viewpoint of IDC-U.S.

14.3.2 Estimation of Parent Cash Flows

From the parent's perspective, additional cash outflows are recorded for any taxes paid to England or the United States on remitted funds. IDC-U.S. has additional cash inflows as well. It receives licensing and overhead allocation fees each year for which it incurs no additional expenses. If it did, the expenses would have to be charged against the fees. IDC-U.S. also profits from exports to its British affiliate.

Loan Payments IDC-U.K. first will make all necessary loan repayments before paying dividends. Specifically, IDC-U.K. will repay the £1.5 million working-capital loan from Lloyds at the end of year 2 and NEB's loan of £5 million at the end of the fifth year. Their dollar repayment costs are estimated at $2.9 million and $9.3 million, respectively, based on the forecast exchange rates. These latter two loan repayments are counted as parent cash inflows because they reduce the parent's outstanding consolidated debt burden and increase the value of its equity by an equivalent amount. Assuming that the parent would repay these loans regardless, having IDC-U.K. borrow and repay funds is equivalent to IDC-U.S. borrowing the money, investing it in IDC-U.K., and then using IDC-U.K.'s higher cash flows (because it no longer has British loans to service) to repay IDC-U.S.'s debts.

Remittances to IDC-U.S. IDC-U.K. is projected to pay dividends equal to 100% of its remaining net cash flows after making all necessary loan repayments. It also pays licensing and overhead allocation fees equal, in total, to 7% of gross sales. On both of these forms of transfer, the British government will collect a 10% withholding tax. These remittances are shown in Exhibit 14.5. IDC-U.S., however, will not owe any further tax to the IRS because the company is assumed to have excess foreign tax credits. Otherwise, IDC-U.S. would have to pay U.S. corporate income taxes on the dividends and fees it receives, less any credits for foreign income and withholding taxes already paid. In this case, IDC-U.K. losses in the first year, combined with the higher British corporate tax rate, will assure that IDC-U.S. would owe minimal taxes to the IRS even if it did not have any excess foreign tax credits.

Earnings on Exports to IDC-U.K. With a 25% margin on its exports, and assuming it has sufficient spare-parts manufacturing capacity, IDC-U.S. has incremental earnings on

		Year				
	1	*2*	*3*	*4*	*5*	*5+*
A. Net cash flow to IDC-U.K. (from Exhibit 17.3, line S)	4.3	6.3	10.6	11.6	11.5	34.5
B. Loan repayments by IDC-U.K.		2.9			9.3	
C. Dividend paid to IDC-U.S. (A − B)	4.3	3.3	10.6	11.6	2.2	34.5
D. Fees and royalties (Exhibit 17.3, line F × line G)	1.0	2.3	2.7	3.0	3.4	15.5*
E. Withholding tax paid to England @ 10% = 0.10 × (C + D)	0.5	0.6	1.3	1.5	0.6	5.0
F. Net income received by IDC-U.S. (C + D − E, in $ millions)	$4.8	$5.1	$11.9	$13.1	$5.1	$45.0
G. Exchange rate	$1.96	$1.92	$1.89	$1.85	$1.82	$1.82

*Estimated present value of future fees and royalties. These were not incorporated in the terminal value figure of $25 million.

EXHIBIT 14.5 • DIVIDENDS AND FEES AND ROYALTIES RECEIVED BY IDC-U.S. (U.S. $ MILLIONS)

	Year					
	1	**2**	**3**	**4**	**5**	**5+**
A. Sales (units)	30,000	66,000	73,000	80,000	88,000	88,000
B. Components purchased from IDC-U.S.						
1. Unit price ($)	60.0	61.8	63.7	65.6	67.5	67.5
2. Total export revenue (A × B1 in $ millions)	1.8	4.1	4.6	5.2	5.9	5.9
C. After-tax cash flow (0.165 × B2 in $ millions)	$0.30	$0.70	$0.80	$0.90	$1.00	$1.00

EXHIBIT 14.6 • NET CASH FLOWS FROM EXPORTS TO IDC-U.K.

sales to IDC-U.K. equaling 25% of the value of these shipments. After U.S. corporate tax of 35%, IDC-U.S. generates cash flows valued at 16.5% (25% × 65%) of its exports to IDC-U.K. These cash flows are presented in Exhibit 14.6.

Estimated Present Value of Project to IDC-U.S.   In Exhibit 14.7, all the various cash flows are added up, net of tax and interest subsidies on debt; and their present value is calculated at $13.0 million. Adding the $5 million in debt-related subsidies ($2.4 million for the interest tax shield and $2.6 million for the NEB loan subsidy) brings this value up to $18.0 million. It is apparent that, despite the additional taxes that must be paid to England and the United States, IDC-U.K. is more valuable to its parent than it would be to another owner on a stand-alone basis. This situation is due primarily to the various licensing and overhead allocation fees received and the incremental earnings on exports to IDC-U.K.

Lost Sales   There is a circumstance, however, that can reverse this conclusion. This discussion has assumed that IDC-U.S. is now producing at capacity and that the 20,000 diesel engines currently being exported to the EC can be sold in the United States, starting in year 2. Should this assumption not be the case (that is, should 20,000 units of IDC-U.K. sales simply replace 20,000 units of IDC-U.S. sales), then the project would have to be charged with the incremental cash flow that IDC-U.S. would have earned on these lost exports. We now see how to incorporate this effect in a capital-budgeting analysis.

Suppose the incremental after-tax cash flow per unit to IDC-U.S. on its exports to the EC equals $180 at present and that this contribution is expected to maintain its value in current dollar terms over time. Then, in nominal dollar terms, this margin grows by 3% annually. If we assume lost sales of 20,000 units per year, beginning in year 2 and extending through year 10, and a discount rate of 12%, the present value associated with these lost sales equals $19.5 million. The calculations are presented in Exhibit 14.8. Subtracting the present value of lost sales from the previously calculated present value of $18.0 million yields a net present value of IDC-U.K. to its parent equal to -$1.5 million (-$6.5 million ignoring the interest tax shield and subsidy).

			Year				
	0	**1**	**2**	**3**	**4**	**5**	**5+**
A. Cash inflows							
1 Loan repayments by IDC-U.K. (from Exhibit 17.4, line B)			2.9			9.3	
2 Dividend paid to IDC-U.S. (from Exhibit 17.4, line C)		4.3	3.3	10.6	11.6	2.2	34.5
3 Fees and royalties paid to IDC-U.S. (from Exhibit 17.4, line D)		1.0	2.3	2.7	3.0	3.4	15.5
4 Net cash flows from exports (from Exhibit 17.5, line C)		0.3	0.7	0.8	0.9	1.0	4.1*
5 Total cash inflows		5.6	9.3	14.0	15.4	15.9	54.1
B. Cash outflows							
1 Plant and equipment	50.0						
2 Working capital	3.0						
3 Withholding tax paid to U.K. (from Exhibit 17.4, line E)		0.5	0.6	1.3	1.5	0.6	5.0
4 Total cash outflows	53.0	0.5	0.6	1.3	1.5	0.6	5.0
C. Net cash flow (A5 − B4)	(53.0)	5.1	8.7	12.7	14.0	15.3	49.1
D. Present value factor at 12%	1.0	0.8929	0.7972	0.7118	0.6355	0.5674	0.5674
E. Present value (C × D)	(53.0)	4.5	6.9	9.0	8.9	8.7	27.9
F. Cumulative present value ($ millions)	−$53.0	−$48.5	−$41.5	−$32.5	−$23.6	−$14.9	$13.0

* Estimated present value of future earnings on export sales to IDC-U.K.

EXHIBIT 14.7 • PRESENT VALUE OF IDC-U.K.: PARENT VIEWPOINT (U.S. $ MILLIONS)

This example points out the importance of looking at incremental cash flows generated by a foreign project rather than total cash flows. An investment that would be marginally profitable on its own, and quite profitable when integrated with parent activities, becomes unprofitable when taking into account earnings on lost sales.

It is apparent from the figures in Exhibit 14.6 that IDC-U.S.'s British investment is quite sensitive to the potential political risks of currency controls and expropriation. The net present value of the project does not turn positive until well after its fifth year of operation (assuming there are no lost sales). Should expropriation occur or exchange controls be imposed at some point during the first 5 years, it is unlikely that the project will ever be viable from the parent's standpoint. Only if compensation is sufficiently great in the event of expropriation, or if unremitted funds can earn a return reflecting their opportunity cost to IDC-U.S. with eventual repatriation in the event of exchange controls, can this project still be viable in the face of these risks.

The general approach recommended previously for incorporating political risk in an investment analysis usually involves adjusting the cash flows of the project (rather than its required rate of return) to reflect the impact of a particular political event on the present value of the project to the parent.

	Year								
	2	**3**	**4**	**5**	**6**	**7**	**8**	**9**	**10**
A. Lost unit sales	20,000	20,000	20,000	20,000	20,000	20,000	20,000	20,000	20,000
B. Cash flow per unit*	185.4	191.0	196.7	202.6	208.7	214.9	221.4	228.0	234.9
C. Total cash flow from exports (A × B)	3.7	3.8	3.9	4.1	4.2	4.3	4.4	4.6	4.7
D. Present value factor at 12%	0.7972	0.7118	0.6355	0.5674	0.5066	0.4523	0.4039	0.3606	0.3220
E. Present value (C × D)	3.0	2.7	2.5	2.2	2.1	1.9	1.8	1.6	1.5
F. Cumulative present value	$3.0	$5.7	$8.2	$10.5	$12.6	$14.5	$16.3	$18.0	$19.5

* The figures in this row grow by 3 percent each year. So, 185.4 = 180(1.03), and so on.

EXHIBIT 14.8 • VALUE OF LOST EXPORT SALES

14.4 ISSUES IN FOREIGN INVESTMENT ANALYSIS

The analysis of a foreign project raises two additional issues other than those dealing with the interaction between the investment and financing decisions:

1. Should cash flows be measured from the viewpoint of the project or that of the parent?
2. Should the additional economic and political risks that are uniquely foreign be reflected in cash flow or discount rate adjustments?

14.4.1 Parent versus Project Cash Flows

A substantial difference can exist between the cash flow of a project and the amount that is remitted to the parent firm because of tax regulations and exchange controls. In addition, project expenses such as management fees and royalties are returns to the parent company. Furthermore, the incremental revenue contributed to the parent of the MNC by a project can differ from total project revenues if, for example, the project involves substituting local production for parent company exports or if transfer price adjustments shift profits elsewhere in the system.

Given the differences that are likely to exist between parent and project cash flows, the question arises as to the relevant cash flows to use in project evaluation. Economic theory has the answer to this question. According to economic theory, the value of a project is determined by the net present value of future cash flows back to the investor. Thus, the parent MNC should value only those cash flows that are, or can be, repatriated net of any transfer costs (such as taxes), because only accessible funds can be used for the payment of dividends and interest, for amortization of the firm's debt, and for reinvestment.

A Three-Stage Approach   A three-stage analysis is recommended for simplifying project evaluation. In the first stage, project cash flows are computed from the subsidiary's standpoint, exactly as if the subsidiary were a separate national corporation. The perspective then shifts to the parent company. This second stage of analysis requires specific forecasts concerning the amounts, timing, and form of transfers to headquarters, as well as information about what taxes and other expenses will be incurred in the transfer process. Finally, the firm must take into account the indirect benefits and costs that this investment confers on the rest of the system, such as an increase or decrease in export sales by another affiliate.

Estimating Incremental Project Cash Flows Essentially, the company must estimate a project's true profitability. **True profitability** is an amorphous concept, but basically it involves determining the marginal revenue and marginal costs associated with the project. In general, as mentioned earlier, incremental cash flows to the parent can be found only by subtracting worldwide parent company cash flows (without the investment) from postinvestment parent company cash flows. This estimating entails the following:

1. Adjust for the effects of transfer pricing and fees and royalties.
   - Use market costs/prices for goods, services, and capital transferred internally.
   - Add back fees and royalties to project cash flows, because they are benefits to the parent.
   - Remove the fixed portions of such costs as corporate overhead.
2. Adjust for global costs/benefits that are not reflected in the project's financial statements. These costs/benefits include
   - Cannibalization of sales of other units
   - Creation of incremental sales by other units
   - Additional taxes owed when repatriating profits
   - Foreign tax credits usable elsewhere
   - Diversification of production facilities
   - Market diversification
   - Provision of a key link in a global service network
   - Knowledge of competitors, technology, markets, and products

The second set of adjustments involves incorporating the project's strategic purpose and its impact on other units. For example, AT&T is investing heavily in the ability to provide multinational customers with seamless global telecommunications services.

Although the principle of valuing and adjusting incremental cash flows is itself simple, it can be complicated to apply. Its application is illustrated in the case of taxes.

Tax Factors Because only after-tax cash flows are relevant, it is necessary to determine when and what taxes must be paid on foreign-source profits. The following example illustrates the calculation of the incremental tax owed on foreign-source earning. Suppose an affiliate remits after-tax earnings of $150,000 to its U.S. parent in the form of a dividend. Assume that the foreign tax rate is 25%, the withholding tax on dividends is 4%, and excess foreign tax credits are unavailable. The marginal rate of additional taxation is found by adding the withholding tax that must be paid locally to the U.S. tax owed on the dividend. Withholding tax equals $6,000 (150,000 × 0.04), and U.S. tax owed equals $14,000. The U.S. tax is calculated as follows: with a before-tax local income of $200,000 (200,000 × 0.75 = 150,000), the U.S. tax owed would equal $200,000 × 0.35, or $70,000. The firm then receives foreign tax credits equal to $56,000—the $50,000 in local tax paid and the $6,000 dividend withholding tax—leaving a net of $14,000 owed to the IRS. This calculation yields a marginal tax rate of 13.33% on remitted profits, as follows:

$$\frac{6,000 + 14,000}{150,000} = 0.1333$$

If excess foreign tax credits are available to offset the U.S. tax owed, then the marginal tax rate on remittances is just the dividend withholding tax rate of 4%.

14.4.2 Political and Economic Risk Analysis

All else being equal, firms prefer to invest in countries with stable currencies, healthy economies, and minimal political risks, such as expropriation. All else is usually not equal, however, and so firms must assess the consequences of various political and economic risks for the viability of potential investments.

The three main methods for incorporating the additional political and economic risks, such as the risks of currency fluctuation and expropriation, into foreign investment analysis are (1) shortening the minimum payback period, (2) raising the required rate of return of the investment, and (3) adjusting cash flows to reflect the specific impact of a given risk.

Adjusting the Discount Rate or Payback Period The additional risks confronted abroad are often described in general terms instead of being related to their impact on specific investments. This rather vague view of risk probably explains the prevalence among multinationals of two unsystematic approaches to account for the added political and economic risks of overseas operations. One is to use a higher discount rate for foreign operations; another is to require a shorter payback period. For instance, if exchange restrictions are anticipated, a normal required return of 15% might be raised to 20%, or a 5-year payback period might be shortened to three years.

Neither of the aforementioned approaches, however, lends itself to a careful evaluation of the actual impact of a particular risk on investment returns. Thorough risk analysis requires an assessment of the magnitude and timing of risks and their implications for the projected cash flows. For example, an expropriation 5 years hence is likely to be much less threatening than one expected next year, even though the probability of its occurring later may be higher. Thus, using a uniformly higher discount rate simply distorts the meaning of the present value of a project by penalizing future cash flows relatively more heavily than current ones, without obviating the necessity for a careful risk evaluation. Furthermore, the choice of a risk premium is an arbitrary one, whether it is 2% or 10%. Instead, adjusting cash flows makes it possible to fully incorporate all available information about the impact of a specific risk on the future returns from an investment.

Adjusting Expected Values The recommended approach is to adjust the cash flows of a project to reflect the specific impact of a given risk, primarily because there is normally more and better information on the specific impact of a given risk on a project's cash flows than on its required return. The cash-flow adjustments presented in this chapter employ only expected values; that is, the analysis reflects only the first moment of the probability distribution of the impact of a given risk. Although this procedure does not assume that shareholders are risk-neutral, it does assume either that risks such as expropriation, currency controls, inflation, and exchange rate changes are unsystematic or that foreign investments tend to lower a firm's systematic risk. In the latter case, adjusting only the expected values of future cash flows will yield a lower bound on the value of the investment to the firm.

Although the suggestion that cash flows from politically risky areas should be discounted at a rate that ignores those risks is contrary to current practice, the difference is more apparent than real: Most firms evaluating foreign investments discount most likely (modal) rather than expected (mean) cash flows at a risk-adjusted rate. If an expropriation or currency blockage is anticipated, then the mean value of the probability distribution of future cash flows will be significantly below its mode. From a theoretical standpoint, of course, cash flows should always be adjusted to reflect the change in expected values caused by a particular risk; however, only if the risk is systematic should these cash flows be further discounted.

14.4.3 Exchange Rate Changes and Inflation

The present value of future cash flows from a foreign project can be calculated using a two-stage procedure: (1) Convert nominal foreign currency cash flows into nominal home currency terms, and (2) discount those nominal cash flows at the nominal domestic required rate of return. In order to properly assess the effect of exchange rate changes on expected cash flows from a foreign project, one must first remove the effect of offsetting inflation and exchange rate changes. It is worthwhile to analyze each effect separately because different cash flows may be differentially affected by inflation. For example, the **depreciation tax shield** will not rise with inflation, while revenues and variable costs are likely to rise in line with inflation. Or local price controls may not permit internal price adjustments. In practice, correcting for these effects means first adjusting the foreign currency cash flows for inflation and then converting the projected cash flows back into dollars using the forecast exchange rate.

ILLUSTRATION   *Factoring in Currency Depreciation and Inflation*

Suppose that with no inflation the cash flow in year 2 of a new project in France is expected to be €1 million, and the exchange rate is expected to remain at its current value of €1 = $1.34. Converted into dollars, the €1, million cash flow yields a projected cash flow of $1,340,000. Now suppose that French inflation is expected to be 6% annually, but project cash flows are expected to rise only 4% annually because the depreciation tax shield will remain constant. At the same time, because of purchasing power parity (and U.S. inflation of 1%), the euro is expected to depreciate at the rate of 5% annually, giving rise to a forecast exchange rate in year 2 of $1.34 \times (1 - 0.05)^2 = \$1.209$. Then the forecast cash flow in year 2 becomes €$1,000,000 \times 1.04^2 = $€$1,081,600$, with a forecast dollar value of $1,307,654 ($1.209 \times 1,081,600$).

An alternative approach to valuing a foreign project's future cash flows is to (1) discount the nominal foreign currency cash flows at the nominal foreign currency required rate of return and (2) convert the resulting foreign currency present value into the home currency using the current spot rate. These two different approaches to valuing project cash flows should give the same results if the international Fisher effect is assumed to hold.

14.5 ESTABLISHING A WORLDWIDE CAPITAL STRUCTURE

In estimating the weighted average cost of capital for an MNC or its affiliates, we took the capital structure as given. However, the capital structure itself should be the outcome of an optimal global financial plan. This plan requires consideration not only of the component costs of capital, but also of how the use of one source affects the cost and availability of other sources. A firm that uses too much debt might find the cost of equity (and new debt) financing prohibitive. The capital structure problem for the multinational enterprise, therefore, is to determine the mix of debt and equity for the parent entity and for all consolidated and unconsolidated subsidiaries that maximizes shareholder wealth.

The focus is on the consolidated **worldwide capital structure**, because suppliers of capital to a multinational firm are assumed to associate the risk of default with its worldwide debt ratio. This association stems from the view that bankruptcy or other forms of financial distress in an overseas subsidiary can seriously impair the parent company's ability to operate domestically. Any deviations from the MNC's target capital structure will cause adjustments in the mix of debt and equity used to finance future investments.

Another factor that may be relevant in establishing a worldwide debt ratio is the empirical evidence that earnings variability appears to be a decreasing function of foreign-source earnings. Because the risk of bankruptcy for a firm is dependent on its total earnings variability, the earnings diversification provided by its foreign operations may enable the multinational firm to leverage itself more highly than can a purely domestic corporation, without increasing its default risk.

14.5.1 Foreign Subsidiary Capital Structure

After a decision has been made regarding the appropriate mix of debt and equity for the entire corporation, questions about individual operations can be raised. How should MNCs arrange the capital structures of their foreign affiliates? And what factors are relevant in making this decision? Specifically, the problem is whether foreign subsidiary capital structures *should*

- Conform to the capital structure of the parent company
- Reflect the capitalization norms in each foreign country
- Vary to take advantage of opportunities to minimize the MNC's cost of capital

Disregarding public and government relations and legal requirements for the moment, we see that the parent company could finance its foreign affiliates by raising funds in its own country and investing these funds as equity. The overseas operations would then have a zero debt ratio (debt/total assets). Alternatively, the parent could hold only one dollar of share capital in each affiliate and require all to borrow on their own, with or without guarantees; in this case, affiliate's debt ratios would approach 100%. Or the parent could itself borrow and relend the monies as intracorporate advances. Here again, the affiliate's debt ratios would be close to 100%. In all these cases, the total amount of borrowing and the debt/equity mix of the consolidated corporation are identical. Thus, the question of an optimal capital structure for a foreign affiliate is completely distinct from the corporation's overall debt/equity ratio.

Moreover, any accounting rendition of a separate capital structure for the subsidiary is wholly illusory *unless* the parent is willing to allow its affiliate to default on its debt.[5] As long as the rest of the MNC group has a legal or moral obligation or sound business reasons for preventing the affiliate from defaulting, the individual unit has no independent capital structure. Rather, its true debt/equity ratio is equal to that of the consolidated group. Exhibits 14.9 and 14.10 show the stated and the true debt-to-equity ratios for a subsidiary and its parent for four separate cases. In cases I, II, and III, the parent borrows $100 to invest in a foreign subsidiary, in varying portions of debt and equity.

---

[5]See, for example, Michael Adler, "The Cost of Capital and Valuation of a Two-Country Firm," *Journal of Finance*, March 1974, pp. 119–132; and Alan C. Shapiro, "Financial Structure and the Cost of Capital in the Multinational Corporation," *Journal of Financial and Quantitative Analysis*, June 1978, pp. 211–226.

i.	**100% Parent Financed**		ii.	**100% Parent Financed**	
$100	D = 50		$100	D = 100	
	E = 50			E = 0	
D/E =	1:1		D/E =	Infinity	

iii.	**100% Parent Financed**		iv.	**100% Bank Financed**	
$100	D = 0		$100	D = 100	
	E = 100			E = 0	
D/E =	0		D/E =	Infinity	

EXHIBIT 14.9 • SUBSIDIARY CAPITAL STRUCTURE: DEBT-TO-EQUITY RATIOS

In case IV, the subsidiary borrows $100 directly from the bank. Depending on what the parent calls its investment, the subsidiary's debt-to-equity ratio can vary from zero to infinity. Despite this variation, the consolidated balance sheet shows a debt-to-equity ratio after the foreign investment of 4:7, regardless of how the investment is financed and what it is called.

Exhibit 14.11 shows that the financing mechanism does affect the pattern of returns, whether they are called dividends or interest and principal payments. It also determines the initial recipient of the cash flows. Are the cash flows from the foreign unit paid directly to the outside investor (the bank), or are they first paid to the parent, which then turns around and repays the bank?

The point of this exercise is to show that unlike the case for the corporation as a whole, an affiliate's degree of leverage does not determine its financial risk. Therefore, the first two options—having an affiliate's financial structures conform to parent or local norms—are unrelated to shareholder wealth maximization.

Multinationals apparently recognize the irrelevance of subsidiary financial structures. In a 1979 survey by Business International of eight U.S.-based MNCs, most of the firms expressed little concern with the debt/equity mixes of their foreign affiliates.[6] (Admittedly, for most of the firms interviewed, the debt ratios of affiliates had not significantly raised the MNCs' consolidated indebtedness.) Their primary focus was on the

	Before Foreign Investment				
	$1,000	D = $300			
		E = $700			
	D/E	3:7			

	After foreign investment				
Domestic	$1,000	D = $400	Domestic	$1,000	D = $400
Foreign	$100	E = 700	Foreign	$100	E = 700
	D/E =	4:7		D/E =	4:7

EXHIBIT 14.10 • CONSOLIDATED PARENT BALANCE SHEET: DEBT-TO-EQUITY RATIOS

---

[6]"Policies of MNCs on Debt/Equity Mix," *Business International Money Report*, September 21, 1979, pp. 319–320.

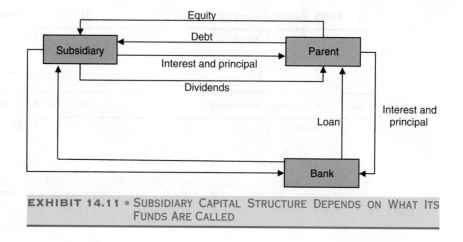

EXHIBIT 14.11 • SUBSIDIARY CAPITAL STRUCTURE DEPENDS ON WHAT ITS FUNDS ARE CALLED

worldwide, rather than individual, capital structure. The third option of varying affiliate financial structures to take advantage of local financing opportunities appears to be the appropriate choice. Thus, within the constraints set by foreign statutory or minimum equity requirements, the need to appear to be a responsible and good guest, and the requirements of a worldwide financial structure, a multinational corporation should finance its affiliates to minimize its incremental average cost of capital.

Political Risk Management   A subsidiary with a capital structure similar to that of its parent may forgo profitable opportunities to lower its cost of funds or its risk. For example, rigid adherence to a fixed debt/equity ratio may not allow a subsidiary to take advantage of government-subsidized debt or low-cost loans from international agencies. Furthermore, it may hamper the subsidiary in designing a financing strategy to mitigate the effects of political risk. The use of financing to reduce political risks typically involves mechanisms to avoid or at least reduce the impact of certain risks, such as those of exchange controls. It may also involve financing mechanisms that actually change the risk itself, as in the case of expropriation or other direct political acts. For example, it may be worthwhile to raise funds locally if the country is politically risky. In the event the affiliate is expropriated, for instance, it would default on all loans from local financial institutions. Similarly, borrowing funds locally will decrease the company's vulnerability to exchange controls. Local currency (LC) profits can be used to service its LC debt.

Another approach used by multinational firms, especially those in the expropriation-prone extractive industries, is to finance their foreign investments with funds from the host and other governments, international development agencies, overseas banks, and customers—with payment to be provided out of production—rather than supplying their own capital. Because repayment is tied to the project's success, the firm(s) sponsoring the project can create an international network of banksf, government agencies, and customers with a vested interest in the faithful fulfillment of the host government's contract with the sponsoring firm(s). Any expropriation threat is likely to upset relations with customers, banks, and governments worldwide. This strategy was employed successfully by Kennecott to finance a major copper mine expansion in Chile. Despite the subsequent rise to power of Salvador Allende, a politician who promised to expropriate all foreign holdings in Chile with "ni un centavo" in compensation, Chile was forced to honor all prior government commitments to Kennecott.

Currency Risk Management   Borrowing in the local currency also can help a company to reduce its foreign exchange exposure. The basic rule is to finance assets that generate foreign-currency cash flows with liabilities denominated in those same foreign currencies. In the case of contractual items—those fixed in nominal terms—this structuring simply involves matching net positive positions (ones with net cash inflows) in each currency with borrowings of similar maturity. The goal here is to offset unanticipated changes in the dollar value of its cash flows with identical changes in the dollar cost of servicing its liabilities.

With noncontractual operating cash flows—those from future revenues and costs—the same financing principle applies: Finance assets that generate foreign currency cash flows with liabilities denominated in those same foreign currencies. Although it is impossible to perfectly hedge operating cash flows in this manner because of the many uncertainties concerning the effects of currency changes on operating flows, the hedging objective at least provides a clear-cut goal that firms should strive for.

On the other hand, forcing a subsidiary to borrow funds locally to meet parent norms may be quite expensive in a country with a high-cost capital market or if the subsidiary is in a tax-loss-carryforward position. In the latter case, because the subsidiary cannot realize the tax benefits of the interest write-off, the parent should make an equity injection financed by borrowed funds. In this way, the interest deduction need not be sacrificed.

Leverage and Foreign Tax Credits   The choice of where to borrow to finance foreign operations is complicated because the distribution of debt between U.S. parents and their foreign subsidiaries affects the use of foreign tax credits. Foreign tax credits (FTCs)—credits that the United States and other home countries grant against domestic income tax for foreign income taxes already paid. The purpose of these FTCs is to eliminate double taxation of foreign-source earnings. In general, if the foreign tax on a dollar earned abroad and remitted to the United States is less than the U.S. corporate tax rate of 35%, then that dollar will be subject to additional tax in order to bring the total tax paid up to 35 cents. If the foreign tax rate is equal to or in excess of 35%, the United States will not impose additional taxes and, in fact, will allow the use of these excess taxes paid as an offset against U.S. taxes owed on other foreign-source income.

The problem for many U.S.-based MNCs is that they are in a position of excess foreign tax credits. One way to use up these FTCs is to push expenses overseas—and thus lower overseas profits—by increasing the leverage of foreign subsidiaries. In the aforementioned example, the U.S. parent may have one of its taxpaying foreign units borrow funds and use them to pay a dividend to the parent. The parent can then turn around and invest these funds as equity in the nontaxpaying subsidiary. In this way, the worldwide corporation can reduce its taxes without losing the benefits of its FTCs.

Leasing and Taxes   As an alternative to increasing the debt of foreign subsidiaries, U.S. multinationals could expand their use of leasing in the United States. Although leasing an asset is economically equivalent to using borrowed funds to purchase the asset, the international tax consequences differ. In the past, U.S. multinationals counted virtually all their interest expense as a fully deductible U.S. expense. Under current tax law, however, firms must allocate interest expense on general borrowings to match the location of their assets, even if all the interest is paid in the United States. This allocation has the effect of reducing the amount of interest expense that can be written off against U.S. income. Rental expense, on the other hand, can be allocated to the location of the leased property.[7] Lease payments on equipment located in the United States, therefore, can be fully deducted.

---

[7]International taxation is an exceptionally complicated subject but here is an indication of its complexity. Interest expenses incurred in the United States are deductible in the United States based on the proportion of U.S.-based assets to the worldwide amount of assets the company owns. So, if 50% of an MNC's assets are in the United States it can only deduct 50% of U.S. interest expenses against U.S. income. But if the equipment being leased is in the United States, 100% of the lease payments associated with that equipment is deductible in the United States.

At the same time, leasing equipment to be used in the United States, instead of borrowing to finance it, increases reported foreign income (because there is less interest expense to allocate against foreign income). The effect of leasing, therefore, is to increase the allowable foreign tax credit to offset U.S. taxes owed on foreign-source income, thereby providing another tax advantage of leasing for firms that owe U.S. tax on their foreign-source income.

Cost-Minimizing Approach to Global Capital Structure   The cost-minimizing approach to determining foreign-affiliate capital structures would be to allow subsidiaries with access to low-cost capital markets to exceed the parent-company capitalization norm, while subsidiaries in higher-capital-cost nations would have lower target debt ratios. These costs must be figured on an after-tax basis, taking into account the company's worldwide tax position.

The basic hypothesis proposed in this section is that a subsidiary's capital structure is relevant only insofar as it affects the parent's consolidated worldwide debt ratio. Nonetheless, some companies have a general policy of "every tub on its own bottom." Foreign units are expected to be financially independent after the parent's initial investment. The rationale for this policy is to "avoid giving management a crutch." By forcing foreign affiliates to stand on their own feet, affiliate managers presumably will be working harder to improve local operations, thereby generating the internal cash flow that will help replace parent financing. Moreover, the local financial institutions will have a greater incentive to monitor the local subsidiary's performance because they can no longer look to the parent company to bail them out if their loans go sour.

Companies that expect their subsidiaries to borrow locally had better be prepared to provide enough initial equity capital or subordinated loans. In addition, local suppliers and customers are likely to shy away from a new subsidiary operating on a shoestring if that subsidiary is not receiving financial backing from its parent. The foreign subsidiary may have to show its balance sheet to local trade creditors, distributors, and other stakeholders. Having a balance sheet that shows more equity demonstrates that the unit has greater staying power.

It also takes more staff time to manage a highly leveraged subsidiary in countries like Brazil and Mexico, where government controls and high inflation make local funds scarce. One treasury manager complained, "We spend 75–80% of management's time trying to figure out how to finance the company. Running around chasing our tails instead of attending to our basic business—getting production costs lower, sales up, and making the product better."[8]

14.5.2 Joint Ventures

Because many MNCs participate in joint ventures, either by choice or necessity, establishing an appropriate financing mix for this form of investment is an important consideration. The previous assumption that affiliate debt is equivalent to parent debt in terms of its impact on perceived default risk may no longer be valid. In countries such as Japan and Germany, increased leverage will not necessarily lead to increased financial risks, due to the close relationship between the local banks and corporations. Thus, debt raised by a joint venture in Japan, for example, may not be equivalent to parent-raised debt in terms of its impact on default risk. The assessment of the effects of leverage in a joint venture requires a qualitative analysis of the partner's ties with the local financial community, particularly with the local banks.

Unless the joint venture can be isolated from its partners' operations, some significant conflicts are likely to be associated with this form of ownership. Transfer pricing, setting royalty and licensing fees, and allocating production and markets among plants are

---

[8]"Determining Overseas Debt/Equity Ratios," *Business International Money Report*, January 27, 1986, p. 26.

just some of the areas in which each owner has an incentive to engage in activities that will harm its partners. These conflicts explain why bringing in outside equity investors is generally such an unstable form of external financing.

Because of their lack of complete control over a joint venture's decisions and its profits, most MNCs will, at most, guarantee joint-venture loans in proportion to their share of ownership. But where the MNC is substantially stronger financially than its partner, the MNC may wind up implicitly guaranteeing its weaker partner's share of any joint-venture borrowings, as well as its own. In this case, it makes sense to push for as large an equity base as possible; the weaker partner's share of the borrowings is then supported by its larger equity investment.

14.6 SUMMARY AND CONCLUSIONS

Capital budgeting for the multinational corporation presents many elements that rarely, if ever, exist in domestic capital budgeting. The primary thrust of this chapter has been to adjust project cash flows, instead of the discount rate, to reflect the key political and economic risks that MNCs face abroad. Tax factors are also incorporated via cash-flow adjustments—preferred on the pragmatic grounds that more and better information is available on the effect of such risks on future cash flows than on the required discount rate. Furthermore, adjusting the required rate of return of a project to reflect incremental risk does not usually allow for adequate consideration of the time pattern and magnitude of the risk being evaluated. Using a uniformly higher discount rate to reflect additional risk involves penalizing future cash flows relatively more heavily than present ones.

Analysis of the available evidence on the impact of foreign operations on firm riskiness suggests that if there is an effect, that effect is generally to reduce both actual and perceived riskiness. These results indicate that corporations should continue investing abroad as long as there are profitable opportunities there. Retrenching because it is believed that investors desire smaller international operations is likely to lead to the forgoing of profitable foreign investments that would be rewarded, instead of penalized, by the firm's shareholders. At the very least, executives of multinational firms should seriously question the use of a higher risk premium to account for the added political and economic risks of overseas operations when evaluating prospective foreign investments.

The use of any added risk premium ignores the fact that the risk of an overseas investment in the context of the firm's other investments, domestic as well as foreign, will be less than the project's total risk. How much less depends on how highly correlated are the outcomes of the firm's different investments. Thus, the automatic inclusion of an added premium for risk when evaluating a foreign project is not a necessary element of conservatism; rather, it is a management shortcut that is unlikely to benefit the firm's shareholders. Some investments, however, are more risk-prone than others, and these risks must be accounted for. This chapter presented a method for conducting the necessary risk analysis for foreign investments when the foreign risks are unsystematic. Also, the chapter showed how the necessary adjustments in project discount rates can be made, using the capital asset pricing model, when those additional foreign risks are systematic in nature. Specifically, the recommended approach to estimating the cost of equity capital for a foreign subsidiary is to find a proxy portfolio in the country in which that subsidiary operates and to calculate its beta relative to the U.S. market. That beta should then be multiplied by the risk premium for the U.S. market. This estimated equity risk premium for the foreign subsidiary would then be added to the U.S. (home country) risk-free rate to compute the dollar (home currency) cost of equity capital.

We assessed the factors that are relevant in determining appropriate parent, affiliate, and worldwide capital structures, taking into account the unique attributes of being a multinational corporation. We saw that the optimal global capital structure entails that mix of debt and equity for the parent entity and for all consolidated and unconsolidated subsidiaries that maximizes shareholder wealth. At the same time, affiliate capital structures should vary to take advantage of opportunities to minimize the MNC's cost of capital.

This chapter showed how cash-flow adjustments can be carried out by presenting a lengthy numerical example. It also discussed the significant differences that can exist between project and parent cash flows and showed how these differences can be accounted for when estimating the value to the parent firm of a foreign investment.

QUESTIONS

1. A foreign project that is profitable when valued on its own will always be profitable from the parent firm's standpoint. True or false. Explain.

2. Early results on the Lexus, Toyota's upscale car, showed it was taking the most business from customers changing from BMW (15%), Mercedes (14%), Toyota (14%), General Motors' Cadillac (12%), and Ford's Lincoln (6%). With what in the auto business is considered a high percentage of sales coming from its own customers (14%), how badly is Toyota hurting itself with the Lexus?

3. What factors should be considered in deciding whether the cost of capital for a foreign affiliate should be higher, lower, or the same as the cost of capital for a comparable domestic operation?

4. According to an article in *Forbes,* "American companies can and are raising capital in Japan at relatively low rates of interest. Dow Chemical, for instance, has raised $500 million in yen. That cost the company over 50% less than it would have at home." Comment on this statement.

5. Boeing Commercial Airplane Company manufactures all its planes in the United States and prices them in dollars, even the 50% of its sales destined for overseas markets. What financing strategy would you recommend for Boeing? What data do you need?

6. United Airlines (UAL) recently inaugurated service to Japan and now wants to finance the purchase of Boeing 747s to service that route. The chief financial officer (CFO) for United Airlines is attracted to yen financing, because the interest rate on yen is 300 basis points lower than the dollar interest rate. Although he does not expect this interest differential to be offset by yen appreciation over the 10-year life of the loan, he would like an independent opinion before issuing yen debt.

a. What are the key questions you would ask in responding to UAL's CFO?

b. Can you think of any other reason for using yen debt?

c. What would you advise him to do, given his likely responses to your questions and your answer to Part b?

7. The CFO of Eastman Kodak is thinking of borrowing Japanese yen because of their low interest rate, currently at 4.5%. The current interest rate on U.S. dollars is 9%. What is your advice to the CFO?

8. What are some of the advantages and disadvantages of having highly leveraged foreign subsidiaries?

9. Compañia Troquelados ARDA is a medium-sized Mexico City auto parts maker. It is trying to decide whether to borrow dollars at 9% or Mexican pesos at 75%. What advice would you give it? What information would you need before you gave the advice?

10. What are the principal cash outflows associated with the IDC-U.K. project?

11. What are the principal cash inflows associated with the IDC-U.K. project?

12. In what ways do parent and project cash flows differ on the IDC-U.K. project? Why?

13. Why are loan repayments by IDC-U.K. to Lloyds and NEB treated as a cash inflow to the parent company?

14. How sensitive is the value of the project to the threat of currency controls and expropriation? How can the financing be structured to make the project less sensitive to these political risks?

15. What options does investment in the new British diesel plant provide to IDC-U.S.? How can these options be accounted for in the traditional capital-budgeting analysis?

PROBLEMS

1. Suppose a firm projects a $5-million perpetuity from an investment of $20 million in Spain. If the required return on this investment is 20%, how large does the

probability of expropriation in year 4 have to be before the investment has a negative NPV? Assume that all cash inflows occur at the end of each year and that the expropriation, if it occurs, will occur just before the year-4 cash inflow or not at all. There is no compensation in the event of expropriation.

2. Suppose a firm has just made an investment in France that will generate $2 million annually in depreciation, converted at today's spot rate. Projected annual rates of inflation in France and in the United States are 7% and 4%, respectively. If the real exchange rate is expected to remain constant and the French tax rate is 50%, what is the expected real value (in terms of today's dollars) of the depreciation charge in year 5, assuming that the tax write-off is taken at the end of the year?

3. A firm with a corporatewide debt-to-equity ratio of 1:2, an after-tax cost of debt of 7%, and a cost of equity capital of 15% is interested in pursuing a foreign project. The debt capacity of the project is the same as for the company as a whole, but its systematic risk is such that the required return on equity is estimated to be about 12%. The after-tax cost of debt is expected to remain at 7%. What is the project's weighted average cost of capital? How does it compare with the parent's WACC?

4. Suppose that a foreign project has a beta of 0.85, the risk-free return is 12%, and the required return on the market is estimated at 19%. What is the cost of capital for the project?

5. IBM is considering having its German affiliate issue a 10-year, $100-million bond denominated in euros and priced to yield 7.5%. Alternatively, IBM's German unit can issue a dollar-denominated bond of the same size and maturity and carrying an interest rate of 6.7%.
   a. If the euro is forecast to depreciate by 1.7% annually, what is the expected dollar cost of the euro-denominated bond? How does this compare to the cost of the dollar bond?
   b. At what rate of euro depreciation will the dollar cost of the euro-denominated bond equal the dollar cost of the dollar-denominated bond?
   c. Suppose IBM's German unit faces a 35% corporate tax rate. What is the expected after-tax dollar cost of the euro-denominated bond?

6. Suppose that the cost of borrowing restricted euros is 7% annually, whereas the market rate for these funds is 12%. If a firm can borrow €10 million of restricted funds, how much will it save annually in before-tax franc interest expense?

7. Suppose that one of the inducements provided by Taiwan to woo Xidex into setting up a local production facility is a 10-year, $12.5 million loan at 8% interest. The principal is to be repaid at the end of the 10th year. The market interest rate on such a loan is about 15%. With a marginal tax rate of 40%, how much is this loan worth to Xidex?

8. Jim Toreson, chairman and CEO of Xebec Corporation, a Sunnyvale, California, manufacturer of disk-drive controllers, is trying to decide whether to switch to offshore production. Given Xebec's well-developed engineering and marketing capabilities, Toreson could use offshore manufacturing to ramp up production, taking full advantage of both low-wage labor and a grab bag of tax holidays, low-interest loans, and other government largesse. Most of his competitors seem to be doing it. The faster he follows suit, the better off Xebec would be according to the conventional discounted cash-flow analysis, which shows that switching production offshore is clearly a positive NPV investment. However, Toreson is concerned that such a move would entail the loss of certain intangible strategic benefits associated with domestic production.
   a. What might be those strategic benefits of domestic manufacturing for Xebec? Consider the fact that its customers are all U.S. firms and that manufacturing technology, particularly automation skills, is key to survival in this business.
   b. What analytical framework can be used to factor these intangible strategic benefits of domestic manufacturing (which are intangible costs of offshore production) into the factory location decision?
   c. How would the possibility of radical shifts in manufacturing technology affect the production location decision?
   d. Xebec is considering producing more sophisticated drives that require substantial customization. How does this possibility affect its production decision?
   e. Suppose the Taiwan government is willing to provide a loan of $10 million at 5% interest rate to Xebec to build a factory there. The loan would be paid off in equal annual installments over a 5-year period. If the market interest rate for such an investment is 14%, what is the before-tax value of the interest subsidy?
   f. Projected before-tax income from the Taiwan plant is $1 million annually, beginning at the end of the first year. Taiwan's corporate tax rate is 25%, and there is a 20% dividend withholding tax. However, Taiwan will exempt the plant's income from corporate tax (but not withholding tax) for the first 5 years. If Xebec plans to remit all income as dividends back to the United States, how much is the tax holiday worth?
   g. An alternative sourcing option is to shut down all domestic production and contract to have Xebec's products built for it by a foreign supplier in a country such as Japan. What are some of the potential advantages and disadvantages of foreign contracting vis-à-vis manufacturing in a wholly owned foreign subsidiary?

BIBLIOGRAPHY

Adler, M. and B. Dumas. "International Portfolio Choice and Corporation Finance: A Synthesis," *Journal of Finance,* June 1983, pp. 925–984.

Agmon, T. and D. R. Lessard, "Investor Recognition of Corporate International Diversification," *Journal of Finance,* September 1977, pp. 1049–1056.

Black, F. "International Capital Market Equilibrium with Investment Barriers," *Journal of Financial Economics,* December 1974, pp. 337–352.

Chan, K. C., G. A. Karolyi, and R. M. Stulz, "Global Financial Markets and the Risk Premium on U.S. Equity," *Journal of Financial Economics,* October 1992, pp. 137–167.

Cho, C. D., C. S. Eun, and L. W. Senbet, "International Arbitrage Pricing Theory: An Empirical Investigation," *Journal of Finance* 41, 1986, pp. 313–330.

Cooper, I. and E. Kaplanis, "What Explains the Home Bias in Portfolio Investment," *Review of Financial Studies* 7, 1994, pp. 45–60.

Cooper, I. and E. Kaplanis, "Home Bias in Equity Portfolios and the Cost of Capital for Multinational Companies," *Journal of Applied Corporate Finance,* Fall 1995, pp. 95–102.

DeSantis, G. and B. Gerard, "International Asset Pricing and Portfolio Diversification with Time-Varying Risk," *Journal of Finance* 52, 1997, pp. 1881–1913.

Fatemi, A. M. "Shareholder Benefits from Corporate International Diversification," *Journal of Finance,* December 1984, pp. 1325–1344.

French, K. R. and J. M. Poterba, "Investor Diversification and International Equity Markets." *American Economic Review, Papers and Proceedings,* 1991, pp. 222–226.

Grauer, F. L. A., R. H. Litzenberger, and R. E. Stehle, "Sharing Rules and Equilibrium in an International Capital Market Under Uncertainty," *Journal of Financial Economics,* June 1976, pp. 233–257.

Harvey, C. R. "The World Price of Covariance Risk," *Journal of Finance* 46, 1991, pp. 111–157.

Hughes, J. S., D. E. Logue, and R. J. Sweeney, "Corporate International Diversification and Market Assigned Measures of Risk and Diversification," *Journal of Financial and Quantitative Analysis,* November 1975, pp. 627–637.

Jacquillat, B. and B. H. Solnik, "Multinationals Are Poor Tools for Diversification," *Journal of Portfolio Management,* Winter 1978, pp. 8–12.

Kester, W. Carl, "Today's Options for Tomorrow's Growth," *Harvard Business Review,* March–April 1984, pp. 153–160.

Kester, W. Carl and T. A. Luehrman, "The Myth of Japan's Low-Cost Capital," *Harvard Business Review,* May–June 1992, pp. 130–138.

Lessard, D. R. "Evaluating Foreign Projects: An Adjusted Present Value Approach." In *International Financial Management,* 2nd ed. Donald R. Lessard, ed. New York: John Wiley & Sons, 1985.

Shapiro, A. C. "Capital Budgeting for the Multinational Corporation," *Financial Management,* Spring 1978, pp. 7–16.

———. "International Capital Budgeting," *Midland Journal of Corporate Finance,* Spring 1983, pp. 26–45.

———. "The Impact of Taxation on the Currency-of-Denomination Decision for Long-Term Borrowing and Lending," *Journal of International Business Studies,* Spring–Summer 1984, pp. 15–25.

———. "Financial Structure and the Cost of Capital in the Multinational Corporation," *Journal of Financial and Quantitative Analysis,* June 1978, pp. 211–226.

Solnik, B. H. "Testing International Asset Pricing: Some Pessimistic Views," *Journal of Finance,* May 1977, pp. 503–512.

Stonehill, A. I. and K. B. Dullum, *Internationalizing the Cost of Capital,* New York: Wiley, 1982.

Stulz, R. M. "A Model of International Asset Pricing," *Journal of Financial Economics,* December 1981, pp. 383–406.

Stulz, R. M. "Globalization of Capital Markets and the Cost of Capital: The Case of Nestlé," *Journal of Applied Corporate Finance,* Fall 1995, pp. 30–38.

Stulz, R. M. "Globalization, Corporate Finance, and the Cost of Capital," *Journal of Applied Corporate Finance,* Fall 1999, pp. 8–25.

Tesar, L. and I. M. Werner, "Home Bias and High Turnover," *Journal of International Money and Finance* 14, 1995, pp. 467–493.

Wheatley, S. "Some Tests of International Equity Integration," *Journal of Financial Economics* 21, 1988, pp. 177–212.

INTERNET RESOURCES

www.standardandpoors.com Web site of Standard & Poor's. Contains data on sovereign risk ratings and spreads.

www.bradynet.com/prices.html Contains information on emerging market debt prices and yields, particularly for Brady Bonds, the most widely traded emerging market debt instrument.

globaledge.msu.edu/ibrd/ibrd.asp Web site run by Michigan State University (MSU) that contains links to various country information helpful for making investment decisions.

www.bloomberg.com Web site of Bloomberg. Contains a wealth of financial and economic information on financial markets and countries worldwide.

www.economist.com Web site of *The Economist*. Contains stories on the economic and political situations of countries and international business developments, along with various national and international economic and financial data.

1. Given exchange rate changes over the past month, how would you revise cash-flow projections for a planned project in Mexico? How would the nature of the project—export-oriented versus producing for the Mexican market—affect your revised cash flows?

2. Based on recent political and economic changes in Mexico gleaned from the MSU, Bloomberg, and/or *The Economist* Web sites, how would you revise cash flows for the project mentioned in the previous question?

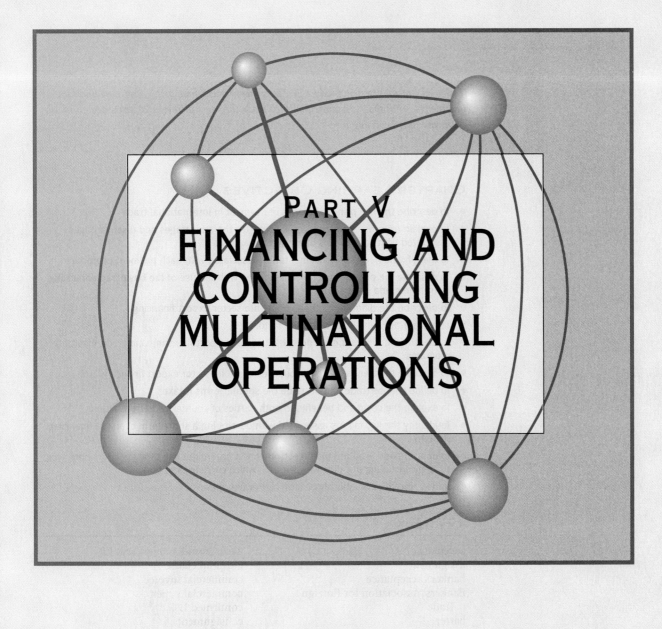

PART V
FINANCING AND CONTROLLING MULTINATIONAL OPERATIONS

FINANCING FOREIGN TRADE

15

The development of a new product is a three-step process: first, a U.S. firm announces an invention; second, the Russians claim they made the same discovery 20 years ago; third, the Japanese start exporting it.

Anonymous

CHAPTER LEARNING OBJECTIVES

- To describe the five principal means of payment in international trade
- To explain from the standpoint of an exporter the advantages and disadvantages associated with each means of arranging payment
- To identify the necessary documentation associated with each payment procedure
- To describe the primary functions associated with the use of the basic trade-financing instruments and documents
- To describe the different methods of private sector export financing
- To explain the benefits and costs of factoring
- To identify the different government-sponsored export-financing and credit insurance programs
- To describe the trends and consequences of public sector export financing
- To define countertrade and describe the specific forms it takes
- To explain the costs and benefits to both parties of countertrade transactions
- To identify the key factors associated with developing a short-term overseas financing strategy
- To describe and evaluate the objectives that a firm might use to arrive at its borrowing strategy, including deciding where and in which currencies to borrow
- To describe the available short-term borrowing options

KEY TERMS

acceptance
assignment
banker's acceptance
Bankers' Association for Foreign
    Trade
barter
bill of exchange
bill of lading (B/L)
buyback
buyer credits
cash in advance
clean B/L
clean draft

clean (nondocumentary) L/C
clean up clause
commercial invoice
commercial paper
confirmed L/C
consignment
consular invoice
counterpurchase
countertrade
discounting
documentary draft
documentary L/C
draft

effective interest rate
export-credit insurance
Export-Import Bank (Eximbank)
factoring
Foreign Credit Insurance Association
   (FCIA)
forfaiting
foul B/L
insurance certificate
intercompany loan
irrevocable L/C
letter of credit (L/C)
line of credit
mixed-credit financing
nonrecourse
on-board B/L
open account selling

order B/L
overdraft
preliminary commitment
Private Export Funding Corporation
   (PEFCO)
received-for-shipment B/L
recourse
revocable L/C
revolving credit agreement
sight draft
straight B/L
supplier credits
term loans
time draft
trade acceptance
transferable L/C
unconfirmed L/C

Most multinational corporations are heavily involved in foreign trade in addition to their other international activities. The financing of trade-related working capital requires large amounts of money as well as financial services such as letters of credit (L/C) and acceptances. It is vital, therefore, that the multinational financial executive does have the knowledge of institutions and documentary procedures that have evolved over the centuries to facilitate the international movement of goods. Much of the material in this chapter is descriptive in nature, but interspersed throughout will be discussions of the role of these special financial techniques and their associated advantages and disadvantages.

This chapter describes and analyzes the various payment terms possible in international trade, along with the necessary documentation associated with each procedure. It examines the different methods and sources of export financing and credit insurance that are available from the public sector. The chapter also discusses the rise of countertrade, a sophisticated word for barter, as well as various short-term financing options available to a multinational corporation.

15.1 PAYMENT TERMS IN INTERNATIONAL TRADE

Every shipment abroad requires some kind of financing while in transit. The exporter also needs financing to buy or manufacture its goods. Similarly, the importer has to carry these goods in inventory until the goods are sold. Then, it must finance its customers' receivables.

A financially strong exporter can finance the entire trade cycle out of its own funds by extending credit until the importer has converted these goods into cash. Alternatively, the importer can finance the entire cycle by paying cash in advance. Usually, however, some in-between approach is chosen, involving a combination of financing by the exporter, the importer, and one or more financial intermediaries.

The five principal means of payment in international trade, ranked in terms of increasing risk to the exporter, are

1. Cash in advance

2. Letter of credit

3. Draft

4. Consignment

5. Open account

As a general rule, the greater the protection afforded to the exporter, the less convenient are the payment terms for the buyer (importer). Some of these methods, however, are designed to protect both parties against commercial and/or political risks. It is up to the exporter when choosing among these payment methods to weigh the benefits in risk reduction against the cost of lost sales. The five basic means of payment are discussed in the following paragraphs.

15.1.1 Cash in Advance

Cash in advance affords the exporter the greatest protection because payment is received either before shipment or upon arrival of the goods. This method also allows the exporter to avoid tying up its own funds. Although less common than in the past, cash payment upon presentation of documents is still widespread.

Cash terms are used when there is political instability in the importing country or when the buyer's credit is doubtful. Political crises or exchange controls in the purchaser's country may cause payment delays or even prevent fund transfers, leading to a demand for cash in advance. In addition, where goods are made to order, prepayment is usually demanded, both to finance production and to reduce marketing risks.

15.1.2 Letter of Credit

Importers often will balk at paying cash in advance and will demand credit terms instead. When credit is extended, the **letter of credit** (**L/C**) offers the exporter the greatest degree of safety.

If the importer is not well known to the exporter or if exchange restrictions exist or are possible in the importer's country, the exporter selling on credit may wish to have the importer's promise of payment backed by a foreign or domestic bank. On the contrary, the importer may not wish to pay the exporter until it is reasonably certain that the merchandise has been shipped in good condition. A letter of credit satisfies both of these conditions.

In essence, the letter of credit is a letter addressed to the seller, written and signed by a bank acting on behalf of the buyer. In the letter, the bank promises it will honor drafts drawn on itself if the seller conforms to the specific conditions set forth in the L/C. (The draft, which is a written order to pay, is discussed in Section 15.1.3.) Through an L/C, the bank substitutes its own commitment to pay for that of its customer (the importer). The letter of credit, therefore, becomes a financial contract between the issuing bank and a designated beneficiary that is separate from the commercial transaction.

The advantages to the exporter are as follows:

1. Most important, an L/C eliminates credit risk if the bank that opens it is of undoubted standing. Therefore, the firm need check only on the credit reputation of the issuing bank.

2. An L/C also reduces the danger that payment will be delayed or withheld because of exchange controls or other political acts. Countries generally permit local banks to honor their letters of credit. Failure to honor them could severely damage the country's credit standing and credibility.

3. An L/C reduces uncertainty. The exporter knows all the requirements for payment because they are clearly stipulated on the L/C.

4. The L/C can also guard against preshipment risks. The exporter who manufactures under contract a specialized piece of equipment runs the risk of contract cancellation before shipment. Opening a letter of credit will provide protection during the manufacturing phase.

5. Last, and certainly not the least, the L/C facilitates financing because it ensures the exporter a ready buyer for its product. It also becomes especially easy to create a banker's acceptance—a draft accepted by a bank.

Most advantages of an L/C are realized by the seller; nevertheless, there are some advantages to the buyer as well.

1. Because payment is only in compliance with the L/C's stipulated conditions, the importer is able to ascertain that the merchandise is actually shipped on, or before, a certain date by requiring an on-board bill of lading. The importer also can require an inspection certificate.

2. Any documents required are carefully inspected by clerks with years of experience. Moreover, the bank bears responsibility for any oversight.

3. An L/C is about as good as cash in advance, so the importer usually can command more advantageous credit terms and/or prices.

4. Some exporters will sell only on a letter of credit. Willingness to provide one expands a firm's sources of supply.

5. L/C financing may be cheaper than the alternatives. There is no tie-up of cash if the L/C substitutes for cash in advance.

6. If prepayment is required, the importer is better off depositing its money with a bank than with the seller because it is then easier to recover the deposit if the seller is unable or unwilling to make a proper shipment.

The mechanics of letter-of-credit financing are quite simple, as illustrated by the case of U.S.A. Importers, Inc., Los Angeles. The company is buying spare auto parts worth $38,000 from Japan Exporters, Inc., Tokyo. U.S.A. Importers applies for, and receives, a letter of credit for $38,000 from its bank, Wells Fargo. The actual L/C is shown in Exhibit 15.1. Exhibit 15.2, in turn, shows the relationships between the three parties to the letter of credit.

After Japan Exporters has shipped the goods, it draws a draft against the issuing bank (Wells Fargo) and presents it, along with the required documents, to its own bank, the Bank of Tokyo-Mitsubishi, which, in turn, forwards the bank draft and attached documents to Wells Fargo; Wells Fargo pays the draft upon receiving evidence that all conditions set forth in the L/C have been met. Exhibit 15.3 details the sequence of steps in the L/C transaction.

Most L/Cs issued in connection with commercial transactions are **documentary**—that is, the seller must submit, together with the draft, any necessary invoices and the like. The documents required from Japan Exporters are listed on the face of the letter of credit in Exhibit 15.1 following the words "accompanied by." A **nondocumentary**, or **clean, L/C** is normally used in other than commercial transactions.

The letter of credit can be revocable or irrevocable. A **revocable L/C** is a means of arranging payment, but it does not carry a guarantee. It can be revoked, without notice, at any time till a draft is presented to the issuing bank. An **irrevocable L/C**, however, cannot be revoked without the specific permission of all parties concerned, including the exporter. Most credits between unrelated parties are irrevocable; otherwise, the advantage of commitment to pay is lost. In the case of Japan Exporters, the L/C is irrevocable.

Although the essential character of a letter of credit—the substitution of the bank's name for the merchant's—is absent with a revocable credit, this type of L/C is useful in some respects. The fact that a bank is willing to open a letter of credit for the importer is in itself an indication of the customer's creditworthiness. Thus, it is safer than sending goods on a collection basis, where payment is made by a draft only after the goods have been shipped. Of equal, if not greater, importance is the probability that imports covered by letters of credit will be given priority in the allocation of foreign exchange should currency controls be imposed.

IRREVOCABLE COMMERCIAL LETTER OF CREDIT

Since 1852

WELLS FARGO BANK N.A.

☐ 475 SANSOME STREET, SAN FRANCISCO, CALIFORNIA 94111

☐ 770 WILSHIRE BLVD. LOS ANGELES CALIFORNIA 90017

INTERNATIONAL DIVISION COMMERCIAL L/C DEPARTMENT CABLE ADDRESS WELLS

OUR LETTER OF CREDIT NO. XYZ9000 AMOUNT US$38,000 DATE MAY 6, 20XX
THIS NUMBER MUST BE MENTIONED ON ALL DRAFTS AND CORRESPONDENCE

. JAPAN EXPORTERS INC.
. TOKYO, JAPAN

. BANK OF TOKYO
. TOKYO, JAPAN

GENTLEMEN:

BY ORDER OF U.S.A. IMPORTERS INC.

AND FOR ACCOUNT OF SAMF

WE HEREBY AUTHORIZE YOU TO DRAW ON OURSELVES

UP TO AN AGGREGATE AMOUNT OF THIRTY EIGHT THOUSAND AND NO/100 U.S. DOLLARS

AVAILABLE BY YOUR DRAFTS AT ON OURSELVES, IN DUPLICATE, AT 90 DAYS SIGHT

ACCOMPANIED BY
SIGNED INVOICE IN TRIPLICATF
PACKING LIST IN CUPLICATE
FULL SET OF CLEAN OCEAN BILLS OF LADING, MADE OUT TO ORDER OF SHIPPER, BLANK ENDORSED, MARKED FREIGHT PREPAID AND NOTIFY: U.S.A. IMPORTERS, INC., LOS ANGFLES, DATED ON BOARD NOT LATER THAN MAY 30, 19XX.
INSURANCE POLICY/CERTIFICATE IN DUPLICATE FOR 110% OF INVOICE VALUE, COVERING ALL RISKS.

COVERING: SHIPMENT OF AUTOMOBILE SPARE PARTS, AS PER BUYER'S ORDER NO. 900 DATED MARCH 15, 20XX FROM ANY JAPANESE PORT C.I.F. LOS ANGELES, CALIFORNIA
PARTIAL SHIPMENTS ARE PERMITTED.
TRANSHIPMENT IS NOT PERMITTED.
DOCUMENTS MUST BE PRESENTED WITHIN 7 DAYS AFTER THE BOARD DATE OF THE BILLS OF LADING, BUT IN ANY EVENT NOT LATER THAN JUNE 6, 20XX.

SPECIMEN

DRAFTS MUST BE DRAWN AND NEGOTIATED NOT LATER THAN JUNE 6, 20XX
ALL DRAFTS DRAWN UNDER THIS CREDIT MUST BEAR ITS DATE AND NUMBER AND THE AMOUNTS MUST BE ENDORSED ON THE REVERSE SIDE OF THIS LETTER OF CREDIT BY THE NEGOTIATING BANK. WE HEREBY AGREE WITH THE DRAWERS, ENDORSERS, AND BONA FIDE HOLDERS OF ALL DRAFTS DRAWN UNDER AND IN COMPLIANCE WITH THE TERMS OF THIS CREDIT, THAT SUCH DRAFTS WILL BE DULY HONORED UPON PRESENTATION TO THE DRAWEE.
THIS CREDIT IS SUBJECT TO THE UNIFORM CUSTOMS AND PRACTICE FOR DOCUMENTARY CREDITS (1974 REVISION). INTERNATIONAL CHAMBER OF COMMERCE PUBLICATION NO. 290.

SPECIMEN
AUTHORIZED SIGNATURE

EXHIBIT 15.1 • LETTER OF CREDIT

(Used by permission from Wells Fargo Bank, N.A.)

A letter of credit can also be confirmed or unconfirmed. A **confirmed L/C** is an L/C issued by one bank and confirmed by another, obligating both banks to honor any drafts drawn in compliance. An **unconfirmed L/C** is the obligation of only the issuing bank.

An exporter will prefer an irrevocable letter of credit by the importer's bank with confirmation by a domestic bank. In this way, the exporter need look no further than a bank in its own country for compliance with terms of the letter of credit. For example, if the Bank of Tokyo-Mitsubishi had confirmed the letter of credit issued by Wells Fargo,

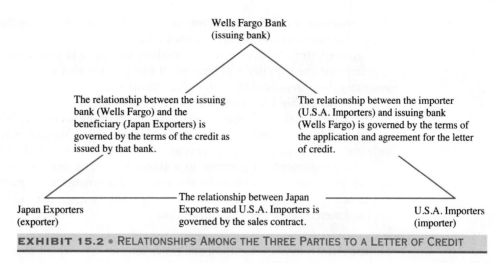

EXHIBIT 15.2 • RELATIONSHIPS AMONG THE THREE PARTIES TO A LETTER OF CREDIT

and Wells Fargo, for whatever reason, failed to honor its irrevocable L/C, Japan Exporters could collect $38,000 from the Bank of Tokyo-Mitsubishi, assuming that Japan Exporters met all the necessary conditions. This arrangement serves two purposes. Most exporters are not in a position to evaluate or deal with a foreign bank directly should difficulties arise. Domestic confirmation avoids this problem. In addition, should the foreign bank fail to fulfill its commitment to pay, owing to foreign exchange controls or political directives, that is of no concern to the exporter. The domestic confirming bank still must honor all drafts in full.

Thus, the three main types of L/C, in order of safety for the exporter, are (1) the irrevocable, confirmed L/C; (2) the irrevocable, unconfirmed L/C; and (3) the revocable L/C. Selecting the type of L/C to use depends on an evaluation of the risks associated with

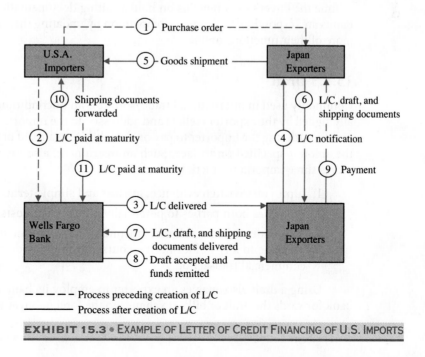

EXHIBIT 15.3 • EXAMPLE OF LETTER OF CREDIT FINANCING OF U.S. IMPORTS

the transaction and the relative costs involved. One of the costs is the possibility of lost sales if the importer can get better credit terms elsewhere.

An exporter who acts as an intermediary may have to provide some assurance to its supplier that the supplier will be paid. It can provide this assurance by transferring or assigning the proceeds of the letter of credit opened in its name to the manufacturer.

A **transferable L/C** is one under which the beneficiary has the right to instruct the paying bank to make the credit available to one or more secondary beneficiaries. No L/C is transferable unless specifically authorized in the credit; moreover, it can be transferred only once. The stipulated documents are transferred along with the L/C.

An **assignment**, in contrast to a transfer, assigns part or all of the proceeds to another party but does not transfer the required documents to the party. This provision is not as safe to the assignee as a transfer because the assignee does not have control of the required merchandise and documentation.

Online Alternatives Creating and processing an L/C, which requires the banks of the buyer and seller to coordinate with each other and exchange documents internationally, can take as much as two weeks–an eternity for cash-strapped companies operating on thin margins and committed to just-in-time manufacturing and inventory management. It is also expensive, with the cost of processing trade documentation estimated at more than 5% of the total annual value of world trade.[1] Moreover, half of all L/C transactions are rejected by banks because of incorrect information from the buyer or seller. Recently, companies have begun to invest in Internet-based platforms that instantly link buyer and seller, cutting down on the paper-processing time and reducing cost. For example, TradeCard (www.tradecard.com) allows a company to connect the flow of physical goods with the flow of electronic funds by handling both through the same electronic document. TradeCard replaces the buyer's and seller's bank with an insurance company that ensures the transaction goes smoothly. UPS Capital (www.upscapital.com), a subsidiary of United Parcel Services, has a similar product that allows it to transport both the hard goods of its clients and the money to pay for them. The increased efficiency of Internet-based alternatives to the traditional L/C lowers processing and financing costs by reducing the amount of time the buyer's cash remains on hold awaiting documentation and approval by banks. Banks are responding to this new competition by updating their L/C processes and putting more of their functions online.

15.1.3 Draft

Commonly used in international trade, a **draft** is an unconditional order in writing—usually signed by the exporter (seller) and addressed to the importer (buyer) or the importer's agent—ordering the importer to pay on demand, or at a fixed or determinable future date, the amount specified on its face. Such an instrument, also known as a **bill of exchange**, serves three important functions:

1. It provides written evidence, in clear and simple terms, of a financial obligation.
2. It enables both parties to potentially reduce their costs of financing.
3. It provides a negotiable and unconditional instrument. (That is, payment must be made to any holder in due course despite any disputes over the underlying commercial transaction.)

Using a draft also enables an exporter to employ its bank as a collection agent. The bank forwards the draft or bill of exchange to the foreign buyer (either directly or through

[1] Andrew Tagart, "Cutting the Costs of Trade Processes," *Trade & Forfaiting Review*, November 2004, vol. 8, issue 2.

a branch or correspondent bank), collects on the draft, and then remits the proceeds to the exporter. The bank has all the necessary documents for control of the merchandise and turns them over to the importer only when the draft has been paid or accepted in accordance with the exporter's instructions.

The conditions for a draft to be negotiable under the U.S. Uniform Commercial Code are that it must be

- In writing
- Signed by the issuer (drawer)
- An unconditional order to pay
- A certain sum of money
- Payable on demand or at a definite future time
- Payable to order of bearer

There are usually three parties to a draft. The party who signs and sends the draft to the second party is called the *drawer*; payment is made to the third party, the *payee*. Normally, the drawer and payee are the same person. The party to whom the draft is addressed is the *drawee*, who may be either the buyer or, if a letter of credit is used, the buyer's bank. In the case of a confirmed L/C, the drawee would be the confirming bank.

In the previous example, Japan Exporters is the drawer, and the Bank of Tokyo-Mitsubishi is the payee. The drawee is Wells Fargo under the terms of the L/C. This information is included in the draft shown in Exhibit 15.4.

Drafts may be either sight or time drafts. **Sight drafts** must be paid on presentation or else dishonored. **Time drafts** are payable at some specified future date and as such become a useful financing device. The maturity of a time draft is known as its *usance* or *tenor*. As mentioned earlier, for a draft to qualify as a negotiable instrument, the date of payment must be determinable. For example, a time draft payable "upon delivery of goods" is not specific enough, given the vagaries of ocean freight; the vague date of payment will likely nullify its negotiability. As shown in Exhibit 15.4, the draft drawn under the letter of credit by Japan Exporters is a time draft with a tenor of 90 days, indicated by the words "at ninety days sight." Thus, the draft will mature on August 24—90 days after it was drawn (May 26).

A time draft becomes an **acceptance** after it is accepted by the drawee. Accepting a draft means writing *accepted* across its face, followed by an authorized person's signature and the date. The party accepting a draft incurs the obligation to pay it at maturity. A draft accepted by a bank becomes a **banker's acceptance**; one drawn on and accepted by a

TOKYO, JAPAN	MAY 26	20 XX No. 712
AT NINETY DAYS	SIGHT OF THIS **ORIGINAL** OF EXCHANGE (DUPLICATE UNPAID)	
PAY TO THE ORDER OF BANK OF TOKYO-MITSUBISHI	U.S. $ 38,000.00	
THE SUM OF THIRTY EIGHT THOUSAND AND NO/100 * U.S. Dollars		

DRAWN UNDER LETTER OF CREDIT NO.	DATED	ISSUED BY
X Y Z 9000	MAY 6, 20XX	WELLS FARGO BANK

To WELLS FARGO BANK
770 WILSHIRE BLVD.
LOS ANGELES, CALIFORNIA

SPECIMEN

JAPAN EXPORTERS INC.

EXHIBIT 15.4 • TIME DRAFT

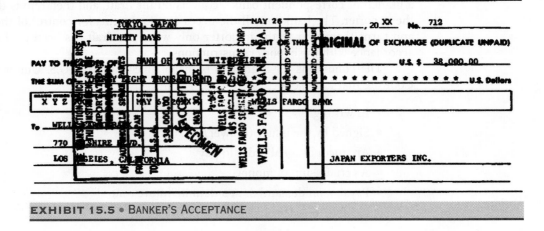

EXHIBIT 15.5 • BANKER'S ACCEPTANCE

commercial enterprise is termed a **trade acceptance**. Exhibit 15.5 is the time draft in Exhibit 15.4 after being accepted by Wells Fargo.

The exporter can hold the acceptance or sell it at a discount from face value to its bank, to some other bank, or to an acceptance dealer. The discount normally is less than the prevailing prime rate for bank loans. These acceptances enjoy a wide market and are an important tool in the financing of international trade. They are discussed in more detail in the next section. An acceptance can be transferred from one holder to another simply by endorsement.

Drafts can be clean or documentary. A **clean draft**, one unaccompanied by any other papers, normally is used only for nontrade remittances. Its primary purpose is to put pressure on a recalcitrant debtor that must pay or accept the draft or else face damage to its credit reputation.

Most drafts used in international trade are documentary. A **documentary draft**, which can be either sight or time, is accompanied by documents that are to be delivered to the drawee on payment or acceptance of the draft. Typically, these documents include the bill of lading in negotiable form, the commercial invoice, the consular invoice where required, and an insurance certificate. The bill of lading in negotiable form is the most important document because it gives its holder the right to control the goods covered. A documentary sight draft is also known as a D/P (documents against payment) draft; if documents are delivered on acceptance, it is a D/A draft.

There are two significant aspects to shipping goods under documentary time drafts for acceptance. First, the exporter is extending credit to the importer for the usance of the draft. Second, the exporter is relinquishing control of the goods in return for a signature on the acceptance to assure it of payment.

Sight drafts are not always paid at presentation, nor are time drafts always paid at maturity. Firms can get bank statistics on the promptness of sight and time draft payments, by country, from bank publications such as Chase Manhattan's *Collection Experience* bulletin.

Unless a bank has accepted a draft, the exporter ultimately must look to the importer for payment. Thus, use of a sight or accepted time draft is warranted only when the exporter has faith in the importer's financial strength and integrity.

15.1.4 Consignment

Goods sent on **consignment** are only shipped, but not sold, to the importer. The exporter (consignor) retains title to the goods until the importer (consignee) has sold them to a third party. This arrangement is normally made only with a related company because of the large risks involved. There is little evidence of the buyer's obligation to pay, and should the buyer default, it will prove difficult to collect.

The seller must carefully consider the credit risks involved as well as the availability of foreign exchange in the importer's country. Imports covered by documentary drafts receive priority to scarce foreign exchange over imports shipped on consignment.

15.1.5 Open Account

Open account selling is shipping goods first and billing the importer later. The credit terms are arranged between the buyer and the seller, but the seller has little evidence of the importer's obligation to pay a certain amount at a certain date. Sales on open account, therefore, are made only to a foreign affiliate or to a customer with which the exporter has a long history of favorable business dealings. However, open account sales have greatly expanded because of the major increase in international trade, the improvement in credit information about importers, and the greater familiarity with exporting in general. The benefits include greater flexibility (no specific payment dates are set) and involve lower costs, including fewer bank charges than incurred with other methods of payment. As with shipping on consignment, the possibility of currency controls is an important factor because of the low priority in allocating foreign exchange normally accorded this type of transaction.

Exhibit 15.6 summarizes some of the advantages and disadvantages associated with the various means of arranging payment in international trade.

Method	Risk*	Chief Advantage	Chief Disadvantages
Cash in advance	L	No credit extension required	Can limit sales potential, disturb some potential customers
Sight draft	M/L	Retains control and title; ensures payment before goods are delivered	If customer does not or cannot accept goods, goods remain at the port of entry and no payment is due
Letters of credit Irrevocable Revocable	M M/H	Banks accept responsibility to pay; payment upon presentation of papers; costs go to buyer	If revocable, terms can change during contract work
Time draft	M/H	Lowers customer resistance by allowing extended payment after receipt of goods	Same as sight draft, plus goods are delivered before payment is due or received
Consignment sales	M/H	Facilitates delivery; lowers customer resistance	Capital tied up until sale; must establish distributor's creditworthiness; need political risk insurance in some countries; increased risk from currency controls
Open account	H	Simplified procedure; no customer resistance	

*L: low risk; M: medium risk; H: high risk.

EXHIBIT 15.6 • International Methods of Payment: Advantages and Disadvantages (Ranked by Risk)

15.1.6 Banks and Trade Financing

Historically, banks have been involved in only a single step in international trade transactions such as providing a loan or a letter of credit. However, as financing has become an integral part of many trade transactions, U.S. banks—especially major money center banks—have evolved as well. They have gone from financing individual trade deals to providing comprehensive solutions to trade needs. Such comprehensive services include combining bank lending with subsidized funds from government export agencies, international leasing, and other nonbank financing sources, along with political and economic risk insurance.

15.1.7 Collecting Overdue Accounts

Typically, 1% to 3% of a company's export sales go uncollected. Small businesses, however, take more risks than do large ones, often selling on terms other than a confirmed letter of credit. One reason is that they are eager to develop a new market opportunity; another reason is that they are not as well versed in the mechanics of foreign sales. Thus, their percentage of uncollected export sales may be higher than that of large companies.

Once an account becomes delinquent, sellers have three options: (1) They can try to collect the account themselves; (2) they can hire an attorney who is experienced in international law; or (3) they can engage the services of a collection agency.

The first step is for sellers to attempt to recover the money themselves. Turning the bill over to a collection agency or a lawyer too quickly will hurt the customer relationship. However, after several telephone calls, telexes, and/or personal visits, the firm must decide whether to write the account off or pursue it further.

The cost of hiring a high-priced U.S. lawyer, who then contacts an expensive foreign lawyer, is a deterrent to following the second option for receivables of less than $100,000. With such a relatively small amount, a collection agency usually would be more appropriate. Unlike lawyers, who charge by the hour for their services, regardless of the amount recovered, collection agencies work on a percentage basis. A typical fee is 20% to 25% of the amount collected, but if the claim is more than $25,000 or so, the agency will often negotiate a more favorable rate.

Even with professional help, there are no guarantees of collecting on foreign receivables. This reality puts a premium on checking a customer's credit before filling an order. But getting credit information on specific foreign firms is often difficult.

One good source of credit information is the U.S. Department of Commerce's International Trade Administration (ITA). Other places to check on the creditworthiness of foreign companies and governments are export management companies and the international departments of commercial banks. Also, Dun & Bradstreet International publishes *Principal International Businesses*, a book with information on about 50,000 foreign enterprises in 140 countries.

The National Association of Credit Management collects data on how much time it takes to collect on the average bill from importers in various foreign countries. Intrum Justitia in the United Kingdom provides credit management services and conducts biannual surveys on the payment habits of businesses in 22 European countries. Exhibit 15.7 shows that the collection times vary widely across the countries surveyed.

15.2 DOCUMENTS IN INTERNATIONAL TRADE

The most important supporting document required in commercial bank financing of exports is the bill of lading. Of secondary importance are the commercial invoice, insurance certificate, and consular invoice.

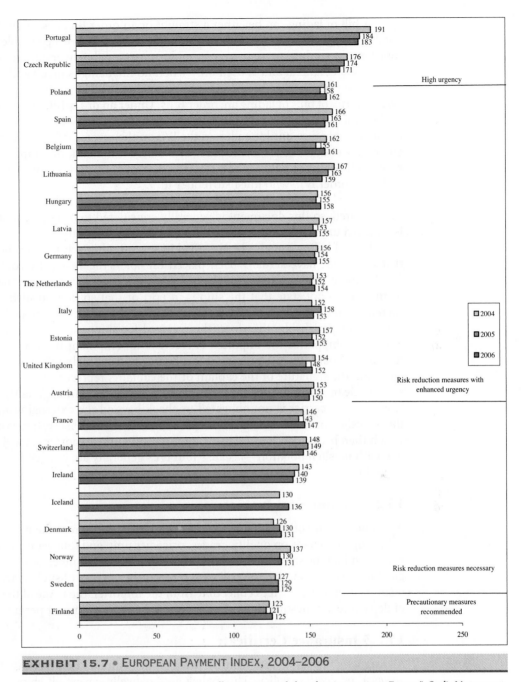

EXHIBIT 15.7 • European Payment Index, 2004–2006

Source: "European Payment Index: Business suffer as payment habits deteriorate across Europe." *Credit Management,* Oct 2006, p. 32.

15.2.1 Bill of Lading

Of the shipping documents, the **bill of lading (B/L)** is the most important. It serves three main and separate functions:

1. It is a contract between the carrier and shipper (exporter) in which the carrier agrees to carry the goods from port of shipment to port of destination.

2. It is the shipper's receipt for the goods.

3. The *negotiable B/L*, its most common form, is a document that establishes control over the goods.

A bill of lading can be either a straight or an order B/L. A **straight B/L** consigns the goods to a specific party, normally the importer, and is not negotiable. Title cannot be transferred to a third party merely by endorsement and delivery; therefore, a straight B/L is not good collateral and is used only when no financing is involved.

Most trade transactions do involve financing, which requires transfer of title, so the vast majority of bills of lading are order B/Ls. Under an **order B/L**, the goods are consigned to the order of a named party, usually the exporter. In this way, the exporter retains title to the merchandise until it endorses the B/L on the reverse side. The exporter's represen-tative may endorse to a specific party or endorse it in blank by simply signing his or her name. The shipper delivers the cargo in the port of destination to the bearer of the endorsed order B/L, who must surrender it.

An order B/L represents goods in transit that are probably readily marketable and fully insured, so this document is generally considered to be good collateral by banks. It is required under L/C financing and for discounting of drafts.

Bills of lading can also be classified in several other ways. An **on-board B/L** certifies that the goods have actually been placed on board the vessel. By contrast, a **received-for-shipment B/L** merely acknowledges that the carrier has received the goods for ship-ment. It does not state that the ship is in port or that space is available. The cargo can, therefore, sit on the dock for weeks, or even months, before it is shipped. When goods are seasonal or perishable, therefore, the received-for-shipment B/L is never satisfactory to either the shipper or the importer. A received-for-shipment B/L can easily be converted into an on-board B/L by stamping it "on-board" and supplying the name of the vessel, the date, and the signature of the captain or the captain's representative.

A **clean B/L** indicates that the goods were received in apparently good condition. However, the carrier is not obligated to check beyond the external visual appearance of the boxes. If boxes are damaged or in poor condition, this observation is noted on the B/L, which then becomes a **foul B/L**. It is important that the exporter get a clean B/L—that is, one with no such notation—because foul B/Ls generally are not acceptable under a letter of credit.

15.2.2 Commercial Invoice

A **commercial invoice** contains an authoritative description of the merchandise shipped, including full details on quality, grades, price per unit, and total value. It also contains the names and addresses of the exporter and importer, the number of packages, any distin-guishing external marks, the payment terms, other expenses such as transportation and insurance charges, any fees collectible from the importer, the name of the vessel, the ports of departure and destination, and any required export or import permit numbers.

15.2.3 Insurance Certificate

All cargoes going abroad are insured. Most of the insurance contracts used today are under an *open*, or *floating*, *policy*. This policy automatically covers all shipments made by the exporter, thereby eliminating the necessity of arranging individual insurance for each ship-ment. To evidence insurance for a shipment under an open policy, the exporter makes out an **insurance certificate** on forms supplied by the insurance company. This certificate con-tains information on the goods shipped. All entries must conform exactly with the informa-tion on the B/L, on the commercial invoice and, where required, on the consular invoice.

15.2.4 Consular Invoice

Exports to many countries require a special **consular invoice**. This invoice, which varies in its details and information requirements from nation to nation, is presented to the local consul in exchange for a visa. The form must be filled out very carefully, for even trivial inaccuracies can lead to substantial fines and delays in customs clearance. The consular invoice does not convey any title to the goods being shipped and is not negotiable.

15.3 FINANCING TECHNIQUES IN INTERNATIONAL TRADE

In addition to straight bank financing, several other techniques are available for trade financing: bankers' acceptances, discounting, factoring, and forfaiting.

15.3.1 Bankers' Acceptances

Bankers' acceptances have played an important role in financing international trade for many centuries. As we saw in the previous section, a banker's acceptance is a time draft drawn on a bank. By "accepting" the draft, the bank makes an unconditional promise to pay the holder of the draft a stated amount on a specified day. Thus, the bank effectively substitutes its own credit for that of a borrower, and in the process it creates a negotiable instrument that may be freely traded.

Creating an Acceptance A typical acceptance transaction is shown in Exhibit 15.8. An importer of goods seeks credit to finance its purchase until the goods can be resold. If the importer does not have a close relationship with and cannot obtain financing from the exporter it is dealing with, it may request acceptance financing from its bank. Under an acceptance agreement, the importer will have its bank issue a letter of credit on its behalf, authorizing the foreign exporter to draw a time draft on the bank in payment for the goods. On the basis of this authorization, the exporter ships the goods on an order B/L made out to itself and presents a time draft and the endorsed shipping documents to its bank. The foreign bank then forwards the draft and the appropriate shipping documents to the importer's bank; the importer's bank accepts the draft and, by so doing, creates a banker's acceptance. The exporter discounts the draft with the accepting bank and receives payment for the shipment. The shipping documents are delivered to the importer, and the importer now may claim the shipment. The accepting bank may either buy (discount) the B/A and hold it in its own portfolio or sell (rediscount) the B/A in the money market. In Exhibit 15.8, the bank sells the acceptance in the money market.

Acceptances also are created to finance the shipment of goods within the United States and to finance the storage of goods in the United States and abroad. However, domestic shipment and storage acceptances have been a small part of the market in recent years. Most acceptances arise from imports into the United States, U.S. exports, and the storage of goods or shipment of goods between foreign countries.

Terms of Acceptance Financing Typical maturities on bankers' acceptances are 30 days, 90 days, and 180 days, with the average being 90 days. Maturities can be tailored, however, to cover the entire period needed to ship and dispose of the goods financed.

For an investor, a banker's acceptance is a close substitute for other bank liabilities, such as certificates of deposit (CDs). Consequently, bankers' acceptances trade at rates very close to those on CDs. Market yields, however, do not give a complete picture of the costs of acceptance financing to the borrower because the accepting bank levies a fee, or commission, for accepting the draft. The fee varies depending on the maturity of the draft as well as the creditworthiness of the borrower, but it averages less than 1% per annum. The bank also receives a fee if a letter of credit is involved. In addition, the bank may hope to realize a profit on the difference between the price at which it purchases and the price at which it resells the acceptance.

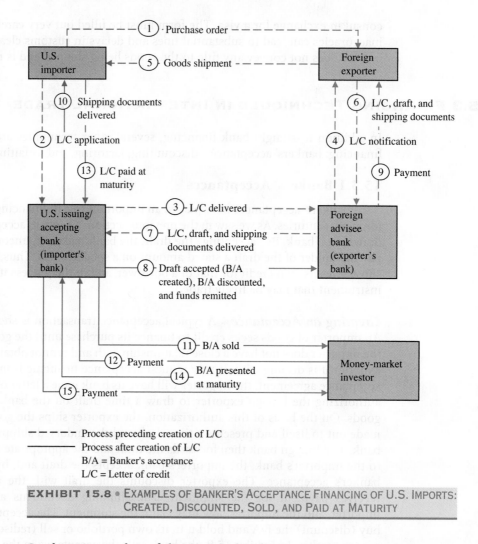

EXHIBIT 15.8 • EXAMPLES OF BANKER'S ACCEPTANCE FINANCING OF U.S. IMPORTS: CREATED, DISCOUNTED, SOLD, AND PAID AT MATURITY

On the maturity date of the acceptance, the accepting bank is required to pay the current holder the amount stated on the draft. The holder of a bank acceptance has recourse for the full amount of the draft from the last endorser in the event of the importer's unwillingness or inability to pay at maturity. The authenticity of an accepted draft is separated from the underlying commercial transaction and may not be dishonored for reason of a dispute between the exporter and importer. This factor significantly enhances its marketability and reduces its riskiness.

In recent years, the demand for acceptance financing has fallen off. One factor has been the increased availability of funding from nonbank investors in the U.S. commercial paper market. **Commercial paper (CP)** is a short-term unsecured promissory note that is generally sold by large corporations on a discount basis to institutional investors and to other corporations. Prime commercial paper generally trades at rates near those on acceptance liabilities of prime banks; for firms with access to this market, the overall cost—including placement fees charged by dealers and fees for backup line of credit—is usually below the all-in cost of acceptance financing.

Evaluating the Cost of Acceptance Financing　Suppose that the discount rate on a $1-million acceptance for 90 days is 9.8% per annum and the acceptance fee is 2% per annum. If the exporter chooses to hold the acceptance, then in 90 days it will receive the face amount less the acceptance fee:

Face amount of acceptance	$1,000,000
Less: 2% per annum commission for 90 days	−5,000
Amount received by exporter in 90 days	$995,000

Alternatively, the exporter can sell the acceptance at a 2.45% discount (9.8%/4) and receive $970,500 immediately:

Face amount of acceptance	$1,000,000
Less: 2% per annum commission for 90 days	−5,000
Less: 9.8% per annum discount for 90 days	−24,500
Amount received by exporter immediately	$970,500

Whether the exporter should discount the acceptance or wait depends on the opportunity cost of money. Suppose that the exporter's opportunity cost of money is 10.2%. Then the present value of holding onto the acceptance is $995,000/[1 + (0.102/4)], or $970,258. In this case, the exporter would come out ahead by selling the acceptance.

15.3.2 Discounting

Even if a trade draft is not accepted by a bank, the exporter still can convert the trade draft into cash by means of **discounting**. The exporter places the draft with a bank or other financial institution and, in turn, receives the face value of the draft less interest and commissions. By insuring the draft against both commercial and political risks, the exporter often will pay a lower interest rate. If losses covered by the insurer do occur, the insuring agency will reimburse the exporter or any institution to which the exporter transfers the draft.

The discount rate for trade paper is often lower than interest rates on overdrafts, bank loans, and other forms of local funding. This lower rate is usually a result of export promotion policies that lead to direct or indirect subsidies of rates on export paper.

Discounting may be done with or without **recourse**. With recourse, the bank can collect from the exporter if the importer fails to pay the bill when due. The bank bears the collection risk if the draft is sold without recourse.

15.3.3 Factoring

Firms with a substantial export business and companies too small to afford a foreign credit and collections department can turn to a *factor*. Factors buy a company's receivables at a discount, thereby accelerating their conversion into cash. Most **factoring** is done on a **nonrecourse** basis, which means that the factor assumes all the credit and political risks except for those involving disputes between the transacting parties. In order to avoid being stuck with only receivables of risky customers (with good credits not being factored), factors usually insist on handling most or all sales. This selection bias is not an issue in factoring *with recourse*, where the exporter assumes all risks.

Factoring is becoming increasingly popular as a trade financing vehicle. The value of world exports financed through factoring now exceeds $10 billion. By using a factor, a firm can ensure that its terms are in accord with local practice and are competitive. For instance, customers can be offered payment on open account rather than being asked for a letter of credit or stiffer credit requirements. If the margin on its factored sales is not sufficiently profitable, the firm can bear the credit risks itself or forgo that business. Even if an exporter chooses not to discount its foreign receivables with a factor, it still can use the factor's extensive credit information files to ascertain the creditworthiness of prospective customers.

An exporter that has established an ongoing relationship with a factor will submit new orders directly to the factor. After evaluating the creditworthiness of the new claim, the factor will make a recourse/nonrecourse decision within two days to two weeks, depending on the availability of information.

Although the factors may consider their fees to be nominal considering the services provided, they are not cheap. Export factoring fees are determined on an individual company basis and are related to the annual turnover (usually a minimum of $500,000 to $1 million is necessary), the average invoice size (smaller invoices are more expensive because of the fixed information-gathering costs), the creditability of the claims, and the terms of sale. In general, these fees run from 1.75% to 2% of sales.

Evaluating the Cost of Factoring   Suppose that a factor will buy an exporter's receivables at a 2.5% per *month* discount. In addition, the factor will charge an extra 1.75% fee for nonrecourse financing. If the exporter decides to factor $1 million in 90-day receivables without recourse, then it will receive $907,500 today:

Face amount of receivable	$1,000,000
Less: 1.75% nonrecourse fee	−17,500
Less: 2.5% monthly factoring fee for three months	−75,000
Amount received by exporter	$907,500

On an annualized basis, factoring is costing this company 41.34%:

$$\text{Annual percentage rate (APR)} = \frac{17,500 + 75,000}{1,000,000 - 17,500 - 75,000} \times \frac{365}{90}$$
$$= 41.34\%$$

Despite these high costs, factoring can be quite worthwhile to many firms for one principal reason: The cost of bearing the credit risk associated with a given receivable can be substantially lower to a factor than to the selling firm. First, the factor's greater credit information makes it more knowledgeable about the actual, as opposed to the perceived, risks involved and thereby reduces its required risk premium. Second, by holding a well-diversified portfolio of receivables, the factor can eliminate some of the risks associated with individual receivables.

In general, factoring is most useful for (1) the occasional exporter and (2) the exporter having a geographically diverse portfolio of accounts receivable. In both cases, it would be organizationally difficult and expensive to internalize the accounts-receivable collection process. Such companies generally would be small or else would be involved on a limited scale in foreign markets.

15.3.4 Forfaiting

The specialized factoring technique known as forfaiting is sometimes used in the case of extreme credit risk. **Forfaiting** is the discounting—at a fixed rate without recourse—of medium-term export receivables denominated in fully convertible currencies (U.S. dollar, Swiss franc, euro). This technique is generally used in the case of capital-goods exports with a 5-year maturity and repayment in semiannual installments. The discount is set at a fixed rate: about 1.25% above the local cost of funds.

Forfaiting is especially popular in Western Europe (primarily in Switzerland and Austria), and many forfaiting houses are subsidiaries of major international banks, such as Credit Suisse, Which also provide help with administrative and collection problems.

15.4 GOVERNMENT SOURCES OF EXPORT FINANCING AND CREDIT INSURANCE

In the race for export orders, particularly for capital equipment and other big-ticket items requiring long repayment arrangements, most governments of developed countries have attempted to provide their domestic exporters with a competitive edge in the form of low-cost export financing and concessionary rates on political and economic risk insurance. Nearly every developed nation has its own export-import agency for development and trade financing.

15.4.1 Export Financing

Procedures for extending credit vary greatly among agencies. Many agencies offer funds in advance of the actual export contract, whereas private sources extend financing only after the sale has been made. Some programs extend credit only to the supplier, called **supplier credits**, to pass on to the importer; others grant credit directly to the buyer—called **buyer credits**–who then pays the supplier. The difference is that in the first arrangement, the supplier bears the credit risk, whereas in the second case, the government is the risk bearer. The government often provides credit insurance in conjunction with supplier credits.

Export-Import Bank The **Export-Import Bank** (**Eximbank**) is the only U.S. government agency dedicated solely to financing and facilitating U.S. exports. Eximbank loans provide competitive, fixed-rate financing for U.S. export sales facing foreign competition backed with subsidized official financing. Evidence of foreign competition is not required for exports produced by small businesses where the loan amount is $2.5 million or less. Eximbank also provides guarantees of loans made by others. The loan and guarantee programs cover up to 85% of the U.S. export value and have repayment terms of one year or more.

Eximbank operations generally conform to five basic principles:

1. Loans are made for the specific purpose of financing U.S. exports of goods and services. If a U.S. export item contains foreign-made components, Eximbank will cover up to 100% of the U.S. content of exports provided that the total amount financed or guaranteed does not exceed 85% of the total contract price of the item and that the total U.S. content accounts for at least half the contract price.

2. Eximbank will not provide financing unless private capital is unavailable in the amounts required. It supplements, rather than competes with, private capital.

3. Loans must have reasonable assurance of repayment and must be for projects that have a favorable impact on the country's economic and social well-being. The host government must be aware of, and not object to, the project.

4. Fees and premiums charged for guarantees and insurance are based on the risks covered.

5. In authorizing loans and other financial assistance, Eximbank is obliged to take into account any adverse effects on the U.S. economy or balance of payments that might occur.

Eximbank extends direct loans to foreign buyers of U.S. exports and intermediary loans to financial institutions that extend loans to the foreign buyers. Both direct and intermediary loans are provided when U.S. exporters face officially subsidized foreign competition.

Eximbank's medium-term loans to intermediaries (where the loan amount is $10 million or less and the term is 7 years or less) are structured as "standby" loan commitments.

The intermediary may request disbursement by Eximbank at any time during the term of the underlying debt obligation.

Eximbank guarantees provide repayment protection for private-sector loans to creditworthy buyers of exported U.S. goods and services. The guarantees are available alone or may be combined with an intermediary loan. Most guarantees provide comprehensive coverage of both political and commercial risks. Eximbank also will guarantee payments on cross-border or international leases.

Exporters may also have access to an Eximbank program that guarantees export-related working-capital loans to creditworthy small and medium-sized businesses. All Eximbank guarantees carry the full faith and credit of the U.S. government, so loans provided under these guarantee programs are made at nearly the risk-free interest rate. In effect, low-cost guarantees are another form of government-subsidized export financing.

Repayment terms vary with the project and type of equipment purchased. For capital goods, long-term credits are normally provided for a period of 5 to 10 years. Loans for projects and large product acquisitions are eligible for longer terms, whereas lower-unit-value items receive shorter terms. Loan amortization is made in semiannual installments, beginning 6 months after delivery of the exported equipment.

In recent years, Eximbank has become more aggressive in fighting perceived abuses by foreign export-credit agencies. One area that Eximbank has targeted is foreign **mixed-credit financing**—the practice of tying grants and low-interest loans to the acceptance of specific commercial contracts. For years, U.S. capital-equipment exporters, engineering firms, and high-tech producers have lost overseas bids to foreign firms backed by government mixed credits. Eximbank now offers its own mixed credits. It will even offer mixed-credit deals before the fact. Any deal that has a chance of attracting a foreign mixed-credit bid is considered. However, an Eximbank spokesperson noted, "This is not an export promotion. We are not out there to match every mixed credit. We're out to end mixed credits, and will only offer one if it helps us to make a specific negotiating point."[2]

Private Export Funding Corporation   The **Private Export Funding Corporation (PEFCO)** was created in 1970 by the **Bankers' Association for Foreign Trade** to mobilize private capital for financing the export of big-ticket items by U.S. firms. It purchases the medium- to long-term debt obligations of importers of U.S. products at fixed interest rates. PEFCO finances its portfolio of foreign importer loans through the sale of its own securities. Eximbank fully guarantees repayment of all PEFCO foreign obligations.

PEFCO normally extends its credits jointly with one or more commercial banks and Eximbank. The maturity of the importers' notes purchased by PEFCO varies from 2.5 years to 12 years; the banks take the short-term maturity and Eximbank takes the long-term portion of a PEFCO loan. Much of this money goes to finance purchases of U.S.-manufactured jet aircraft and related equipment such as jet engines.

Trends   There are several trends in public-source export financing, including:

- *A shift from supplier to buyer credits*: Many capital goods exports that cannot be financed under the traditional medium-term supplier credits become feasible under buyer credits, where the payment period can be stretched up to 20 years.

- *A growing emphasis on acting as catalysts to attract private capital*: This action includes participating with private sources, either as a member of a financial consortium or as a partner with an individual private investor, in supplying export credits.

---

[2] "How U.S. Firms Benefit from Eximbank's War on Foreign Mixed Credits," *Business International Money Report*, February 10, 1986, p. 41.

- *Public agencies as a source of refinancing*: Public agencies are becoming an important source for refinancing loans made by bankers and private financiers. Refinancing enables a private creditor to discount its export loans with the government.

- *Attempts to limit competition among agencies*: The virtual export-credit war among governments has led to several attempts to agree upon and coordinate financing terms. These attempts, however, have been honored more in the breach than in the observance.

15.4.2 Export Credit Insurance

Export financing covered by government credit insurance, also known as **export-credit insurance**, provides protection against losses from political and commercial risks. It serves as a collateral for the credit and is often indispensable in making the sale. The insurance does not usually provide an ironclad guarantee against all risks, however. Having this insurance results in lowering the cost of borrowing from private institutions because the government agency is bearing those risks set forth in the insurance policy. The financing is nonrecourse to the extent that risks and losses are covered. Often, however, the insurer requires additional security in the form of a guarantee by a foreign local bank or a certificate from the foreign central bank that foreign exchange is available for repayment of the interest and principal.

The purpose of export-credit insurance is to encourage a nation's export sales by protecting domestic exporters against nonpayment by importers. The existence of medium- and long-term credit insurance policies makes banks more willing to provide nonrecourse financing of big-ticket items that require lengthy repayment maturities, provided the goods in question have been delivered and accepted.

Foreign Credit Insurance Association In the United States, the export-credit insurance program is administered by the **Foreign Credit Insurance Association (FCIA)**—a cooperative effort of Eximbank and a group of approximately 50 of the leading marine, casualty, and property insurance companies. FCIA insurance offers protection from political and commercial risks to U.S. exporters. The private insurers cover commercial risks, and the Eximbank covers political risks. The exporter (or the financial institution providing the loan) must self-insure that portion not covered by the FCIA.

Short-term insurance is available for export credits up to 180 days (360 days for bulk agricultural commodities and consumer durables) from the date of shipment. Coverage is of two types: comprehensive (90%–100% of political and 90%–95% of commercial risks) and political only (90%–100% coverage). Coinsurance is required presumably because of the element of moral hazard: The possibility that exporters might take unreasonable risks knowing that they would still be paid in full.

Rather than sell insurance on a case-by-case basis, the FCIA approves discretionary limits within which each exporter can approve its own credits. Insurance rates are based on terms of sale, type of buyer, and country of destination and can vary from a low of 0.1% to a high of 2%. The greater the loss experience associated with the particular exporter and the countries and customers it deals with, the higher the insurance premium charged. The FCIA also offers preshipment insurance up to 180 days from the time of sale.

Medium-term insurance, guaranteed by Eximbank and covering big-ticket items sold on credit usually from 181 days to 5 years, is available on a case-by-case basis. As with short-term coverage, the exporter must reside in, and ship from, the United States. However, the FCIA will provide medium-term coverage for that portion only of the value added that originated in the United States. As before, the rates depend on the terms of sale and the destination.

Under the FCIA lease insurance program, lessors of U.S. equipment and related services can cover both the stream of lease payments and the fair market value of products leased outside the United States. The FCIA charges a risk-based premium that is determined by country, lease term, and the type of lease.

15.4.3 Taking Advantage of Government-Subsidized Export Financing

Government-subsidized export-credit programs often can be employed advantageously by multinationals. The use will depend on whether the firm is seeking to export or import goods or services, but the basic strategy remains the same: Shop around among the various export-credit agencies for the best possible financing arrangement.

ILLUSTRATION *Texas Instruments Searches for Low-Cost Capital*

Texas Instruments (TI) is seeking to finance an aggressive capital spending program through a series of joint ventures and other cooperative arrangements with foreign governments and corporations. In Italy, TI received a package of development grants and low-cost loans from the government that offset more than half of TI's investment in a state-of-the-art semiconductor plant there—an investment expected to total more than $1 billion over many years. TI was able to negotiate the incentive package because the Italian government was seeking to improve its technological infrastructure in the area selected by TI for the new plant.

In Taiwan, TI and a Taiwanese customer, Acer Computer Company, established a joint venture in which Acer's majority stake is financed with Taiwanese equity capital that would be unavailable to a U.S. company acting alone. In Japan, TI entered into a joint venture with Kobe Steel, a company seeking diversification. Here, too, TI relies on its foreign partner to supply a majority of the equity. In both Asian joint ventures, however, TI has an option to convert its initial minority stake into a majority holding.

Export Financing Strategy   Massey-Ferguson (now Varity Corporation), the multinational Canadian farm-equipment manufacturer, illustrates how MNCs are able to generate business for their foreign subsidiaries at minimum expense and risk by playing off national export-credit programs against each other.

The key to this *export financing strategy* is to view the foreign countries in which the MNC has plants not only as markets but also as potential sources of financing for exports to third countries. For example, in early 1978, Massey-Ferguson was looking to ship 7,200 tractors (worth $53 million) to Turkey, but it was unwilling to assume the risk of currency inconvertibility.[3] Turkey at that time already owed $2 billion to various foreign creditors, and it was uncertain whether it would be able to come up with dollars to pay off its debts (especially because its reserves were at about zero).

Massey solved this problem by manufacturing the tractors at its Brazilian subsidiary, Massey-Ferguson of Brazil, and selling them to Brazil's Interbras—the trading arm of Petrobras, the Brazilian national oil corporation. Interbras, in turn, arranged to sell the tractors to Turkey and pay Massey in cruzeiros. The cruzeiro financing for Interbras came from Cacex, the Banco do Brazil department that is in charge of foreign trade. Cacex underwrote all the political, commercial, and exchange risks as part of the Brazilian government's intense export promotion drive. Before choosing Brazil as a supply point, Massey made a point of shopping around to get the best export-credit deal available.

---

[3] "Massey-Ferguson's No-Risk Tractor Deal," *Business International Money Report*, February 3, 1978, pp. 35–36.

Item	Total Project	United States	France	Germany	Japan	United Kingdom	Sweden	Italy
Mine Equipment								
Shovels	$12	$12	$8	$12	$12	$12	$10	—
Trucks	20	20	—	20	20	10	20	12
Other	8	8	5	3	6	8	—	4
Mine Facilities								
Shops	7	7	7	7	3	7	5	6
Offices	3	3	3	3	2	3	3	2
Preparation Plan								
Crushers	11	11	8	11	11	11	—	—
Loading	15	15	10	10	15	12	15	7
Environmental	13	13	5	8	5	10	7	5
Terminal								
Ore Handling	13	13	10	13	13	13	8	9
Shiploader	6	6	6	6	6	6	2	4
Bulk Commodities								
Steel	20	20	20	20	20	15	8	20
Electrical	17	17	12	14	10	15	5	8
Mechanical	15	15	8	—	12	10	6	—
Total Potential Foreign Purchases	$160	$160	$102	$127	$135	$132	$89	$77

EXHIBIT 15.9 • ALTERNATIVE SOURCES OF PROCUREMENT: HYPOTHETICAL COPPER MINE (U.S. $ MILLIONS)

Import Financing Strategy   Firms engaged in projects that have sizable import requirements may be able to finance these purchases on attractive terms. A number of countries, including the United States, make credit available to foreign purchasers at low (below-market) interest rates and with long repayment periods. These loans are almost always tied to procurement in the agency's country; thus, the firm must compile a list of goods and services required for the project and relate them to potential sources by country. Where there is overlap among the potential suppliers, the purchasing firm may have leverage to extract more favorable financing terms from the various export-credit agencies involved. This strategy is illustrated by the hypothetical example of a copper mining venture in Exhibit 15.9.

Perhaps the best-known application of this *import financing strategy* in recent years was the financing of the Soviet gas pipeline to Western Europe. The former Soviet Union played off various European and Japanese suppliers and export financing agencies against each other and managed to get extraordinarily favorable credit and pricing terms.

15.5 COUNTERTRADE

In recent years, more and more multinationals have had to resort to **countertrade** to sell overseas: purchasing local products to offset the exports of their own products to that market. Countertrade transactions often can be complex and cumbersome. They may involve two-way or three-way transactions, especially where a company is forced to accept unrelated goods for resale by outsiders.

If swapping goods for goods sounds less efficient than using cash or credit, that is because it is less efficient, but it is preferable to having no sales in a given market. More firms are finding it increasingly difficult to conduct business without being prepared to countertrade. Although precise numbers are impossible to come by, this transaction is growing in importance. One estimate placed countertrade volume at from 20% to 30% of all international trade.[4]

When a company exports to a nation requiring countertrade, it must take back goods that the country cannot (or will not try to) sell in international markets. To unload these goods, the company usually has to cut the prices at which the goods are nominally valued in the barter arrangement. Recognizing this necessity, the firm typically will pad the price of the goods it sells to its countertrade customer. When a German machine-tool maker sells to Romania, for instance, it might raise prices by 20%. Then, when it unloads the blouses it gets in return, the premium covers the reduction in price.

Usually, an exporting company wants to avoid the trouble of marketing those blouses, so it hands over the 10% premium to a countertrade specialist. This middleman splits the premium with a blouse buyer, keeping perhaps 2% and passing the remaining 8% along in price cuts. The result: Romania pays above the market for imports, making international trade less attractive than it should be, and dumps its own goods through backdoor price shaving. In the long run, however, the practice is self-defeating. Having failed to set up continuing relationships with customers, Romania never learns what the market really wants—what style blouses, for instance—or how it might improve its competitiveness.

Countertrade takes several specific forms.

- **Barter** is a direct exchange of goods between two parties without the use of money. For example, Iran might swap oil for guns.

- **Counterpurchase**, also known as parallel barter, is the sale and purchase of goods that are unrelated to each other. For example, PepsiCo sold soft drinks to the former Soviet Union for vodka.

- **Buyback** is repayment of the original purchase price through the sale of a related product. For example, Western European countries delivered various pipeline materials to the former Soviet Union for construction of a gas pipeline from Siberian gas fields and in return agreed to purchase 28 billion cubic meters of gas per year.

The unanswered question in countertrade is: Why go through such a convoluted sales process? Why not sell the goods directly at their market price (which is what ultimately happens anyway) using experts to handle the marketing? One argument is that countertrade enables members of cartels such as OPEC to undercut an agreed price without formally doing so. Another argument is that countertrade keeps bureaucrats busy in centrally planned economies. Countertrade also may reduce the risk faced by a country that contracts for a new manufacturing facility. If the contractor's payment is received in the form of goods supplied by the facility, the contractor has an added incentive to do quality work and to ensure that the plant's technology is suitable for the skill levels of the available workers.

Regardless of reasons for its being, countertrading is replete with problems for the firms involved. First, the goods that can be taken in countertrade are usually undesirable. Those that could be readily converted into cash have already been converted, so, although a firm shipping computers to Brazil might prefer to take coffee beans in return, the only goods available might be Brazilian shoes. Second, the trading details are difficult to work

---

[4] Thomas R. Hofstedt, "An Overview of Countertrade," July 29, 1987, unpublished.

out. (How many tons of naphtha is a pile of shoddy Eastern European goods worth?) The inevitable result is a very high ratio of talk to action, with only a small percentage of deals that are talked about getting done. And lost deals cost money.

Until recently, most countertrade centered on government foreign trade organizations (FTOs) of Eastern European countries. In order to sell a machine or an entire plant to an FTO, a western firm might be required to accept at least some of its payment in goods (for example, tomatoes, linen, and machine parts). Sometimes these deals will stretch over several years. Centered in Vienna, the countertrade experts in this business use their contacts with Eastern European officials and their knowledge of available products to earn their keep. However, the downfall of communism and restructuring currently taking place in Eastern Europe have eliminated most FTOs and thereby reduced the scale and profitability of the countertrade business.

The loss of Eastern European business, however, has been more than offset by the explosive growth in countertrade with Third World countries. The basis for the new wave of countertrade is the cutting off of bank credit to developing nations. Third World countertrade involves more commodities and fewer hard-to-sell manufactured goods. A typical deal, arranged by Sears World Trade, involved bartering U.S. breeding swine for Dominican sugar. Another countertrader swapped BMWs for Ecuadoran tuna fish. The dissolution of the Soviet Union also has created new opportunities for countertrade as the following convoluted example illustrates.

ILLUSTRATION   *Marc Rich & Co. Recreates the Former Soviet Union's Supply System*

In 1992, Marc Rich & Co., a giant Swiss-based commodity trader, engineered a remarkable $100 million deal involving enterprises and governments in five newly independent countries. This deal essentially pieced together shattered supply links that Moscow controlled when the U.S.S.R. was one giant planned economy.

Here's how the deal worked. Marc Rich bought 70,000 tons of raw sugar from Brazil on the open market. The sugar was shipped to Ukraine, where through a "tolling contract" it was processed at a local refinery. After paying the sugar refinery with part of the sugar, Marc Rich sent 30,000 tons of refined sugar east to several huge Siberian oil refineries, which need sugar to supply their vast workforces.

Strapped for hard currency, the oil refineries paid instead with oil products, much of it low-grade A-76 gasoline, which has few export markets. But one market is Mongolia, with which Marc Rich has long traded. The company shipped 130,000 tons of oil products there; in payment, the Mongolians turned over 35,000 tons of copper concentrate. The company sent most of that back across the border to Kazakhstan, where it was refined into copper metal. Then the metal was shipped westward to a Baltic seaport and out to the world market where, several months after the deal began, Marc Rich earned a hard currency profit.

In an effort to make it easier for Third World countries to buy their products, big manufacturers—including General Motors, General Electric, and Caterpillar—have set up countertrading subsidiaries. Having sold auto and truck parts to Mexico, for example, GM's countertrade subsidiary, Motors Trading Corporation, arranged tour groups to the country and imported Mexican slippers and gloves. Similarly, arms manufacturers selling to developing countries are often forced to accept local products in return—for example, Iraqi oil for French Exocet missiles or Peruvian anchovies for Spanish Piranha patrol boats.

Authorities in countertrading countries are concerned that goods taken in counter-trade will cannibalize their existing cash markets. Proving that countertrade goods go to new markets is difficult enough in the area of manufactured goods; it's impossible for commodities, whose ultimate use cannot be identified with its source. For example, some Indonesian rubber taken in countertrade inevitably will displace rubber that Indonesia sells for cash.

Interest in countertrade and its variations appears to be growing, even among devel-oped countries, despite the obvious difficulties it presents to the firms and countries involved. For example, to sell F-15s to the Japanese air force, McDonnell Douglas had to offset the cost to Japan in currency and jobs by agreeing to teach Japanese manufacturers to make military aircraft.

The growth in countertrade is reflected in the scramble for experienced specialists. It has been said that a good countertrader combines the avarice and opportunism of a commodities trader, the inventiveness and political sensitivity of a crooked bureaucrat, as well as the technical knowledge of a machine-tool salesperson.

15.6 SHORT-TERM FINANCING

Financing the working capital requirements of a multinational corporation's foreign affil-iates poses a complex decision problem that stems from the large number of financing options available to the subsidiary of an MNC. Subsidiaries have access to funds from sis-ter affiliates and the parent, as well as from external sources. This section is concerned with the following four aspects of developing a short-term overseas financing strategy: (1) identifying the key factors, (2) formulating and evaluating objectives, (3) describing available short-term borrowing options, and (4) developing a methodology for calculat-ing and comparing the effective dollar costs of these alternatives.

15.6.1 Key Factors in Short-Term Financing Strategy

Expected costs and risks, the basic determinants of any funding strategy, are strongly influenced in an international context by six key factors.

1. If forward contracts are unavailable, the crucial issue is whether differences in nominal interest rates among currencies are matched by anticipated changes in the exchange rate. For example, is the difference between an 8% dollar interest rate and a 3% Swiss franc interest rate due solely to expectations that the dollar will devalue by 5% relative to the franc? The key issue here, in other words, is whether there are deviations from the international Fisher effect. If deviations do exist, then expected dollar borrowing costs will vary by cur-rency, leading to a decision problem. Trade-offs must be made between the expected borrowing costs and the exchange risks associated with each financ-ing option.

2. The element of exchange risk is the second key factor. Many firms borrow locally to provide an offsetting liability for their exposed local currency assets. On the other hand, borrowing a foreign currency in which the firm has no exposure will increase its exchange risk. That is, the risks associated with borrowing in a spe-cific currency are related to the firm's degree of exposure in that currency.

3. The third essential element is the firm's degree of risk aversion. The more risk averse the firm (or its management) is, the higher the price it should be willing to pay to reduce its currency exposure. Risk aversion affects the company's risk-cost trade-off and consequently, in the absence of forward contracts, influences the selection of currencies it will use to finance its foreign operations.

4. If forward contracts are available, however, currency risk should not be a factor in the firm's borrowing strategy. Instead, relative borrowing costs, calculated on a covered cost basis, become the sole determinant of which currencies to borrow in. The key issue here is whether the nominal interest differential equals the forward differential—that is, whether interest rate parity holds. If it does hold, then the currency denomination of the firm's debt is irrelevant. Covered costs can differ among currencies because of government capital controls or the threat of such controls. Because of this added element of risk, the annualized forward discount or premium may not offset the difference between the interest rate on the LC loan versus the dollar loan—that is, interest rate parity will not hold.

5. Even if interest rate parity does hold before tax, the currency denomination of corporate borrowings does matter where tax asymmetries are present. These tax asymmetries are based on the differential treatment of foreign exchange gains and losses on either forward contracts or loan repayments. For example, English firms or affiliates have a disincentive to borrow in strong currencies because Inland Revenue, the British tax agency, taxes exchange gains on foreign currency borrowings but disallows the deductibility of exchange losses on the same loans. An opposite incentive (to borrow in stronger currencies) is created in countries such as Australia that may permit exchange gains on forward contracts to be taxed at a lower rate than the rate at which forward contract losses are deductible. In such a case, even if interest parity holds before tax, after-tax forward contract gains may be greater than after-tax interest costs. Such tax asymmetries lead to possibilities of borrowing arbitrage, even if interest rate parity holds before tax. The essential point is that, in comparing relative borrowing costs, firms must compute these costs on an after-tax covered basis.

6. A final factor that may enter into the borrowing decision is **political risk**. Even if local financing is not the minimum cost option, multinationals often will still try to maximize their local borrowings if they believe that expropriation or exchange controls are serious possibilities. If either event occurs, an MNC has fewer assets at risk if it has used local, rather than external, financing.

15.6.2 Short-Term Financing Objectives

Four possible objectives can guide a firm in deciding where and in which currencies to borrow.

1. *Minimize expected cost*: By ignoring risk, this objective reduces information requirements, allows borrowing options to be evaluated on an individual basis without considering the correlation between loan cash flows and operating cash flows, and lends itself readily to breakeven analysis (see Chapter 14, Section 14.2).

2. *Minimize risk without regard to cost*. A firm that followed this advice to its logical conclusion would dispose of all its assets and invest the proceeds in government securities. In other words, this objective is impractical and contrary to shareholder interests.

3. *Trade off expected cost and systematic risk*. The advantage of this objective is that, like the first objective, it allows a company to evaluate different loans without considering the relationship between loan cash flows and operating cash flows from operations. Moreover, it is consistent with shareholder preferences as described by the capital asset pricing model. In practical terms, however, there is probably little difference between expected borrowing costs adjusted for systematic risk and expected borrowing costs without that adjustment. The reason for this lack of difference is that the correlation between currency fluctuations and a well-diversified portfolio of risky assets is likely to be quite small.

4. *Trade off expected cost and total risk.* The theoretical rationale for this approach was described in Chapter 1. Basically, it relies on the existence of potentially substantial costs of financial distress. On a more practical level, management generally prefers greater stability of cash flows (regardless of investor preferences). Management typically will self-insure against most losses but might decide to use the financial markets to hedge against the risk of large losses. To implement this approach, it is necessary to take into account the covariances between operating and financing cash flows. This approach (trading off expected cost and total risk) is valid only where forward contracts are unavailable. Otherwise, selecting the lowest cost borrowing option, calculated on a covered after-tax basis, is the only justifiable objective (for the reason why, see Chapter 9, Section 9.4).[5]

15.6.3 Short-Term Financing Options

Firms typically prefer to finance the temporary component of current assets with short-term funds. The three principal short-term financing options that may be available to an MNC include: (1) the intercompany loan, (2) the local currency loan, and (3) commercial paper.

Intercompany Financing A frequent means of affiliate financing is to have either the parent company or sister affiliate provide an **intercompany loan**. At times, however, these loans may be limited in amount or duration by official exchange controls. In addition, interest rates on intercompany loans are frequently required to fall within set limits. The relevant parameters in establishing the cost of such a loan include the lender's opportunity cost of funds, the interest rate set, tax rates and regulations, the currency of denomination of the loan, and expected exchange rate movements over the term of the loan.

Local Currency Financing Like most domestic firms, affiliates of multinational corporations generally attempt to finance their working capital requirements locally, for both convenience and exposure management purposes. All industrial nations and most LDCs have well-developed commercial banking systems, so firms seeking local financing generally turn there first. The major forms of bank financing include overdrafts, discounting, and term loans. Nonbank sources of funds include commercial paper and factoring (see Section 15.3).

Bank Loans Loans from commercial banks are the dominant form of short-term interest-bearing financing used around the world. These loans are described as *self-liquidating* because they are generally used to finance temporary increases in accounts receivable and inventory. These increases in working capital soon are converted into cash, which is used to repay the loan.

Short-term bank credits are typically unsecured. The borrower signs a note undertaking its obligation to repay the loan when it is due, along with accrued interest. Most notes are payable in 90 days; the loans must, therefore, be repaid or renewed every 90 days. The need to periodically roll over bank loans gives a bank substantial control over the use of its funds, reducing the need to impose severe restrictions on the firm. To further ensure that short-term credits are not being used for permanent financing, a bank will usually insert a **cleanup clause** requiring the company to be completely out of debt to the bank for a period of at least 30 days during the year.

---

[5] These possible objectives are suggested by Donald R. Lessard, "Currency and Tax Considerations in International Financing," Teaching Note No. 3, Massachusetts Institute of Technology, Spring 1979.

Forms of Bank Credit. Bank credit provides a highly flexible form of financing because it is readily expandable and, therefore, serves as a financial reserve. Whenever the firm needs extra short-term funds that cannot be met by trade credit, it is likely to turn first to bank credit. Unsecured bank loans may be extended under a line of credit, under a revolving credit arrangement, or on a transaction basis. Bank loans can be originated in either the domestic or the Eurodollar market.

1. *Term loans*: **Term loans** are straight loans, often unsecured, that are made for a fixed period of time, usually 90 days. They are attractive because they give corporate treasurers complete control over the timing of repayments. A term loan typically is made for a specific purpose with specific conditions and is repaid in a single lump sum. The loan provisions are contained in the promissory note that is signed by the customer. This type of loan is used most often by borrowers who have an infrequent need for bank credit.

2. *Line of credit*: Arranging separate loans for frequent borrowers is a relatively expensive means of doing business. One way to reduce these transaction costs is to use a **line of credit**. This informal agreement permits the company to borrow up to a stated maximum amount from the bank. The firm can draw down its line of credit when it requires funds and pay back the loan balance when it has excess cash. Although the bank is not legally obligated to honor the line-of-credit agreement, it almost always does so unless it or the firm encounters financial difficulties. A line of credit is usually good for one year, with renewals renegotiated every year.

3. *Overdrafts*: In countries other than the United States, banks tend to lend through overdrafts. An **overdraft** is simply a line of credit against which drafts (checks) can be drawn (written) up to a specified maximum amount. These overdraft lines often are extended and expanded year after year, thus providing, in effect, a form of medium-term financing. The borrower pays interest on the debit balance only.

4. *Revolving credit agreement*: A **revolving credit agreement** is similar to a line of credit except that now the bank (or the syndicate of banks) is *legally committed* to extend credit up to the stated maximum. The firm pays interest on its outstanding borrowings plus a commitment fee, ranging between 0.125% and 0.5% per annum, on the *unused* portion of the credit line. Revolving credit agreements are usually renegotiated every two or three years.

   The danger that short-term credits are being used to fund long-term requirements is particularly acute with a revolving credit line that is continuously renewed. Inserting an out-of-debt period under a cleanup clause validates the temporary need for funds.

5. *Discounting*: The **discounting** of trade bills is the preferred short-term financing technique in many European countries—especially in France, Italy, Belgium, and, to a lesser extent, Germany. It is also widespread in Latin America, particularly in Argentina, Brazil, and Mexico. These bills often can be rediscounted with the central bank.

Discounting usually results from the following set of transactions. A manufacturer selling goods to a retailer on credit draws a bill on the buyer, payable in, say, 30 days. The buyer endorses (accepts) the bill or gets his or her bank to accept it, at which point it becomes a **banker's acceptance**. The manufacturer then takes the bill to his or her bank, and the bank accepts it for a fee if the buyer's bank has not already accepted it. The bill is then sold at a discount to the manufacturer's bank or to a money-market dealer. The rate of interest varies with the term of the bill and the general level of local money-market interest rates.

The popularity of discounting in European countries stems from the fact that according to European commercial law, which is based on the Code Napoleon, the claim of the bill holder is independent of the claim represented by the underlying transaction. (For example, the bill holder must be paid even if the buyer objects to the quality of the merchandise.) This right makes the bill easily negotiable and enhances its liquidity (or tradability), thereby lowering the cost of discounting relative to other forms of credit.

Interest Rates on Bank Loans. The interest rate on bank loans is based on personal negotiation between the banker and the borrower. The loan rate charged to a specific customer reflects that customer's creditworthiness, previous relationship with the bank, maturity of the loan, and other factors. Ultimately, bank interest rates are based on the same factors as the interest rates on the financial securities issued by a borrower: the risk-free return, which reflects the time value of money, plus a risk premium based on the borrower's credit risk. However, there are certain bank-loan pricing conventions that you should be familiar with.

Interest on a loan can be paid at maturity or in advance. Each payment method gives a different effective interest rate, even if the quoted rate is the same. The **effective interest rate** is defined as follows:

$$\text{Effective interest rate} = \frac{\text{Annual interest paid}}{\text{Funds received}}$$

Suppose you borrow $10,000 for one year at 11% interest. If the interest is paid at maturity, you owe the lender $11,100 at the end of the year. This payment method yields an effective interest rate of 11%, the same as the stated interest rate:

$$\text{Effective interest rate when interest is paid at maturity} = \frac{\$1,100}{\$10,000} = 11\%$$

If the loan is quoted on a *discount basis*, the bank deducts the interest in advance. On the $10,000 loan, you will receive only $8,900 and must repay $10,000 in one year. The effective rate of interest exceeds 11% because you are paying interest on $10,000 but have the use of only $8,900:

$$\text{Effective interest rate on discounted loan} = \frac{\$1,100}{\$8,900} = 12.4\%$$

An extreme illustration of the difference in the effective interest rate between paying interest at maturity and paying interest in advance is provided by the Mexican banking system. In 1985, the nominal interest rate on a peso bank loan was 70%, about 15 percentage points higher than the inflation rate. But high as it was, the nominal figure did not tell the whole story. By collecting interest in advance, Mexican banks boosted the effective rate dramatically. Consider, for example, the cost of a Ps 10,000 loan. By collecting interest of 70%, or Ps 7,000, in advance, the bank actually loaned out only Ps 3,000 and received Ps 10,000 at maturity. The effective interest rate on the loan was 233%:

$$\text{Effective interest rate on Mexican loan} = \frac{\text{Ps } 7,000}{\text{Ps } 3,000} = 233\%$$

Many banks require borrowers to hold from 10% to 20% of their outstanding loan balance on deposit in a non-interest-bearing account. These **compensating balance requirements** raise the effective cost of a bank credit because not all of the loan is available to the firm:

$$\text{Effective interest rate with compensating balance requirement} = \frac{\text{Annual interest paid}}{\text{Usable funds}}$$

Usable funds equal the net amount of the loan less the compensating balance requirement.

Returning to the previous example, suppose you borrow $10,000 at 11% interest paid at maturity, and the compensating balance requirement is 15%, or $1,500. Thus, the $10,000 loan provides only $8,500 in usable funds for an effective interest rate of 12.9%:

$$\text{Effective interest rate when interest is paid at maturity} = \frac{\$1,100}{\$8,500} = 12.9\%$$

If the interest is prepaid, the amount of usable funds declines by a further $1,100—that is, to $7,400—and the effective interest rate rises to 14.9%:

$$\text{Effective interest rate on discounted loan} = \frac{\$1,100}{\$7,400} = 14.9\%$$

In both instances, the compensating balance requirement raises the effective interest rate above the stated interest rate. This higher rate is the case even if the bank pays interest on the compensating balance deposit because the loan rate invariably exceeds the deposit rate.

Commercial Paper   One of the most favored alternatives for MNCs to borrowing short term from a bank is to issue commercial paper. As defined earlier in this chapter, **commercial paper (CP)** is a short-term unsecured promissory note that is generally sold by large corporations on a discount basis to institutional investors and to other corporations. Because commercial paper is unsecured and bears only the name of the issuer, the market has generally been dominated by the largest, most creditworthy companies.

Available maturities are fairly standard across the spectrum, but average maturities—reflecting the terms that companies actually use—vary from 20 to 25 days in the United States to more than three months in the Netherlands. The minimum denomination of paper also varies widely: In Australia, Canada, Sweden, and the United States, firms can issue CP in much smaller amounts than in other markets. In most countries, the instrument is issued at a discount, with the full face value of the note redeemed upon maturity. In other markets, however, interest-bearing instruments are also offered.

By going directly to the market rather than relying on a financial intermediary such as a bank, large, well-known corporations can save substantial interest costs, often on the order of 1% or more. In addition, because commercial paper is sold directly to large institutions, U.S. CP is exempt from SEC registration requirements. This exemption reduces the time and expense of readying an issue of commercial paper for sale.

There are three major noninterest costs associated with using commercial paper as a source of short-term funds: (1) backup lines of credit, (2) fees to commercial banks, and (3) rating service fees. In most cases, issuers back their paper 100% with lines of credit from commercial banks. Because its average maturity is very short, commercial paper poses the risk that an issuer might not be able to pay off or roll over maturing paper. Consequently, issuers use backup lines as insurance against periods of financial stress or tight money, when lenders ration money directly rather than raise interest rates. For example, the market for Texaco paper, which provided the bulk of its short-term financing, disappeared after an $11.1 billion judgment against the company. Texaco replaced these funds by drawing on its bank lines of credit.

Backup lines usually are paid for through compensating balances, typically about 10% of the unused portion of the credit line plus 20% of the amount of credit actually used. As an alternative to compensating balances, issuers sometimes pay straight fees ranging from 0.375% to 0.75% of the line of credit; this explicit pricing procedure has been used increasingly in recent years.

Another cost associated with issuing commercial paper is fees paid to the large commercial and investment banks that act as issuing and paying agents for the paper issuers and handle all the associated paperwork. Finally, rating services charge fees ranging from $5,000 to $25,000 per year for ratings, depending on the rating service. Credit ratings are not legally required by any nation, but they are often essential for placing paper.

In Chapter 12, we saw that alternatives to commercial paper issued in the local market are Euronotes and Euro-commercial paper (Euro-CP). The Euronotes are typically underwritten, whereas Euro-CP is not.

15.6.4 Calculating the Dollar Costs of Alternative Financing Options

This section presents explicit formulas to compute the effective dollar costs of a local currency loan and a dollar loan.[6] These cost formulas can be used to calculate the least expensive financing source for each future exchange rate. A computer can easily perform this analysis, called *breakeven analysis*, and determine the range of future exchange rates within which each particular financing option is cheapest.

With this breakeven analysis, the treasurer can readily see the amount of currency appreciation or depreciation necessary to make one type of borrowing less expensive than another. The treasurer will then compare the firm's actual forecast of currency change, determined objectively or subjectively, with this benchmark.

To illustrate breakeven analysis and show how to develop cost formulas, suppose that Du Pont's Mexican affiliate requires funds to finance its working capital needs for one year. It can borrow pesos at 45% or dollars at 11%. To determine an appropriate borrowing strategy, we will develop explicit cost expressions for each of these loans using the numbers just given. Expressions then will be generalized to obtain analytical cost formulas that are usable under a variety of circumstances.

Case 1: No Taxes. Absent taxes and forward contracts, costing these loans is relatively straightforward.

1. *Local currency loan:* We saw in Chapter 14 (Section 14.2) that, in general, the dollar cost of borrowing local currency (LC) at an interest rate of r_L and a currency change of c is the sum of the dollar interest cost plus the percentage change in the exchange rate:

$$\begin{aligned}\text{Dollar cost} \atop \text{of LC loan} &= \text{Interest cost} + \text{Exchange rate change} \\ &= r_L(1 + c) + c\end{aligned} \qquad (15.1)$$

Employing Equation 15.1, we compute an expected U.S. dollar cost of borrowing Mexican pesos for Du Pont's Mexican affiliate of $0.45 \times (1 + c) + c$, or $0.45 + 1.45c$. For example, if the Mexican peso is expected to fall by 20% ($c = -0.20$), then the effective dollar interest rate on the Mexican loan will be 16% ($0.45 + 1.45 \times -0.20$).

2. *Dollar loan:* The Mexican affiliate can borrow dollars at 11%. In general, the cost of a dollar (HC) loan to the affiliate is the interest rate on the dollar (HC) loan r_H.

Analysis. The peso loan costs $0.45(1 + c) + c$, and the dollar loan costs 11%. To find the breakeven rate of currency depreciation at which the dollar cost of peso borrowing is just equal to the cost of dollar financing, equate the two costs—$0.45(1 + c) + c = 0.11$—and

---

[6] This section draws on material in Alan C. Shapiro, "Evaluating Financing Costs for Multinational Subsidiaries," *Journal of International Business Studies*, Fall 1975, pp. 25–32.

solve for c:

$$c = -\frac{(0.45 - 0.11)}{1.45} = -0.2345$$

In other words, the Mexican peso must devalue by 23.45% before it is less expensive to borrow pesos at 45% than dollars at 11%. Ignoring the factor of exchange risk, the borrowing decision rule is as follows:

> If $c < -23.45\%$, borrow pesos.
> If $c > -23.45\%$, borrow dollars.

In the general case, the breakeven rate of currency change is found by equating the dollar costs of dollar and local currency financing—that is, $r_H = r_L(1 + c) + c$—and solving for c:

$$c^* = \frac{r_H - r_L}{1 + r_L} \tag{15.2}$$

If the international Fisher effect holds, then we saw in Chapter 4 (Equation 4.15) that c^*, the breakeven amount of currency change, also equals the expected LC devaluation (revaluation); that is, the expected peso devaluation should equal 23.45% unless there is reason to believe that some form of market imperfection is not permitting interest rates to adjust to reflect anticipated currency changes.

Case 2: Taxes. Taxes complicate the calculating of various loan costs. Suppose the effective tax rate on the earnings of Du Pont's Mexican affiliate is 40%.

1. *Local currency loan*: Chapter 14 presented the after-tax dollar cost of borrowing in the local currency for a foreign affiliate as equaling the after-tax interest expense plus the change in the exchange rate, or

$$\frac{\text{After-tax dollar}}{\text{cost of LC loan}} = \text{Interest cost} + \text{Exchange rate change}$$

$$= r_L(1 + c)(1 - t_a) + c \tag{15.3}$$

where t_a is the affiliate's marginal tax rate. Employing Equation 15.3, we can calculate the after-tax dollar cost of borrowing pesosas equaling $0.45 \times (1 + c)(1 - 0.40) + c$, or $0.27 + 1.27c$.

2. *Dollar loan*: The after-tax cost of a dollar loan equals the Mexican affiliate's after-tax interest expense, $0.11(1 - 0.40)$, minus the dollar value to the Mexican affiliate of the tax write-off on the increased number of pesos necessary to repay the dollar principal following a peso devaluation, $0.4c$.

In general, the total cost of the dollar loan is the after-tax interest expense less the tax write-off associated with the dollar principal repayment, or

$$\frac{\text{After-tax dollar}}{\text{of dollar loan}} = \frac{\text{Interest cost}}{\text{to subsidiary}} - \text{Tax gain(loss)}$$

$$= r_H(1 - t_a) + ct_a \tag{15.4}$$

Substituting in the relevant parameters to Equation 15.4 yields an after-tax cost of borrowing dollars equal to $0.11 \times (1 - 0.40) + 0.4c$, or $0.066 + 0.4c$.

Analysis. As in case 1, we will set the cost of dollar financing, $0.066 + 0.4c$, equal to the cost of local currency financing, $0.27(1 + c) + c$, in order to find the breakeven rate of peso depreciation necessary to make the firm indifferent to borrowing in dollars or peso.

The breakeven value of c occurs when $0.066 + 0.4c = 0.27(1 + c) + c$, or

$$c^* = -0.2345$$

Thus, the peso must devalue by 23.45% before it is cheaper to borrow pesos at 45% than dollars at 11%. This is the same breakeven exchange rate as in the before-tax case. Although taxes affect the after-tax costs of the dollar and LC loans, they do not affect the relative desirability of the two loans. That is, if one loan has a lower cost before tax, it will also be less costly on an after-tax basis.

In general, the breakeven rate of currency appreciation or depreciation can be found by equating the dollar costs of local currency and dollar financing and solving for c:

$$r_H(1 - t_a) + ct_a = r_L(1 + c)(1 - t_a) + c$$

or

$$c^* = \frac{r_H(1 - t_a) - r_L(1 - t_a)}{(1 + r_L)(1 - t_a)} = \frac{r_H - r_L}{1 + r_L} \tag{15.5}$$

The tax rates cancel out and we are left with the same breakeven value for c as in the before-tax case (see Equation 15.2).

15.7 SUMMARY AND CONCLUSIONS

In this chapter, we examined different financing arrangements and documents involved in international trade. The most important documents encountered in bank-related financing are the draft, which is a written order to pay; the letter of credit, which is a bank guarantee of payment provided that certain stipulated conditions are met; and the bill of lading, the document covering actual shipment of the merchandise by a common carrier and title. Documents of lesser importance include commercial and consular invoices and the insurance certificate.

These instruments serve four primary functions. They

1. Reduce both buyer and seller risk;
2. Define who bears those risks that remain;
3. Facilitate the transfer of risk to a third party; and
4. Facilitate financing.

Each instrument evolved over time as a rational response to the additional risks in international trade posed by the greater distances, lack of familiarity between exporters and importers, possibility of government imposing exchange controls, and greater costs involved in bringing suit against a party domiciled in another nation. Were it not for the latter two factors and publicly financed export-promotion programs, we might expect that, with the passage of time, the financial arrangements in international trade would differ little from those encountered in purely domestic commercial transactions.

We also examined some of the government-sponsored export financing programs and credit insurance programs. The number of these institutions and their operating scope have grown steadily, in line with national export drives. From the standpoint of international financial managers, the most significant difference between public and private sources of financing is that public lending agencies offer their funds and credit insurance at lower than normal commercial rates. The multinational firm can take advantage of these subsidized rates by structuring its marketing and production programs in accord with different national financial programs.

We also examined the various short-term financing alternatives available to a firm, focusing on parent company loans, local currency bank loans, and commercial paper. We saw how factors such as relative interest rates, anticipated currency changes, the existence of forward contracts, and economic exposure combine to affect a firm's short-term borrowing choices. Various objectives that a firm might use to arrive at its borrowing strategy were evaluated. It was concluded that if forward contracts exist, the only valid objective is to minimize covered interest costs. In the absence of forward contracts, firms can either attempt to minimize expected costs or establish some trade-off between reducing expected costs and reducing the degree of cash-flow exposure. The latter goal involves offsetting operating cash inflows in a currency with financing cash outflows in that same currency.

This chapter also developed formulas to compute effective dollar costs of loans denominated in dollars (home currency) or local currency were also developed in this chapter. These formulas were then used to calculate the breakeven rates of currency appreciation or depreciation that would equalize the costs of borrowing in the local currency or in the home currency.

QUESTIONS

1. What are the basic problems arising in international trade financing, and how do the main financing instruments help solve those problems?

2. The different forms of export financing distribute risks differently between the exporter and the importer. Analyze the distribution of risk in the following export financing instruments.
   a. Confirmed, revocable letter of credit
   b. Confirmed, irrevocable letter of credit
   c. Open account credit
   d. Time draft, D/A
   e. Cash with order
   f. Cash in advance
   g. Consignment
   h. Sight draft

3. Describe the different steps and documents involved in exporting motors from Kansas to Hong Kong using a confirmed letter of credit, with payment terms of 90 days sight. What alternatives are available to the exporter to finance this shipment?

4. Explain the advantages and disadvantages of each of the following forms of export financing:
   a. Bankers' acceptances
   b. Discounting
   c. Factoring
   d. Forfaiting

5. What are the potential advantages and disadvantages of countertrade for the parties involved?

6. What are the three principal short-term financing options?

PROBLEMS

1. Texas Computers (TC) recently has begun selling overseas. It currently has 30 foreign orders outstanding, with the typical order averaging $2,500. TC is considering the following three alternatives to protect itself against credit risk on these foreign sales:
   - *Request a letter of credit from each customer.* The cost to the customer would be $75 plus 0.25% of the invoice amount. To remain competitive, TC would have to absorb the cost of the letter of credit.
   - *Factor the receivables.* The factor would charge a nonrecourse fee of 1.6%.
   - *Buy FCIA insurance.* The FCIA would charge a 1% insurance premium.

   a. Which of these alternatives would you recommend to Texas Computers? Why?
   b. Suppose that TC's average order size rose to $250,000. How would that affect your decision?

2. L.A. Cellular has received an order for phone switches from Singapore. The switches will be exported under the terms of a letter of credit issued by Sumitomo Bank on behalf of Singapore Telecommunications. Under the terms of the L/C, the face value of the export order, $12 million, will be paid 6 months after Sumitomo accepts a draft drawn by L.A. Cellular. The current discount rate on 6-month acceptances is 8.5% per annum, and the acceptance fee is 1.25% per annum. In

addition, there is a flat commission, equal to 0.5% of the face amount of the accepted draft, that must be paid if it is sold.

   a. How much cash will L.A. Cellular receive if it holds the acceptance until maturity?

   b. How much cash will it receive if it sells the acceptance at once?

   c. Suppose L.A. Cellular's opportunity cost of funds is 8.75% per annum. If it wishes to maximize the present value of its acceptance, should it discount the acceptance?

3. Suppose Minnesota Machines (MM) is trying to price an export order from Russia. Payment is due 9 months after shipping. Given the risks involved, MM would like to factor its receivable without recourse. The factor will charge a monthly discount of 2% plus a fee equal to 1.5% of the face value of the receivable for the nonrecourse financing.

   a. If Minnesota Machines desires revenue of $2.5 million from the sale, after paying all factoring charges, what is the minimum acceptable price it should charge?

   b. Alternatively, CountyBank has offered to discount the receivable, but with recourse, at an annual rate of 14% plus a 1% fee. What price will net MM the $2.5 million it desires to clear from the sale?

   c. On the basis of your answers to Parts a and b, should Minnesota Machines discount or factor its Russian receivables? MM is competing against Nippon Machines for the order, so the higher MM's price, the lower the probability that its bid will be accepted. What other considerations should influence MM's decision?

   d. What other alternatives might be available to MM to finance its sale to Russia?

7. Apex Supplies borrows £1 million at 12%, payable in one year. If Apex is required to maintain a compensating balance of 20%, what is the effective percentage cost of its loan (in pounds)?

8. The Olivera Corporation, a manufacturer of olive oil products, needs to acquire €1 million in funds today to expand a pimiento-stuffing facility. Banca di Roma has offered the company a choice of an 11% loan payable at maturity or a 10% loan on a discount basis. Which loan should Olivera choose?

9. If Consolidated Corporation issues a Eurobond denominated in Japanese yen, the 7% interest rate on the $1 million, 1-year borrowing will be 2% less than rates in the United States. However, ConCorp would have to pay back the principal and interest in yen. Currently, the exchange rate is ¥123 = $1. By how much could the yen rise against the dollar before the Euroyen bond would lose its advantage to ConCorp?

10. Ford can borrow dollars at 12% or Swiss francs at 80% for 1 year. The peso:dollar exchange rate is expected to move from $1 = Fr 1.24 currently to $1 = Fr 1.25 by year's end.

   a. What is the expected after-tax dollar cost of borrowing dollars for one year if the Swiss corporate tax rate is 35%?

   b. What is Ford's expected after-tax dollar cost of borrowing Swiss francs for one year?

   c. At what end-of-year exchange rate will the after-tax Swiss franc cost of borrowing dollars equal the after-tax Swiss franc cost of borrowing francs?

BIBLIOGRAPHY

Abdul J. and H. Saboor, "ExIm Helps SMEs Who Help Themselves," *World Trade*, 19 (April), 2006, pp. 30–34.

Business International Corporation. *Financing Foreign Operations*. New York: BIC, various issues.

Chase World Information Corporation. *Methods of Export Financing*, 2nd ed. New York: Chase World Information Corporation, 1976.

Schneider, G. W. *Export-Import Financing*. New York: The Ronald Press, 1974.

INTERNET RESOURCES

   http://www.export.gov/ Web site that is dedicated to helping U.S. firms learn the costs and risks associated with exporting and develop a strategy for exporting. Contains detailed information on all aspects of exporting, including setting payment terms, financing, logistics, and so on.

   www.exim.gov Web site of the U.S. Export-Import Bank (Eximbank). Contains detailed information on the Eximbank and its various programs.

   www.countertrade.org Web site of the American Countertrade Association (ACA). Contains information on countertrade and links to other relevant Web sites.

www.bloomberg.com Web site of Bloomberg. Contains a wealth of financial and economic information on financial markets and countries worldwide.

www.nacm.org Web site of the National Association of Credit Management (NACM). Provides news and publications on domestic and international credit. Also offers courses and certificate programs in credit management.

INTERNET EXERCISES

1. What programs does the U.S. Eximbank have available to help U.S. exporters?

2. What issues are countertraders currently grappling with?

3. Go to the Web site of a major international bank such as Citigroup (www.citigroup.com) or Bank of America (www.bankofamerica.com). What international trade financing services does this bank provide? How can these services be of value to a multinational company?

4. Using data from Bloomberg, what is the relative cost of short-term borrowing for the countries listed there? Which country has the highest and which has the lowest rates? What might account for the differences in interest rates among these countries?

5. Based on the interest rates found on the Bloomberg Web site, where would you invest excess cash for the next 3 months? What other factors would you want to take into account besides relative interest rates?

6. Go to the Web site of a major international bank such as Citigroup (www.citigroup.com) or Bank of America (www.bankofamerica.com). What treasury services does this bank provide? How can these services be of value to a multinational company?

MANAGING THE MULTINATIONAL FINANCIAL SYSTEM

An injudicious tax offers a great temptation to smuggling. But the penalties of smuggling must rise in proportion to the temptation. The law, contrary to all the ordinary principles of justice, first creates the temptation, and then punishes those who yield to it.

Adam Smith (1776)

The Eiffel Tower is the Empire State Building after taxes.

Anonymous

CHAPTER LEARNING OBJECTIVES

- To identify the principal transfer mechanisms that multinational corporations (MNCs) can use to move money and profits among their various affiliates and to describe their tax, currency control, and cash management implications

- To identify the three principal arbitrage opportunities available to MNCs that stem from their ability to shift profits and funds internally

- To describe the costs and benefits associated with each transfer mechanism, as well as the constraints on their use

- To identify the factors that affect a multinational firm's ability to benefit from its internal financial transfer system

- To describe the information an MNC needs to take full advantage of its internal financial system

KEY TERMS

ad valorem tariff
advance pricing agreement
 (APA)
arm's-length prices
back-to-back loan
dividends
exchange controls
fees and royalties
financial channels
financial market arbitrage
foreign tax credit (FTC)

interaffiliate trade credit
intercompany fund flows
intercompany loan
leading and lagging
multinational financial system
parallel loan
regulatory system arbitrage
Section 482
Subpart F income
tax arbitrage
transfer prices

From a financial management standpoint, one of the distinguishing characteristics of the multinational corporation, in contrast to a collection of independent national firms dealing at arm's length with one another, is its ability to move money and profits among its affiliated companies through internal financial transfer mechanisms. Collectively, these mechanisms make up the **multinational financial system**. These mechanisms include transfer prices on goods and services traded internally, intercompany loans, dividend payments, leading (speeding up) and lagging (slowing down) intercompany payments, and fee and royalty charges. Together, they lead to patterns of profits and movements of funds that would be impossible in the world of Adam Smith.

These internal financial transfers are inherent in an MNC's global approach to international operations, specifically the highly coordinated international interchange of goods (material, parts, subassemblies, and finished products), services (technology, management skills, trademarks, and patents), and capital (equity and debt) that is the hallmark of the modern multinational firm. Indeed, over 38% of U.S. imports and exports are transactions between U.S. firms and their foreign affiliates or parents.[1] Intercompany trade is not confined to U.S. multinationals. Nearly 80% of the two-way trade between the United States and Japan goes from parent to foreign subsidiary or vice versa. So too does 40% of U.S.-European Community trade and 55% of EC-Japan trade. Similarly, nearly 90% of U.S. imports from Ireland are such "related party" trade, as are 75% from Singapore, 62% from Germany, and 61% from Mexico.

This chapter analyzes the benefits, costs, and constraints associated with the multinational financial system. This analysis includes (1) identifying the conditions under which use of this system will increase the value of the firm relative to what it would be if all financial transactions were made at arm's length (that is, between unrelated entities) through external financial channels, (2) describing and evaluating the various channels for moving money and profits internationally, and (3) specifying the design principles for a global approach to managing international fund transfers. We will examine the objectives of such an approach and the various behavioral, informational, legal, and economic factors that help determine its degree of success.

16.1 THE VALUE OF THE MULTINATIONAL FINANCIAL SYSTEM

Financial transactions within an MNC result from the internal transfer of goods, services, technology, and capital. These product and factor flows range from intermediate and finished goods to less tangible items such as management skills, trademarks, and patents. Those transactions not liquidated immediately give rise to some type of financial claim, such as royalties for the use of a patent or accounts receivable for goods sold on credit. In addition, capital investments lead to future flows of dividends and interest and principal repayments. Exhibit 16.1 depicts some of the myriad financial linkages possible in an MNC.

Although all the links portrayed in Exhibit 16.1 can and do exist among independent firms, the MNC has greater control over the mode and timing of these financial transfers.[2]

---

[1] In 2004, Intra-MNC trade accounted for 38.5% of all MNC-associated exports and 41.6% of all MNC-associated imports. See Raymond J. Mataloni, Jr. and Daniel R. Yorgason, "Operations of U.S. Multinational Corporations: Preliminary Results from the 2004 Benchmark Survey," *Survey of Current Business*, November 2006, pp. 37–68.

[2] See Donald R. Lessard, "Transfer Prices, Taxes, and Financial Markets: Implications of Internal Financial Transfers within the Multinational Firm," in *The Economic Effects of Multinational Corporations*, edited by Robert G. Hawkins. (Greenwich, Conn.: JAI Press, 1979); and David P. Rutenberg, "Maneuvering Liquid Assets in a Multinational Company," *Management Science*, June 1970, pp. B671–B684. This section draws extensively from Lessard's article.

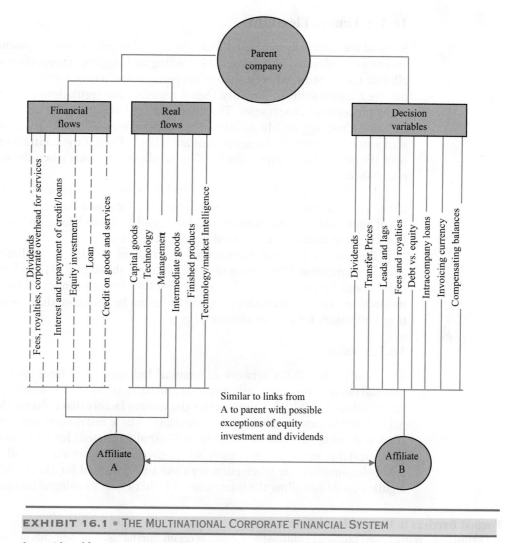

EXHIBIT 16.1 • THE MULTINATIONAL CORPORATE FINANCIAL SYSTEM

Source: Adapted from Figure 1 in Donald R. Lessard, "Transfer Prices, Taxes, and Financial Markets: Implications of Internal Financial Transfers withn the Multinational Firm," in *The Economic Effects of Multinational Corporations*, edited by Robert G. Hawkins (Greenwich, Conn,: JAI Press, JAI Press, 1979), with permission of the author and the publisher.

16.1.1 Mode of Transfer

An MNC has considerable freedom in selecting the **financial channels** through which funds and allocated profits or both are moved. For example, patents and trademarks can be sold outright or transferred in return for a contractual stream of royalty payments. Similarly, an MNC can move profits and cash from one unit to another by adjusting **transfer prices** on intercompany sales and purchases of goods and services. With regard to investment flows, capital can be sent overseas as debt with at least some choice of interest rate, currency of denomination, and repayment schedule, or as equity with returns in the form of dividends. Multinational firms can use these various channels, singly or in combination, to transfer funds internationally, depending on the specific circumstances encountered. Furthermore, within the limits of various national laws and with regard to the relations between a foreign affiliate and its host government, these flows may be more advantageous than those that would result from dealings with independent firms.

16.1.2 Timing Flexibility

Some of the internally generated financial claims require a fixed payment schedule; others can be accelerated or delayed. This **leading and lagging** is most often applied to **inter-affiliate trade credit**, where a change in open account terms, say from 90 to 180 days, can involve massive shifts in liquidity. (Some nations have regulations about the repatriation of the proceeds of export sales. Thus, they do not have complete freedom to move funds by leading and lagging.) In addition, the timing of fee and royalty payments may be modified when all parties to the agreement are related. Even if the contract cannot be altered once the parties have agreed, the MNC generally has latitude when the terms are initially established.

In the absence of **exchange controls**—government regulations that restrict the transfer of funds to nonresidents—firms have the greatest amount of flexibility in the timing of equity claims. The earnings of a foreign affiliate can be retained or used to pay dividends that in turn can be deferred or paid in advance.

Despite the frequent presence of government regulations or limiting contractual arrangements, most MNCs have some flexibility in the timing of fund flows. This latitude is enhanced by the MNC's ability to control the timing of many of the underlying real transactions. For instance, shipping schedules can be altered so that one unit carries additional inventory for a sister affiliate.

16.1.3 Value

The value of the MNC's network of financial linkages stems from the wide variations in national tax systems and significant costs and barriers associated with international financial transfers. Exhibit 16.2 summarizes the various factors that enhance the value of internal, relative to external, financial transactions. These restrictions are usually imposed to allow nations to maintain artificial values (usually inflated) for their currencies. In addition, capital controls are necessary when governments set the cost of local funds at a lower-than-market rate when currency risks are accounted for, that is, when government regulations do not allow the international Fisher effect or interest rate parity to hold.

Formal Barriers to International Transactions
Quantitative restrictions (exchange controls) and direct taxes on international movements of funds
Differential taxation of income streams according to nationality and global tax situation of the owners
Restrictions by nationality of investor and/or investment on access to domestic capital markets

Informal Barriers to International Transactions
Costs of obtaining information
Difficulty of enforcing contracts across national boundaries
Transaction costs
Traditional investment patterns

Imperfections in Domestic Capital Markets
Ceilings on interest rates
Mandatory credit allocations
Limited legal and institutional protection for minority shareholders
Limited liquidity due to thinness of markets
High transaction costs due to small market size and/or monopolistic practices of key financial institutions
Difficulty in obtaining information needed to evaluate securities

Source: Donald R. Lessard, "Transfer Prices, Taxes, and Financial Markets: Implications of Internal Financial Transfers within the Multinational Firm," in *The Economic Effects of Multinational Corporations*, edited by Robert G. Hawkins (Greenwich, Conn,: JAI Press, 1979), with permission by Donald R. Lessard and JAI Press.

EXHIBIT 16.2 • MARKET IMPERFECTIONS THAT ENHANCE THE VALUE OF INTERNAL FINANCIAL TRANSACTIONS

Consequently, the ability to transfer funds and to reallocate profits internally provides multinationals three different types of arbitrage opportunities.

1. **Tax arbitrage**: MNCs can reduce their global tax burden by shifting profits from units located in high-tax nations to those in lower-tax nations. Or they may shift profits from units in a taxpaying position to those with tax losses.

2. **Financial market arbitrage**: By transferring funds among units, MNCs may be able to circumvent exchange controls, earn higher risk-adjusted yields on excess funds, reduce their risk-adjusted cost of borrowed funds, and tap previously unavailable capital sources.

3. **Regulatory system arbitrage**: When subsidiary profits are a function of government regulations (e.g., when a government agency sets allowable prices on the firm's goods) or union pressure, rather than the marketplace, the ability to disguise true profitability by reallocating profits among units may give the multinational firm a negotiating advantage.[3]

A fourth possible arbitrage opportunity is the ability to permit an affiliate to negate the effect of credit restraint or controls in its country of operation. If a government limits access to additional borrowing locally, then the firm able to draw on external sources of funds may not only achieve greater short-term profits but also a more powerful market position over the long term.

At the same time, we must recognize that because most of the gains derive from the MNC's skill at taking advantage of openings in tax laws or regulatory barriers, governments do not always appreciate the MNC's capabilities and global profit-maximizing behavior. MNCs must be aware of the potentially controversial nature of some of these maneuvers and must not put themselves in a position where they lose the goodwill necessary to make them welcome citizens of their host countries.

16.2 INTERCOMPANY FUND-FLOW MECHANISMS: COSTS AND BENEFITS

The MNC can be visualized as *unbundling* the total flow of funds between each pair of affiliates into separate components that are associated with resources transferred in the form of products, capital, services, and technology. For example, dividends, interest, and loan repayments can be matched against the capital invested as equity or debt; fees, royalties, or corporate overhead can be charged for various corporate services, trademarks, or licenses.

The different channels available to the multinational enterprise for moving money and profits internationally include transfer pricing, fee and royalty adjustments, leading and lagging, intercompany loans, dividend adjustments, and investing in the form of debt versus equity. This section examines the costs, benefits, and constraints associated with each of these methods of effecting **intercompany fund flows**. It begins by sketching out some of the tax consequences for U.S.-based MNCs of interaffiliate financial transfers.

16.2.1 Tax Factors

Total tax payments on intercompany fund transfers are dependent on the tax regulations of both the host and the recipient nations. The host country ordinarily has two types of taxes that directly affect tax costs: corporate income taxes and withholding taxes on

---

[3] See Ibid.

dividend, interest, and fee remittances. In addition, several countries, such as Germany and Japan, tax retained earnings at a different (usually higher) rate than earnings paid out as dividends.

Many recipient nations, including the United States, tax income remitted from abroad at the regular corporate tax rate. Where this rate is higher than the foreign tax rate, dividend and other payments will normally entail an incremental tax cost. A number of countries, however, such as Canada, the Netherlands, and France, do not impose any additional taxes on foreign-source income.

As an offset to these additional taxes, most countries, including the United States, provide tax credits for affiliate taxes already paid on the same income. For example, if a subsidiary located overseas has $100 in pretax income, pays $30 in local tax, and then remits the remaining $70 to its U.S. parent in the form of a dividend, the U.S. Internal Revenue Service (IRS) will impose a $35 tax ($0.35 \times \$100$) but will then provide a dollar-for-dollar **foreign tax credit (FTC)** for the $30 already paid in foreign taxes, leaving the parent with a bill for the remaining $5. Excess foreign tax credits from other remittances can be used to offset these additional taxes. For example, if a foreign subsidiary earns $100 before tax, pays $45 in local tax, and then remits the remaining $55 in the form of a dividend, the parent will wind up with an excess FTC of $10, the difference between the $35 U.S. tax owed and the $45 foreign tax paid.

16.2.2 Transfer Pricing

The pricing of goods and services traded internally is one of the most sensitive of all management subjects, and executives typically are reluctant to discuss it. Each government normally presumes that multinationals use *transfer pricing* to its country's detriment. For this reason, a number of home and host governments have set up policing mechanisms to review the transfer pricing policies of MNCs.

The most important uses of transfer pricing include (1) reducing taxes, (2) reducing tariffs, and (3) avoiding exchange controls. Transfer prices also may be used to increase the MNC's share of profits from a joint venture and to disguise an affiliate's true profitability.

Tax Effects The following scenario illustrates the tax effects associated with a change in transfer price. Suppose that affiliate A produces 100,000 circuit boards for $10 apiece and sells them to affiliate B, which, in turn, sells these boards for $22 apiece to an unrelated customer. As shown in Exhibit 16.3, pretax profit for the consolidated company is $1 million regardless of the price at which the goods are transferred from affiliate A to affiliate B.

Nevertheless, because affiliate A's tax rate is 30% whereas affiliate B's tax rate is 50%, consolidated after-tax income will differ depending on the transfer price used. Under the low-markup policy, in which affiliate A sets a unit transfer price of $15, affiliate A pays taxes of $120,000 and affiliate B pays $300,000, for a total tax bill of $420,000 and a consolidated net income of $580,000. Switching to a high-markup policy (a transfer price of $18), affiliate A's taxes rise to $210,000 and affiliate B's decline to $150,000, for combined tax payments of $360,000 and consolidated net income of $640,000. The result of this transfer price increase is to lower total taxes paid by $60,000 and raise consolidated income by the same amount.

In effect, profits are being shifted from a higher to a lower tax jurisdiction. In the extreme case, an affiliate may be making a loss because of high startup costs, heavy depreciation charges, or substantial investments that are expensed. Consequently, it has a zero effective tax rate, and profits channeled to that unit can be received tax-free. The basic rule of thumb to follow if the objective is to minimize taxes is as follows: If affiliate A is

	Affiliate A	*Affiliate B*	*A + B*
Low-Markup policy			
Revenue	1,500	2,200	2,200
Cost of goods sold	1,000	1,500	1,000
Gross profit	500	700	1,200
Other expenses	100	100	200
Income before taxes	400	600	1,000
Taxes (30%/50%)	120	300	420
Net income	280	300	580
High-Markup policy			
Revenue	1,800	2,200	2,200
Cost of goods sold	1,000	1,800	1,000
Gross profit	800	400	1,200
Other expenses	100	100	200
Income before taxes	700	300	1,000
Taxes (30%/50%)	210	150	360
Net income	490	150	640

EXHIBIT 16.3 • Tax Effect of High versus Low Transfer Price ($ thousands)

selling goods to affiliate B, and t_A and t_B are the marginal tax rates of affiliate A and affiliate B, respectively, then

If $t_A > t_B$, set the transfer price as low as possible.
If $t_A < t_B$, set the transfer price as high as possible.

Tariffs   The introduction of tariffs complicates this decision rule. Suppose that affiliate B must pay **ad valorem tariffs**—import duties that are set as a percentage of the value of the imported goods—at the rate of 10%. Then, raising the transfer price will increase the duties that affiliate B must pay, assuming that the tariff is levied on the invoice (transfer) price. The combined tax-plus-tariff effects of the transfer price change are shown in Exhibit 16.4.

Under the low-markup policy, import tariffs of $150,000 are paid. Affiliate B's taxes will decline by $75,000 because tariffs are tax-deductible. Total taxes plus tariffs paid are $495,000. Switching to the high-markup policy raises import duties to $180,000 and simultaneously lowers affiliate B's income taxes by half that amount, or $90,000. Total taxes plus tariffs rise to $450,000. The high-markup policy is still desirable, but its benefit has been reduced by $15,000 to $45,000. In general, the higher the ad valorem tariff relative to the income tax differential, the more likely it is that a low transfer price is desirable.

There are some costs associated with using transfer prices for tax reduction. If the price is too high, tax authorities in the purchaser's (affiliate B's) country will see revenues forgone; if the price is too low, both governments might intervene. Affiliate A's government may view low transfer prices as tax evasion at the same time that the tariff commission in affiliate B's country sees dumping or revenue foregone or both. These costs must be paid for in the form of legal fees, executive time, and penalties.

Most countries have specific regulations governing transfer prices. For instance, **Section 482** of the U.S. Revenue Code calls for **arm's-length prices**—prices at which a willing buyer and a willing unrelated seller would freely agree to transact. The four

	Affiliate A	*Affiliate B*	*A + B*
Low-Markup policy			
Revenue	1,500	2,200	2,200
Cost of goods sold	1,000	1,500	1,000
Import duty (10%)	0	150	150
Gross profit	500	550	1,050
Other expenses	100	100	200
Income before taxes	400	450	850
Taxes (30%/50%)	120	225	345
Net income	280	225	505
High-Markup policy			
Revenue	1,800	2,200	2,200
Cost of goods sold	1,000	1,800	1,000
Import duty	0	180	180
Gross profit	800	220	1,020
Other expenses	100	100	200
Income before taxes	700	120	820
Taxes (30%/50%)	210	60	270
Net income	490	60	550

EXHIBIT 16.4 • Tax Effect of High versus Low Transfer Price ($ thousands)

alternative methods for establishing an arm's-length price, in order of their general acceptability to tax authorities, are as follows:

1. *Comparable uncontrolled price method*: Under this method, the transfer price is set by direct references to prices used in comparable bona fide transactions between enterprises that are independent of each other or between the multinational enterprise group and unrelated parties. In principle, this method is the most appropriate to use, and the easiest. In practice, however, it may be impractical or difficult to apply. For example, differences in quantity, quality, terms, use of trademarks or brand names, time of sale, level of the market, and geography of the market may be grounds for claiming that the sale is not comparable. There is a gradation of comparability: Adjustments can be made easily for freight and insurance but cannot be made accurately for trademarks.

2. *Resale price method*: Under this method, the arm's-length price for a product sold to an associate enterprise for resale is determined by reducing the price at which it is resold to an independent purchaser by an appropriate markup (that is, an amount that covers the reseller's costs and profit). This method is probably most applicable to marketing operations. However, determining an appropriate markup can be difficult, especially where the reseller adds substantially to the value of the product. Thus, there is often quite a bit of leeway in determining a standard markup.

3. *Cost-plus method*: This method adds an appropriate profit markup to the seller's cost to arrive at an arm's-length price. This method is useful in specific situations, such as where semifinished products are sold between related parties or where

one entity is essentially acting as a subcontractor for a related entity. However, ordinarily it is difficult to assess the cost of the product and to determine the appropriate profit markup. In fact, no definition of full cost is given, nor is there a unique formula for prorating shared costs over joint products. Thus, the markup over cost allows room for maneuver.

4. *Another appropriate method*: In some cases, it may be appropriate to use a combination of the above methods, or still other methods (e.g., comparable profits and net yield methods) to arrive at the transfer price. In addition, the U.S. Treasury regulations are quite explicit that while a new market is being established, it is legitimate to charge a lower transfer price.

In light of Section 482 (and the U.S. government's willingness to use it) together with similar authority by most other nations, the current practice of MNCs appears to be setting standard prices for standardized products. However, the innovative nature of the typical multinational ensures a continual stream of new products for which no market equivalent exists. Hence, some leeway is possible on transfer pricing. In addition, although finished products do get traded among affiliates, trade between related parties increasingly is in high-tech, custom-made components and subassemblies (e.g., automobile transmissions and circuit boards) where there are no comparable sales to unrelated buyers. Firms also have a great deal of latitude in setting prices on rejects, scrap, and returned goods. Moreover, as trade in intangible services becomes more important, monitoring transfer prices within MNCs has become extraordinarily complex, creating plentiful opportunities for multinationals to use transfer pricing to shift their overall taxable income from one jurisdiction to another.

ILLUSTRATION   *President Clinton Seeks $45 Billion from Foreign Companies*

One of the linchpins of President Bill Clinton's economic revival plan was a proposal to extract billions from foreign companies doing business in the United States. By closing loopholes and instituting more vigorous enforcement, Clinton said he believed that the federal government could raise $45 billion over 4 years from foreign companies, which take in nearly $1 trillion in U.S. revenue annually. Clinton's contention was based on a view prevalent in the IRS that foreign multinationals were manipulating their transfer prices on goods they sold to their U.S. subsidiaries to avoid paying U.S. tax. For example, IRS data for 1989 showed that the 44,480 domestic companies controlled by foreign entities generated $1 trillion of worldwide sales and had total assets of $1.4 trillion but reported net income of only $11.2 billion, a return on assets of under 1%. However, many analysts are skeptical that much is to be gained by tougher enforcement of Section 482. For example, one government study reportedly found that the IRS had only limited success in recovering additional taxes in transfer pricing cases involving foreign MNCs. From 1987 through 1989, the IRS got only 26.5% of the $757 million it sought.

In addition, the circumstantial evidence the IRS relied on to support its case was suspect. For example, in 1990, the IRS cited as evidence of transfer pricing manipulation the fact that over a 10-year period foreign-controlled companies' (1) gross income had more than doubled and (2) the taxes paid by these companies had hardly changed. However, this argument made no sense because on U.S. tax returns, "gross income" is "sales" less "cost of sales"; thus transfer price manipulation, if any, would reduce "gross income" (by raising the cost of goods sold). Therefore, a doubling of "gross income" could not indicate transfer price manipulation.

One means of dealing with the U.S. government's crackdown on alleged transfer pricing abuses is greater reliance on **advance pricing agreements** (APAs). The APA procedure allows the multinational firm, the IRS, and the foreign tax authority to work out, in advance, a method to calculate transfer prices. APAs are expensive, can take quite a while to negotiate, and involve a great deal of disclosure on the part of the MNC, but if a company wants assurance that its transfer pricing is in order, the APA is a useful tool.

Exchange Controls   Another important use of transfer pricing is to avoid currency controls. For example, in the absence of offsetting foreign tax credits, a U.S. parent will wind up with $\$0.65Q_0$ after tax for each dollar increase in the price at which it sells Q_0 units of a product to an affiliate with blocked funds (based on a U.S. corporate tax rate of 35%). Hence, a transfer price change from P_0 to P_1 will lead to a shift of $0.65(P_1 - P_0)Q_0$ dollars to the parent. The subsidiary, of course, will show a corresponding reduction in its cash balances and taxes, due to its higher expenses.

Bypassing currency restrictions to explains the seeming anomaly whereby subsidiaries operating in LDCs with low tax rates are sold overpriced goods by other units. In effect, companies appear to be willing to pay a tax penalty to access otherwise unavailable funds.

Joint Ventures   Conflicts over transfer pricing often arise when one of the affiliates involved is owned jointly by one or more partners. The outside partners are often suspicious that transfer pricing is being used to shift profits from the joint venture, where they must be shared, to a wholly owned subsidiary. Although there is no pat answer to this problem, the determination of fair transfer prices should be resolved before the establishment of a joint venture. Continuing disputes may still arise, however, over the pricing of new products introduced to an existing venture.

Disguising Profitability   Many LDCs erect high tariff barriers in order to develop import-substituting industries. However, because they are aware of the potential for abuse, many host governments simultaneously attempt to regulate the profits of firms operating in such a protected environment. When confronted by a situation in which profits depend on government regulations, the MNC can use transfer pricing (buying goods from sister affiliates at a higher price) to disguise the true profitability of its local affiliate, enabling it to justify higher local prices. Lower reported profits also may improve a subsidiary's bargaining position in wage negotiations. It is probably for this reason that several international unions have called for fuller disclosure by multinationals of their worldwide accounting data.

Evaluation and Control   Transfer price adjustments will distort the profits of reporting units and create potential difficulties in evaluating managerial performance. In addition, managers evaluated on the basis of these reported profits may have an incentive to behave in ways that are suboptimal for the corporation as a whole.

16.2.3 Reinvoicing Centers

One approach used by some multinationals to disguise profitability, avoid government scrutiny, and coordinate transfer pricing policy is to set up reinvoicing centers in low-tax nations. The reinvoicing center takes title to all goods sold by one corporate unit to another affiliate or to a third-party customer, although the goods move directly from the factory or warehouse location to the purchaser. The center pays the seller and, in turn, is paid by the purchasing unit.

With price quotations coming from one location, it is easier and quicker to implement decisions to have prices reflect changes in currency values. The reinvoicing center also provides a firm with greater flexibility in choosing an invoicing currency. Affiliates can be ordered to pay in other than their local currency if required by the firm's external currency obligations. In this way, the MNC can avoid the costs of converting from one currency to another and then back again.

Having a reinvoicing center can be expensive, however. There are increased communications costs due to the geographical separation of marketing and sales from the production centers. In addition, tax authorities may be suspicious of transactions with an affiliated trading company located in a tax haven.

Before 1962, many U.S. multinationals had reinvoicing companies located in low- or zero-tax countries. By buying low and selling high, U.S. MNCs could siphon off most of the profit on interaffiliate sales with little or no tax liability because the U.S. government at that time did not tax unremitted foreign earnings. This situation changed with the passage of the U.S. Revenue Act of 1962, which declared that reinvoicing-center income is Subpart F income. **Subpart F income** is a category of foreign-source income that is subject to U.S. taxation immediately, whether or not remitted to the United States. For most U.S.-based multinationals, this situation negated the tax benefits associated with a reinvoicing center.

A 1977 ruling by the IRS, however, has increased the value of tax havens in general and reinvoicing centers in particular. That ruling, which allocates to a firm's foreign affiliates certain parent expenses that previously could be written off in the United States, has generated additional foreign tax credits that can be utilized only against U.S. taxes owed on foreign-source income, increasing the value of tax-haven subsidiaries.

A reinvoicing center, by channeling profits overseas, can create Subpart F income to offset these excess FTCs. In effect, foreign tax credits can be substituted for taxes that would otherwise be owed to the United States or to foreign governments. Suppose a firm shifts $100 in profit from a country with a 50% tax rate to a reinvoicing center where the tax rate is only 10%. If this $100 is deemed Subpart F income by the IRS, the U.S. parent will owe an additional $25 in U.S. tax (based on the U.S. corporate tax rate of 35% and the $10 foreign tax credit). However, if the company has excess foreign tax credits available, then each $100 shift in profits can reduce total tax payments by $25, until the excess FTCs are all expended.

16.2.4 Fees and Royalties

Management services such as headquarters advice, allocated overhead, patents, and trademarks are often unique and, therefore, are without a reference market price. The consequent difficulty in pricing these corporate resources makes them suitable for use as additional routes for international fund flows by varying the **fees and royalties** charged for using these intangible factors of production.

Transfer prices for services or intangible assets have the same tax and exchange control effects as those for transfer prices on goods. However, host governments often look with more favor on payments for industrial know-how than for profit remittances. Where restrictions do exist, they are more likely to be modified to permit a fee for technical knowledge than to allow for dividends.

For MNCs, these charges have assumed a somewhat more important role as a conduit for funneling remittances from foreign affiliates. To a certain extent, this trend reflects the fact that many of these payments are tied to overseas sales or assets that increased very rapidly over the past 50 years, as well as the growing importance of tax considerations and exchange controls. For example, by setting low transfer prices on intangibles to manufacturing subsidiaries in low-tax locations such as Puerto Rico or Singapore, multinationals can receive profits essentially tax free.

In recognition of this possibility, the United States in 1986 amended Section 482 to provide that the transfer price of an intangible asset must be "commensurate with the income" the intangible generates. This means in practice that the IRS will not consider a related-party transfer price for an intangible arm's length unless it produces a split in profits between transferor and transferee that falls within the range of profits that unrelated parties realize (1) on similar intangibles, (2) in similar circumstances. Armed with this amendment, the IRS now carefully scrutinizes the pricing of intangibles.

ILLUSTRATION   *Glaxo Gets an Ulcer from the IRS*

In January 2005, GlaxoSmithKline, the world's second largest pharmaceutical company, received a bill from the IRS for almost $5 billion. Glaxo, based in London, said it had paid all its taxes in full to the U.S. government. The dispute centered around what made Zantac–Glaxo's hugely profitable ulcer drug—so valuable. Glaxo claims that Zantac's value largely derived from R&D, because the drug was different enough from its competition to make the U.K. patent that Glaxo U.K. holds the key to its success. According to the IRS, however, as the second ulcer drug in the market (after the pioneer, Tagamet), Zantac's success in the U.S. market was largely attributable to the marketing acumen and distribution capabilities of its U.S. affiliate. This difference of opinion translates into a major transfer pricing issue as the IRS contended that Glaxo U.K. overcharged Glaxo U.S. for the Zantac patent and undercompensated Glaxo U.S. for its valuable marketing and distribution services, thereby artificially reducing U.S. profits subject to U.S. tax. In other words, the dispute revolved around how to divvy up the profits on Zantac between fees to Glaxo U.K. for R&D and fees to Glaxo U.S. for marketing services. The relative value of various intangibles, such as brand names, technology, and know-how, and the appropriate compensation for these intangibles, had become a major area of contention between MNCs and the IRS. On September 11, 2006, while still maintaining the strength of its position, GlaxoSmithKline settled the dispute by agreeing to pay $3.4 billion to the IRS and also dropping its own refund claim of $1.8 in overpaid income taxes. This settlement was the largest in IRS history.

The most common approach to setting fee and royalty charges is for the parent to decide on a desired amount of total fee remittances from the overseas operations, usually based on an allocation of corporate expenses, and then to apportion these charges according to subsidiary sales or assets. This method, which sometimes involves establishing identical licensing agreements with all units, gives these charges the appearance of a legitimate and necessary business expense, thereby aiding in overcoming currency restrictions.

Governments typically prefer prior agreements and steady and predictable payment flows; a sudden change in licensing and service charges is likely to be regarded with suspicion. For this reason, firms try to avoid abrupt changes in their remittance policies. However, where exchange controls exist or are likely, or if there are significant tax advantages, many firms will initially set a higher level of fee and royalty payments while still maintaining a stable remittance policy.

Special problems exist with joint ventures because the parent company will have to obtain permission from its partner(s) to be able to levy charges for its services and licensing contributions. These payments ensure the parent of receiving at least some compensation for the resources it has invested in the joint venture, perhaps in lieu of dividends over which it may have little or no control.

16.2.5 Leading and Lagging

A highly favored means of shifting liquidity among affiliates is an acceleration (**leading**) or delay (**lagging**) in the payment of interaffiliate accounts by modifying the credit terms extended by one unit to another. For example, suppose affiliate A sells goods worth $1 million monthly to affiliate B on 90-day credit terms. Then, on an average, affiliate A has $3 million of accounts receivable from affiliate B and is, in effect, financing $3 million of working capital for affiliate B. If the terms are changed to 180 days, there will be a one-time shift of an additional $3 million to affiliate B. Conversely, reducing credit terms to 30 days will create a flow of $2 million from affiliate B to affiliate A, as shown in Exhibit 16.5.

Shifting Liquidity The value of leading and lagging depends on the opportunity cost of funds to both the paying unit and the recipient. When an affiliate already in a surplus position receives payment, it can invest the additional funds at the prevailing local lending rate; if it requires working capital, the payment received can be used to reduce its borrowings at the borrowing rate. If the paying unit has excess funds, it loses cash that it would have invested at the lending rate; if it is in a deficit position, it has to borrow at the borrowing rate. Assessment of the benefits of shifting liquidity among affiliates requires that these borrowing and lending rates be calculated on an after-tax dollar (HC) basis.

Suppose, for example, that a multinational company faces the following effective, after-tax dollar borrowing and lending rates in Germany and the United States:

	Borrowing Rate (%)	**Lending Rate (%)**
United States	3.8	2.9
Germany	3.6	2.7

Both the U.S. and German units can have either a surplus (+) or deficit (−) of funds. The four possibilities, along with the domestic interest rates (U.S./German) and interest differentials (U.S. rate − German rate) associated with each state, are as follows:

Affiliate A Sells $1 Million in Goods Monthly to Affiliate B

	Credit Terms		
Balance Sheet Accounts	*Normal* *(90 days)*	*Leading* *(30 days)*	*Lagging* *(180 days)*
Affiliate A Accounts receivable from B	$3,000,000	$1,000,000	$6,000,000
Affiliate B Accounts payable to A	$3,000,000	$1,000,000	$6,000,000
Net cash transfers From B to A		$2,000,000	$0
From A to B		$0	$3,000,000

EXHIBIT 16.5 • FUND-TRANSFER EFFECTS OF LEADING AND LAGGING

		Germany	
		+	−
United States	+	2.9%/2.7% (0.2%)	2.9%/3.6% (−0.7%)
	−	3.8%/2.7% (1.1%)	3.8%/3.6% (0.2%)

For example, if both units have excess funds, then the relevant opportunity costs of funds are the U.S. and German lending rates of 2.9% and 2.7%, respectively, and the associated interest differential (in parentheses) is 0.2%. Similarly, if the U.S. unit requires funds while the German affiliate has a cash surplus, then the relevant rates are the respective U.S. borrowing and German lending rates of 3.8% and 2.7% and the interest differential is 1.1%.

If the interest rate differential is positive, the MNC as a whole—by moving funds to the United States—will either pay less on its borrowing or earn more interest on its investments. This move can be made by leading payments to the United States and lagging payments to Germany. Shifting money to Germany—by leading payments to Germany and lagging them to the United States—will be worthwhile if the interest differential is negative.

Based on the interest differentials in this example, all borrowings should be done in Germany, and surplus funds should be invested in the United States. Only if the U.S. unit has excess cash and the German unit requires funds should money flow into Germany.

For example, suppose the German unit owes $2 million to the U.S. unit. The timing of this payment can be changed by up to 90 days in either direction. Assume that the U.S. unit is borrowing funds, and the German unit has excess cash available. According to the prevailing interest differential of 1.1%, given the current liquidity status of each affiliate, the German unit should speed up, or lead, its payment to the U.S. unit. The net effect of these adjustments is that the U.S. firm can reduce its borrowing by $2 million, and the German unit has $2 million less in cash—all for 90 days. Borrowing costs for the U.S. unit are pared by $19,000 ($2,000,000 × 0.038 × 90/360), and the German unit's interest income is reduced by $13,500 ($2,000,000 × 0.027 × 90/360). There is a net savings of $5,500. The savings could be computed more directly by using the relevant interest differential of 1.1% as follows: $2,000,000 × 0.011 × 90/360 = $5,500.

Advantages   A leading and lagging strategy has several advantages over direct intercompany loans.

- No formal note of indebtedness is needed, and the amount of credit can be adjusted up or down by shortening or lengthening the terms on the accounts. Governments do not always allow such freedom on loans.

- Governments are less likely to interfere with payments on intercompany accounts than on direct loans.

- Section 482 allows intercompany accounts up to six months to be interest free. In contrast, interest must be charged on all intercompany loans. The ability to set a zero interest rate is valuable if the host government does not allow interest payments on parent company loans to be tax deductible or if there are withholding taxes on interest payments.

Government Restrictions As with all other transfer mechanisms, government controls on intercompany credit terms are often tight and are given to abrupt changes. Although appearing straightforward on the surface, these rules are subject to different degrees of government interpretation and sanction. For example, in theory Japan permits firms to employ leads and lags. In reality, however, leading and lagging is very difficult because regulations require that all settlements be made in accordance with the original trade documents unless a very good reason exists for an exception. On the contrary, Sweden, which prohibits import leads, will often lift this restriction for imports of capital goods.

16.2.6 Intercompany Loans

A principal means of financing foreign operations and moving funds internationally is to engage in intercompany lending activities. The making and repaying of **intercompany loans** is often the only legitimate transfer mechanism available to the MNC.

Intercompany loans are more valuable to the firm than arm's-length transactions only if at least one of the following market distortions exist: (1) credit rationing (due to a ceiling on local interest rates), (2) currency controls, or (3) differential tax rates among countries. This list is not particularly restrictive because it is rare the MNC faces none of these situations in its international operations.

Although various types of intercompany loans exist, the most important methods at present are direct loans, back-to-back financing, and parallel loans. *Direct loans* are straight extensions of credit from the parent to an affiliate or from one affiliate to another. The other types of intercompany loans typically involve an intermediary.

Back-to-Back Loans. **Back-to-back loans**, also called *fronting loans* or *link financing*, are often employed to finance affiliates located in nations with high interest rates or restricted capital markets, especially when there is a danger of currency controls or when different rates of withholding tax are applied to loans from a financial institution. In the typical arrangement, the parent company deposits funds with a bank in country A that in turn lends the money to a subsidiary in country B. These transactions are shown in Exhibit 16.6. By contrasting these transactions with a direct intercompany loan, the figure reveals that, in effect, a back-to-back loan is an intercompany loan channeled through a bank. From the bank's point of view, the loan is risk free because the parent's deposit fully collateralizes it. The bank simply acts as an intermediary or a front; compensation is provided by the margin between the interest received from the borrowing unit and the rate paid on the parent's deposit.

A back-to-back loan may offer several potential advantages when compared with a direct intercompany loan. Two of the most important advantages are as follows:

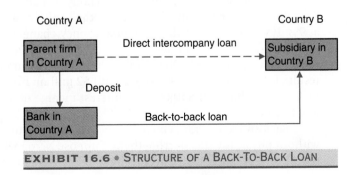

EXHIBIT 16.6 • STRUCTURE OF A BACK-TO-BACK LOAN

1. Certain countries apply different withholding-tax rates to interest paid to a foreign parent and interest paid to a financial institution. A cost saving in the form of lower taxes may be available with a back-to-back loan.

2. If currency controls are imposed, the government usually will permit the local subsidiary to honor the amortization schedule of a loan from a major multinational bank, as stopping payment would hurt the nation's credit rating. Conversely, local monetary authorities would have far fewer reservations about not authorizing the repayment of an intercompany loan. In general, back-to-back financing provides better protection than does a parent loan against expropriation and/or exchange controls.

Some financial managers argue that a back-to-back loan conveys another benefit: The subsidiary seems to have obtained credit from a major bank on its own, possibly enhancing its reputation. However, this appearance is unlikely to be significant in the highly informed international financial community.

The costs of a back-to-back loan are evaluated in the same way as any other financing method (i.e., by considering relevant interest and tax rates and the likelihood of changes in currency value). To see how these calculations should be made, assume that the parent's opportunity cost of funds is 10%, and the parent's and affiliate's marginal tax rates are 34% and 40%, respectively. Then, if the parent earns 8% on its deposit, the bank charges 9% to lend dollars to the affiliate, and the local currency devalues by 11% during the course of the loan, the effective cost of this back-to-back loan equals

Interest cost to parent		Interest income to parent		Interest cost to subsidiary		Tax gain on exchange loss
0.10(0.66)	−	0.08(0.66)	+	0.09(0.6)	−	0.40(0.11) = 2.32%

Variations on the back-to-back loan include the parent depositing dollars while the bank lends out local currency, or a foreign affiliate placing the deposit in any of several currencies with the bank loan being denominated in the same or a different currency. To calculate the costs of these variations would require modifying the methodology shown previously, but the underlying rationale is the same: Include all interest, tax, and currency effects that accrue to both the borrowing and the lending units and convert these costs to the home currency.

Users of the fronting technique include U.S. companies that have accumulated sizable amounts of money in "captive" insurance firms and holding companies located in low-tax nations. Rather than reinvesting this money overseas (assuming that is the intent) by first paying dividends to the parent company and incurring a large tax liability, some of these companies attempt to recycle their funds indirectly via back-to-back loans.

For example, suppose affiliate A, wholly owned and located in a tax haven, deposits $2 million for one year in a bank at 7%; the bank, in turn, lends this money to affiliate B at 9%. If we assume that there are no currency changes, and if B has an effective tax rate of 50%, then its after-tax interest expense equals $90,000 ($2,000,000 × 0.09 × 0.5). The return to A equals $140,000 ($2,000,000 × 0.07), assuming that A pays no taxes. The net result of this transaction has been to shift $2 million from A to B while realizing a net gain to A + B combined of $50,000 (A's interest income of $140,000 less the after-tax cost to B of $90,000).

Back-to-back arrangements also can be used to access blocked currency funds without physically transferring them. Suppose Xerox wishes to use the excess reais (the plural of *real*, the Brazilian currency) being generated by its Brazilian operation to finance a needed plant expansion in the Philippines, where long-term money is virtually unobtainable. Xerox prefers not to invest additional dollars in the Philippines because of the high probability of a Philippine peso devaluation. Because of stringent Brazilian exchange controls, however, this movement of reais cannot take place directly. However, Xerox may be able to use the worldwide branching facilities of an international bank as a substitute for an internal transfer. For example, suppose the Brazilian branch of J.P. Morgan Chase Bank needs deposits of reais to continue funding its loans in a restrictive credit environment. Chase may be willing to lend Xerox long-term pesos through its branch in the Philippines in return for a deposit of equivalent maturity of reais in Brazil.

In this way, Xerox gets the use of its funds in Brazil and at the same time receives locally denominated funds in the Philippines. Protection is provided against a peso devaluation, although Xerox's funds in reais are, of course, still exposed. The value of this arrangement is based on the relative interest rates involved, anticipated currency changes, and the opportunity cost of the funds being utilized. Given the exchange and credit restrictions and other market imperfections that exist, it is quite possible that both the bank and the client can benefit from this type of arrangement. Negotiation between the two parties will determine how these benefits are to be shared.

Parallel Loans   A **parallel loan** is a method of effectively repatriating blocked funds (at least for the term of the arrangement), circumventing exchange control restrictions, avoiding a premium exchange rate for investments abroad, financing foreign affiliates without incurring additional exchange risk, or obtaining foreign currency financing at attractive rates. As shown in Exhibit 16.7, it consists of two related but separate—that is, parallel—borrowings and usually involves four parties in at least two different countries. In Exhibit 16.7a, a U.S. parent firm wishing to invest in Spain lends dollars to the U.S. affiliate of a Spanish firm that wants to invest in the United States. In return, the Spanish parent lends euros in Spain to the U.S. firm's Spanish subsidiary. Drawdowns, payments of interest, and repayments of principal are made simultaneously. The differential between the rates of interest on the two loans is determined, in theory, by the cost of money in each country and anticipated changes in currency values.

Exhibit 16.7b shows how a parallel loan can be used to access blocked funds. In this instance, the Brazilian affiliate of ITT is generating reais that it is unable to repatriate. It lends this money to the local affiliate of Dow Chemical, which in turn, lends dollars to ITT in the United States. Hence, ITT would have the use of dollars in the United States and Dow would obtain reais in Brazil. In both cases, the parallel transactions are the functional equivalent of direct intercompany loans.

Fees to banks brokering these arrangements usually run from 0.25% to 0.5% of the principal for each side. (Chapter 8 discussed currency swaps, which are an outgrowth of parallel loans.)

16.2.7 Dividends

Dividends are by far the most important means of transferring funds from foreign affiliates to the parent company, typically accounting for more than 50% of all remittances to U.S. firms. Among the various factors that MNCs consider when deciding on dividend payments by their affiliates are taxes, financial statement effects, exchange risk, currency controls, financing requirements, availability and cost of funds, and the parent's dividend payout ratio. Firms differ, however, in the relative importance they place on these variables, as well as in how systematically the variables are incorporated in an overall remittance policy.

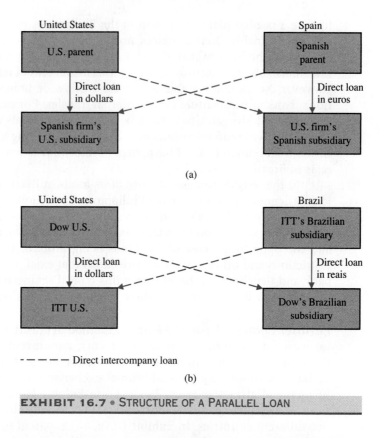

EXHIBIT 16.7 • STRUCTURE OF A PARALLEL LOAN

The parent company's *dividend payout ratio* often plays an important role in determining the dividends to be received from abroad. Some firms require the same payout percentage as the parent's rate for each of their subsidiaries; others set a target payout rate as a percentage of overall foreign-source earnings without attempting to receive the same percentage from each subsidiary. The rationale for focusing on the parent's payout ratio is that the subsidiaries should contribute their share of the dividends paid to the stockholders. Thus, if the parent's payout rate is 60%, then foreign operations should contribute 60% of their earnings toward meeting this goal. Establishing a uniform percentage for each unit, rather than an overall target, is sometimes helpful in persuading foreign governments, particularly those of less-developed countries, that these payments are necessary rather than arbitrary.

Tax Effects   A major consideration behind the dividend decision is the effective tax rate on payments from different affiliates. By varying payout ratios among its foreign subsidiaries, the corporation can reduce its total tax burden.

Once a firm has decided on the amount of dividends to remit from overseas, it can then reduce its tax bill by withdrawing funds from those locations with the lowest transfer costs. Here is a highly simplified example. Suppose a U.S. company, International Products, wishes to withdraw $1 million from abroad in the form of dividends. Each of its three foreign subsidiaries—located in Germany, the Republic of Ireland, and France— has earned $2 million before tax this year and, hence, all are capable of providing the funds. The problem for International Products is to decide on the dividend strategy that will minimize the firm's total tax bill.

The German subsidiary is subject to a split corporate tax rate of 50% on undistributed gross earnings and 36% on dividends, as well as a dividend withholding tax of 10%.

As an export incentive, the Republic of Ireland grants a 15-year tax holiday on all export profits. Because the Irish unit receives all its profits from exports, it pays no taxes. There are no dividend withholding taxes. The French affiliate is taxed at a rate of 45% and must also pay a 10% withholding tax on its dividend remittances. It is assumed that there are no excess foreign tax credits available and that any credits generated cannot be used elsewhere. The U.S. corporate tax rate is 35%. Exhibit 16.8 summarizes the relevant tax consequences of remitting $1 million from each affiliate in turn.

These calculations indicate that it would be cheapest to remit dividends from Germany. By paying this $1 million dividend with its associated total worldwide tax cost of $1.86 million, International Products is actually reducing its worldwide tax costs by $40,000, compared to its total tax bill of $1.9 million in the absence of any dividend.[4] This result is due to the tax penalty that the German government imposes on retained earnings.

Financing Requirements   In addition to their tax consequences, dividend payments lead to liquidity shifts. The value of moving these funds depends on the different opportunity costs of money among the various units of the corporation. For instance, an affiliate that must borrow funds will usually have a higher opportunity cost than a unit with excess cash available. Moreover, some subsidiaries will have access to low-cost financing sources, whereas others have no recourse but to borrow at a relatively high interest rate.

All else being equal, a parent can increase its value by exploiting yield differences among its affiliates—that is, setting a high dividend payout rate for subsidiaries with relatively low opportunity costs of funds while requiring smaller dividend payments from those units facing high borrowing costs or having favorable investment opportunities.

Exchange Controls   Exchange controls are another major factor in the dividend decision. Nations with balance-of-payments problems are apt to restrict the payment of dividends to foreign companies. These controls vary by country, but in general they limit the size of dividend remittances, either in absolute terms or as a percentage of earnings, equity, or registered capital.

Many firms try to reduce the danger of such interference by maintaining a record of consistent dividends. The record is designed to show that these payments are part of an established financial program rather than an act of speculation against the host country's currency. Dividends are paid every year, whether or not they are justified by financial and tax considerations, just to demonstrate a continuing policy to the local government and central bank. Even when they cannot be remitted, dividends are sometimes declared for the same reason, namely, to establish grounds for making future payments when these controls are lifted or modified.

Some companies even set a uniform dividend payout ratio throughout the corporate system to set a global pattern and maintain the principle that affiliates have an obligation to pay dividends to their stockholders. If challenged, the firm then can prove that its French or Brazilian or Italian subsidiaries must pay an equivalent percentage dividend. MNCs often are willing to accept higher tax costs to maintain the principle that dividends are a necessary and legitimate business expense. Many executives believe that a record of paying dividends consistently (or at least declaring them) helps in getting approval for further dividend disbursements.

---

[4] In fact, paying a dividend from Germany could reduce International Products' tax bill even further. As shown in Exhibit 1620.8, International Products will receive a foreign tax credit of $240,351 on the German dividend. To the extent that International Products can use this credit, it can reduce its worldwide tax bill by an additional $240,351.

Location of Foreign Affiliate	Dividend Amount	Host Country Income Tax if Dividend Paid	Host Country Withholding Tax	U.S. Income Tax	Total Taxes if Dividend Paid	Host Country Income Tax if No Dividend Paid	Worldwide Tax Liability if Dividend Paid*
Germany	$1,000,000	$360,000 / 500,000 / $860,000	$100,000	0[1]	$960,000	$1,000,000	$1,860,000
Republic of Ireland	$1,000,000	$0	$0	$350,000	$350,000	$0	$2,250,000
France	$1,000,000	$900,000	$100,000	$0	$1,000,000	$900,000	$2,000,000

[1]Computation of U.S. tax owed

Profit before tax	$2,000,000
Tax ($1,000,000 × 0.50 × $1,000,000 × 0.36)	860,000
Profit after tax	$1,140,000
Dividend paid to U.S. parent company	$1,000,000
Less withholding tax @ 10%	$100,000
Net dividend received in the United States	$900,000
Include in U.S. income	
Gross dividend received	$1,000,000
Foreign indirect tax deemed paid[2]	$754,386
U.S. gross dividend included	$1,754,386
U.S. tax @ 35%	$614,035
Less foreign tax credit[2]	$854,386
Net U.S. tax cost (credit)	$240,351
U.S. tax payable	$0

[2]Computation of indirect and total foreign tax credit

(a) Direct credit for withholding tax	$100,000
(b) Indirect foreign tax credit	

$$\frac{\text{Dividend paid}}{\text{Profit after tax}} \times \text{Foreign tax} = \frac{1,000,000}{1,140,000} \times 860,000 = 754,386$$

Total tax credit	$854,386

EXHIBIT 16.8 • TAX EFFECTS OF DIVIDEND REMITTANCES FROM ABROAD

* Worldwide tax liability if dividend paid equals tax liability for foreign affiliate paying the dividend plus tax liabilities of nondividend-paying affiliates plus any U.S. taxes owed.

Joint Ventures The presence of local stockholders may constrain an MNC's ability to adjust its dividend policy in accordance with global factors. In addition, to the extent that multinationals have a longer term perspective than their local partners, conflicts might arise, with local investors demanding a shorter payback period and the MNC insisting on a higher earnings-retention rate.

16.2.8 Equity versus Debt

Corporate funds invested overseas, whether they are called debt or equity, require the same rate of return, namely, the firm's marginal cost of capital. Nonetheless, MNCs generally prefer to invest in the form of loans rather than equity for several reasons.

First, a firm typically has wider latitude to repatriate funds in the form of interest and loan repayments than as dividends or reductions in equity because the latter fund flows are usually more closely controlled by governments. In addition, a reduction in equity may be frowned upon by the host government and is likely to pose a real problem for a firm trying to repatriate funds in excess of earnings. Withdrawing these funds by way of dividend payments will reduce the affiliate's capital stock, whereas applying this money toward repayment of a loan will not affect the unit's equity account. Moreover, if the firm ever desired to increase its equity investment, it could relatively easily convert the loan into equity.

A second reason for the use of intercompany loans over equity investments is the possibility of reducing taxes. The likelihood of a tax benefit is due to two factors: (1) Interest paid on a loan is ordinarily tax-deductible in the host nation, whereas dividend payments are not; and (2) unlike dividends, principal repayments on the loan do not normally constitute taxable income to the parent company.

For example, suppose General Foods Corporation (GFC) is looking for a way to finance a $1 million expansion in working capital for its Danish affiliate, General Foods Denmark (GFD). The added sales generated by this increase in working capital promise to yield 20% after local tax (but before interest payments), or $200,000 annually, for the foreseeable future. GFC has a choice between investing the $1 million as debt, with an interest rate of 10%, or as equity. GFD pays corporate income tax at the rate of 50% as well as a 10% withholding tax on all dividend and interest payments. Other assumptions are that the parent expects all available funds to be repatriated and that any foreign tax credits generated are unusable.

If the $1 million is financed as an equity investment, the Danish subsidiary will pay the full return as an annual dividend to GFC of $200,000—of which GFC will receive $180,000 net of the withholding tax. Alternatively, if structured as a loan, the investment will be repaid in 10 annual installments of $100,000 each with interest on the remaining balance. Interest is tax-deductible, so the net outflow of cash from GFD is only half the interest payment. It is assumed that the parent does not have to pay additional tax to the United States on dividends received because of the high tax rate on GFD's income. In addition, the interest is received tax-free because of the availability of excess foreign tax credits. All funds remaining after interest and principal repayments are remitted as dividends. In year 5, for example, $100,000 of the $200,000 cash flow is sent to GFC as a loan repayment and $60,000 as interest (on a balance of $600,000). The $30,000 tax saving on the interest payment and the remaining $40,000 on the $200,000 profit are remitted as dividends. Hence, GFC winds up with $217,000 after the withholding tax of $13,000 (on total dividend plus interest payments of $130,000).

The evaluation of these financing alternatives is presented in Exhibit 16.9. If we assume a 15% discount rate, the present value of cash flows under the debt financing plan is $1,102,695. This amount is $199,275 more over the first 10 years of the investment's life than the $903,420 present value using equity financing. The reason for this disparity

			Debt				Equity	
	(1)	(2)	(3)	(4)	(5)	(6)	(7)	(8)
					Cash Flow			Cash Flow
	Principal			Withholding	to Parent		Withholding	to Parent
Year	Repayment	Interest	Dividend	Tax	(1+2+3−4)	Dividend	Tax	(6−7)
1	100,000	100,000	50,000	15,000	235,000	200,000	20,000	180,000
2	100,000	90,000	55,000	14,500	230,500	200,000	20,000	180,000
3	100,000	80,000	60,000	14,000	226,000	200,000	20,000	180,000
4	100,000	70,000	65,000	13,500	221,500	200,000	20,000	180,000
5	100,000	60,000	70,000	13,000	217,000	200,000	20,000	180,000
6	100,000	50,000	75,000	12,500	212,500	200,000	20,000	180,000
7	100,000	40,000	80,000	12,000	208,000	200,000	20,000	180,000
8	100,000	30,000	85,000	11,500	203,500	200,000	20,000	180,000
9	100,000	20,000	90,000	11,000	199,000	200,000	20,000	180,000
10	100,000	10,000	95,000	10,500	194,500	200,000	20,000	180,000
Present value discounted at 15%					$1,102,695			$903,420

EXHIBIT 16.9 • DOLLAR CASH FLOWS UNDER DEBT AND EQUITY FINANCING

is the absence of withholding tax on the loan repayments and the tax deductibility of interest expenses. It is apparent that the higher the interest rate that can be charged on the loan, the larger the cash flows will be. After 10 years, of course, the cash flows are the same under debt and equity financing because all returns will be in the form of dividends.

Alternatively, suppose the same investment and financing plans are available in a country having no income or withholding taxes. This situation increases annual project returns to $400,000. Because no excess foreign tax credits are available, the U.S. government will impose corporate tax at the rate of 35% on all remitted dividends and interest payments. The respective cash flows are presented in Exhibit 16.10. In this situation, the present value under debt financing is $175,657 more ($1,480,537 − $1,304,880) than with equity financing.

Firms do not have complete latitude in choosing their debt-to-equity ratios abroad, though. This subject is frequently open for negotiation with the host governments. In addition, dividends and local borrowings often are restricted to a fixed percentage of equity. A small equity base also can lead to a high return on equity, exposing a company to charges of exploitation.

Another obstacle to taking complete advantage of parent company loans is the U.S. government. The IRS may treat loan repayments as constructive dividends and tax them if it believes the subsidiary is too thinly capitalized. Many executives and tax attorneys feel that the IRS is satisfied as long as the debt-to-equity ratio does not exceed 4 to 1.

Firms normally use guidelines such as 50% of total assets or fixed assets in determining the amount of equity to provide their subsidiaries. These guidelines usually lead to an equity position greater than that required by law, causing MNCs to sacrifice flexibility and pay higher taxes than necessary.

The IRS also has gone after foreign companies operating in the United States that it accuses of "earnings stripping." Earnings stripping occurs when a foreign company uses parent loans instead of equity capital to fund its U.S. activities. The resulting interest payments, particularly on loans used to finance acquisitions in the United States, are deducted from pretax income, leaving minimal earnings to tax.

| | Debt | | | | | Equity | | |
| | (1) | (2) | (3) | (4) | (5) | (6) | (7) | (8) |
Year	Principal Repayment	Interest	Dividend	Withholding Tax	Cash Flow to Parent (1+2+3−4)	Dividend	Withholding Tax	Cash Flow to Parent (6−7)
1	100,000	100,000	200,000	105,000	295,000	400,000	140,000	260,000
2	100,000	90,000	210,000	105,000	295,000	400,000	140,000	260,000
3	100,000	80,000	220,000	105,000	295,000	400,000	140,000	260,000
4	100,000	70,000	230,000	105,000	295,000	400,000	140,000	260,000
5	100,000	60,000	240,000	105,000	295,000	400,000	140,000	260,000
6	100,000	50,000	250,000	105,000	295,000	400,000	140,000	260,000
7	100,000	40,000	260,000	105,000	295,000	400,000	140,000	260,000
8	100,000	30,000	270,000	105,000	295,000	400,000	140,000	260,000
9	100,000	20,000	280,000	105,000	295,000	400,000	140,000	260,000
10	100,000	10,000	290,000	105,000	295,000	400,000	140,000	260,000
Present value discounted at 15%				$1,480,537				$1,304,880

EXHIBIT 16.10 • DOLLAR CASH FLOWS UNDER DEBT AND EQUITY FINANCING

Congress tried to control earnings stripping with a law that took effect in 1989. Under this law, if a heavily indebted U.S. unit pays interest to its foreign parent, the interest deduction is limited to 50% of the unit's taxable income. But that still left a large loophole. The foreign-owned companies continued to take big interest deductions by arranging loans through banks rather than through their parent companies. To reassure the banks, the parent companies provided guarantees.

A law that came into effect in 1994 attempts to close this loophole by treating guaranteed loans as if they were loans from the parent company. U.S. officials expected that foreign companies would convert their loans to their U.S. units into equity, thus generating taxable dividends. But most companies seem to have found new ways to avoid taxes. Some sold assets and leased them back, replacing loans with leases. Others factored accounts receivable or turned mortgages into securities. The net result so far has been few new taxes collected.

16.3 DESIGNING A GLOBAL REMITTANCE POLICY

The task facing international financial executives is to coordinate the use of the various financial linkages in a manner consistent with value maximization for the firm as a whole. This task requires these four interrelated decisions: (1) how much money (if any) to remit, (2) when to do so, (3) where to transmit these funds, and (4) which transfer method(s) to use.

In order to take proper advantage of its internal financial system, the firm must conduct a systematic and comprehensive analysis of the available remittance options and their associated costs and benefits. It also must compare the value of deploying funds in affiliates other than just the remitting subsidiary and the parent. For example, rather than simply deciding whether to keep earnings in Germany or remit them to the U.S. parent, corporate headquarters must consider the possibility and desirability of moving those funds to, say, Italy or France via leading and lagging or transfer price adjustments.

In other words, the key question to be answered is: Where and how in the world can available funds be deployed most profitably? Most multinationals, however, make their dividend remittance decision independently of, say, their royalty or leading and lagging decision rather than considering what mix of transfer mechanisms would be best for the company overall. Given the complexity of determining an optimal allocation across all the financial links with all the affiliates, most parents allow their affiliates to keep just enough cash on hand to meet their fund requirements and require them to send the rest back home.

This limited approach to managing international financial transactions is understandable in view of the tangled web of interaffiliate connections that already has been depicted. Still, compromising with complexity ought not to mean ignoring the system's profit potential. Instead, the MNC should search for relatively high-yield uses of its internal financial system. This task often is made easier by choices that are generally more limited in practice than in theory.

First of all, many of the potential links will be impossible to use because of government regulations and the specifics of the firm's situation. For example, two affiliates might not trade with each other, eliminating the transfer pricing link. Other channels will be severely restricted by government controls.

Furthermore, in many situations, it is not necessary to develop an elaborate mathematical model to figure out the appropriate policy. For example, where a currency is blocked and investment opportunities are lacking or local tax rates are quite high, it normally will be in the company's best interest to shift its funds and profits elsewhere. Where credit rationing exists, a simple decision rule usually suffices: maximize local borrowing. Moreover, most MNCs already have large staffs for data collection and planning, as well as some form of computerized accounting system. These elements can form the basis for a more complete overseas planning effort. In addition, for most multinationals, fewer than 10 affiliates account for an overwhelming majority of intercompany fund flows. Recognizing this situation, several firms have developed systems to optimize fund flows among this limited number of units.

16.4.1 Prerequisites

A number of factors strongly affect an MNC's ability to benefit from its internal financial transfer system. These include the (1) number of financial links, (2) volume of interaffiliate transactions, (3) foreign-affiliate ownership pattern, (4) degree of product and service standardization, and (5) government regulations.

Because each channel has different costs and benefits associated with its use, the wider the range of choice, the greater a firm's ability to achieve specific goals. For example, some links are best suited to avoiding exchange controls, and others are most efficiently employed in reducing taxes. In this vein, a two-way flow of funds will give a firm greater flexibility in deploying its money than if all links are in only one direction. Of course, the larger the volume of flows through these financial arteries, the more funds that can be moved by a given adjustment in intercompany terms. A 1% change in the transfer price on goods flowing between two affiliates will have a 10 times greater absolute effect if annual sales are $10 million rather than $1 million. Similarly, altering credit terms by 30 days will become a more effective means of transferring funds as the volume of intercompany payables and receivables grows.

A large volume of intercompany transactions is usually associated with the worldwide dispersal and rationalization of production activities. As plants specialize in different components and stages of production, interaffiliate trade increases, as do the accompanying financial flows. Clearly, 100% ownership of all foreign affiliates removes a major impediment to the efficient allocation of funds worldwide. The existence of joint ventures is likely to confine a firm's transfer activities to a set of mutually agreed rules, eliminating its ability to react swiftly to changed circumstances.

The more standardized its products and services are, the less latitude an MNC has to adjust its transfer prices and fees and royalties. Conversely, a high-technology input, strong product differentiation, and short product life cycle enhance a company's ability to make use of its mechanisms for transfer pricing and fee adjustments. The latter situation is more typical of the MNC, so it is not surprising that the issue of transfer pricing is a bone of contention between multinationals and governments.

Last, and most important, government regulations exert a continuing influence on international financial transactions. It is interesting to note that government tax, credit allocation, and exchange control policies provide firms the principal incentives to engage in international fund maneuvers while at the same time government regulations most impede these flows.

16.4.2 Information Requirements

In order to take full advantage of its global financial system, a multinational firm needs detailed information on affiliate financing requirements, sources and costs of external credit, local investment yields, available financial channels, volume of interaffiliate transactions, all relevant tax factors, and government restrictions and regulations on fund flows.

Without belaboring the points already made, it is clear that the costs and benefits of operating an integrated financial system depend on the funds and transfer options available, as well as on the opportunity costs of money for different affiliates and the tax effects associated with these transfer mechanisms. Hence, the implementation of centralized decision making requires information concerning all these factors.

16.4.3 Behavioral Consequences

Manipulating transfer prices on goods and services, adjusting dividend payments, and leading and lagging remittances lead to a reallocation of profits and liquidity among a firm's affiliates. Although the aim of this corporate intervention is to boost after-tax global profits, it may actually destroy incentive systems based on profit centers and cause confusion and computational chaos. Subsidiaries may rebel when asked to undertake actions that will benefit the corporation as a whole but will adversely affect their own performance evaluations. To counter this reaction, a firm must clearly spell out the rules and adjust profit center results to reflect true affiliate earnings rather than the distorted remnants of a global profit-maximizing exercise.

16.4 SUMMARY AND CONCLUSIONS

This chapter examined a variety of fund-shifting mechanisms. Corporate objectives associated with the use of these techniques include financing foreign operations, reducing interest and tax costs, and removing blocked funds.

It is apparent after examining these goals that there are trade-offs involved. For instance, removing blocked funds from a low-tax nation is likely to raise the firm's worldwide tax bill. Similarly, reducing exchange risk often results in higher interest expenses and adds to the financing needs of affiliates in soft-currency nations. The realistic weight that should be assigned to each of these goals depends on the individual impact of each goal on corporate profitability. Focusing on just one or two of these goals, such as avoiding exchange risk or minimizing taxes, to the exclusion of all others will probably lead to suboptimal decisions.

The recommended global approach to managing fund transfers is best illustrated by the creative use of financial linkages, whereby one unit becomes a conduit for the movement of funds elsewhere. For example, requiring affiliate A to remit dividends to its parent while financing this withdrawal by lowering transfer prices on goods sold to affiliate A by affiliate B will reduce income taxes and/or customs duties in the process. Or cash can be shifted from A to B through leading and lagging, with these same funds moved on to affiliate C by adjusting royalties or repaying a loan. Taking advantage of being multinational means remitting funds to the parent and other affiliates via royalties and licensing fees from some countries, dividend payments from other nations, and loan repayments from still others. All these maneuvers are to be coordinated with an eye toward maximizing corporate benefits.

It is apparent that the major benefit expected from engaging in these maneuvers comes from government actions that distort the risk-return trade-offs associated with borrowing or lending in different currencies or that alter after-tax returns because of tax asymmetries. The fact that a particular action is legal and profitable, however, does not necessarily mean it should be undertaken. When devising currency, credit, and tax regulations, governments obviously have other goals in mind besides creating profitable arbitrage opportunities for multinational firms. A company that consistently attempts to apply a "sharp pencil" and take maximum advantage of these arbitrage opportunities may optimize short-run profits, but this "penciling" is likely to be done at the expense of long-run profits.

The notion of being a good corporate citizen may be an amorphous concept, but firms that are perceived as being short-run profit-oriented may face questions regarding their legitimacy. More and more, multinationals are dependent on the goodwill of home and host governments, and actions that undermine this key factor may reduce the viability of their foreign operations.

Thus, it may well be worthwhile to pass up opportunities to make higher profits today if those profits are gained at the expense of the corporation's long-run international existence. As in all business decisions, of course, it is important to evaluate the costs and benefits associated with particular actions. Such evaluation has been the goal of this chapter in the area of intercompany fund flows.

QUESTIONS

1. a. What is the internal financial transfer system of the multinational firm?

   b. What are its distinguishing characteristics?

   c. What are the different modes of internal fund transfers available to the MNC?

2. How does the internal financial transfer system add value to the multinational firm?

3. California, like several other states, applies the unitary method of taxation to firms doing business within the state. Under the unitary method, a state determines the tax on a company's worldwide profit through a formula based on the share of the company's sales, assets, and payroll falling within the state. In California's case, the share of worldwide profit taxed is calculated as the average of these three factors.

   a. What are the predictable corporate responses to the unitary tax?

   b. What economic motives might help explain why Oregon, Florida, and several other states have eliminated their unitary tax schemes?

4. In comparisons of a multinational firm's reported foreign profits with domestic profits, caution must be exercised. This same caution must also be applied when analyzing the reported profits of the firm's various subsidiaries. Only coincidentally will these reported profits correspond to actual profits.

   a. Describe five different means that MNCs use to manipulate reported profitability among their various units.

   b. What adjustments to its reported figures would be required to compute the true profitability of a firm's foreign operations so as to account for these distortions?

c. Describe at least three reasons that might explain some of these manipulations.

5. It has been found that U.S.-controlled companies, on the average, earned higher returns on their assets as compared to their foreign-controlled counterparts. A number of American politicians have used these figures to argue that there is widespread tax cheating by foreign-owned multinationals.

a. What are some economically plausible reasons (other than tax evasion) that would explain the low rates of return earned by foreign-owned companies in the United States? Consider the consequences of the debt-financed U.S.-investments made by foreign companies as well as the depreciation of the U.S. dollar.

b. Could the differences in returns be attributed to the risks faced by U.S.-controlled companies outside of the U.S. and the foreign-controlled companies operating in the U.S.? Explain.

c. A study reveals that a majority of foreign-controlled companies in the U.S. started their U.S. operations only during the late-1980s, while U.S. controlled companies had been operating abroad for decades before that. Could the difference in returns be explained by experience? If not, why not?

PROBLEMS

1. Suppose Navistar's Canadian subsidiary sells 1,500 trucks monthly to the French affiliate at a transfer price of $27,000 per unit. Assume that the Canadian and French marginal tax rates on corporate income equal 45% and 50%, respectively.

a. Suppose the transfer price can be set at any level between $25,000 and $30,000. At what transfer price will corporate taxes paid be minimized? Explain.

b. Suppose the French government imposes an ad valorem tariff of 15% on imported tractors. How would this tariff affect the optimal transfer pricing strategy?

c. If the transfer price of $27,000 is set in euros and the euro revalues by 5%, what will happen to the firm's overall tax bill? Consider the tax consequences both with and without the 15% tariff.

d. Suppose the transfer price is increased from $27,000 to $30,000 and credit terms are extended from 90 days to 180 days. What are the fund-flow implications of these adjustments?

2. Suppose a U.S. parent owes $5 million to its English affiliate. The timing of this payment can be changed by up to 90 days in either direction. Assume the following effective annualized after-tax dollar borrowing and lending rates in England and the United States.

	Lending (%)	Borrowing (%)
United States	3.2	4.0
England	3.0	3.6

a. If the U.S. parent is borrowing funds while the English affiliate has excess funds, should the parent speed up or slow down its payment to England?

b. What is the net effect of the optimal payment activities in terms of changing the units' borrowing costs and/or interest income?

3. Suppose that DMR SA, located in Switzerland, sells $1 million worth of goods monthly to its affiliate DMR Gmbh, located in Germany. These sales are based on a unit transfer price of $100. Suppose the transfer price is raised to $130 at the same time that credit terms are lengthened from the current 30 days to 60 days.

a. What is the net impact on cash flow for the first 90 days? Assume that the new credit terms apply only to new sales already booked but uncollected.

b. Assume that the tax rate is 25% in Switzerland and 50% in Germany and that revenues are taxed and costs deducted upon sale or purchase of goods, not upon collection. What is the impact on after-tax cash flows for the first 90 days?

4. Suppose a firm earns $1 million before tax in Spain. It pays Spanish tax of $0.52 million and remits the remaining $0.48 million as a dividend to its U.S. parent. Under current U.S. tax law, how much U.S. tax will the parent owe on this dividend?

5. Suppose a French affiliate repatriates as dividends all the after-tax profits it earns. If the French income tax rate is 50% and the dividend withholding tax is 10%, what is the effective tax rate on the French affiliate's before-tax profits, from the standpoint of its U.S. parent?

BIBLIOGRAPHY

Arpan, J. S. *International Intracorporate Pricing*. New York: Praeger; 1972.

Lessard, D. R. Transfer Prices, Taxes, and Financial Markets: Implications of International Financial Transfers within the Multinational Firm. In *The Economic Effects of Multinational Corporations*. Robert G. Hawkins, ed. Greenwich, Conn.: JAI Press; 1979.

Obersteiner, E. Should the Foreign Affiliate Remit Dividends or Reinvest? *Financial Management*, Spring 1973, pp. 88–93.

Robbins, S. M., R. B. Stobaugh, *Money in the Multinational Enterprise*. New York: Basic Books; 1973.

Rutenberg, D. P. Maneuvering Liquid Assets in a Multinational Company. *Management Science*, June 1970, pp. B671–B684.

Zenoff, D. B. Remitting Funds from Foreign Affiliates. *Financial Executive*, March 1968, pp. 46–63.

INTERNET RESOURCES

www.irs.gov Official Web site of the Internal Revenue Service. Provides extensive information on the APA program as well as the APA Study Guide as well as information on tax treaties with various countries.

www.kpmg.com Web site of KPMG, the global accounting and consulting company. Contains information on the various international tax and transfer pricing services it provides. The latest edition of their transfer pricing guide is also available from the site.

http://www.deloitte.com Web site of Deloitte Touche Tohmatsu, another global accounting and consulting firm, that contains information on international tax issues as well as information about the tax and investment climate in several countries. Their publication, "Strategy Matrix for Global Transfer Pricing" can be downloaded from the site.

http://www.ey.com Web site of Ernst & Young. Provides information on foreign taxation and transfer pricing guidelines. The latest version of their "Transfer Pricing Global Reference Guide" is available from the site.

http://www.taxsites.com/international.html Web site that contains links to tax authorities worldwide as well as to other international tax information.

http://www.oecd.org Web site of the Organisation for Economic Co-operation and Development. Provides discussion, documents, statistics, and policy guidelines for transfer pricing and avoiding double taxation in its Center for Tax Policy and Administration site.

INTERNET EXERCISES

1. Based on materials found at the KPMG and Deloitte Web sites, what are some international tax issues that multinationals are concerned about? Which tax issues are the national tax authorities concerned about?

2. Go to the Web site of a major international bank such as Citigroup (www.citigroup.com) or Bank of America (www.bankofamerica.com). What financial services does this bank provide that would be of value to an MNC in managing its multinational financial system?

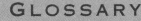

Acceptance A time draft that is accepted by the drawee. Accepting a draft means writing *accepted* across its face, followed by an authorized person's signature and the date. The party accepting a draft incurs the obligation to pay it at maturity.

Accounting Exposure The change in the value of a firm's foreign-currency-denominated accounts due to a change in exchange rates.

Adjusted Present Value The net present value of a project using the all-equity rate as a discount rate. The effects of financing are incorporated in separate terms.

Administrative Pricing Rule IRS rules used to allocate income on export sales to a foreign sales corporation.

Advance Pricing Agreement (APA) Procedure that allows the multinational firm, the IRS, and the foreign tax authority to work out, in advance, a method to calculate transfer prices.

Adverse Incentives *See* moral hazard.

Adverse Selection The possibility that only the highest-risk customers will seek insurance.

Agency Costs Costs that stem from conflicts between managers and stockholders and between stockholders and bondholders.

All-Equity Beta The beta associated with the unleveraged cash flows of a project or company.

All-Equity Rate The discount rate that reflects only the business risks of a project and abstracts from the effects of financing.

All-In Cost The effective interest rate on a loan, calculated as the discount rate that equates the present value of the future interest and principal payments to the net proceeds received by the borrower; it is the internal rate of return on the loan.

American Depository Receipt (ADR) A certificate of ownership issued by a U.S. bank as a convenience to investors in lieu of the underlying foreign corporate shares it holds in custody.

American Option An option that can be exercised at any time up to the expiration date.

American Shares Securities certificates issued in the United States by a transfer agent acting on behalf of the foreign issuer. The certificates represent claims to foreign equities.

American Terms Method of quoting currencies; it is expressed as the number of U.S. dollars per unit of foreign currency.

Appreciation *See* revaluation.

Arbitrage The purchase of securities or commodities on one market for immediate resale on another in order to profit from a price discrepancy.

Arm's-Length Price Price at which a willing buyer and a willing unrelated seller would freely agree to transact (i.e., a market price).

Asiacurrency (or Asiadollar) Market Offshore financial market located in Singapore that channels investment dollars to a number of rapidly growing Southeast Asian countries and provides deposit facilities for those investors with excess funds.

Ask The price at which one can sell a currency. Also known as the offer price.

At-the-Money An option whose exercise price is the same as the spot exchange rate.

Back-to-Back Loan An intercompany loan, also known as a *fronting loan* or *link financing,* that is channeled through a bank.

Balance of Payments Net value of all economic transactions—including trade in goods and services, transfer payments, loans, and investments—between residents of the same country and those of all other countries.

Balance of Trade Net flow of goods (exports minus imports) between countries.

Balance-Sheet Exposure *See* accounting exposure.

Bank Capital The equity capital and other reserves available to protect bank depositors against credit losses.

Bank Draft A draft addressed to a bank. *See also* draft.

Bankers' Acceptance Draft accepted by a bank: *See also* draft.

Bank for International Settlements (BIS) Organization headquartered in Basel that acts as the central bank for the industrial countries' central banks. The BIS helps central banks manage and invest their foreign exchange reserves and also holds deposits of central banks so that reserves are readily available.

Bank Loan Swap *See* debt swap.

Barrier Option *See* knockout option.

Basis Point One hundred basis points equal one percent of interest.

Basis Swap Swap in which two parties exchange floating interest payments based on different reference rates.

Bearer Securities Securities that are unregistered.

Bear Spread A currency spread designed to bet on a currency's decline. It involves buying a put at one strike price and selling another put at a lower strike price.

Beggar-Thy-Neighbor Devaluation A devaluation that is designed to cheapen a nation's currency and thereby increase its exports at others' expense and reduce imports. Such devaluations often led to trade wars.

Beta A measure of the systematic risk faced by an asset or project. Beta is calculated as the covariance between returns on the asset and returns on the market portfolio divided by the variance of returns on the market portfolio.

Bid The price at which one can buy a currency.

Bid-Ask Spread The difference between the buying and selling rates.

Bill of Exchange *See* bank draft.

Bill of Lading A contract between a carrier and an exporter in which the former agrees to carry the latter's goods from port of shipment to port of destination. It is also the exporter's receipt for the goods.

Black Market An illegal market that often arises when price controls or official rationing lead to shortages of goods, services, or assets.

Blocked Currency A currency that is not freely convertible to other currencies due to exchange controls.

Branch A foreign operation incorporated in the home country.

Bretton Woods System International monetary system established after World War II under which each government pledged to maintain a fixed, or pegged, exchange rate for its currency vis-à-vis the dollar or gold. As one ounce of gold was set equal to $35, fixing a currency's gold price was equivalent to setting its exchange rate relative to the dollar. The U.S. government pledged to maintain convertibility of the dollar into gold for foreign official institutions.

Bull Spread A currency spread designed to bet on a currency's appreciation. It involves buying a call at one strike price and selling another call at a higher strike price.

Call Provision Clause giving the borrower the option of retiring the bonds before maturity should interest rates decline sufficiently in the future.

Capital Account Net result of public and private international investment and lending activities.

Capital Asset Pricing Model (CAPM) A model for pricing risk. The CAPM assumes that investors must be compensated for the time value of money plus systematic risk, as measured by an asset's beta.

Capital Flight The transfer of capital abroad in response to fears of political risk.

Capital Market Imperfections Distortions in the pricing of risk, usually attributable to government regulations and asymmetries in the tax treatment of different types of investment income.

Capital Market Integration The situation that exists when real interest rates are determined by the global supply and global demand for funds.

Capital Market Segmentation The situation that exists when real interest rates are determined by local credit conditions.

Capital Productivity The ratio of output (goods and services) to the input of physical capital (plant and equipment).

Cash-Flow Exposure Used synonymously with economic exposure, it measures the extent to which an exchange rate change will change the value of a company through its impact on the present value of the company's future cash flows.

Cash Pooling   *See* pooling.

Central Bank   The nation's official monetary authority.

Chicago Mercantile Exchange (CME)   The largest market in the world for trading standardized futures and options contracts on a wide variety of commodities, including currencies and bonds.

CHIPS   *See* Clearing House Interbank Payments System.

Clean Draft   A draft unaccompanied by any other papers; it is normally used only for nontrade remittances.

Clean Float   *See* free float.

Cleanup Clause   A clause inserted in a bank loan requiring the company to be completely out of debt to the bank for a period of at least 30 days during the year.

Clearing House Interbank Payments System (CHIPS)   A computerized network for transfer of international dollar payments, linking about 140 depository institutions that have offices or affiliates in New York City.

Commercial Invoice   A document that contains an authoritative description of the merchandise shipped, including full details on quality, grades, price per unit, and total value, along with other information on terms of the shipment.

Commercial Paper (CP)   A short-term unsecured promissory note that is generally sold by large corporations on a discount basis to institutional investors and to other corporations.

Compensating Balance   The fraction (usually 10% to 20%) of an outstanding loan balance that a bank requires borrowers to hold on deposit in a non-interest-bearing account.

Concession Agreement   An understanding between a company and the host government that specifies the rules under which the company can operate locally.

Consignment   Under this selling method, goods are only shipped, but not sold, to the importer. The exporter (consignor) retains title to the goods until the importer (consignee) has sold them to a third party. This arrangement is normally made only with a related company because of the large risks involved.

Consular Invoice   An invoice, which varies in its details and information requirements from nation to nation, that is presented to the local consul in exchange for a visa.

Controlled Foreign Corporation (CFC)   A foreign corporation whose voting stock is more than 50% owned by U.S. stockholders, each of whom owns at least 10% of the voting power.

Convertible Bonds   Fixed-rate bonds that are convertible into a given number of shares prior to maturity.

Corporate Governance   The means whereby companies are controlled.

Correspondent Bank   A bank located in any other city, state, or country that provides a service for another bank.

Cost of Equity Capital   The minimum rate of return necessary to induce investors to buy or hold a firm's stock. It equals a basic yield covering the time value of money plus a premium for risk.

Countertrade   A sophisticated form of barter in which the exporting firm is required to take the countervalue of its sale in local goods or services instead of in cash.

Country Risk   General level of political and economic uncertainty in a country affecting the value of loans or investments in that country. From a bank's standpoint, it refers to the possibility that borrowers in a country will be unable to service or repay their debts to foreign lenders in a timely manner.

Covered Interest Arbitrage   Movement of short-term funds between two currencies to take advantage of interest differentials with exchange risk eliminated by means of forward contracts.

Covered Interest Differential   The difference between the domestic interest rate and the hedged foreign interest rate.

Cross-Default Clause   Clause in a loan agreement which says that a default by a borrower to one lender is a default to all lenders.

Cross-Hedge   Hedging exposure in one currency by the use of futures or other contracts on a second currency that is correlated with the first currency.

Cross-Rate   The exchange rate between two currencies, neither of which is the U.S. dollar, calculated by using the dollar rates for both currencies.

Currency Arbitrage   Taking advantage of divergences in exchange rates in different money markets by buying a currency in one market and selling it in another.

Currency Call Option   A financial contract that gives the buyer the right, but not the obligation, to buy a specified number of units of foreign currency from the option seller at a fixed dollar price, up to the option's expiration date.

Currency Collar   A contract that provides protection against currency moves outside an agreed-upon range. It can be created by simultaneously buying an out-of-the-money put option and selling an out-of-the-money call option of the same size. In effect, the purchase of the put option is financed by the sale of the call option.

Currency Controls   *See* exchange controls.

Currency Futures Contract   Contract for future delivery of a specific quantity of a given currency, with the exchange rate fixed at the time the contract is entered. Futures contracts are similar to forward contracts except that they are traded on organized futures exchanges and the gains and losses on the contracts are settled each day.

Currency of Denomination   Currency in which a transaction is stated.

Currency of Determination   Currency whose value determines a given price.

Currency Option   A financial contract that gives the buyer the right, but not the obligation, to buy (call) or sell (put) a specified number of foreign currency units to the option seller at a fixed dollar price, up to the option's expiration date.

Currency Put Option   A financial contract that gives the buyer the right, but not the obligation, to sell a specified number of foreign currency units to the option seller at a fixed dollar price, up to the option's expiration date.

Currency Risk Sharing   An agreement by the parties to a transaction to share the currency risk associated with the transaction. The arrangement involves a customized hedge contract imbedded in the underlying transaction.

Currency Spread   An options position created by buying an option at one strike price and selling a similar option at a different strike price. It allows speculators to bet on the direction of a currency at a lower cost than buying a put or a call option alone but at the cost of limiting the position's upside potential.

Currency Swap   A simultaneous borrowing and lending operation whereby two parties exchange specific amounts of two currencies at the outset at the spot rate. They also exchange interest rate payments in the two currencies. The parties undertake to reverse the exchange after a fixed term at a fixed exchange rate.

Current Account   Net flow of goods, services, and unilateral transactions (gifts) between countries.

Current Assets   Short-term assets, including cash, marketable securities, accounts receivable, and inventory.

Current Exchange Rate   Exchange in effect today.

Current Liabilities   Short-term liabilities, such as accounts payable and loans expected to be repaid within one year.

Current/Noncurrent Method   Under this currency translation method, all of a foreign subsidiary's current assets and liabilities are translated into home currency at the current exchange rate while noncurrent assets and liabilities are translated at the historical exchange rate (that is, at the rate in effect at the time the asset was acquired or the liability incurred).

Current Rate Method   Under this currency translation method, all foreign currency balance-sheet and income items are translated at the current exchange rate.

Cylinder   The payoff profile of a currency collar created through a combined put purchase and call sale.

Debt Relief   Reducing the principal and/or interest payments on LDC loans.

Debt Swap   A set of transactions (also called a debt-equity swap) in which a firm buys a country's dollar bank debt at a discount and swaps this debt with the central bank for local currency that it can use to acquire local equity.

Depreciation   *See* devaluation.

Depreciation Tax Shield   The value of the tax write-off on depreciation of plant and equipment.

Derivatives   Contracts that derive their value from some underlying asset (such as a stock, bond, or currency), reference rate (such as a 90-day Treasury bill rate), or index (such as the S&P 500 stock index). Popular derivatives include swaps, forwards, futures, and options.

Devaluation   A decrease in the spot value of a currency.

Direct Quotation   A quote that gives the home currency price of a foreign currency.

"Dirty" Float   *See* managed float.

Discount Basis   Means of quoting the interest rate on a loan under which the bank deducts the interest in advance.

Discounting   A means of borrowing against a trade or other draft. The exporter or other borrower places the draft with a bank or other financial institution and, in turn, receives the face value of the draft less interest and commissions.

Documentary Draft   A draft accompanied by documents that are to be delivered to the drawee on payment or acceptance of the draft. Typically, these documents include the bill of lading in negotiable form, the commercial invoice, the consular invoice where required, and an insurance certificate.

Down-and-In Option   An option that comes into existence if and only if the currency weakens enough to cross a preset barrier.

Down-and-Out Call   A knockout option that has a positive payoff to the option holder if the underlying currency strengthens but is canceled if it weakens sufficiently to hit the outstrike.

Down-and-Out Put   A knockout option that has a positive payoff if the currency weakens but is canceled if it weakens beyond the outstrike.

Draft   An unconditional order in writing—signed by a person, usually the exporter, and addressed to the importer—ordering the importer or the importer's agent to pay, on demand (sight draft) or at a fixed future date (time draft), the amount specified on its face. Accepting a draft means writing *accepted* across its face, followed by an authorized person's signature and the date. The party accepting a draft incurs the obligation to pay it at maturity.

Dragon Bond   Debt denominated in a foreign currency, usually dollars, but launched, priced, and traded in Asia.

Drawdown   The period over which the borrower may take down the loan.

Dual Currency Bond   Bond that has the issue's proceeds and interest payments stated in foreign currency and the principal repayment stated in dollars.

Dual Syndicate Equity Offering   An international equity placement where the offering is split into two tranches—domestic and foreign—and each tranche is handled by a separate lead manager.

EAFE Index   The Morgan Stanley Capital International Europe, Australia, Far East Index, which reflects the performance of all major stock markets outside of North America.

Economic Exposure   The extent to which the value of the firm will change due to an exchange rate change.

Economies of Scale   Situation in which increasing production leads to a less-than-proportionate increase in cost.

Economies of Scope   Scope economies exist whenever the same investment can support multiple profitable activities less expensively in combination than separately.

Effective Interest Rate   The true cost of a loan; it equals the annual interest paid divided by the funds received.

Efficient Frontier   The set of portfolios that has the smallest possible standard deviation for its level of expected return and has the maximum expected return for a given level of risk.

Efficient Market   One in which new information is readily incorporated in the prices of traded securities.

Electronic Trading System   A system used in the foreign exchange market that offers automated matching. Traders can enter buy and sell orders directly into their terminals on an anonymous basis, and these prices will be visible to all market participants. Another trader, anywhere in the world, can execute a trade by simply hitting two buttons.

Emerging Markets A term that encompasses the stock markets in all of South and Central America; all of the Far East with the exception of Japan, Australia, and New Zealand; all of Africa; and parts of Southern Europe, as well as Eastern Europe and countries of the former Soviet Union.

Equity-Related Bonds Bonds that combine features of the underlying bond and common stock. The two principal types of equity-related bonds are convertible bonds and bonds with equity warrants.

Equity Warrants Securities that give their holder the right to buy a specified number of shares of common stock at a specified price during a designated time period.

Euro New currency created for members of the European Monetary Union and issued by the European Central Bank. Coins and bills denominated in the euro will be unavailable until 2002.

Eurobank A bank that accepts and makes loans in Eurocurrencies.

Eurobond A bond sold outside the country in whose currency it is denominated.

Eurobond Market Market in which Eurobonds are issued and traded.

Euro-Commercial Paper (Euro-CP) Euronotes that are not underwritten.

Eurocurrency A currency deposited in a bank outside the country of its origin.

Eurocurrency Market The set of banks that accept deposits and make loans in Eurocurrencies.

Eurodollar A U.S. dollar on deposit outside the United States.

Eurodollar Future A cash-settled futures contract on a three-month, $1,000,000 Eurodollar deposit that pays LIBOR.

Euroequity Issue A syndicated equity offering placed throughout Europe and handled by one lead manager.

Euro-Medium Term Note (Euro-MTN) A non-under-written Euronote issued directly to the market. Euro-MTNs are offered continuously rather than all at once like a bond issue. Most Euro-MTN maturities are under five years.

Euronote A short-term note issued outside the country of the currency it is denominated in.

Europe, Australia, Far East (EAFE) Index An index put out by Morgan Stanley Capital International which tracks the performance of the 20 major stock markets outside of North America.

European Central Bank The central bank for the European Monetary Union. It has the sole power to issue a single European currency called the euro.

European Currency Unit (ECU) A composite currency, consisting of fixed amounts of 12 European currencies.

European Investment Bank (EIB) A development bank that offers funds for certain public and private projects in European and other nations associated with the European Community.

European Monetary System (EMS) Monetary system formed by the major European countries under which the members agree to maintain their exchange rates within a specific margin around agreed-upon, fixed central exchange rates. These central exchange rates are denominated in currency units per ECU.

European Monetary Union Eleven members of the European Community who have joined together to establish a single central bank (the European Central Bank) that issues a common European currency (usually referred to as the euro).

European Option An option that can be exercised only at maturity.

European Terms Method of quoting currencies; it is expressed as the number of foreign currency units per U.S. dollar.

European Union Organization of fifteen European nations whose purpose is to promote economic harmonization and tear down barriers to trade and commerce within Europe.

Exchange Controls Restrictions placed on the transfer of a currency from one nation to another.

Exchange Rate Mechanism (ERM) Arrangement at the heart of the European Monetary System which allows each member of the EMS to determine a mutually agreed-on central exchange rate for its currency; each rate is denominated in currency units per ECU.

Exchange Risk The variability of a firm's (or asset's) value that is due to uncertain exchange rate changes.

Exercise Price The price at which an option is exercised. Also known as strike price.

Export-Import Bank (Eximbank) U.S. government agency dedicated to facilitating U.S. exports, primarily through subsidized export financing.

Exposure Netting Offsetting exposures in one currency with exposures in the same or another currency, where exchange rates are expected to move in such a way that losses (gains) on the first exposed position should be offset by gains (losses) on the second currency exposure.

Expropriation The taking of foreign property, with or without compensation, by a government.

Factor Specialized buyer, at a discount, of company receivables.

FASB No. 8 *See* Statement of Financial Accounting Standards No. 8.

FASB No. 52 *See* Statement of Financial Accounting Standards No. 52.

FASB No. 133 *See* Statement of Financial Accounting Standards No. 133.

FedWire The Federal Reserve network for transferring fed funds.

Fiat Money Nonconvertible paper money.

Financial Accounting Standards Board Organization in the United States that sets the rules that govern the presentation of financial statements and resolves other accounting issues.

Financial Channels The various ways in which funds, allocated profits, or both are transferred within the multinational corporation.

Financial Deregulation The dismantling of various regulations that restrict the nature of financial contracts that consenting parties, such as borrowers and lenders, could enter into.

Financial Economics A discipline that emphasizes the use of economic analysis to understand the basic workings of financial markets, particularly the measurement and pricing of risk and the intertemporal allocation of funds.

Financial Innovation The process of segmenting, transferring, and diversifying risk to lower the cost of capital as well as creating new securities that avoid various tax and regulatory costs.

Fisher Effect States that the nominal interest differential between two countries should equal the inflation differential between those countries.

Fixed Exchange Rate An exchange rate whose value is fixed by the governments involved.

Fixed-Rate Bonds Bonds that have a fixed coupon, set maturity date, and full repayment of the principal amount at maturity.

Floating Currency A currency whose value is set by market forces.

Floating Exchange Rate An exchange rate whose value is determined in the foreign exchange market.

Floating-Rate Bond A bond whose interest rate is reset every three to six months, or so, at a fixed margin above a mutually agreed-upon interest rate "index" such as LIBOR for Eurodollar deposits, the corresponding Treasury bill rate, or the prime rate.

Foreign Bank Market That portion of domestic bank loans supplied to foreigners for use abroad.

Foreign Bond Market That portion of the domestic bond market that represents issues floated by foreign companies or governments.

Foreign Credit Insurance Association The FCIA is a cooperative effort of Eximbank and a group of approximately 50 of the leading marine, casualty, and property insurance companies that administers the U.S. government's export-credit insurance program. FCIA insurance offers protection from political and commercial risks to U.S. exporters: The private insurers cover commercial risks, and the Eximbank covers political risks.

Foreign Direct Investment The acquisition abroad of physical assets such as plant and equipment, with operating control residing in the parent corporation.

Foreign Equity Market That portion of the domestic equity market that represents issues floated by foreign companies.

Foreign Exchange Brokers Specialists in matching net supplier and demander banks in the foreign exchange market.

Foreign Exchange Market Intervention Official purchases and sales of foreign exchange that nations undertake through their central banks to influence their currencies.

Foreign Exchange Risk *See* exchange risk.

Foreign Market Beta A measure of foreign market risk that is derived from the capital asset pricing model and is calculated relative to the U.S. market in the same way that individual asset betas are calculated.

Foreign Sales Corporation (FSC) A special type of corporation created by the Tax Reform Act of 1986 that is designed to provide a tax incentive for exporting U.S.-produced goods.

Foreign Tax Credit Home country credit against domestic income tax for foreign taxes already paid on foreign-source earnings.

Forfaiting The discounting—at a fixed rate without recourse—of medium-term export receivables denominated in fully convertible currencies (e.g., U.S. dollar, Swiss franc, Deutsche mark).

Forward Contract Agreement between a bank and a customer (which could be another bank) that calls for delivery, at a fixed future date, of a specified amount of one currency against dollar payment; the exchange rate is fixed at the time the contract is entered into.

Forward Differential The forward discount or premium on a currency expressed as an annualized percentage of the spot rate.

Forward Discount A situation that pertains when the forward rate expressed in dollars is below the spot rate.

Forward Forward A contract that fixes an interest rate today on a future loan or deposit.

Forward Market Hedge The use of forward contracts to fix the home currency value of future foreign currency cash flows. Specifically, a company that is long a foreign currency will sell the foreign currency forward, whereas a company that is short a foreign currency will buy the currency forward.

Forward Premium A situation that pertains when the forward rate expressed in dollars is above the spot rate.

Forward Rate The rate quoted today for delivery at a fixed future date of a specified amount of one currency against dollar payment.

Forward Rate Agreement (FRA) A cash-settled, over-the-counter forward contract that allows a company to fix an interest rate to be applied to a specified future interest period on a notional principal amount.

Free Float An exchange rate system characterized by the absence of government intervention. Also known as a **clean float**.

Functional Currency As defined in FASB 52, an affiliate's functional currency is the currency of the primary economic environment in which the affiliate generates and expends cash.

Fundamental Analysis An approach to forecasting asset prices that relies on painstaking examination of the macroeconomic variables and policies that are likely to influence the asset's prospects.

Funds Adjustment A hedging technique designed to reduce a firm's local currency accounting exposure by altering either the amounts or the currencies (or both) of the planned cash flows of the parent or its subsidiaries.

Futures Contracts Standardized contracts that trade on organized futures markets for specific delivery dates only.

Futures Option An option contract calling for delivery of a standardized IMM futures contract in the currency rather than the currency itself.

G-5 Nations The United States, France, Japan, Great Britain, and Germany.

G-7 Nations The G-5 nations plus Italy and Canada.

Global Capital Asset Pricing Model (Global CAPM) Implementation of the CAPM in which the base portfolio against which beta is estimated is the global market portfolio and the market risk premium is based on the expected return on the global market portfolio. This model is appropriate if capital markets are globally integrated.

Global Fund A mutual fund that can invest anywhere in the world, including the United States.

Gold Standard A system of setting currency values whereby the participating countries commit to fix the prices of their domestic currencies in terms of a specified amount of gold.

Good Funds Funds that are available for use.

Government Budget Deficit A closely watched figure that equals government spending minus taxes.

Growth Options The opportunities a company may have to invest capital so as to increase the profitability of its existing product lines and benefit from expanding into new products or markets.

Hard Currency   A currency expected to maintain its value or appreciate.

Hedge   To enter into a forward contract in order to protect the home currency value of foreign-currency-denominated assets or liabilities.

Herstatt Risk   Named after a German bank that went bankrupt, this is the risk that a bank will deliver currency on one side of a foreign exchange deal only to find that its counterparty has not sent any money in return. Also known as settlement risk.

Historical Exchange Rate   In accounting terminology, it refers to the rate in effect at the time a foreign currency asset was acquired or a liability incurred.

Home Bias   The tendency of investors to hold domestic assets in their investment portfolios.

Hyperinflationary Country   Defined in FASB-52 as one that has cumulative inflation of approximately 100% or more over a three-year period.

IFC Emerging Markets Index   An index of developing country stock markets published by the International Finance Corporation.

Import-Substitution Development Strategy   A development strategy followed by many Latin American countries and other LDCs that emphasized import substitution—accomplished through protectionism—as the route to economic growth.

Indexed Bond   Bond that pays interest tied to the inflation rate. The intent is to fix the real interest rate on the bond.

Indirect Quotation   A quote that gives the foreign currency price of the home currency.

Inflation   Change in the general level of prices.

Inflation Risk   Refers to the divergence between actual and expected inflation.

Interbank Market   The wholesale foreign exchange market in which major banks trade currencies with each other.

Intercompany Loan   Loan made by one unit of a corporation to another unit of the same corporation.

Intercompany Transaction   Transaction, such as a loan, carried out between two units of the same corporation.

Interest Rate/Currency Swap   Swap that combines the features of both a currency swap and an interest rate swap. It converts a liability in one currency with a stipulated type of interest payment into one denominated in another currency with a different type of interest payment.

Interest Rate Parity   A condition whereby the interest differential between two currencies is (approximately) equal to the forward differential between two currencies.

Interest Rate Swap   An agreement between two parties to exchange interest payments for a specific maturity on an agreed upon principal amount. The most common interest rate swap involves exchanging fixed interest payments for floating interest payments.

Interest Tax Shield   The value of the tax write-off on interest payments (analogous to the depreciation tax shield).

International Bank for Reconstruction and Development (IBRD)   Also known as the World Bank, the IBRD is owned by its member nations and makes loans at nearly conventional terms to countries for projects of high economic priority.

International Banking Facility (IBF)   A bookkeeping entity of a U.S. financial institution that is permitted to conduct international banking business (such as receiving foreign deposits and making foreign loans) largely exempt from domestic regulatory constraints.

International Diversification   The attempt to reduce risk by investing in more than one nation. By diversifying across nations whose economic cycles are not perfectly in phase, investors can typically reduce the variability of their returns.

International Fisher Effect   States that the interest differential between two countries should be an unbiased predictor of the future change in the spot rate.

International Fund   A mutual fund that can invest only outside the United States.

International Monetary Fund (IMF)   International organization created at Bretton Woods, N.H., in 1944 to promote exchange rate stability, including the provision of temporary assistance to member nations trying to defend their currencies against transitory phenomena.

International Monetary Market (IMM)   The IMM is a market created by the Chicago Mercantile Exchange for the purpose of trading currency futures.

International Monetary System   The set of policies, institutions, practices, regulations, and mechanisms that determine the rate at which one currency is exchanged for another.

In-the-Money   An option that would be profitable to exercise at the current price.

Intrinsic Value   The value of an option that is attributable to its being in-the-money. An out-of-the money option has no intrinsic value.

Investment Banker   A financing specialist who assists organizations in designing and marketing security issues.

Irrevocable Letter of Credit   An L/C that cannot be revoked without the specific permission of all parties concerned, including the exporter.

J-Curve   Theory that says a country's trade deficit will initially worsen after its currency depreciates because higher prices on foreign imports will more than offset the reduced volume of imports in the short run.

Keiretsu   The large industrial groupings—often with a major bank at the centers—that form the backbone of corporate Japan.

Knockout Option   An option that is similar to a standard option except that it is canceled—that is, knocked out—if the exchange rate crosses, even briefly, a pre-defined level called the outstrike. If the exchange rate breaches this barrier, the holder cannot exercise this option, even if it ends up in-the-money. Also known as barrier options.

Law of One Price   The theory that exchange-adjusted prices on identical tradeable goods and financial assets must be within transaction costs of equality worldwide.

L/C   *See* letter of credit.

LDC Debit-Equity Swap   *See* debt swap.

LDC Debt Swap   *See* debt swap.

Leading and Lagging   A means of shifting liquidity by accelerating (leading) and delaying (lagging) international payments by modifying credit terms, normally on trade between affiliates.

Lean Production   Ultra-efficient manufacturing techniques pioneered by Japanese industry that gave it a formidable competitive edge over U.S. rivals.

Lender of Last Resort   Official institution that lends funds to countries or banks that get into financial trouble. It is designed to avert the threat of a financial panic.

Letter of Credit   A letter addressed to the seller, written and signed by a bank acting on behalf of the buyer, in which the bank promises to honor drafts drawn on itself if the seller conforms to the specific conditions contained in the letter.

Line of Credit   An informal agreement that permits a company to borrow up to a stated maximum amount from a bank. The firm can draw down its line of credit when it requires funds and pay back the loan balance when it has excess cash.

Link Financing   *See* back-to-back loan.

Liquidity   The ability to readily exchange an asset for goods or other assets at a known price, thereby facilitating economic transactions. It is usually measured by the difference between the rates at which dealers can buy and sell that asset.

Listed Options   Option contracts with prespecified terms (amount, strike price, expiration date, fixed maturity) that are traded on an organized exchange.

Loan Syndication   Group of banks sharing a loan.

Lock Box   A postal box in a company's name to which customers remit their required payments.

London Interbank Bid Rate (LIBID)   The rate paid by one bank to another for a deposit.

London Interbank Offer Rate (LIBOR)   The deposit rate on interbank transactions in the Eurocurrency market.

Long Position   In the foreign exchange market, it means that one has more assets in a particular currency than liabilities.

Look-Thru   A method for calculating U.S. taxes owed on income from controlled foreign corporations that was introduced by the Tax Reform Act of 1986.

Louvre Accord   Named for the Paris landmark where it was negotiated, this accord called for the G-7 nations to support the falling dollar by pegging exchange rates within a narrow, undisclosed range, while they also moved to bring their economic policies into line.

Maastricht Criteria   Tough standards on inflation, currency stability, and deficit spending established in the Maastricht Treaty that European nations must meet in order to join EMU.

Maastricht Treaty Agreement under which the EC nations would establish a European Monetary Union with a single central bank having the sole power to issue a single European currency called the euro.

Managed Float Also known as a "dirty" float, this is a system of floating exchange rates with central bank intervention to reduce currency fluctuations.

Market Efficiency A market in which the prices of traded securities readily incorporate new information.

Market Risk Premium The difference between the required return on a particular stock market and the risk-free interest rate.

Marking to Market A daily settlement feature in which profits and losses of futures contracts are paid over every day at the end of trading. More generally, this term refers to pricing assets at their market value rather than their book value.

Monetary/Nonmonetary Method Under this translation method, monetary items (for example, cash, accounts payable and receivable, and long-term debt) are translated at the current rate while nonmonetary items (for example, inventory, fixed assets, and longterm investments) are translated at historical rates.

Monetary Union A group of states that join together to have a single central bank that issues a common currency.

Money-Market Hedge The use of simultaneous borrowing and lending transactions in two different currencies to lock in the home currency value of a foreign currency transaction.

Moral Hazard The tendency to incur risks that one is protected against.

Morgan Stanley Capital International World Index An internationally diversified index of developed country stock markets that combines the EAFE index with the U.S. market index.

Multicurrency Clause This clause gives a Eurocurrency borrower the right to switch from one currency to another when the loan is rolled over.

Multinational Cash Mobilization A system designed to optimize the use of funds by tracking current and near-term cash positions and redeploying those funds in an efficient manner.

Multinational Financial System The aggregate of the internal transfer mechanisms available to the MNC to shift profits and money among its various affiliates. These transfer mechanisms include transfer price adjustments, leading and lagging interaffiliate payments, dividend payments, fees and royalties, intercompany loans, and intercompany equity investments.

Nationalization The taking of property, with or without compensation, by a government.

Net Liquidity Balance The change in private domestic borrowing or lending that is required to keep payments in balance without adjusting official reserves. Nonliquid, private, short-term capital flows and errors and omissions are included in the balance; liquid assets and liabilities are excluded.

Netting *See* exposure netting; payments netting.

No-Arbitrage Condition The relationship between exchange rates such that profitable arbitrage opportunities don't exist. If this condition is violated on an ongoing basis, we would wind up with a money machine.

Nominal Exchange Rate The actual exchange rate; it is expressed in current units of currency.

Nominal Interest Rate The price quoted on lending and borrowing transactions. It is expressed as the rate of exchange between current and future units of currency unadjusted for inflation.

Nonrecourse Method of borrowing against an asset, such as a receivable, under which the lender assumes all the credit and political risks except for those involving disputes between the transacting parties. The lender has no recourse to the borrower.

Note Issuance Facility (NIF) A facility provided by a syndicate of banks that allows borrowers to issue short-term notes, which are then placed by the syndicate providing the NIF. Borrowers usually have the right to sell their notes to the bank syndicate at a price that yields a prearranged spread over LIBOR.

Notional Principal A reference amount against which the interest on a swap is calculated.

Official Reserves Holdings of gold and foreign currencies by official monetary institutions.

Official Reserve Transactions Balance The adjustment required in official reserves to achieve balance-of-payments equilibrium.

Offshore Finance Subsidiary A wholly owned affiliate incorporated overseas, usually in a tax-haven country, whose function is to issue securities abroad for use in either the parent's domestic or foreign business.

Open Account Selling   This selling method involves shipping goods first and billing the importer later.

Open Interest   The number of futures contracts out-standing at any one time.

Open-Market Operation   Purchase or sale of government securities by the monetary authorities to increase or decrease the domestic money supply.

Operating Exposure   Degree to which an exchange rate change, in combination with price changes, will alter a company's future operating cash flows.

Optimum Currency Area   Largest area in which it makes sense to have only one currency. It is defined as that area for which the cost of having an additional currency—higher costs of doing business and greater currency risk—just balances the benefits of another currency—reduced vulnerability to economic shocks associated with the option to change the area's exchange rate.

Option   A financial instrument that gives the holder the right—but not the obligation—to sell (put) or buy (call) another financial instrument at a set price and expiration date.

Out-of-the-Money   An option that would not be profitable to exercise at the current price.

Outright Rate   Actual forward rate expressed in dollars per currency unit, or vice versa.

Outsourcing   The practice of purchasing a significant percentage of intermediate components from outside suppliers.

Outstrike   Pre-defined exchange rate at which a knockout option is canceled if the spot rate crosses this price even temporarily.

Overdraft   A line of credit against which drafts (checks) can be drawn (written) up to a specified maximum amount.

Overseas Private Investment Corporation (OPIC) Agency of the U.S. government that provides political risk insurance coverage to U.S. multinationals. Its purpose is to encourage U.S. direct investment in less-developed countries.

Over-the-Counter Market (OTC)   A market in which the terms and conditions on contracts are negotiated between the buyer and seller, in contrast to an organized exchange where contractual terms are fixed by the exchange.

Over-the-Counter Options   Option contracts whose specifications are generally negotiated as to the amount, exercise price, underlying instrument, and expiration. They are traded by commercial and investment banks.

Parallel Loan   Simultaneous borrowing and lending operation usually involving four related parties in two different countries.

Payments Netting   Reducing fund transfers between affiliates to only a netted amount. Netting can be done on a bilateral basis (between pairs of affiliates) or on a multilateral basis (taking all affiliates together).

Pegged Currency   A currency whose value is set by the government.

Peso Problem   Reference to the possibility that during the time period studied investors anticipated significant events that didn't materialize, thereby invalidating statistical inferences based on data drawn from that period.

Plaza Agreement   A coordinated program agreed to in September 1985 that was designed to force down the dollar against other major currencies and thereby improve American competitiveness.

Political Risk   Uncertain government action that affects the value of a firm.

Pooling   Transfer of excess affiliate cash into a central account (pool), usually located in a low-tax nation, where all corporate funds are managed by corporate staff.

Price Elasticity of Demand   Percentage change in the quantity demanded of a particular good or service for a given percentage change in price.

Price-Specie-Flow Mechanism   Adjustment mechanism under the classical gold standard whereby disturbances in the price level in one country would be wholly or partly offset by a countervailing flow of specie (gold coins) that would act to equalize prices across countries and automatically bring international payments back in balance.

Private Export Funding Corporation (PEFCO) Company that mobilizes private capital for financing the export of big-ticket items by U.S. firms by purchasing at fixed interest rates the medium- to long-term debt obligations of importers of U.S. products.

Private Placements Securities that are sold directly to only a limited number of sophisticated investors, usually life insurance companies and pension funds.

Privatization The act of returning state-owned or state-run companies back to the private sector, usually by selling them off.

Product Cycle The time it takes to bring new and improved products to market. Japanese companies have excelled in compressing product cycles.

Property Rights Rights of individuals and companies to own and utilize property as they see fit and to receive the stream of income that their property generates.

Protectionism Protecting domestic industry from import competition by means of tariffs, quotas, and other trade barriers.

Purchasing Power Parity The notion that the ratio between domestic and foreign price levels should equal the equilibrium exchange rate between domestic and foreign currencies.

Put-Call Option Interest Rate Parity A parity condition that relates put and call currency options prices to the interest differential between two currencies and, by extension, to their forward differential.

Quota Government regulation specifying the quantity of particular products that can be imported to a country.

Range Forward *See* currency collar.

Rational Expectations The idea that people rationally anticipate the future and respond to what they see ahead.

Real Exchange Rate The spot rate adjusted for relative price level changes since a base period.

Real Interest Rate The nominal interest rate adjusted for expected inflation over the life of the loan; it is the exchange rate between current and future goods.

Real or Inflation-Adjusted Exchange Rate Measured as the nominal exchange rate adjusted for changes in relative price levels.

Regional Fund A mutual fund that invests in a specific geographic areas overseas, such as Asia or Europe.

Regulatory Arbitrage The process whereby the users of capital markets issue and trade securities in financial centers with the lowest regulatory standards and, hence, the lowest costs.

Reinvoicing Center A subsidiary that takes title to all goods sold by one corporate unit to another affiliate or to a third-party customer. The center pays the seller and in turn is paid by the buyer.

Reporting Currency The currency in which the parent firm prepares its own financial statements; that is, U.S. dollars for a U.S. company.

Revaluation An increase in the spot value of a currency.

Revolving Credit Agreement A line of credit under which a bank (or syndicate of banks) is *legally committed* to extend credit up to the stated maximum.

Revolving Underwriting Facility (RUF) A note issuance facility that includes underwriting services. The RUF gives borrowers long-term continuous access to short-term money underwritten by banks at a fixed margin.

Right of Offset Clause that gives each party to a swap or parallel loan arrangement the right to offset any nonpayment of principal or interest with a comparable nonpayment.

Risk Arbitrage The process that leads to equality of risk-adjusted returns on different securities, unless market imperfections that hinder this adjustment process exist.

Rollover Date Date on which the interest rate on a floating-rate loan is reset based on current market conditions.

Rule 144A Rule adopted by the Securities and Exchange Commission (SEC) in 1990 that allows qualified institutional investors to trade in unregistered private placements, making them a closer substitute for public issues.

Same-Day Value Funds that are credited and available for use the same day they are transferred.

Samurai Bonds Yen bonds sold in Japan by a non-Japanese borrower.

Secondary Market   The market where investors trade securities already bought.

Section 482   United States Department of Treasury regulations governing transfer prices.

Securitization   The matching up of borrowers and lenders wholly or partly by way of the financial markets. This process usually refers to the replacement of nonmarketable loans provided by financial intermediaries with negotiable securities issued in the public capital markets.

Seigniorage   The profit to the central bank from money creation; it equals the difference between the cost of issuing the money and the value of the goods and services that money can buy.

Settlement Risk   *See* Herstatt risk.

Shogun Bonds   Foreign currency bonds issued within Japan by Japanese corporations.

Shogun Lease   Yen-based international lease.

Short Position   In the foreign exchange market, it means that one has more liabilities in a particular currency than assets.

Sight Draft   A draft that must be paid on presentation or else dishonored.

Single-Country Fund   A mutual fund that invests in individual countries outside the United States, such as Germany or Thailand.

Smithsonian Agreement   After the currency turmoil of August 1971, the United States agreed in December 1971 to devalue the dollar to 1/38 of an ounce of gold, and other countries agreed to revalue their currencies by negotiated amounts vis-à-vis the dollar.

Society for Worldwide Interbank Financial Telecommunications (SWIFT)   A dedicated computer network to support funds transfer messages internationally between more than 900 member banks worldwide.

Soft Currency   A currency expected to depreciate.

Sovereign Risk   The risk that the country of origin of the currency a bank is buying or selling will impose foreign exchange regulations that will reduce or negate the value of the contract: also refers to the risk of government default on a loan made to it or guaranteed by it.

Special Drawing Rights (SDR)   A new form of international reserve assets, created by the IMF in 1967, whose value is based on a portfolio of widely used currencies.

Spot Rate   The price at which foreign exchange can be bought or sold with payment set for the same day.

Statement of Financial Accounting Standards No. 8   This is the currency translation standard previously in use by U.S. firms.

Statement of Financial Accounting Standards No. 52   This is the currency translation standard currently in use by U.S. firms. It basically mandates the use of the current rate method.

Statement of Financial Accounting Standards No. 133 (FASB 133)   Statement issued by the Financial Accounting Standards Board that establishes accounting and reporting standards for derivative instruments and for hedging activities that U.S. firms must use.

Statistical Discrepancy   A number on the balance-of-payments account that reflects errors and omissions in collecting data on international transactions.

Sterilized Intervention   Foreign exchange market intervention in which the monetary authorities have insulated their domestic money supplies from the foreign exchange transactions with offsetting sales or purchases of domestic assets.

Strike Price   *See* exercise price.

Structured Notes   Interest-bearing securities whose interest payments are determined by reference to a formula set in advance and adjusted on specified reset dates.

Subpart F   Special category of foreign-source "unearned" income that is currently taxed by the IRS whether or not it is remitted back to the United States.

Subsidiary   A foreign-based affiliate that is a separately incorporated entity under the host country's law.

Swap   A foreign exchange transaction that combines a spot and a forward contract. More generally, it refers to a financial transaction in which two counterparties agree to exchange streams of payments over time, such as in a currency swap or an interest rate swap.

Swap Rate The difference between spot and forward rates expressed in points (e.g., $0.0001 per pound sterling or DM 0.0001 per dollar).

SWIFT *See* Society for Worldwide Interbank Financial Telecommunications.

Systematic (Nondiversifiable) Risk Marketwide influences that affect all assets to some extent, such as the state of the economy.

Systematic Risk That element of an assets risk that cannot be eliminated no matter how diversified an investor's portfolio.

Target-Zone Arrangement A monetary system under which countries pledge to maintain their exchange rates within a specific margin around agreed-upon, fixed central exchange rates.

Tariff A tax imposed on imported products. It can be used to raise revenue, to discourage purchase of foreign products, or some combination of the two.

Tax Arbitrage The shifting of gains or losses from one tax jurisdiction to another to profit from differences in tax rates.

Tax Haven A nation with a moderate level of taxation and/or liberal tax incentives for undertaking specific activities such as exporting.

Tax Reform Act of 1986 A 1986 law involving a major overhaul of the U.S. tax system.

Technical Analysis An approach that focuses exclusively on past price and volume movements— while totally ignoring economic and political factors—to forecast future asset prices.

Temporal Method Under this currency translation method, the choice of exchange rate depends on the underlying method of valuation. Assets and liabilities valued at historical cost (market) are translated at the historical rate (current rate).

Term Loan A straight loan, often unsecured, that is made for a fixed period of time, usually 90 days.

Terms of Trade The weighted average of a nation's export prices relative to its import prices.

Time Draft A draft that is payable at some specified future date and as such becomes a useful financing device.

Time Value The excess of an option's value over its intrinsic value.

Total Dollar Return The dollar return on a non-dollar investment, which includes the sum of any dividend/interest income, capital gains (losses), and currency gains (losses) on the investment.

Trade Acceptance A draft accepted by a commercial enterprise. *See also* draft.

Trade Draft A draft addressed to a commercial enterprise. *See also* draft.

Transaction Exposure The extent to which a given exchange rate change will change the value of foreign-currency-denominated transactions already entered into.

Transfer Price The price at which one unit of a firm sells goods or services to an affiliated unit.

Translation Exposure *See* accounting exposure.

Treasury Workstation A software package implemented on a computer that treasurers use to run their cash management systems.

Triangular Currency Arbitrage A sequence of foreign exchange transactions, involving three different currencies, that one can use to profit from discrepancies in the different exchange rates.

Unbiased Nature of the Forward Rate (UFR) States that the forward rate should reflect the expected future spot rate on the date of settlement of the forward contract.

Underwriting The act by investment bankers of purchasing securities from issuers for resale to the public.

United Currency Options Market (UCOM) Market set up by the Philadelphia Stock Exchange in which to trade currencies.

Universal Banking Bank practice, especially in Germany, whereby commercial banks perform not only investment banking activities but also take major equity positions in companies.

Unsterilized Intervention Foreign exchange market intervention in which the monetary authorities have not insulated their domestic money supplies from the foreign exchange transactions.

Unsystematic (Diversifiable) Risk Risks that are specific to a given firm, such as a strike.

Up-and-In Option An option that comes into existence if and only if the currency strengthens enough to cross a preset barrier.

Up-and-Out Option   An option that is canceled if the underlying currency strengthens beyond the outstrike.

Value-Added Tax   Method of indirect taxation whereby a tax is levied at each stage of production on the value added at that specific stage.

Value Additivity Principle   The principle that the net present value of a set of independent projects is simply the sum of the NPVs of the individual projects.

Value-at-Risk (VAR)   A calculation which allows a financial institution to estimate the maximum amount it might expect to lose in a given time period with a certain probability.

Value Date   The date on which the monies must be paid to the parties involved in a foreign exchange transaction. For spot transactions, it is set as the second working day after the date on which the transaction is concluded.

Value-Dating   Refers to when value (credit) is given for funds transferred between banks.

Virtual Currency Option   A foreign currency option listed on the Philadelphia Stock Exchange which is settled in U.S. dollars rather than in the underlying currency.

Weighted Average Cost of Capital (WACC)   The required return on the funds supplied by investors. It is a weighted average of the costs of the individual component debt and equity funds.

Working Capital   The combination of current assets and current liabilities.

World Bank   *See* International Bank for Reconstruction and Development.

Yankee Bonds   Dollar-denominated foreign bonds sold in the United States.

Yankee Stock Issues   Stock sold by foreign companies to U.S. investors.

SELECTED CURRENCIES AND SYMBOLS

Country	Currency	Symbol	Country	Currency	Symbol
Afganistan	Afghani	Af	Egypt	pound	LE
Albania	lek	lek	European Monetary Unit	euro	€
Algeria	dinar	DA			
Antigua and Barbuda	E.C. Dollar	E.C.$	Estonia	Kroon	F$
Argentina	peso	Arg$	Fiji	dollar	F$
Australia	dollar	$A	Finland	euro	€
Austria	euro	€	France	euro	€
Bahamas	dollar	BS	Germany	euro	€
Bahrain	dinar	BD	Greece	euro	€
Barbados	dollar	BDS$	Guatemala	quetzal	Q
Belgium	euro	€	Honduras	lempira	LE
Belize	dollar	BZ$	Hong Kong	dollar	HK$
Bermuda	dollar	Ber$	Hungary	forint	Ft
Bolivia	boliviano	Bs	India	rupee	Rs
Botswana	pula	P	Indonesia	rupiah	Rp
Brazil*	real	R$	Iran, Islamic Republic of	rial	Rls
Cambodia	riel	CR			
Canada	dollar	$ or Can$	Ireland	euro	€
Cayman Islands	dollar	KY$	Israel	new sheqel	NIS
Chile	peso	Ch$	Italy	euro	€
China, People's Republic of*	yuan	Y	Jamaica	dollar	J$
			Japan	yen	¥
Colombia	peso	Col$	Kenya	shilling	KSh
Costa Rica	colon	C	Korea, Republic of	won	W
Cyprus	pound	£ or C£	Kuwait	dinar	KD
Denmark	krone	DKr	Liberia	dollar	L$
Dominican Republic	peso	RD$	Liechtenstein	franc	Sw F
Ecuador	sucre	S/.	Luxembourg	euro	€

*The currency is the renminbi, whereas the currency unit is the yuan.